T0351251

Innovative Automatic Identification and Location–Based Services:
From Bar Codes to Chip Implants

Katina Michael
University of Wollongong, Australia

M.G. Michael
University of Wollongong, Australia

Information Science REFERENCE

INFORMATION SCIENCE REFERENCE

Hershey · New York

Director of Editorial Content: Kristin Klinger
Senior Managing Editor: Jamie Snavely
Managing Editor: Jeff Ash
Assistant Managing Editor: Carole Coulson
Typesetter: Chris Hrobak
Cover Design: Lisa Tosheff
Printed at: Yurchak Printing Inc.

Published in the United States of America by
        Information Science Reference (an imprint of IGI Global)
        701 E. Chocolate Avenue,
        Hershey PA 17033
        Tel: 717-533-8845
        Fax: 717-533-8661
        E-mail: cust@igi-global.com
        Web site: http://www.igi-global.com/reference

and in the United Kingdom by
        Information Science Reference (an imprint of IGI Global)
        3 Henrietta Street
        Covent Garden
        London WC2E 8LU
        Tel: 44 20 7240 0856
        Fax: 44 20 7379 0609
        Web site: http://www.eurospanbookstore.com

Library of Congress Cataloging-in-Publication Data

Innovative automatic identification and location-based services : from bar codes to chip implants / Katina Michael and M.G. Michael, author.

    p. cm.

  Includes bibliographical references and index.

  Summary: "This book emphasizes the convergence and trajectory of automatic identification and location-based services toward chip implants and real-time positioning capabilities"--Provided by publisher.

  ISBN 978-1-59904-795-9 (hardcover) -- ISBN 978-1-59904-797-3 (ebook) 1. Bar coding equipment industry. 2. Automatic data collection systems. 3. Location-based services. I. Michael, Katina, 1976- II. Michael, M. G.   HD9801.6.P762I56 2009

   303.48'3--dc22

                            2008055307

British Cataloguing in Publication Data
A Cataloguing in Publication record for this book is available from the British Library.

All work contributed to this book is new, previously-unpublished material. The views expressed in this book are those of the authors, but not necessarily of the publisher.

To the cherished memory of Michael Michael (1962-1995)
and Andrew Michael (1978-1999).

Yea, though I walk through the valley
of the shadow of death,
I will fear no evil;
For you are with me
Your rod and your staff,
they comfort me.

Psalm 23:4

Table of Contents

Section II:
Auto-ID and LBS Innovation

Section III:
The Social Implications of Auto-ID and LBS Technology

Foreword

The rapid pace of technology change and adoption has led to the fear that our 21st century societies are now approaching the nightmare scenarios that were once predicted in such dystopian and futuristic novels as George Orwell's *1984* and Ben Elton's *Blind Faith*. The specter of terrorism has presented governments with the justification to introduce surveillance of the citizenry on an unprecedented scale. It is therefore timely that Katina and Michael have written this book which examines the trajectory of automatic identification and location-based services (LBS) from bar codes to chip implants. Of course, not all of these innovative techniques should be viewed negatively. Electronic health monitoring solutions, for instance, are helping doctors gather accurate and timely medical data about their patients and their needs. In the area of criminal intelligence, GPS tracking units are being used by law enforcement agencies to gather evidence toward convicting suspects of criminal activities or keeping track of parolees who have been released from prison.

I have had the pleasure of working with Katina and Michael for many years now. Katina provided the many thought-provoking case studies for the 3rd edition of my book *Internet Commerce: Digital Models for Business*. It was also my pleasure to be on the panel that examined her first class PhD where she initially investigated many of the technologies that appear in this book. With Michael, I have presented at a number of international conferences where his stimulating presentations are evidence of his broad education and intelligent projections.

The authors have developed a valuable and constructive conceptual framework that serves to allow for the proper analysis and critique of the rapid advances made in LBS. The historical presentation of these technological advances provides for an expert insight into how we have arrived at the respective innovations. Each of the case studies serves to illustrate the usage of the luggable, wearable and implantable devices for a diverse range of sectors, and the predictive chapter on uberveillance serves as a warning of what a number of thinkers are now increasingly beginning to agree, could become a reality. Indeed, it is not surprising that *uberveillance* was one of ninety-two words from around the English-speaking world, chosen to enter the Macquarie Dictionary in 2008 and in the running for Word of the Year. The authors have also tackled the all important social and ethical issues before presenting this glimpse into a potentially ominous future.

Original contributions of this cross-disciplinary work include: the extension of the terms technological trajectory and selection environment from the innovation literature as applied to automatic identification and location-based services; the introduction of the new concepts of *electrophorus* (as opposed to cyborg) and *uberveillance* (an above and beyond, exaggerated surveillance); and the unique reflections of the expert interviewees that strike at the core of current and future possibilities. Given that serious and restrained publications on this contentious subject of humancentric implants are in the main terribly scant, *Innovative Automatic Identification and Location-Based Services (LBS): From Bar Codes to Chip Implants* is a major addition to international bibliography.

I congratulate Katina and Michael on the writing of this well-timed and important book- it is vital that we learn to recognize the impact of emerging technologies such as the ones which have been addressed, so we can keep what is best and refuse that which is destructive to ourselves and to our society. One way or another, for better or for worse, the applied consequences of these decisions especially at the practical level will be for the greater part, if not entirely, irreversible.

Associate Professor Elaine Lawrence
Head of Department of Computer Systems
Faculty of Information Technology
University of Technology Sydney, Australia

Preface

INTRODUCTION

This book serves as a critical piece of documentary evidence for automatic identification and location-based services from its inception until today. Automatic identification (auto-ID) is the act of identifying a living or nonliving thing without direct human intervention. Location-based services (LBS) are the ability for an information system to denote the position of a user, based on a device they are carrying, or their position in a given context. Automatic identification technologies and location-based services are both complementary and supplementary technologies. Being able to identify and locate someone on the same device is powerful for different types of requests. But even more powerful is the ability to imply someone's identity by their location. The latter has critical implications for the way law enforcement is conducted, emergency services are deployed, and loved ones are notified of your given circumstances. Indeed this book is about the social implications of technology, and how new emerging innovations are completely changing the rules of engagement.

The great bulk of the research for this book was conducted between 1998 when the first person (a British researcher, Professor Kevin Warwick) was officially chip implanted for the Cyborg 1.0 project, and 2003 with the Jacobs family who were the first family to officially receive the commercial VeriChip implant for an emergency service application. Much has happened since 2003 and this book also attempts to capture the major events since that time, that together, have acted to change the way consumers live, employees work, and companies and governments do business. It therefore follows, that the book could be utilized as a historical source, as a reader on the broad topic of automatic identification and location-based services innovation, but it could also be credited with a futurist perspective, predictive in nature, and multidisciplinary in source and content.

The book was largely written during a time of global geo-political and economic turbulence when the world witnessed a rise in a new kind of terrorism and also large-scale emergencies related to natural disasters. In this time of evident technological advancement, many have questioned, why in such a period of rapid scientific progress are we so incapable of preventing, mitigating, and recovering from catastrophic events. The Hurricane Katrina disaster of 2005 stands as a signpost more than any other event in modern day United States, in the land of the free, where communications and technology abound, millions of people were left without food and water for days after the hurricane ravaged the Atlantic coastline. Government agencies, whether in the business of strategic intelligence or emergency management or securitization, are seeking new ways to protect their nation's borders. In doing so, they have turned to technology for the answers and realized (even if it has not yet been communicated) that technology is only a partial solution if correctly deployed, and that it is humans working together that ultimately provide the real effective solutions in the long term.

The audience for this book is wide-reaching. In its original form, as a dissertation submitted within the field of Information Technology by Katina Michael, it attempted to demystify the innovation of auto-ID and location-based services, focusing on the firm as the central actor in the process of innovation. Beyond the dissertation, as opportunities arose for Katina to collaborate with husband M.G. Michael, who had a background in the humanities, the focus shifted from a purely technical work, to one that incorporated the socio-ethical component, legal, philosophical, cultural, and religious issues. Here there was an emphasis in informing the general public of the current state of affairs, in providing material that was written in an accessible language, in invigorating debate, and pondering the automatic identification trajectory. Questions of the place of auto-ID and LBS within society, then led to even grander questions related to the role of new technologies within public administration, which then led to the big picture question of the social impact of technology upon citizens and business. This book is about considering where we are headed, why we are headed that way, how fast we will get there, and trying to make sense of what it all could mean. It is in a sense, a one big "what if" scenario which is meant to stir the thinking of the general public, as well as a plea to practitioners to consider the social implications of their research, the development, and its application.

For now, the trajectory we are on seems to be one of aiming to control the masses using technologies we ourselves have created and instituted. The question is whether this is the kind of world we want to live in, filled with smart sensors, smart objects, and real-time analytics. On face value, most perceive competitive advantages in terms of cost savings in business or at least emphasize the convenience factor for the individual or family. Wouldn't it be a great life if I could walk up to my house door and not have to fiddle with keys to gain entry? Or wouldn't it be great if my house knew what temperature I liked the air-conditioning set to, or could just sense my level of discomfort and act appropriately? Or better still, wouldn't it be great if I could just communicate with others just by thinking about them, and never have to lift a handset? All these kinds of potential lifestyle options seem great but what of the continual decline of the individual to live, act, and to make decisions within a discernible physical space? Have we seriously considered the extensive implications that this "new order" of existence might have on our general well being? And these are real consequences (not simply imagined ones) both on the physical and mental levels. Are we knowingly fooling ourselves that such things are the "holy grail" to contentment, to happiness, to the idealized, if not *ideal* life? The oft quoted Latin phrase is certainly not out of place here: *Caveat emptor* (Let the buyer beware).

The consequences of these initiatives will take some time to be felt but already we can predict with some confidence what some of the shortfalls will be. Postmodernist theory might have us believe that the profession of history is in crisis and that its methods are outmoded, but as Richard Evans and others have effectively argued, the discipline can teach us many lessons and provide us with "genuine insights". In the context of technology itself, thinkers in the sociological tradition of Lewis Mumford and Jacques Ellul continue to challenge us to stop for a moment and to critically evaluate the unchecked consequences upon our civilization of an "artificial environment". Whatever happens, whatever road is taken or "not taken", the irreversible consequences of our "technicized" society will be felt by future generations. This is perhaps a traditional problem that has less to do with technology and more to do with people. Are we continually building new defenses with a "catch me if you can" way of thinking, and "here, try penetrating my latest solutions", or are we genuine about peaceful resolutions which look at the root causes of national security concerns? The question is how much room are we truly leaving ourselves for future modification and change, if we go ahead and implement what we are proposing today? For the record, no one is debunking technology; there are no *neo-Luddites* here. The basic point is to remain the masters over that which we create, and to not allow for the *machine* to dictate the terms and boundaries of our existence.

ORGANIZATION OF THE BOOK

This book is divided into three main sections. Section I provides a background and context for the study. Section II introduces the reader to the technology and representative applications while examining distinct innovation processes. Secion III explores the social implications of auto-ID and LBS technology.

Section I: Background and Context

Chapter I defines automatic identification and location-based services, describes why these technologies are significant and how they are closely allied, and describes the gap this book will fill in the literature. The introduction will also provide an overview of the conceptual framework used for the whole study, the general methodological approach and the multiple sources of evidence used to gather data.

Chapter II presents an overview of relevant literature in the field of innovation studies. The chapter presents theories and frameworks that have been tried and tested against a backdrop of previous qualitative innovation studies. The systems of innovation (SI) framework which has emerged from the contemporary evolutionary economic theory is used in this study to capture both time and context. It is a holistic framework which does not underestimate the study of an innovation from a variety of perspectives including: organizational, institutional, regulatory, technical, social, political, and so forth. This chapter introduces the reader to important innovation concepts including, technological trajectory, selection environment, path dependency, technological guideposts and much more. These basic definitions are used inherently to study the technologies throughout the book, providing a setting for interpretation.

Chapter III takes the reader as far back as antiquity, so they can better appreciate the evolution of the technology and the potential and realized impacts of auto-ID and LBS on today's society. Being able to identify someone or something or to locate someone, something or a physical structure is *not* a new phenomenon. People have always had a need to make correlations between the people they know and the people they do not, between those things that belong to them and those things that do not. In fact, the idea of belonging to a group in a variety of contexts was prevalent in ancient times. However, as places became more urbanized and new inventions changed the way we worked (e.g. the Industrial Revolution) and the way we traveled, moved goods, and communicated (e.g. the invention of the steam train and electricity), automated means of identification and location determination became increasingly important. Understanding the beginnings, how the technologies (even in their manual forms) have been applied in the past, helps to shed light on the present and future possibilities. What has in truth changed since automated methods of identification were introduced? And what of location-based services in their infancy at present? Have these technologies had revolutionary consequences? What can we learn from history? And why is auto-ID or LBS any different to other information technologies?

Interview 3.1 is conducted with a Holocaust survivor, Mrs. Judy Nachum, who was forced to wear the Yellow Star pointing to the potential for more sophisticated means of auto-ID and LBS to be used to segregate a populace today in the framework of "social sorting". This interview explores some of the issues raised in the preceding chapter, however in more detail. The interview brings to life the potential for technology to be misused by persons in position of power. The interview presents examples of how simple manual identification techniques were first used to identify the Jewish populations during World War II, to gather these people into concentration camps, and then used in the calculated process of dehumanization. The interview is explicit in stating how the Nazis were meticulous record keepers, and how identification numbers granted them the ability to link numerous pieces of information together which was initially paper-based and "off-line". The interview demonstrates that there are clear limits to how present day governments should use computers to record citizen information. It also suggests that while another type of *holocaust* of similar proportions to the persecution of the Jewish people is improbable, that the power of the digital medium to control and to sort, if ever unleashed, would be even more punishing and exacting in pinpointing its desired minority.

Chapter IV is about placing the research study in a background setting. The chapter focuses on issues pertaining to national security for the purposes of border control and counter-terrorism. The dilemma is presented as the trade-off between the collective security of a nation and the right to individual privacy. In this chapter the usefulness of providing strict controls for all citizens via technologies which inherently identify or locate or surveil is questioned, especially when such measures can also be adopted by transnational criminal groups. The speed of deploying new technologies for public administration is also questioned especially given the sweeping legislative changes that were enacted post the September 11, 2001 terrorist attacks.

Section II: Auto-ID and LBS Innovation

Chapter V is dedicated to the rise of bar code innovations particularly in the retail sector. Objects have been identified with labels since herbs and spices were placed in silos for storage. In the 1970s the universal produce code (UPC) revolutionized the checkout at supermarkets and ever since almost every consumable packaged item has been bar coded. The chapter traverses from the first bar code developments in the 20th Century, to modern day two-dimensional bar code advances with biometrics onboard. The limitations of bar code are outlined as are the fundamental issues surrounding its widespread usage. Technically bar code has worked on the principles of symbology, black and white contiguous lines that digitally represent 1s and 0s. In favor of the bar code as an identification technique is that it is relatively cheap, is well established standards-wise, and enjoys worldwide end-user acceptance. The case studies presented in this chapter include the retail and educational sectors indicating how pervasive the technology actually is. Bar code remains the most widespread auto-ID technique in use today, despite its much touted rival, RFID, receiving a great deal of attention and publicity in recent times.

Chapter VI explores the magnetic-stripe card which has not only revolutionized the face of banking but also many other industries, including ticketing and transportation. They were responsible for the move away from cash towards a *cashless* society, a future state where money would become altogether obsolete. Despite magnetic-stripe cards having significant drawbacks, namely that they are subject to counterfeiting, skimming and other criminal practices, the technology is still very popular in a large number of markets. The technology has also been responsible for the growing physical infrastructure that has supported its inception. ATM machines, global interbank agreements, credit card companies, and standard devices have all lead to the success of magnetic-stripe cards. Today instead of wallets bulging with lose change and bank notes, they are bulging with plastic cards. While many would consider magnetic-stripe card a dying technology, some research has been conducted in the United States in an attempt to make the technique more secure. Admittedly, making magnetic-stripe card "more secure" is an expensive business. This is considered, however, in light of the requirement to update a whole lot of existing infrastructure to meet the technical demands of more robust technologies like smart cards. Similarly to bar codes, magnetic-stripes are here for the long-haul despite better, more secure, technologies being available today.

Chapter VII explores the smart card. In the mid-1980s much was promised about smart card and its pending proliferation but the forecasts missed their mark. Was it an expensive manufacturing process that stifled the card's diffusion, or was it that cardholders were simply not ready for the chip-on-a-card technology? This chapter tells the smart card story from its development in the mid-1970s and traces its use in the medical and telecommunications sectors. Smart cards have had their greatest impact in Europe, although the adoption of the mobile phone has meant that smart cards have become widespread through the use of subscriber identity modules (SIM) for communications. Smart cards have many technical advantages including that they are multiapplication/multifunction capable and have onboard cryptographic abilities and sizeable storage space. Despite the fact that smart card enjoyed a large institutional network that helped the technology receive world-wide coverage and publicity, the network failed to project the smart card into fundamental markets like credit card companies. This is not to say that these companies have abandoned the smart card, on the contrary, many have projected that it will become the preferred technology before too long (e.g. banking industry).

Chapter VIII is about biometric technologies. Biometrics was the first auto-ID technology that displaced the use of cards or ID numbers altogether. It changed the face of identification- a human's physical characteristic, trait or behavior could now identify him/her. In the 1600s, a fingerprint was accepted in place of a signature on title deeds, and criminals had long been fingerprinted right back to the early days of Scotland Yard. But it was not until the 1970s that criminal fingerprints were placed on automatic systems for cross-matching purposes. Biometric technology of the 1980s was both clunky and expensive. Today, biometric technology is easy to install and multi-modal biometrics (the use of more than one physical characteristic) is standard practice in large-scale implementations. The role of government in using biometrics for citizen applications is also discussed in this chapter, as are the use of biometrics for entertainment applications such as fun parks. The use of biometrics, such as DNA, raises a great number of ethical issues which are explored in detail. Contradictions in laws and regulations are studied, as the question of the rightful ownership of a biometric is considered.

Chapter IX is about RFID tag and transponder innovations. Radio-frequency is a capability that was prevalent since before World War II, however as an identification technology in the modern context, RFID has only been trialed and used in niche applications since the late 1990s. Today, RFID has made major inroads into the retail bar code market, initially considered as a replacement technology by its proponents, and then recognized as a complementary technology to bar code. RFID is being heralded as a future supply chain enabler. The push is toward having the ability to identify and locate products at the item level as opposed to the larger pallet level. Emerging standards such as the Electronic Product Code (EPC) are promising an "Internet of Things", allowing ordinary objects to come "alive" using wireless triggers. Animal centric and human-centric RFID tag and transponder applications are also presented in this chapter. In Europe and many other parts of the world, governments have introduced new regulations and directives in an attempt to contain and eradicate virus outbreaks in livestock. Local councils have also imposed mandatory chip implanting of cats and dogs to limit the number of stray pets and identify ownership. Innovative auto-ID and LBS applications are being used to increase milk production in cow herds, track species that are close to extinction, and for breeding purposes. Commercial applications now exist to tag and track people. In some parts of the world, their entry have meant the establishment of anti-chipping acts, such as in cases throughout the United States. Over time auto-ID technologies have become more invasive, and in some instances technologies are not only worn externally, but implanted into the body. The first human-centric implant experiment was conducted by Professor Kevin Warwick in 1998. RFID implants for humans pose a great number of socio-ethical issues, cultural, religious, and philosophical.

Chapter X analyses the patterns and trends that emerge in Section II in a bid to understand the auto-ID innovation process. Early in Chapter X the complexity of auto-ID is shown by examining the interactions between stakeholders. The auto-ID innovation process is also described and linked to a generic auto-ID product lifecycle. The time between auto-ID inventions also depicts how individual auto-ID technologies have not been invented to make existing techniques obsolete, but have acted as complementary and supplementary technologies. In addition, the frequency of the introduction of major new auto-ID techniques is about a ten year window meaning that the industry is only going to expand over time, probably with developments in the area of nanotechnology next. The auto-ID product lifecycle is also examined and detailed. This lifecycle shows the typical issues that the technologies come up against after their inception and how future technologies could be introduced with a shorter lead time and with greater emphasis on the technology's implications, beyond discussion on plain system design needs. Prevalent trends in the information and communication technology (ICT) sector have shown migration, integration and convergence patterns. Within the auto-ID industry, these patterns are easily identifiable, especially as emerging techniques lend themselves more to not only the function of identification but also the function of location. RFID for instance, can act to identify a thing, in addition to being able to locate it precisely if the corresponding wireless infrastructure is available.

Chapter XI is dedicated to defining geographic information systems (GIS) in the context of location-based services. A GIS is a system of storing information linked to geographic details such as objects (pinpoint locations using an X and Y coordinate), lines (such as roads, and other topographic and human-made features that have a bearing and distance value), and regions (such as administrative, political or council boundaries that can be measured in surface area). The concept of geocoding is integral to a GIS. A telecommunications operator for example could store millions of records of information, including asset data such as their infrastructure's physical lifetime, photos of their telephone exchanges, as well as customer billing data per individual householder. Geocoding allows organizations to conduct exact matching or fuzzy matching on large datasets and to visualize them to differing geographic levels of detail in a GIS. As a presentation tool, a GIS can be used to conduct districting or target marketing via thematic mapping. Today, such LBS applications as *Google Earth* and *Google Street View* have revolutionized the way people conduct navigation activities and also reconnaissance for personal or competitive business reasons. Such new technologies are clashing with cultural ideals and testing the limits of definitions of personal versus public space in the field of privacy law.

Interview 11.1 consists of an interview with Professor Alan Brimicombe of the Centre for Geo-Information Studies at the University of East London. Brimicombe describes the strengths of today's geographic information systems (GISs), as they are used in tandem with other technologies such as location-based services and data warehouses. He is well known for work in the area of location-based services and geo-information engineering. For Brimicombe the future is not only in the collection of data via satellite imagery or GPS from the tops of cars but in Web crawlers that go out and check spatial databases for information that is already out there waiting to be harvested and used.

Section III: The Social Implications of Auto-ID and LBS Technology

Chapter XII explores the trajectory of an innovation related to which path or course it may follow over time. Having already studied in earlier chapters, where auto-ID and LBS came from, and understanding where it is now, one should be able to gain insight about its future direction and use value. This chapter illuminates the short-term trajectory of auto-ID and LBS without the hysteria and sensationalism that so often plagues predictive studies in the field. It is based on sober analysis of the current research in universities, patents on the United States database, and worldwide commercial ventures. This chapter has a predictive element running right through it and presents a number of mini embedded cases. It begins with wearable technologies (e.g. industrial application), e-wallets (e.g. medical application) and smart clothes (e.g. military application). The merging of a number of disciplines ranging from engineering, computing, and medical is prevalent in this chapter.

Interview 12.1 consists of an interview with Professor Christofer Toumazou, a former telecommunications engineer and now the Chair of the Biomedical Institute at Imperial College, London, who speaks with compelling insight and a globally recognized authority on the current state of development of biomedical devices. Through his extensive record of research he has invented innovative electronic devices ranging from dual mode cellular phones to ultra-low power devices for both medical diagnosis and therapy.

Chapter XIII discusses the socio-ethical implications and the dilemmas surrounding an environment of uberveillance, an emerging age of omnipresent embedded surveillance which is increasingly introducing us to lots of grey areas. These have to do with the fundamental rights of an individual, the powers of commercial enterprises and government agencies, about underlying philosophies, ideologies, religious beliefs, cultures, and inherent freedoms. It has to do with the legal framework, the law, and a consensus approach to juridical action. Technology must be understood within a social context, and not solely as a dumb artifact with no trajectory. Beyond guidelines, standards for product development are needed, as are appropriate regulations supported by governments. Without these vital safeguards society runs the actual risk of being overridden and destroyed by the very things that it has set out to create to make the world "a better and safer place". The debate has little to do with "stopping science" and "progress" and more to do with attempting to curb the potential problems that may arise as a consequence of a "harmful" technique's widespread use. The question is not whether one can prejudge ethics, but more about circumspectly considering the long-term impacts and implications of that which we plan to create and to unleash into the world.

Interview 13.1 provides the perspective of Professor Ian Angell of the Department of Management, Information Systems and Innovation Group at the London School of Economics. Professor Angell is one of the world's most recognized forecasters of the socio-political and business consequences of information and communication technologies. He gives his thought-provoking views on the current state of play between the quest for national security *contra* terrorism and the rights to individual privacy. He emphasizes not only the darker implications of auto-ID but that the whole motivation for mass market citizen auto-ID technologies has essentially to do with economics.

Chapter XIV points to the rise of the *Electrophorus*. It is predicted that the ultimate trajectory of auto-ID and LBS in humans is encapsulated in the emerging concept of "Electrophorus". Far from the notion of "cyborg" meaning part human and part machine, the notion of Electrophorus refers to a bearer of an embedded electric technology. In short, we do hold that embedded technologies for predisposition and healing of illness or for prosthesis is indeed acceptable, but that humans should not too quickly rush into these technologies for "bionic" enhancement or auto-amplification without first carefully examining the potential pitfalls. Questions of applied ethics are raised as the potential to use auto-ID and other advanced nanotechnologies to unite flesh and machine or at least to make the experience between the virtual and physical space indistinguishable. What type of person is the *Electrophorus*, if indeed he/she still belongs to that family called Homo sapiens. At what point is a person who adopts embedded technologies for enhancement, something other than a human being?

Interview 14.1 for the most part investigates the usability context of control with respect to human-centric microchip implants. Professor Kevin Warwick from the University of Reading is generally the first acknowledged "implantee"/"cyborg" who amongst other research endeavors (e.g. robotics) studies the direct interfaces between computer systems and the human nervous system. The interview captures the essence of the proposed Electrophorus concept and in general raises concerns about the potential of the Electrophorus in society. Kevin is best known for his pioneering experiments involving a neuro-surgical implantation into the median nerves of his left arm to link his nervous system directly to a computer to assess the latest technology for use with the disabled. He was successful with the first extra-sensory (ultrasonic) input for a human and with the first purely electronic telegraphic communication experiment between the nervous systems of two humans.

Interview 14.2 predominantly investigates the usability context of convenience with respect to human-centric microchip implants in a straightforward and revealing interview with arguably the world's most recognizable "do-it-yourselfer" RFID implantee, Amal Graafstra of the United States and author of *RFID Toys*. He is the owner of several technology and mobile communications companies and is presently the Director of Information Technology for *OutBack Power Systems*. Amal loves thinking up interesting ways to combine and apply various technologies in his daily life.

Interview 14.3 investigates the usability context of care with respect to auto-ID and location-based services. This is done with in an interview of Mr. Kenneth Lea, a carer of an Alzheimer's sufferer. Mr. Lea considers the possibilities for identifying, tracking and tracing people who have a tendency to wander using location-based services and provides insights from his first hand experience as a carer. Mr. Lea speaks honestly and frankly about the major safety issue related to people suffering with dementia and the possible technological solutions that might aid carers and sufferers. Kenneth feels that the current information and communication technology (ICT) solutions are inadequate to support members of society who require 24x7 care.

Chapter XV describes *uberveillance* and argues that it is a more suitable concept in the context of the auto-ID trajectory than dataveillance given the pervasiveness of the emerging embedded surveillance technologies. Uberveillance is defined as an above and beyond, an exaggerated, an omnipresent 24/7 embedded in the body surveillance. Uberveillance is more than just data-surveillance, it encompasses an ethereal presence, is not measured just by bits and bytes, although almost certainly begins at that basic level of detail. Computers, however, are not omniscient, although they might be "always on" and accessible at "any time." And that is one of the problems which we explore. Uberveillance is more than just ubiquity. It has a motive, a purpose, an agenda; is governed by someone/ something; and does not just exist due to evolutionary forces of nature. It is not simply about being able to determine whether someone owes the tax office money by using data-matching techniques, to mine their personal data. Uberveillance has the potential to control the masses. In its ultimate form, it is *Big Brother* on the inside looking out from the microchipped human working in concert with existing wholesale surveillance and auto-ID infrastructure.. In this mode, there can be no place to hide, everything is recorded and society is impartially dissected between the haves and have-nots. Also pervasive computing within the context of eHealth raises some complex questions about the value and use of uberveillance within a given application, but it remains that any type of intrusive surveillance within the body must be considered with caution regardless.

Chapter XVI is the conclusion to *Innovative Auto-ID and LBS applications: from Bar Codes to Chip Implants* which was chiefly about exposing the reader to a synthesized account of literature on the topic and raising awareness of the many possibilities in the field. Some readers would have been surprised to learn that RFID implants and advanced location-based service (A-LBS) applications are now realities, and indeed commercial realities with a number of companies already listed on stock exchanges across the world. These technologies - and many others about to make their mark, such as nanotechnology - are beginning to permeate global cultures, initiating changes that will become irreversible before too long. It is one thing to use technology to help grant someone sight, hearing, speech, and mobility, a different thing to willingly invite technology into the body as a fashion statement, or to extend basic human function beyond natural measure, or in the hope of becoming an immortal. *Re-designing* the human species before we know much more could inevitably lead us down a path of extinction electronic viruses will have the potential to cause virtual pandemics which no security patch will be able to fix. One need only consider what happens to animals when the ecosystem within which they reside is disrupted ... "mutations", "recombination" and "hybrids" will not only describe different types of inventions, but different forms of "somewhat" human existence. While these technologies are often purported to be enabling technologies- in the sense of progress, improvement and wonder- in actual fact they will herald a loss of control of our own autonomy and be subject to abuse. Beyond what technology promises or hopes to achieve, the basic premise remains that the end-user should be in control of their world and not a third party or system extension. If we think that a future vision of people and machines being fused is farfetched, we need only look at the evidence provided in this book and in others to understand that we are at the brink of another revolution, this time a *hyper*-revolution. How we respond, both individually and collectively to these super changes which we are only now getting a good glimpse, will go a long to determining the eschatology of our planet.

CONCLUSION

When the research project was first established while the primary author was working at Nortel Networks in 1996, the possibility of microchip implants in humans seemed remote if not impossible. Even though Nortel were original part-sponsors of the Cyborg 1.0 experiment, the vast majority of employees in the company still had little if any idea of the potential possibilities to implant humans. When discussing the research project with peers (mostly engineers), the primary author was often lightheartedly mocked for taking on such a "far-fetched" and futuristic type project. "C'mon Katina, microchips in humans, that's the stuff of the *Six Million Dollar Man*." Of course Nortel supported the Warwick initiative as members of British Telecom also touted it groundbreaking for its sheer potential to change how people could communicate with one another in deference to the use of physical telephone handsets. Many academics today, deemed experts in the field of mobile commerce, are still too commonly unaware or misinformed to the current microchipping of humans. This not only highlights the importance of predictive studies in the high-tech field and also the rapid change of pace technology is instilling in our everyday lives, but that investigation based on cutting edge research is paramount. Most of this cutting edge research is not found in refereed journal papers or in large volumes dedicated to special topics- these simply take too long to get through the publication process. We find the future is here in sci-fi, popular media, through newspaper articles, the World Wide Web (WWW), and small snippets of university and commercial media releases. The use of popular media is not without caution however- all *claims* need to be substantiated and exaggerations tempered with the appropriate evidence. It is from within such a context that the reader of this book should expect to learn about auto-ID innovation and LBS, through a mixture of academic and non-academic sources, used together to shed light on a topic that has the propensity to change just about everything.

Acknowledgment

This multidisciplinary study began over a decade ago, and there are many who joined us at different legs of the journey.

Thank you to our colleagues at the University of Wollongong, especially to those from the School of Information Systems and Technology in the Faculty of Informatics, including the head of school, associate professor Peter Hyland, and the dean, professor Philip Ogunbona. Your backing and encouragement, your willingness to listen to our research findings, but also to offer ideas and corrections has proven invaluable during these years that we have been investigating the social implications of automatic identification technologies, and more recently advanced location-based services. To professor Joe Chicharo, Pro-Vice Chancellor (International), who was the brain child of the IP Location Based Services Research Program, we wish to acknowledge your great support and encouragement in our research endeavors. Despite your internationally recognized engineering background, you could see the importance of bringing together seemingly disparate fields in the pursuit of knowledge.

A special thank you to associate professor Robyn Lindley who agreed to supervise Katina's PhD on the topic of the auto-ID trajectory in 1996- you had and still have such incredible foresight- thank you for sharing your insights and for diving into the original draft manuscript with pencil in hand before heading off into industry. And to professor Joan Cooper, Pro-Vice Chancellor (Students) and Registrar at the University of New South Wales, and associate professor Carole Alcock, the former Head of the School of Computer and Information Science at the University of South Australia, who made sure that Katina completed her PhD sooner rather than later.

A big thank you to our very keen and enthusiastic students, both at undergraduate and postgraduate levels. We love being in the classroom with you and teaching you about Information and Communication Security Issues, eBusiness, Location-Based Services, IT & Innovation, Professional Practice and Ethics, and the Social Impacts of Technology. Of particular note are our PhD, Masters by Research and Honors Bachelors graduates (at last count approaching thirty). Thank you for enriching our lives in so many different ways, and for allowing us to explore specific topics that have contributed to the sharpness and focus of our work through your well-informed questioning. The fruits of our work continue to be published, fuelling public and academic debate across the broad community. In the early stages you placed enormous trust in our academic research direction. We cherished every meeting with each and every one of you and the life-long contact that has ensued. A special mention must go to Ms Amelia Masters, Ms Laura Perusco and Mr. Andrew McNamee who co-authored papers with us in the initial stages when much of this research was in its embryonic stage.

To the Convener Professor Priyan Mendis of the ARC-funded (Australian Research Council), Research Network for a Secure Australia (RNSA), thank you for recognizing the significance of the *Social Implications of National Security* workshops (three altogether so far) and for the trust you placed in us to both organize the gatherings and to edit the proceedings which have been referenced and cited internationally. The workshop is presently in its fourth year and now affiliated with the ARC Center of Excellence in Policing and Security (CEPS). Our meetings have attracted a truly national audience from a variety of disciplines that have understood that no one group holds the monopoly on wisdom and knowledge. Together with the fantastic support of Mr. Athol Yates of the Australian Homeland Security Research Centre (AHSRC) the workshop has stood its ground on an international arena. We thank here our colleagues in this endeavor, especially Miss Roba Abbas, Professor Simon Bronitt, Mr. Mark Burdon, Professor Roger Clarke, Ms Suzanne Lockhart, Professor Brian Martin, Dr Lauren May, Mr. George Mickhail, Mr. Rob Nicholls, Associate Professor Nicholas O'Brien, Dr Lucy Resnyansky, Dr Mark Rix, Ms Michelle Rowland, Dr Holly Tootell, Professor Marcus Wigan, and Professor Jennifer Seberry for her seen and unseen support from day one. And to all of our many colleagues who joined us at different times during this demanding but enjoyable undertaking that both reviewed papers and presented their work.

Thank you to the conveners of the international forums and conferences who have accepted our papers and who have invited us to present our research in Asia, Eurasia, North and South America, Scandinavia, and Europe. We especially appreciate the support of our colleagues in the *IEEE International Conference on Mobile Business (ICMB)*, the *International Symposium on Technology and Society (ISTAS)*, and *Cultural Attitudes Towards Technology and Communication (CATaC)*. An important presentation on our research on uberveillance was also made at the *29th International Conference of Data Protection and Privacy Commissioners* in 2007 for which both authors were especially grateful to have been invited to participate. These were critical opportunities for us to present our results to colleagues of worldwide standing and to receive crucial feedback. Likewise we thank the editors of *IBM Systems Journal, Computer Communications, Electronic Commerce Research and Applications*, and *Quadrant* for accepting select works, and the editors of *Prometheus*, the *IEEE Technology and Society Magazine*, and *Intelligence and National Security* for publishing special issues and special sections on our work.

To our interviewees for their generosity to willingly participate in this complex project. You placed your trust in us, embraced us, and took time out of your busy lives to contribute to this study. On some occasions we know it was not easy for you to elaborate on issues that were close to your hearts, but you were guided with the knowledge that it would help others better understand the context of the challenges which we are facing today and those which we will have to face well into the future. We present your names in the order our interview transcripts appear: Mrs. Judith Nachum, Professor Alan Brimicombe, Professor Christofer Toumazou, Professor Ian Angell, Professor Kevin Warwick, Mr. Amal Graafstra and Mr. Kenneth Lea.

Many thanks also to all the organizations and persons who granted us permission to use photographs and images from their archives. You are listed here in alphabetical order: AirData Pty Ltd. a Motorola Premier Business Partner, Argus Solutions Limited, Cochlear Limited, MapInfo Australia, McGraw-Hill, Mr. Adam Trevarthen, Mr. Amal Graafstra, Mr. Gary Elfring, Mr. Dane Hamilton, Mr. Jason Paul Sargent, NXP Semiconductors, Professor Kevin Warwick, Professor Steven Mann, Toumaz Technology

Limited, U.S. Army, United States Holocaust Memorial Museum (USHMM), Wherify Wireless Location Services and Xybernaut Corporation. Of course the context within which these images are reproduced is not meant to suggest that the providers are not engaged with a socially-aware innovation process.

We thank also those research assistants who helped us prepare the manuscript in one way or another. Mr. Ramin Mostaghimi who labored for weeks on transferring citations into EndNote, Miss Sarah Jane Fusco, Miss Stephanie Lee Fusco, Mr. Rodney Ip, and Mr. Hussein Abbas for transcribing sections of interviews, and for Associate Professor Greg Rose for double-checking the transcription of Mrs. Judith Nachum's interview to ensure place names and other sensitive details were correct.

Needless to say we are grateful to our publishers IGI Global for the belief and trust they placed in both our work and in our ability to deliver. A well deserved thanks and a bouquet of flowers to our primary contact, Development Editor, Ms Julia Mosemann, for reinforcing to us why this book had to come out -now-, and especially for never giving up hope that the manuscript would finally arrive after so many near misses! Thank you also to Associate Professor Elaine Lawrence for her generous and insightful remarks in the preface. You were one of the first to link the concept of uberveillance to your own vital research in eHealth. Your conviction in the importance of this book meant a whole lot to the both of us.

Four people who remained with us from beginning to end were our parents. We acknowledge the enormous support of George and Helen Michael, and George and Vasiliki Vlahos. They have been completely selfless of their giving in whatever capacity they might have been called upon. We could *not* have done this without you. Thank you also to Katina's siblings Christine, Athanasius, Dianne, and to members of our extended families for expressing their support in numerous ways and for their genuine interest in our work. But we also extend our embrace to a very special group of friends (they do *know* who they are), and whom Michael has often referred to as 'ministering angels'. Your succor, steadfastness, and prayers are a precious balm and a treasure beyond price. From this list of names honorable mention must go to Michael's PhD supervisor Professor Pauline Allen, Director of the Centre for Early Christian Studies of the Australian Catholic University, who represents all that is best in an educated and spiritual soul, and to an exceptional and highly literate man who has played a distinct part in each of our lives, Dr Nicholas Kyriacos. When we ponder on the mystery of true friendship it is difficult to go past the Proverbs, "A friend loves at all times..." (Prov 17:17).

Oh yes, the best of cheers and lots of hugs to the Big Cherubs- Annie, Kellie, Pat, Shaz, Maria, Chris, Sharlene, and Nicole! And, of course, last but certainly not least, thank you to our two greatest fans, our little children, George Gabriel Michael and Eleni Keziah Michael. We love you more than you will ever know and say sorry for those times when either one of us had to be away. You inspire us, strengthen us, and help us to make better sense of why we are here.

Our debt to all of the above-mentioned is continuing and enormous.

Katina Michael & M.G. Michael
University of Wollongong, Australia

Please Note:
Any photo that is not attributed to any organisation or individual has been taken by Katina Michael.

Section I
Background and Context

Chapter I
Introduction

AUTO-ID TECHNOLOGIES

This study is concerned with the automatic identification (auto-ID) industry which first came to prominence in the early 1970s. Auto-ID belongs to that larger sector known as information technology (IT). As opposed to manual identification, auto-ID is the act of identifying a living or nonliving thing without direct human intervention. Of course, the process of auto-ID data capture and collection requires some degree of human intervention, but the very act of authenticating or verifying an entity can now be done automatically. An entity can possess a unique code indicating personal identification or a group code indicating conformity to a common set of characteristics. Some of the most prominent examples of auto-ID techniques that will be explored in this book include bar code, magnetic-stripe, integrated circuit (IC), biometric and radio-frequency identification (RFID). The devices in which these techniques are packaged include a variety of form factors such as labels and tags, card technologies, human feature recognition, and implants. Generally the devices are small in size, not larger than that of a standard credit card. There has been a visible trend towards miniaturization through the development of mini-cards and tiny RFID tags (some even as minute as pinheads).

Auto-ID Applications

Traditionally auto-ID has been synonymous with bar code labels on supermarket store items, financial transaction cards (FTCs) used to withdraw money from automatic teller machines (ATMs), and subscriber identity module (SIM) cards in mobile phones. Today auto-ID devices are being applied in very different ways to what they were originally intended. For instance, frequent air travelers can bypass immigration queues using their biometric trait, prisoners can serve their sentences from home by wearing electronic tags and animals can be identified by implanted transponders. While the nature of auto-ID is one that is innately compatible to mass market diffusion, it does also accommodate well for niche applications where for instance security is paramount and access is limited to only a few authorized persons. Auto-ID has also become an integral part of electronic commerce (EC) applications, particularly those related to e-government. Increasingly we are seeing bar code scanners and RFID readers integrated onto mobile devices.

The Significance of Auto-ID

Prior to the 1970s who could have envisaged that every packaged item sold on a supermarket shelf would be equipped with a bar code label. And that by the early 1990s the majority of the population in more developed countries (MDCs) would be carrying a magnetic-stripe or smart card to conduct financial transactions, without having to visit a bank branch. And furthermore, by the turn of the twenty-first century that it would be enforceable by law to implant domesticated animals with a microchip. These examples not only indicate the pervasiveness of auto-ID but also how reliant the world has become upon the technology, including public and private enterprise. The impact of auto-ID is irreversible, an essential part of life. It is interwoven in a highly structured manner with the way we live and work and is a seamless part of our day-to-day routine activities. The technology is so widespread and diffused that it seems to possess an almost omnipresent quality.

Auto-ID Innovation

Auto-ID technologies are complex artifacts. In their natural state they are simply inventions seeking an economically significant purpose. Only when the devices are applied to a given context as part of an information system (IS), and they achieve a desired result, can they be considered product innovations. For example, a plastic card with a magnetic-stripe is quite useless unless it grants the cardholder the ability to make an EFTPOS (electronic funds transfer point-of-sale) transaction at a restaurant to pay for a meal. Furthermore, one need only consider just how complex an auto-ID system is: first cards need to be produced by a manufacturer based on a common set of standards; second the cards need to be acquired by a financial institution and set up with the appropriate parameters; third an end-user with that financial institution must adopt the card and be inclined to make an EFTPOS transaction; and fourth the merchant must accept EFTPOS payments and have predefined agreements with the appropriate financial institutions to enact a valid transaction. The auto-ID innovation process requires that there be dynamic interaction among numerous stakeholders including technology providers, service providers and customers. All too often studies will only focus on the first of these, neglecting to understand that the other stakeholders are equally important to the innovation process. It is the premise of this book that the citizen perspective not be ignored; citizens must be active participants in the design of systems related to e-government (Kumar & Vragov, 2009).

LOCATION-BASED SERVICE

Location-Based Services (LBS) is a branch of m-Commerce that has revolutionized the way people communicate with others or gather timely information based on a given geographic location. Everything living and nonliving has a location on the earth's surface, a longitude and latitude coordinate that can be used to provide a subscriber with a wide range of value added services (VAS). Subscribers can use their mobile phone, personal digital assistant (PDA) or laptop to find information relating to their current location. Commercial applications that utilize positioning technologies are diverse and range from child monitoring devices used to ensure safety to care-related devices for Alzheimer's sufferers who may lose their way. Typical LBS consumer applications include roadside assistance, who is nearest, where is, and personal navigation. Humans are not the only living recipients of positioning technologies; animals too are now implanted or tagged to prevent the extinction of species, to encourage better agricultural practices and even to track food down the chain to the point of consumption. Objects are also being equipped with GPS receivers and RFID tags. It is now possible to get directions from in-car GIS applications, objects on-the-move, and from stolen vehicles being tracked. LBS business applications differ in their focus and many are linked to core business challenges such as optimizing supply chain management (SCM) and enhancing customer relationship management (CRM). There exist niche LBS companies that specialize in offering fleet management services incorporating vehicle navigation and property asset tracking via air, ship and road.

Positioning Technologies

Positioning technologies differ in their capacity to locate. Some technologies work well outdoors while others are tailor-made for the in-building environment. Independent of the positioning technology application, location information is being sought to allow the furthering of processes such as the ostensibly simple "am I on the right track" or "where am I" queries. In some instances the value returned to the end-user is a latitude and longitude coordinate, in other instances it is the nearest base transmission station (BTS), nearest building or a specific location within an area. Spatial data plays an important role in visualizing location information, whether this is in hardcopy or on digital maps. Knowing where things are, where one has been, and where one is going can be vital. Defense has long realized this potential and was preoccupied with positioning techniques even before digital technologies became available. Mobile handsets can even be tracked, either by the use of an in-house GPS chipset receiver or by the current zonal information acquired by nearby base transmission stations. Initially, the general method of network triangulation could only identify a mobile device as being inside a particular BTS coverage area, however, over time, algorithms became increasingly sophisticated and could denote whether the phone was right next to a BTS or over 30 kilometers away.

The emergency services sector in the United States (US) was responsible for driving the first pin-point location service, demonstrating to the world the potentially life-saving functionality of the technology. In 2003 the Federal Trade Commission (FTC) in the U.S. asked that wireless operators provide Automatic Location Identification (ALI) for persons making emergency services calls. The resultant Public Service Answering Point (PSAP) now allows wireless operators to accurately identify the location of an individual to between 50-150 meters (Gabber & Wool, 1998, p. 145). ALI standards designate that more than two-thirds of emergency calls received require the location of the individual to be accurate to within 50 meters, and 95 per cent of calls to within 150 meters. The technology is available for potential mass market deployment, how feasible it is however is a separate issue altogether.

By 2010, Nokia has estimated that fifty per cent of all its mobile phones will contain GPS chipset receivers which will be able to locate individuals to 15 meters on average (Choney, 2008). In some place in Europe and Asia, penetration of GPS chipsets in mobile phones is much higher, at around eighty percent. And in some countries like Japan, RFID readers have been integrated into mobile phones with astonishing user adoption levels over 50 million people in a just a little more than two years (Das, 2008, p. 11). LBS have been a catalyst towards the integration and convergence of various technologies including automatic identification techniques, wireless telecommunications, sensor networks, location positioning technologies and spatial content. The next generation of advanced location-based services (A-LBS) will be those linked to social networking applications, such as Google Latitude (Labrador, Michael & Kuepper, 2008).

Auto-ID + LBS = ALI (Automatic Location Identification)

Most books and papers published on the topic of auto-ID are either wholly focused on presenting technical aspects of a particular device or architecture or show how it is being applied commercially. Experts continue to publish new material on niche topics related to auto-ID but few offer a holistic approach to understanding the industry. Contributions are primarily aimed at making the wider community, including potential customers of auto-ID, aware of what technology options are available to them. The vast majority of refereed publications focus on only one technology. However, more recently a few contributions have appeared making reference to multiple auto-ID technologies. For instance, in 2003, the development that received most attention surrounded the storage of a biometric pattern onto a bar code or smart card. And today, the integration of GPS chipsets with RFID readers is in an early concept stage. This indicates that auto-ID and LBS organizations, specializing in a given technique, are at least beginning to consider themselves as members of a larger value chain system, that being the auto-ID industry. In 2003, the notion of an auto-ID technology system (TS) within which organizations and institutions could innovate together dynamically was lacking. Today, we are witnessing the emergence of such a system, and a willingness of various stakeholders to at least be on speaking terms. No doubt the vital question of the *interoperability* of their respective systems has been a prime motivator.

At the same time one might be led to consider whether or not a location-based services technology system exists. LBS are complex; the value chain for LBS is even more meshed and detailed than that of auto-ID. So why explore both these technologies in the one research project? What do auto-ID and LBS actually have in common? How are they complementary to one another? How may they be exploited together to provide powerful functionality for advanced services? What do they tell us together, that they do not reveal if used in a stand-alone fashion? Fundamentally automatic identification, *identifies* a living or nonliving thing, while location based services can provide a physical *position* of a living or nonliving thing. Consider a large group of employees who are all located in the confines of a single multi-story building. Their approximate position may be very similar in terms of coordinates, but their personal identification is unique. On the other hand I may have personal information designating that a particular individual made a given transaction but without location services I do not know categorically where that transaction actually took place. Auto-ID together with LBS is powerful because it can tell us more about a given situation or context, i.e. we have a more complete picture than if the technologies were used on their own. Few works to date (which include those that have been written by the authors of this book) actually address the use of auto-ID techniques and location-based services in the same space.

LANDMARK STUDIES ON AUTO-ID AND INNOVATION

Until 2003, only one author had written an extensive work directly on the topic of innovation as related to one auto-ID technology, i.e. smart cards. Robyn A. Lindley used socio-technical theory and a case study method to come out with her overall conclusions in her book *Smart Card Innovation* (1997). It was an exploratory study that thoroughly examined the interaction between smart card users, the technology and the organization. Lindley was not the only researcher who believed that there was a growing need to develop our understanding of new and complex technologies within the scope of the field of innovation. However, she was the first to put forward a concise volume on innovation and any type of auto-ID technology. This investigation takes the next step forward in exploring that cluster of innovations known as auto-ID.

The need for this study has been steadily increasing over the last decade as many researchers have begun to not only compare one auto-ID technology to another, but to consider new combinations of existing innovations. This can be seen within the context of magnetic stripe cards and smart cards. Lindley (1997, p. 18) writes: *"There is also now little doubt among leaders in the banking industry that smart card will take over from magnetic-stripe card technology because of its ability to reduce fraud. The main advantage of smart card compared to other technologies is that it does provide a large range of design and service options with a high degree of security which is required when monetary or secret information exchanges are to occur. The old card technologies are rapidly being made obsolescent as the rate and level of sophistication of fraudulent use are rapidly approaching unacceptable levels. It is therefore now seen by many as only a matter of when, and how the services will be differentiated."*

Thus, examining auto-ID innovations is beneficial in understanding the industry trends. Hewkin (1989) and Swartz (1999) realized this need earlier than most and were compelled to write about it. Hewkin saw the industry-wide need for an understanding of the auto-ID innovation process but presented scattered thoughts and did not follow up with other complimentary publications in the field. He also used a neo-classical model of interpretation based on the price mechanism. He did however allude to the future evolution of new auto-ID technologies. Swartz in particular provided some helpful concise insights (1999, p. 21). *"Today, many of us see Auto ID technologies as "complementary," with each filling a space in the market defined by the fit between its strengths and weaknesses, and the requirements of target applications. And looking forward, I believe we'll evolve from a "coexistence" model to one that leverages the many converging opportunities around the intersections and in the gaps between those technologies."*

Understanding Convergence

Four works that should be consulted regarding the notion of "convergence" in technology studies include: 'A definition of convergence in the area of information and telecommunication technologies' (Radinger & Goeschka, 2002), *Digital Convergence* (Covell, 2000, ch. 7), *Competing in the Age of Digital Convergence* (Yoffie, 1997, ch. 5), *Convergence: Integrating media, information and communication* (Baldwin et al., 1996, ch. 5). The term "convergence" means different things to different people and can be used at different levels. In some instances, the term has been used too loosely in high-tech with reference to digital or technological convergence, e.g. the "combination of computing, communications, and digital media technologies" (Covell, 2000, p.161). It is not that Covell's definition is wrong but it is perhaps somewhat too all-encompassing for this study of auto-ID innovation. Convergence in the context of this study is not anything and everything coming together. Radinger and Goeschka (2002, p. 88) define convergence for the area of technology as "...the multidisciplinary integration of inhomogeneous methods, systems, views, knowledge areas and other disciplines of technology with the aim to reach an added value."

A more sophisticated definition for convergence is that given by Greenstein and Khanna (1997, pp. 203-205). They suggest there are two kinds, convergence in substitutes and convergence in complements. *"Two products converge in substitutes when users consider either product interchangeable with the other. Convergence in substitutes occurs when different firms develop products with features that become increasingly similar to the features of certain other products... Two products converge in complements when the products work better together than separately or when they work better together now than they worked together formerly. Convergence in complements occurs when different firms develop products or subsystems within a standard bundle that can increasingly work together to form a larger system... [D]epending on the level at which a computing system or communications system is analyzed, a particular instance of convergence may be construed as being of either kind. It may be interpreted as a convergence in substitutes at one level of analysis and, equally appropriately, as a convergence in complements at a different level."*

The Emergence of the Auto-ID Paradigm

It is surprising to note that from the thousands of articles reviewed for this research project, that until 2003, the term automatic identification had appeared in the titles of only a limited number of publications including: Moran (n.d.), Berge (1987), K. R. Sharp (1987), Schwind (1987), Gold (1988), Hewkin (1989), I. G. Smith (1990), Adams (1990), J. Cohen (1994), LaMoreaux (1998), O'Gorman and Pavlidis (1999), and Swartz (1999). And it should be noted that most of these works were republished in 1990 collectively in a book edited by Ron Ames titled, *Perspectives on Radio Frequency Identification: what is it, where is it going, should I be involved?* This does not mean that the term *automatic identification* is not popular for it is continually used in the main body of papers, irrespective of the type of technique being discussed. Rather what it may indicate is that the term auto-ID carries a loaded meaning when it is used in a paradigmatic fashion. Perhaps as a concept that has industry-wide applicability, admitting to the reality that numerous auto-ID solutions are co-existing and that there are common experiences that can be shared between stakeholders in the innovation process.

Four works must be especially highlighted here in support of the emerging auto-ID paradigm described previously. While these works point to the emergence of an auto-ID paradigm, it is not to be assumed that this was the conscious intent of each of the authors. The first is *Automatic Identification and Data Collection Systems*, by Jonathan Cohen (1994). Its contribution to the field is its attempt to give a thorough industry-wide perspective, though it falls short of its aim in terms of its unbalanced focus on bar code technology. It also does not compare auto-ID technologies and dedicates little space in the form of predictions about the future of the industry. The second work is by Hewkin (1989), 'Future Automatic Identification Technologies'; and the third by Swartz (1999), 'The Growing "MAGIC" of Automatic Identification'. These works are both short articles centered on the need to understand auto-ID innovation.

One will note a ten year interval between these publications. Neither goes into great depth but both offer insights worthy of research efforts yet to be entirely realized. There is an apparent need for research in auto-ID innovation and the characterization and prediction of the auto-ID industry. It is in response to this pressing need that this book is making one its principal contributions to knowledge. Hewkin understood the auto-ID market well and emphasized the need for industry-wide communication flows between the different auto-ID players, independent of their major auto-ID product focus. Swartz, on the other hand, who had been able to witness the changes in the industry over the decade between 1989 and 1999), analysed the most prominent auto-ID technologies and offered a brief but useful description of the emerging auto-ID paradigm. His insights are very important in that they assist and garner support for some of the findings of this investigation. Finally, I.G. Smith (1990, pp. 49, 52) presents the AIM (automatic identification manufacturers) activity group in a brief article, stipulating that their focus is broader than just bar code, "[s]o the automatic identification industry has an almost unique global communication network... The members of AIM collectively cover all the established technologies as well as most of the emerging ones". What is apparent is that AIM is promoting the idea of one auto-ID industry sharing in common resources. This is further reflected on their web site which is all inclusive of auto-ID technologies (Beauchamp, 2007).

The Gap in the Literature

At the macro level there is a requirement for a well-researched, up-to-date work that traces the evolution of the auto-ID industry; a summation of the last forty years of change. This book offers an intricately interwoven discussion on the history, background, development and likely future directions of auto-ID. Currently researchers are normally offering fragmented perspectives on the auto-ID selection environment by focusing on a given technology and mostly neglecting the rest or at best mentioning them in passing. At the micro level the key issues that have affected auto-ID innovation and its ancillary extensions need to be explored. Demystifying the complex auto-ID innovation process is important as well and has not been adequately explored. Another gap in the literature is predicting the trajectory of auto-ID. This is perhaps where the least work has been done in the field. The outcomes of a study such as this current one have far-reaching implications, both to practitioners and end-users, of a technical and social nature. For example, how does one understand competition in the auto-ID industry? Are new electronic commerce application requirements driving the path of auto-ID? How will auto-ID technology be used in the future? What are some of the long-term impacts of the widespread introduction of auto-ID devices? And how are new technologies such as location positioning systems going to affect auto-ID?

The Auto-ID Trajectory

One of the fundamental questions this study seeks to answer is what is the *auto-ID trajectory*? The question requires an interdisciplinary approach and is intended to allow for the characterization of devices from their inception into the market to the present day, in a hope to predict future trends in the industry. In other words, what is the destiny of auto-ID and just how intertwined will it become to applications that everyone relies on? How far can the human-computer metaphor be taken, now that the prospects of chip implants for auto-ID have been confirmed? And what risks or benefits may this pose to humans and the general economy? How much further can engineers develop individual auto-ID technologies and how will these advancements be affected by other breakthroughs in the IT sector, such as location-based services? The nature of these questions implies a holistic methodology to understanding the auto-ID technology system- a novel approach seeking to discover new facts. Location-based services are integral to the trajectory of auto-ID as we will later discover.

The other purpose of this study is to establish the auto-ID paradigm. It is to convey to stakeholders that the dynamics within the technology system (TS) are paramount to the success of individual auto-ID devices. It is also important to determine how one auto-ID device should be considered within the wider auto-ID selection environment. In addition, forecasting the auto-ID trajectory is not only meant to assist technology and service providers but also to prepare end-users for potential change. The book is designed to also bring to the fore thought-provoking and challenging philosophical questions that are often neglected at the expense of other topics centered almost exclusively on technical breakthroughs. How will the auto-ID trajectory affect our everyday lives? What could the impacts be on our culture, society, and even on our metaphysics? How can the impact of the trajectory be tempered and safeguards established to ensure their use as opposed to their potential misuse? What are we to make of all this technological development in the context of our intellectual development? Today most high-tech complex technology innovation is perceived as 'useful', 'progressive', 'awe-inspiring', a step toward a better future. This book challenges the notion that *all* developments are necessarily useful (Mills, 1997). The authors are mindful that some technologies can be used toward both positive and negative ends, ethical and unethical means, for productive and counter-productive objectives. Technology is not so neutral as we might have been led to believe. There is a strong socio-ethical component running throughout the whole study in an attempt to harmonize opposing forces. For foundation principles on ethics in information technology and social informatics see: Tavani, 2007; Quinn, 2006; Morris & Zuluaga, 2006; Reynolds, 2006; Edgar, 2003; Hester & Ford, 2001; Ermann, Williams, & Shauf, 1997; Kling, 1996.

THE SYSTEMS OF INNOVATION CONCEPTUAL FRAMEWORK

Traditionally studies in innovation have followed one of two theories, the neo-classical or the more recent evolutionary. Compare for instance the works of Schumpeter (1934) with those of Nelson and Winter (1982). Neo-classical economic theory focuses on the production function as the major indicator of product/process innovation. On the other hand, the evolutionary theory of innovation is characterized by the concepts of reproduction, variety and selection (Andersen, 1997, p. 175). It is considered by many that the former theory has depreciated as a tool for investigating modern product and process innovations. Among its primary limitations is that technological change is treated as an exogenous factor (Edquist, 1997, p. 16). The more recent evolutionary theory of innovation has become increasingly accepted in that it is an interdisciplinary approach with the ability to bring within a "...single framework the institutional/organizational as well as cognitive/cultural aspects of social and economic change" (Carlsson, 1995, p. 23). It is this conceptual framework which will be used to set the system bounds of this present research.

Founded on the principles of evolutionary theory, is the systems of innovation (SI) approach. SI is a conceptual framework rather than an established theory in which most innovation investigations that have taken place in the 1990s have followed empirically. Researchers in Europe, Asia and North America have used this approach to study technology, especially advanced technologies. Since the early 1990s, national, regional, sectoral and technological systems investigations in innovation have shifted from a product-focused view, to a view that incorporates the whole process of innovation including the institution, organization and market orientation. It is in this light that the research will be conducted, deviating from the norm only on the condition that a micro-level investigation focusing on the auto-ID industry will be conducted. While other schools of thought are presently emerging, particularly in the field of information technology methodologies and socio-technical theory, none offer such a complete interdisciplinary understanding of technological change. *"The systems of innovation approach also allows for the inclusion not only of economic factors influencing innovation but also of institutional, organizational, social and political factors"* (Edquist, 1997, p. 17). This will allow for the investigation of previously neglected material important to understanding auto-ID innovation.

The available SI literature helps the researcher to seek out specific references and sources that are relevant to the dimensions of innovation, for instance, what is meant by the factor "organizational" as opposed to "institutional" and "economic". For example, the key words searched for three of the most important SI dimensions considered in the investigation included:

- "**Organizational:** Public organizations, policy, political bodies, regulatory agencies, organizations for higher education, technology support entities (e.g. training), patent offices, standards setting organizations, consulting agencies, knowledge production, universities, organizations with formal structures, explicit purpose, players or actors, other firms
- **Institutional:** Norms, habits, practices, routines, laws, interaction, often no specific purpose, form spontaneously, relations between groups, research and development links, consumer reactions, conflicts and cooperation, reduction in uncertainty, technical standards, rules of the game, framework conditions
- **Economic:** Infrastructure, physical infrastructure, knowledge infrastructure, standards, formal knowledge, tacit knowledge, explicit knowledge, research councils, standard setting organizations, libraries, databases, skilled/technical personnel, routine, industry associations, conferences, training centers, trade publications, research laboratories, public agencies."

Throughout chapters five to nine entire sections are dedicated to discussing SI dimensions. Headings such as "Committees, Subcommittees and Councils", "Public Policy", "Clusters of Knowledge and a Growing Infrastructure", "Setting Standards", "A Patchwork of Statutes" and so forth, can be found to reflect direct SI concepts. In concluding chapters, key terms from evolutionary theory are used to discuss patterns and trends in the auto-ID industry.

Qualitative research expert John Creswell (1998, p. 15) emphasizes the requirement for exploratory research to possess this "holistic picture". He believes this whole view "...takes the reader into the multiple dimensions of a problem or issue and displays it in all of its complexity" (Creswell, 1998, p. 15). In fact, what attracts researchers to SI is that it is indeed a "holistic and interdisciplinary" approach which "encompasses all or most determinants of innovation" (Edquist, 1998a, p. 20). Creswell (1998, p. 13) himself believes that it is the application of appropriate frameworks that "hold qualitative research together". He uses the following metaphor to convey the importance of frameworks: *"I think metaphorically of qualitative research as an intricate fabric composed of minute threads, many colors, different textures, and various blends of material. The fabric is not explained easily or simply. Like the loom on which the fabric is woven, general frameworks hold qualitative research together."*

METHODOLOGY

Case Studies and Usability Context Analyses

Due to the exploratory nature of this research, the most appropriate methodology to use is that of multiple embedded case studies. The five auto-ID technology case studies form the main unit of analysis: bar codes, magnetic stripe cards, smart cards, biometrics, radio-frequency identification (RFID) tags and transponders. The order in which the cases are presented is chronological in terms of the way one technology has impacted on the innovation and diffusion of subsequent technologies. This historical perspective helped to draw out the pattern of technical change that occurred in auto-ID since its commercial introduction. Chapter three especially is dedicated to tracing the historical perspective of identification, from manual to automatic. In fact, the whole study has a historical element attached to it.

Similarly, in the research conducted by Edquist et al. (1998, p. 17) "...case studies within the sub-project employed a historical approach, and many covered processes of technological development spanning several decades."

Industry dynamics happen over time, thus history is very important. Coincidentally, the chronological manner in which the devices have been presented has also corresponded to a growing level of technological invasiveness. From bar codes attached to non-living things; to magnetic-stripe cards and smart cards carried by humans; to the biometrics of humans; to RFID tags and transponders implanted in animals and people. The researchers describe this development as the "human evolution". The term is derived from numerous sources. However two phrases 'Human Metaphor' and 'New Age Systems' from Tren (1995) have influenced the researchers the most. Auto-ID was initially developed to identify packaged goods at the checkout counter, now it is being used increasingly to monitor and track animals and humans.

The sub-unit of analysis is the usability context which can be considered a context within which a given technology can be applied. For each of the technologies, space is dedicated to two main usability contexts. For example, in the chapter 7 on smart card innovation, the telecommunications usability context is studied as is health care. It is well-known in the auto-ID industry that these contexts as applied to smart card have led to widespread diffusion of the technology. Traditionally, retail also has been synonymous with bar code technology and financial services with magnetic-stripe card technology. As there were five auto-ID technologies chosen for the research, a maximum of ten electronic commerce (EC) applications were potentially feasible within the scope of this study. The ten applications cover a wide variety of vertical sectors specifically to address the growing pervasiveness of auto-ID technology. Within each application area (e.g. telecommunications) there can be literally thousands of product innovations, e.g., pre-paid telephone cards, subscriber identity module (SIM) cards, virtual private network (VPN) cards, cable television (CATV) cards. Several innovations are documented within each sub-unit. The number of different product innovations discussed varies dependent on the available literature and space constraints. It should also be pointed out that the innovation system studied is 'supranational' (i.e. global), concentrating on the technological system rather than the geographical dimension. Location-based services and respective applications, while not strictly automatic identification innovations, were added to the study after the bulk of the research was completed in 2003.

Data Collection and Data Analysis

This study adopts a qualitative research strategy (Flick, 2002) that uses some elements of descriptive research to enhance the central usability context analyses. These analyses are similar to case studies as they investigate "a contemporary phenomenon within its real life context when the boundaries between phenomenon and context are not clearly evident" (Yin, 1998, p. 123). They also similarly use multiple sources of evidence, however are differentiated on the basis of the unit of analysis. In a usability context analysis methodology, units are not individuals, groups or organizations but are applications or application areas for a product, where 'product' is defined as "any interactive system or device designed to support the performance of users' tasks" (Thomas & Bevan, 1996). The results of multiple analyses are more convincing than a singular study, and the broad themes identified cover the major fields of current auto-ID development. Further, the usability context analyses in this study are supplemented by a discussion of surrounding social, legal and ethical ambiguities. By this means, the addition of a narrative analysis to the methodology ensures a thorough investigation of usage and context (Masters & Michael, 2007).

Documentation

Traditionally books in the field of auto-ID contain a brief historical introduction about one or more technologies and give examples of applications without going into too much depth. Auto-ID books show static representations of technologies at a given point in time, however, they are useful in that they make the researcher aware of the incremental changes that have occurred over the years. They also familiarize the researcher with the more important auto-ID definitions and concepts and raise some very important issues. General computing or engineering journal articles and reports have much the same function as books but with the advantage that they are more frequent and up-to-date pieces of research. Auto-ID industry articles are also able to focus on aspects of the technology and are usually written by experts who have had professional experience in the field. There were also the specific auto-ID journals and magazines which provided industry insights which could not be found elsewhere. These were excellent and reliable sources of evidence that included relevant industry contact names and telephone numbers for further investigation.

Conference proceedings are also particularly useful in a study such as this that is exploratory and requires empirical evidence to justify its findings. A researcher can expect to find in conference proceedings, information about the newest auto-ID innovations. Leading edge case studies and surveys are usually compiled by consultants who are at the forefront of the industry and have had real-life experiences implementing auto-ID solutions. Press releases are also crucial- though brief they are a good way of tracking developments in specific product innovations throughout the year. One criticism of press releases is that they are sometimes written by product marketers or communications employees who have the interests of the corporation at heart. Nevertheless they do indicate changes that are occurring in auto-ID.

Newspaper articles about auto-ID are usually not technical in nature and are often written by journalists who do not have experience in the field. However, they do act to raise issues that are not dealt with in mainstream journals and magazines. They have predominantly reported on the social implications of the technology with a view to capturing the interests and imaginations of readers. However, while one must be careful to separate sensational material from scientific fact, it does not mean that popular material cannot be used in an investigation such as this. Often these articles are surprisingly up-to-date and offer different perspectives than would otherwise be found in scientific journals. The popular media- newspapers, radio, television- have long been used as an open forum to gauge political and social responses to technological developments before they are actually introduced. A classic example of this is the Australia Card debate of 1987. All forms of media were heavily involved in the debate; from front page headlines, to letters to the editor, to polls taken during current affairs shows, to talk-back radio comments. See Smith (1989) who gave a first-hand account of the Australia Card and the story of its defeat, especially chapter 8 titled '[t]he day of the media' and chapter 9 titled '[t]he role of the press'. In the latter, Smith (p. 150) writes: *"[i]f one accepts the Australia Card as a matter of great importance, the bringing about of its demise... must rank as foremost in the achievements of ordinary people. And the events of September would not have occurred but for the part played by the media, and in particular the press... in my opinion the role of the press was paramount... The newspapers responded to the groundswell of public opinion."*

Archival Records

The archival records used in this study are in the form of electronic information sources, publicly available on the Internet. Web site information is a newfound source of evidence that many researchers have simply ignored in the past. At each web site it is commonplace to find a myriad of press releases dating back to the mid-90s, a historical overview of the technology, product-specific technical information, case studies of the latest applications, as well as customer testimonials. The information in these web sites has been largely sidelined by researchers in the field but should be given attention based on their individual merit. It is here that many references were gathered with respect to the auto-ID trajectory. In this study auto-ID web sites have been chosen, after being identified in the documentation collected or by querying a variety of search engines. These web sites include: auto-ID companies such as manufacturers, value-added resellers (VARs) and system integrators; customers such as private organizations; auto-ID research centers such as universities; service providers; and auto-ID-related associations. By visiting web sites, further electronic links to other sites containing valuable information were also found.

Company web sites are very informative containing a huge amount of information that cannot be found elsewhere. Private companies, organizations, even government agencies are now placing internal articles, product technical specifications, marketing brochures, whitepapers, press releases and other auto-ID information on the Internet for wider readership and greater accessibility to employees and customers. It is estimated that around 2500 web sites were visited by the researchers over a period of 5 years between 1998 and 2003. At least 200 of these web sites were exclusive auto-ID technology providers. In the field of technological innovation especially, the Internet is an invaluable data gathering tool. Patent databases can be searched, government policies reviewed, standards bodies referenced and academic research laboratories consulted for future directions, among many other capabilities. Wherever applicable the content analysis tool *Leximancer* was used in analyzing large volumes of data in digital format.

e-Research

The researchers used a variety of means to identify relevant Internet sites. Initially generic searches were conducted based on the key words defined by major categories, such as "bar code", "magnetic-stripe card" etc. A variety of popular search engines were used, such as *Yahoo!* and *Google*. The hits returned were then examined for relevance and accuracy. The researchers periodically performed these searches and downloaded files in text format, HTML but largely targeted Microsoft Word and Powerpoint and PDF formats, storing them in digital folders with meaningful names. With each periodic search performed, categories were refined and new subcategories defined. The key words used to search became more targeted and granular with each iteration and instead of thousands of web links being returned, a few hundred would result (Michael, Fusco & Michael, 2008, p. 1192).

The guidelines for which web pages were included in the data collection were not inflexible however there were several overriding controls the researchers used. First, there had to be an author of the web page or site, whether this was an individual, group or company. Second, the content of the web page had to be accurate. Accuracy was established by cross-referencing similar web pages or documentation on the exact same topic(s). Third, a date on the material viewed also added weight to what was being conveyed as well as a date for the period the web site was last updated (Yule & Hewson, 2003, pp. 11f). As much as was possible the researchers attempted to verify the authority of documents where content or sourcing was potentially dubious.

Apart from the exhaustive searches that were performed on the major categories, auto-ID company marketing lists were publicly obtained from magazines such as the *Automatic ID News* and individual company web sites searched and further recommended links on these sites followed through. It soon becomes apparent to the researchers which sites are those considered significant to the industry (e.g. AIM Global), as numerous companies reference the same link on their respective web sites. In addition, the experienced Internet researcher who has spent thousands of hours searching for relevant online material is able to quickly discern between web content that is of value to their investigation and that which should be set aside.

Validating the Outcomes with Interviews

The semi-structured interviews were chosen to validate the outcomes of the secondary data collection completed in 2003. It is important to note that the interviews were conducted by Katina Michael and M.G. Michael almost four years after the initial data collection of documents, archival data, and e-research. They took place between 12 October 2006 and 11 December 2007. In total, seven interviews were conducted to shed light onto the current state of development in the auto-ID industry and emerging location-based services. The interviews could have been used as individual case studies, with the interviewee being the main unit of analysis but in the context of this study, the interviews were used to validate the author's projections of the auto-ID trajectory.

The choice of academic interviewees was based on several factors including: (i) the main field of research of the individual researcher, (ii) the track record of the individual researcher, (iii) and the need for the study to explore interdisciplinary perspectives. Telephone and in-person interviews in Australia, the United Kingdom, and United States were conducted with Professor Allan Brimicombe of the University of East London, Professor Christofer Toumazou of Imperial College, Professor Ian Angell of the London School of Economics and Political Science and Professor Kevin Warwick of the University of Reading. The interviews varied in length from thirty-five minutes to seventy-five minutes.

As the study sought to emphasize the role of citizens in the auto-ID and LBS innovation process, three interviews were also conducted with members of the general public. These interviewees were also handpicked and could be considered key informants in the debate over the social implications of technology. Mrs Judy Nachum, Mr Amal Graafstra and Mr Kenneth Lea, represent three very diverse perspectives: historical, techno-ethical, and life-world. These interviews varied in length, between sixty and one hundred and twenty minutes. Mr Graafstra commented that it was the most comprehensive interview he had ever conducted with any academic or journalist. He wrote in his blog: *"[w]e covered implants, automatic identification, location based services, and biometrics... with a bit of security and privacy issues sprinkled in for flavor. Basically, this phone interview is the current state of my thoughts on these subjects all laid out in conversation. She thanked me for my time, but frankly I was glad to get it all out... maybe now when someone wants to interview me for a magazine or newspaper or something, I can point them to the recording and if they have any more questions to shoot me an email"(Graafstra, 2007).* In comparing the sentiments of the researchers with those of the general public, great synergy can be found, not only regarding the future projections made by the authors on the auto-ID trajectory but on those specific questions we need to critically address at the very least during the course of the next decade..

Each of the interviewees was asked a different set of questions related to their specific field or area of concern, though there were some 'typical' questions that we might be able to trace any common discernment. The level of technical response was commensurate to the background of the interviewee. A brief biography of the interviewee can be found in the section titled: "About the Contributors" before the Index.. Each interview serves a unique role in the study, complementing specific chapters in the book. A key words definition section is also included to help readers with understanding specialist concepts discussed in each interview. Nevertheless every interview is predominantly preoccupied by questions related to the trajectory of auto-ID and LBS technology. Of emphasis in most of the interviews was the question of microchip implants for humans, the ability to locate humans, and the socio-ethical implications of the technology. It was particularly reassuring when Professor Toumazou and Professor Warwick supported the concept of *Electrophorus* put forward to them by the authors.

Professor Allan Brimicombe is the Head of Geo-Information Studies specializing in spatial data analysis, data mining and location-based services. Professor Kevin Warwick is a professor of cybernetics and renowned for his Cyborg 1.0 and Cyborg 2.0 chip implant experiments. Professor Christofer Toumazou is the director of the New Institute of Biomedical Engineering at Imperial College and founder of the company Toumaz specializing in health monitoring devices. Professor Ian Angell, department convener of the Information Systems and Innovation group at LSE, is a well-known expert in the global consequences of information and communication technologies (ICT), specializing in national IT policies. Mrs Judy Nachum is a WWII holocaust survivor. Mr Amal Graafstra is a do-it-yourselfer hobbyist and entrepreneur who has two RFID tag implants, one in each hand. Mr Kenneth Lea is a carer of a sufferer of Alzheimer's disease. The interviews have not been explicitly analyzed; they stand in their original complete transcription form, serving as primary evidence in their own right.

A NOTE ON FORECASTING

Since one of the aim's of this study is to "characterize" as well as to "predict" the path of auto-ID, some space must be given to that body of literature encompassing the prediction of future events. Braun (1995, p. 133) writes that "[f]orecasts do not state what the future will be... they attempt to glean what it might be." In this study to 'predict' means to look at 'past' and 'present' trends and use these for providing a road map of future possibilities. Such a projection can take the form of an extensive technology assessment (TA) or technology forecast. TA as defined by Braun (1995, p. 129) "...is the activity of describing, analyzing and forecasting the likely effects of a technological change on all spheres of society, be it social, economic, environmental or any other." TAs are usually armored with their own methodologies and are conducted over a short period involving a group of experts, government policy officials, and other interested parties from the field. Although the scope of this research did not allow for a genuine TA to be conducted, it did allow for auto-ID technology forecasting. "Here the emphasis is on predicting the development of the technology and assessing its potential for adoption, including an analysis of the technology's market" (Westrum, 1991, p. 328). It was not the intention of the researchers to predict extraordinary things, it was to predict with the use of reliable evidence that was accessible. Kaku (1998, p. 14) advises, "[i]n making predictions about the future, it is crucial to understand the time frame being discussed, for, obviously, different technologies will mature at different times... These are not absolute time frames; they represent only the general period in which certain technologies and sciences will reach fruition".

Auto-ID forecasts may not eventuate but are still more likely to happen than 'predictions in their pure form' and for this reason they are more valuable. Even the founder of *Microsoft*, Bill Gates (1995, p. 274) accepted that his predictions may not come true. But his insights in the *Road Ahead* are to be commended, even though they are broad. "The information highway will lead to many destinations. I've enjoyed speculating about some of these. Doubtless I've made some foolish predictions, but I hope not too many." In the quest to prove or disprove forecasts or predictions, "[s]cientific understanding can lead to practical uses. With the first such application, the quest for further understanding intensifies, leading to even more advanced applications" (Queisser, 1985, pp. viif). Allaby (1996, p. 206) writes "[f] orecasts deal in possibilities, not inevitabilities, and this allows forecasters to explore opportunities." In speculating about the next 500 years Berry (1996, p. 1) writes, "[p]rovided the events being predicted are not physically impossible, then the longer the time scale being considered, the more likely they are to come true... if one waits long enough everything that can happen will happen."

Thus the term "forecaster" rather than such loaded terms as "futurist", "visionary" or "secular prophet" is to be preferred. Someone who predicts, at any rate in the classical sense of the foreknowledge of future events, is being prophetic. In the traditional meaning, The Seer of Patmos, the author of the *Book of Revelation* (*c.* CE 95), can be considered a prophet an a predictor of events, but a modern day forecaster like Nicholas Negroponte, for example, is not being prophetic. It can be said that there are many forecasters and very few prophets. History is proof enough, *vaticinium ex eventu* not withstanding! Forecasters, as it will be seen in the brief review of works to follow, usually use trends or patterns or present-day findings to make projections. Forecasters are more *likely* to make predictions about new innovations rather than new inventions. For the greater part, they raise challenging issues that are thought provoking, about how existing inventions or innovations will impact society. They give scenarios for the technology's projected pervasiveness, how they may affect other technologies, what potential benefits or drawbacks they may introduce, how they will affect the economy, etc. And it is here that a robust framework like the systems of innovation approach can assist a researcher in making predictions, as it looks at the whole system, not just a single fragment.

Michio Kaku (1998, p. 5) argued, "that predictions about the future made by professional scientists tend to be based much more substantially on the realities of scientific knowledge than those made by social critics, or even those by scientists of the past whose predictions were made before the fundamental scientific laws were completely known". He believes that among the scientific body today there is a growing concern regarding predictions that for the greater part come from consumers of technology (writers, sociologists etc.) rather than those who shape and create it. Kaku is of course correct in so far that scientists should be consulted as well, since they are the ones *actually* making things possible after discoveries have occurred. But to these researchers, a balanced view is necessary, encompassing various perspectives of different disciplines is extremely important. In the 1950s for instance, when technical experts forecasted improvements in computer technology they envisaged even larger machines but science fiction writers predicted microminiaturization. They "[p]redicted marvels such as wrist radios and pocket-sized computers, not because they foresaw the invention of the transistor, but because they instinctively felt that some kind of improvement would come along to shrink the bulky computers and radios of that day" (Bova, 1988 quoted in Berry, 1996, p. 18). The methodologies used as vehicles to predict in each discipline should be respected. The question of who is more correct in terms of predicting the future is perhaps the wrong question. For example, some of Kaku's own predictions in *Visions* can be found in science fiction movies dating back to the 1960s.

Prominent Technology Forecasters

Forecasters have diverse backgrounds. The contemporaries include a long list of scientists, engineers, physicists, biologists, mathematicians, entrepreneurs, lawyers, economists, geographers, sociologists, historians, philosophers, religious thinkers, science fiction writers, culture critics, ethicists and others. While all of them cannot be mentioned here, some of the more prominent and representative 'technology-focused' forecasters (i.e. automated machinery, computers, networks, digital media technologies, artificial intelligence, etc.) and their important works include: Ellul (1964), McLuhan (1962; 1964), A. C. Clarke (1968), Toffler (1970; 1981), Minsky (1985), Moravec (1988, 1999), Kelly (1994), Gates (1995), Negroponte (1995), Kaku (1998), Cochrane (1999), Mann (2001), Warwick (2002), Crichton (2006), and Dvorsky (2009). In making predictions these forecasters are required to not only draw on their own expertise, but to also utilize sources outside their own disciplines in order to effect a more complete picture of their projections (and to avoid potentially embarrassing errors)..Of topical relevance here in the bringing together of seemingly disparate fields, is William A. Stahl's (1999) *God and the Chip: Religion and the Culture of Technology*. In providing evidence for the likelihood of their future predictions, forecasters often use the work of other forecasters to support their own positions. These works also track the changes that have occurred over time, setting their findings in the context of larger events in history, and then making predictions. See especially the brilliant timeline compiled and presented by Ray Kurzweil (1999, pp. 261-280) in *The Age of Spiritual Machines* and his further considerations of our destiny in *The Singularity is Near* (2005).

Often forecasters need to use an interdisciplinary approach to successfully bring together related projections. For instance the founding members of the Media Lab were made up *"of a filmmaker, a graphic designer, a composer, a physicist, two mathematicians, and a group of research staff who, among other things, had invented multimedia in preceding years. We came together... [t]he common bond was not a discipline, but a belief that computers would dramatically alter and affect the quality of life through their ubiquity, not just in science, but in every aspect of living"* (Negroponte, 1995, p. 225). Professor Steve Mann (2009) is possibly our greatest living example of this diverse talent- inventor, engineer, developer, philosopher, filmmaker, artist, instrumentalist, author, photographer, actor, and much more. This resonates of Toffler's (1970, p. 463) assertion that the "...world's biggest and most tough-minded corporations... today hire intuitive futurists, science fiction writers and visionaries as consultants. A gigantic European chemical company employs a futurist who combines a scientific background with training as a theologian. An American communications empire engages a future-minded social critic..." Seeing the same problem from different perspectives is crucial, and pondering the future armored with skills in completely different disciplines offers unique insights.

A spate of publications predicting future technical breakthroughs were published prior to the onset of the new millennium. Most of these touched upon topics to do with advancements in computer technology, cybernetics, economic change, cloning, and space exploration. The following works are quite challenging in terms of the predictions they present: Knoke (1996), Paul and Cox (1996), Berry (1996), Stork (1997), Robertson (1998), Cetron and Davies (1998), Gershenfeld (1999), Johnscher (1999), Canton (1999), Rantala and Milgram (1999), Kurzweil (1999, 2005).

From "Electronic Banks" to "Digital Money"

When Jacques Ellul predicted the use of "electronic banks" in his ground-breaking book, *Technological Society* (1964, p. 432), he was not referring to the computerization of financial institutions, ATMs or EC (electronic commerce). Rather it was in the context of the possibility of the dawn of a new entity- "the coupling of man and machine". Ellul (1964, pp. 395, 414, 430) was predicting that one day knowledge would be accumulated in electronic banks and "transmitted directly to the human nervous system by means of coded electronic messages… What is needed will pass directly from the machine to the brain without going through consciousness…" As unbelievable as this "man-machine" complex may have sounded at the time, over forty years later forecasters are still predicting such scenarios will be possible by the turn of the 22nd century. Today, of course they have a better understanding of the issues at hand and write with a clearer road map of how to get there. Kaku (1998, p. 112) observes that: *"[s]cientists are proceeding to explore this possibility with remarkable speed. The first step in attempting to exploit the human brain is to show that individual neurons can grow and thrive on silicon chips. Then the next step would be to connect silicon chips directly to a living neuron inside an animal, such as a worm. One then has to show that human neurons can be connected to a silicon chip. Last… in order to interface directly with the brain, scientists would have to decode millions of neurons which make up our spinal cord"*. The main obstacle at present is the complexity of the brain. *"The brain's wiring is so complex and delicate that a bionic connection with a computer or neural net is something that is, at present, seemingly impossible without causing permanent damage…. Nonetheless, this has not prevented some individuals from making certain conjectures about mind/machine links, which properly belong in the far future"* (Kaku, 1998, p. 115).

One can trace the predictions of these forecasters over time and see that the *predictions* themselves are evolving as new discoveries are made to defend or attack a given forecast (see table 1). In like manner this is precisely how the present writers wish to make predictions about auto-ID; by using existing

Table 1.

1950
Alan Turing… considered …machine intelligence in his 1950 paper, "Computer Machinery and Intelligence". (Negroponte 1995, p. 156)

1953
Pierre de Latil, in his La Pensee artificielle, gives an excellent characterization of some of these machines…"In the machine, the notion of finality makes its appearance, a notion sometimes attributed in living beings to some intelligence inherent in the species, innate to life itself. Finality is artificially built into the machine… Errors are corrected without human analysis, or knowledge without even being suspected. The error itself corrects the error… For the machine, as for animals, error is fruitful; it conditions the correct path". (Ellul 1964, p. 430)

1964
Knowledge will be accumulated in "electronic banks" and transmitted directly to the human nervous system by means of coded electronic messages. (Ellul 1964, p. 432)

McLuhan argued that "physiologically, man in the normal use of technology (or his variously extended body) is perpetually modified by it and in turn finds ever new ways of modifying his technology." Having extended ourselves through "auto-amputation," we become whole again by reintegrating our technologies into our physiologies: the toolmaker becomes one with his tools… "We have to numb our central nervous system when it is extended and exposed," argues McLuhan, "or we will die." (Dery 1996, pp. 117, 165)

1984
The best descriptions of VR actually come from so-called cyberpunk science fiction like that written by William Gibson. Rather than putting on a bodysuit, some of his characters "jack in" by plugging a computer cable directly into their central nervous systems. It will take scientists a while to figure out how this can be done, and when they do, it will be long after the highway is established..It will probably first be used to help people with physical disabilities (Gates 1995, p. 133).

1987
Still others dream of the distant day when cyborgs will walk the earth, the ultimate merger of humans with their electronic creation. Marvin Minsky of MIT even believes that cyborgs may represent the next stage in human evolution! Then we would achieve true immortality, replacing flesh with steel and silicon. (Kaku 1998, p. 94)

1988
In his 1988 book, *Mind Children*, Hans Moravec imagines that a bionic merger of this sort between humans and machines will lead to "immortality" of sorts. He envisions humans in the distant future being able to gradually transfer their consciousness from their bodies to a robot, without ever losing consciousness. Each time a tiny clump of neurons is removed, a surgeon will connect it to a clump of neural nets in a metal hull which duplicates the precise firing of the original clump. Fully conscious, the brain could be gradually replaced, piece by piece, by a mechanical mass of electronic neurons. Upon completion, the robot brain will have all memories and thought patterns of the original person, but will be housed in a mechanical body of silicon and steel which can potentially live forever (Kaku 1998, p. 116).

1991
Alvin Toffler believes that miniaturized computers "will not only be implanted [in our bodies] to compensate for some physical defect but eventually will be implanted to enhance human capability, and computer at some point will become completely blurred." (Dery 1996, p. 231)

[Rosen and Chase claim that] "[t]he possibility of interfacing elements of the peripheral nervous system with a silicon chip has become a reality… (Dery 1996, p. 291)

[According to Stelarc,] "EVOLUTION ENDS WHEN TECHNOLOGY INVADES THE BODY. Once technology provides each person with the potential to progress individually in its [sic] development, the cohesiveness of the species is no longer important." (Dery 1996, p. 161)

1995
It is time to make computers see and hear. (Negroponte 1995, p. 128).

The best metaphor I can conceive of for a human-computer interface is that of a well-trained English butler. The "agent" answers the phone, recognises the callers, disturbs you when appropriate, and may even tell a white lie on your behalf. (Negroponte 1995, p. 150)

Little by little, computers are taking on personalities…This is not as frivolous as it sounds. The persona of a machine makes it fun, relaxing, usable, friendly, and less "mechanical" in spirit…We will see systems with humour, systems that nudge and prod, even ones that are as stern and disciplinarian as a Bavarian nanny. (Negroponte 1995, p. 218)

1998
Logically, a better scheme would be a chip implant. Just a small slice of silicon under the skin is all it would take for us to enjoy the freedom of no cards, passports, or keys… (Cochrane 1998, p. 8)

Beyond 2020
If these difficulties can be overcome, then the period 2020 to 2050 may mark the entrance into the marketplace of an entirely new kind of technology: true robot automatons that have common sense, can understand human language, can recognise and manipulate objects in their environment, and can learn from their mistakes. It is a development that will likely alter our relationship with machines forever. (Kaku 1998, p. 16)

Some scientists feel the ultimate direction of scientific research would be the merger of all three scientific revolutions in the far future. The quantum theory would provide us with microscopic quantum transistors smaller than a neuron. The computer revolution would give us neural networks as powerful as those found in the brain. And the biomolecular revolution would give us the ability to replace the neural networks of our brain with synthetic ones, thereby giving us a form of immortality. (Kaku 1998, p. 116) findings as a 'launch-pad' for building likely future scenarios (Perusco & Michael, 2007). The main point of this example is to demonstrate that some very credible persons have made what many may believe (or used to believe) to be some very incredible predictions about the future. But they can do this with authority because their predictions are supported by work that is being conducted in universities and commercial research laboratories around the world. Berry (1996, p. 5) is quite right when he comments that "[e]vents only seem extraordinary at the time when they are predicted, never after they have happened."

In terms of auto-ID, several forecasters have made predictions about technologies and applications. Gates, Negroponte and Kaku all agree that auto-ID technologies, especially smart cards and biometrics, will have a great impact on society in the next twenty years. Gates places much emphasis on the wallet PC, Negroponte on wearable devices and Kaku on ubiquitous computing (see table 2). Simply by analyzing these three positions one can trace an evolution of ideas. From devices that one carries, to those that one wears, to those that are everywhere. Additionally in terms of auto-ID-related electronic commerce applications, all three forecasters are in agreement that these are going to become increas-

Table 2.

Bill Gates (1995), *The Road Ahead*	Nicholas Negroponte (1995), *Being Digital*	Michio Kaku (1998), *Visions*
Rather than holding paper currency, the new wallet will store unforgeable digital money... Your wallet will link into a store's computer to allow money to be transferred without any physical exchange at a cash register. Digital cash will be used in interpersonal transactions, too. When wallet PCs are ubiquitous we can eliminate the bottlenecks that now plague airport terminals, theatres, and other locations where people queue to show identification or a ticket. You won't need a key or magnetic card key to get through the doors either. You wallet PC will identify you to the computer controlling the lock. (pp. 74f)	Early in the next millennium your right and left cuff links or earrings may communicate with each other by low-orbiting satellites and have more computing power than your present PC. (p. 6)

Computers are getting smaller and smaller. You can expect to have on your wrist tomorrow what you have on your desk today, what filled the room yesterday. (p. 146)

Wearing one of their badges allows the building to know where you are. When you have a call, the phone you're nearest rings. In the future, such devices will not be tacked on with a clip or safety pin but securely attached or woven into your clothes. (p. 210) | By 2020, microprocessors will likely be as cheap and plentiful as scrap paper, scattered by the millions into the environment, allowing us to place intelligent systems everywhere. This will change everything around us... the nature of commerce, the wealth of nations, and the way we communicate, work, play, and live. This will give us smart homes, TVs, clothes, jewelry, and money. We will speak to our appliances and they will speak back. (p. 14) |
| Another option, which could eliminate the need for you to remember a password, is the use of biometric measurements. Individual biometric measurements are more secure and almost certainly will be eventually included in some wallet PCs. (p. 75) | | The first step in the long but exciting journey toward ubiquitous computing is to create marketable computer devices called tabs, pads, and boards which are roughly an inch, a foot, and a yard size... Tabs are tiny, inch-size clip-on badges that employees will wear- |
| Wallet PCs with the proper equipment will be able to tell you exactly where you are anyplace on the face of the Earth (p. 75)

I think of the wallet PC as the new Swiss Army knife. (p. 76) | Computer corduroy, memory muslin, and solar silk might be the literal fabric of tomorrow's digital dress. Instead of carrying your laptop, wear it. While this may sound outrageous, we are already starting to carry more and more computing and communications equipment on our body. The wristwatch is the most obvious. It is certain to migrate from a mere timepiece today to a mobile command-and-control centre tomorrow. It is worn so naturally that many people sleep with it on. An all-in-one, wrist-mounted TV, computer, and telephone is no longer the exclusive province of Dick Tracy, Batman, or Captain Kirk. Within the next five years, one of the largest areas of growth in consumer products is likely to be such wearable devices. (pp. 210f) | similar to an employee's ID badge, except that they will carry an infrared transmitter and have the power of a PC... As an employee moves around the building, the tabs can keep track of his or her precise location. Doors magically open up when they are approached, lights come one as people enter a room... (p. 32)

These crude beginnings that make us part of the Wearable Computers project of the Media Lab will ultimately make any individual a walking node of the World Wide Web... Wearable Computers in many respects represent a merger of cellular phones with the laptop computer... Some day wearable computers may even save lives. (p. 36) |
| The smart card of the future will identify its owner and store digital money, tickets, and medical information... (p. 77) | | |
| There will be less need for cash because most purchases will be handled with a wallet PC or an electronic "smart card" that will combine the features of a credit card, automatic teller machine card, and checkbook (p. 181) | | |
| Your wallet PC will be able to keep audio, time, location, and eventually even video records of everything that happens to you. It will be able to record every word you say and every word said to you, as well as body temperature, blood pressure, barometric pressure, and a variety of other data about you and your surroundings... [t]he technology required is not too difficult. (p. 267) | Also the form factor of most antennas lends itself to being woven into fabric or worn like a tie... (p. 211)

The ubiquity of each person's computer presence will be driven by various and disconnected computer processes in their current lives (airline reservation systems, point-of-sales data, on-line service utilisation, metering, messaging). These will be increasingly interconnected. If your early-morning flight to Dallas is delayed, your alarm clock can ring a bit later and the car service automatically notified in accordance with traffic predictions. (p. 212) | In the years ahead..there will be enormous economic pressure for people to convert to smart cards and digital money. This is because maintaining a society based on cash is very expensive... In the future, smart cards will replace ATM cards, telephone cards, train and transit passes, credit cards, as well as cards for parking meters, petty cash transactions, and vending machines. They will also store your medical history, insurance records, passport information... They will even connect to the Internet. (pp. 37f) |

ingly interconnected over the Internet. Thus, there is an underlying synergy between the predictions, especially in the context of *trend curves* and *growth curves*, which puts what the forecasters are saying inside the margins of the probable.

It is the intention of the authors however, to offer more detailed evidence for the predictions regarding the auto-ID trajectory. For instance, Gates (1995, p. 77) stated that "[t]he smart card of the future will identify its owner and store digital money, tickets, and medical information..." Kaku (1998, p. 37f) agreed that *"[t]here will be enormous economic pressure for people to convert to smart cards and digital money... In the future, smart cards will replace ATM cards, telephone cards, train and transit passes, credit cards, as well as cards for parking meters, petty cash transactions, and vending machines. They will also store your medical history, insurance records, passport information, and your entire family photo album. They will even connect to the Internet."* But the evidence they offer in their books for these particular outcomes is quite scarce. Of course the overall scope of their books does not allow for such inquiry, but this presents an adequate gap in the literature to be filled by this study, offering a unique contribution to knowledge.

CONCLUSION

Innovative Auto-ID and Location Based Services: From Bar Codes to Chip Implants is sure to take the reader on a grand tour of more than just the future trajectory of automatic identification technologies, but the big picture question of the social impact of technology. What began as a study in the confines of innovation within an information technology dissertation has grown to become a detailed inquiry that has reached out to multiple disciplines including philosophy, ethics, culture, religion, sociology, political science, law and economics. The authors clearly do not proclaim to have profound expertise in all of these fields but their research is informed by decades of study in tertiary institutions beginning in the early 1980s. This study has further been supported by decades of relevant practical work experience in information and communication technology, theology, policing and defense, and vocational instruction. There is much more to say on this topic but alas one has to stop somewhere: *Ars longa, vita brevis.*

REFERENCES

Adams, R. (1990). *Sourcebook of Automatic Identification and Data Collection*. New York: Van Nostrand Reinhold.

Allaby, M. (1996). *Facing The Future: the case for science*. London: Bloomsbury.

Andersen, E. S. (1997). Innovation systems: evolutionary perspectives. In C. Edquist (Ed.), *Systems of Innovation: technologies, institutions and organizations* (pp. 174-179). London: Pinter.

Baldwin, T. F., McVoy, D. S., & Steinfield, C. W. (1996). *Convergence: integrating media, information & communications*. London: Sage Publications.

Banbury, C. M. (1997). *Surviving Technological Innovation in the Pacemaker Industry 1959-1990*. New York: Garland Publishing.

Beauchamp, M. (2007). Association for Automatic Identification and Mobile Data Capture. *AIM UK* Retrieved 31 January 2009, from http://www.aimuk.org/

Berge, P. (1987). *IATA and Automatic Identification Standards for the Airlines*. London: AIM.

Berry, A. (1996). *The Next 500 Years: life in the coming millennium*. New York: Gramercy Books.

Braun, E. (1995). *Futile Progress: technology's empty promise*. London: Earthscan Publications Ltd.

Brodsky, I. (1995). *Wireless: the revolution in personal telecommunications*. London: Artech House.

Canton, J. (1999). *Technofutures*. New York: Hay House.

Carlsson, B. (Ed.). (1995). *Technological Systems and Economic Performance: the case of factory automation*. Dordrecht: Kluwer.

Cetron, M., & Davies, O. (1998). *Cheating Death: the promise and the impact of trying to live forever*. New York: St Martin's Press.

Choney, S. (2008). Cell phone want list: Finding some GPS. *msnbc.com* Retrieved 31 January 2009, from http://www.msnbc.msn.com/id/24728056/

Clarke, A. C. (1968). *2001: a space odyssey*. London: Orbit.

Cochrane, P. (1999). *Tips For Time Travelers: visionary insights into new technology, life, and the future on the edge of technology*. New York: McGraw-Hill.

Cohen, J. (1994). *Automatic Identification and Data Collection Systems*. London: McGraw-Hill Book Company.

Covell, A. (2000). *Digital Convergence: how the merging of computers, communications, and multimedia is transforming our lives*. Rhode Island: Aegis Publishing.

Creswell, J. W. (1998). *Qualitative Inquiry and Research Design: choosing among five traditions*. London: Sage Publications.

Crichton, M. (2006). *Next*. USA: HarperCollins.

Das, R. (2008). NFC-enabled phones and contactless smart cards 2008–2018. *Card Technology Today, 20*(7/8), 11-13.

Dvorsky, G. (2009). Transhumanist perspectives on science, philosophy, ethics and the future of intelligent life. *Sentient Developments* Retrieved 30 January 2009, from http://www.sentientdevelopments.com/

Edgar, S. L. (2003). *Morality and Machines* (2nd ed.). Toronto: Jones and Bartlett Computer Science.

Edquist, C. (1998). Findings and conclusions of ISE case studies on public technology procurement. *Innovation Systems and European Integration (ISE)*(April), 1-39.

Edquist, C. (Ed.). (1997). *Systems of Innovation: Technologies, Institutions and Organizations*. London: Pinter.

Ellul, J. (1964). *The Technological Society*. New York: Vintage Books.

Ermann, M. D., Williams, M. B., & Shauf, M. S. (1997). *Computers and Ethics, and Society* (2nd ed.). Oxford: Oxford University Press.

Flick, U. (2002). *An Introduction to Qualitative Research*. London: Sage.

Gabber, E., & Wool, A. (1998). *How to prove where you are: tracking the location of customer equipment.* Paper presented at the Proceedings of the 5th ACM Conference on Computer and Communications Security.

Gates, B. (1995). *The Road Ahead*. New York: The Penguin Group.

Gellersen, H.-W. (1999). *Handheld and Ubiquitous Computing.* Paper presented at the First International Symposium HUC '99 September 1999 Proceedings, Karlsruhe, Germany.

Gershenfeld, N. (1999). *When Things Start to Think*. New York: An Owl Book.

Gold, A. E. (1988). An overview of automatic identification technologies'. In R. Ames (Ed.), *Perspectives on Radio Frequency Identification: what is it, where is it going, should I be involved?* (pp. 1-2- 1-8). New York: Van Nostrand Reinhold.

Graafstra, A. (2007). Interview with Katina Michael. *Amal Graafstra: An object at rest cannot be stopped!* Retrieved 24 May 2007, from http://blog.amal.net/?p=36

Greenstein, S., & Khanna, T. (1997). What does industry convergence mean? In D. B. Yoffie (Ed.), *Competing in the Age of Digital Convergence* (pp. 201-226). Massachusetts,: Harvard Business School.

Harmon, C. K., & Adams, R. (1989). *Reading Between the Lines- An Introduction to Bar Code Technology*. New Hampshire

Helmers Publishing Inc.

Hester, M., & Ford, P. J. (2001). *Computers and Ethics in the Cyberage*. New York: Prentice Hall.

Hewkin, P. F. (1989). Future automatic identification technologies. *Colloquium on the Use of Electronic Transponders in the Automation*, 6/1-6/10.

Johnscher, C. (1999). *The Evolution of Wired Life*. UK: John Wiley & Sons.

Kaku, M. (1998). *Visions: how science will revolutionize the 21st century and beyond*. Oxford: Oxford University Press.

Keenan, W. (1997). Components of the business proposition: the consumer demand proposition:the consumer demand proposition. In C. A. Allen & W. J. Barr (Eds.), *Smart Cards: Seizing Strategic Business Opportunities* (pp. 21-43). New York: McGraw-Hill.

Kelly, K. (1994). *Out of Control: the new biology of machines, social systems and the economic world*. Massachusetts: Perseus Books.

Kling, R. (1996). *Computerization and Controversy: value conflicts and social choices*. New York: Academic Press.

Knoke, W. (1996). *Brave New World: the essential roadmap for the twenty-first century.* New York: Kodansha International.

Kumar, N., & Vragov, R. (2009). Active citizen participation using ICT tools. *Communications of the ACM, 52*(1), 118-121.

Kurzweil, R. (1999). *The Age of Spiritual Machines.* New York: Penguin Books.

Kurzweil, R. (2005). *The Singularity is Near.* New York: Penguin.

Labrador, M., Michael, K., & Kuepper, A. (2008). Advanced Location-Based Services. *Computer Communications, 31*(6), 1053-1054.

LaMoreaux, R. D. (1998). *Barcodes and Other Automatic Identification Systems.* New York: Pira International.

Lindley, R. A. (1997). *Smart Card Innovation.* Australia: Saim.

Mann, S. (2009). WearComp.org, WearCam.org... Retrieved 31 January 2009, from http://genesis.eecg. toronto.edu/

Mann, S., & Niedzviecki, H. (2001). *Cyborg: Digital Destiny and Human Possibility in the Age of the Wearable Computer* Toronto: Random House.

Marriot, M. (1987). *International Bar Code Standards: Bar Code Symbologies, Standards and Technology Updates.* London: AIM.

Masters, A., & Michael, K. (2007). Lend Me Your Arms: the Use and Implications of Humancentric RFID. *Electronic Commerce Research and Applications, 6*(1), 29-39.

McLuhan, M. (1962). *The Gutenberg Galaxy: The Making of Typographic Man.* Toronto: University of Toronto Press.

McLuhan, M. (1964). *Understanding Media: the extensions of man.* Cambridge: MIT Press.

Michael, K., & Masters, A. (2004, 18-21 July). *Applications of human transponder implants in mobile commerce.* Paper presented at the The 8th World Multiconference on Systemics, Cybernetics and Informatics, Orlando, Florida.

Michael, M. G., Fusco, S. J., & Michael, K. (2008). A Research Note on Ethics in the Emerging Age of Uberveillance (Überveillance). *Computer Communications, 31*(6), 1192-1199.

Mills, S. (Ed.). (1997). *Turning Away From Technology: a new vision for the 21st century.* San Francisco: Sierra Club Books.

Minsky, M. (1985). *Society of Mind.* New York: A Touchstone Book.

Moran, R. (n.d.). *Automatic Identification Systems: growth markets- a major enabling technology for the 90s.* New York: Business Communications Co.

Moravec, H. (1988). *Mind Children: the future of robot and human intelligence.* Cambridge: Harvard University Press.

Moravec, H. (1999). *Robot: mere machine to transcendent mind*. Oxford: Oxford University Press.

Morris, E., & Zuluaga, C. (2006). *Information Technology Issues: Ethical and Legal*. Sydney: Pearson Education.

Moutray, R. E., & Ponsford, A. M. (2003). Integrated maritime surveillance: protecting national sovereignty. *Radar*, 385-388.

Negroponte, N. (1995). *Being Digital*. Australia: Hodder and Stoughton.

Nelson, R. R., & Winter, S. G. (1982). *An Evolutionary Theory of Economic Change*. Cambridge: Harvard University Press.

O'Gorman, L., & Pavlidis, T. (1999). Auto ID technology: From barcodes to biometrics. *IEEE Robotics & Automation Magazine, 6*(1), 4-6.

Paul, G. S., & Cox, E. D. (1996). *Beyond Humanity: cyberevolution and future minds*. Massachusetts: Charles River Media.

Pavlidis, T. (1996). *Challenges in document recognition bottom up and top down processes*. Paper presented at the IEEE Proceedings of ICPR '96.

Perusco, L., & Michael, K. (2007). Control, Trust, Privacy, and Security: Evaluating Location-Based Services. *IEEE Technology and Society, 26*(1), 4-16.

Perusco, L., Michael, K., & Michael, M. G. (2006). *Location-based Services and the Privacy-Security Dichotomy*. Paper presented at The Third International Conference on Mobile Computing and Ubiquitous Networking (ICMU 2006), London, UK.

Queisser, H. (1985). *The Conquest of the Microchip: science and business in the silicon age*. Cambridge: Harvard University Press.

Quinn, M. J. (2006). *Ethics for the Information Age* (2nd ed.). Sydney: Pearson International.

Radinger, W., & Goeschka, K. M. (2002). *A definition of convergence in the area of information and telecommunication technologies* Paper presented at the Conference on Object Oriented Programming Systems Languages and Applications, Seattle, Washington

Rantala, M. L., & Milgram, A. J. (Eds.). (1999). *Cloning: for and against*. Chicago: Open Court.

Reynolds, G. (2006). *Ethics in Information Technology* (2nd ed.). New York: Thomson Course Technology.

Robertson, D. S. (1998). *The New Renaissance: computers and the next level of civilisation*. New York: Oxford University Press.

Saxenian, A. (1994). *Regional Advantage: culture and competition in Silicon Valley and Route 128*. Cambridge: Harvard University Press.

Schumpeter, J. A. (1934). *The Theory of Economic Development*. Cambridge: Harvard University Press.

Schwind, G. (1990). Electronic codes for automatic identification. In R. Ames (Ed.), *Perspectives on Radio Frequency Identification: What is it, Where is it going, Should I be Involved?* (pp. 1-19- 11-27). New York: Van Nostrand Reinhold.

Sharp, K. R. (1987). Automatic identification improves the bottom line. In R. Ames (Ed.), *Perspectives on Radio Frequency Identification: What is it, Where is it going, Should I be Involved?* (pp. 1-9- 1-18). New York: Van Nostrand Reinhold.

Smith, E. (1989). *The Australia Card: the story of its defeat.* Australia: Macmillan.

Smith, I. G. (1990). AIM- an industry activity group for automatic identification. *Computing & Control Engineering Journal, 11,* 49-52.

Stahl, W. A. (1999). *God and the Chip: religion and the culture of technology.* Canada: Canadian Corporation for Studies in Religion.

Stork, D. G. (Ed.). (1997). *Hal's Legacy.* Massachusetts: MIT Press.

Swartz, J. (1999). The growing 'MAGIC' of automatic identification. *IEEE Robotics & Automation Magazine,* 20-22, 56.

Tavani, H. T. (2007). *Ethics & Technology: Ethical Issues in An Age of Information and Communication Technology.* New York: John Wiley & Sons.

Thomas, C., & Bevan, N. (1996). *Usability Context Analysis: A Practical Guide.* Middlesex: National Physical Laboratory DITC.

Toffler, A. (1970). *The Third Wave.* London: Pan Books.

Toffler, A. (1981). *Future Shock.* New York: Bantam Books.

Tren, R. (1995). Trends in the Cards Industry. *Andersen Consulting,* 1-99.

Warwick, K. (2002). *I, Cyborg*: Century.

Westrum, R. (1991). *Technologies and Society: the shaping of people and things.* California: Wadsworth Publishing Company.

Yin, R. (1998). The Case Study Method As A Tool For Doing Evaluation. *Current Sociology, 40*(1), 123.

Yoffie, D. B. (Ed.). (1997). *Competing in the Age of Digital Convergence.* Massachusetts: Harvard Business School.

Yule, P., & Hewson, C. (2003). *Internet Research Methods: a practical guide for the social and behavioral sciences.* London: Sage Publications.

Chapter II
Innovation Studies

INTRODUCTION

This chapter will explore literature in the field of innovation in order to establish a conceptual framework for the auto-ID trajectory research. The primary aim of this review is to provide a critical response to the literature on technological innovation. The review will also serve to: (i) identify and understand widely accepted definitions, concepts and terms, born from past innovation research as a guide for further research; (ii) review theories, theoretical frameworks and methods adopted by other researchers doing similar innovation studies (especially in the area of information technology) in order to choose an appropriate approach for this study; (iii) understand what aspects of complex high technologies (high-tech) have already been explored by researchers and what aspects have been neglected and to discover any similarities or differences in existing findings.

Previous research will be examined in this chapter using a two-tiered approach; topical at the surface layer and chronologically organized therein. This type of analytical strategy is advantageous because similar patterns, trends, or findings can be uncovered and organized into clusters over time. Each study will be categorized according to the theory and research method used by the author(s). Additionally, findings of each study will be briefly highlighted for comparison. Seminal works will be treated at a greater length than smaller studies. The same emphasis will be attached to reporting accurate summaries, and responding critically to previous research. Overall, greater consideration will be given to reviewing contemporary innovation literature, as opposed to outdated research that was never conducted with the knowledge of information technologies.

FUNDAMENTAL DEFINITIONS IN THE INNOVATION PROCESS

Invention, Innovation and Diffusion

This section will be dedicated to defining the fundamental links between invention, innovation and diffusion as it applies to this research. The three terms are different, however, as Lindley (1997, p. 19) observes at the same time, the terms are also closely allied. Sahal (1981, p. 41) makes the distinction that an invention is the creation of a "new device" and an innovation is the "commercial application" of that device. Similarly Braun (1984, p. 39) argues that "...an invention is merely an idea for a prototype of a new product or process and does not become an innovation until it reaches the market [diffusion]." Most inventions never become innovations; they fall by the wayside on the long road from idea to marketable product (Westrum, 1991, p. 150). For a thorough introduction into the diffusion of innovations see Rogers (1995).

Invention: Mutation, Recombination, Hybrid

As suggested by Jacob Schmookler, a patentable invention is a new product or process that shows a significant degree of originality and has some future use (1966, p. 6). A question often asked is, do all inventions fall into the same category? The answer according to Farrell (1993) and Mokyr (1996) is no: inventions may differ depending on how their formation came about. Table 1 shows that invention can be classified into three types, mutation, recombination, and hybrid (Mokyr, 1996, p. 69). Without reference to Farrell or Mokyr, Edquist (1997, p. 1) states, "[i]nnovations are new creations of economic significance... [that] may be brand new but are more often new combinations of existing elements."

Innovation: Radical vs. Incremental

Generally, an innovation can be described as "...a process or a product, a technical or an organizational change, an incremental improvement or a radical breakthrough" (Deideren, 1990, p. 123 quoted in Lindley 1997, p. 20). Since the 1900s the term innovation has undergone many revisions with the emergence of new theories in the field of economics. Schumpeter's (1939, p. 87f) well-known definition of innovation is directly linked to neoclassical economic theory by means of the production function: "*...we will simply define innovation as the setting up of a new production function. This covers the case of a new commodity as well as those of a new form of organization... this function describes the way in which quantity of product varies if quantities of factors vary. If, instead of quantities of factors, we vary the form of the function, we have an innovation... we may express the same thing by saying that innovation combines factors in a new way, or that it consists in carrying out New Combinations.*" The production function indicates the "*maximum amount* of product that can be obtained from any specific combination

Table 1. Types of inventions

Type of Invention	Description
Mutation	"Of course, mutations are variations on existing material. Most of the genetic material in every mutant is not new..."
Recombination	"Because technological recombination is multiparental, the opportunities for innovation through novel combinations of existing knowledge are a function of the complexity and diversity of the economy."
Hybrid	"The difference between a hybrid and a recombinant invention is that a hybrid is a combination of two (or more) *artefacts*, rather than the information embedded in them... In most cases, hybrid inventions require complementary types of invention that are necessary if the pieces are to work together and the new device is to be made operational."

The definitions for the different types of inventions have been taken from Mokyr (1996, pp. 70-73).

of inputs, given the current state of knowledge. That is, it shows the *largest* quantity of goods that any particular collection of inputs is capable of producing" (Baumol & Blinder, 1992, pp. 507-510).

As Saviotti (1997, p. 184) comments, for Schumpeter new combinations gave rise to new products and processes that were qualitatively different from those preceding them. However, while the phrase 'new combinations' is still widely used today within the evolutionary theory of economics by researchers such as Lundvall (1992, p. 8) and Elam (1992, p. 3), innovation is no longer attributed to the setting up of a new production function. Rather, innovation is a natural process of 'technical progress,' a technology-specific process of 'learning by experience' (see Sahal, 1981, p. 37). Nelson and Rosenberg (1993, pp. 4f) interpret innovation broadly, adding an optional geographic context: *"...to encompass the processes by which firms master and get into practice product designs and manufacturing processes that are new to them, whether or not they are new to the universe, or even to the nation."*

There is some value in this geographic perspective either at the local, regional, or national level. In *National Innovation Systems*, Nelson and Rosenberg (1993, p. 3) state that "[t]here is a new spirit of what might be called "technonationalism" in the air, combining a strong belief that the technological capabilities of a nation's firms are a key source of their competitive prowess, with a belief that these capabilities are in a sense national, and can be built by national action." In selecting a preferred definition of innovation for this book, the more contemporary and balanced definition given by Edquist (1997, p. 16) is appropriate: "[t]echnological innovation is a matter of producing new knowledge or combining existing knowledge in new ways- and of transforming this into economically significant products and processes."

It is often important to classify the impact of a product or process innovation in a way that can be useful for comparing one or more technologies. Admittedly this is very difficult, since the extent of an innovation is dependent upon the perspective taken by the researcher. However, using Braun's terse definitions (see Table 2) one can distinguish one type of innovation from the other. Similarly Landau (1982, p. 54) believes that there are "...fundamentally two kinds of innovation: 1. The 'breakthrough'; 2. The 'improvement'."

Diffusion

According to Rogers (1995, p. 5), "diffusion is the process by which an innovation is communicated through certain channels over time among the members of a social system. It is a special type of communication, in that the messages are concerned with new ideas." Diffusion is characterized by a two way channel, where ideas are exchanged and feedback is provided. For Rogers, diffusion means a kind

Table 2. Types of innovations

Type of Innovation	Description
Radical	"[a] cluster of related innovations which together form a technology which differs considerably from previous technologies..."
Incremental	"[o]ne which offers a relatively small technical improvement without changing the nature of the technology."

The definitions for the two types of innovations have been taken from Braun (1984, p. 42).

of "social change." There are four main elements in diffusion including, innovation, communication channels, time, and the social system. For the application of the diffusion of innovation (DOI) theory to information technology, see Prescott (1995) and Prescott and Cogner (1995). The elements of DOI are similar to the qualities inherent in the systems of innovation framework, especially that element of time, feedback mechanisms, and change.

The Innovation Process: Product vs. Process

Throughout innovation literature there is some confusion over the terms innovation process, product innovation and process innovation. First, the innovation process can refer to either products or processes. It is the stages or phases involved with getting an idea for an invention to a 'finished product' or 'finished process' to operation. Braun (1995, p. 61f) outlines these phases as: the idea or invention; development of the product; prototype; production; and marketing and diffusion. An example of a product innovation is the semiconductor microchip. An example of a process innovation is the automated assembly line, set up at an automobile manufacturing plant. However, it is not always clear whether a given innovation should be categorized as either a product or process; this is especially true in the IT sector (Edquist et al., 1998, p. 12). Irrespective, today it is more relevant to be concerned with the actual system of innovation. Now that the relationship between invention, innovation and diffusion has been presented it is necessary to allocate space to the actual innovation studies themselves. By reviewing the various types of conceptual frameworks and methodologies applied by other researchers, an appropriate approach can be chosen for this investigation. Significant findings in the way of emergent patterns or events in the innovation process will also be highlighted and explained.

SETTING THE STAGE- KARL MARX ON TECHNOLOGY

Marx was a philosopher, sociologist and economist considered by many to be one of the most influential persons of all time. In his classic work *Capital*, Karl Marx (1818-1883) writes about the importance of products in the labor process. He stated that the result of this process was "...a use-value, a piece of natural material adapted to human needs by means of a change in its form..." (Marx, 1976, p. 287). Products were "...not only the results of labor, but also its essential conditions." For instance, a finished product could assist in the innovation process of another new product. In this manner technological change was the force behind process changes within existing institutions or the force behind the establishment of new institutions. It seemed obvious to Marx that for economic growth to be achieved product and process innovations were required. In commenting on the capitalist system he wrote that: *"...the capitalist has two objectives: in the first place, he wants to produce a use-value which has exchange-value, i.e. an article destined to be sold, a commodity; and secondly he wants to produce a commodity greater in value than the sum of the values of the commodities used to produce it, namely the means of production and the labor-power he purchased with his good money on the open market. His aim is to produce not only a use-value, but a commodity; not only use-value, but value; and not just value, but also surplus-value" (Marx, 1976, p. 293).*

Marx's long-lasting contribution was recognizing that product and process innovations had a social impact. Technology could be used to oppress a class or to empower an individual. This is an important observation that Marx has made about the power of technology. When considering auto-ID today this question is still relevant. In the Introduction, the growing dependence of humans on auto-ID devices was highlighted for this very reason. In discussing the evolution of digital technologies, Covell (2000, p. 5) notes a fundamental shift in the nature of the evolution: "[t]he difference is that digital technology is now being applied to enhance and extend human interaction." Accompanied by Friedrich Engels (1825-1895), Marx conducted historical research on process innovations in England. He used original factory documents to draw conclusions on the life of a worker who was driven by the capitalist to create surplus value. Modern interpretations of Marx's ideology have sought to reassess parts of his labor theory of value as a means to reveal its limitations (Habermas, 1981, p. 159).

NEOCLASSICAL ECONOMIC THEORY (1870 - 1960)

As defined by Cohendet and Llerena (1997, p. 226) neoclassical economics "...examines the way through which market mechanisms select new technologies and eliminate those that have become obsolete." One shortcoming of studies using neoclassical economic theory is that they focus primarily on business process innovations. Neoclassical studies are concerned with the manner in which technological innovations can enhance the productivity of a firm and decrease employment per unit of output (Edquist, 1997, p. 22). A fundamental weakness of neoclassical economic theory is that "[e]xchange takes place without any specification of its institutional setting. Only prices and volumes matter" (Edquist & Johnson, 1997, p. 48).

Joseph Alois Schumpeter

In the year that Marx died Schumpeter was born (1883-1950). While he was to eventually share many of Marx's beliefs, particularly in the self-destruction of capitalism, he focused his efforts on the statistical analysis of the capitalist process. What he is probably best remembered for are his studies on the production function and his book titled *Theory of Economic Development* (1934). Schumpeter was a neoclassical economist who attributed higher amounts of capital per worker to technological change, which resulted in more for the profit receivers. Throughout his professional career, he was preoccupied with innovation as the main agent for entrepreneurial profit. Like Marx he too focused on business process innovations. The production function that Schumpeter wrote about "...expresses the relationship between various technically feasible combinations of inputs, or factors of production, and output... it is a specification of all conceivable modes of production in the light of the existing technical knowledge about input-output relationships" (Sahal, 1981, p. 16). However, discontent with the production function has led many economists to abandon the neoclassical approach. This study also, does not lend itself to this type of rigid analysis as the questions it asks are more exploratory than computational. Neoclassical economic theory allows only for purely economic factors to be considered, neglecting other significant aspects of innovation.

EVOLUTIONARY ECONOMIC THEORY (1980 - 1990)

Evolutionary economic theory has not achieved the degree of articulation corresponding to neoclassical economic theory (Saviotti, 1997, p. 181). For one simple reason, it is more recent. It is an alternative to understanding technical change as something other than an attempt to maximize profits (Nelson & Winter, 1982). Unlike neoclassical economics, evolutionary theory is suited to both process and product innovations. It is also more contemporary, developed with an understanding of modern technological innovations. It has been applied to product innovations, such as semiconductors and satellites in the high-tech industry and is more suited to the investigation of auto-ID technologies. Numerous recent theoretical and empirical studies performed, have been conducted with the notion that technical change is an evolutionary process.

Devendra Sahal in his book *Patterns of Technological Innovation* (1981, p. 64) commented that evolution was not just a matter of 'chop and change'; it related to the "...very structure and function of the object." He stated that innovation was "...inherently a continuous process that [did] not easily lend itself to description in terms of discrete events" (1981, p. 23). Sahal is best remembered for his quantitative diffusion analytical strategies. While he made excellent evolutionary theoretical discoveries his methodology differs from contemporary researchers in innovation. In that same year Richard Nelson also suggested that due to the randomness and the time-consuming nature of innovation processes, evolutionary models of technological change were more realistic in understanding innovations than the models provided by neoclassical economics (Nelson, 1981, 1059f).

Perhaps one of the most significant publications, as suggested by Saviotti (1997, p. 181) was Nelson and Winter's, *An Evolutionary Theory of Economic Change* (1982). It was not until this time, that a researcher had concretely stipulated that "technical change [was] clearly an evolutionary process" (Nelson, 1987, p. 16). While many innovation studies had challenged neoclassical economic assumptions during the 1970s, none had been so game as to suggest that evolutionary economic theory was more appropriate. At the time, Nelson (1987, p. 16) believed that the innovation generator kept making technologies superior to those in earlier existence. However, as later clarified by Charles Edquist (1997, p. 6) "...only superior in a relative sense, not optimal in an absolute sense." Edquist affirms that "...technological change is an open-ended and path-dependent process where no optimal solution to a technical problem can be identified" (Edquist, 1997, p. 6). This perspective is embraced throughout this research study. It has very important implications as it shapes the context in which auto-ID is to be understood. Rather than concentrating on the progression from one auto-ID technology to the next in terms of 'superiority', the question is more about the actual path taken to develop, by firms, government and consumers. Who drives this path and the dynamic interaction between the stakeholders then becomes of interest. This idea is quite different and challenging.

In contrast refer to Charles Darwin's (1809-1882) writings (ch. 4) on 'Natural Selection; or the Survival of the Fittest' (1960, p. 53). His fundamental argument is "...[t]hat as new species in the course of time are formed through natural selection, others will become rarer and rarer, and finally extinct. The forms which stand in closest competition with those undergoing modification and improvement will naturally suffer most." Refer also to the sections in ch. 4 on "divergence of character" (p. 53) and "convergence of character" (p. 62). When this Darwinist approach is applied to economic affairs, Allaby (1996, pp. 130-132) calls it "social Darwinism". He believes that this theory is deeply flawed: "[i]ts first error lies in its equation of evolution with progress, the idea that later forms are better than earlier ones. This is a value judgment, for what do we mean by 'better'? If we mean 'better at surviving' we are being tautologous." More recent observations by Dr Jerome Swartz (1999), founder and former CEO of Symbol Technologies, present a whole new approach to understanding auto-ID technologies. He writes (p. 21): *"[n]ot long ago, I recall the heated debates about which technology was best- which would bring the most benefits, prove the most reliable or the cheapest. The implied question was, "Which will emerge as the real winner at the end of the day?" I believe that "competitive" framework asked all the wrong questions and clouded a better understanding of how the technologies could exist side-by-side."* These most insightful observations serve as a calling for further research to be conducted in the field of auto-ID innovation using evolutionary economic theory.

Case Studies and Qualitative Research

A landmark study becomes obvious to the researcher who has read a plethora of literature in the field he or she is studying. Margaret Sharp's, *Europe and the New Technologies: Six Case Studies in Innovation & Adjustment* (1985), is one of these landmark studies. She later follows up with *Strategies for New Technologies: Case Studies from France and Britain* (1989) that is equally impressive. Space will be dedicated to the former because it was without a doubt a paragon for future research in the field. Sharp uses evolutionary theory and a case study methodology to examine six new technologies in Europe. The methodology chosen for this study is advantageous in that it gives Sharp and her fellow contributors the flexibility to explore the many diverse issues surrounding the central thesis. New industrial activities are examined rather than individual industries or sectors. The research which was focused on computer-aided design (CAD), advanced machine tools and robotics, telecommunications, videotext, biotechnology and offshore supplies was very successful, and finally conclusions were drawn from recurring themes identified in the case studies. In summary, Sharp (1985, p. 271) concludes that: *"[t] he process of change is evolutionary- new industrial activities emerge from the body of old industrial activities, the decisions are incremental as firms adjust their product/process mix to opportunities which present themselves, and, as this happens, so firms progressively redefine the nature and boundaries of the industry itself."*

More precisely, Sharp believes that the concept, technological trajectory, is useful in the context of her case studies. Her discovery is very significant and is quoted in full as follows. *"A new technology very often, and certainly, in the cases we have been studying, is subject to continuous improvement over a number of years. Firms which develop the capability to make these continuous improvements, that is to move along the trajectory, are often the most successful. As well as continuities, there are discontinuities. Major new technical or marketing innovations present such discontinuities. A discontinuity halts progress along the existing trajectory but simultaneously opens up a new one. In assimilating major technological change, a firm in effect changes gear and shifts to a new trajectory. In this sense, the discontinuity may be regarded as a revolution. Whereas evolution, development along the trajectory, is an everyday occurrence, revolutions are quite rare"* (Sharp, 1985, p. 272).

Sharp's study is an excellent model for this investigation. It shows how a research project such as the one that these researchers are undertaking, is likely to lead to some valuable results. And results, that are applicable to more than just that group of technologies (in this case auto-ID) being investigated. The key terms that Sharp uses, evolutionary, continuous improvement, discontinuity, technological change, technological trajectory, will be used throughout the main body of this work. Friedman (1994), like Sharp (1982) applies evolutionary concepts to his study on the IT field. Of particular interest is his emphasis on the technological trajectory of IT which he breaks down into four phases of historical change: 1) hardware capacity constraints, 2) software productivity constraints, 3) user relations constraints, and 4) the future. Friedman also makes the useful distinction between a technology field and technological paradigm. *"First, the focus of the technology field is on people, institutions, and organizations. The focus of the technological paradigm is on designs or patterns of solutions. The technology field encourages a much wider set of people to be analyzed. The technological paradigm contains practitioners working in organizations supplying the technology, and possibly scientists and technologists working in associated research institutes and universities (Clark, 1987)."*

Fundamental Concepts

As identified by Carlsson and Stankiewicz (1995, p. 23) the major strength of the evolutionary approach is its "...ability to bring within a single framework the institutional/organizational as well as cognitive/ cultural aspects of social and economic change". This corresponds with the second objective of this book, in that many issues, not just economic will be analyzed to identify the factors influencing auto-ID innovation. The key terms used in this framework are highlighted in Table 3.

Technological Trajectories

The term technological trajectories, also known as natural trajectories, can be attributed to Dosi (1982) as being a pattern of innovation. While there have been several definitions given for this term, in the context of this book von Hippel's interpretation (1988) is appropriate: "[t]echnological trajectories consist in the continuous improvements of products in terms of performance and reliability and in the tailoring of products to specific users' needs, within specific application contexts." For a thorough explanation of the term technological trajectory see Durand (1991). He makes the important link between the terms technological trajectory and technological forecasting which is extremely pertinent to this study. In quoting Dosi (1982), Durand makes the distinction between continuous changes along the same paradigm versus discontinuities which are associated with a new emerging paradigm. Hirooka (1998) makes the distinction between the technological trajectory of a product and its diffusion trajectory. The paper focuses on three cases of innovation paradigm, synthetic dyestuffs, electronics and biotechnology. Through these examples Hirooka provides evidence that the technological trajectory of an innovation spans about 20-30 years upon which point it joins the diffusion period. Banbury (1997, p. 13) writes "[t] he concept of a technological paradigm enables us to delineate the boundaries of technological change cycles (paradigms) and to delineate the direction of change (trajectories)".

Table 3. Important terms and concepts in the innovation literature

Term	Description
Technological Guidepost	- Basic design of a technology acts as a guidepost charting the course of future innovations
Selection Environment	- The choice between a number of other innovations in the same firm/industry - Acts to influence the path of innovation and the rate of diffusion - Feedback to influence the direction of R&D programs that firms invest in
Creative Symbiosis	- The case where two or more technologies combine in an integrative fashion - The overall system is simplified
Path Dependency	- A map of the impact of auto-ID technology - What are the long-range effects of the technology
Technological Trajectories	- A pattern of innovation - Continuous improvement of products in terms of performance and reliability
Technology Forecasting	- Predicting the development of the technology and assessing its potential for adoption

What should be highlighted here is the focus on products and their continuous improvements, tailored to specific users' needs for specific applications. Each firm follows a technological trajectory in search of improvements to their existing products (Breschi & Malerba, 1997, p. 146f). In this manner a firm's technological understanding is enhanced and one dominant design can emerge. Each firm pursues "...a single technical option and, over time, become[s] increasingly committed to a single technological trajectory" (Saxenian, 1994, p. 112). The case study that Saxenian examines is the regional economy of Silicon Valley. In this instance, learning and technological change are cumulative in nature. Firms secure their knowledge base and then attempt to build upon it seeking new opportunities. In contrast the emerging auto-ID industry has a knowledge base that is still in its early development and the future impact of auto-ID product innovations is still very much speculative. Thus the need has arisen to look ahead and propose a map or attempt to understand the path dependency of these technologies. Foresight is necessary because it also allows us to see the potential long-range effects of technical change (Westrum, 1991, p. 344). The question of why it is important to forecast and what is to be gained by it, is very important to this investigation. The researchers believe that forecasting is essential, even if the predictions arrived at may not eventuate or even if some unexpected events happen that were not anticipated. It is better to make some logical predictions based on the evidence one has and be prepared for what lies ahead, than to find oneself completely unprepared.

Selection Environment and Other Terms

Having revealed the importance of technological trajectories, it is now appropriate to understand the concept of selection environment. As the term suggests it is the process that involves the interaction between the product and its environment. Lindley (1997, p. 25) phrases it well when she states that: *"[t]he selection environment acts to influence the path of innovation and the rate of diffusion generated by any given innovation, and at the same time generate feedback to strongly influence the direction and type of R&D programs that firms might invest in."* Sahal can be credited with the popularization of the term technological guidepost. He stated that the basic design of a technological innovation acts as a guidepost charting the course of future innovation activity. To prove this he used an arbitrary example, highlighting that one or two early models of a product or process usually stand out above all the others in the history of an industry and their design becomes the foundation for the evolution of many innovations. "In consequence, they leave a distinct mark on a whole series of observed advances in technology" (Sahal, 1981, p. 33; see also Anderson & Tushman, 1990). This led Sahal to the principle of creative symbiosis, the case where "...two or more technologies combine in an integrative fashion such that the outline of the overall system is greatly simplified... when it [happens], totally new possibilities for further evolution present themselves" (Sahal, 1981, p. 75). This phenomenon has occurred in the auto-ID industry and will be discussed in the main body of the book.

THE EMERGENCE OF THE SYSTEMS OF INNOVATION APPROACH (1990-)

The systems of innovation (SI) approach is a conceptual framework that can be used to study technological innovations. See *Systems of Innovation: Technologies, Institutions and Organizations*, edited by Edquist (1997) and *Systems of Innovation: Growth, Competitiveness and Employment*, edited by Edquist and McKelvey (2000). The approach, admittedly not an established theory, has been gaining prominence in the last decade. SI defines innovation as an evolutionary process, not as a process for achieving optimality. Edquist et al. (1998, p. 21) explain that "the notion of optimality is absent from the SI approach. The notion of optimality stems from static equilibria and therefore is not applicable to processes of technological change... [this] is a major contribution of evolutionary theory, which the SI approach has adopted." SI is described well in the 'Innovation Systems and European Integration Policy Statement' (Edquist et al., 1998b, p. 3f): *"The Systems of Innovation (SI) approach for understanding innovations in the economy stresses that firms do not normally innovate in isolation but in interaction with other organizational actors (other firms, universities, standard setting organizations, etc.) within the framework of existing institutional rules (laws, norms, technical standards, etc.). Institutions are not organizations. Rather, they constitute the rules of the game or framework conditions for interaction. In contrast, organizations are the entities (actors) that interact. From this perspective, innovation is a matter of interactive learning."*

The origin of this approach is well documented as proceeding from theories of interactive learning and evolutionary theories of technical change. Among researchers like Carlsson and Stankiewicz, Nelson and Rosenberg, as well as Lundvall and his colleagues, there is support for this approach stemming from its close affinity with the evolutionary theory (Edquist, 1997, p. 7). The "system" that Sahal once referred to has been defined in the SI approach (Edquist, 1997, p. 14f): *"One way of specifying 'system' is to include in it all important economic, social, political, organizational, institutional, and other factors that influence the development, diffusion, and use of innovations. Potentially important determinants cannot be excluded a priori if we are to be able to understand and explain innovation. Provided that the innovation concept has been specified, the crucial issue then becomes one of identifying all those important factors. This could- in principle- be done by identifying the determinants of (a certain group of) innovations. If, in this way, innovations could be causally explained, the explanatory factors would define the limits of the system. The problem of specifying the extent of the system studied would be solved- in principle."* Using these definitions it becomes a simpler task to understand auto-ID innovation. These factors could be causally explained, limiting the scope of the actual system and thus presenting a conceptual framework within which to perform the research.

The Value of the SI Approach

The attractiveness of the SI framework is that it is a "holistic and interdisciplinary" approach which "encompasses all or most determinants of innovation" (Edquist et al., 1998, p. 20). Fundamental to its doctrine is that "history matters" since innovation processes take time to evolve. Queisser's (1985) historical account of *The Conquest of the Microchip* highlights this point well. In the Foreword of this book, Robert Noyce (p. viii) writes regarding the microchip: *"[t]hose of us who have been involved in the development of this technology recognize that the terms technological revolution and breakthroughs are used to attract public attention to the progress being made, in reality progress is almost seamless, with pieces of the puzzle continually being put in place until a coherent picture emerges."* Noyce is suggesting that the microchip revolution happened through evolutionary steps, i.e. the notion of revolution through evolution. These two words are often used at different levels by technologists in auto-ID. One expert may refer to the smart card revolution and another may refer to the evolution of card technology from magnetic-stripe to smart card.

Thus by understanding the past one is better equipped for the current and future patterns of innovation. This approach is also used by some futurists like Adrian Berry. He writes "[s]o that my subsequent chapters will be intelligible, I must explain what has been happening in the past five hundred years and how it relates to the present" (Berry, 1996, p. 19). In a paper titled 'Unfaithful offspring? Technologies and their trajectories', S. Hong (1998, p. 262) challenges the notion that a technology's trajectory is autonomous or its development unpredictable and uncontrollable. Hong (1998) chooses to examine three technologies including the Triode, the numerically controlled (NC) machine tool and the Internet. He concurs with an underlying philosophy of SI; that it is rather an "imperfect historical understanding of a technology [that] largely contributes to the idea that the technological trajectory is uncertain, and, therefore, autonomous." In examining the high-tech industry in Sweden, McKelvey et al. (1998) traced the historical changes that occurred in the Swedish mobile telecommunication system from the 1970s till the 1990s to attain a better understanding of the industry dynamics. More recently McKelvey has shifted her focus to studying modern biotechnology (McKelvey, 2000; McKelvey, Rickne, & Laage-Hellman, 2004; McKelvey & Orsenigo, 2006). In like manner this study will explore auto-ID innovation. The SI approach embodies nine characteristics, among which is that they may "employ historical perspectives" (Edquist 1998, p. 8).

The SI approach successfully brings together the conventional teachings of various experts in the innovation field from all over the world. It has not only been adopted by the Europeans but also by researchers in Asia and North America. To understand its origin one must first look at the many case studies that have been conducted using a systems view of evolutionary theory. The term 'national systems of innovation' was first used by Chris Freeman in 1987. Lundvall then used it as a chapter heading in Dosi (1988). In 1989, Brown and Karagozoglu published a paper titled, 'A systems model of technological innovation'. Following in 1992, Lundvall titled his book, *National Systems of Innovation: Towards a Theory of Innovation and Interactive Learning*.

The research that acted to launch the SI framework was *National Systems of Innovation: A Comparative Study* (1993) by Nelson and Rosenberg that will be critically analyzed to follow. Lipsett and Smith (1995) then published a paper titled, 'Cybernetics and (real) National Innovation Systems' challenging some of the ways that Nelson and Rosenberg treated their subject matter. The former made some very good points that are worthwhile noting but were supportive of the approach used overall. They called for researchers using the national systems of innovation to improve their information base and chosen metrics of analysis, and for more participants to get involved in discussions. They also emphasized the need to understand that system dynamics are different when humans are involved and relationships are established. In 1995, Carlsson and Stankiewicz completed defining the technological systems (TS) approach. The TS program focused on both theoretical studies and empirical studies. At the fifth *International Conference on FACTORY 2000*, Keating, Stanford and Cope (1997) also contributed to the idea of systematic technology innovation.

In retrospect most of these publications carried the word 'national' in their titles. See also the ISE policy statement (Edquist et al., 1998, p. 20): *"[i]nitially the SI approach was dominated by the national level. However, other systems of innovation than those defined by a country criterion, should be, and are being, identified and studied... Leaving the geographical dimension, we can also talk about 'sectoral' systems of innovation (i.e. 'technological' systems that include only a part of a regional, national or international system)."* The focus of this book is to make an enquiry at the specific auto-ID 'technology system' (TS) level. More recently, the validity of national innovation studies has been questioned (Edquist, 1997, p. 11). The terms sectoral innovation system (SIS) and technological system (TS) are often used interchangeably by researchers. The reason for this is that both focus on the firm as the central actor. There is however a subtle difference, TS is in actual fact a subset of SIS. For instance, auto-ID is the TS system being analyzed in this book and the industry belongs to the larger sector of electronics and IT. See examples of SIS case studies in section two of Henry (1991, pp. 129-239) and part three of Rosenberg (1994, pp. 159-250). It is the opinion of these researchers that TS studies can influence organizations more directly than national studies which are often aimed at government bodies. It is much easier to shape an industry than a whole nation.

What is so special about SI is that it "...allows for the inclusion not only of economic factors influencing innovation but also of institutional, organizational, social, and political factors. In this sense it is an interdisciplinary approach" (Edquist, 1997, p. 17). SI should be looked at as a whole system because its elements are directly or indirectly related to each other. One advantageous aspect of SI is that each part of the system can be examined on its own or in relation to another one. To study one subsystem can also contribute to the understanding of the whole, to deal with individual elements whether they are technological, educational, organizational, social, cultural, economic or institutional in nature.

National Systems of Innovation and Other Technology Systems

National Systems of Innovation: A Comparative Study (1993), edited by Nelson and Rosenberg, was another landmark study propelling innovation thought forward. Like Sharp, Nelson and Rosenberg used a case study methodology but instead of choosing specific new technologies, the national systems of innovation of fifteen countries were investigated. Most of the case studies were conducted by resident researchers in each country. This may have complicated matters a little because different authors held different interpretations of the same concept of 'national system of innovation' (Edquist, 1997, p. 4). Nevertheless, the book was intended to emphasize empirical evidence first, then to confirm theory. This research spanning fifteen countries was a much larger undertaking than Sharp's earlier projects in 1985 and 1989. The resources and efforts required, to collect the data and present it in a coherent way with a set number of features for each country was a mammoth task, obviously outside the scope of this study.

Findings from the case studies suggested that it did make sense to think of national innovation systems although there was some problem with identifying national borders (Nelson & Rosenberg, 1993, pp. 20, 506). Other difficulties included comparing and contrasting countries with varying economic and political circumstances, and distinguishing cross-border operations such as with transnational firms. At the conclusion, there was evidence to suggest that the technological capabilities of a nation's firms do have an impact on its ability to remain competitive globally. However not all research tasks can produce results at this macro-level, nor is it a requirement. In 1998, Choung authored an article titled, 'Patterns of innovation in Korea and Taiwan', examining thirty-four technical fields among which were telecommunications; semiconductors; electrical devices and systems; and calculators computers and other office systems. While Choung identifies Korea and Taiwan as the geographic settings for his study, the focus is on the thirty-four technical fields not on the actual countries.

Micro-level projects have their benefits also. They are likely to uncover more detailed results and recommendations that are easier to implement within a firm or industry. The issue with a national comparative study is, who are the results aimed at and what types of organizations are willing to react to the findings? Consequently the term systems of innovation without the word 'national' has become more acceptable as a framework, giving the researcher the flexibility he or she needs to work at any level; national, regional, sectoral or industry-specific. Evidence of the SI framework is particularly apparent throughout Nelson and Rosenberg's (1993, p. 15) introduction: *"Technological advance proceeds through the interaction of many actors. Above we have considered some of the key interactions involved, between component and system producers, upstream and downstream firms, universities and industry, and government agencies and universities and industries. The important interactions, the networks, are not the same in all industries or technologies."*

Contrary to both studies conducted by Sharp and, Nelson and Rosenberg, this investigation will focus on a single industry, i.e. auto-ID. Nelson and Rosenberg (1993, p. 13) themselves deem this to be positive, acknowledging that "...there are important interindustry differences in the nature of technical change, the sources, and how the involved actors are connected to each other..." Carlsson and Stankiewicz (1991, p. 111) are also in agreement with a technology and industry specific focus. As mentioned, they have termed this idea "technology system" (TS) where upon a "...greater emphasis is placed on the way specific clusters of firms, technologies, and industries are related in the generation and diffusion of new technologies and on the knowledge flows that take place among them" (Breschi & Malerba, 1997, p. 130).

Empirical Studies at the Sectoral Level

In Henry (1991), some very interesting papers were published in *Forecasting Technological Innovation*; proceedings of the Eurocourse lectures delivered in Italy the previous year. Many of the case studies presented used a sector-level approach and investigated high technologies such as advanced materials (Malaman), machinery and automation (Parker), electronics and information technology (Drangeid), telecommunications (Bigi & Cariello), transport (Marchetti) and biotechnology (Roels). The study on telecommunications is the one with which this forthcoming auto-ID study will be most closely aligned stylistically. Rosenberg (1994) also uses a sectoral approach in his case studies of technological change in energy, chemical processing, telecommunications, and forest products. Banbury's 1997 study however, *Surviving Technological Innovation in the Pacemaker Industry, 1959-1990*, is that study that can be considered a precursor to this book. Banbury's work shows the validity of a micro-level investigation on an individual industry and the excellent results which can be achieved.

In so far as the method is concerned for this research project, case studies will be more exploratory in the style of Sharp than Nelson and Rosenberg. The results of the study are not meant to be quantifiable (e.g. how many patents, how many firms) but rather qualitative (e.g. what are the organizational and institutional dynamics). In terms of the structure of the literature review, this now concludes the space dedicated to the review of theories, theoretical frameworks and methods adopted by other researchers doing similar innovation and diffusion studies.

CONCLUSION

The fundamental purpose of the review on innovation literature was to establish a plausible conceptual framework within which to study auto-ID innovation. This study will use key terms and concepts defined by researchers in evolutionary theory, to describe trends that are occurring in the auto-ID industry. In approach, it will incorporate the interdisciplinary SI framework to identify the factors affecting innovation and diffusion in the auto-ID industry. As shown from the critical review, the framework of SI is very flexible. It allows the researcher to include and exclude data dependent on the scope of the problem, macro or micro in level. By collecting the data using a case study methodology, this study will also be adopting the example of many other researchers (e.g. Sharp, Nelson and Rosenberg) in the field of innovation. Case studies are compatible with the kind of research that requires exploration and are common in books on automatic identification. Indicative of the widespread applicability of the SI framework is the support it has gained from researchers all over Europe especially. Researchers in business, economics, sociology, industrial management and information technology have contributed to its development (see Edquist, 1997). While some may regard this to be a disadvantage, interdisciplinary research has boomed in the 1990s and has even been adopted by researchers in Asia and North America.

REFERENCES

Allaby, M. (1995). *Facing The Future: the case for science*. London: Bloomsbury.

Anderson, P., & Tushman, M. L. (1990). Technological discontinuities and dominant designs. A cyclical model of technological change. *Administrative Science Quarterly, 35*(4), 604-633.

Banbury, C. M. (1997). *Surviving Technological Innovation in the Pacemaker Industry 1959-1990*. New York: Garland Publishing.

Baumol, W., & Blinder, A. S. (1992). *Economics: principles and policy*. Sydney: HBJ.

Berry, A. (1996). *The Next 500 Years: life in the coming millennium*. New York: Gramercy Books.

Bijker, W. E. (1995). *Of Bicycles, Baekelite and Bulbs: towards a theory of sociotechnical change*. Cambridge: MIT Press.

Bijker, W. E., & Law, J. (Eds.). (1992). *Shaping Technology/Building Society: studies in sociotechnical change*. Massachusetts: The MIT Press.

Braun, E. (1984). *Wayward Technology*. London: Frances Pinter.

Breschi, S., & Malerba, F. (1997). Sectoral innovation systems: technological regimes, Schumpeterian dynamics, and spatial boundaries. In C. Edquist (Ed.), *Systems of Innovation: technologies, institutions and organizations* (pp. 130-156). London: Pinter.

Brown, G. B., & Karagozoglu, N. (1989). A systems model of technological innovation. *IEEE Transactions on Engineering Management, 36*(1), 11-16.

Carlsson, B. (Ed.). (1995). *Technological Systems and Economic Performance: the case of factory automation*. Dordrecht: Kluwer.

Carlsson, B., & Stankiewicz, R. (1991). On the nature, function and composition of technological systems. *Journal of Evolutionary Economics, 1*(2), 93-118.

Choung, J.-Y. (1998). Patterns of innovation in Korea and Taiwan. *IEEE Transactions on Engineering Management, 45*(4), 357-365.

Clark, N. (1987). Similarities and differences between scientific and technological paradigms. *Futures* (19), 1-24.

Cohendet, P., & Llerena, P. (1997). Learning, technical change, and public policy: how to create and exploit diversity. In C. Edquist (Ed.), *Systems of Innovation: technologies, institutions and organizations* (pp. 223-241). London: Pinter.

Covell, A. (2000). *Digital Convergence: how the merging of computers, communications, and multimedia is transforming our lives.* Rhode Island: Aegis Publishing.

Darwin, C. (1960). The origin of species by means of natural selection. In *Great Books of the Western World* (Vol. 49). London: Encyclopedia Britannica.

Dosi, G. (1982). Technological paradigms and technological trajectories: a suggested interpretation of the determinants and directions of technical change. *Research Policy, 2*(3), 147-162.

Dosi, G. (Ed.). (1988). *Technical Change and Economic Theory.* London: Pinter.

Durand, T. (1991). Forecasting the strategic impact of technological innovation on competitive dynamics in industries. In B. Henry (Ed.), *Forecasting Technological Innovation* (pp. 41-54). Boston: Kluwer Academic Publishers.

Edquist, C. (1998a). Findings and conclusions of ISE case studies on public technology procurement. *Innovation Systems and European Integration (ISE)*(April), 1-39.

Edquist, C. (1998b). The ISE policy statement. *Innovation Systems and European Integration (ISE),* 1-26.

Edquist, C. (Ed.). (1997). *Systems of Innovation: Technologies, Institutions and Organizations.* London: Pinter.

Edquist, C., & Johnson, B. (1997). Institutions and organizations in systems of innovation. In C. Edquist (Ed.), *Systems of Innovation: Technologies, Institutions and Organizations* (pp. 36-63). London: Pinter.

Edquist, C., & McKelvey, M. (2000). *Systems of Innovation: Growth, Competitiveness and Employment.* London: Edward Elgar Publishing.

Elam, M. (1992, 12-15 August). *National systems of innovation in social and political theory.* Paper presented at the EASST/4S Conference, Sweden.

Elliot, B. (1988). *Technology and Social Process.* Edinburgh: Edinburgh University Press.

Farrell, C. J. (1993). Survival of the fittest technologies. *New Scientist.*

Fox, R. (Ed.). (1996). *Technological Change: methods and themes in the history of technology.* Australia: Harwood Academic Publishers.

Freeman, C. (1987). *Technology Policy and Economic Performance: lessons from Japan.* London: Pinter.

Friedman, A. L. (1994). The information technology field: using fields and paradigms for analyzing technological change. *Human Relations, 47*(4), 367-393.

Habermas, J. (1981). Ideology. In T. Bottomore (Ed.), *Modern Interpretations of Marx* (pp. 155-170). Oxford: Basil Blackwell.

Henry, B. (Ed.). (1991). *Forecasting Technological Innovation*. Boston: Kluwer Academic Publishers.

Hirooka, M. (1998). *Business opportunity and technology fusion in terms of innovation dynamism*. Paper presented at the IEMC '98.

Hong, S. (1998). Unfaithful offspring? Technologies and their trajectories. *Perspectives on Science, 6*(3), 259-269.

Keating, D. A. (1997). *Leadership of systematic technology innovation and the advanced professional education of engineers*. Paper presented at the Fifth International Conference on FACTORY 2000.

Landau, R. (1982). The innovative milieu. In S. B. Lundstedt & E. W. Colgazier (Eds.), *Managing Innovation: the social dimensions of creativity, invention and technology* (pp. 53-74). New York: Pergamon Press.

Lindley, R. A. (1997). *Smart Card Innovation*. Australia: Saim.

Lipsett, M. S., & Smith, R. K. (1995). *Cybernetics, and (real) National Innovation Systems*. Paper presented at the IEEE International Conference on Intelligent Systems for the 21st Century.

Lundvall, B.-A. (Ed.). (1992). *National Systems of Innovation: towards a theory of innovation and interactive learning*. London: Pinter.

MacKenzie, D. (1996). *Knowing Machines: essays on technological change*. Cambridge: MIT.

MacKenzie, D., & Wajcman, J. (Eds.). (1999). *The Social Shaping of Technology*. Buckingham: Open University Press.

Marx, K. (1976). *Capital* (Vol. 1). New York: Penguin Books.

McKelvey, M. (2000). *Evolutionary Innovations: The Business of Biotechnology*. Oxford: Oxford University Press.

McKelvey, M., & Orsenigo, L. (2006). *The Economics of Biotechnology: A Reference Collection* Cheltenham: Edward Elgar Publishers.

McKelvey, M., Rickne, A., & Laage-Hellman, J. (2004). *The Economic Dynamics of Modern Biotechnology*. Cheltenham: Edward Elgar Publishers.

McKelvey, M., Texier, F., & Alm, H. (1998). The dynamics of high tech industry: Swedish firms developing mobile telecommunication systems. *Innovation Systems and European Integration (ISE), Sub-project 3.5.2: Technological Diversification Vs. New Innovators*, 1-72.

Mokyr, J. (1996). Evolution and technological change: a new metaphor for economic history? In R. Fox (Ed.), *Technological Change: methods and themes in the history of technology* (pp. 63-83). Australia: Harwood Academic Publishers.

Molina, A. H. (1989). *The Social Basis of the Microelectronics Revolution*. Edinburgh: Edinburgh University Press.

Nelson, R. R. (1981). Research on productivity growth and productivity differences: dead ends and new departures. *Journal of Economic Literature, 19*, 1029-1064.

Nelson, R. R. (1987). *Understanding Technical Change as an Evolutionary Process.* Amsterdam: Elsevier.

Nelson, R. R., & Rosenberg, N. (1993). Technical innovation and national systems. In R. R. Nelson (Ed.), *National Systems of Innovation: A Comparative Study* (pp. 3-21). Oxford: Oxford University Press.

Nelson, R. R., & Winter, S. G. (1982). *An Evolutionary Theory of Economic Change.* Cambridge: Harvard University Press.

Pool, R. (1997). *Beyond Engineering: how society shapes technology.* New York: Oxford University Press.

Prescott, M. B. (1995). Diffusion of innovation theory: borrowings, extensions, and modifications from IT researchers. *ACM SIGMIS Database, 26*(2/3), 16-19.

Prescott, M. B., & Conger, S. A. (1995). Information technology innovations: a classification by IT locus of impact and research approach *SIGMIS Database, 26*(2/3), 20-41.

Queisser, H. (1985). *The Conquest of the Microchip: science and business in the silicon age.* Cambridge: Harvard University Press.

Rogers, E. M. (1962). *Diffusion of Innovations.* New York: The Free Press.

Rosenberg, N. (1994). *Exploring the Black Box: technology, economics, and history.* Great Britain: Cambridge University Press.

Sahal, D. (1981). *Patterns of Technological Innovation.* Massachusetts: Addison-Wesley Publishing Company, Inc.

Saviotti, P. P. (1997). 'Innovation systems and evolutionary theories. In C. Edquist (Ed.), *Systems of Innovation: Technologies, Institutions and Organizations* (pp. 180-199). London: Pinter.

Saxenian, A. (1994). *Regional Advantage: culture and competition in Silicon Valley and Route 128.* Cambridge: Harvard University Press.

Schmookler, J. (1966). *Invention and Economic Growth.* Cambridge: Harvard University Press.

Schumpeter, J. A. (1934). *The Theory of Economic Development.* Cambridge: Harvard University Press.

Schumpeter, J. A. (1939). *Business Cycles: A Theoretical, Historical and Statistical Analysis of the Capitalist Process.* New York: McGraw Hill.

Sharp, M. (Ed.). (1985). *Europe and the New Technologies: six case studies in innovation and adjustment.* Ithaca: Cornell University Press.

Sharp, M., & Holmes, P. (Eds.). (1989). *Strategies for New Technologies: case studies from France and Britain.* Hertfordshire: Philip Allan.

Swartz, J. (1999). The growing 'MAGIC' of automatic identification. *IEEE Robotics & Automation Magazine,* 20-22, 56.

von Hippel, E. (1988). *The Sources of Innovation.* Oxford: Oxford University Press.

Westrum, R. (1991). *Technologies and Society: the shaping of people and things.* California: Wadsworth Publishing Company.

Chapter III
Historical Background:
From Manual Identification to Auto-ID

INTRODUCTION

This chapter takes the reader through a historical tour of identification techniques from ancient times to the present. The histories shed light on how the purpose of citizen identification (ID) has changed as it has been impacted by complementary and supplementary innovations. The chapter provides a thorough exploration of government-to-citizen (G2C) ID systems, so as to better understand the possible uses or potential misuses of current and future mandatory ID schemes. It also presents some of the evolutionary changes that have taken place in the nature and scope of citizen ID, and their subsequent potential implications on society. Historically governments have requested the registering of their population for census collection and more recently the need to know what social benefits accrue to each household. Nowadays, however, citizen ID numbers are even used to open bank accounts and to subscribe to mobile services, among many other things. In addition, auto-ID techniques are not only pervasive but are increasingly becoming invasive. The chapter draws examples from history and emphasizes the types of issues that should be carefully deliberated in the introduction of any new national ID-based scheme. These schemes need forward planning and safeguards beyond those currently provided.

Defining Identification

Identification is defined in several ways, dependent on what aspect is being considered; it is "the act of identifying, the state of being identified [or] something that identifies one" (Macquarie Dictionary, 1998, p. 1062). The verb *identify* is linked to the noun *identity*, such as in the case of the term identity card which can be used to identify someone belonging to a particular group. Founded in Europe (from the Late Latin *identitas*) the word identity became noticeable in the English-speaking world around 1915, primarily through Freud (Pollock, 1993, pp. 1-20). The preferred definition for identity within the context of this book is the "condition, character, or distinguishing features of person or things effective as a means of identification" (Macquarie Dictionary, 1998, p. 1062).

MANUAL IDENTIFICATION

Early Identification Techniques

Before the introduction of computer technology the various means of external identification were greatly limited. The most commonly used method was relying on one's memory to identify the distinguishing features and characteristics of other humans, such as their outward appearance or the sound of their voice. However, relying solely on one's memory had many pitfalls and thus other methods of identification were introduced. These included marks, stamps, brands, cuts or imprints engraved directly onto the skin, which were to be later collectively referred to as tattooing. A tattoo is defined as "...permanent marks or designs made on the body by the introduction of pigment through ruptures in the skin..." (Encyclopedia Britannica, 1983c, p. 841). Tattooing is considered to be the human's first form of expression in written form (Cohen, 1994; Delio, 1993; Gell, 1993; Jaguer, 1990; Sanders, 1989; Rubin, 1988; Jones, 1987).

"All the nomadic peoples try to distinguish themselves from the rest, to make themselves unique and also to establish a means of recognizing their kinsmen in the various clans. In order to achieve this, they resort to the resource which is the most accessible and the most lasting: their skin. This decorated skin defines the boundary against the hostility of the outside world, for it is visible to everyone and it accompanies the individual everywhere" (Grognard, 1994, p. 19).

Historical records date the first tattoo about 2000 BC to Ancient Egypt, though there is evidence to suggest that tattooing was introduced by the Egyptians as early as 4000 BC (Cohen, 1994, p. 25). Tattoos and/or marks on humans were considered both disapprovingly and in some instances (which were not lacking) quite acceptable. An example of the former is in the *Old Testament* in the Book of Leviticus 19:28, where God commands Moses: "You shall not make any cuttings in your flesh on account of the dead or tattoo any marks upon you". Similarly in the *New Testament* in the Book of Revelation 13:16-17, there is the ill-omened passage about the beast who forces everyone "...both small and great, both rich and poor, both free and slave, to be marked on the right hand or the forehead, so that no one can buy or sell unless he has the mark..." Though, strictly speaking, the mark [*charagma*] is not necessarily a tattoo per se. It can be a mark or stamp, engraved, etched, branded, cut, imprinted (Gingrich & Danker, 1958, p. 876). In classical literature, however, tattooing could serve to identify the bearer's rank, status or membership in a group or profession. The historian, Herodotus (c. 484 - c. 425 BC) writes concerning the Thracians, "[t]hey consider branding a mark of high birth, the lack of it a mark of low birth..." (Herodotus, 1972, p. 282). The mark was usually visible for others to recognize. M.G. Michael (1998, pp. 278-301) has written extensively on the topic of tattooing and marking with reference to the Bible. In addition, for a complete guide to tattooing as a form of body art, particularly by people in Africa, Asia and Oceania, see Rubin (1988).

The Misuse of Manual ID

Branding as a method of identification (especially of minority groups) continued throughout history. In antiquity tattooing was generally held in disrepute, "[t]he ancient Greeks branded their slaves (*doulos*) with a delta, and the Romans stamped the foreheads of gladiators, convicted criminals sentenced to the arena, for easy identification" (Cohen, 1994, p. 32). According to Paoli (1990, p. 140), "...the Romans fastened to the necks of slaves who were liable to run away an iron collar with a disc (bulla) firmly attached to it bearing the owner's name and address." Even until 1852, the French penal system would identify thieves by "...a V tattooed on the right shoulder, and galley slaves by the three letters GAL" (Grognard, 1994, p. 25). United States convicts and British Army deserters were similarly treated (Jones, 1987, pp. 148-150).

During the Holocaust

In recent times however, society has become intolerant of tattooing as a means of enforced segregation where the act is committed without the permission of the bearer, and with dubious intent. Nazi dictator Adolf Hitler in his planned genocide of the Jewish people during World War II (1939-1945) enforced various methods of identification to separate them from the rest of the population (Figure 1). There is evidence to suggest that punch cards originally intended to help in the tabulation of census data, were used instead to help segregate the Jewish people from the rest of the German and Polish populations (Black, 2001, pp. 22, 58) (Figure 2). On September of 1941, an order was issued that all Jews were to "...wear a Star of David badge" (Kitchen, 1995, p. 202) (Figure 3). Those who did not comply with such orders were sent to Nazi extermination camps immediately where they were "...branded like animals. A registration number, corresponding to the camp, was stamped on the left forearm. This was preceded with a "D" if the person was Jewish..." (Grognard, 1994, p. 21).

In the *Drowned and the Saved*, Primo Levi (1986, p. 118f), an Auschwitz survivor, writes of the mandatory tattooing of individuals that occurred in the concentration camp:

...a true and proper code soon began to take shape: men were tattooed on the outside of the arm and women on the inside; the numbers of the Zigeuner, the gypsies, had to be preceded by a Z. The number of a Jew, starting in May 1944... had to be preceded by an A, which shortly after was replaced by a B... After this date, [September 1944] there began to arrive entire families of Poles... all of them were tattooed, including newborn babies.

Figure 1. An identification card bearing a photo of a child holding a cup and a piece of bread in the Kielce ghetto. An official ID card was required to receive food rations at the soup kitchen organized by the Jewish Social Self-help Committee of the Jewish Council. The ID card was issued for the month of May 1941, and was valid only for breakfast. The inscription in Polish reads, "1,600 morning meals served daily."

Courtesy of the US Holocaust Memorial Museum

Figure 2. Buchenwald Concentration Camp Prisoner Data Card for Symcho Dymant. Symcho Dymant arrived in Buchenwald on December 12, 1944. The data card indicates that Dymant's personal data had been transferred onto a Hollerith machine punch card.

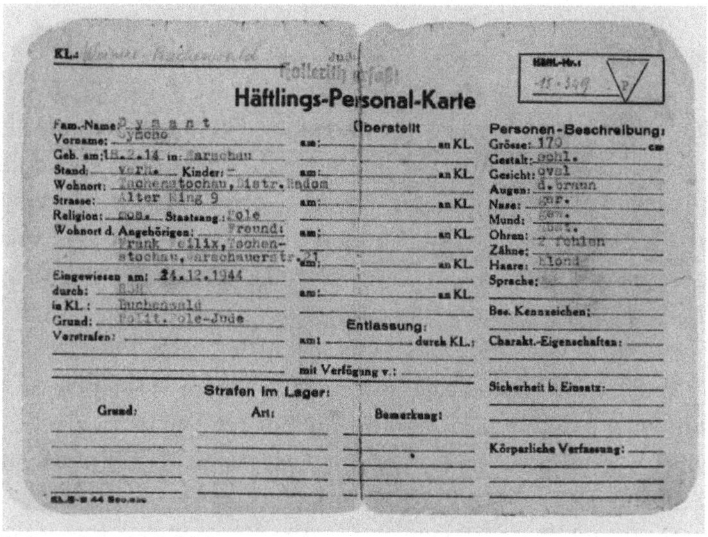

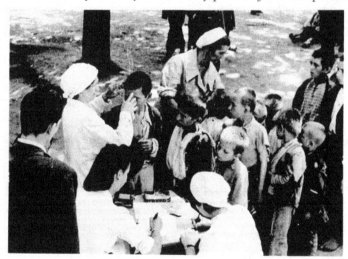

KL.:

Hollerith erfaßt

Häftlings-Personal-Karte

Häftl.-Nr.:

Fam.-Name: Dymant
Vorname: Symcho
Geb. am: 18.2.14 in: Warschau
Stand: verh. Kinder: -
Wohnort: Tschenstochau, Distr. Radom
Strasse: Alter Ring 9
Religion: mos. Staatsang.: Pole
Wohnort d. Angehörigen: Freund: Frank Feilix, Tschenstochau, Warschauerstr. 21
Eingewiesen am: 24.12.1944
durch:
in KL.: Buchenwald
Grund: Polit. Pole-Jude
Vorstrafen:

Überstellt
am: an KL.
am: an KL.
am: an KL.
am: an KL.
am: an KL.
am: an KL.

Entlassung:
am: durch KL.:
mit Verfügung v.:

Personen-Beschreibung:
Grösse: 170 cm
Gestalt: schl.
Gesicht: oval
Augen: d. braun
Nase: gr.
Mund:
Ohren:
Zähne:
Haare: blond
Sprache:
Bes. Kennzeichen:
Charakt.-Eigenschaften:
Sicherheit b. Einsatz:
Körperliche Verfassung:

Strafen im Lager:

Grund:	Art:	Bemerkung:

Courtesy of the US Holocaust Memorial Museum

Figure 3. Children are led through a registration process at the Stara Gradiska concentration camp before being transported to Zagreb. Jasenovac was a complex of five concentration camps established between August 1941 and February 1942 by the security police of the Independent State of Croatia.

Source: "Jasenovac," Holocaust Learning Center, (28 August 2002); Savich, Carl; Lituchy, Barry, brochure of the Jasenovac Research Institute, c.2000, http://www.logon.org/_domain/holocaustrevealed.org/Jasenovac/Jasenovac.htm (28 August 2002)]

Courtesy of the US Holocaust Memorial Museum

In this case both the character and the number were used for identification. The character indicated the group the individual was linked to and the number uniquely identified the individual. The numbers were serialized numerically and accompanied by shapes, symbols and letters which identified the prisoner's status, nationality, or religion (Rosenthal, 2008). Women were not issued numbers from the same series as the men. Another survivor was quoted in *The Nazi Doctors: medical killing and the psychology of genocide,*

"I remember when… that thing [the number tattooed on each prisoner's forearm] was put on" (Lifton, 1986, p. 165). That thing according to another account stood for dehumanization. "And as they gave me my tattoo number, B-4990, the SS man came to me, and he says to me,| "Do you know what this number's all about?"| I said, "No, sir."| "Okay, let me tell you now. You are being dehumanized." (Michael Berenbaum, 1993, p. 147 quoted in Dery, 1996, p. 311)

There were various methods of applying the tattoo as described by Rosenthal (2008), in addition to placing the tattoo on differing locations on the body, based on the group the individual belonged to. For some Soviet prisoners-of-war (POWs) captured by the Nazis in 1941, a number was tattooed "by means of a metal plate with interchangeable needles attached to it; the plate was impressed into the flesh on the left side of their chests and then dye would be rubbed into the wound." After a month of interrogation and inspection, the POWs were then placed into sub-groups such as "fanatic Communist", "politically suspect", "not politically suspect" or "suitable for reeducation". This was a type of manual-based social sorting (Lyon, 2004) which for instance, identified 300 "fanatic Communists" (Czech, 1990, p. 102). Later in 1942, the practice of tattooing on the forearm of individuals was done with pen and ink, mainly to Jewish persons, and only systematically at the Auschwitz Concentration Camp Complex. The practice of branding was not confined to the Nazis. Up until the fall of Communism the practice was even continued by the former Soviet Union on exiled criminals and political prisoners in Siberia, for security purposes.

The Importance of Context

The wearing of a badge does not immediately imply the misuse of ID- it all depends on the context and who it is that has requested this manner of identification and for what purpose. For instance, European migrants in the early 1900s traveling by ship to New York City were given a badge to wear to make identification easier while going through immigration (Marcantonio, 1940). The badge was either pinned on clothing or as in the majority of cases tied to a cotton necklace. After undergoing a medical examination certain letters would be recorded on the badge to identify the condition of the immigrant, especially if further screening was required. Those suspected of suffering from mental illness or other health concerns not acceptable to authorities were separated from larger groups and sent back to their homeland. There was simply no other manner in which hundreds of thousands of people could be processed efficiently in such a short period (Figure 10). The badge also alleviated the requirement for the migrant to communicate with officials, especially because the majority did not know English.

One can see that the early identification techniques, while primitive in nature, could be hideously misused against minority groups in helpless situations. Plainly, when a technique becomes available it is applied wherever it is required, "without distinction of good or evil" by whomever has the capability and authority (Ellul, 1964, pp. 98-100). There has been much written on whether technology or techniques, possess a "moral neutrality" (Brown, 1990, ch. 2). Mumford and Gideon hold the stance that "if a technology fails to alleviate misery, but only compounds it… the blame falls not on the tools, which are themselves neutral" but upon external factors such as historical circumstances (Kuhns, 1971, pp. 82-83). Ellul on the other hand, believes that the technique itself has an autonomous mandate, that

"...once man has given technique its entry into society, there can be no curbing of its gathering influence, no possible way of forcing it to relinquish its power. Man can only witness and serve as the ironic beneficiary-victim of its power". That being true, advances in data collection techniques have even greater far-reaching effects.

ADVANCES IN RECORD KEEPING

As manual record keeping procedures evolved, identification became an integral part of the data collection process. Widespread branding of people was unacceptable and thus other means had to be developed to allow authorities to keep track of individuals. These means varied drastically throughout the ages but increased in sophistication especially after the Industrial Revolution. When computerization occurred most of the manual techniques were ported into an electronic environment (Figure 4). This part of the chapter sheds light on some of the incremental innovations that led to the development of automatic identification.

The Registering of People and the Census

The registering of people dates back to ancient times, see for example, 1 Chronicles 21:1, 7 and Esther 6:1. Also, in 2 Samuel 24:2, "Go through all the tribes of Israel, from Dan to Beer-sheba, and number the people, that I may know the number of the people." And in Luke 2:1-3, "In those days a decree went out from Caesar Augustus that all the world should be enrolled. This was the first enrolment, when Quirin'i-us was governor of Syria. And all went to be enrolled, each to his own city." The Romans were

Figure 4. Naturalization certificate issued to Sylvia Amar, a Greek-Jewish immigrant. On the line marked visible distinctive marks is written her Auschwitz tattoo number. USHMM, courtesy of Meryl Menashe.

particularly advanced in their data collection requirements, wishing not only to count but to gather additional information about their citizens (Scullard, 1981, pp. 232f):

A periodic census of Roman citizens was held... every four years, but from 209 BC onwards... every five years... This was a reflection of the mustering of the army into centuries, and it was these men, grouped in the five classes, that were the chief concern of the censors who had to register them in their tribes and assess their property in order to assign them to the correct classes for purposes of both taxation and military services. The head of each family had to answer questions about the property and age of all its members...

Censors had to rely on manual identification techniques to ensure the accuracy of inventories. This was a very difficult and time-consuming task, especially since "...houses had no numbers, and many streets were nameless. The ancients had not discovered the countless practical advantages of numbers" (Paoli, 1990, p. 138). An error made by the censor could impact the life of a citizen since,

early inventories were made to control particular individuals- for example, to identify who should be taxed, inducted into military service, or forced to work... Strictly speaking, the modern population census began in the 17th century. Before then, inventories of people, taxpayers, or valuables were made; but the methods and purposes were different to modern ones. (Britannica Encyclopedia, 1983a, p. 679)

As can be seen, over time newer more advanced techniques were developed which ultimately served to change the purpose of the population census. More automated means of identification and data collection made it possible for census surveys to be extended. For example, in the U.S. Census of 1890, part of the process of classifying and counting the data collected was automated (Comppile, 2004). Herman Hollerith invented a method that allowed census takers to punch holes in predetermined locations to represent various characteristics. The holes were then processed by a machine. As elementary as this may seem, such advances led to subsequent breakthroughs in the field (Austrian, 1982). Of course, this does not mean that errors in the data collection of personal information are no longer incurred.

Record-Keeping by the Church and State

The overall intent of a census was to determine the aggregate profile of people residing within a defined geographic region so that authorities could address their needs appropriately. Census statistics,

"*are used as the basis for estimating the population at the national, state and local government levels, for electoral purposes and the distribution of government funds. They are used by individuals and organizations, in the public and private sectors, for planning, administration, research, and decision making*" (Castles, 1993, p. 35).

However with advances in social welfare, authorities required to know more specific details about their citizens and their individual circumstances. In establishing an official relationship with the citizen, identification and specialized record keeping practices became important from the perspective of the state (i.e. for the purpose of citizenship). A variety of paper-based documentation was instituted; in some cases special seals or ink-based stamps were used to indicate legality. Examples of official documentation included land title deeds, birth certificates and bank account records. These were among the most common proofs of identity but this varied dependent on the state in question and period of history.

The Notion of a Personal Document File

The importance of the Church in the evolution of record-keeping should also be highlighted. In many parts of the world the local church was a thorough documenter of events and very much an integral part of government until about the Middle Ages. For instance, church laws and state laws ran in parallel until the Middle Ages. Church and State had their own law and court systems and there were often issues over jurisdictional rights (Anglim, 1999). The interaction of the Church and State led to developments in the centralization of government and bureaucracy (Caenegem, 1988). With the centralization of power came a need for the centralization of citizen information which led to the creation of personal files. Churches also provided proofs of identity, such as marriage and baptismal certificates. Some churches even kept records of disputes or wrong-doings and how victims had been recompensed. Given that the size of towns was relatively small compared to today, names could be used to identify individuals. But the Industrial Revolution was set to change things dramatically, especially as mass production drew large groups of people (in most cases from surrounding towns) closer towards employment opportunities in factories. Given names and surnames were not always unique. In some instances the name was accompanied by the paternal lineage, or an address location, or by a nickname. However even address locations in ancient times were for the greater part difficult to precisely identify. In ancient Rome for instance, roads were nameless "and were referred to simply by such expressions as 'The road to'... a few of the more important had names..." (Paoli, 1990, p. 141).

One of the earliest modern day responses to improved identification techniques and record keeping standards came in 1829. In that year, British Parliament made a decision to enact the reforms of Prime Minister Robert Peel who wanted more emphasis to be placed on printed police records. In this manner relevant data could be stored in a personal document file and linked back to individuals using a unique value. In many ways these records were forerunners to government databases that were linked to ID cards. During this same period, photographic technology was invented but it was not until 1840 that amateur scientist William Henry Fox Talbot developed the negative-positive photographic system which eventually became a useful police identification tool. In an age of computers, humans generally take for granted the invention of the still-shot camera and motion camera because the technology is so readily available. But a simple ID badge with a photograph on it really did not become widespread until after the turn of the 20th century. Photographs fastened to cards were excellent manual identifiers before the proliferation of cameras which then enabled fake IDs to be developed by criminals. As soon as this occurred an additional measure was required to ensure positive identification.

Signatures were about the most unique method of cross-checking someone's identity between original and duplicate copies. This was all dependent on the literacy level of the individual, though unique markings were accepted as substitutes. By the late 1870s, a significant breakthrough in identification came about in India. Sir William Herschel (a British 'Magistrate and Collector') had made a defendant's fingerprint part of court records. Ron Benrey also reported that Herschel used fingerprints as manual signatures on wills and deeds (Connecticut Dept, 1998). For the first time, a biometric had officially become a means of precise identification. In 1901, police technology had advanced so much that Scotland Yard had introduced the Galton-Henry system of fingerprint classification (Lee & Gaensslen, 1994). To the present times, fingerprints have been associated with crime for this reason. The system did not become widespread because the practicality of taking fingerprints of all citizens and cross-matching records for individual transactions was not viable.

The Evolution of the Citizen ID Number

Unique citizen identification numbers were adopted by numerous countries around the period of the Great Depression in the 1930s. Unique identifiers in the context of citizen numbers are known by a variety of names. These include: identification number (IN), personal identification number (PIN), uniform personal identification mark (UPIM), national identification number (NIN), universal identification number (UIN), unique identification system (UIS), universal identifiers (UID), unique personal identifier (UPI), single identifying number (SIN), standard universal identifier (SUI), universal multipurpose identifier (UMI), universal personal number (UPN), unique lifetime identifier (ULI). The majority of these nation-wide numbering schemes have been maintained, relatively unchanged, till today. Some of the national numbering schemes include: the Person Number (PN) system of Norway, the Central Register of Persons (CRP) in Denmark, the German Insurance Number (GIN), the Social Account Number (SAN) of Austria, the Insurance Number (IN) of the former Czechoslovakia, the French Identification Number (FIN), the Insured Persons Number (IPN) of Switzerland and the National Insurance Number (NIN) of the United Kingdom (New Zealand Computer Society, 1972).

The initial person registration system used in Sweden dates back about three hundred years when the process involved the Church of Sweden. Local parishes were considered to be like regional administration offices. But in 1947 each person was assigned a PN that was recorded electronically in 1967 from metal plates to magnetic tape. The Netherlands used the census of 1849 as a starting point for there decentralized PN system. But in 1940 personal cards with unique numbers were issued to the whole population that acted as lifetime identifiers. In Israel a PN was allotted in 1948 via a census after the State of Israel was officially established. A Population Registry Law in 1965 established the basic information that had to be collected when registering. This involved disclosing details about the ethnic group that one belonged to, as well as religious beliefs and past and present nationalities. In 1966, this information was computerized. Iceland has used a population register since 1953. When a citizen reaches the age of twelve they are given a number that is based on the alphabetical sequence of a person's name in the total population. In 1964, Norway's Central Bureau of Statistics was asked to establish a national identification numbering system as the world learnt of the potential of electronic data processing (EDP). In 1968, Denmark followed in Norway's footsteps by computerizing their records as well. France has used numbering systems for individuals and organizations since 1941. The system was computerized in 1973 after existing records were put on magnetic tape and adapted to include check digits. Finland introduced their personal identification code (PIC) system in 1964 (Lunde et al. 1980).

The potential for a globally implemented unique national identifier (UNI) is realistic. This could be tied in with the concept of a follow-me telephone number such as that defined in Universal Personal Telecommunications (UPT). UPT "...will enable each user to participate in a user-defined set of subscribed services and to initiate and receive calls on the basis of a personal, network-transparent UPT Number across multiple networks and any terminals, fixed or mobile, irrespective of geographic location limited only by terminal and network capabilities and restrictions imposed by the network operator" (ITC, 1992). For the purpose of showing the evolution of the citizen ID number, one of the oldest schemes, the United States social security number (SSN), will be discussed in more detail. The maturation of the SSN is representative of many person number schemes worldwide.

CASE STUDY: THE U.S. SOCIAL SECURITY ADMINISTRATION (SSA)

By the 1920s, countries such as Britain, Germany and France were using personal document files to administer specific government assistance schemes for unemployment, worker's compensation, health, pensions and child endowment (Clark, 1943, p. 9). Western European countries had established population registers that were updated continually to include the name, residence, age, sex and marital status of an individual. The registers were administered at a municipal or county level initially but towards the mid-1900s they became more centralized. There was an increasing demand for the registers by government for voting, education, welfare, police and the courts (Lunde et al., 1980, p. 1). In observing the processes of the European governments, the United States (U.S.) sought even more efficient methods of identification. Thus the Social Security Administration (SSA) was formed, a centrally managed scheme, supported by an official Act in 1935. The SSA was instituted by President Roosevelt after the impact of the Great Depression in the early 1930s. This act was designed to protect individuals and their families from unemployment, old age, sickness etc (SSA, 2003). Setting up the program was a daunting task. The U.S. government was dealing with a large group of people (five million elderly people alone), each personal record attached to several applications (pension, medicare, family allowance etc.), and individuals were geographically dispersed. Since money and benefits were being distributed at a cost to taxpayers, the government was obligated to establish guidelines as to eligibility, proof of identity and citizenship to keep track of funds.

The SSN Gathers Momentum – More than Just a Number

As government policies became more sophisticated, administrators required a mechanism for the unique identification of individuals to improve the efficiency of operations. In 1938 the social security number

Figure 5. "U.S. Army Photo" Console of BRLESC-II computer, front view, from the archives of the ARL Technical Library. At the console: Alexander V. Kurian Note high-speed card reader in foreground, high-speed line printer behind CPU. BRLESC (Ballistic Research Laboratory's Electronic Scientific Computer) 1966-1978. This is the type of computer that the SSA would have first used.

(SSN) was introduced. The SSN was phased in to reduce the incidence of duplicate records, allow for more accurate updates and ensure that entitlements were received by the bona fide. With the introduction of the SSN came the social security card. Each card contained the nine digit SSN and the cardholder's name. The card (with the printed number on it) was useful in that cardholders could carry it with them and quote it freely when requested to fill out government forms. It meant that citizens did not have to memorize the number and risk referencing it incorrectly. The card also acted as a proof of identity. This deterred many people from making fraudulent claims, yet the quality of the paper card was poor and susceptible to damage. Thus the need for cards to be made out of more durable material. Cards made out of cardboard were initially introduced, followed by plastic cards with embossing. By 1943, President Roosevelt had signed "...Executive Order 9397 (EO9397) which required federal agencies to use the number [SSN] when creating new record-keeping systems" (Hibbert, 1996, p. 693).

In the early fifties the insurance and banking sector also adopted the SSN and requested it from each individual who wanted to open a bank account and make monetary transactions. By 1961, the Internal Revenue Service (IRS) was also using the SSN as a taxpayer identification number (TIN) (SSA, 2002). It can be seen that knowledge gained from the improved administration of government services was applied to other sectors, such as finance. Thus the ID number itself, had two important uses when the computer age arrived. First it could be used as a primary key for storing personal information in databases. "The PN, as a computer file key, has the characteristics of uniqueness, permanence, reliability, and universality" (Lunde et al., 1980, p. 2). Second it could be linked with any identification technique for authentication or verification. It was the ID itself that was fundamental to these applications whether in the form of a unique number, character set, symbol or image. The ID device accompanying the ID was more a facilitator. What should be observed is that even without advanced machinery and automatic identification techniques, the underlying information systems concept had been born.

The Computerization of Records

The proportion of recorded transactions was now reaching new limits in the United States. Written records had served their purpose but could no longer effectively support the collection, storage and processing of data. Government agencies were plagued by such problems as limited physical storage space for paper documentation; slow response times to personal inquiries; inaccurate information stored in personal records; difficulties in making updates to records; duplicate information existing for a single person; and illegal and fraudulent claims for benefits by persons. By 1970 the SSA had set up its headquarters in Baltimore. The basic data stored there included the "...social security status of every citizen with a social security registration... and equivalent records on all phases of the Medicare program." The SSA had established 725 field offices and citizen transactions were communicated to SSA headquarters via dedicated circuits where it was received on magnetic tape ready for input into the SSA computer (Miller, 1970, p. 77) (Figure 5).

Initially the types of analysis that could be performed on the records were limited (Lipetz, 1966). By 1977 however, the government had not only computerized its paper records but had even developed computer matching applications (Figure 6). The Public Law 95-216 "mandated that state welfare agencies use stage wage information in determining eligibility for Aid to Families with Dependent Children (ADFC). Subsequent legislation also required similar wage matching for the Food stamp program" (Kusserow, 1984). By the early 1980s it was common for data matching programs to check personal records between social security, other federal agencies and the banking sector. In this manner the government could determine whether a citizen was receiving legitimate funds and contributing to the nations numerous taxes.

The emergence of the microprocessor and the development of electronic storage devices enabled the invention of information technologies that could automate the process of identifying living and non-living things (Yoffie, 1997, pp. 41-110). Historically, auto-ID systems have been constrained by the capabilities of other technologies they have been dependent upon. Limitations in network infrastructure, central processing unit (CPU) speeds, electronic storage space, microchip miniaturization, application software and data collection devices are just some of the components that have impacted auto-ID. For example, it has already been noted in this chapter that the first biometric manually recorded for criminal records was the fingerprint as far back as the 1870s. However, it took more than one hundred years to develop a commercial electronic fingerprint recognition system that had the ability to store thousands of fingerprint minutiae and cross-match against a large database of records with a workable response time.

Problems with Some Government Citizen Identifiers

The U.S. social security number ultimately became a multi-purpose identifier though originally it was only meant to be used for social security purposes. As paper records were transferred into a machine-readable format and simple searches performed it became apparent that there were duplicate SSNs. One must note that the SSN was created without the knowledge of how computer technology would revolutionize the government's processes. By the time computers and networks were introduced into the SSA's practices, the SSN was a legacy system that maintained numerous well-established problems. At the center of these problems was that the identifier's composition was not unique; neither was it randomly or sequentially generated. The nine digit SSN was broken up into three sections: area number assigned to states on a population basis, group number (2 digits), serial number assigned sequentially (4 digits) which was controlled by the first six letters of the person's surname (New Zealand Computer Society, 1972, p. 28). When the regional-based ID numbers were pooled together to form a central population register (CPR) the IDs were found not to be unique. As Hibbert (1996, pp. 686-696) critically pointed out, "[m]any people assume that Social Security numbers are unique, but the SSA didn't take sufficient precautions to ensure that it would be so". In addition to this, the SSA itself was forced to admit that more than four million people had two or more SSNs (Westin & Baker, 1972, pp. 396-400).

This immediately posed a problem for both authorities and citizens. The computer system could not handle cases adequately whereby there were more than 999 persons with a surname beginning with the exact same 6 letters living in the same area (as defined by the SSA). While this may sound impossible to achieve some names are very common and a lot of surnames are shorter than 6 characters in length. In other cases the problems that some citizens have endured after their SSN has been stolen, have been well-documented on current affairs programs. The call for some other means of identification, automatic in nature, was heeded and many states more recently have acted to implement state-of-the-art biometric and smart card-based systems to alleviate issues of duplication and crime. The rest of the world have followed the U.S. example, more recently even those countries considered as either lesser developed (LDC) or newly industrialized countries (NIC).

As of 2003, those LDCs and NICs that had PNs for over twenty years included: Argentina (Documento Nacional de Identidad DNI), Chile (Rol Unico Nacional RUN), Colombia, Peru (Event Identification Number EIN), Uruguay and Jordan. The need for PN systems in LDCs and NICs are considered as greater than those in MDCs. Usually LDCs in particular, have very large populations and huge data management problems. In terms of planning for such things as basic infrastructure (e.g. housing, education, employment, health) the task becomes even more difficult without a PN. For example, the distribution of benefits like food, if not handled properly, could become life-threatening to citizens. Thus the recent introduction of smart cards for food rations in many LDCs, as the global economy experiences rises in food prices given the looming oil crisis. Most cards also store a photograph of an individual as well as a biometric. Many countries in Asia also, are now beginning to introduce auto-ID devices for government administration. Examples include Cambodia, Taiwan and China.

THE RISE OF AUTOMATIC IDENTIFICATION TECHNIQUES

The Commercialization of Identification

New technological innovations originally intended for government often find themselves being applied commercially within a short period of time. The lessons of the SSN and other early identification systems were used to improve processes in banking and retail from the 1970s onwards, as a variety of auto-ID technologies became available to implement. The introduction of the bar code and magnetic-stripe card especially was noticeable because it directly impacted the way people shopped and banked. Consumers now had the ability to withdraw funds without having to visit a bank branch. Shop store owners could use bar codes on products to improve their inventory control and employ fewer workers because of the speed of checking-out customers. These innovations were not only targeted at what one would term mass market but they affected every single person in the community. The bar code was linked to the purchasing of food and other goods, and the magnetic-stripe card to money that is required for survival in a modern society. As one scientist wrote in 1965 "...the impact of automation on the individual involve[d] a reconstruction of his values, his outlook and his way of life" (Sacleman, 1967, pp. 36, 552-560).

Too Many IDs?

As government and enterprise databases became widespread and increased in sophistication, particularly after the introduction of the desktop computer in 1984, implementing auto-ID solutions became possible for even the smallest of businesses. Auto-ID could be applied to just about any service. The vision of a cashless society gained momentum as more and more transactions were being made electronically and the promise of smart cards was being publicized. But instead of wallets and purses becoming thinner since the need to carry cash was supposedly diminishing, the number of cards and pieces of identification people had to carry increased significantly. Citizens were now carrying multiple devices with multiple IDs: ATM cards, credit cards, private and public health insurance cards, retail loyalty cards, school student cards, library cards, gym cards, licenses to drive automobiles, passports to travel by air and ship, voting cards etc. Dependent on the application and the auto-ID device being used, passwords were also required as an additional security measure. But since passwords such as Personal Identification Numbers (PINs) were never meant to be recorded, expecting consumers to remember more than one PIN was cumbersome. But as Davies pointed out (1996, p. 121f), while "[m]anaging all these numbers is a chore… it's a state of affairs most of us have learned to accept." This statement was probably an interim truism until the turn of the 21st century. Today, more than ever, most likely due to major technical breakthroughs, there is an underlying view that computers are supposed to make life less complicated rather than more complicated.

The vision is still one where cards (probably multiapplication and multifunctional in nature) will play an important role in identification but whereby other advances such as biometric recognition systems will be an integral part of the solution to ID. Consider the Access Card proposal of 2006 in Australia where it was suggested that 17 different existing benefit cards would be linked and integrated onto the one smart card (Jackson and Ligertwood, 2006, pp. 45-55). Now compare, the contactless rechargeable smart card, known as the Octopus Card that was deployed in Hong Kong in 1994 (Chau and Poon, 2003). Initially, the Octopus Card was used to allow commuters to pay for all modes of public transport (rail, bus, ferry, mini-van). The card then found its way to becoming a citizen identity card with more than 70 per cent of the population subscribed to the e-cash system.

Numbers Everywhere

In his book, *Rome: its people, life and customs*, Ugo E. Paoli (1990, ch. XIII) emphasizes the significance of numbers by describing what it was like in ancient Roman times without street addresses. He contrasts this setting, i.e. the streets without names and the houses without numbers, by referring to how numbers are used profusely today in modern civilization. It is worth quoting Paoli at length (1990, p. 139).

When we travel, our train has a number, as do the carriages, the compartments, the seats, the ticket-collector, the ticket and the note with which we buy our ticket. When we reach the station we take a taxi which is numbered and driven by a driver similarly numbered; on arrival at our hotel we become a number ourselves. Our profession, age, date of arrival and departure are all reckoned in numbers. When we have booked a room, we become a number, 42 perhaps, and if we are so unfortunate as to forget our number we seem to have forgotten ourselves. If we mistake it, we run the risk of being taken for a thief, or worse. The number is on the disc hanging from the key in our room; it is above the letter rack in the hall; every morning we find it chalked on the soles of our shoes, and we continually see it on the door of our room, and, finally, we find it on the bill. We grow so used to our number that it becomes part of us; if we have a parcel sent to the hotel, we give the number 42; however important we may be, to the porter and the chambermaid we are simply No. 42.

Everything is indeed numbered (Figure 6). Even we ourselves are numbered. And as Paoli (1990, p. 140) continues, this great ease in identifying everything is supposedly "a result of our position as modern civilized men." These ubiquitous ID numbers (which include addresses) follow us everywhere, and not

Figure 6. Numbered identification tag worn by Henry Schmelzer when he was a member of a Kinder-transport sent from Austria to England in December 1938

Courtesy of the US Holocaust Memorial Museum

unexpectedly as Paoli also reckons, have almost become a part of our personalities. On extending this notion Paoli (1990, p. 140) reminds us that even if one finds themselves homeless, without an income, without any hope for the future, they still have their ID number. In a similar light what should be underscored is the increasing requirement today towards obligatory practices to do business with one's ID number(s). Whether making a transaction over the counter, through the mail, or on the telephone, service providers have become more interested in our customer reference number than our name. One is led to a justifiable conclusion of whether in amongst all of these manufactured numbers, we are little by little, losing our natural right to be called by our given name, and hence allowing for the overthrow of our identity.

CONCLUSION

Tracing the path from manual identification through to automatic identification some conclusions may be drawn. First, the practice of identification can be sourced to very ancient times. Second, throughout history manual ID of humans was not always a voluntary modus operandi, especially in the enforced tattooing of individuals in authority. Third, the identification processes and procedures that were developed before automation were replicated after automation, and dramatically enhanced because computer technology allowed for more powerful processing of information. Legacy systems however did impact automation. Fourth, the success of auto-ID was dependent on the rise of information technology. In many ways auto-ID was limited by a variety of hardware and software system components. As soon as these became feasible options for service providers, both in affordability and usability, auto-ID flourished. Fifth, the widespread adoption and acceptance of auto-ID by citizens is indicated in that people carry so many different ID devices for different applications. And finally, and most importantly, national ID schemes are becoming increasingly pervasive, complemented by increasingly invasive ID technologies. Governments need to be forward-thinking in introducing privacy and security safeguards when introducing new schemes and/or new devices, or extending existing schemes to new application areas, particularly of a commercial nature such as banking. No one can predict the future but one thing is certain, if a technology (high-tech or other) is open to misuse, it will eventually be abused.

The following chapter is a full-length interview with Mrs Judith Nachum, a Holocaust survivor. The interview presents examples of how simple manual identification techniques were used to identify the Jewish populations during WWII and to gather them into concentration camps (i.e. a type of manual-based social sorting, Lyon, 2004) and then rigorously applied to dehumanize the targeted people. The interview is explicit in stating how the Nazis were meticulous record keepers, and how identification numbers granted them the ability to link numerous pieces of information together. The Nazis were well-known for keeping detailed hand-written registers, including of Jewish-owned property for each family. The interview with Mrs Nachum, demonstrates that there should be limits as to how governments use "technique" to record citizen information. It also suggests while another similar type of 'holocaust' might seem unlikely, that the power of the digital medium to control, if ever unleashed, would be even more exacting in the pinpointing of its desired minority.

REFERENCES

Anglim, C. T. (1999). *Religion and the Law: a dictionary*. California: ABC-CLIO.

Austrian, G. D. (1982). *Herman Hollerith: forgotten giant of information processing*. New York: Columbia University Press.

Berenbaum, M. (1993). *The History of the Holocaust as Told in the United States Holocaust Memorial Museum*. Boston: Little, Brown and Company.

Black, E. (2001). *IBM and the Holocaust*. UK: Little, Brown and Company.

Brown, G. (1990). *The Information Game: ethical issues in a microchip world*. New Jersey: Humanities Press International.

Castles, I. (1993). *CDATA91 Data Guide: 1991 census of population and housing*: Australian Bureau of Statistics Canberra.

Clark, C. (1943). *The advance to social security*. Carlton: Melbourne University Press.

Cohen, T. (1994). *The Tattoo*. Sydney: Savvas.

Comppile. (2004). CompPanels: Images from the annals of the composition #17 (Race Categories and Hollerith Machines). Retrieved 21 April 2008, from http://comppile.tamucc.edu/comppanel_17.htm

Connecticut Dept. (1998). Understanding public perception. *Connecticut Department of Social Services*, from http://www.dss.state.ct.us/faq/disuppt.htm

Czech, D. (1990). *Auschwitz Chronicle 19391945*. New York: Henry Holt.

Davies, S. (1996). *Monitor: extinguishing privacy on the information superhighway*. Sydney: PAN Macmillan.

Delio, M. (1993). *The Tattoo: the exotic art of skin decoration*. New South Wales: Sun.

Ellul, J. (1964). *The Technological Society*. New York: Vintage Books.

Encyclopedia Britannica (Ed.). (1983a). *Census* (Vol. II). Sydney.

Encyclopaedia Britannica (Ed.). (1983b). *Common Law* (Vol. IV). Sydney.

Encyclopaedia Britannica (Ed.). (1983c). *Tattoo* (Vol. IX). Sydney.

Gates, B. (1995). *The Road Ahead*. New York: The Penguin Group.

Gell, A. (1993). *Wrapping in Images*. Oxford: Clarendon Press.

Gingrich, F. W., & Danker, F. W. (1958). *A Greek-English Lexicon of the New Testament and Other Early Christian Writers*. Chicago: University of Chicago Press.

Grognard, C. (1994). *The Tattoo: graffiti for the soul*. Spain: The Promotional Reprint Company.

Herodotus. (1972). *The Histories*. London: Penguin Books.

Hibbert, C. (1996). What to do when they ask for your social security number. In R. Kling (Ed.), *Computerization and Controversy: value conflicts and social choices* (pp. 686-696). New York: Academic Press.

The Holy Bible: Revised Standard Version containing the Old and New Testaments with the Apocrypha/Deuterocanonical Books, Expanded Edition. (1973). New York: Collins.

Identification. (1998). (1998). In *Macquarie Dictionary* (pp. 1062). Sydney: Macquarie.

Identity. (1998). (1998). In *Macquarie Dictionary* (pp. 1062). Sydney: Macquarie.

ITC. (1992, October 12-14). *'Address Note', Proceedings ITC*. Paper presented at the 8th ITC Specialist Seminar on Universal Personal Telecommunications.

Jackson, M., & Ligertwood, J. (2006). Identity management: is an identity card the solution for Australia? In K. Michael & M. G. Michael (Eds.), *The Social Implications of Information Security Measures on Citizens and Business* (pp. 45-55). Wollongong: Wollongong University.

Jaguer, J. (1990). *The Tattoo: a pictorial history*. Great Britain: Milestone Publications.

Jones, C. P. (1987). Stigma: tattooing and branding in Graeco-Roman antiquity. *The Journal of Roman Studies, 77*, 139-155.

Kaku, M. (1998). *Visions: how science will revolutionize the 21st century and beyond*. Oxford Oxford University Press.

Kitchen, M. (1995). *Nazi Germany at War*. Essex: Longman.

Kuhns, W. (1971). *The Post-Industrial Prophets: interpretations of technology*. New York: Harper Colophon Books.

Kusserow, R. P. (1996). The government needs computer matching to root out waste and fraud. In Rob Kling (Ed.), *Computerization and Controversy: value conflicts and social choices* (Vol. part 6 section E, pp. 653f). New York: Academic Press.

Lee, H. C., & Gaensslen, R. E. (Eds.). (1994). *Advances in Fingerprint Technology (CRC Series in Forensic and Police Science)*. New York: CRC Press.

Levi, P. (1988). *The Drowned and the Saved, trans. Raymond Rosenthal*. London: Summit Books.

Lifton, R. J. (1986). *The Nazi Doctors: medical killing and the psychology of genocide*. New York: Basic Books.

Lipetz, B.-A. (1966). *Information storage and retrieval*. London: W. H. Freeman.

Lunde, A. S., Lundeborg, S., Lettenstrom, G. S., Thygesen, L., & Huebner, J. (1980). *The Person-Number Systems of Sweden, Norway, Denmark, and Israel*. Maryland: DHSS.

Lyon, D. (2004). Surveillance Technologies: Trends and Social Implications. In OECD (Ed.), *The Security Economy* (pp. 127-148): OECD.

Marcantonio, V. (1940). *The registration of aliens*. New York American Committee for Protection of Foreign Born.

Meissner, D. (2000, 9 June). Tattoos, police instinct used in hunt for snakeheads: Mountie. *The Globe and Mail,* p. A5.

Michael, M. G. (1998). *The Number of the Beast, 666 (Revelation 13:16-18): Background, Sources and Interpretation.* Macquarie University, Sydney, Australia.

Miller, A. (1971). *The Assault on Privacy: computers, databanks and dossiers.* London: New American Library.

New Zealand Computer Society. (1972). *Investigation of a unique identification system.*

Office of Technology Assessment. (1981). Government Involvement in the Innovation Process. New York: Congress of United States.

Paoli, U. E. (1990). *Rome: its people, life and customs.* London: Bristol Classical Press.

Pollock, G. H. (Ed.). (1993). *Pivotal Papers on Identification.* Connecticut: International Universities Press.

Rosenthal, G. (2008). The Evolution of Tattooing in the Auschwitz Concentration Camp Complex. Retrieved 15 May 2008, from http://www.jewishvirtuallibrary.org/jsource/Holocaust/tattoos1.html

Rubin, A. (Ed.). (1988). *Marks of Civilization: artistic transformations of the human body.* Los Angeles: Museum of Cultural History.

Sacleman, H. (1967). *Computers, System Science, And Evolving Society: the challenge of man-machine digital systems.* New York: Wiley.

Sanders, C. R. (1989). *Customizing the Body: the art and culture of tattooing.* Philadelphia: Temple University Press.

Scullard, H. H. (1981). *Festivals and Ceremonies of the Roman Republic.* London: Thames and Hudson.

Society., N. Z. C. (1972). *Investigation of a unique identification system.*

SSA. (2002). Social security numbers. from http://www.socialsecurity.gov/history/ssn/ssnforms.html

SSA. (2003). Historical development. from http://www.ssa.gov/history/brief.html

Stallings, W., & van Slyke, R. (1994). *Business Data Communications.* New York: Macmillan Publishing Company.

van Caenegem, R. C. (1988). *The Birth of the English Common Law.* Cambridge: Cambridge University Press.

Westin, A. F., & Baker, M. A. (1972). *Databanks in a free society.* New York: Quadrangle Books.

Westrum, R. (1991). *Technologies and Society: the shaping of people and things.* California: Wadsworth Publishing Company.

Yoffie, D. B. (Ed.). (1997). *Competing in the Age of Digital Convergence.* Massachusetts: Harvard Business School.

Interview 3.1
The Holocaust Survivor

Mrs. Judith Nachum, Sydney, Australia
Interview conducted by Katina Michael on 5 March 2008.

INTERVIEW

Katina Michael: Mrs. Nachum, how old were you during the Holocaust, and where were you?

Judith Nachum: I was ten years old when we had to move from the city where I was born to Prague. So I can say that my childhood stopped when I was ten years old. When we were taken to camp, I was about thirteen and a half.

Katina Michael: Which camp Mrs. Nachum?

Judith Nachum: First it was Theresienstadt, then Auschwitz, from Auschwitz to Oederan, and from Oederan back to Theresienstadt. And that was the end of the war in 1945.

Katina Michael: Mrs. Nachum, I will now ask you a series of questions related to how identification was used to segregate people during the

Figure 1. Mrs Judith Nachum in her home in Bondi Junction, New South Wales, Australia. She is pictured here with a tapestry she made of her former Rabbi from Israel. Photo taken in 2008.

Holocaust. Could you please describe the Yellow Star to us? For instance, its symbolism, and why it was used?

Judith Nachum: First of all, the Star of David, in Hebrew it is מָגֵן דָּוִד, and the translation of it means the Shield of David. By David, I mean King David. It was his shield and so it stayed with the Hebrews. In 1948 when Israel came into being the symbol was used widely. But in Europe, the Germans, knew very well what the דָּוִד מָגֵן (pronounced ma'gen da'vid in modern Hebrew) meant and so therefore as a symbolism to show that we are Jews, we had to wear that Star of David (Figure 2). And you know, I was at the Holocaust Museum on Monday because usually when there are young children, they call me because apparently I know how to talk with younger children and somebody asked me, one girl from a Catholic private school, whether it was difficult for me to be Jewish and to wear the Star of David. And I very quickly said "No". That it really did not bother me, and that it never bothered me to be Jewish, and in general, I feel that we have to be comfortable in our own skin.

Figure 2. The Star of David which by order of the Nazis, all Jews had to stitch onto the left hand side of their outer garment. Courtesy of The Sydney Jewish Museum.

And no matter what I went through in my life, I always felt comfortable in my own skin. And that was it, I was born Jewish, I stayed Jewish, and I had to go through the consequences.

Katina Michael: Mrs. Nachum, do you recall how you received the badge?

Judith Nachum: All the Jewish populations received it, populations I say because wherever Germany occupied territory, the Jews had to wear it. *In France they had written "Juif" in the French way. And in Holland with two "O's" in Dutch they had written "Jood". And so we had to pick them up from the Gestapo. As many members of the family, as many stars you got, and we had to put it on the left-hand side of every overcoat, on every jacket that we wore.* And because we did not get enough, I remember my mother used to put a lining underneath the star, and put small buttons, so we could transfer the star from one coat to the other because we did not have enough stars to put on all our clothes. Even when we were already in the camp at Theresienstadt, we still had to wear the Star.

Katina Michael: What would happen if a Jewish person didn't wear the Star and they were found out?

Judith Nachum: Oh, if as a child, nothing very much would happen to you, but your parents would have been taken away on the next transport to the "East" as they called it. We never knew where those transports were going.

Katina Michael: We have seen in many photographs that there were persons in the camps that were tattooed or branded. Can you tell me why all people were not tattooed? What was the motivation for this do you think?

Judith Nachum: I know what the motivation was… I wasn't tattooed. It depended when you arrived at Auschwitz. When there was enough time you got a tattoo. We came in 1944 when the Germans nearly lost the war. Once they lost it in Russia, they lost it. And so the Nazi's had one thing in their mind, to kill as many Jews as possible. And so there wasn't really very much time to tattoo everyone at that point. Either you went to the gas chambers- which in our case there were 2,500 taken to Auschwitz and after the first selection there were 200 women and 50 men left alive. My mother, elder sister and I were not in Auschwitz very long, as we were sent to Germany to work … they shaved our heads, yes, took our hair off completely, and so you couldn't run away because everyone would know. Yes, now it is a fashion, men shave their hair off but not in those days.

Katina Michael: Do you know if the tattoo itself had a code, was it a specific sequence for specific types of people- young, married, elderly, men and women?

Judith Nachum: That I really don't know. You see there is a general term, Auschwitz, but Auschwitz was divided. I was in the camp which was called Birkenau, that is where the gas chambers were, and again there you had different groups divided with electric wire. We were in a camp that was called B2BLAGER, that means B2B. So most probably, and this is my guess, the code of the tattoo was made up of the first few letters of the name of the camp followed by the number of people in that camp. But believe you me, you didn't ask very many questions.

Figure 3. Women display their tattoos which were marked onto their skin at Nazi concentration camps for the purpose of identification and dehumanization. Courtesy of the US Holocaust Memorial Museum.

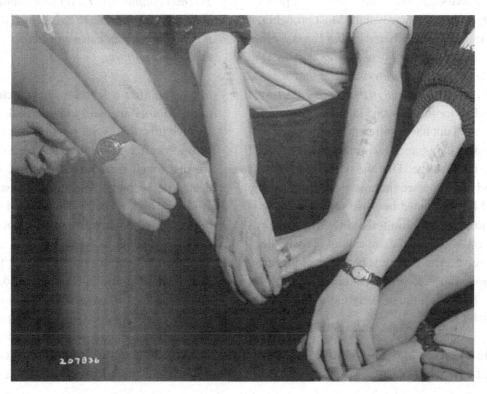

Katina Michael: Did you have any friends or family in the camp that were tattooed?

Judith Nachum: Heaps… heaps… just not in the transport that I came to Auschwitz with. I didn't have one [tattoo], my mother didn't, my sister didn't, and all the others because there were only 200 left and we were sent altogether to Germany. None of us was tattooed. But of course, in the other camps, the people that were in Auschwitz before me were all tattooed, but those people that came after me were not (Figure 3). After I was at the camp there were only two more transports and that was the end.

Katina Michael: Could you describe how the mark, the tattoo, makes you feel as a Jewish person, having seen this mark tattooed on friends and family.

Judith Nachum: That is very very hard to answer. For me personally, if I would have been tattooed most probably, I would have been proud of it, and I would have said, "there look." But other people, I cannot speak on their behalf. Most probably, it did hurt them, or they hated it. *And I am sure that there would have been people after the war who tried to get rid of the tattoo, maybe they went to doctors and had it cut out (if that is possible, I don't know).* But for me, as I said in the beginning, for me it would not have mattered. This is who I am, this is who I was, and I was marked for it. See, I wasn't the bad one. The one who did it, he was the bad one. You see there is a difference. Why should I be ashamed because somebody else is bad and does something- the sin is his, not mine. And very often people are asking me whether I can forgive. And I say, it is not for me to forgive, it is God who is forgiving… forget, I can never forget, but I can forgive every German who was born after me.

Katina Michael: May I ask how was the tattoo applied?

Judith Nachum: Like any other tattoo is applied nowadays.

Katina Michael: Here is a terribly powerful excerpt written by Michael Berenbaum with extensive connotations: could I ask you to reflect on this? Can you add to it? Explain it a little more? "And as they gave me my tattoo number, B-4990, the SS man came to me, and he says to me,| "Do you know what this number's all about?"| I said, "No, sir."| "Okay, let me tell you now. You are being dehumanized."

Judith Nachum: *Oh… I could talk about that for the next half an hour… that is so true because you tattoo animals, you tattoo cows, you tattoo whatever animal so that they are unable to run away. This tattoo is only one small thing in dehumanizing, there were so many other things- to shave your hair, to make you undress as a female in front of men, to have your whole body shaven… Why? This was all to make you not human… You lost your name, you were not called by name… You had a number here, on your clothes you had a number, and you were called by that number… it is just my number was not tattooed but it was still on my uniform.*

My sister, after a few days in Auschwitz, went to my mother and said to her: "look, we cannot survive this, this is not possible, why should we go on to suffer. If we go to this electric wire and we just touch it (it was 240 volts), we will be dead in a second." And my mum said: "Okay. And how about Yuci?" They called me Yuci at home [Judy]. And so my mum came to me and said Gerti wants to do so and so… And I said, "no". And my mum said "You want to suffer all this, the dirt… and all?" And I said, "I am not going to commit suicide, I am not going to make the job easier for the Germans. If they want to kill me, they will have to try. I am not going to do their job for them." And so my mother said to my sister, she is the younger one and we can't leave her here by herself… So they did not go through with it, and the three of us survived. I am not a person who gives in very very easily…

And dehumanized? We definitely were. But I knew who I was. And just, for me, it was out of the question to crawl, not even to the SS. And I am telling you, somehow, and this is already my philosophy, because as you get older you are trying to understand or feel an excuse, how come that you are here, and there were 1.5 million children that went to the gas chambers… and so, you know, I just have to say that I was a toughy… and I think that even the Germans somehow felt that I was a strong person, that they would have to reckon with me… I mean, I did my work properly, I worked hard, and kept my head up… I would not have given them that satisfaction that I would kill myself for them.

Katina Michael: Did prisoners in the camp wear different colored clothing depending on why and when they were drafted into the camp?

Judith Nachum: In Auschwitz most prisoners had striped uniforms with different colored triangles so they could be easily identified, in terms of their reason for being there. Red was used for political prisoners, pink for homosexuals, yellow for the Jews, etc (Figure 4). We in Birkenau wore only rags. That is we only had one outer garment, and they gave us no other apparel- no undergarments, no socks, nothing else.

Katina Michael: Edwin Black describes that IBM's Hollerith machine which was used to collect census information was actually used in the Holocaust to identify Jewish persons?

Judith Nachum: I don't know anything about that… I don't think I had even heard the word "computer" until I came to Australia…

Figure 4. Two concentration camp badges bearing purple triangles worn by Jehovah's Witnesses. The badge with prisoner number 46436 was issued in Sachsenhausen to Albert Jahndorf; the badge with prisoner number 1989 was issued in Ravensbrueck to Luise Jahndorf. USHMM, courtesy of Annemarie & Waltraud Kuesserow.

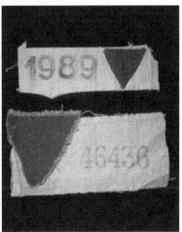

Katina Michael: Okay, but on reflection how do you feel about technology being used specifically in a context like this- for the purposes of segregation?

Judith Nachum: In this context, of course, it is dreadful. But you have got to understand that in Western Europe, for sure in Austria, for sure in Germany, and for sure in Czechoslovakia, we all had ID cards. You were born and you were registered by the police. You had to tell them that you were Jewish (Figure 5). You went to the nearest board of deputies which every city and every state had. So you could not deny that you were Jewish or Catholic or Protestant because that went for everybody. So the Nazis just had to go to every police station and just have a look. Your religion was recorded on your birth certificate. So you know why they would have needed a machine, I have got no idea because it was very, very easy to access information. My father lost his life because they took his pants down and saw he was

Figure 5. A police form stamped with a red letter J for Jude, that registers the residence of the Jewish child, Hannah Kastan, at the home of her grandparents in Berlin. USHMM, courtesy of Hannah Kastan Weiss.

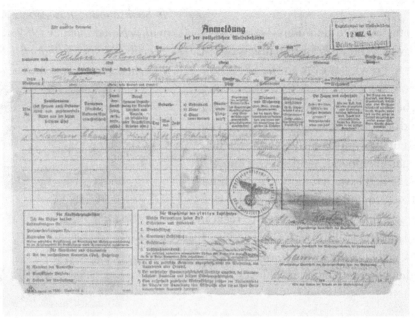

circumcised… we Jews make it easy for others to recognize us. So I really cannot tell you why the use of automatic technology was necessary. I just don't know.

Katina Michael: Yes, the information existed already...

Judith Nachum: *The information existed, from one country to the other. They found it all out so quickly. And we had to keep repeating it to them. We had to give up first the fur coats (and it was so, so cold), then it was jewelry besides the wedding ring, and then it was watches, then it was radios… and every time you went and you filled in forms you would give things away. So they knew fifty times over who you were and that you were Jewish and they could cross-check it. The Germans were so meticulous.*

After the war, when I came to Australia, I tried very hard to get a pension from the Germans.

There was an office I visited, and I saw a lady who had a book that was very thick, and there were all the concentration camps written down that existed. And she went through this book, and there came a camp which was called Niederhagen where I was… a lousy little camp, not thousands and thousands like Flossenbürg (the mother's camp), and there it was in the book. My name was also in that book. They had the transport number, and with which number I went to Auschwitz, and under what number I went to Auschwitz to Germany. You know they had everything. It took them days and nights and weeks to burn all these papers, well as many as they could in Auschwitz and then they blew the chimneys, the gas chambers. So you know they were and they are perfectionists, the Germans. They were high culture, Beethoven etc., and they were absolutely perfect in killing.

I always thought that Zyklon B was the first, and that the gas chambers started in Auschwitz. Not so. First they killed "in" Germany all the crazies, all the "sub-normal" people, all the sick ones like mongoloids. And they had people like this in the camps, and in the beginning they would take them by train from the camp back to Germany and put them in a special building with cellars, which they called Sunshine House, and they killed them with carbon-monoxide. And then someone thought that carbon-monoxide would be a good way to kill the Jews, and they started by putting the Jews on trucks in Russia, already half-dead and they finished them off in the trucks. But you needed vehicles and so it was costly to them, and then only, they said in this one place in Auschwitz where they were holding Polish prisoners, political prisoners who they had killed (some of whom were hung)... One Nazi SS opened the door in one of these old buildings (Block 11), and found a whole heap of old clothing, hundreds of pieces, that were worn by the Polish prisoners. And on the door, was the sign of the *skull and crossbones* which represented poison and infection. So you had these little platelets that you would light up the gas with, and they were used to kill vermin, it killed all these things. And that gave them the idea- vermin here, and here you've got the vermin, the Jews. And that is how they made these gas chambers. That was the Zyclon B, and this is how they did it.

So first they killed the sick in Germany. An official SS man was interviewed. And he admitted to the killings. And the lady who interviewed him asked "what did you feel? What did you feel in taking hundreds of people and you let them dig a trench and you put them in the trench and then you shot them." And he said, "I didn't feel a thing." She said "how is it possible"? And he said, "because I hate the Jews so much... I hate them even today". She then asks, "what is the reason"? And he says, "I don't know... when I was a kid everyone says it was because of the Jews that we lost World War One... because the Jews had all the money, and this is why we were starving, and this is why my parents did not have any money, and so I hated them all my life." And the woman asks, "do you have any proof, any evidence"? And he says, "no, that was enough, I hate them even now." You have got all kinds of people on this earth...

Katina Michael: I find it abhorrent that the sick were taken first to be killed, then those who they considered "not normal," and that then they also began to kill the Jews.

Judith Nachum: Also the Slavs. The Russians were even considered on a lower level, they wanted them dead. The Germans planned the war into Russia, they hated communists. I do not think you will find this in any book. If they wanted to win the war against Russia, Russia had to feed the German Army. That meant that they were going to take away all their food... and that is what they did, they starved millions of Russians... they starved them to death.

Katina Michael: Can I digress slightly and ask you whether Stalin was any better than Hitler?

Judith Nachum: In this way not. But you know, no dictator is better. I ran away from Czechoslovakia, I just made it in 1948. In July of that year I was 20 years old, by August I was gone. My mother had to give me permission in the court because you had to be 21 years old to travel on your own. I said, I am not going to stay under the communist regime; I'd had enough brown, I did not want red. All my life I worked with my hands, but I cannot even say the word "labor" because "labor" equates to "communism". My poor brother-in-law was locked up for 2 years because my mother and I exchanged letters with him because they were spying on us... definitely, they were not any better....

Katina Michael: Do you think automatic identification devices like biometrics or smart cards could—

Judith Nachum: I'm looking at it in a different way. I would feel quite happy to have an ID card. For instance, I am going to the post office to send a parcel, and they say "any ID, driver's license?". There you go. What do I do if I don't drive, I would have to have a passport, I would have to have something with a photo on it. So what is it? I am asking you? That is identification. You have got your papers, your name is in the bank, everywhere. Supermarkets, department stores, they pay for your name and your address, that is why you get all that rubbish in the letterbox. So you know, it is a fallacy to say we don't need ID. So as long as I don't do anything bad, which 99 per cent I do not do, I really don't care… I don't care.

Katina Michael: Do you think it would make it easier to gather information however, to segregate persons in the future—

Judith Nachum: *You know there may be thousands of Jews in Australia, who in a Census will not put down their religion for that exact reason. I know people who will not provide that information in the Census. All the other questions you must fill in, but this information they do not give. And I don't blame them. It is in them, and to a degree it is in me to be wary.*

Katina Michael: If I told you that today people can receive implants that contain ID chips and can be used for location tracking, how does that make you feel? For instance, today we have a digital brand, a high-tech brand that is currently being used for medical purposes so if someone has an allergic reaction to penicillin, emergency doctors can quickly find out about it if the patient is unconscious.

Judith Nachum: I don't think this is a bad idea—

Katina Michael: You mean, for medical applications?

Judith Nachum: For medical, yes. Look, they do it for dogs and they do it for cats. A dog gets lost and it runs away and they reunite it with their owner. So I don't feel that that is a bad idea. I would not want to be tattooed today, you know, that "no". But if it is for medical reasons, and the person wants to do it, that is okay. They wouldn't do it to me because I am too old for it- nobody would try to save my life in that context…

Katina Michael: But they are even tracking patients who have Alzheimer's now, in case they wander, so they can be found by loved ones.

Judith Nachum: Yes, this is a positive application.

Katina Michael: What if I was to say to you… let me give you a scenario… tomorrow it is announced that implants are to become the defacto ID card. And they tell us we no longer require an ID card- what would you say to that?

Judith Nachum: *No… No! Definitely NOT implant… we are not going to the moon or something, definitely no… no.*

Katina Michael: Okay. Would your religion forbid the use of microchip implants in general?

Judith Nachum: I don't know. That I would have to ask my Rabbi. We have very strict laws about things like Euthanasia… that is a no-no… for organ donations there are Rabbis who say we cannot do that. The more orthodox, the more they say no, as we are supposed to go in our grave in one piece so when the Messiah comes we can rise. There are orthodox rabbis that are more modern, who say that it is the first law in the Torah to save a life. You save one life, you save the world. So if you donate an organ that will save somebody's life, like a heart, a lung, a kidney, you do a *mitzva* (a good deed), that is allowed. You want to give a retina or hair or something, no. Just to save a life.

There are a lot of rabbis who say it is okay but they leave it up to your own conscience.

Katina Michael: You have mentioned previously to me that you have nothing to hide because you have not done anything bad—

Judith Nachum: Yes…

Katina Michael: And that Australia you are certain is a carefree country where our rights will always be preserved?

Judith Nachum: I am not so sure today anymore. I live here, my grandchildren were born here, and my great grandchildren… so there are already four generations here- but, Israel for me is extremely important. And most of the articles that you read in the newspapers today are very very anti-Israel. And to me anti-Israel is anti-Semitic. You cannot divide one from the other.

And I am now digressing… years ago the first Prime Minister, Ben Gurion always said we won't be a nation till we are like any other nation. That means we have got to have thieves, and we have prostitution, etc. I don't agree with him, there are a lot of things we should not do, according to our laws, there are things we should plainly just not do. For example, men should not hit their wives and women should not hit their husbands. If you had told me even three or four years ago that there are Jewish women bashers, I would have said, "no, just go, you must be crazy, Jews don't do that"… Jews don't harm children, you know there are certain things that we plainly don't do. We are not drunk… but now… the kids take drugs and men hit their wives, and there are people in prison who murder… you know I have to change my opinion about Jews in Israel.
And a kid asked me yesterday what is going to happen- will people deny the Holocaust? And I said, yes, we won't be here, there are so few of us who survived the Holocaust and are now volunteering our time to give talks at Jewish Museums. Once we are all gone, yes, they will deny- this is why I am lecturing to you, so that you look at this old Auntie and that you know "she was"… and then later on in a couple of years they can say, "I have seen one who was". The Holocaust did exist, it does exist… There are plenty of those people who say the Holocaust never happened… plenty…
So to answer your question, I am unsure whether countries like Australia will have peace always, for good…

Katina Michael: You have told me that you find direct marketing very annoying. Is it because the companies have not given you a choice when they send you something?

Judith Nachum: Just before you came I ordered a dust buster. In fact, I ordered it three weeks ago. And so I rang them again today and told them I want this… and then it started. If you pay only thirty dollars more we will give you a second one free. And I said but I don't need it. They said, you can give it to someone… I said, somebody else should buy their own. And then he said, how about a charger? I said I don't need a charger, I can give you a charger- I've got so many chargers I can give you chargers to sell! I've thrown out half a dozen chargers recently, I don't want a charger. He went on and on… and I in the end said, "listen, I have a sore throat, I can hardly talk, you take my number and you send me what I ordered. I don't want anything else." But there are people unlike me, who would buy things pushed on them… this is why we are all in such a financial mess and people are losing houses and taking mortgages out on their homes and they cannot make repayments. So I don't like direct marketing to answer your question!

Katina Michael: I've learnt that some ways Jewish people survived during World War Two was because of the Resistance Movement. Where siblings were separated and assimilated into other families, for example with some Catholic families. And these individuals were constantly moved around so as not to muster suspicion by the local police. Today we have other technologies like location tracking techniques using the mobile phone that can find people, Internet email addresses, and a number of other digital footprints that can pinpoint where you are. Do you think that anyone can physically hide today?

Judith Nachum: This is a difficult question to answer because honest to God, I don't know. I am computer illiterate…. I am so illiterate with regards to technology that I only know how to switch a television on and off… this is completely a foreign language… I know this is a physical footprint [pointing to her foot], nothing more or less, but you are using the term in a completely different context. You have you own linguae that I cannot understand. I feel awful if I have a letterbox full with advertisements or people who tell me I should shop and I should buy something that I don't need. It should be prohibited.

Katina Michael: Do you hold any fears for the current national security climate, globally?

Judith Nachum: *Plenty. Yes, I do. And that is surely natural. See, in my humble opinion as soon as religion becomes political it is dangerous. As long as you believe in God, and I believe in God and you will wear a cross and I will wear a 'chai', and I will honor your cross, and I will take it that you honor that which I have hanging around my neck- well this is perfectly alright…* You know there will never be peace in Israel, no matter how much the Israeli's try, as long as there is a political party who don't do anything else but stir… that is their life, they make money through that. And they will send other people to die, usually children. So long as they misuse religion, we are in terrible danger.

Katina Michael: Are there any other comments you'd like to make about anything we've spoken about, or anything else you'd like to add?

Judith Nachum: I don't know if I have much else to add, besides the fact that I like to live. I know that I am old and that I am not going to be here forever. I would like to add, that in 47 years of living in Australia, I personally have never encountered anti-Semitism and I think it is because other people knew I felt comfortable in my own skin. I always admitted, I never denied who I was, and it was always respected by everyone.

I've been working in the Holocaust Museum in Sydney for 15 years, I'm doing my best there and I've done upteen interviews and when my life finishes I hope I would've left something behind because otherwise I would not know why God left me here instead of taking me when I was thirteen years old like all the others. So I have to give myself a reason why I survived, and that would be the only reason. It is not because I had to have children, and grandchildren, and a family- everyone can have children. The reason for my survival was to bear witness to the events of the Holocaust…

Dr Katina Michael: Thank you very much for your time.

KEY TERMS

Anti-Semite: An individual hostile towards the Jews.

Auschwitz: A town in south-western Poland and site of the Nazi concentration camp during World War II.

Chai: In the Hebrew language, the word chai means "living" and is connected to the term for "life", chaim. Characteristically it also appears in the cry "àm yisrael chai!", that is, "The nation of Israel lives!"

Gestapo: The Secret State Police of Nazi Germany which acted to suppress all opposition to Hitler's regime.

Holocaust: The genocidal murder of Jews by the Nazis in World War II.

Rabbi: The principal religious official of a synagogue and the spiritual leader of a Jewish community.

Resistance Movement: A secret organization in an enemy-occupied country working to maintain hostilities unofficially after a formal capitulation.

SS: An elite military unit of the Nazi party which served as Hitler's bodyguard and as a special police force.

Star of David: Also known as מָגֵן דָּוִד. A star-shaped figure with six points, formed of two interlaced equilateral triangles, used as a symbol of Judaism.

Tattoo: The act of marking the skin with indelible patterns, etc., by making punctures in it and inserting pigments.

Zyklon B: Also spelled Cyclon B, was the tradename of a cyanide-based insecticide notable for its use by Nazi Germany against civilians in the gas chambers of the Extermination camps during the Holocaust.

Chapter IV
Globalization and the Changing Face of IDentification

INTRODUCTION

National security measures can be defined as those technical and non-technical measures that have been initiated as a means to curb breaches in national security, irrespective of whether these might occur by nationals or aliens in or from outside the sovereign state. National security includes such government priorities as maintaining border control, safeguarding against pandemic outbreaks, preventing acts of terror, and even discovering and eliminating identification fraud. Governments worldwide are beginning to implement information and communication security techniques as a way of protecting and enhancing their national security. These techniques take the form of citizen identification card schemes using smart cards, behavioral tracking for crowd control using closed-circuit television (CCTV), electronic tagging for mass transit using radio-frequency identification (RFID), ePassports for travel using biometrics (Figure 1), and 24×7 tracking of suspected terrorists using global positioning systems (GPS).

The electorate is informed that these homeland security techniques are in actual fact deployed to assist government in the protection of its citizenry and infrastructure. The introduction of these widespread measures, however, is occurring at a rapid pace without equivalent deliberation over the potential impacts in the longer term on both citizens and business. This chapter explores the background context to the proliferation of automatic identification and location-based service techniques post September 11, 2001. Such themes as globalization, the role of intelligence in preserving national security, the rise of new terrorism, and the ability to securitize a nation state are explored.

THE IMPACT OF GLOBALIZATION

Globalization is defined by Findlay (1998, p. viii) as "...the collapsing of time and space – the process whereby, through mass communication, multinational commerce, internationalized politics and transnational regulation, we seem to be moving inexorably towards a single culture..." For Findlay, crime (and more specifically transnational crime), "its representation and its impact are part of globalization." Some scholars have even gone as far as to pronounce that globalization is a facilitator of modern transnational

Figure 1. The chip centre page of the ePassport. Over 50 million e-Passports have now been issued. Even though the e-Passport was introduced to 'enhance security', some authorities recommend shielding the contactless microchip in a metal jacket to prevent the chip from being read when the passport is closed. If not provided, a sheet of aluminum foil will equally prevent unauthorized access of personal data on the e-Passport. Courtesy of Australian Government.

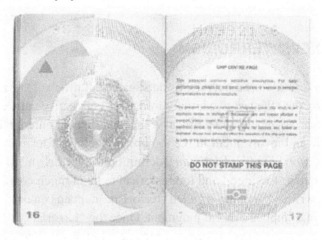

crime (TNC). Globalization is a paradox and reflexive concept. It generates two opposing forces. At first it attempts to bring together people of all nations, to break down borders and barriers alike. Globalization is about coordination, integration and harmonization in a bid to reduce global insecurity by increasing knowledge sharing activities. Yet this same openness and interdependence enables "various risks to destabilize the international economy" (Bruck, 2004, p. 116). For the greater part, modern TNC is piggybacking on global supply chains (Shelley, 2006); in this manner, organized crime groups can quickly form, act, and then disband after fulfilling an objective.

Terrorist organizations engaged in transnational crime (TNC) for instance, like any other transnational company, can take advantage of open markets, global reach of customers, technological innovation, new recruits (of all backgrounds and talent), international financing sources etc. There is a type of convergence which is occurring between criminal groups, between crime types and between crime regions which has been facilitated by globalization. Some of these TNC groups also claim that their involvement in organized crime is a direct response to globalization pressures. Buzan, Wæver and de Wilde (1998, p. 4) call this the "dark side" of globalization, "where criminal organizations are said not only to have benefited from the increasingly open global economy, but to have developed powerful tools, techniques and relationships to thwart the state." Barrie Stevens (2004, p. 10) calls this view the "flip side of the coin" where transnational organized criminal groups use the very same channels (i.e. transport and communications) to conduct their illegal activities, as if they were legal entities. These channels are "vulnerable to abuse through theft, fraud, the trafficking of humans and animals, terrorist operations and so on" (Stevens, 2004, p. 21).

In summary, there have been structural changes in transnational organized crime as a result of globalization. Transnational criminal groups now reflect a typical business set-up with established "core competencies"- they are cellular, small and flat as opposed to hierarchically structured and focus on their strengths in a given service (i.e. transnational crime). The groups form temporary alliances, form rapidly, so as to go undetected. Members of specific groups are also sub-contracted, rather than recruiting permanent staff, analogous to the notion of virtual teams in corporations. Globalization, it should be noted, is often cited as one of the "root causes" for terrorism today, as the rich-poor divide continues to widen. According to Paul Rogers (2007), "...the combination of a widening rich-poor gap with an increasingly knowledgeable poor, is leading to a 'revolution of unfulfilled expectations', a prominent feature of many insurgencies and instability in Latin America, North Africa and the Middle East."

THE RISE OF "NEW" TERRORISM

The key difficulties in formulating a universally acceptable definition of "terrorism" include: (a) fluidity of the term particularly over the last two hundred years; (b) subjective nature of the definition based on the biases of individuals or agencies; (c) political vernacular that has entered the discourse on terrorism; and (d) media rhetoric and involvement in the too broad labeling of terrorist acts. On commenting on the much-venerated *Oxford English Dictionary* definition of "terrorism", Bruce Hoffman (2006, p. 3) states that the definition is "too literal and too historical to be of much contemporary use..."

Brian Jenkins has written that what is called "terrorism" depends on one's point of view. The term is inherently 'negative' and implies a moral judgment. Once the "terrorist" tag is given to an opponent, it is highly likely that others will also be persuaded to use it in the same manner. *"Hence the decision to call someone or label some organization "terrorist" becomes almost unavoidably subjective, depending largely on whether one sympathizes with or opposes the person/group/cause concerned. If one identifies with the victim of the violence, for example, then the act is terrorism. If, however, one identifies with the perpetrator, the violent act is regarded in more sympathetic, if not positive... light, and it is not terrorism"* (Hoffman, 2006, p. 23). Consider that terrorist organizations themselves today will never use the term "terrorist" in any form to describe themselves or their activities. Terrorists do not see themselves as "terrorists" but as "reluctant warriors, driven by desperation" (Hoffman, 2006, p. 22).

In addition what is disturbing is that the United Nations and other organizations have taken action against terrorism even while not being able to agree on a definition (Boulden & Weiss, 2004, p. 4). In the United States definitions of "terrorism" abound, each agency (and even each department within an agency) chooses a construct that caters to their main objectives. The depth of the problem of definition can be seen in the aphorism that "my freedom fighter is your terrorist" (Ganor, 2002, p. 287). As Hoffman (2006, p. 23) elaborates, he who has been called a terrorist will almost always claim that the real terrorist is the 'system'– whether society, law or government– that they are fighting against. What the media often labels as terrorism is not truly representative of what a terrorist act is. The term "terrorism" seems to be thrown about by the media loosely to depict wide ranging acts of violence. Hoffman points to the role of the news media that divided the United Nations in the 1970s and continues to do so today. He believes that the news media "...has further contributed to the obfuscation of the terrorist/"freedom fighter" debate, enshrining imprecision and implication as the lingua franca of political violence in the name of objectivity and neutrality" (Hoffman, 2006, p. 28).

Characteristics of the New Terrorism

Hoffman (2006, p. 19) has written that the terrorist attacks of September 11, 2001 "redefined terrorism yet again... more than twice as many Americans perished on 9/11 than had been killed by terrorists since 1968- the year acknowledged as marking the advent of modern, international terrorism." This redefined terrorism has been given the name "new terrorism" by Simon and Benjamin (2000, p. 12), among others. The increasing trend is towards mass-casualty terrorism, a significantly more lethal preference than in the past (Figures 2 and 3). According to Dolnik and Fitzgerald (2008), "new terrorism" as opposed to "traditional terrorism" is characterized by: increasing lethality, religion replacing politics, mass casualty justification, a reduction of "taboo targets", transnational networks, advanced technologies, decentralized leadership, ad hoc groups, one-off events; and increased prominence of suicide terrorism.

What we are witnessing today, are terrorists attempting to out-do previous attacks in a bid to intensify their campaign and muster support for their plight by those who are sympathetic in the international

Figure 2. International airport terminals have been a common target for terrorism for the main reason that they provide an international theatre for the terrorist cause. Photo taken in 2005.

Figure 3. Authorities claim that by utilizing the appropriate intelligence sources that they are able to foil terrorist attacks which are often aimed at dense urban areas and points of interest with sentimental value. Photo taken in 2007.

arena. Not only are the new terrorists attempting to 'shock' their audience, but as the audience continues to become desensitized given wide media coverage of past attacks (Ben-Shaul, 2006), each new attack must become more and more violent to maintain the same level of fear and panic in society. The incidence of suicide operations is indicative of the new terrorism.

The increasing lethality of the new terrorism is also an attractive tool for the recruitment of new members into terrorist organizations, and even the formation of new splinter groups that end up being even more radical than their predecessors. Another important characteristic of the "new terrorism" is the expansion of target categories and a reduction of taboo targets. In the past there were certain groups that were plainly considered "off-limits" but today anyone can be a legitimate target including women and children, the elderly and the young, even members of the same constituency depending on their place of residence and to whom their taxes are paid. This all has to do with terrorists enforcing a "common grief" on their victims.

Another characteristic of the "new terrorism" is the advanced technologies that are at the disposal of today's terrorist organizations for the careful planning, operation and execution of violent acts (McNeal, 2007, p. 789). Among these technologies, can be included specific Internet applications such as electronic mail, bulletin boards, social networking sites and web sites (Table 1). Today it is possible to do meter-by-meter reconnaissance of targets via virtual tours freely available for viewing on the Internet. It is these types of technologies which are also said to be responsible for the rise of "home grown terrorism". Pre-paid mobile phones are even being used to detonate bombs remotely. Analogous to the network-centric nature of the Internet, the structures of terrorist organizations have also transformed into loose networks of cells which operate without any real central command.

Suicide Missions

The most popular and rapidly proliferating terrorist tactic today is suicide missions (Dolnik & Fitzgerald, 2008, p. 14). Suicide missions are defined as an act where a suicide bomber attaches explosives to themselves or a vehicle driven by him/her and with complete premeditated knowledge approaches a chosen target and detonates the bomb, and thus kills himself/herself to cause maximum damage. Lucia Ricolfi (2006, p. 103) categorizes suicide missions into three levels based on the count of deaths caused by the attack: high efficiency attacks (e.g. al-Qaeda style), medium efficiency attacks (e.g. Hamas style), and low efficiency attacks (e.g. PKK style).

Suicide attacks have become the modern day symbol of terrorism. "More than any other form of terrorism these attacks demonstrate terrorists' determination and devotion, to the extent of killing themselves for their cause" (Merari, 2005). Bruce Hoffman, citing a Rand Corporation report, also rightly points to the effectiveness of suicide attacks, noting that such missions on average kill four times as many people as other terrorist acts (Holmes, 2006, p. 158).

Suicidal terrorism also attracts a great deal of public attention with the added value that so-called 'martyrdom' places on it, further attracting new recruits into terrorist organizations. *"Etymologically, a 'martyr' is a witness giving testimony before listeners on a jury or tribunal. Their desire to bear witness before a world audience seems to be an essential reason why 9/11's planners decided to mount an exploit of such staggering magnitude. Referring to the attacks as 'speeches', bin Laden himself boasted that 'The speeches are understood by both Arabs and non-Arabs- even the Chinese"* (Holmes, 2006, p. 159)

The organizers of 9/11 were strategic in choosing their targets, mounting a spectacular operation in one of America's busiest cities that was to wreak as much havoc as possible and was destined to receive long-term coverage on global television and media. Dolnik and Fitzgerald (2008, p. 15) rightly point out that this type of coverage may even spur on popular inquiry by the international community into the motivations behind such attacks. These attacks also ensure that enemy despair is long-lasting.

Suicide attacks show that *David can defeat Goliath* (Rogers, 2007), that the 'system' in its very core is still weak and that by throwing a small stone and avalanche can be let loose to crush the giant super-power, delivering a "knockout blow" that has the ability to excite the desire of the warriors (Holmes, 2006, p. 161). In this way, suicide attacks deliver a psychological victory because the brave terrorist is ready to sacrifice his life for their cause. In contrast the enemy is seen scurrying in fear from death and destruction.

INTELLIGENCE FAILURE

According to Hannah, O'Brien and Rathmell (2005, p. iii) of the Rand Corporation, *"[i]ntelligence is a special kind of knowledge, a specialized subset of information that has been put through a systematic analytical process in order to support a state's decision and policy makers. It exists because some states or actors seek to hide information from other states or actors, who in turn seek to discover hidden information by secret or covert means."* Intelligence failure can be defined within organizational, political and even psychological parameters. Copeland (2007, pp. 4-8) provides numerous definitions of "intelligence failure" from a variety of perspectives, pointing to well-known events in American history such as Pearl Harbor, the placement of Soviet missiles in Cuba, and the Iraqi invasion of Kuwait (Higgins, 1987; Matthias, 2001; Griffin, 2004). While it is difficult to find one definition of intelligence failure the following is offered as being all-inclusive of the literature. Intelligence failures occur when a policy maker or analyst knows something or should have known something, given the amount of information available to them, to accurately assess the probability and consequences of an event taking place, and they do not act according to that knowledge (Copeland, 2007, p. 6).

Intelligence fails because of failures of "communication, of bureaucratic structure and behavior, of estimation and analysis, of warning, of policy, or of judgment... [it incorporates] leadership failures, organizational obstacles, problems of warning information, and analytical challenges" (Copeland, 2007, pp. 19-20). Many still believe that the Sept 11, 2001 terrorist attacks could have been prevented if appropriate measures had been taken in response to intelligence information available prior to the attack (Wilkie, 2004; Hersh, 2005; and Neumann & Smith, 2005). Scholars often point to policy failures as the main cause of intelligence failures. How often have intelligence analysts assessed the likelihood of a terrorist event and their warnings have gone unheeded? As Matthias (2001, p. 12) highlights, "[t]he intelligence "failure," if there was such, lay in the question of warning: how soon was it given, to whom, with what degree of alarm, and from what level of command."

Despite the hundreds of millions of dollars that are being invested in the development and implementation of intelligent collection systems- for the analysis of phone calls, e-mails, financial transactions- terrorists, for the greater part, have been able to bypass these measures. One has to query whether the information revolution has led to information overload- too much information and too little knowledge. That is, we can collect the data we need, we can pull all the facts together but we cannot appropriately make sense of them to extract that which is useful and to subsequently take appropriate action. It is what Roberta Wohlstetter called "the problem of signals vs. noise ratio" in the 1960s (Copeland, 2007, p. 13).

In the context of terrorism and today's climate of asymmetric warfare, there is nothing to stop a suicide bomber who is "working alone" from detonating a device in a busy street (Posner, 2005). It would have to be a very lucky analyst to pinpoint this kind of incident. Thus we can speak of this kind of element of surprise as being beyond the capability of any intelligence organization. We cannot yet enter into people's personal thoughts and mind. Larger terrorist plots like the Mumbai Attacks (26-29 November 2008) however, can be foiled by law enforcement agencies if the right sources of intelligence are made available to relevant authorities in time. But it must be underscored that adding layer upon layer of digital touch-points on the humble citizen is not the way to foil potential attacks; it is not a solution to a problem.

INTELLIGENCE REFORMS

A number of improvements were made to the way intelligence was conducted post the 9/11 terrorist attack, which may be collectively regarded as intelligence reforms. Intelligence reform is not a new concept- the U.S. has been practicing 'reform' since intelligence legislation was first instituted in World War II- it is a continuous process (Taylor & Goldman, 2004). The Reagan and Clinton Administrations for instance, were well-known for their efforts to reform intelligence. According to Berkowitz (1996, p. 40), '[t]he Clinton administration concentrated on two areas of intelligence reform: making the intelligence organization more efficient and responsive and defining roles, missions and priorities within the intelligence community." What is ironic is that President Clinton instituted efficiency studies, called for better streamlining between agencies, better prioritization and planning during his time in office. Where he fell short of succeeding in his reform plans was in thinking that there was nothing wrong with the administration of intelligence and that better management would fix any shortcoming of the highly strung bureaucracy that had amassed during the Reagan era. The 9/11 attacks however triggered new questions about intelligence agencies in the U.S. and a variety of studies proposed new types of reforms: structural (reorganization), and process-oriented reforms. It should be noted however, different studies pointed to different recommendations. Among the only thing the studies all agreed on was that the mission of the intelligence community remains the same, but that the intelligence "agenda and priorities" changed after 9/11 (Lowenthal, 2006, pp. 232-3).

Given the events of 9/11 and Iraq, the intelligence cycle is moving away from a "linear and single tracked" model which was about defining requirements, assigning collection responsibilities, getting a technician to process the collected data and then using analysts to produce products that would later be disseminated to consumers. The new model which has been used by the U.S. military is more about dispersed intelligent networks where the intelligence consumers are directly linked to the intelligence collectors. The new intelligence model is less centralized and more flexible and allows every intelligence consumer to speak directly to an intelligence collector, increasing communications and coordination efforts. The information and communication technologies exist to facilitate this kind of 'real-time' collaborative exchange. According to Goodman (2003, p. 60), "[w]e now know from the preliminary report that the timely use and distribution of intelligence data could have prevented the terrible acts of terrorism in 2001. And the refusal of the White House and the CIA to declassify the information…" In fact, one major criticism of intelligence agencies is that they have locked themselves into technologies and cannot keep pace with the changes to information and communication technology (ICT). For instance, some American collection systems date back to 1970s, and there is some resistance to bringing new technology on board. However, when compared with process, technological changes are much easier to effect- process tends to be deeply rooted in the intelligence culture.

Inexorably linked to the alternative intelligence cycle which seeks to be effective in real-time, are structural changes to intelligence agencies which have traditionally not moved fast enough. It has to be an organizational approach that will "readily adapt as requirements for information change and as the ability of the outside world to meet these requirements improve" (Berkowitz, 1996, p. 42). After 9/11, the U.S. attempted to circumvent the silo intelligence problem by creating the Department of Homeland Security (DHS) which included an Office of Intelligence and Analysis. According to Chalk and Rosenau (2004, p. xi), *"[p]roponents argue that establishing an agency that is solely concerned with information gathering, analysis, assessment, and dissemination would decisively ameliorate the type of hybrid reactive-proactive mission that so often confounds police-based intelligence units. Opponents counter that an institution of this sort would merely undermine civil liberties, unduly hinder interagency communication and coordination, and create additional barriers between intelligence and law enforcement."* The office is now responsible for funneling intelligence from the CIA, FBI and other agencies and is responsible for data analysis and ensuring that important knowledge does not slip between the "foreign intelligence-domestic intelligence divide" (Lowenthal, 2006, p. 235). Goodman (2003, p. 67) calls this "demilitarizing the intelligence community" and calls for a resolution of key turf issues between agencies. But he believes that even if the thirteen agencies and departments were willing to share information under the same umbrella agency that their "anachronistic computer systems would not allow it."

While it was recognized that technology plays a crucial role in conducting intelligence, a debate regarding the balance between human intelligence (HUMINT) and technical intelligence (TECHINT) resurfaced post 9/11. Claims were made that the U.S. was becoming too reliant on TECHINT and needed more HUMINT and should reexamine its position regarding how best to combat terrorism. But this in itself did not stop the U.S. from continuing to invest in operational level technology towards the unique identification of every citizen, beyond the often unreliable Social Security Number (SSN). Chambliss (2005, p. 5) agreed that HUMINT needed to get the right emphasis in the intelligence reform debate. The increased role of open source intelligence (OSINT) was also highly reported on, some even questioning the role of intelligence analysts altogether. In summary, proposals to reform intelligence include: sweeping administrative changes, better correlation between strategy and intelligence, removal of analytical redundancy between agencies, better quality analysis by expert intelligence analysts, and an improvement in the intelligence collection process itself. Reforms that were not considered appealing included: boosting the number of intelligence agencies, and increasing funding for the U.S. intelligence community.

THE NATIONAL SECURITY AGENDA

Towards the Securitization of "All" Things

Securitization means taking a broader view of security, beyond just military force and war, to include issues such as transnational crime. Securitization of transnational crime, is trying to understand why it happens and how best to combat it within the context of a state, a region, and the globe. One of the major talking points as identified is the purported linked between transnational crime and terrorism. About preventing terrorism Schmid (2005, p. 223) writes: *"...there is really no way that one can disregard the conditions that enable terrorism, whether these are called breeding grounds of terrorism or root causes... The root causes of terrorism are a subject that offers some intellectual challenges. When the United Nations first took up the issue of terrorism in 1972, there were two schools of thought. On the one hand there were those who were primarily interested in addressing the causes of terrorism. On the other hand, there were those who were more concerned with fighting the manifestations of terrorism itself. The second school of thought has become more prominent over the last three decades."*

After the Cold War ended many scholars believed in the expansion of the notion of "security" to include transnational crime matters, among numerous others (Gromes & Bonacker, 2007, p. 2). Buzan, Wæver and de Wilde (1998) identified five distinguishing sectors as viewed by the initiators of the securitization concept. Among them were: the military sector, the political sector, the societal sector, the economic sector and the environmental sector. Thus we can now speak of military security, political security, societal security, economic security and environmental security. Plainly, securitization can be considered an "all-hazards" approach to security. Allan Castle (1997, p. 4) regards securitization as "survival across a number of dimensions."

To some in the traditionalists field of security studies this was considered a backward step; a watering down of the discipline to the point of rendering "security" meaningless. Ralph Emmers (2002, p. 6) has written on this diverging point: *"The question which arises is why we should bother cataloguing a whole series of new concerns, to be christened "security issues," when such a practice may render our use of the term so loose as to make it meaningless. Why not simply state that security issues promise to be increasingly minimized amongst the core states? For the traditionalist, if one adds the contribution to this debate of Ole Waever, for whom the securitization of non-military issues seems closer to a subjective manipulation of language rather than the objective emergence of new threats to core values comparable to previous military threats, the picture becomes even muddier, and may raise the suspicion that security is now what one makes of it."* [underline ours]

For Bruck (2004, p. 103), the security economy has to do with "activities preventing, dealing with and mitigating insecurity in the economy. That broad definition would include private and public activities in both legal and illegal areas of the economy." For Stevens (2004, p. 8) the idea of a security economy "attempts to describe a kaleidoscope cluster of activities concerned with preventing or reducing the risk of deliberate harm to life and property." In the same light then, we can speak of military security "relationships of force; the reference object usually is the state and the survival of the armed forces"; political security which has to do with "relations of authority, governance, and recognition, where an existential threat concerns a state's sovereignty and ideology" and societal security which has to do with "collective identities" (Buzan, 1998, pp. 5-8, 21-3). In this study it is the latter notion of security which is most relevant.

Wensink (2009) from Brandeis University believes that collective identity has been a major catalyst for change throughout history. The concept more explicitly refers to *"the component of one's identity held in common with a larger group. It manifests as a shared feeling of "we" or "groupness," and often coalesces around common social or political objectives. These common goals derive in part from the group's shared sense of identity, and also contribute, in circular fashion, to binding and reinforcing the group's sense of solidarity and collective identity. This mutual reinforcement between identity and goals may help explain the tremendous transformative power collective identity has historically produced."* Among the social and political movements of the 20th century, Wensink (2009) cites: the

Bolshevik revolution, the Nazis, movements for colonial independence, civil rights, feminist and gay pride, and various movements involved in conflict in the Middle East. Collective identity is something different to individual identity (i.e. comprised of personal traits unique to the individual such as one's physical characteristics) and social identity (i.e. interactions of individuals in society, such as the class of a family or employment in a given profession).

Questioning the Role of Auto-ID and LBS Technologies in National Security

Automatic identification technologies can and have been instituted by governments to either include or exclude someone from a group (e.g. in relation to citizenship, permanent residency, refugee status or alien). In the United States, after the terrorist attacks of Sept 11 in 2001, several bills were passed in Congress to allow for the creation of three new Acts related to biometric identification of citizens and aliens- the *Patriot Act*, *Aviation and Transport Security Act*, and the *Enhanced Border Security and Visa Entry Reform Act*. Many civil libertarians were astounded at the pace at which these bills were passed and related legislation was created. The USA has even placed pressure on international travelers and their respective countries to comply with biometric passports or forgo visiting altogether. To some degree national security measures are moving from a predominantly "internalized" perspective to one that is transnational. With this change has been a re-shaping of nation-specific requirements for citizens both in-country and outside its borders to comply with obligatory conditions.

Heightened national security sensitivities have meant a reorganization of our priorities and values, especially when it has come to identification. It seems we have now become obsessed with identifying as a means to providing additional security, as if this is the answer to national security. This is not to say that clear advantages do not exist in the use of automated systems. For example, in 2004, unidentified Tsunami victims who lost their lives in Thailand were actually fitted with RFID chips so that their loved ones might have been able to identify them later (Smith, 2005). But by and large governments are now introducing sweeping changes to citizen ID systems without considering the probable repercussions into the future, and doing so under the guise of a national security agenda. The rhetoric is the same in all instances- we need to do 'x' to ensure effect 'y' is achieved. The only problem with this line of thinking is that the evidence for such claims is almost non-existent. New technologies are introduced with little proof of their success to combat a given national problem (Michael & Michael, 2008).

What started out as a need to identify individuals within one's borders (i.e., personal identification for the self) has now evolved into a national-wide scheme and is poised to make a debut as an international-based solution (personal identification for the 'collective'). It is difficult not to compare these shifts in government policy with those of political movements of the twentieth century. The collective (i.e. co-operation between individuals) was considered by Karl Marx to hold civil society together (Humphrey, 1983). More explicitly for Marx, "only in the community is personal freedom possible" (Rick, 2003).

Blocks forming like the European Union with a single currency are potentially the first test-beds for the larger scale ID and location-based schemes (Michael & Michael, 2009). The trend began in the early 1990s with livestock, and humancentric schemes followed a decade later. EU legislative directives were clear in their requirements for livestock to be identified uniquely based on a common standardized approach. Today, it is people, especially persons who are suspected of crimes, who are being tracked (Michael and Michael, 2009) via a host of surveillance techniques (Laidler, 2008; Lyon, 2002; Garfinkel, 2001; Norris & Armstrong, 1999; Whitaker, 1999; Brin, 1998). The future of homeland security is draped in even more invasive technology, nanotechnology (Ratner & Ratner, 2004). The question to ask, however, is who can ensure that current and future schemes are not misused by any ruling individual or power base? And more importantly, do these schemes really work? Have technologies like ePassports, really kept the terrorists and criminals out (Hunt, Puglia & Puglia, 2007)? And what of homegrown terrorists (Figure 4)? How does a national identity card prevent a given individual who is a legitimate citizen from causing harm to others?

Bruce Schneier (2009) writes of the current dilemmas facing society with regards to open access sources of intelligence. It is worth quoting him at length: *"[i]t regularly comes as a surprise to people that our own infrastructure can be used against us... According to officials investigating the Mumbai attacks, the terrorists used Google Earth to help find their way around... Such incidents have led many governments to demand that Google removes or blurs images of sensitive locations: military bases, nuclear reactors, government buildings, and so on."* We can ponder whether or not the good uses of infrastructure far outweigh the bad uses but Schneier (2003) argues that Schneier (2003) is correct in arguing that the good uses of infrastructure far outweigh the bad uses and that by threatening to dismantle systems like Google Earth that we are only harming ourselves. Thus, Schneier is correct in his assessment, for the main reason that once a capability diffuses, it is almost impossible to go back to the way it was before. And this is all the more the imperative to test, debate, forecast, and view the challenges ahead from multiple disciplines. Law enforcement personnel for instance, rely on location-based services to help them conduct covert policing (Harfield & Harfield, 2008). We cannot switch off the mobile phone network because of the possibility that terrorists may use it to detonate a bomb remotely (Michael & Masters, 2006). However this can never mean that we abandon ethical debate on the consequences of innovation or stop short of arguing for the introduction of technological safeguards; or as Sara Baase (2008, p. 479) underlines, "we must always be alert to potential risks."

Figure 4. Flight boarding passes are still based on old magnetic-strip technology. A number of home-grown terrorists in the United States or United Kingdom have obtained legitimate boarding passes over the counter for travel and attempted terrorist attacks in mid air. Authorities have boosted security measures on airplanes, including the use of armed "air marshalls." In this scenario, the usefulness of a national ID card is questionable.

The Privacy Risk vs. the Security Risk

While automatic identification schemes purportedly offer convenience, speed, higher productivity, better accuracy and efficiency, they are in their very nature "controlling" techniques- they either grant access or deny it (Figure 5 and 6). They inevitably suffer from problems related to function creep (Hayes,

Figure 5. Just like so many other motorways, the Sydney Harbour Bridge became completely cashless in January 2009. The Road Transport Authority (RTA) of New South Wales ran a successful campaign spearheaded by the words: "TimE to tag along." As vehicles enter and exit a RFID gantry, a unique ID number is transmitted and the respective details are logged.

Figure 6. On the "road" to a cashless society. The e-tag RFID device which is installed in all vehicles whose drivers decide to opt-in to paying electronically for road tolling. As devices become more sophisticated, so do intelligence efforts and the rich data that is made available regarding space and time, acquired by law enforcement agencies who are investigating crimes or for evidence in court. Several high profile cases in the United States have already been decided based on information gathered by EZ-Pass and made available to authorities. Courtesy of Mr Jason Paul Sargent.

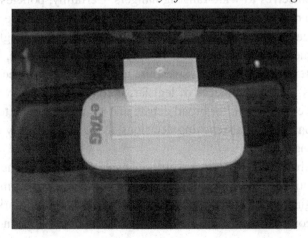

2004). History has also shown what was possible with largely manual-based techniques during WWII; auto-ID techniques at the disposal of a similar head of state could be manifold more intrusive. One need ask now, what safeguards have been put in place to prevent the misuse or abuse of one's personal ID (Tootell, 2007). Some auto-ID technologies even pose legal dilemmas. One could claim that biometric techniques for instance, and beneath-the-skin RFID transponders, do encroach on an individual's privacy when used for ID. Biometrics like fingerprints or DNA are wholly owned by the individual yet requested and stored by the state on large citizen databases.

While in today's society the need for ID is unquestionable, we need to ensure we do not enforce changes that are irreversible and perhaps even uncontrollable. While national ID schemes were introduced by a number of countries after the Great Depression of the 1930s, what has changed since their inception are the technological capabilities that we have (often quite literally) at our fingertips. These auto-ID technologies are manifold more powerful and when enjoined to other automated processes are a magnitude more invasive. The periodic census is a fine example of something that was introduced by the church and state to collect data in order to help provision services for citizens. Today, however, aggregated census data is being sold as a commodity to help private organizations perform more precise "target marketing". Perhaps it is not too long before our "private" IDs also undergo a similar transformation- "DNA for sale, anyone?" But what of the rhetoric that in order to enhance our personal security we must give up certain privacy rights to the collective, for the common good, so to speak (Perusco, Michael & Michael, 2006). Certainly, ID systems and location systems are useful in emergency management situations such as that played out during Hurricane Katrina which struck New Orleans in 2005 and affected millions of lives (Tootell, 2008; Aloudat, Michael & Yan, 2007). The case for all pervasive systems however, which require citizen blanket coverage for the sake of potentially apprehending only a few suspects is less appealing. This is the very topic of an excellent dissertation completed by Holly Irene Tootell at the University of Wollongong in 2007, titled: *The Social Impact of Auto-ID and Location Based Services in National Security.*

CONCLUSION

The growing interconnectedness of systems means that any ICT solution proposed by powerful nation states will be rapidly adopted by other nations. Truly global solutions, while seemingly convenient on the surface, lend themselves to wide-ranging dangers. Certainly, policies and procedures are important, so are laws and regulations, and standards, and guidelines but these all seem to be more exactly 'reactionary' to the status quo. Studies have recently shown that at the height of terrorist events or other national security issues, public sentiment is swayed by media coverage, the public perception itself, and government statements. As a result sweeping changes are introduced in a short period of time, particularly 'changes' with large pieces of legislative content. There never seems to be enough time for additional public consultation, for broad debate and discussion; time to consider the consequences of the implementation of these far-reaching decisions and for the scrutiny of their overall effect on the community in the long-term.

We seem to have become captive to a whirlpool cycle of surplus change, a capital accumulation of power house capabilities without the follow-on forethought. New government and business challenges are created as emerging technologies are prematurely released to the market; still newer technologies are invented to overcome the challenges, laws are instituted to set the bounds of how technology should and should not be used and people are ultimately expected to learn to live with the implications and complications. Information and communication security measures adopted in haste in response to terrorism and other national security breaches have only acted to increase this cycle of change. There is also an underlying paradox in all of this which political skeptics would have already noted: though in recent years governments have been ostensibly committed to reducing state power, they have in reality increased it massively.

REFERENCES

Aloudat, A., Michael, K., & Yan, J. (2007). Location-Based Services in Emergency Management- from Government to Citizens: Global Case Studies. In P. Mendis, J. Lai, E. Dawson & H. Abbass (Eds.), *Recent Advances in Security Technology* (pp. 190-201). Melbourne: Australian Homeland Security Research Centre.

Baase, S. (2008). *A Gift of Fire: Social, Legal, and Ethical Issues for Computing and the Internet* (3rd ed.). New Jersey: Prentice Hall.

Ben-Shaul, N. S. (2006). *A violent world: TV news images of Middle Eastern terror and war.* Lanham, Maryland: Rowman & Littlefield.

Berkowitz, B. D. (1996). Information age intelligence. *Foreign Policy, 103,* 35-50.

Boulden, J., & Weiss, T. G. (2004). *Terrorism and the UN: before and after September 11.* Bloomington, IN: Indiana University Press.

Brin, D. (1998). *The Transparent Society: will technology force us to choose between privacy and freedom?* Massachusetts: Perseus Books.

Bruck, T. (2004). Assessing the Economic Trade-offs of the Security Economy. In OECD (Ed.), *The Security Economy* (pp. 101): OECD.

Buzan, B., Wæver, O., & Wilde, J. d. (1998). *Security: A New Framework for Analysis.* Boulder: Lynne Rienner Publishers.

Castle, A. (1997). Transnational Organized Crime and International Security. *Institute of International Relations* Retrieved 9 September 2008

Chalk, P., & Rosenau, W. (2004). *Confronting the Enemy Within: Security Intelligence, the Police, and Counterterrorism in Four Democracies.* Santa Monica, California: RAND Corp.

Chambliss, S. (2005). We Have Not Correctly Framed the Debate on Intelligence Reform. *Parameters, 35*(1), 5-13.

Copeland, T. E. (2007). *Fool me twice: intelligence failure and mass casualty terrorism.* Leiden: Martinus Nijhoff.

Dolnik, A., & Fitzgerald, K. M. (2008). *Negotiating hostage crises with the new terrorists.* Westport, Conn.: Praeger Security International.

Emmers, R. (2002). The Securitization of Transnational Crime in ASEAN. *Institute of Defence and Strategic Studies Singapore Working Series No. 39* Retrieved 9 September 2008, from www.rsis.edu. sg/publications/WorkingPapers/WP39.pdf

Findlay, M. (1998). *The globalization of crime: understanding transitional relationships in context.* Cambridge: Cambridge University Press.

Ganor, B. (2002). Defining Terrorism: Is One Man's Terrorist another Man's Freedom Fighter? *Practice and Research, 3*(4), 287-304.

Garfinkel, S. (2001). *Database Nation: The Death of Privacy in the 21st Century.* New York: O'Reilly Media.

Goodman, M. A. (2003). 9/11: The Failure of Strategic Intelligence. *Intelligence and National Security, 18*(4), 59-71.

Griffin, D. R. (2004). *The New Pearl Harbor: Disturbing Questions About the Bush Administration and 9/11.* Northampton, Mass.: Olive Branch Press.

Gromes, T., & Bonacker, T. (2007). The Concept of Securitization as a Tool for Analysing the Role of Human-Rights-Related Civil Society in Ethno-Political Conflicts. *SHUR Working Paper Series* Retrieved 9 September 2008, from http://www.luiss.it/shur/wp-content/uploads/2007/05/shurwp05-07.pdf

Hannah, G., O'Brien, K. A., & Rathmell, A. (2005). *Intelligence and Security Legislation for Security Sector Reform.* Europe: RAND Corp.

Harfield, C., & Harfield, K. (2008). *Covert Investigation* (2nd ed.). Oxford: Oxford University Press.

Hayes, B. (2004). From the Schengen Information System to SIS II and the Visa Information (VIS): the proposals explained *Statewatch Analysis, 3*.

Hersh, S. M. (2005). *Chain of command.* London: Penguin.

Higgins, T. (1987). *The perfect failure: Kennedy, Eisenhower, and the CIA at the Bay of Pigs* (1st ed.). New York: Norton.

Hoffman, B. (2006). *Inside Terrorism.* New York: Columbia University Press.

Holmes, S. (2006). Al-Qaeda, September 11, 2001. In D. Gambetta (Ed.), *Making Sense of Suicide Missions* (pp. 131-172). Oxford: Oxford University Press.

Humphrey, C. (1983). *Karl Marx Collective: Economy, Society and Religion in a Siberian Collective Farm.* Cambridge: Cambridge University Press.

Hunt, V. D., Puglia, A., & Puglia, M. (2007). RFID Technology in Homeland Security, Law Enforcement, and Corrections. In V. D. Hunt, A. Puglia & M. Puglia (Eds.), *RFID-A Guide to Radio Frequency Identification* (pp. 67-82): John Wiley- Inderscience.

Knudsen, O. F. (2001). Post-Copenhagen Security Studies: Desecuritizing Securitization. *Security Dialogue, 32*(3), 355-368.

Laidler, K. (2008). *Surveillance Unlimited: How We've Become the Most Watch People on Earth*. Cambridge: Icon Books.

Lowenthal, M. M. (2006). *Intelligence: from secrets to policy* (3rd ed.). Washington, DC: CQ Press.

Lyon, D. (2002). *Surveillance as Social Sorting: Privacy, Risk and Automated Discrimination*. London: Routledge.

Matthias, W. C. (2001). *America's Strategic Blunders: Intelligence Analysis and National Security Policy, 1936-1991*. Pennsylvania: The Pennsylvania State University Press.

McNeal, G. S. (2007/2008). Cyber Embargo: Countering the Internet Jihad. *Case Western Reserve Journal of International Law, 39*(3), 789.

Merari, A. (2005). Social, organizational and psychological factors in suicide terrorism. In T. Bjorgo (Ed.), *Root causes of terrorism: Myths, reality and ways forward* (pp. 70-86). London: Routledge.

Michael, K., & Masters, A. (2006). Realized Applications of Positioning Technologies in Defense Intelligence. In H. Abbass & D. Essam (Eds.), *Applications of Information Systems to Homeland Security and Defense* (pp. 167-195). Hershey, USA: Idea Group Publishing Press.

Michael, K., & Michael, M. G. (2008). *Australia and the New Technologies: Evidence Based Policy in Public Administration*. Wollongong: University of Wollongong.

Michael, K., & Michael, M. G. (2009). Schengen Information System II: The Balance Between Civil Liberties, Security & Justice. *Intelligence and National Security, in press*.

Neumann, P. R., & Smith, M. L. R. (2005). Missing the Plot? Intelligence and Discourse Failure. *Orbis, Winter*, 95-107.

Norris, C., & Armstrong, G. (1999). *The Maximum Surveillance Society: CCTV in Britain*. London: Berg.

Perusco, L., Michael, K., & Michael, M. G. (2006). *Location-based Services and the Privacy-Security Dichotomy*. Paper presented at the Third International Conference on Mobile Computing and Ubiquitous Networking (ICMU 2006), London, UK.

Posner, R. (2005). *Preventing Surprise Attacks: Intelligence Reform in the Wake of 9/11*. Stanford: Hoover Institution Press.

Ratner, D., & Ratner, M. A. (2004). *Nanotechnology and Homeland Security: New Weapons for New Wars*. New Jersey: Pearson Education.

Rick, J. (2003). Human Nature According to Niccolò Machiavelli, Karl Marx and Ayn Rand. *jonathanrick. com* Retrieved 29 December 2009, from http://jonathanrick.com/2003/05/human-nature-according-to-niccolo-machiavelli-karl-marx-and-ayn-rand/

Ricolfi, L. (2006). Palestinians, 1981-2003. In D. Gambetta (Ed.), *Making Sense of Suicide Missions* (pp. 77-130). Oxford: Oxford University Press.

Rogers, P. (2007). *Global security and the War on Terror: elite power and the illusion of control*. Abingdon ; New York, NY: Routledge.

Schmid, A. P. (2005). Prevention of terrorism: Towards a multi-pronged approach. In T. Bjorgo (Ed.), *Root causes of terrorism: Myths, reality and ways forward* (pp. 223-240). London: Routledge.

Schneier, B. (30 January 2009). Don't let terrorists strip us of our technological rights. *Sydney Morning Herald* Retrieved 31 January 2009, from http://www.smh.com.au/text/articles/2009/01/29/1232818630291. html

Schneier, B. (2003). *Beyond Fear: Thinking Sensibly about Security in an Uncertain World*. New York: Springer-Verlag.

Shelley, L. (2006). The Globalization of Crime and Terrorism.   Retrieved 11 September 2008, from http://usinfo.state.gov/journals/itgic/0206/ijge/shelley.htm

Simon, S., & Benjamin, D. (2000). America and the new terrorism. *Survival, 42*(1), 59-75.

Smith, J. (2005). Too many corpses to count. *DailyRecord*   Retrieved January 1, from http://www. dailyrecord.co.uk

Stevens, B. (2004). The Emerging Security Economy: An Introduction. In OECD (Ed.), *The Security Economy* (pp. 7): OECD.

Taylor, S. A., & Goldman, D. (2004). Intelligence Reform: Will More Agencies, Money, Personal Help. *Intelligence and National Security, 19*(3), 416-435.

Tootell, H. (2008). The Social Impact of National Security Technologies: ePassports, E911 and mobile alerts. In K. Michael & M. G. Michael (Eds.), *Australia and the New Technologies: Evidence Based Policy in Public Administration* (pp. 87-99): University of Wollongong.

Tootell, H. I. (2007). *The Social Impact of Using Automatic Identification Technologies and Location-Based Services in National Security*. University of Wollongong, Wollongong.

V. Daniel Hunt, A. P., Mike Puglia. (2007). RFID Technology in Homeland Security, Law Enforcement, and Corrections. In V. D. Hunt, A. Puglia & M. Puglia (Eds.), *RFID-A Guide to Radio Frequency Identification* (pp. 67-82): John Wiley- Inderscience.

Wensink, J. (2009). Collective Identity. *MCRI Globalization and Autonomy* Retrieved 28 January 2009, from http://www.globalautonomy.ca/global1/glossary_entry.jsp?id=CO.0075

Whitaker, R. (1999). *The End of Privacy: how total surveillance is becoming a reality*. New York: The New Press.

Wilkie, A. (2004). Intelligence Failures. In A. Wilkie (Ed.), *Axis of Deceit* (pp. 150-166). Melbourne, Victoria: Black Inc.

Section II
Auto-ID and LBS Innovation

Chapter V
Barcode:
The Pioneer Auto-ID Technology

BARCODE TECHNOLOGY

Historical Overview

Of all the auto-ID technologies in the global market today, barcode is the most widely used. In 1994, Cohen (p. 55) wrote "...barcode technology is clearly at the forefront of automatic identification systems and is likely to stay there for a long time." It is estimated by GS1, that there are over 5 billion barcode reads each day. Despite complementary and supplementary technologies entering the barcode space, Cohen's statement still holds true. Palmer (p. 9) agreed in 1995, that "barcode ha[d] become the dominant automatic identification technology". Ames (1990, p. G-1) defines the barcode as: *"an automatic identification technology that encodes information into an array of adjacent varying width parallel rectangular bars and spaces."*

The technology's popularity can be attributed to its application in retail, specifically in the identification and tracking of consumer goods. Before the barcode, only manual identification techniques existed. Handwritten labels or carbon-copied paper were attached or stuck to 'things' needing identification. In 1932 the first study on the automation of supermarket checkout counters was conducted by Wallace Flint. Subsequently in 1934 a patent was filed presenting barcode-type concepts (Palmer, 1995, p. 11) by Kermode and his colleagues. The patent described the use of four parallel lines as a means to identify different objects.

In 1959 a group of railroad research and development (R&D) managers (including GTE Applied Research Lab representatives) met in Boston to solve some of the rail industry's freight problems. By 1962 Sylvania (along with GTE) had designed a system which was implemented in 1967 using color barcode technology (Collins & Whipple, 1994, p. 8). In 1968, concentrated efforts began to develop a standard for supermarket point-of-sale which culminated in the RCA developing a bull's eye symbol to be operated in the Kroger store in Cincinnati in 1972 (Palmer, 1995, p. 12). Until then, barcodes in retail were only used for order picking at distribution centers (Collins & Whipple, 1994, p. 10). But it was not the bull's eye barcode that would dominate but the Universal Product Code (UPC) standard. The first UPC barcode to cross the scanner was on a packet of Wrigley's chewing gum at Marsh's supermarket in Ohio in June 1974 (Brown, 1997, p. 5). Within two years the vast majority of retail items in the United States carried a UPC.

The Barcode System

Barcode technology increased in popularity throughout the 1980s as computing power and memory became more affordable, and consumer acceptance increased. This enabled programs and peripheral devices (complementary innovations) to be built to support barcodes for the identification and capture of data. A barcode can only work within a systems environment. Barcode labels in themselves are useless without peripheral equipment. The components required in a barcode system include: a barcode label (encoded with a symbology), a scanner, a decoder, a computer with a database, and a printer. Additional components include software, monitors, and networks which are used to complement most systems (Jesse & Rosenbaum, 2000). Simply put, a scanner reads the label using a given symbology, a decoder then converts this signal into a digital form so that a computer can perform its functions.

The Importance of Symbologies

When examining the technical features of the barcode it is important to understand symbologies, also known as configurations. There are many different types of symbologies that can be used to implement barcodes, each with its distinct characteristics. New symbologies are still being introduced today. Cohen (1994, p. 55) explains a symbology is a language with its own rules and syntax that can be translated into ASCII code.

Common to all symbologies is that the barcode is made up of a series of dark and light contiguous bars (Collins & Whipple, 1994, pp. 20-24). Each barcode differs based on the width of the bars. Of particular importance is the width of the narrowest bar which is called the 'X dimension' (usually measured in millimeters) and the number of bar widths. Essentially, this defines the character width- the amount of bars needed to encode data. When the barcode is read by a device called a scanner, light is illuminated onto the bars. This pattern of black and white spaces is then reflected (like an OFF/ON series) and decoded using an algorithm. This special pattern equates to an identification number but can be implemented using any specification. For instance, the major linear barcode symbologies include: Interleaved 2 of 5, Code 39 (also known as code 3-of-9), EAN 13, U.P.C. 8 and Code 128. Major two-dimensional symbologies, known also as area symbologies, include Data Matrix, MaxiCode, and PDF417.

Interleaved 2 of 5 is based on a numeric character set only. Two characters are paired together using bars. The structure of the barcode is made up of a start quiet zone, start pattern, data, stop pattern and trail quiet zone. According to Palmer (1995, p. 29) it is mainly used in the distribution industry. Code 39 is based on a full alphabet, full numeric and special character set. It consists of a series of symbol characters represented by five bars and four spaces. Each character is separated by an intercharacter gap. This symbology was widely used in non-retail applications. The barcode is made up of light and dark bars representing 1s and 0s. The structure of the barcodes includes three guard bars (start, centre and stop), and left and right data. The barcodes can be read in an omni-directional fashion as well as bi-directional. Allotted article numbers are only unique identification numbers in a standard format and do not classify goods by product type. Like the Interleaved 2 of 5 symbology, EAN identification is exclusively numerical. The structure of the EAN and U.P.C. includes (i) the prefix number that is an organization number that has been preset by EAN, and (ii) the item identification that is a number that is given to the product by the country-specific numbering organization. The U.P.C. relevant only to the U.S. and Canada does not use the prefix codes as EAN does but denotes the prefix by 0, 6, or 7.

According to Palmer (1995, p. 37), Code 128 was increasingly adopted throughout the 1990s because it was a highly-dense alphanumeric symbology that allowed for variable length and multiple element widths. With the introduction of the Data Matrix symbology even more information could be packed onto a square block. Since the symbology is scalable it is possible to fit hundreds of thousands of characters on a block. Data Matrix used to be a proprietary technology until it became public in 1994. As opposed to the light and dark bars of the EAN symbology, MaxiCode is a matrix code which is made up of a series of square dots, an array of 866 interlocking hexagons. On each 3cm by 3cm square block, about 100 ASCII characters can be held. It was developed by the United Parcel Service for automatic identification of packages. Like the MaxiCode symbology, PDF417 is stacked. The symbology consists of 17 modules each containing 4 bars and spaces. The structure allows for between 1000 and 2000 characters per symbol. Collins and Whipple (1994, p. 41) suggest a maximum of 50 characters when using linear symbologies.

The 2D barcode configuration has increased the physical data limitations of the linear configurations. Users are now able to store larger quantities of information on barcodes with many company-defined fields. Contrarily, linear barcodes should never extend to more than 20 characters as they become difficult to read by scanners. Other linear and 2D barcode symbologies include: Plessey Code, Matrix 2 of 5, Nixdorf Code, Delta Distance A, Codabar, Codablock, Code 1, Code 16K, Code 11, Code 39, Code 49, Code 93, Code 128, DataGlyphs, Datastrip Code, InterCode, MSI Code, Snowflake Code USD-5, UnisCode, Vericode, ArrayTag, Dotcode.

Choosing a Symbology

Each symbology has benefits and limitations. It is important for the adopter of barcode technology to know which symbologies are suitable to their particular industry. Standards associations and manufacturers can also help with a best-fit recommendation (Grieco et al., 1989, pp. 43-45). Considerations may include: what character sets are required by the company, what the required level of accuracy of the symbology should be, whether the symbology allows for the creation and printing of a label (in terms of density), and whether the symbology has specifications that make it intolerant to particular circumstances.

Sometimes there may also be pressure by industry groups for users to conform to certain symbologies. As Cohen (1994, p. 99f) points out, there are some bodies that have created industrial barcode standards such as: ODETTE (Organization for Data Exchange by Tele Transmission in Europe) that adopted Code 39; IATA (International Air Transport Authority) that adopted Interleaved 2 of 5; HIBCC (Health Industry Business Communication Council) that adopted Code 39 as well as Code 128; and LOGMARS (Logistic Applications of Automated Marking and Reading Symbols) that has also adopted Code 39. It should be noted that even if a symbology is created for a particular industry group, it does not mean it is highly sophisticated. For example, Codabar developed in 1972 is used today in libraries, blood banks and certain parcel express applications although it is not considered a sophisticated symbology, despite that it has served some industry groups well for decades (Collins and Whipple, 1994, p. 28).

About Scanners

The barcode scanner, also known as a reader, takes that which has been encoded in a symbology and converts it to a digital format to be read by software on a computer or software resident on the scanner itself. The reader uses an electro-optical system as a type of transducer so that it can analyze the optical symbol using the reader's processing electronics (Palmer, 1995, p. 79). The electro-optical system both illumines the symbol and determines how much light has been reflected once a symbol is read. The analog voltage coming out from the electro-optical system is then converted to digital format by the analog-to-digital (A/D) converter and outputted to a processor. According to LaMoreaux (1998, p. 144) eight basic functions are performed by the scanner: *"(1) shine light on the barcode; (2) collect the reflected light, convert it into plus and minus electricity; (3) process the signal; (4) analyze the relative width of the light and dark areas; (5) compare the signal from the barcode symbol to the symbology standards in memory; (6) if it corresponds to a known symbology, continue; (7) decode the barcode; (8) transmit the information as usable for the rest of the system."*

There are different ways you can categorize scanner types. One way is by separating the types based on readers that require human intervention and those that do not. Attended barcode scanners include input devices like lightpens, wand scanners or hand-held laser guns. These scanners can be further categorized into those that require the scanner's physical contact with the barcode label, and those that do not (i.e. non-contact). Some practice is required by attendees using handheld, fixed beam contact devices. These scanners, also known as charge-coupled devices (CCD), are pixel readers with very little depth of field capability. Common errors in reading a barcode include the operator scanning the barcode label too slowly, or the operator stopping or starting the scan outside the quiet zones. Handheld fixed beam noncontact devices require the attendee to manually provide the scanning motion and are typically used for soft or irregular surfaces. Handheld, moving beam scanners, also known as laser scanners are usually found at supermarket stores and are more expensive than wands. They can scan at more than a thousand times per second, and require little operator training. They are preferred because they are non-contact, they have a greater range of distance and depth of field, and are rugged able to be used in harsh environments (Figure 1).

Conveyor barcode scanners, which do not require human intervention at the point of scanning can be divided into orientation-dependent laser scanners and omnidirectional laser scanners. These scanners are used in automated material handling systems and dominate manufacturing floors in an attempt to speed the flow of goods, decrease the amount of inventory stored and increase industrial productivity. High speed conveyors are used in concert with diverters, packaging lines and transfer machines (Palmer,

Figure 1. Symbol's handheld scanner for radio-frequency data capture (RFDC) and barcode collection. Courtesy AirData Pty Ltd, Motorola Premier Business Partner.

1995, p. 117). Orientation-dependent scanners require the symbol orientation to be precisely fixed in a given application whereas omni-directional scanners do not. Omni-directional scanners are growing in sophistication, and while they are more expensive, are advantageous especially for parcels which come in different shapes and sizes, from different countries, and have to be sorted quickly. There are also vision-based scanners which can belong to either aforementioned category. The vision-based scanners are currently being used to read 2D symbologies to overcome some of the problems associated with using omnidirectional laser scanning technology. Advances in digital signal processing (DSP) chips, high resolution imagers, and pattern recognition software have made it possible to read 2D stacked symbologies and 2D matrix symbologies with even the smallest of aspect ratios.

Printer Types and Labels

Choosing printer technology is similar in a way to choosing a symbology, it is heavily dependent on the application context. Barcode printers broadly fall into two classifications: off-site and on-site printing. Basically, labels are printed on the site they will be used, or they are printed off-site where production is done separate to a location where they will be applied. Off-site printing is usually for large volumes of barcode labels either with the same symbols or sequenced. With on-site printing, the data encoded in each symbol is different and is usually entered manually for small counts of items, or electronically by an attached computer, if the batch is larger. On-site printing techniques are especially good for applications where the user cannot predict in advance their label printing requirements.

LaMoreaux (1995, p. 170) identifies no less than 11 different types of printing systems including: *electrostatic* for the printing of high-speed large labels, *impact* for high-quality printing which is dedicated to one code, *dot matrix* which is ideal for multi-part forms and infinite variable formats, *thermal* printers which are quiet and inexpensive, *thermal transfer* which has a high-quality print and is permanent, *ink jet* which is fast and silent but which suffers from low corrugated quality, *ink jet (hot melt)* which has excellent quality and high density, laser etch on things which will print on most surfaces but is expensive, *laser* toner on labels which is fast and has superior quality, *letterpresses/flexo* which are cheap but labor intensive, and *hotstamp* which allows for multi-color prints. In 2007, linear imaging was surpassing laser scanning as the preferred scan engine for its performance and durability.

The group of off-site printers which consist of the letterpress, offset lithography, flexography, rotogravure, and the inking wheel are all known as wet ink techniques. The more money that is spent for the purchase of an on-site printer, the better the quality of the barcode label, and the greater its readability and lifetime. Since the mid-90s, the range of printers for bar coding has increased as the size of the printers has decreased. There are now a number of powerful barcode labeling programs granting businesses the functionality to create customized labels (Figure 2). For example, BarTender is considered the leading Windows barcode labeling program which is developed by Seagull Scientific. The quality of the label is dependent upon the quality of materials used, among which are paper, vinyl, mylar, and acetate. The quality of the printer cartridges, ribbons, toners is also important, as is how the labels are stuck onto items by hand or using applicators.

Communications

Local area networks (LANs) are a key part of any automatic identification system, whether they are wireline or wireless. Increasingly, data communications are not being done using the traditional model

Figure 2. A screenshot from the Barcodingfonts software developed by Gary Elfring for making barcodes using the UPC symbology. Courtesy of Gary Elfring http://www.elfring.com/

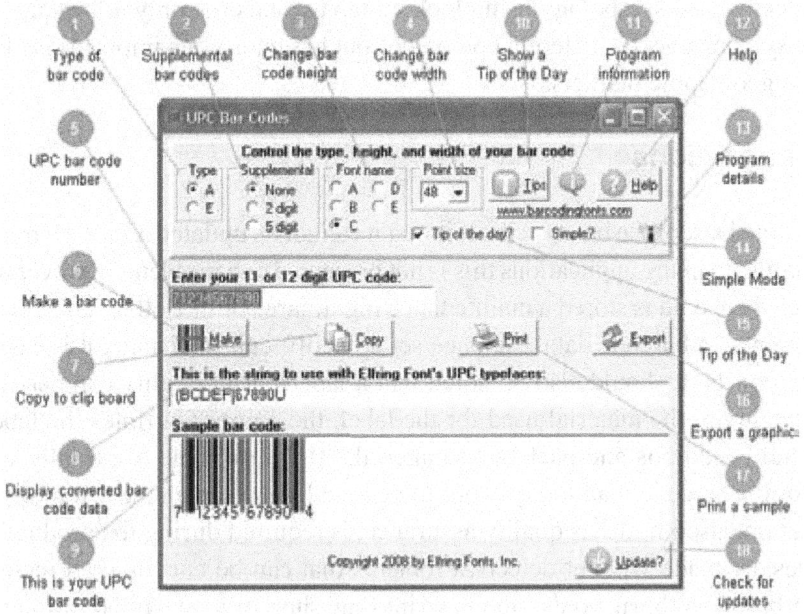

linking the labeling and reading equipment with the data processing resource using cable. Instead radio frequency data capture (RFDC) is being used taking advantage of the electromagnetic spectrum. The RF-based data collection network has many advantages over the wireline network, the greatest of which are the use of portable terminals. However, small-to-medium sized companies who prefer the wireless environment must invest in a network which employs a base station unit which controls remote units and large sized companies might use multiple base stations which is driven by a single network controller to ensure complete coverage.

Incremental Innovations

Of the significant incremental innovations to barcode technology has been bar coding small sized objects and the reading of different symbologies using a single hardware device. In 1996 the Uniform Code Council (UCC) and EAN (European Article Number) International recognized the need for a symbology that could be applied to small-sized products such as microchips and health care products. The UCC and EAN Symbol Technical Advisory Committee (STAC) identified a solution that was able to incorporate the benefits of both linear (1D) and 2D barcodes. The symbol class is called Composite Symbology (CS), and the family of barcodes is called GS1 DataBar (formerly known as Reduced Space Symbology (RSS)). GS1 DataBar provides *"product identification for hard-to-mark items like fresh foods and can carry information such as supplier identification, lot numbers, and expiration dates. This new technology also creates the opportunity for solutions supporting product authentication and traceability, product quality and effectiveness, variable measure product identification, and couponing" GS1, 2008)*. It has been heralded as the new generation of barcodes because it allows for the co-existence of symbologies already in use (Moore & Albright, 1998, pp. 24-25). The biggest technical breakthrough (conceived prior to the 1990s) was *autodiscrimination*. This is the ability for a barcode system to read more than one symbology by automatically detecting which symbology has been used and converting the data to a relevant locally-used symbology using look-up tables. This not only allows the use of several different types of symbologies by different companies but has enormous implications for users trading their goods across geographic markets.

Barcode Limitations

A technical drawback of the barcode itself is that it cannot be updated. Once a barcode is printed, it is the identifier for life. In many applications this is not presented as a problem, however it does make updating the database where data is stored a maintenance nightmare. Unlike other auto-ID technologies that can be reprogrammed, a barcode database once set up is difficult to change; it is easier in some instances to re-label products. It should also be noted that a label's print quality can decline with age, depending on the quality of the material used for the label, the number of times the label has been scanned, environmental conditions and packaging material. "[I]t is possible (especially with marginal quality barcodes) for the barcode read today... not to be read by the same reader tomorrow" (Cohen, 1994, p. 93). Verification, also known as quality assurance, is required during the production process to ensure that barcodes are made without defects. Problems that can be encountered include: undersized quiet zones, underburn/ overburn, voids, ribbon wrinkling, short or long barcodes, transparent or translucent backgrounds, missing information which is human-readable, symbol size or font is incorrect, spread or overlays, location on packaging, and roughness and spots. Another limitation of the technology is that it is insecure. Anyone with the right scanner can read a barcode and decode it effortlessly.

THE BARCODE INNOVATION SYSTEM

Committees, Subcommittees and Councils

As LaMoreaux (1998, p. 51) points out, "[n]o invention comes in a flash. Each is built on many minds sharing ideas and working towards the same goals." At first, the auto-ID industry had very few innovators, most of who were involved in barcode development. It was around 1970 that product coding started to be noticed by retail and manufacturing companies, especially in the U.S. Until that time, individual innovators in small firms were attempting to offer solutions to companies in isolation. These solutions were dissimilar because they were based on proprietary solutions. At the time the retail industry especially feared that barcode might cause more problems than it would solve through incompatible check-out systems and the implementation of a number of different product coding schemes (Brown, 1997, p. 39).

Firms had valuable ideas regarding the direction of barcode but were not able to share these with each other as there was no common body linking everyone together. This eventually led to the urgent formation of the Ad Hoc Committee in 1970. The committee was made up of ten chief executive officers. Five would come from grocery manufacturers and another five from distributor associations. Trade associations collectively posed five questions to this committee. These included (Brown, 1997, pp. 42f): *"(1) is a standard industry product code worthwhile even if it not feasible to devise a standard symbol? (2) If so, what should that code be? (3) How can widespread acceptance of the industry standard be obtained? (4) How shall the code be managed? (5) Should there be a standard symbol representing the code, and if so what should it be?"* As can be seen, these questions were all concerned with the barcode technology itself, not about such things as end-user acceptance. This is characteristic of a technology in its early adoption phase. The technology must work properly and must make sense economically before it can enjoy widespread adoption. In this manner, progress is connected to technology itself, "vorsprung durch Technik" [[p]rogress through technology].

In 1971 the Symbol Selection Subcommittee was formed, aided by the Ad Hoc Committee. The Committee was made up of young, intense and brilliant individuals who were committed to the cause. Meetings were "electric as idea fed upon idea" (Brown, 1997, p. 58). Many skilful people committed large amounts of time to the committee while holding full-time positions during the day. The Symbol Committee enthusiastically sought help from anyone that was willing and so attracted a wider group of players who brought with them a great number of diverse issues, many of which were not technical in nature. The focus was now on how to get barcode successfully to market. Key tasks included to: *"(1) Develop alternate agreements to license and/or put selected symbol in public domain; (2) Visit key equipment companies; (3) Initiate and coordinate special studies; (4) Contact other affected groups, e.g., printer... manufacturers; (5) Develop test parameters and formats; (6) Develop environment guidelines; (7) Interview and decide on special consultants; (8) Develop press releases"* (Brown, 1997, pp. 61f).

This was an important point in the history of barcode because the Committee encouraged firm-to-firm and firm-to-agency interaction. For the first time, industry stakeholders could voice their concerns about the proposed standard. Representatives from companies could also share their visions about the technology and potential applications. This kind of information exchange was fruitful in that it encouraged participatory behavior by stakeholders, giving the Committee the ability to address critical issues in a timely manner. For instance, food wholesaler *Jewel*, voiced their concerns through formal letters to the Committee. In one such letter to the Symbol Committee the company president listed seven main concerns about the work, including, whether the standard defined in 1971 would soon become obsolete, that the ten-digit code would not stand the test of time and that the lack of compatibility with other codes would be a major problem. *Jewel* believed that technological innovation was inevitably a continual process and that it was up to the Ad Hoc Committee to make decisions on key issues (Brown, 1997, p. 84).

Determined to complete its mission the Symbol Committee finished its two-year investigation in 1973 announcing a suitable standard- the UPC (Universal Product Code) was officially born. A spin-off of the Symbol Committee was the formation of the Symbol Technical Advisory Committee (STAC) and later the Universal Product Code Council (UPCC). Seeing the invaluable work done by the UPCC, other standards-setting organizations were also subsequently formed such as EAN (Electronic Article Numbering) and AIM (Automatic Identification Manufacturers). It is through these well-known organizations, councils and committees that international standards are set via ISO (International Standards Organization) today. While barcode enjoyed steady growth after the mid 1970s, it was only when mass merchants like KMart and Wal-Mart committed to U.P.C. scanning that adoption boomed. This is when barcode started to become noticeable to the general public.

Public Policy: Labor Unions and the Consumer Response

The primary aim of the barcode was to improve the efficiency and productivity of the checkout process-it was oriented towards savings for business. Increased consumer convenience was a by-product but not something that preoccupied the attention of the Ad Hoc or Symbol Committees in the U.S. Very early on in the development of barcode, labor unions and consumer activist groups joined forces to oppose the new technology. In 1998 Lamoreaux (pp. 17-19) wrote that the "...fears of barcodes, today, are more psychological and economic. People are afraid they will be cheated... or that they will be used for spying. Trade unions still fight barcoding if they perceive that it will negatively affect members' jobs".

First and foremost, any level of automation at the check out counter equated to job losses. Labor unions were quick to highlight the inevitabilities and journalists were quick to report on them. Second, consumers were very skeptical about the removal of price tags on supermarket store items. Historically, consumers were used to purchasing goods with a price tag on the item itself. At the check-out counter, a sales assistant would then key in the price of the item and the consumer would pay the amount. The introduction of barcodes changed the way people shopped. Many shoppers had never seen electronic devices at that time, so the scanner at the check-out was treated apprehensively. The light emitting from the scanner, and the beeps heard when an item was entered contributed to some of the customer feeling. A lot of doubt initially crept in regarding the accuracy of the new technology. Brown (1997, p. 128) described the deep mistrust consumers held of business: "[f]rom their perspective, of course industry wanted to remove prices from items: using computer technology would enable prices to be manipulated without fear of detection". It was difficult for many consumers to understand how a bar with black and white lines imprinted on products could equate to a cost for the good they were purchasing or a decrease in queuing time. While the barcode did act to increase productivity levels, some consumers could argue that they are still queuing up at large supermarkets for the same amount of time, as less staff is hired offset by the productivity gains (Figure 3). Also, the need for a single item to be scanned, like a packet of chewing gum, is debatable. It would be faster to pay for the item and leave.

Political games eventuated from the polemical situation between consumer activists and the Committee. Members of the Public Policy Committee (for barcode) even ended up at state legislatures and finally succumbed to the demands of consumers by putting forward several proposals for itemized

Figure 3. German supermarket chain, ALDI at Shellharbour Stockland, New South Wales, Australia. A self-service supermarket, known for its low prices, and 'faster' checkout- no plastic bags, the goods are scanned, and go straight into the trolley. Photo taken in 2007.

pricing as well as the establishment of by-laws. Accuracy issues related to barcode in the United States were finally put to rest in 1996 when the Federal Trade Commission (FTC) published its findings on the impacts of barcodes on pricing. The FTC report revealed that on average most supermarkets will undercharge rather than overcharge when an error has occurred in the price: "[c]heckout scanners result in fewer errors than manual entry of prices at the checkout" (Reeves, 1996, p. 41).

By the late 1970s politicians had grown weary of the debate and abandoned it altogether. The Public Policy Committee ceased to exist in 1977 but served a crucial role in the early stages of barcode development as a mechanism to encourage interaction between various stakeholders. Yet this was not the end of public policy issues related to barcode. By the 1990s, labor unions and other independent bodies were now pointing to serious injuries suffered by employees who had to repetitively scan products for long periods of time with awkward equipment and heavy supermarket store items. Repetitive strain injury (RSI) received a lot of media attention and affected employees sought compensation.

The U.P.C. also received attention from religious groups who saw the bar coding of products as a movement towards the fulfillment of prophecies in the Book of Revelation (Hristodoulou, 1994). There are still groups, especially some monastic communities who refuse to purchase goods that are marked with the barcode. This would surely limit their ability to survive on anything, save subsistence farming practices. Members of these groups link the U.P.C. with the infamous "number of the beast" (666). A plethora of web sites have noted the uncanny coincidence between the number of the beast "666" (Revelation 13:18) and the left (101), centre (01010) and right (101) border codes of the U.P.C. equating to "6, 6, 6". Some of the more prominent end-time web sites that discuss the U.P.C. include: Ministries (1995), An Apocalyptic Warning (2003), Greater Things (2003), BibleTruthOnline (2006). At first the sites focused on barcode technology, now they have grown to encompass a plethora of auto-ID technologies, especially biometrics and chip implants.

More recently, the work of Katherine Albrecht offers an educated response to the normally "fundamentalist" positions of the websites. Albrecht similarly believes that those who said bar code labels and Social Security numbers were *the mark of the beast* were not completely wrong. She considers these technologies as precursors to radio frequency identification (RFID) and steps towards a totalitarian regime (Albrecht & McIntyre, 2005; 2006). In an interview with Baard (2006) for *Wired* she states: "[a]ll of these technologies are of concern… I'd like to think I'd be speaking out against them, too, if I was around at the time they were introduced."

Barcode Fever Spreads in Supply Chains

As more and more distributors, suppliers and retailers implemented barcode solutions, the word spread about the significant gains offset by the technology. It caused a ripple effect in company supply chains especially. As a result, a greater number of customer inquiries were made to technology providers who were only too willing to answer queries from prospective customers. With each new request for information (RFI), technology providers could understand the needs of customers better and feed this knowledge back into the development process. The future was thus being molded by the learning gained from each successive customer engagement. The evolution of barcode innovations became an interactive experience. As the awareness grew that barcode could be used not only for product coding but for literally thousands of other applications, barcode suppliers became inundated with requests and the rate of barcode-related patents increased substantially. For a representative list of relevant patents in the U.S. beginning in 1995, see Palmer (1995, pp. 361-369). Auto-ID firms, therefore, no longer solely relied on their own knowledge production but also on the interaction between the various players in the industry such as issuers of barcode cards, merchants and consumers for valuable feedback. Cooperatives and alliances began to emerge to support and promote activities for auto-ID product innovation such as AIM. Among numerous other associations and forums, AIM assisted to catapult barcode and other auto-ID technologies into the fore.

Clusters of Knowledge and a Growing Infrastructure

Formal knowledge generated and documented by councils, standards bodies, patent offices, universities and R&D programs became of growing importance, especially to new barcode company entrants who relied on existing infrastructure to start their operations. Associations like AIM Global provided support by publishing important documents and specifications for members. In addition, a great deal of explicit knowledge continues to be produced by students and staff doing research at universities on behalf of private enterprise or government who funded their work. In July 2002, TEKLYNX donated fifteen thousand dollars worth of software (CODESOFT) to the University of Ohio and another fourteen universities for education research purposes across North and South America. Among the prominent research hubs in this field, are the Centre for Auto-ID at Ohio University, the Auto-ID Centre at MIT, the Automatic Data Capture Laboratory at the University of Pittsburgh, the NCTU Automatic Information Processing Lab in Taiwan, InsightU.org- an on-line university, the Information Management Institute (IMI), the Automatic Identification and Data Capture Program at Purdue University and the Robert W. Rylander Corporation that has numerous collaborative projects with universities throughout the U.S. It should be noted that many of these universities specialize in a variety of auto-ID technology.

University researchers have the opportunity to exchange information with private enterprise via auto-ID conferences, trade publications and industry associations. Knowledge distribution in this environment has been among the most useful. Both manufacturers and VARs (Value Added Resellers) are able to exhibit their product innovations and attract interested customers to view a range of possible solutions. Valuable feedback is often gained from such events. The proceedings of these conferences are usually published. What all these stakeholders understand is that communication about barcode technology and its future direction is paramount to its continued success. Universities are also excellent locations to store archival information as they have public libraries and other specialized facilities. At Stony Brook State University in New York an automatic identification and data capture industry archive was launched in October 2002. The AIDC 100 Archive at Stony Brook University includes *"documents, financial reports, conference proceedings, market studies, periodicals, books and prototype hardware... AIDC 100 is an organization founded in 1997 by industry leaders... the vision of the leaders was to create an intellectual gathering place for those business professionals who have made significant contributions... AIDC archive is constantly growing"* (Media Relations, 2002).

Setting Standards

Today each individual barcode application requires numerous standards considerations. Before a barcode can be used, a symbology for the product innovation must be chosen along with the rules for information content, the barcode label, where the label is to be placed, the electronic data interchange (EDI) standard and verification standard. "[I]n some industries not only does the barcode label need to meet the required quality in terms of printing standards, but the data conveyed by the barcode also has to conform to a required structure" (Cohen, J., 1994, p. 100; see also Palmer, 1995, pp. 159-174). Even the way barcode information is collected using data terminal equipment (DTE), transmitted over a network and stored in a relational database is standardized (Collins & Whipple, 1994, ch. 5-7).

Barcode standards have also been established by voluntary committees which over time have assisted in convincing other companies in the same industry to follow similar practices. Some standards-setting organizations like UCC/EAN are heavily oriented towards offering specific solutions to retail and have in some respect ignored the needs of non-retail members who are not commodity oriented (Moore, 1998, p. 6). Depending on the barcode aspect to be standardized the process can be as simple as an employee presenting their findings to their immediate manager or as complex as multiple presentations to AIM International by technology providers, proceeding to global standardization through ISO. According to Bert Moore (1998, p. 3), former director of AIM technical communications, it already takes an average of one to two years to create a standard which is pan-national. At the international level it takes at least 50 per cent longer to accomplish anything.

UCC and EAN

Standards differ in type and importance. LaMoreaux (1998, pp. 213-214) distinguishes between major, mid-level, industry, company and lower level barcode standards. Examples of each can be found in Table 1. Perhaps the most influential standards in the world today are industry-specific. Two examples of this in the retail industry are the U.P.C. and EAN. The U.P.C., a subset of EAN, is used to identify supermarket goods. First a manufacturer's number must be obtained to ensure uniqueness between say one can of pet food and another from a different manufacturer. Second each product is allotted a number. When combined, manufacturer number and product number uniquely represent a particular product. In the case of EAN-13, the aforementioned U.P.C. numbers apply, plus an additional first two digits which identify the country of origin in which the manufacturer's number was allocated. EAN has now been implemented in over 70 countries worldwide. Although they seem to have struck a reasonable alliance, "[t]he growing use of UCC-EAN standards across industries and borders continues to test the relationship between the two organizations" (Brown, 1997, p. 201). Overall, the aims of barcode standards bodies as outlined by J. Cohen (1994, p. 99) include: *"(1) multiple use of a single symbology by a number of different users in the same industry; (2) reduce the amount of research needed by any single user to implement a barcode system; (3) encourage the development of standardized data collection systems within any one industry; and (4) meet the majority of needs of all users within any one user group or industry."*

Electronic Data Interchange (EDI)

The gradual industry movement has been towards the tracking of products throughout the enterprise (e.g. Enterprise Resource Planning, ERP) and the supply chain (SCM). The eventual goal is to implement true EDI using barcode technology to take advantage of value added services (VAS) over the company extranet. TRADANET, the UK data network formed in 1982 is based on specific standards now able to offer EDI to international companies. *"Joining forces are the Article Numbering Association (ANA), the standards authority for bar coding and electronic data interchange (EDI) and the Electronic Commerce Association (ECA), which offers guidance and solutions to businesses seeking to take up paperless trading"* (Jones ed., 1998, p. 13). However, not all industries want to conform to a single major barcode standard. While EDI has matured within the UCC there are quite a few historical issues which have caused friction between EDI leaders and UPC pioneers. Brown (1997, p. 173) believes that "time... will bring new understanding and cooperation" between the two groups as has been witnessed today.

In a move that could have a major impact on the global barcode market, the UCC and NATO (North Atlantic Treaty Organization) are believed to have been working together to reach a consensus on shipment identification codes in the form of the SSCC-18 (Serialized Shipping Container Code) standard. This caused a ripple effect which took place throughout NATOs supply chain. From NATO supplier companies to other government agencies it has been predicted that "every industry segment would, of necessity, adopt UCC/EAN coding and marking" (Moore, 1998, p. 6). This would place immense pressure on barcode suppliers specializing in custom symbologies to conform to a potential super-standard. It should be noted however, that organizations like NATO and government agencies like the United States Department of Defense (DOD), have very different bargaining power than other members of the open market.

The Rise of GS1

In 2005 EAN International changed its name to GS1, being the global office for more than one hundred member organizations in the world. The Uniform Code Council (UCC) responsible for numbering in the US and managing the EAN.UCC system, soon after also changed its name, to GS1 US. It only made sense that the two organizations come together, given they were responsible for the world's supply chain standards across multiple sectors. In addition, GS1 Canada was formed when the Electronic Commerce Council of Canada (ECCC) got on board as well. GS1's main activity is the development of the GS1 System, a family of standards designed for the improvement of supply chain practices globally. The GS1 System has four arms: barcodes, eCom, GDSN (Global Data Synchronization Network) and EPCglobal (Electronic Product Code global, linked to radio-frequency identification). GS1's mission for barcodes is to enable businesses to respond to the challenges of the global supply chain by increasing their efficiency and helping them to maximize profitability. The new DataBar is smaller than its predecessor barcode but it can store a lot more information (GS1, 2008).

Legal Aspects

Barcode developers once placed symbologies in the public domain, granting access to whoever needed them, at no cost. As Palmer (1995, p. 243) recollects early on there was a spirit of openness, even between competitors who often assisted one another in an effort to get their products to work with new symbologies. Early developers could see the long-term benefit for all concerned of such cooperation. Today, that same spirit of openness does not exist. Barcode is a mature technology and there are a lot more players in the global market than there used to be, all vying for a share of the profits. By patenting barcode inventions manufacturers have realized that as well as protecting their intellectual property (IP) rights, they can also collect money via royalties from license agreements and other contracts.

The Public Domain vs. Over-Patenting

One criticism of recent behavior has been the incidence of over-patenting, especially by barcode manufacturers. Some inventors are taking advantage of the patent process in some countries and even patenting ideas that are intuitively obvious. According to Palmer (1995, p. 241) these instances have been counter-productive to the real spirit of innovation and ultimately end-users end up paying for the costs, and technical progress in some areas of development is stifled as a result. For instance, in 2000, Hutchison reported that PSC and Symbol Technologies were embroiled in yet another patent-infringement suit over a portable barcode scanner named the Grocer e-Scan. The reporter noted that the two companies had a history of litigation.

Patents in the field of barcode are usually related to symbologies, hardware or applications. It is important for all stakeholders to be aware of what is happening in the industry because they do not want to find themselves having to pay large amounts of money to inventors who are mostly concerned with royalty revenues than solutions. Formal challenges have been launched against a variety of committees, other manufacturers, and even end-users in the past. In some of the more prominent barcode-related legal battles, can be included Walter Kaslow's coupon validation system (1976), Ilhan Bilgutay's challenge on the UPC symbol (1985) and IAMPO's UPC definition (1992).

BARCODE APPLICATIONS

Overview

Supply Chain Management

Over the years barcodes have been applied to many different applications. For an extensive list of uses of barcodes and a diverse range of case studies see LaMoreaux (1995, pp. 10-11; 22-50), Palmer (1995, pp. 225-239; 2007), Grieco et al. (1989, pp. 135-168) and Collins and Whipple (1994, pp. 187-251) who cover barcode solutions for inventory control systems, retail, and tracking. The biggest adopter of barcode technology is the retail industry. Via the retail industry alone, the barcode had permeated a global population in just a short period of time. It can be credited as being the first sector to establish symbologies for product marking. The first symbology to be widely adopted was the UPC. However, European interest in the UPC led to the adoption of the EAN symbology in 1976. Today there exist several different versions of UPC and EAN, each with its own characteristics. The changes in the check-out process did not go unnoticed. It changed the way consumers bought goods and the way employees worked. It also had a major impact on how businesses functioned and related to one another, i.e. supplier-customer relations. In terms of barcode developments, the 1990s have been characterized by an attempt to evolve standards and encourage uniformity. This has been particularly important in the area of supply chain management (SCM).

Enterprise Resource Planning

Another application of barcode is in manufacturing where it has acted to increase productivity levels significantly. Specific part types can now be identified automatically. The label is used in the sorting and tracking of parts until the finished product is completed and dispatched, using various checkpoints throughout assembly (Wamba, Lefebvre & Lefebvre, 2006). This work-in-process innovation also acts as an order entry system and quality control measure. In shipping, delivery errors have been reduced because of barcode labels on individual packaging items, resulting in goods getting to their correct destinations on time. Such practices are saving large companies millions of dollars annually. Barcode systems can also transmit order information and other data using electronic data interchange (EDI). This allows for international operations worldwide to be linked together. Executives can now receive timely and accurate sales and inventory data and have an ability to exercise a just-in-time (JIT) strategy in their operations (Johnston & Lee, 1997). Highly automated systems have reduced labor costs and increased productivity. Quick response (QR) and direct store delivery (DSD) have lead to better customer relations that have helped companies achieve a competitive edge (Figure 4). Expensive goods are also asset-tagged with barcodes to reduce the incidence of theft, shoplifting or illegal imitation.

Other Applications

The versatile nature of barcode to be imprinted on just about any type of surface meant that its application on plastic cards or paper forms was inevitable (Figure 5). Acting as an automatic identifier for low-risk

Figure 4. Barcodes printed on individual packaged items on pallets. Order information is shown on the fork-lift's on-board laptop and the driver scans items that are being prepared for shipping using a handheld gun to update inventory records wirelessly. Courtesy AirData Pty Ltd, Motorola Premier Business Partner.

Figure 5. A vending machine dispensing bar coded booking taxi paper-based cards outside the Queensland University of Technology (QUT), Brisbane City, Queensland, Australia. Photo taken in 2006.

applications barcode is renowned for being an effective solution. In 1994, Cohen (p. 63) believed that barcode had the highest accuracy amongst auto-ID technologies: "…barcode technology is seen today as the most reliable of all auto-ID technologies, that is, the one with the lowest substitution error rate." This statement has to be taken in context. It is now commonplace to find libraries issuing cards with barcodes to borrowers, as are school administrations to their students and staff. In fact, a student's absenteeism or individual class attendance can also be monitored. In the workplace, attendance hours can be logged using barcode to indicate an employee's hours of work. Barcode access control cards can grant privileges to employees who are authorized to use work facilities. Tracking people is also possible using wearable tags with the barcode imprinted on the tag. Barcodes can also be used for crowd control, particularly for highly publicized events where large numbers of people are expected. And barcodes they have long been used for baggage handling and collection at airports throughout the world (Figure 6).

Other applications include bar coding every publication using the International Standard Book Number (ISBN), direct mailing systems that insert barcodes on forms or brochures to keep track of information gathered in order to perform target marketing. Invoices sent out can also be barcoded for tracking goods sent and used in the returns or damaged items process. In the health industry hospital patients can be identified by barcodes that are securely attached to them via a plastic bracelet. Laboratory samples are also labeled with barcodes for tracking purposes (Figure 7). In agriculture barcodes are used in the process of cattle breeding as well. The barcode today continues to be the standard auto-ID technique of choice. The infrastructure for barcode is well-established, the technology is well-understood, and it is relatively cheap to implement and operate. Post the year 2000, new applications of barcode are

Figure 6. A baggage bar code label provided by the Cathay Pacific airline routing the customer's bags from Sydney to Hong Kong.

Figure 7. Symbol's handheld device used in an ehealth application. A doctor inputs a blood sample which is to be used on her patient, using a PDA-based camera phone which acts as a scanner. Courtesy AirData Pty Ltd, Motorola Premier Business Partner.

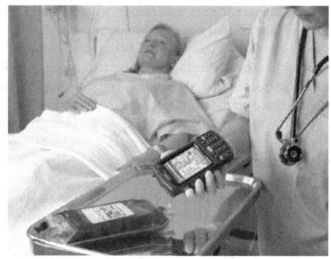

continually being invented, as is demonstrated by its potential to even be used as a tracking instrument for even the smallest of insects.

Case 1: Barcodes in Manufacturing

The greatest impact that barcodes have made in the retail sector has been in the production process and distribution of goods. Two examples of this can be found in Bobson, a Japanese-based manufacturer of casual apparel and R. M. Palmer, a US-based leading confectionary manufacturer. Both manufacturers have been able to achieve quick response (QR) because of the barcode. "Stage one is exemplified by the use of U.P.C., EDI for purchase orders and invoices and, lastly, the UCC/EAN-128 shipping label standard for container marking" (McInerney, 1998, p. 33). Bobson has the capacity to cater for up to 60000 apparel items on a daily basis and has over 1300 customers. Using the Interleaved 2 of 5 symbology, products are organized into barcoded collapsible totes that have a unique identification. Placed on an automated conveyer belt barcodes are scanned updating Bobson's inventory file. Orders are then sorted by destination automatically using a cross-belt sorter. The automated system eliminates sales losses and allows Bobson "...to compete effectively against lower cost apparel from overseas" (Automatic ID, 1998b, p. 31). Suppliers of goods, like R. M. Palmer, have also had to meet customer compliance demands. The candy producer created its own automated labeling system: "[it] has moved from stenciling cartons to ordering preprinted labels to hand-applying pressure-sensitive labels printed on site" (Automatic ID, 1998a, p. 30). Today Palmer has the capability to produce a different label for each of its customers utilizing Code 128 barcodes. It additionally produces Interleaved 2 of 5 barcodes for internal purposes and UPC for preprinted labels. Similar to Bobson, Palmer places cartons on conveyors that must pass through barcode laser scanners. The equipment scans the barcode labels after they are applied, ensuring quality control and that a customer order was satisfied receiving the correct Code 128 barcode (Automatic ID, 1998a, pp. 31f).

Similar to the Japanese-based manufacturer Bobson discussed in the previous section, an auto-ID system is also in place at Calvin Klein's Italian European Jeans warehouse. This particular warehouse is responsible for the distribution of Calvin Klein sportswear for all its outlets outside North America. It is estimated that the 12000 square meter storage area handles more than 10 million items per year. As Beale (1998, p. 1) reported: *"...Calvin Klein receives finished goods (jeans, shirts, sweatshirts, hats, and tennis shirts) from its subcontractors and readies them for shipment to retailers. Each day, between 30000 and 40000 individual garments (roughly 2000 to 2500 pallets) are transported through the facility."* There is one noticeable difference between the Bobson warehouse and that of Calvin Klein. The latter heavily relies on radio-frequency data communication (RFDC) technology, not only barcode. Like Calvin Klein, the Alto Group in Australia, Panasonic Logistics in England and Toyota in the U.S. have incorporated barcodes and RF/DC technology into their operations.

In the case of the Alto Group which holds an inventory of 100000 line items valued at 5.5 million dollars with 4000 different lines of parts, warehouse personnel also use Janus 2020 handheld terminals to receive data and instructions using wireless means via the management system called STOCK*MAN. Incoming inventory is barcode labeled and STOCK*MAN provides putaway instructions by a RF transmission. Order processing is also simplified when an item is picked and scanned the inventory is updated in real-time. Alto Parts claims it has increased its parts putaway by 300 per cent and its parts delivery rate by 150 per cent. Additionally 50 per cent less stock is held in the warehouse which has freed up finances. In the case of the Panasonic Logistics, the distribution arm of Panasonic an automatic data capture (ADC) facility has been built at the Northampton center. With 80000 different product lines and 23000 pallet locations the plant is significantly bigger than the Alto Parts of Australia but works on the same principles. It uses about 50 radio terminals for picking, almost one for each of its employees. The ADC system is so efficient that the work force at the center was envisaged to be reduced by 25 per cent in 1999.

RFID: Complementary or Replacement Technology?

The Toyota case differs significantly from the former cases. Instead of using barcode, the automotive manufacturer chose a fully-fledged radio-frequency identification (RFID) system instead. Whereas the previous three cases integrated barcodes and RFID into one system, Toyota has opted to use RFID in place of barcode. The manufacturer is probably using the most advanced methods in its plant to implement JIT and EDI (J. Cohen, 1994, ch. 14). The facility produces more than 550000 engines and 475000 vehicles annually. The old system could not ensure that the right trailers went to the right dock at the right time. The new system using TIRIS passive RFID tags from Texas Instruments has eliminated delays and mistakes that total into the hundreds of thousands of dollars. Each of the 200 trailers is tagged permanently. Prior to the truck's arrival at the gate, the management system receives information about the trailer's contents and arrival times via EDI. A gate antenna is used to read the tag as it arrives and departs checking it against the appropriate database that contains the trailer number, gate number, date and time of arrival.

While the mass introduction of RFID tags was still a number of years away at the turn of the millennium, primarily due to cost, some companies decided to migrate part or all of their operations to take advantage of RF functionality. The launch of TROLLEYPONDER RFID by Trolley Scan, a South African-based company, caused much debate over the future of barcodes in the late 1990s. It is not surprising that the managing director and inventor, Mike Marsh has touted the RFID technology as a replacement for the barcode marking of products. Marsh is convinced that this is the way of the future and is currently forming agreements with commercial partners globally. While some observers believe that the technology is only useful for niche markets, Trolleyponder is heavily targeting the retail market, particularly supermarket chains and their suppliers. The technology has the potential to be used for everything from manufacturing, warehousing and logistics with the added benefits of Electronic Article Surveillance (EAS) and putaway. Trolley Scan has also initiated a Development Users Group, an informal collection of about 60 companies and organizations that would like to contribute or be informed of Trolleyponder developments. It is envisaged that RFID may be ultimately used in retail for customer self-service check-out such as in the system developed by University of New South Wales called BRANDERS Point of Sale. The Metro conglomerate, the sixth largest retailer in the world, opened one of the first fully-fledged RFID-enabled future stores in Rheinberg, Germany, in 2003 (Kanellos, 2003) which among smart shelves and antitheft systems had self-checkout lanes.

Kroger's supermarket in Louisville started trialling the U-Scan Express system in 1997. The trials were reportedly so successful that the company considered rolling out the PSC and Optimal Robotics technology to more stores. In this instance customers approached an aisle passage that had a restricted exit. Upon scanning all their goods the customer then made an EFTPOS transaction to pay for the items purchased and received a receipt. Upon EFTPOS authorization, the trolley was allowed to go through and a secure EAS system was used to assure the retailer that nothing had been accidentally left unpaid or deliberately stolen. If such a system was to be introduced widely, the impact on workers and customers would be huge; the former from a mass reduction in staffing requirements and the latter from a shift in responsibility at the check-out. Yet it is also currently possible for consumers not even to have to visit a supermarket but transmit their requirements from home (Abass, 1996; and LaPlante, 1999). While Internet grocery shopping can be a little tedious, Hutchison (2000) shows how the Grocer e-Scan portable handheld barcode scanner device could save customers time and trouble. Grayson (1998) reviews an all-in-one barcode scanner, microwave, and television, developed by NCR's Knowledge Labs. One can use the microwave to cook, conveniently watch television while preparing food, and after dinner use the barcode scanner to order new grocery items.

Case 2: Barcodes in Education

The versatility of barcode has seen the device proliferate in the education sector. Primary, secondary and tertiary educational institutions are using the barcode on a plastic card, replacing traditional cardboard cards. The card systems are commonly known as campus cards. *"The all-campus card- now finding its way onto an increasing number of college campuses- can provide access to everything from elevators, doors and garages, to vending machines, library books, and clothing at the campus store" (Facilities Design, 1997, p. 20).* In Australia, Knox Grammar School, Beverly Hills Girls' High School, and the University of Wollongong are just three institutions that have introduced barcode cards. Typically campus cards at schools and universities operate in a closed systems environment. That is, they are only useful within the bounds of the campus of a single institution.

In 1996, Knox Grammar issued 1400 students and staff with Knox Cards. Each Knox card is "... complete with barcode, date of birth, photo and magnetic strip" (Knox Grammar, 1996, p. 43). The Knox Card was originally introduced for the library so that each title catalogued could be tracked. It could also serve the purpose of giving each student a unique identifier and automatically monitoring overdue books, library fines or limits of books being borrowed. The card showed the way for Knox to become a micro-cashless society. Students and staff could use the card for photocopying in the library and for other future purchases such as textbooks and stationery or school uniforms (Knox Grammar, 1996, p. 43). While Knox Grammar students use the barcode card primarily as a borrowing device in the library, Beverly Hills Girls' High School use it to record attendance, "[i]nstead of teachers marking rolls, students swipe a barcoded card through a machine" (Raethel, 1997, p. 1). Teachers can then check to see whether all pupils are present or not via a printout. The 20000 dollar system has increased attendance from 85 per to 95 per cent in only one year and reduced both absenteeism and truancy. While there has been some criticism of the school for introducing an electronic monitoring system, many other schools have planned to trial or install such a system. The card also helps to know where students are when they have free periods during the day. Although obviously these types of systems are not foolproof given students could swipe cards for one another secretly.

The Old Dominion University (ODU) also trialed such a system (Walzer, 1996) to ensure attendance at lectures in a bid to reduce the failure rate of first year students, who are generally under the misconception that they can get through a course without attending the majority of classes. Alamo Community College District (ACCD) also monitored student interactions using barcode ID cards (Madaras, 1993). At the University of Wollongong, student identification cards were introduced in 1994. The barcodes on the student ID are primarily used for borrowing purposes in the library. The unique barcode ID number also grants student access to the University's Student Online Kiosk (SOLs) where individuals can enroll in subjects, download their assessment results and receive important messages, among other things. The University of Wollongong campus card also comes equipped with a photograph which acts as proof of identity, particularly useful during examinations when hundreds of students are present in large halls. The magnetic strip on the card is predominantly for access to computer laboratories (Carroll, 1994, p. 8). The image of each student is stored in a database for the instance that a card needs to be replaced, or so instructors can put an ID number to a face in an online teaching environment.

Smart Card or Hybrid Card: More Flexible and Secure

Barcode cards have been the most popular cost-effective identification solution for educational institutions. Magnetic-stripes have been complimentary to the plastic cards, sometimes serving little or no purpose at all. In those cases where the magnetic-stripe is utilized however, it is likely related to stored value (i.e. money) or some other application requiring a higher level of security than the barcode can offer. Due to their student population, colleges and universities have often looked to adopt other auto-ID solutions such as smart cards and biometric devices. In addition, at tertiary institutions more money is transacted per student for higher education fees, text books, stationary, photocopying, printing and the purchase of food. Coupled with the monetary aspect is that of student identification for examinations, attendance to classes, resource borrowing allowances and access to computer rooms. The cards could also be used to store student results etc. Table 2 shows how smart cards were introduced into institutions prior to 2003.

Some of the campus schemes include hybrid cards while others rely only on the smart card technology (Omar & Djuhari, 2004). The University of Michigan smart card scheme, known as M-Card, is in the former category. Faced with making a significant investment in equipment in 1995 to provide a single card with multi-functionality, smart card was chosen over barcode and magnetic-stripe cards as the ultimate solution that would keep pace with future innovation. In the short term the new smart card scheme was integrated into the legacy systems but eventually everything on the card was migrated to smart card. Smith and Cunningham (1997, pp. 228-229) describe this evolution. *"The situation at the university was typical. They had several "legacy" or existing systems using different card technologies such as barcode and magnetic stripe. Their approach was to use existing systems when feasible, and to implement new services with smart cards. This was achieved by including OCR, barcode, and magnetic-stripe on the student identity card as well as the integrated chip. Over time, all services are likely to be migrated to the chip."* By 1999 there were more than 94000 active M-cards that could be used at 56 merchants, 340 cash points with 23 available reload devices. "While it is primarily used as a photo ID, the M-Card may also be used for banking purposes, making small purchases from participating merchants, library services, and secure entrances to buildings." The M-Card went beyond a closed campus system implementation.

Cards developed in the 1980s were more likely to be used on-campus rather than off-campus. Today universities are establishing partnerships and alliances with banks, health insurance companies and telephone operators allowing students and staff to use their card in an open system with commercial supplier agreements. Leading the way in campus smart card innovation is a group at the Florida State University (FSU) which is developing a card that can act as more than just a prepaid card. The team located at the Card Application Technology Center on campus at FSU, includes such sponsor companies as MCI, V-One, Debitek, PTI and Gemplus (now Gemalto). Gemplus had a large piece of the education market. The company's cards were also used at the University Jannus Pannonius, the University of Medicine of Pécs and the University of Aix-Marseille (France) to name a few. The scheme has developed a multipurpose card that can handle money transfers, payment for stationary, text books, laundry, public transport, food and vending. In Australia, the incumbent telephone operator Telstra is funding a smart card scheme for the University of Adelaide, TAFE NSW (Lidcombe) and the Australian Defense Force Academy (ADFA). The single card is being heralded as a replacement for the older student ID photo card, barcode library card and magnetic-stripe photocopy card (Creed, 1999). The Vice Chancellor of the University of Adelaide believes the scheme will reduce costs associated with the annual issue of cards and will benefit students by offering them loyalty discounts for phone calls and other services. More recently an ID card for school children was launched in Australia supported by the Victorian government. The card contains personal information and emergency contact details.

Barcodes Today

For some time it seemed that the much touted radio-frequency identification tag would displace the barcode (McCathie & Michael, 2005). This has not eventuated as yet, despite the forecasts. Instead the barcode is making a resurgence in a range of application areas. Not only have institutes spent more time on incremental barcode innovations, but the barcode has now been coupled with other mobile commerce devices to offer solutions to even high security applications. The 2D barcode has been among the most successful innovations (Editor, 2005; Chu, Yang & Cheng, 2007). Coupled with devices like the mobile phone (Gao, Prakash, & Jagatesan, 2007), scanners, cameras and biometrics, the 2D barcode is now providing solutions for secure drivers licenses (Hagman, Hendrickson, & Whitty, 2003), voting applications (Adida & Rivest, 2006), and even automated storage and retrieval systems (Sriram et al., 1996). The barcode is "piggybacking" on the success of other well-diffused technologies (Chu, Yang, & Chen, 2007; Kato & Tan, 2005; Ohbuchi, Hanaizumi, & Hock, 2004). Given it already has such a widespread reach in retail, global companies are still taking advantage of industry-wide economies of scale.

Applications for Mobile Commerce

As the number of consumers who are equipped with more sophisticated mobile phones increases rapidly, the potential for launching mobile commerce applications also increases. Not only are newer phones today Internet-enabled but they are also equipped with Bluetooth capabilities, in-built cameras, and global positioning system (GPS) chipsets. Of relevance in this chapter is how the camera phone will be used in the not-to-distant future by consumers to access information about retail products, simply by taking a picture of a 2D barcode on an item. In actual fact, consumers will soon be using their phones to 'scan' barcodes to request information to be pulled to their mobile phones or handsets such as: information related to allergens, ingredients and nutritional facts; service prices, recipes, access to coupon offers; and other packaging-related information (Horwood, 2008a). The consumer, is thus becoming an operator, an attendee, but using their own relatively inexpensive device to read a barcode. The initiative was begun by GS1 Mobile Com in June 2007, and has now gathered momentum with other players also getting involved (CTIA, 2008). Currently the recommendation by the GS1 Mobile Com group is that only approved standards (e.g. ISO or GS1 that are royalty-free) and specified barcodes be used (e.g. GS1 EAN/UPC, 2D and QR code) for testing and implementing applications (Horwood, 2008b, p. 1). CTIA (2008) describe that a mobile commerce transaction using the camera phone and barcode can take place in only three simple steps: (1) the consumer scans the 2D bar code and makes a decision to connect or not to connect to associated data; (2) scan information is sent to a clearing house for processing; and (3) information is sent to the consumer's handset and a target action is launched. Integrating this mobile commerce capability with location services, will mean that manufacturers and retailers will gain additional knowledge about their customers, even information related to the whereabouts of the customer making the purchase.

CONCLUSION

Looking back at the major innovations of the 20th century, the unassuming barcode may not obviously rank as one of the technologies that revolutionized the way we live and work but on second glance its impact has been significant to every facet of our life. One could argue that originally it was the conception of the identification number itself, that was fundamentally responsible for the rapid changes that followed after computerization, but it was the barcode that applied to an industry, was able to really harness the power of computerization, and more specifically the importance of serialization to people and products. It was the aspect of automated data capture that convinced enterprises all over the world to invest in this technology. Automated data capture was appealing for more than the benefits of production savings and the like; it was about processing large amounts of data in a short time and organizing things in a way that would advance operational processes. Today most consumers do not even notice barcodes on supermarket store items, unless the attendee at the checkout is having trouble scanning the item, or a barcode label has fallen off the packaging and we hear the words "price check for granny smith apples" over the loudspeaker. If we can talk of e-business in the context of supply chains, we have the barcode to thank for it.

REFERENCES

Abass, K. (1996). The grocery supply chain: manufacturers, retailers and technology. *IEE Colloquium on Next Generation Manufacturing*, pp. 6/1-6/4.

Adida, B., & Rivest, R. L. (2006). *Scratch & vote: self-contained paper-based cryptographic voting* Paper presented at the Proceedings of the 5th ACM workshop on Privacy in electronic society.

Albrecht, K., & McIntyre, L. (2005). *SPYCHIPS: How Major Corporations and Government Plan to Track your Every Move with RFID*. United States: Nelson

Albrecht, K., & McIntyre, L. (2006). *The Spychips Threat: Why Christians Should Resist RFID and Electronic Surveillance*. United States: Nelson.

Ames, R. (Ed.). (1990). *Perspectives on Radio Frequency Identification: what is it, where is it going, should I be involved?* New York: Van Nostrand Reinhold.

An Apocalyptic Warning. *666soon*, from http://www.666soon.com

Automatic ID. (1998a). Candy maker tastes sweet success. *Automatic I.D. News Asia*(March/April), 29-32.

Automatic ID. (1998b). High-speed retail distribution centre ensures Quick Response for Bobson. *Automatic I.D. News Asia* (May/June), 30-31.

Baard, M. (2006). RFID: Sign of the (End) Times? *Wired* Retrieved 5 March 2007, from http://www.wired.com/science/discoveries/news/2006/06/70308

Beale, S. (1998). Calvin Klein's warehouse is designed for success. *ID Systems: The European Source for Auto ID*, 1-4.

BibleTruthOnline. (2006). Bible Truth Online.

Brown, S. A. (1997). *Revolution at the Checkout Counter: the explosion of the bar code*. London: Harvard University Press.

Carroll, R. (1994). New ID cards. *Tertangala*.

Chu, C.-H., Yang, D.-N., & Chen, M.-S. (2007). Image stabilization for 2D barcode in handheld devices *Proceedings of the 15th international conference on Multimedia*

Cohen, J. (1994). *Automatic Identification and Data Collection Systems*. London: McGraw-Hill Book Company.

Collins, D. J., & Whipple, N. N. (1994). Using Bar Code- Why It's Taking Over. Massachusetts: Data Capture Institute.

Creed, A. (1999). Australian students issued reloadable smart cards. *Newsbytes*.

CTIA. (9 September 2008). Camera-Phone Based Barcode Scanning. *CTIA- The Wireless Association* Retrieved 26 September 2008, from http://files.ctia.org/pdf/WhitePaper_CTIA_WIC_CodeScan_9_08.pdf

Editor. (2005). The 2D data matrix barcode. *Computing & Control Engineering Journal, 16*(6), 39.

Elliot, J. (1999). The one-card trick multi-application smart card e-commerce prototypes. *Computing & Control Engineering Journal*(June), 121-128.

Facilities Design. (1997). All-campus cards open many doors. *Facilities Design & Management, 16*(2), 20.

Gao, J. Z., Prakash, L., & Jagatesan, R. (2007, 24-27 July). *Understanding 2D-BarCode Technology and Applications in M-Commerce - Design and Implementation of A 2D Barcode Processing Solution.* Paper presented at the 31st Annual International Computer Software and Applications Conference.

Grayson, I. (1998, 29 September). NCR cooks up a non-PC. *The Australian,* p. 37.

Greater Things. (2003). Modern Parables for the Lord's People. from http://www.greaterthings.com/

Grieco, P. L., Gozzo, M. W., & Long, C. J. (1989). *Behind Bars: bar coding principles and applications.* Florida: PT Publications.

GS1. (2008). GS1 DataBar. *GS1 Bar Codes* Retrieved 28 September 2008, from http://www.gs1.org/productssolutions/barcodes/databar/

Hagman, J., Hendrickson, A., & Whitty, A. (2003). What's in a barcode? informed consent and machine scannable driver licenses *CHI '03 extended abstracts on Human factors in computing systems.*

Horwood, J. (2008a). Can Mobile Phones Read Barcodes? Retrieved 26 September 2008, from http://www.gs1.org/docs/media_centre/gs1_pr_110908_mobile_com_barcodes.pdf

Horwood, J. (2008b). GS1 Mobile Com Group recommends barcodes for mobile applications to promote early development, piloting and standardization. Retrieved 26 September 2008, from http://www.gs1.org/docs/mobile/GS1_Mobile_Com_Barcodes_Position_Paper.pdf

Hristodoulou, M. H. (1994). In the last days. In *Geron Paisios* (pp. 181-192). Mount Athos, Greece, (in Greek).

Hutchison, K. (2000, 1 June). Handheld bar-code scanners pitched as e-tailing savior. *The Globe and Mail.*

Jesse, R., & Rosenbaum, O. (2000). *Barcode: Theorie, Lexikon, Software.* Germany: Verlag Technik.

Johnston, R. B., & Lee, R. P. W. (1997). *The role of electronic commerce technologies in Just-in-Time replenishment.* Paper presented at the IEE Proceedings of the Thirtieth Hawaii International Conference System Sciences.

Jones, D. (1998). Electronic Commerce in Government. *Card Technology Today, 10*(2), 13-16.

Kanellos, M. (23 April 2003). Intel, SAP shop 'store of the future'. *CNET News* Retrieved 25 April 2003, from http://news.cnet.com/Intel%2C-SAP-shop-store-of-the-future/2100-1006_3-998038.html?tag=mncol;txt

Kaplan, J. M. (1996). *Smart Cards: the global information passport- managing a successful smart card program.* London: International Thomson Computer Press.

Kato, H., & Tan, K. T. (2005, 15-17 November). *2D barcodes for mobile phones.* Paper presented at the 2nd International Conference on Mobile Technology, Applications and Systems.

Knox Grammar. (1996, 23 July). Students swipe away cash. *The Daily Telegraph,* p. 43.

LaMoreaux, R. D. (1998). *Barcodes and Other Automatic Identification Systems.* New York: Pira International.

LaPlante, A. (1999). The battle for the fridge; the food industry is looking to hook up your home to the supply chain, *Computerworld* (pp. 52).

Madaras, W. (1993). Live data student information kiosk built using EDA/SQL. *Information Builder News (IBN)*(Fall/Winter), 14-16.

Marsh, M. (1998). BRANDERS point of sale system developed by University of New South Wales, Australia. Retrieved 4 December 1998, from http://rapidttp.co.za/transponder/presre29.html

McCathie, L., & Michael, K. (2005, 3-5 October). *Is it the end of barcodes in supply chain management?* Paper presented at the Collaborative Electronic Commerce, Talca, Chile.

McInerney, J. (1998). Real companies are saving real money with quick response. *Automatic I.D. News Asia,* pp. 32-35.

Media Relations. (2002). Stony Brook University inaugurates automatic identification and data capture industry archive. *Stony Brook NEWS,* pp. 1-3.

Meyers, R. B. (2000). The ten commandments of bar coding. *Frontline Solutions*(August), A-5- A-22.

Ministries. (1995). Dial-the-Truth Ministries. from http://www.av1611.org/

Moore, B. (1998). Developments in bar code readers. *Automatic I.D. News Asia*(March/April), 35-38.

Moore, B., & Albright, B. (1998). EAN/UCC create new item marking symbologies. *Automatic I.D. News Asia*(August/September), 24-25.

Ohbuchi, E., Hanaizumi, H., & Hock, L. A. (2004, 18-20 November). *Barcode readers using the camera device in mobile phones.* Paper presented at the 2004 International Conference on Cyberworlds.

Omar, S., & Djuhari, H. (2004, 31 May-2 June). *Multi-purpose student card system using smart card technology.* Paper presented at the Proceedings of the Fifth International Conference on Information Technology Based Higher Education and Training.

Palmer, R. C. (1995). *The Bar Code Book- Reading, Printing and Specification of Bar Code Symbols.* New Hampshire: Helmers Publishing Inc.

Raethel, S. (1997). Late? The micro-chip won't be pleased. *The Sydney Morning Herald.*

Reeves, T. (1996, 29 October). The checkout checks out okay. *The Australian,* p. 41.

Sharp, K. R. (1998). Selecting inventory control (pp. 1-3): ID Systems: The European Source for Auto ID.

Smith, M., & Cunningham, D. (1997). Education. In C. A. Allen & W. J. Barr (Eds.), *Smart Cards: Seizing Strategic Business Opportunities* (pp. 224-233). New York: McGraw-Hill.

Sriram, T., Vishwanatha Rao, K., Biswas, S., & Ahmed, B. (1996, 5-10 August). *Applications of barcode technology in automated storage and retrieval systems.* Paper presented at the 22nd International Conference on Industrial Electronics, Control, and Instrumentation.

Thompson, A. R. (1996). Campus card. *Security Management, 40*(5), 19-20.

Walzer, P. (1996). ODU planning to test scanner to keep tabs on class attendance. *V.P.*

Wamba, S. F., Lefebvre, L. A., & Lefebvre, E. (2006). *Enabling intelligent B-to-B eCommerce supply chain management using RFID and the EPC network: a case study in the retail industry.* Paper presented at the Proceedings of the 8th international conference on Electronic commerce: The new e-commerce: innovations for conquering current barriers, obstacles and limitations to conducting successful business on the internet.

Yang, C.-H. (1999). *On the design of campus-wide multi-purpose smartcard systems.* Paper presented at the IEEE 33rd Annual 1999 International Carnahan Conference on Security Technology.

Chapter VI
Magnetic–Stripe Cards:
The Consolidating Force

MAGNETIC-STRIPE CARD TECHNOLOGY

Almost simultaneously that the retail industry underwent revolutionary changes with the introduction of bar code, the financial industry adopted magnetic-stripe card technology. What is of interest is that both bar code and magnetic-stripe card enjoyed limited exposure when they were first introduced in the late 1960s. It took at least a decade for the technologies to become widespread. Each overcame a variety of obstacles. Coupled together the two techniques were major innovations that affected the way that consumers carried out their day-to-day tasks. The technologies were complementary; on the one hand were the actual commodities consumers purchased and on the other was the means with which they purchased them. Yet, the bar code differed from magnetic-stripe card in that it was more a service offered by retailers to consumers, with the primary focus being to make business back-end operations more efficient. The magnetic-stripe card however, had a more direct and personal impact on the card-holder, as it was the individual's responsibility to maintain it. The consumer had to carry it, use it appropriately, and was liable for it in every way. Certainly bar codes on cards were being used early on but they were far less secure than magnetic stripe cards and therefore not adopted by financial institutions. Before too long, magnetic-stripe cards became synonymous with the withdrawal of cash and the use of credit which acted to heighten the importance of the auto-ID technology. Even today, magnetic-stripe cards for financial transaction cards dominate the market.

Historical Overview

Plain card (i.e. blank paper card) issuing became popular in the 1920s when some United States retailers and petrol companies began to offer credit services to their customers. McCrindle (1990, p. 15) outlines the major developments that led to the first magnetic-stripe being added to embossed cards in 1969. *"By the 1920s the idea of a credit card was gaining popularity... These were made of cardboard and engraved to provide some security... The 1930s saw the introduction of some embossed metal and plastic cards... Embossed cards could be used to imprint information on to a sales voucher... Diners Club introduced its charge card in 1950 while the first American Express cards date from the end of the 1950s."* Magnetic-stripe cards made their debut more than a decade after computer technology was introduced into the banking system in the 1950s (Mee & Daniel, 1996). Until that time computers were chiefly used for automating formerly manual calculations and financial processes rather than offering value-added benefits to bank customers (Essinger, 1999, p. 66). One of the first mass mail-outs of cards to the public was by credit card pioneer, Chuck Russell, who launched the Pittsburgh National Charge Plan. Out of the one hundred thousand cards that were sent to households about fifty per cent of them were returned, primarily because consumers did not know what to do with them or how to use them. Cash remained the preferred method of payment for some time. Armed with this experience, Russell went on to become the chairman of Visa International in the 1980s.

Historically, embossed cards had made an impact on the market, particularly on the financial services industry. Financial transaction cards (FTC) were widespread by the late 1970s and large firms that had invested heavily in embossed-character imprinting devices needed time to make technological adjustments (Bright, 1988, p. 13). Jerome Svigals (1987, p. 28f) explained the integration of the embossed card and the new magnetic-stripe as something that just had to happen: *"It would take a number of years before an adequate population of magnetic-stripe readers became available and were put into use. Hence, providing both the embossing and stripe features were a transition technique. It allowed issued cards to be used in embossing devices while the magnetic-stripe devices built up their numbers."*

Today magnetic-stripe cards are still the most widely used card technology in the world, and they still have embossed characters on them for the cardholder's name, card expiry date, and account or credit number. This is just one of many examples showing how historical events have influenced future innovations. As Svigals (1987, p. 29) noted more than twenty years ago, it is not clear when or even if, embossing will eventually be phased out. Hence, his prediction that the smart card would start its life as "...a carrier of both embossed and striped media." These recombinations are in themselves new innovations even though they are considered interim solutions at the time of their introduction; they are a by-product of a given transition period that continues for a time longer than expected. Perhaps here also can be found the reason why so many magnetic-stripe cards still carry bar codes also. The bar code on the same card can be advantageous to the card issuer. For instance, in an application for a school it can serve a multifunctional purpose: the bar code can be used for a low risk application such as in the borrowing of books, the magnetic-stripe card in holding student numbers, and the embossing can also be used for back up if on-line systems fail.

Essinger (1999, p. 80) describes this phenomenon by describing technology as being in a constant state of change. No sooner has a major new innovation been introduced than yet another incremental change causes a more powerful, functional, and flexible innovation to be born. Essinger uses the example of the magnetic-stripe card and subsequent smart card developments, cautioning however, that one should not commit the "cardinal sin of being carried away by the excitement of new technology and not stopping to pause to ask whether there is a market for it." He writes (1999, p. 80) "what matters is not the inherent sophistication of technology but the usefulness it offers to customers and, in extension, the commercial advantage it provides".

The Magnetic-Stripe Card System

Encoding the Magnetic-Strip

The magnetic stripe technology had its beginnings during World War II (Svigals, 1987, p. 170). Magnetic-stripe cards are composed of a core material such as paper, polyester or PVC. Typically, plastic card printers use either thermal transfer or dye sublimation technology. The advantage of dye sublimation over thermal transfer is the millions of colors that can be created by heat intensity. If color is required by the operator on both sides then one side of the card is colored first before the other but this is expensive. The process as outlined on a manufacturer's web page is quite basic (Eltron, 1998): *"...you simply insert the ribbon and fill the card feeder. From there, the cards are pulled from the card feeder to the print head with rollers. When using a 5 panel color ribbon the card will pass under the print head and back up for another pass 5 times. When all the printing is complete, the card is then ejected and falls into the card hopper."*

Finally, the magnetic-strip (similar to that of conventional audio tapes) is applied to the card and a small film of laminated patches is overlaid. The magnetic-strip itself is typically gamma ferric oxide "... made of tiny needle-shaped particles dispersed in a binder on a flexible substrate" (Zoreda & Oton, 1994, p. 16). The strip is divided laterally into three tracks, each track designed for differing functions (Table 1). Track 1 developed by IATA, is used for transactions where a database requires to be accessed such as an airline reservation. Track 2, developed by the ABA contains account or identification number(s). This track is commonly used for access control applications and is written to before the card is dispatched to the cardholder so that every time it is presented it is first interrogated by the card reading device. As Bright (1988, p. 14) explains: *"...[t]he contents, including the cardholder's account number, are transferred directly to the card issuer's computer centre for identification and verification purposes. This on-line process enables the centre to confirm or deny the terminal's response to the presenter..."* Finally, Track 3 is used for applications that require data to be updated with each transaction. It was introduced some time after Tracks 1 and 2. It contains an encoded version of the personal identity number (PIN) that is private to each individual card. The cardholder must key in the PIN at a terminal that is then compared with the PIN verification value (PVV) to verify a correct match.

Each magnetic-stripe card is magnetically encoded with a unique identification number. This unique number is represented in binary on the strip. This is known as biphase encodation. When the strip is queried, the 1s and 0s are sent to the controller in their native format and converted for visual display only into decimal digits. When magnetic-stripe cards are manufactured they do not have any specific polarity. Data is encoded by creating a sequence of polarized vertical positions along the stripe. An important concept in understanding how tracks are triggered to change polarity is coercivity (measured in Oersted, Oe). This can be defined as the amount of magnetic energy or solenoid required which can be broadly defined as low (about 300 Oe) and high (3000-4000 Oe). Most ATM cards are said to have

Table 1. Magnetic-strip track description

Track Number	Description
Track 1 (read only)	▪ 210 bits/inch; 79 characters (alpha/numeric) ▪ Used mainly by airline developers (IATA) ▪ First field for account number (up to 19 digits) ▪ Second field for name (up to 26 alphanumerics)
Track 2 (read only)	▪ 75 bits/inch; 40 digits (numeric only) ▪ Developed by American Bankers Association on-line ▪ First field for account number (up to 19 digits)
Track 3 (read/write)	▪ 210 bits/inch; 107 digits (numeric only) ▪ Higher density achieved by later technology ▪ Rewritten each use. Suitable for off-line ▪ Uses PIN verification value (encoded)

low coercivity (*loco*) while access control cards have high coercivity (*hico*) to protect against accidental erasure. Here is one reason why embossed account numbers still appear on ATM or credit cards; if the card has been damaged, information can be manually retrieved and identified (from the front of the card) while the replacement card is dispatched.

Mercury Security Corporation (1998) explain this process in more detail: *"[t]he magnetic media is divided into small areas with alternating polarization; the first area has North/South polarization, and the next has South/North, etc. In order to record each "0" and "1" bit in this format, a pattern of "flux" (or polarity) changes is created on the stripe. In a 75bpi (bits per inch) format, each bit takes up 1/75th (0.0133) of an inch. For each 0.0133" unit of measure, if there is one flux change, then a zero bit is recorded. If two flux changes occur in the 0.0133" area, then a one bit is recorded."* When choosing a magnetic-stripe card for an application the following issues should be taken into consideration. First, should the magnetic-stripe be loco or hico. Hico stripes can typically withstand 10 times the magnetic field strength of loco stripes. Most stripes today are hico so that they are not damaged by heat or exposure to sunlight and by other magnets. Second, which track should the application use to encode data, track one, two or three. One should be guided by ANSI/ISO standards here that recommend particular applications to particular tracks. Other considerations include whether the card requires lamination, to be embossed or watermarked and whether the card will follow ISO card dimensions. The cost of the card chosen should also be considered as it can vary significantly.

Automated Teller Machines (ATMs)

An automated teller machine is an unattended computer which is located in a public space, accessible twenty-four hours a day, and seven days a week by bank customers (Figure 1). The electronic machine is connected to a data network and other peripheral devices and activated by a consumer to obtain transac-

Figure 1. A magnetic-stripe cardholder making a cash withdrawal at a HongkongBank ATM in Hong Kong. Note the words "electronic money" above the ATM machine and the general topper (i.e. signage). Photo taken in 1998.

tion information in the form of mini-statements, to deposit or to make a withdrawal of cash, or to make a basic enquiry about their account(s). Don Wetzel is credited as the inventor of the 'networked' ATM. He created the machine while working for the Docutel Company in Dallas, Texas, during the 1960s. Today there are more than 1.5 million ATMs worldwide. ATMs are always positioned in a convenient location close to banks, shopping centers, petrol stations or where large numbers of people congregate. ATM installations are considered to be located either on premises or off premises. On premise ATMs are usually more advanced and offer a range of services just like a customer would enjoy in a bank branch. Off premise ATMs are cheaper models which serve the primary purpose of allowing customers to withdraw cash.

Hardware and Software

An ATM is much like a standard computer, although historically ATMs had custom hardware architectures using microcontrollers. A modern ATM has a central processing unit (CPU) that controls the user interface and handles transaction requests. It has a display that the customer reads when making a transaction in order to follow simple commands. Customers enter details such as a PIN, the amount of cash to be withdrawn using a dedicated PIN pad and access special features through function key buttons (e.g. OK and Cancel). Customers insert their magnetic-stripe card into a card reader, and also can request a printout of a receipt or specialized transactional query. The ATM uses a cash dispenser to provide the money to the customer. When a transaction is complete, typically, the user will receive their card back first, then they can receive their cash, then finally a printout of their receipt. Some ATMs have features like voice commands, useful for the blind or are housed in sunken units to help shorter persons. What makes ATMs different to computers is a purpose-built secure cryptoprocessor and vault which is not accessible to the general public. Mechanisms in the vault ay include: dispensing, deposit, security sensors, and locks. Most vaults are attached to the ground so they cannot be stolen. The operating systems utilized on ATMs are again similar to those available in standard computers. ATM applications built on these standard operating systems (eg Microsoft Windows) are vulnerable to the same attacks, as those in computers. Common application layer transaction protocols include Diebold 912, IBM PBM, and NCR NDC.

Networks

ATMs are directly linked to an ATM Transaction Processor via a network link such as a leased line. Dial-up modems have traditionally been used in the past but with increasing bandwidth, leased lines are used because they establish a connection faster. In Australia for instance, the cost of leasing an E1 (i.e. 2 Mbps made up of 32 channels at 64 Kbps) is still expensive, so the promise of high-speed Internet Virtual Private Networks (VPNs) are solutions that customers are demanding from banks. It is not uncommon still to find ATMs in developing countries that use lower-level layer communication protocols to communicate back to the bank such as X.25 and Frame Relay. The Secure Socket Layer (SSL) protocol is used to encrypt information going between the ATM and the ATM Transaction Processor to ensure that all transaction information remains secure.

Security

Given ATMs are located in a public space, physical security of the actual machine is paramount. Ramraids are not unheard of, and are an attempt for thieves to crash into the ATM and literally carry it away with them using a heavy vehicle. ATMs can also be subject to tampering, surveillance by professional fraudsters, and other problems. Essinger (1999, pp. 162f) is correct in highlighting that cardholders need to adhere to the bank's instructions of never writing a PIN down. However recent attacks against magnetic-stripe cards have focused on using tiny secret cameras or other equipment to steal cardholder PINs as they are entering them onto the ATM keypad (Smith, 2002, p. 3). In 1994, fraud on Visa was about 0.4 per cent of total credit card transactions (Harris, 1994). By 2005, this figure had grown to 0.7 per cent, much higher when one considers that the number of credit card transactions had also increased substantially overall.

Personal information is secured using Triple DES encryption in most cases to ensure that transactional integrity is enforced. Alarm sensors are also located within the ATM itself to alert operators when illegal access has occurred. Security surveillance cameras are usually located near ATMs, recording consumer behavior. In some countries, like Chile and the Philippines, security guards stand watch over ATMs.

Card Processing

So magnetic stripe cards are issued by financial institutions and can be used to withdraw money or when a customer pays for products or services with a credit card. In the latter case, the card information needs to be recorded either manually, using a card imprinter or at a point of sale (POS) terminal which is then verified so that the merchant can ensure that they receive payment. Typically in any credit transaction there are five stakeholder types: the cardholder, merchant, acquirer, card association and issuer. The cardholder owns the card which is used to make a purchase. The issuer is the financial institution that issued the credit card to the cardholder. The merchant is the business accepting the credit card payment for particular goods or services sold to the cardholder. Now for a consumer to purchase a product with a credit card, a card processing service needs to be made available to a merchant via a financial institution, known as the acquirer in this context. A card association, such as VISA or MasterCard, acts as a gateway between the acquirer and issuer to authorize and fund a given transaction. The flow of information and money between the stakeholders is known as the process of *interchange* and involves the following steps: authorization, batching, clearing and settlement, and funding (Hendry, 2007).

Magnetic-Stripe Drawbacks

The durability of magnetic-stripe cards often comes into question: "[m]agnetic stripes can be damaged by exposure to foreign magnetic fields, from electric currents or magnetized objects, even a bunch of keys" (Cohen, 1994, p. 27). This is one reason why so many operators have expiry dates on cards they issue. According to Svigals (1987, p. 185), "[m]agnetic stripes have been tested and are generally specified to a two-year product life by the card technology standards working groups." Another drawback is that once a magnetic-stripe has been damaged, data recovery is impossible (Cohen, 1994, p. 29). Another way that a magnetic-stripe card can be worn out is if it has been read too many times by a reader. The read head has a small surface window, known as the *field of view*, that comes into direct contact with the magnetic-stripe. When a card is passed through or inserted in a reader a read head generates a series of electrical pulses. These alternating voltages correspond to alternating polarities on the magnetic-stripe. Per bit length, the reader counts the changes in polarity that are then decoded by the reader's electronics to recover the information that is hidden on the card.

Svigals (1987, p. 36) is more explicit in describing the limitations of magnetic-stripe by writing that "[m]ost knowledgeable tape experts readily admit that the magnetic stripe content is: readable, alterable, modifiable, replaceable, refreshable, skimmable, counterfeitable, erasable, simulatable." Jose and Oton (1994, p. 20) identify the primary methods of magnetic-stripe fraud as being theft, counterfeit, buffering, and skimming. The magnetic-stripe has rewrite capability and data capacity ranges from 49-300 characters. The latter is clearly a handicap when a chosen application(s) requires the addition of new data or features. While linear bar codes are even more limited, magnetic-stripe may still not be the right solution for a given service. Another issue that requires some attention is security. As Bright explains (1998, p. 15): *"[t]he primary problem may be described with one word 'passivity'; lacking any above board intelligence, the magnetic stripe card must rely on an external source to conduct the positive checking/ authentication of the card and its holder. This exposes the system to attack. The scale of the problem exacerbated by the relative ease of obtaining a suitable device with which to read and amend the data stored in the stripe."* Consider the case in the United Kingdom were hundreds of cards were skimmed at Shell Service stations in 2006. While the UK press claimed that it was the EMV card that criminals were targeting, it was in fact the older EMV magnetic-stripe cards that were vulnerable to the attack (Aconite, 2006). There are however, numerous innovators that continue to believe that magnetic-stripe technology still has a future and they are researching means to make the technology more secure.

THE MAGNETIC-STRIPE CARD INNOVATION SYSTEM

Retail and Banking Associations Join Forces

The rise of the magnetic-stripe card, as we know it today, can be attributed to the collaborative efforts between the banking and transport associations, namely the American Banking Association (ABA) and the International Air Transport Association (IATA). It is commonly stated that an American National Standards Institute (ANSI) publication in 1973, developed jointly by ABA and IATA for a plastic credit card with a magnetic-stripe, laid the foundations for widespread diffusion. By banding together, the two associations were able to present a positive case for standardization. Banking and transport are two broad application areas that affect the masses, so the influence of the organizations on the direction of the magnetic-stripe card cannot be underestimated. Early on however, magnetic-stripe technology like bar code was hampered by a lack of standards: "[a]s has so often been the case with the commercialization of new ideas, one of the delaying factors was the absence of recognized international standards during its early existence" (Bright, 1988, p. 14). ISO finally resolved this issue through its Technical Committee for information processing standards (TC 97). International Standards (IS) 7810 and 7811 were published outlining definitions about the physical dimensions of the magnetic-stripe card, embossing, layout and reading requirements. Magnetic-stripe can boast a 35 year stockpile of documentation. ISO and ANSI have published a plethora of information on the topic, together with IATA and ABA. With input from the IATA, ABA and the Thrift industry, specific tracks were defined on the magnetic-stripe for specific uses. Track 2 for instance, reserved for banking applications, contained a field for the primary account number (PAN) of 19 digits. Another field for additional data such as the expiration date (4 digits) of the card, restriction or type (3 digits), offset or PVV (5 digits) or discretionary data is available, as well as control characters for the start and end sentinel, field separator and redundancy check character.

From Exclusivity to Interoperability

Solutions for magnetic-stripe cards based on proprietary schemes were initially used strategically by banks and other companies to secure a loyal customer base. Cash dispensers were not plentiful initially, so banks were able to attract customers by being the first to market. Louderbacker (1980, p. 40) recounts that one of the first cash dispensers was installed by the Chemical Bank in New York City in 1969. By early 1970, other banks began planning for full-service ATM (Automatic Teller Machine) installations. By the late 1970s bank card technology became a mechanism for differentiating financial institutions. If a bank was able to offer the card linked to its existing portfolio of services it was considered technologically advanced. Egner (1991, p. 56) wrote that ATM services were exclusive, and institutions like Citibank were actually able to shift market share by their promotion. The same could be said for Barclays Bank in the UK. According to Essinger (1999, pp. 172-173), the United Kingdom's first cash dispensers were installed by Barclay's bank in 1967 and branded *Barclaycash*. *"They were not strictly speaking ATMs, as their function was restricted to providing cash. They were only open for limited periods in the day and were off-line (i.e. not connected to the central computer in real time)... The first implementation in the UK of a machine which was recognizably an... ATM rather than simply a cash dispenser is regarded as having taken place on 30 June 1975".*

There was often friction between the major bank players who had reaped the rewards for taking the risk with the new technology versus the banking association that wished to exercise authority on behalf of all the other (and in most cases smaller) banks to make it a level playing field. In fact Citibank, so protective of its market share, vehemently challenged magnetic-stripe standardization. Yet the bank soon realized that if it did not commit to the changes that it would be left behind, eventually becoming the minority. In essence, what Citibank and others in a similar position were afraid of was losing their competitive advantage to interoperability. Interoperability "...[r]elates to a situation whereby a card issued by one organization, e.g. a bank, can be used in an ATM belonging to another" (Bright, 1988, p. 15). Today most major service provider's cards can be used in each others' ATMs. In Australia customers were only able to access funds from the ATMs of different banks in 1992. The National Bank's corporate affairs manager was quoted as saying: "[t]he attitude of the 1980s has certainly changed for the better and it's only a matter of time before a uniform system comes into being" (Daily Telegraph, 1992).

Today, banks across the world have forged stronger relationships, as can be seen by international ATM sharing schemes (Essinger, 1999, p. 160). And all this is possible because of the PAN that is defined in Track 2 of the magnetic stripe. All PANs contain an industry code for the issuer (1 digit), an issuer identification (5 digits), customer identification (12 digits) and check digit. It was this very field that enabled different banks to accept magnetic-stripe cards at ATMs, regardless the operator. The PAN can identify the card issuer and cardholder, thus making interoperability possible via advanced card readers. It is important to note, that not all applications require a standardized magnetic-stripe card format, especially for 'closed' systems like amusement parks. In fact there are some instances when a non-ISO design would be more appropriate, acting to increase security by non-conformity. This usually makes counterfeiting or fraudulent alterations to the card difficult (Mullen & Sheppard, 1998, p. 1).

The ATM Economic Infrastructure

As ATM machines began to sprout up all over North America and the UK in the 1980s, a physical infrastructure began to grow to support the banking sector. It should be noted however that this infrastructure was very expensive and it took about 16 years for the first one hundred thousand ATMs to be installed. First and foremost, magnetic-stripe cards without ATMs were almost entirely useless: "[i]mprovements in card technology would not be particularly valuable without reader technology" (Browne & Cronin, 1996, p. 102). Second, internal bank equipment needed to be able to communicate with ATMs. A physical network was required for this to become possible, and telecommunication data providers quickly sought these opportunities as they became available using protocols such as X.25. Here is perhaps one reason why smart cards have not yet replaced magnetic-stripe cards in North America- the physical infrastructure in terms of the installed base of ATMs and POS equipment kept growing and growing throughout the 1990s. For instance, in 1997, NCR installed three thousand units (ATMs) in just 150 days for Banc One (Korala & Basham, 1999, p. 6-7).

In the 1970s and 1980s ATM volumes boomed but in the 1990s manufacturers turned their attention to adding POS functionality (Mitchell, 1996, p. 57). In some parts of the world like the United States, Japan and Hong Kong large investments in magnetic-stripe equipment have tied card issuing organizations to the technology. Apart from the initial investment it should also be considered that ATMs also incur ongoing rental space costs (Godin, 1995, p. 178). Weighing up the total potential losses as a direct result of fraud and other drawbacks of magnetic-stripe cards, against the potential multi-million dollar investment of upgrading readers and writers for smart cards worldwide; one is able to understand how physical infrastructure directly affects innovations. Smart cards are also more complicated to produce and need more expertise than magnetic-stripe. And the more complicated the production process, the harder it is produce large quantities. Murphy (1996, p. 82) outlines the intricate process by which one can only assume that the person in charge must have acquired some first hand experience previously. "Converting to smart card production is no easy task. Not only does a company need state-of-the-art printing presses, it must upgrade its plastics to a thickness that can accommodate the computer chip that makes a smart card 'smart,' as well as ensure the cards are temperature resilient; it needs special machines to drill holes for the chips, and another set of machines to place computer chips in those holes..." Economies of scale are necessary here.

The Global Inter-Bank Network

The success of magnetic-stripe card technology can be measured by the increasing need for the interconnection of thousands of banks across every continent in the world. Colton and Kraemer (1980, pp. 22-23) list some of the major centralized network operations. *"Federal Reserve System (FedWire) manages Federal reserve banks across the US interconnecting 275 banks; Clearinghouse Interbank Payment System (CHIPS) has the capability to execute international transactions among 62 financial institutions in New York; interbank switching in Japan is provided by Zenginkyo and the National Cash Service (NCS) network systems; the UK clearing banks have formed a company called Bankers Automated Clearing Services (BACS); Society for Worldwide International Financial Telecommunications (SWIFT) links more than 239 banks."*

SWIFT stands for the Society for World-wide Interbank Financial Telecommunications. It was established in 1973, and by 1984 it enveloped 1,104 banks in 49 countries (Dean, 1984). Dean's article on the cashless society raises ethical issues about the power of an organization like SWIFT (see also Kirkman, 1987, pp. 224-227). As of November 2008, the SWIFTNet FIN network had corporate customers from 209 countries on its network, 2,272 full members, 3,303 sub-members, 3,146 participants and 8,721 live users. The users are typically banking organizations, securities institutions or private enterprise and exchange millions of standardized financial messages every day (SWIFT, 2008). SWIFT believes that its role is two-fold. First they provide a proprietary communications platform, products and services that allow their customers to exchange financial information securely and reliably. Second, they act as a hub to bring the financial community together to work towards defining standards and mutually beneficial financial solutions.

One can only begin to guesstimate the number of agreements that are in place between so many different entities to allow it all to work properly. This kind of meshed structure cannot be established instantaneously but only after years of formal exchanges. The European Union is another example of inter-bank data transfer standardization that requires thousands of banks to agree on a particular type of electronic payment system (EPS) that goes beyond even SWIFT (Central Banks, 1989, p. 102; Radu, 2002). Of course to understand the extent of sharing, of not only data but of physical resources such as ATMs, one must consider the networks of the large credit card and banking associations of Visa, MasterCard, Cirrus, PLUS, GlobalAccess, ATM™, AutoCash. What is worthy of noting here is the support structure that has been built around the magnetic-stripe functionality, i.e. being able to withdraw, deposit and transfer funds almost anywhere in the world. Without this infrastructure in place, the magnetic-stripe card would not have become as prolific as it has. Brands like Visa and Mastercard would not have had in excess of twenty million members each.

Calculated Social Change

"Twenty-five years ago, the very idea of going to a machine in order to withdraw money from a bank seemed outlandishly fanciful. Yet, with the rapidity so often associated with technological change, it soon became just another part of everyday life" (Korala & Basham, 1999, p. 6-1). The same could be

Figure 2. A customer purchasing apparel at a Giordano store in Singapore using Electronic Funds Transfer Point of Sale (EFTPOS) equipment. The customer is entering her Personal Identification Number (PIN) and when the transaction is authorized she will be given a receipt. Photo taken in 2002.

said for Electronic Funds Transfer at Point of Sale (EFTPOS) (Figure 2). Numerous business people were convinced during the mid 1980s that EFTPOS would be an unsuccessful application and yet it is increasingly being used today (Essinger, 1999, p. 9). It is important to note however, that while change was "rapid", it still took a considerable amount of time for end-users to come to terms with the fact that they did not have to physically enter a branch to withdraw money. Essinger regards ATMs to be the "[m]ost visible, and perhaps most revolutionary, element of the virtual banking revolution" (Essinger, 1999, p. 159). He believes that ATMs changed the way we lived forever and that every day throughout the world millions of people in *thousands of walks of life* rely on the convenience of the cash machines to gain access to money.

Governments across the globe committed resources to investigating the potential impact of the technical change of ATMs, EFT, and EFTPOS. In Australia, a Technological Change Committee investigated the possible changes EFT would initiate (ASTEC, 1986). One of the earliest EFT trials in Australia was conducted in 1982 between the Whyalla Credit Union and the G.J. Coles Company (S.A. Council of Technology, 1983, pp. 21-25). The government had a role to play in regulating EFT transactions but before doing so it had to ensure that it had adequately researched the implications of the new technology. Worldwide studies were also conducted on EFT by the OECD in particular (OECD, 1989; Revell, 1983, pp. 108-110).

As in the case of bar code, labor unions and other groups were again quick to point out that the automation would mean job losses for bank staff. The technology appealed more to the needs of business, as they sought ways to operate more efficiently. Learning about consumer spending habits through transaction history records was also important. Both banks and retailers saw the advantages that had to be gained by using financial transaction cards. Speed and security were among the most important attributes. Retailers also saw a reduction in the amount of cash-on-hand they required to handle. Many bank branches have been closed as a result of the automation and face-to-face over the counter staff numbers have been significantly reduced, driving consumers to change their habits for the sake of minimizing bank fees and charges. Stephen Bennett (1995, p. 10) a senior manager with KPMG wrote: *"[e] lectronic transactions are considerably more cost effective than the counter based equivalent. This led to banks in the U.S. charging fees for branch based transactions and providing "free" transactions via telephone, ATM's and EFTPOS, a concept that is now being embraced in Australia."*

As part of their marketing campaign in the 1970s credit companies mailed out plastic cards to consumers and in the early 1980s banks mailed out magnetic-stripe cards to prospective cardholders. For many of the recipients, it was unclear what added benefit the card could provide, although this was later realized. Essinger (1999, p. 8) wrote: *"...it is likely that the availability of the new technology, and the fact that someone had decided to create it, is what is determining the application, rather than the customer need for it. In effect, after the invention has been put on the market, the customer demand is created for it."* He continues by pointing out that *"...the cash machine was not an instant success; people needed to get used to the idea. However, once they had, the cash machine rapidly became an essential part of the customer service armory of any bank..."* (p. 68).

Big Brother and the Privacy Invasion

At the time, some consumers believed that the new magnetic-stripe technology would eventually lead to breaches in privacy, especially by government agencies. Watts (1997) highlights that breaches in privacy have more to do with government outsourcing contracts than auto-ID itself. For a comprehensive overview of issues such as those related to the invasion of privacy see Rothfeder (1995, pp. 152-162), Colton and Kraemer (1980, pp. 28-30), Campbell et al. (1994), Wacks (1993), Tucker (1992), Young (1978), Federal Department of Communications and Justice in Canada (1974), Madgwick and Smythe (1974) and Cowen (1972). The rise of magnetic-stripe cards coincided with numerous Big Brother predictions made by Orwell and others. Compare Will's *The Big Brother Society* (1983) with 'Big Brotherdom has benefits' (MIS, 1994, p. 80): "[i]t is a mistake to believe that the information supplied to such public and private organizations, or to the tax commissioner or to your employer, is your property..." Other authors that reference the term 'big brother' as related to auto-ID include: Thompson (1997), Andersen (1995), Conolly (1995), Martin (1995), Privacy Committee of NSW (1995), Smith (1995a), Vincent (1995), Crosby (1994), Stix (1994), Davies (1992; 1996), Hogarth (1987), Donelly (1986). It was also at this stage of the magnetic-stripe card product lifecycle, that many countries across the globe formulated Privacy Acts. Citizen identity cards were also a topical issue in which civil libertarians became involved. The Australia Card debate is a fascinating case to reflect on (Clarke, 1987; Greenleaf, 1988).[1]

There are still people today who refuse to use plastic cards to make any sort of transactions, though it is becoming more and more difficult for them to continue this practice. The younger generations, who have been brought up surrounded by technology like the Internet are far less cynical about technology in general. Internet banking (Yan, Paradi & Bhargava, 1997, pp. 275-284) has been adopted by a technology-savvy population that appreciates the convenience of banking from anywhere/ anytime. There is now an established customer base with which to leap into the new-age authentic cashless society (Egner, 1991, pp. 105-109; Husemann, 1999; Smith, 1998). Some countries like Singapore disclosed their agenda to abandon cash by the year 2000, thus preparing all consumers for the change, even though this has not obviously eventuated as yet. "In France, an agreement has been signed that forms the basis of a nationwide, electronic replacement for cash" (O'Sullivan, 1997, p. 57; Fisher, 1996, Pope, 1990). While the cashless society is not completely here yet, many countries and consumers have made substantial inroads into the virtual world. According to most it is just a matter of time.

A Patchwork of Statutes

Current laws worldwide have lagged behind technological innovation. US privacy law, for instance, has been developed in a piecemeal fashion and in a case-by-case mode. It is little wonder that some types

Table 2 U.S. Federal law statutes

Examples of Federal Law Statutes in the U.S.
▪ Fair Credit Reporting Act (Credit records)
▪ Internal Revenue Code (Tax return)
▪ Electronic Funds Transfer Act (Banking records)
▪ Electronic Communications Privacy Act (Information transmitted electronically)
▪ National Labour Relations Act (Labour-related records)
▪ Computer Security Act (Benefits-related records)
▪ Video Privacy Protection Act (Video rental or sale records)
▪ Cable Communications Privacy Act (Subscriber records)
▪ Family Educational Rights and Privacy Act (Educational records) (see Barr et al. 1997, p. 75)
▪ Credit Card Abuse Laws
▪ Wire Fraud Act
▪ The National Stolen Property Act
▪ U.S. Copyright Act
▪ Electronic Communications Privacy Act
▪ State Computer Crime Laws (see Cavazos & Morin 1995, pp. 109-117)
▪ Computer Matching and Privacy Protection Act (see O'Connor 1998, p. 10).

of personal information that have been enabled mostly by auto-ID techniques, such as supermarket transaction records, are still unprotected (Barr et al., 1997, p. 75). As can be seen from Table 2, U.S. privacy-related laws are a patchwork of statutes addressing specific areas and specific types of data. There is, however, no structure or governing authority in place to enforce these statutes. This means that not only can laws vary between states but with respect to the global arena, laws in other countries are also disparate, if existent at all. A similar problem is faced in Australia. Harris (1994) reported that "[t]he Australian Federal Police Association (AFPA) [was] calling for national legislation to curb credit card fraud... [as] officials find themselves virtually powerless..." In 1994, counterfeit cards accounted for $US260 million of credit card fraud worldwide, i.e. one quarter of the world's credit card fraud. Cornford (1995) reported that Australian *"[f]ederal police fear that our laws are inadequate to deal with this type of crime. The Indonesian criminal caught with the card encoder was set free on a legal technicality. Two Americans who used counterfeit cards to steal $250,000 and then sent it back to the US could be charged only with illegal transfer... A Malaysian is awaiting trial after being arrested with 77 counterfeit Visa cards. A Hong Kong criminal was jailed for nine months after using three counterfeit credit cards to get $40,000 in Sydney... The Chinese Public Security Bureau raided factories in Beijing and Shantau, which together made more than 110,000 counterfeit Visa and MasterCard holograms."*

Consider the case where a traveler to a foreign country had their credit card stolen and misused by a perpetrator. Where does the liability lie- with the traveler, with the credit card company, with the perpetrator? "In most national jurisdictions, once the customer has notified the bank of the loss or theft, the customer is then no longer liable for any withdrawals made by a third party, although sometimes the liability remains if the customer has disclosed the PIN to somebody else" (Essinger, 1999, p. 27). Whatever the perspective, for those unfortunate persons who have found themselves in this predicament (and these are not isolated incidences) the experience can be daunting as they attempt to gather evidence.

Regulation E

Regulation E implements the Electronic Fund Transfer Act (EFTA). The act and regulation cover the following consumer electronic funds transfer systems: ATM, POS, automated clearinghouse, telephone bill-payment system, or remote banking programs. Regulation E provides the rules that restrict unsolicited issuance of ATM cards, the need for financial institutions to disclose terms and conditions of EFT services, the provision for receipts and account statements to be given to cardholders, limitations in consumer liability in the case of unauthorized transfers and procedures for error resolution. It has to be said, that most consumers do not consider the implications of Regulation E, until they fall victim to unauthorized transfers or disputes in banking errors (FDIC, 2008).

In the U.S. there is no law governing electronic payments; these aspects are covered by provisions in the Civil Code (Central Banks, 1989, p. 217). Regulation E under the Electronic Funds Transfer Act of 1978 does not include check guarantee and authorization services, transmission of data between banks and any transaction that is about the purchase or sale of securities (Scott, M.D., 1994, p. 497). Canada has also followed the United States by setting up a voluntary code of practice for debit card issuers, retailers, and consumer associations, as well as the federal and provincial regulatory bodies. In 1992 the code for Consumer Debit Card Services was introduced by the Canadian Bankers Association (CBA). However, it would be essential to remember, *"[t]he code applies only to services which use debit cards and personal identification numbers (PINs) to access automated banking machines and point of sale terminals in Canada. It does not apply to cross-border transactions. The code establishes a code of practice for the issuance, use, and security of PINs. It sets the general requirements for cardholder agreements, transaction records, and transaction security, and is intended to set a minimum standard which participating organizations meet or exceed. It does not preclude protection given by other laws and standards. The code deals with the theft, fraud, technical malfunction, and other losses, and requires card issuers to establish fair and timely procedures for resolving disputes"* (Campbell, 1994, p. 44).

Numerous associations have endorsed the code. The most prominent members include: the Canadian Payments Association, the Trust Companies Association of Canada, Credit Union Central of Canada, Retail Council of Canada, Canadian Federation of Independent Business and Consumers' Association Canada. Other innovations like EFTPOS require long-term commitments to improvements to rules and regulations if they are to continually evolve to meet the needs of the end-user and withstand the test of time. The Commonwealth of Australia wrote a detailed report on the rights and obligations of users and providers of EFT systems in 1986, however much of what was documented was voluntary codes of practice like in the case of Canada and the United States.

In a recent article by Geva (2006), three topics are explored on the common theme of changes in the law due to the developments in electronic banking. These topics include: checks, payment cards, and securities transfers. Checks once considered purely paper-based payment systems are now being transmitted either in whole or in part, electronically. This process is called *check truncation*. The question of whether checks are now recognized under Regulation E is discussed by Geva, as are other more advanced devices used for payment.

Incremental Innovations

A number of incremental innovations to the basic magnetic-stripe card have been introduced since its inception (Ross, 2003). Developers in magnetic-stripe have primarily aimed to increase basic track capacity and protect data content with some form of encryption (Smith et al., 1996). While some of these improvements are theoretically possible many hold that the widespread introduction of these techniques is not economically viable and not worth pursuing. Consider the example of Washington University's Magnetics and Information Science Centre (MISC) that has discovered a way of protecting the magnetic-stripe card against fraud. "The biggest expense of deploying Magneprint will be replacing or modifying card readers so they can read the magnetic wave patterns" (Stroud, 1998, p. 2). This is not to discount the efforts of MISC or other commercial manufacturers.

There is evidence to suggest that companies are still investing R&D dollars into magnetic-stripe. For example refer to the new developments listed by IPC (2001). Other experts, particularly those in smart card, believe that the costs of delivering projected magnetic-stripe innovations are too high and fall short when compared to smart card solutions which are already proven and on offer now. Svigals (1987, p. 146) predicted that if smart card was to replace magnetic-stripe cards that "...the economic and functional break-even point might be reached within a five-year period." Svigals did not believe that the incremental density changes to the magnetics would come close to even challenging the advantages of the smart card. Yet these and other predictions made in the late 1980s and early 1990s have not eventuated and those that were quick to publicize the demise of the magnetic-stripe card have been left wondering where things went wrong.

It is true that smart card has now reached economies-of-scale and is becoming more affordable but this does not necessarily equate to the total extinction of magnetic-stripe (Nickel, 1999, pp. 1-2; Holland, 2004). Even Svigals (1987, p. 175f) himself, acknowledged that: *"[a]ll evidence suggests that the magnetic-stripe FTC will have a place in the future. A financial institution with a static market, a significant investment in magnetic-stripe work stations, a very low card acceptance rate and/or rapid customer turnover, and little prospect of additional types of electronic services will probably stay with the magnetic-stripe FTC... At the other end of the spectrum is the institution with a large stable of aggressive magnetic-stripe FTC users, a fast-growing range of electronic services, an increasing set of interchange and sharing arrangements, and a growing concern about magnetic-stripe-based losses and frauds. That institution will take an early look at Smart Cards... In between the two extremes are the majority of institutions... In the final analysis, an active effort to accommodate both types of financial transaction cards appears to be the appropriate action path" (Svigals, 1987, p. 175f).* In the case of the current global EMV migration, some regions have been slow to take-up the new chip and pin card. Analysts have noted that the slow uptake has been due to the complexity of replacing the entire card and terminal base, coupled with changes to the networks and bank issuer systems to deal with processing requirements (Aconite, 2006, p. 12). Fraudsters can still continue to target EMV cards, so long as the magnetic stripe is present on the back.

The new-found relationship between the magnetic-stripe and biometrics techniques has also opened a plethora of new opportunities for the technology. The University of Kent began to conduct research on encoding facial images on blocks of data small enough to fit on a magnetic-stripe in (Middleton, 1998). In addition manufacturers of numerous auto-ID devices have even seen a possible convergence between the bar code, magnetic-stripe and integrated circuit (IC) onto the one device (de Bruyne, 1990; Magbar, 2000).

Collaborative Research

Together with firms and standards-setting organizations, universities are also investing research dollars in developing further magnetic-stripe innovations, admittedly however many of these projects are sponsored. Yet it is firms that are generally more overprotective about their intellectual property (IP). But as Bright (1988, p. 136) does rightly point out, the reluctance on the part of potential suppliers to disclose their techniques and progress is understandable, granted the commercial sensitivity. Even universities, that were once considered fairly open institutions, have now jumped on the commercialization bandwagon, in order to attract even bigger funding opportunities to support laboratories and centers. For instance, MISC has developed MAGNEprint to increase the security of magnetic-stripe technology. Previously, this had been one of the technology's technical limitations, making smart card technology more favorable for access control applications (Magneprint, 1999; Batterson, 2002): *"Researchers at Washington University have invented a method for the positive identification of any piece of magnetic recording medium. The innovation permits a reading device to verify the authenticity of a document bearing magnetically recorded information, and to reject unauthorized copies... The innovation eliminates all types of magnetic fraud."* This innovation can now be implemented by manufacturers of magnetic-stripe cards to increase the attractiveness of magnetic-stripe technology compared to other card technologies. The innovation was first presented at a number of technical forums. Thereafter an article was published in a recognized journal and in 1993 became protected through worldwide patenting. With further trials conducted the university licensed Magneprint to Mag-Tek Incorporated, a firm that makes electronic readers (Stroud, 1998, p. 1). This is yet another sign that the technique is continuing to evolve and will continue to meet the needs of a variety of applications.

MAGNETIC-STRIPE CARD APPLICATIONS

Overview

Financial Transaction Cards

A cursory glance at the content of one's wallet will reaffirm why "[f]inancial cards are by far the main application of magnetic stripe cards" (Zoreda & Oton, 1994, p. 20). The finance sector, have been responsible for the FTC explosion in the form of debit and credit cards which have paved the way towards an evolving cashless society.[2] The two types of cards differ in that debit cards require the cardholder to enter a personal identification number (PIN) at unsupervised terminals (known as automatic teller machines ATMs) whereas credit cards only require signature verification at supervised terminals (known as electronic funds transfer at point of sale EFTPOS). Financial transactions can even be carried out from the home using a PC (personal computer) or a touchtone telephone. For the present however, ATMs and EFT terminals can be viewed as the most popular complementary innovations to magnetic-stripe cards that have changed the face of banking. For instance, between 1990 and 1994 the number of EFTPOS transactions worldwide increased from 61 million to 245 million (Federal Bureau of Consumer Affairs, 1995, p. 6). In the same period EFTPOS terminals grew annually at a rate of 38 per cent as compared to ATM terminals which only experienced an annual growth of 4 per cent. The trends as identified by Tren (1995, p. 42) can be attributed to the early adoption of ATMs by North America, Canada and Japan versus the adoption of EFTPOS by European countries to handle multi-currency payments.

Wallets Bulging with Plastic not Cash

The magnetic-stripe card was heralded as the technology that would see an end to the large bulging wallet containing copper coins and paper money (Johnstone, 1999). For a fascinating study on what consumers actually store in their wallet and the shifting uses for wallets over time see L. Cooper (1999, pp. 87-93). Financial objects in wallets include: receipts, money (cash and coins), loyalty cards, debit cards, bank cards, credit cards, charge (smart cards) and checks. Non-financial objects include: membership cards, business cards, drivers license, telephone numbers, ID cards, postage stamps, lottery tickets, coupons, photographs, national insurance card, medical prescriptions, train tickets and a calendar. While the magnetic-stripe card has successfully acted to reduce the amount of money people carry, the technology has attracted other countless product innovations. Unfortunately, the reality is that wallets and purses are still bulging but not with money, instead with numerous plastic cards. It is not unusual to be held up in a shopping queue while someone is shuffling through their collection of magnetic-stripe cards searching for the right one to make their transaction. It is not out of the ordinary for a consumer to possess a separate ATM savings card, several credit cards, a frequent flyer card, a phone card, a discounted travel card, an employee identification card, a library photocopy card, a driver's license and several different loyalty retail cards (Cox, 1997, pp. 28-31).

There are presently several billion magnetic-stripe cards in circulation in the United States alone (Blank, 2007). This is testament to the increase in consumer acceptance of card technology and the marketing efforts of large corporations to sell the benefits of the card. In addressing the issue of the magnetic-stripe card taking the form of an electronic purse, Peter Harrop (1992, p. 227) describes the main applications other than the FTC. He makes the observation that: *"[s]o far, payphones are the*

Figure 3. Purchasing a pre-paid parking ticket that features a magnetic-stripe card at a supermarket parking lot in Canberra, ACT, Australia. Photo taken in 2006

commonest application... Mass transit, particularly 'stored-value tickets' for trains and buses, is the second largest application... Prepayment cards are widely used for taxis, road tolls, parking [Figure 3], vending, payment in canteens and small shops, purchase of electricity and gas at the home meter, in launderettes and many other applications."

The Plastag Corporation, a card manufacturer approved by MasterCard and Cash Station have put together an imaginative range of product solutions. While producing the standard line of bank cards and blank cards, they are also the largest supplier of casino cards in the U.S. Other Plastag (1998) products include:

- **Pre-paid phone cards:** Phone cards are one of the most popular and effective promotional tools to build traffic in a business
- **Membership/I.D. cards:** An important record-keeping tool for hospitals, nursing homes, other health providers, insurance companies and colleges/universities
- **Keylock cards:** All over the world, hotels and resorts are changing the traditional door locks to electronic swipe key cards... they keep guests safe... [Figure 4]

It is important to keep in mind that not all applications require the same level of security as the FTC-it all depends on the application. For instance, paper bus and rail travel tickets featuring a magnetic-stripe are highly negotiable (i.e. they do not require a PIN or user ID and can be interchanged between persons).

Case 1: Magnetic-Stripe Cards for Financial Transactions

Some may have thought it more valuable to relate financial services to smart cards but the reality is that widespread usage of smart cards by most banks is still some time away, especially in North America. *"...Less than 5% of smart cards worldwide are issued by banks... Mass rollout of smart cards is years away because of the cost to convert magnetic-strip credit, debit and ATM card systems to chip technology" (Bank Sys., 1997, p. 21).* Presently, it is the plastic embossed card with the magnetic stripe and

Figure 4. A magnetic stripe card acting as a keylock card at Swissotel | The Stamford in Singapore. Many hotels are now using these cards to save on energy expenses as well. Upon entry, the card is placed in a reader to enable electricity in the hotel room, upon exit, the card is removed and all electricals disabled. Photo taken in 2002.

signature that has permeated most countries around the world. The card is used to perform transactions for various types of electronic funds transfer systems (EFTS): ATMs, CDs (cash dispensers), EFTPOS and remote banking. As one report noted these 'profound changes' linked for the first time the consumer directly to the computer. Prior to magnetic-stripe cards, consumers depended upon the services of an intermediary at the counter but now the consumer is able to perform operations that were previously conducted by a bank clerk (OECD, 1989, p. vi).

Magnetic-stripe cards have been able to offer the dual function of paper-based and paper-less transactions. This is important because it has enabled the cardholder the ability not only to withdraw or transfer cash but also to use 'plastic money' with the same card. For instance, in Australia the St George Bank Freedom MultiAccess Visa magnetic-stripe card (with hologram) allows the cardholder to visit ATM machines to withdraw cash using a PIN and also to purchase goods and services by credit using the cardholder's signature. International credit card corporations like American Express (AMEX), Bank Americard, Cartasi and Diners Club which are offering credit-based financial services are still using magnetic-stripe cards with embossed writing and signature though they have signaled their intention to migrate cards over time. While this type of system is obviously convenient for the cardholder, questions are continually being raised about the vulnerability of the cards to fraud and theft. More recently in Australia, credit card companies are linking PINs to cardholder accounts to eliminate the possibility of fraudsters giving false signatures at point of sale.

Are Magnetic-Stripe Cards Outdated Technology?

While most banks and financial institutions still utilize magnetic-stripe on their customer FTCs, particularly in the U.S., all of the banks in France are reaping the benefits of smart card. "All bankcards in France have a chip imbedded in them... When a French cardholder makes a purchase, the transaction is processed at the point of service using the chip and not the magnetic stripe" (Ayer & McKenna, 1997, p. 50). The Dutch have followed the example of the French. Each of the French chip cards carry a payment application known as B0'. "Dutch banks are poised to become the first in the world to introduce computer smart cards on a nationwide scale this year, eventually giving 15 million people the possibility of living without cash" (van Grinsven, 1996, p. 32).

Smart cards have always been a dormant threat to magnetic-stripe but in most countries it has taken until the year 2000 for noticeable migration from the magnetic-stripe card to the smart card to happen. It took almost 40 years to distribute plastic payment cards widely; it will probably take another 10 years before consumers worldwide are comfortable with the multiapplication smart card. Even though the card is a more secure technology enabling the reduction of fraud, many consumers are concerned with the card's potential uses. It is the information centralization to one unique ID per person that consumers find uncomfortable. Some banks have already issued multiple application cards but consumers still fear security breaches.

Many banks have conducted feasibility studies on smart cards, either by doing secondary research or conducting pilot studies. They are presently, albeit seamless to the consumer, considering a transition between auto-ID devices. Customers are being supplied with hybrid cards until the migration from magnetic-stripe to smart cards is complete. In the former case, major banks across the world have begun marketing the smart card concept to consumers. In Australia for instance in 1997, the ANZ bank advertised the change from magnetic-stripe to smart card in full-page advertisements. One of these announcements is worth noting in full- a magnetic-stripe bankcard appears on the left page and a VISA card (with IC) on the right:

October 1974. There it was in your letterbox. Whether you wanted it or not. A Bankcard. They all looked the same and their new owners likewise, were all treated the same. You were told where to use it and how much you could spend. All that changed. At ANZ it changed faster than most. To the point where you can now enjoy ANZ cards that not only provide credit... Cards that are aligned to your telecommunications company, your airline, and many other major companies you do business with on a daily basis. What next? Well, we're currently at the forefront of smart card technology. Cards that use a microchip to record details of transactions and the balance on the card. Now won't that be a nice change? (The Australian, 1997, pp. 6-7)

Globally and throughout the 1990s banks conducted widespread smart card trials. In the U.S., Citibank and Chase Manhattan conducted a trial in 1997 covering New York City and some 50000 consumers. In 1993, National Westminster Bank and Midland Bank teamed up to trial the Mondex card in Swindon, including 40000 consumers. In the same year, the three largest credit card giants, Europay, MasterCard and Visa, implemented a global standard generally known as the EMV specification for smart card credit cards as they considered future migration paths (D.S. Gold, 1999). VISA was the first of the trio to distribute smart cards to their customers. American Express has also made inroads to developing EMV standard credit services. As Ayer and McKenna from VISA International reported (1997, p. 49), the EMV specification is truly global. It allows for the same terminal to accept a variety of payment cards. The aim is to expand the usefulness of payment cards to be able to do much more with them. In France there are even migrations occurring from smart bank cards developed in the 1980s to newer smart cards that adhere to the EMV standard and are based on the MULTOS operating system. Clearly this has been an unsettling period for banks and merchants as the costs to upgrade or replace existing ATM, EFTPOS, electronic cash registers, self-service fuel dispensers and other such terminals to make them smart card-ready are very high. Some have therefore chosen to remain with the magnetic-stripe technology for the interim and may well suffer for it later. In 2000, "Visa USA estimated it would cost $11.1 billion US to convert to smart cards in the United States alone, with $7 billion of that cost borne by merchants" (Blank, 2007).

From Electronic Purse to a Cashless Society

The first well-known electronic purse trial was conducted in Denmark, Noestved in 1992. The prepaid card system was called Danmønt A/S. The integrated circuit card (ICC) was used for the payment of small amount transactions such as at vending machines, payphones and transportation. By 1993 the card was rolled out to several large cities, and terminals were located at payphones, parking meters, kiosks and railway. In 1996, there were over 600,000 cards in circulation in 50 Danish cities. The next step for Danmønt was to introduce more sophisticated SVCs that could be used for bigger transactions that require more security. Danmønt's strategy is to heighten consumer awareness and acceptance (PBS, 1998; Kaplan, 1996, pp. 150-152; Ferrari, 1998, pp. 196-197). In Portugal the SIBS (Sociedade Interbancaria de Servicos) have introduced the Multibanco electronic purse, yet another hybrid card incorporating a microprocessor for purse applications and magnetic-stripe for credit facilities. Close to 7000 smart card terminals have been introduced, the majority are off-line and about one-third can read both magnetic-stripe and smart card technology.

Two years after the Danmønt card was introduced, the Mondex card made its debut in the UK. "Enter electronic cash. The idea of digital money is simple enough: instead of storing value on paper, find a way to wrap it in a string of digits that's more portable" (Ramo, 1998, p. 50). It is interesting to note that both Danmønt and Mondex were initiatives of large banks and telephone companies, although the two cards differ in principle. While Danmønt was designed for the payment of small transactions, Mondex was designed for the replacement of cash altogether. Mondex is also designed to leave an 'untraceable' audit trail. Since its inception in 1993, Mondex International (now a subsidiary of MasterCard International), has rapidly begun to roll-out trials all over the world. Mondex is being marketed as convenient for consumers and merchants. Some of its differentiators from ATM magnetic-stripe cards include: access to electronic money via public or private telephones, its ability to carry up to 5 currencies, an electronic wallet which allows card-to-card transactions, lock-code functions and instant statements. In the English town of Swindon, Godin writes (1995, p. 84), *"...customers at the local McDonald's buy Big Macs without touching a bank note; pub crawlers at Bass Taverns keep the taps running without tapping their wallets; and grocery shoppers pay for their provisions without currency changing hands. Citizens of Swindon... are participating in a pilot project testing Mondex, a smart card for dispensing digital cash."*

In 1994, Mondex was heralded as having the potential to become a global payment system and banks rushed to become a franchisee of the company. Mondex International has been hailed as the "evangelist" of the smart card world (Mitchell, 1996b, p. 52). More recently Mastercard International has reached an agreement to assume full ownership of Mondex International (Mei, 2001, p. 10). In Asia, HongKong Shanghai Bank along with Hang Seng Bank are serving Hong Kong, China, Singapore, Taiwan, Philippines and other surrounding countries with Mondex cards. Chase Manhattan and Wells Fargo along with the Royal Bank of Canada and the Canadian Imperial Bank of Commerce (CIBC) are trialing Mondex in the U.S. and Canada respectively. The Australian banks, National Australia Bank (NAB), Westpac, ANZ and Commonwealth Bank have paid ten million Australian dollars for their right to issue Mondex smart cards to consumers (Moreira, 1997, p. 45). Clearly, there is a movement away from the traditional magnetic-stripe FTC and a move towards both the electronic purse and electronic cash. The latter, of course, meaning a world without paper money- a cashless society. However, Mondex officials are still cautious about predicting the demise of cash completely. "They see digital money as an alternative to cash, another option among many options for consumers. Mondex has estimated that e-cash will carve out 30 percent of the payments market" (Godin, 1995, p. 97).

DigiCash is another company that is focused on delivering smart card solutions. The company established by David Chaum, a cryptography expert, is part of the consortium of firms that is involved in developing the electronic-wallet for the CAFE project (Conditional Access for Europe). A trial is already underway in the European Commission in Brussels. Other companies which are making their mark in the digital cash arena include: CyberCash, First Virtual, Michigan National, BankOne, CheckFree, CommerceNet, NetCash, Smart Cash, Telequip and NetMarket. These companies have developed solutions for purchasing goods and services over the Internet and conducting money transfers using electronic cash (Brands, 1995; Godin, 1995; and Essinger, 1999, ch. 10). Other well-known solutions include the Proton cash card (Proton, 1999) from Banksys in Belgium that is closely linked to American Express, and the Visa Cash card which is being tested by Visa International. Other schemes worth noting, which are trialling types of electronic purses include: Transcard, Quicklink & MasterCard (Australia), Balkan-Card (Bulgaria), EltCard (Estonia), Avant (Finland), SEPT (France), Chip Knip (Holland), Eximsmart (Indonesia), LINK (Lebanon), Interpay (Netherlands), Bankaxept (Norway), SIBS (Portugal), NETS & CashCard (Singapore), UEPS (South Africa), SEMP (Spain), POSTCARD (Switzerland), FISC (Taiwan), VISA SVC (USA). This signifies a truly global reach.

According to Hendry (2007, pp. 144-162) the drawbacks of electronic purse schemes such as the Danish Danmønt, the Portuguese PMB, VisaCash and Mondex were three fold. Transaction times were usually felt to be slower taking up to several seconds, and a separate transaction was required for loading the card which was inconvenient for the user. In addition, there were problems with the cost of the schemes which were highly customized and proprietary in nature. When the Internet became a plausible avenue to making payments, either from a fixed or mobile device, electronic purse schemes became less popular as a longer term solution.

Biometrics and Beyond – Why Carry Cards at All?

"Automatic teller machines that identify users just by looking at them are expected to make PIN numbers and ATM cards obsolete" (Johnson, 1996, p. 11). Several systems have been developed by U.S. companies using iris identification. The Sensar Corporation, have already installed IrisIdent units in parts of North America and Asia. Citibank liked the idea so much, that it prematurely invested $US3 million into Sensar back in 1997. Nationwide Building Society, Britain's largest mortgage lender is also trialing Sensar's product in Britain, using NCR-built ATMs (Brown, 1998, p. 52). Oki Electric, a Japanese ATM manufacturer has agreed to buy at least $US35 million in Sensar products within 5 years (Fernandez, 1997, p.13). It is significant to note that even if biometric ATMs are phased in, that most banks will still continue to issue customers with some type of card device which will store the individual's biometric. Diebold Incorporated have developed a multimodal biometric system for making transactions that incorporates both face and voice recognition. Using face recognition software by Visionics and voice-verification from Keyware Technologies, the face and voice must match an image and voice sample in a database for a customer to make a transaction (Belsie, 1997, p. 1; S. Gold, 1999). Even as far back as 1992 an Australian company, Bio Recognition, developed FingerScan for ATM transactions (Gora,

1992, p. 3). Biometric systems do seem to remove the need for remembering passwords and account numbers or carrying several cards with expiration dates etc, but they do require each customer to willingly provide a biometric (Wahab, Tan & Heng, 1999; Essick, 1998). The up-front cost of installing a biometric system is still not viable for most companies.

Biometrics is also more complex than solutions like RFID transponders. Recently, the advantages of transponders with respect to animal identification have been highlighted by print media. Some advocates of the technology say, if chip implants work for animals then they should also work for people. A number of respected scientists see it as a gradual progression to better efficiency and security. Others nervously acknowledge that mass trials are already technologically feasible. One of the earliest references to a type of auto-ID device that would herald in a cashless society was recorded in *The New Westralian Banker*, an official publication of the Australian Bank Employees Union. The article (Devereux, 1984, p. 5) was titled "1984 IS HERE!" and highlights a new system that supposedly does not require a bankcard or credit card or check or cash. *"This is the crux of an experiment begun in Sweden starting March, 1983. 6,000 people have agreed to take part in this experiment. Each person involved has received a special mark (shot on to the relevant area with a special, painless ray gun) and is now marked for life (it doesn't come off.) The mark is registered in a computer and will register in banks or wherever those marked decide to shop. The shopkeeper simply runs an electronic pen over the mark and it instantly sends that person's number to a computer center from where all information of their transactions is sent to their bank. No money needs to be touched."*

The technology depicted suggests that some kind of human bar code trial occurred in Sweden. The technology did exist in 1984 to run this trial; however we have not been able to verify the authenticity of the content of the article. Whether Devereux had a wry sense of humor or the article content is true, still makes one wonder where the technology could be headed. In making reference to electronic cash, a *Time Magazine* reporter commented, "Your daughter can store the money any way she wants- on her laptop, on a debit card, even (in the not too distant future) on a chip implant under her skin" (Ramo, 1998, p.51). U.K. Professor Kevin Warwick, the first man to be implanted with a chip, has also said: *"[i]n five years' time, we will be able to do chip with all sorts of information on them. They could be used for money transfers [Figure 5], medical records, passports, driving licenses, and loyalty cards. And if they are implanted they are impossible to steal. The potential is enormous"* (Dennis, 1998, p. 2).

Case 2: Magnetic-Stripe Cards in Transportation

Electronic Ticketing

Electronic ticketing systems based on magnetic-stripe technology are now widespread. Most tickets issued for a variety of transportation are made of a thin cardboard containing a magnetic-stripe down one side. They are known as 'prepayment cards'. While these tickets are highly negotiable, consumers seem to be relatively unconcerned with loss or theft of a ticket. The cost to manufacture and purchase a ticket is relatively low compared to other card types. The movement away from traditional cardboard-only tickets only raised the price of a fare by a few cents and increased revenue manifold. In the U.S. the push toward transit fare automation began in 1972 when BART (Bay Area Rapid Transit) in the San Francisco Bay area was introduced. The process is as follows: *"[t]ickets are dispensed by machines in stations that accept coins and bills. Ticket value is recorded on the mag stripe. When a rider enters the system the turnstile read-write unit records the place and time of entry. Upon exit, the turnstile*

Figure 5. The queue at the National Australia Bank (NAB) automatic teller machines located on the University of Wollongong Campus (NSW, Australia) are in great demand during session. Advocates of a cash-less society, in particular proponents of chip implant solutions, always point to the convenience of not having to carry cash at all, and never having to queue.

computes and subtracts the price of the trip based on length of trip, and in some systems, the time of day" (Holmstrom, 1996, p. 1).

One of the successes of the introduction of magnetic-stripe ticketing is that it has allowed for the operation of a unified and standard metropolitan transport system. In Sydney, Australia, the State Rail Authority, the State Transit Authority and Ferry Authority have standardized their magnetic-stripe ticketing system. The Washington transit system also uses a similar set-up (Harrop, 1989, p. 342). Weekly or daily tickets can be purchased with ease and used for different types of transport (Figure 6). Consumers who purchase pre-paid tickets for multiple journeys usually receive price discounts (Todd, 1990). The short-comings of the ticket include that they are disposable (i.e. paper waste) and the ability to check whether an individual has purchased the right trip for their destination requires human intervention.

When standards for magnetic-stripe were being developed the International Air Transport Industry ensured that Track 2 was dedicated solely to air travel. Before any domestic or international flight, the traveler is issued with a boarding pass. Without this pass he or she cannot board the airplane even if their passport has been stamped by immigration. A boarding pass contains flight and seating information, the traveler's name and flight class in the front and a magnetic stripe at the back. If a traveler has luggage to check-in bar code labels are attached to the bags so that they can be read later and routed to the correct destination (LaMoreaux, 1995, pp. 12-14). Today integrated RFID tags are used for baggage handling in many international airports, such as Hong Kong.

Loyalty Card Schemes

One of the biggest boosts to the magnetic-stripe card industry was the introduction of loyalty cards attached to air transportation especially. The idea has been around since the late 1980s but it picked up momentum in the late 1990s with frequent flyer card programs linked up with hotel chains and rental

Figure 6. The electronic ticketing vending machine at the Hauptbahnhof in München, Germany. The MVV magnetic-stripe tickets can be purchased using cash. The intention is to introduce a smart card in the MVV region, but this initiative is not being supported. A lot of additional infrastructure would be needed and MVV would have to shoulder the costs. At present 70% of all passengers are seasonal ticket holders and the proposed contact-free smart card would mean to them a retrograde step, involving many more procedures. Photo taken in 2005.

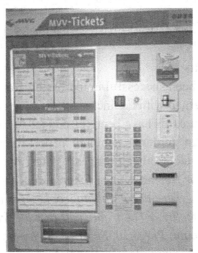

car companies. As far back as in 1987, the Airplus Company (initially backed by the top 13 European airlines) launched its loyalty card. It was one of the first companies to offer such a service but it found it very difficult to continue in the short-term as projected card targets were continually not met. The card was initially misunderstood by observers as a type of credit card but David Huemer (the CEO at the time) clearly stated that the service the card provided was the purchase of business travel for the frequent traveler. By 1988 Airplus was forced to change its strategy. The company restructured and successfully entered into the co-brand market directly featured on a host of Airplus-linked family cards like Austrian Airlines. Similarly in 1989, the Alitalia airline was offering a twenty per cent discount on full-fare domestic flights in Italy for Alicard cardholders. *"Alicard, which is personalized and carries a magnetic stripe (the stripe is inactive and for 'image' purposes only), is being produced by a Rome-based subsidiary... Air industry observers consider Alitalia's foray into the plastic card business part of an overall attempt to build itself an image as an innovator and improve its level of service"* (Card World, 1990, p. 44).

The new loyalty card market is booming in that more and more consumers are subscribing to programs. Cross (1996, pp. 30-34) discusses how intelligent shoppers can benefit from loyalty programs. See the agreement between Mondex and beenz.com for loyalty points (D. Jones, 2000). Another example is the Australian loyalty card program called Ezy Rewards offers points for shopping at the Woolworths retailer, banking with the Commonwealth Bank, flying with Qantas, visiting particular entertainment venues and booking particular holiday packages. Under the guise of Club Miles, Frequent-Flyer, Fly-buys, Air Miles, The Travel Club, Reward Card, Premier Points, Executive Club and other so-named programs, consumers are rewarded for their loyalty by discounted or free flights, upgrades to flight class or airline lounges or hotel rooms etc. Companies from all types of industries are enjoying the co-branding concept, especially airlines that have teamed with large hotel chains, credit card corporations and telecommunications operators. What is important to highlight, however, is that the cost of these programs to airlines, hotels, and card companies is high and the return questionable. "The current process is inconvenient for the consumer, costly for the travel company to administer, and a nightmare for a corporate travel and finance department to manage" (Wesley & Wilkey, 1997, p. 201). In some cases, travel companies have abandoned loyalty programs altogether.

Are Smart Cards the Smart Choice for Contactless Ticketing?

At Airports and Checkpoints

Magnetic-stripe tickets have been successful in increasing commuter throughput at peak hour periods but many operators are concerned with the increasing means to counterfeit this media (Dinning, 1997, p. 186). For this reason, smart cards have been introduced to many transit systems all over the world. Since the Schengen Treaty, Amsterdam's Schiphol airport has introduced a 100 million guilder smart card system for members of eight other European states that have agreed to scrap identity checks. *"The plastic cards... allow for free movement for travelers through a special gate without having to show passports or ID cards... there are no photographs of travelers, passport numbers or any other safeguards in the card's microchip... The treaty will provide free passage of citizens through France, the Netherlands, Germany, Spain, Portugal, Belgium, Luxemburg, Italy and Greece" (European, 1993, p. 3).* More recently Iceland's Keflavik International Airport upgraded its CCTV (closed circuit television) system with facial recognition technology to guard against terrorism, since its inception into the European Schengen Agreement (Lockie, 2001).

For Metropolitan Bus, Rail and Ferry Services

Among the most advanced is that established in Hong Kong. The consortium Creative Star has integrated the ticketing system for trains, buses, taxis, trams and ferries. The Octopus Card (Kwok, 2001, p. A4) is used to collect payment for taxi fares and other transport services (Wallis, 2001, p. B5). Consumers are charged a small levy for using the card to offset overall costs. This is how Creative Star as the service provider makes money and how merchants can recover their costs for buying specialized readers (Chan, 2001, p. 6). The contactless card allows commuters to pass through turnstiles without having to insert it in a reader. The consumer has the choice between a personalized and non-personalized card (Chau & Poon, 2003).

In the U.K., Transys began to develop the Oyster Card for London Transport (LT) in the 1990s. It was proposed that (Jones, 1998, p. 4): *"[a]utomatic gating will be extended to all the London Underground stations and existing automatic gates will be upgraded to read smart cards. Electronic ticketing machines will be introduced in all buses operating in London. Transys will also take over the operation of London Transport's Pass Agent ticket retailing network operated confectioners, newsagents and tobacconists and collect revenue from them. Some 2,300 retail outlets will have the equipment for issuing smart cards."* Today we know this scheme as the Oyster Card (London Transport, 2008). An Oyster card can store up to £90 of credit, which can on bus, Tube, trams, DLR, London Overground and some National Rail services in London.

The Washington Metropolitan Area Transit Authority (WMATA) trialed contactless smart cards in 1995. The 'Go Card' as it was named, could also be used to pay for commuter parking. German Autobahns used the chip-ticket system from about the mid-1990s (Wenter, 1994, pp. 50-54). The Tapei City government implemented a Mass Rapid Transport (MRT) system using contactless smart cards for payment on buses, the subway and a number of car parks. The MAPS concept called for the ability to pay for all transit purchases from bus fairs to parking fees and tolls (Cunningham, 1993, pp. 021-025). Additionally, smart transit cards have been used in agreement with universities and other applications.

The smart card is not only convenient for the consumer but provides a wealth of knowledge for operators in terms of resource allocation and transport network optimization (Blythe, 1996; Blythe & Holland 1998). For the advantages and disadvantages of smart card fare collection media refer to Okine and Shen (1995, pp. 524-525). Zlatinov (2001, pp. 35-36) reported on the next generation of transit cards. Readers linked to an information system can gather important statistical data that can assist with planning present and future transport services. For example, an operator has the ability to count the number of passengers that use particular bus, train and ferry routes at particular times of the day.

Road Tolling Applications

In Singapore, this idea has been taken one step further with the fully operational ERP (Electronic Road Pricing) system and contact-based electronic purse 'CashCard' (LTA, 2008). Drivers do not only go through toll gates without stopping but information collected allows operators to locate congested areas at peak traffic times, plan for new roads or redirect traffic through other routes (Figure 7). The RFID-based system even has the capability to charge drivers according to the route they have taken, to ensure a smooth flow of traffic (Kristoffy, 1999). Drivers who do not wish to pay higher levies may use non-direct routes which take longer to get them to their destination. For an overview of RFID toll applications refer to Gerdeman (1995, ch. XI). This type of system has enormous implications for congested and polluted cities such as Athens in Greece. In London in the United Kingdom instead of RFID a network of camera sites monitors every entrance and exit to the Congestion Charging Zone (CCZ). High quality digital images are taken of vehicles through a process called Automatic Number Plate Recognition (ANPR) which reads and records each number plate and charges vehicle registrations accordingly.

Figure 7. Singapore's ERP (Electronic Road Pricing) system "In Operation." The ERP uses a dedicated short-range radio communication system to deduct ERP charges from CashCards. These are inserted in the in-vehicle units (IUs) of vehicles before each journey. Each time vehicles pass through a gantry when the system is in operation, the ERP charges are automatically deducted. Photo taken in 2003.

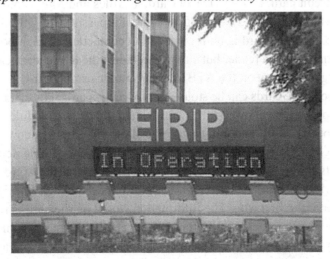

In understanding the flow of traffic, new bus routes could be setup to encourage people to take public transport instead of their own car. The terms 'smart city', 'smart vehicles', 'smart roads' are beginning to surface in transport and telematics. Komanecky & Claus (1991), and Gerdeman (1995, ch. XII) refer to this type of RFID application as an Intelligent Vehicle Highway System (IVHS). Choi et al. (1995) discuss a real-time moving automotive vehicle identification system (AVIS) that uses bar codes at toll gates to measure city traffic. In the Italian city of Turin, the public transport company ordered a Confident RFID system (TagMaster AB) for its 900 buses, 300 trams and drivers. "[T]he ID tags in the system will also make it possible to get information about mileage, fuel consumption and service interval status of the vehicles" (M. Marsh, 1998, p. 1).

Boarding Passes and the Airline Industry
In October 1995, at the *Passenger Services Conference*, a smart card subcommittee was established to develop an airline industry smart card standard. Problems envisaged with electronic ticketing, namely how to identify a passenger quickly without a paper boarding pass, led to the formation of the subcommittee. In Australia QANTAS allows for 'e-check ins' for domestic flights. A traveler is required to use his/her credit card at a check-in kiosk at the airport and a boarding pass is provided after the consumer enters their itinerary details. Flight times, seat changes and baggage check-in are all automated through this process. Delta Airlines, Lufthansa and Air France are now using IATA standard smart cards. The results of the Smart Card Subcommittee were IATA resolution 791 and ATA resolution 20.204- 'Specifications for Airline Industry Integrated Circuit Cards (ICC)'. The resolution made effective in 1997, means that cards are interoperable at gates which have upgraded their read/write hardware. It is expected that most of the airline cards will be co-branded cards. Credit card companies like Visa, MasterCard and American Express showed immediate interest. For a list of airlines that provide an e-ticket services refer to the IATA web site (IATA, 1999). Delta Airlines have issued smart cards to frequent flyers between New York, Boston and Washington.[3] The contactless chip card is swiped by the passenger at the boarding gate for authorization to board the plane. The card not only acts as the ticket but serves the other functions of a Frequent Flyer Card and credit card.

Lufthansa have already issued hundreds of thousands of smart cards to its frequent flyers and Senator cardholders. Known as the ChipCard, the card is used on all German domestic flights as well as from London and Paris. The card is truly a multiapplication card, as it can be used for making telephone calls in Germany, as a credit card, and Air Travel Card, a 'Miles and More' frequent flyer card, a membership card for airport lounges, and a boarding authority for passengers. Different from the Delta Airlines frequent flyer card, the ChipCard is both contact and contactless. When boarding the passenger does not need to insert the card in a reader but simply walk past the RF reader near the gate. Air France also records the passenger itinerary on the ATB Pectab Gemplus smart card.

Just as magnetic-stripe cards can be stolen, so can smart cards. For that reason, it is possible that an unauthorized person may be allowed to travel accidentally or by fraudulent intent. After the terrorist attacks of September 11, 2001, and numerous other foiled attempts to down passenger airliners in the UK and US, numerous governments have either investigated or implemented biometric schemes or electronic Passports known as ePassports. Some authorities around the world have even integrated smart cards with biometrics (Halpin, 1999). As the traveler passes through immigration, he/she must insert a card into a reader at the first gate. The information stored on the card is read and verified. Different airports around the world are using different human characteristics, varying from fingerprints, hand geometry or a combination of both. The sample taken is then matched with a record in the database and the image on the card. If there is an exact match, the passenger is allowed to travel. Such a system is being promoted by IATA and is already in use in Australia, Belgium, Canada, France, Germany, Hong Kong, Netherlands, Switzerland and Taiwan and the U.S.

CONCLUSION

Magnetic-stripe cards are now considered a mature auto-ID technique, a catalyst for the highly complex physical and logical infrastructural interconnectivity that exists in the banking sector today. While the technology itself has not undergone revolutionary changes to its make-up, simple incremental innovations have been introduced in a bid to minimize fraudulent activities, especially where credit cards are concerned (Berghel, 2007). The predicted demise of the magnetic-stripe card in the mid-to-late 1980s did not eventuate. Cost and first-to-market principles seem to have overridden any attempt for the smart card to overtake the magnetic-stripe card in market share, despite its superiority in terms of security and functionality. While magnetic-stripe card fraud continues to be a global problem for credit card companies especially, the transition to another card technology is riddled with obstacles. Namely, transitioning requires a change in physical infrastructure, a shift in consumer mindset, agreement in card standardization focused on security and interoperability, all of which seem too difficult to institute. For now at least, the industry seems complacent, willing to live with the multi-billion dollar problem of fraud rather than to make radical changes. Outside the financial sector, magnetic-stripe cards have prospered in terms of their utility, effectiveness and versatility. They have acted primarily to verify a cardholder's identity, linking an embossed number or barcode also present on the card to specific applications. While we can lay claim to the fact that we are now living in a relatively cash-*less* society, today's wallets and purses are still bulging, only now bulging with strips of plastic, rather than strips of reinforced paper.

REFERENCES

Aconite. (2006). Mag-stripe's the problem. *Card Technology Today, July/August,* 11-12.

Allard, T. (1995, 28 October). Get ready to kiss your cash goodbye. *The Sydney Morning Herald,* pp. 1, 44.

Allard, T. (1997, 10 April). Smart cards the key to a cashless society of future. *The Sydney Morning Herald,* p. 1.

ASTEC. (1986). *Towards a Cashless Society? A report to the Prime Minister.* A.C.T: Australian Government Publishing Service.

AT&T Universal MasterCard. AT&T universal card services. Retrieved 20 November 1996, from http://public.att.com/ucs/card/card.html

Australian. (1981, 4 September). The cashless society. *The Australian.*

Ayer, K., & McKenna, J. (1997). Worldwide developments and player motivations. In C. A. Allen & W. J. Barr (Eds.), *Smart Cards: Seizing Strategic Business Opportunities* (pp. 44-56). New York: McGraw-Hill.

Bank Systems. (1997). Move to chip technology still a ways off. *Bank Systems & Technology, 34*(6), 21.

Barr, W. J. (1997). Shifting boundaries. In C. A. Allen & W. J. Barr (Eds.), *Smart Cards: Seizing Strategic Business Opportunities* (pp. 57-78). New York,: McGraw-Hill.

Batterson, R. (2002). MasterCard International tests Magneprint. *Washington University in St Louis: News & Information*, from http://news-info.wustl.edu/tips/2002/business-law/indeck.html

Belsie, L. (1997). Coming soon: ATMs that Recognise your Eyes. pp. 1-2.

Bequai, A. (1980). America's cashless society: the problem of crime in the electronic society. *Journal of Media and Law Practice*(1), 154-166.

Berghel, H. (2007). Credit Card Forensics. *Communications of the ACM, 50*(12).

Blank, A. (2007). Millions of Cardholders Can't be Wrong. *Arthur Blank & Co Online*   Retrieved 28 November 2008, from http://www.arthurblank.com/article_details.asp?ID=4

Blythe, P. (1996). Global view of transport applications. *Smart Card News*, 1-7.

Blythe, P. T. (1991). *The use of transponder technology in road traffic control.* Paper presented at the Eighth International Conference on Automotive Electronics.

Blythe, P. T., & Holland, R. (1998). *Integrated ticketing smart cards in transport.* Paper presented at the IEE Colloquium: Using ITS in Public Transport and in Emergency Services

Bowne, A. (1984). Westpac leads the race to a cashless society. -Electronic funds transfer point of sale. *Business Review Weekly, 17-23 March.*

Brands, S. (1995). *Electronic cash on the Internet.* Paper presented at the IEEE Proceedings of the Symposium on Network and Distributed System Security.

Bright, R. (1988). *Smart Cards: principles, practice, applications.* New York: John Wiley & Sons.

Brooks, A. (1995). Cashless' future in the cards with UK and Canadian pilots. *Computing Canada, 21*, 33, 36.

Brown, S. F. (1998, Feb 16). Robots don't blink. *Time Magazine*, 50-52.

Browne, F. X., & Cronin, D. (1996). Payment technologies, financial innovation, and laissez-faire banking. *Cato Journal, 15*(1), 101-116.

Campbell, D. C. (Ed.). (1994). *Data Transmission and Privacy.* Canada: Martinus Nijhoff Publishers.

Card World (Ed.). (1990). *ITALY- Slowed by cultural resistance.* Surrey.

Central Banks. (1989). Payment Systems: in eleven develop countries. *Bank Administration Institute United States.*

Chan, F. (2001, 11 January). Octopus extends tentacles to taxis. *South China Morning Post*, p. 6.

Chau, P. Y. K., & Poon, S. (2003). Octopus: An E-Cash Payment System Success Story. *Communications of the ACM, 46*(9), 129-133.

Choi, M.-Y. (1995). Real-time moving automotive vehicle identification (AVIS). *Proceedings of the Intelligent Vehicles Symposium*, 241-246.

Clarke, R. (1987). Just Another Piece of Plastic for your Wallet: The 'Australia Card' Scheme Retrieved 4 December 2008, from http://www.anu.edu/people/Roger.Clarke/DV/OzCard.html

Clarke, R. (1991). The Tax File Number Scheme: A Case Study of Political Assurances and Function Creep. Retrieved 4 December 2008, from http://www.anu.edu/people/Roger.Clarke/DV/PaperTFN.html

Cohen, J. (1994). *Automatic Identification and Data Collection Systems*. London: McGraw-Hill Book Company.

Collier, I., & Hill, J. (1987, 24 September). Privacy lawyer's shock claim: I.D. card not dead. *The Sun*, p. 1.

Colton, K. W., & Kraemer, L. (1980). *Computers and banking: electronic funds transfer systems and public policy*. New York: Plenum Press.

Commonwealth Department of Health. (1987). *Towards Fairness and Equity: the Australia Card program*: Australian Government Publishing Service, Canberra.

Computergram. (1999). Late-running cashless society dependent on transport. *Computergram International*.

Conolly, C. (1995). *Smart Cards: big brother's little helpers*. Sydney.

Cooper, L. (1999). *A run on Sterling- personal finance on the move*. Paper presented at the The Third International Symposium on Wearable Computers.

Cornford, P. (1995, 25 March 1995). $100m sting forecast as gangs plan Olympic credit fraud blitz. *The Sydney Morning Herald*.

Cowen, Z. (1972). *The Private Man: the Boyer lectures 1969*. Sydney: Australian Broadcasting Commission.

Cox, R. J. (1997). Hold onto your wallet! *Information Technology & People, 11*(4), 28-31.

Crosby, L. (1994). Electronic leash: the implantable bio-chip is already here. Is Big Brother just around the corner? *Tuscon [AZ] Weekly, 11*(14).

Cross, R. (1996). Smart cards for the intelligent shopper. *Direct Marketing, 58*(12), 30-34.

Cumming, F. (1986, August). ID card's impact on fraud under fire. *Daily Telegraph*.

Cunningham, R. F. (1993). *Smart card applications in integrates transit fare, parking fee and automated toll payment systems- the MAPS concept*. Paper presented at the Telesystems Conference Commercial Applications and Dual-Use Technology 93CH3318-3.

Davies, S. (1992). *Big Brother: Australia's growing web of surveillance*. Australia: Simon and Schuster.

Davies, S. (1996). *Monitor: extinguishing privacy on the information superhighway.* Sydney: PAN Macmillan.

Davies, S. G. (1993, 22 March 1997). Campaigns of opposition to ID card schemes. *Privacy International*, from http://www.privacy.org/pi/activities/idcard/campaigns.html

Davies, S. G. (1996). Identity cards: Frequently asked questions. *Privacy International*, from http://www.privacy.org/pi/activities/idcard/idcard_faq.html

Dawes, P. (1986, 21 November). ID Card: one number will reveal all. *Sydney Morning Herald.*

de Bruyne, P. (1990). *New technologies in credit card authentication.* Paper presented at the IEEE International Carnahan Conference on Security Technology.

Dean, W. (1984, 15 February). Cashless, paperless defenceless? *The Sydney Morning Herald*, p. 9.

Dennis, S. (1998). UK professor implants chip, turns himself into Cyborg. *Newsbytes*, from http://www.newsbytes.com/pubNews/110782.html

Devereux, M. (1984). 1984 IS HERE. *The New Westralian Banker, 4*(2), 5.

Dinning, M. (1997). Transportation. In C. A. Allen & W. J. Barr (Eds.), *Smart Cards: Seizing Strategic Business Opportunities* (pp. 177-198). New York: McGraw-Hill.

Donnelly, M. (1986, 22 June). Big brother- it is closer than you think. *The Sunday Telegraph.*

Eaton, J. W. (1986). *Card-carrying Americans: privacy, security, and the national ID card debate.* New Jersey: Rowman & Littlefield Publishers.

Economist. (1995). On a card and a prayer. *Economist, 334*(7900), 60.

Egner, F. E. (1991). *The Electronic Future of Banking: succeeding in the new electronic age for tomorrow's financial institutions.* Illinois: Financial Sourcebooks.

Eltron. Plastic card printing technology. from http://www.eltron.com/Support/a-faq_card.htm

Essick, K. (1998). Biometrics, e-cash to gain ground in '98, Gartner says. *InfoWorld Electric*, 1-2.

Essinger, J. (1999). *The Virtual Banking Revolution: the customer, the bank and the future.* London: International Thomson Business Press.

European. (1993). Airport card proves the passport to freedom. *The European*, 3.

Evans, D. (1987, 12 August). Everything you wanted to know about the Australia Card... but were afraid to ask. *The Daily Mirror.*

FDIC. (2008). 6500 - FDIC Consumer Protection: PART 205—ELECTRONIC FUND TRANSFERS (REGULATION E). *FDIC Law, Regulations, Related Acts* Retrieved 28 November 2008, from http://www.fdic.gov/regulations/laws/rules/6500-3100.html

Federal Bureau of Consumer Affairs. (1995). A Cashless Society? Electronic banking and the consumer. In Federal Bureau of Consumer Affairs (Ed.). Canberra: Australian Government Publishing Service.

Federal Department of Communications and Justice. (1974). Privacy and Computers. In F. D. o. C. a. Justice (Ed.): Information Canada Ottawa.

Fernandez, B. (1997, 15 April). Bank keeps eye on iris technology. *The Australian.*

Ferrari, J., Mackinnon, R., Poh, S., & Yatawara, L. (1998). *Smart Cards: a case study*: Research Triangle Park.

Fewster, A. (1986, October). ID card: $20,000 penalty for non-compliance. *Telegraph Mirror.*

Financial. (1995). AT&T backs cashless society. *Financial Technology International Bulletin, 12*(6), 6.

Fisher, R. L. (1996). The future of money in the information age. *New Payments Technology* Retrieved 4 April 1997, from http://www.cato.org/moneyconf/14mc-10.html

Freeze, C. (2000, 21 July). Keep your credit card in sight: detective. *The Globe and Mail*, p. A5.

Gerdeman, J. D. (1995). *Radio Frequency Identification Application 2000: a guide to understanding and using radio frequency identification*. North Carolina: Research Triangle Consultants.

Geva, B. (2006). Recent International Developments in the Law of Negotiable Instruments and Payment and Settlement Systems. *Texas International Law Journal, 42*, 685-726.

Glynn, A. J. (1987, 18 September). Poor, dumb and forced to join the herd. *The Sun*, p. 17.

Godin, S. (1995). *Presenting Digital Cash*. Indiana: sams.net publishing.

Gold, D. S. (1999, April 6). Global e-purse specification revealed. *Newsbytes.*

Gold, S. (1999, 13 April). Diebold launches iris recognition ATM banking. *Newsbytes.*

Gora, B. (1992, 17 May). Fingerprint plan to beat ATM cheats. *The Telegraph Mirror.*

Graham, G. (1996, 20 August). You can bank on the Internet- for growth. *The Australian*, p. 4.

Greenfield, P. (1996). London prepares to get smart. *Professional Engineering, 9*(12), 20.

Greenleaf, G. (1988). Lessons from the Australia Card -- deux ex machina? *The Computer Law and Security Report, 3*(6), 6.

Halpin, J. (1999). Bio-Identity, *Computer Shopper* (Vol. 19, pp. 390).

Harmelink, M. D. (1993). *Smart trucking in Ontario.* Paper presented at the IEEE Vehicle Navigation & Information Systems Conference.

Harris, S. (1994, 22 May). Credit card fraud set to explode, say police. *Sunday Telegraph.*

Harrop, P. (1992). The electronic purse prepayment cards. *IEE Review, 38*(6), 227-231.

Helm, L. (1995). Cashless society gets closer with plans for electronic currency. *Los Angeles Times*, p. D4.

Hendrickson, R. (1972). *The Cashless Society*. New York: Dodd, Mead and Company.

Hendry, M. (2007). *Multi-application Smart Cards: Technology and Applications*. Cambridge: Cambridge University Press.

Hogarth, M. (1987, 30 August). Big Brother rules when your number's up. *Times on Sunday*, p. 4.

Holland, N. (2004). Through the Looking Glass. *Smart Card News* Retrieved 4 December 2008, from http://www.smartcard.co.uk/articles/through_the_looking_glass_nh.htm

Holmstrom, F. R. (1996). *Tech brief: smart fare payment systems for public transit* (No. DTS-38).

Hurry, K. (1987, 10 July). I am very angry. *The Daily Telegraph*.

Husemann, D. (1999). The smart card: don't leave home without it. *IEEE Concurrency, 7*(2), 24-27.

IATA. Airline industry smart card developments. *IATA*, from http://www.iata.org/smartcard/

IATA. (1998). Passenger Services Conference. from http://www.iata.org/smartcard/

IATA. (1999, 19 April). Airline industry ET developments. from http://www.iata.org/eticket/eticket.htm

ID-TECH. (27 November 2001). About Magnetic Stripe Technology: ID-TECH's Guide to Magnetic Encoding on Cards. from http://www.idt-net.com/magnetic/index.cfm

IPC. (2001). International Plastic Cards. 2003, from http://www.ipccards.com/developments/developments_main.htm

Johnson, L. (1996, 16 June). Iris ATM only a blink away. *The Sunday Telegraph*.

Johnstone, B. (1998, 3 May). Really smart card. *Forbes*, 198.

Joint Select Committee. (1986). Report of the Joint Select Committee on an Australia Card: Australian Government Publishing Service Canberra.

Jones, B. (1987a, 6 September). Australia Card: secret plan to push ID on you. *The Sun-Herald*, p. 1.

Jones, B. (1987b, 6 September). Hawke sets date for ID card laws. *The Sun-Herald*, p. 2.

Jones, D. (1998). Electronic Commerce in Government. *Card Technology Today, 10*(2), 13-16.

Jones, D. (2000). Mondex cards serve up beenz.com loyalty points. *Ctt, 11*(6), 4-5.

Kaplan, J. M. (1996). *Smart Cards: the global information passport- managing a successful smart card program*. London: International Thomson Computer Press.

Keir, M. (1986). On the way to a cashless society. *Technological Change: impact of information technology*, 79-88.

Keir, M. (1987). *Issues for a Cashless Society*. Retrieved. from.

Kirkmann, P. (1987). *Electronic Funds Transfer*. USA: Library Cataloguing in Publication Data.

Komanecky, M. R., & Claus, D. M. (1991, 20-23 October). *IVHS applications of smart cards*. Paper presented at the Vehicle Navigation and Information Systems Conference.

Korala, A., & Basham, P. (1999). The Self-Service Revolution: Harnessing the Power of Kiosks and ATMS. In J. Keyes (Ed.), *Banking Technology Handbook* (pp. 6-1- 6-7). London: CRC Press.

Kosmos. (1987, 17 September (in Greek)). Identity card: number or Big Brother? *O Kosmos,* pp. 20-21.

Kristoffy, A. (1999). *IEE driver information systems.* Paper presented at the Telematics Conference.

Kwok, A. (2001, 11 January). Octopus card users face having to pay taxi tip. *Hong Kong iMail,* p. A4.

LaMoreaux, R. D. (1998). *Barcodes and Other Automatic Identification Systems.* New York: Pira International.

Lasky, H. (1984). The cashless society: reality or myth? -Argument for the continued use of cash. *Law Institute Journal, 58*(10), 1206-1207.

Lockie, M. (2001). New AfB sets its sights on international status, *Biometric Technology Today* (July/August ed., Vol. 9, pp. 1,12).

London Transport. (2008). Transport for London: Oyster Online. Retrieved 28 November 2008, from https://oyster.tfl.gov.uk/oyster/entry.do

Louderback, P. D. (1980). Status of EFT: an assessment of services and a review of EFT in the fifty states. In K. W. Colton & L. Kraemer (Eds.), *Computers and banking: electronic funds transfer systems and public policy* (pp. 39-52). New York: Plenum Press.

LTA. (2008). Electronic Road Pricing: How it works? *Land Transport Authority* Retrieved 28 November 2008, from http://www.lta.gov.sg/motoring_matters/index_motoring_erp.htm

Madgwick, D., & Smythe, T. (1974). *The Invasion of Privacy.* Oxford: Pitman Publishing.

Magbar. (2000). ID Tech. from http://www.idt-net.com/products/mag_stripe/magbar.cfm

Magneprint. (1999). MISC. 2003, from http://www.magneprint.earth.wustl.edu/maneprint/

Manchester, D. (1997). Smart cards: key to cashless economy? *Futurist, 31*(1), 29-32.

Marsh, M. (1998). Is it possible to scan a supermarket trolley using RFID? *Transponder News,* pp. 1-5.

Marsh, M. (1998). Tagmaster AB - Electronic access system makes parking operations simpler and more profitable. *Transponder News,* 1-2.

Martin, B. (1997). *Challenging Bureaucratic Elites.* Wollongong: Schweik Action.

Martin, S. E. (1995). *Bits, Bytes and Big Brother: federal information control in technological age.* Westport: Praeger.

Mee, C. D., & Daniel, E. D. (1996). *Magnetic Recording Technology.* New York: McGraw-Hill Professional.

Mei, L. Y. (2001). Mastercard, the ruler of Mondex. *Cards Now Asia*(July/August), 10.

Mercury Security Corp. ANSI specification for encoding ABA track 2 data. from http://www.mercury-security.com/ansi.htm

Middleton, G. (1998). Researchers encode faces on mag-stripe cards. *TechWeb* Retrieved 4 December 2002, from http://www.techweb.com/wire/story/TWB19980907S0009

MIS. (1993). Big Brotherdom has benefits. *MIS*(December/January), 80.

Mitchell, R. (1996a). Beyond the basics of ATMs. *Credit Card Management, 9*(4), 57-62.

Mitchell, R. (1996b). The evangelist of the smart card world. *Credit Card Management, 9*(5), 52.

Moore, P. (1996, 17 September). Banks launch a money highway. *The Australian,* p. 41.

Moreira, P. (1997, 18 February). Mondex speeds up its cash card launch. *The Australian,* p. 45.

Muhammad, T. K. (1996). Toward a cashless society. *Black Enterprise, 26*(11), 58.

Mullen, D., & Sheppard, J. (1998). Magnetic stripe cards: giving 'credit' to everyone. *Automatic I.D. News,* 1-3.

Murphy, P. A. (1996). Does plastic still have a great future? *Credit Card Management, 9*(3), 80-90.

Newton, J. (1995). Reducing 'plastic' counterfeiting. *European Convention on Security and Detection, 408*, 198-201.

Nickel, L. (1999). Why use magnetic-stripe cards? *Mercury Security Corp: OEA Hardware for Access Control,* 1-2.

NSW Combined Community Legal Centres Group. (1988). *A National Identification System for Australia.* Kensington: Communications Law Centre.

O'Sullivan, O. (1997). From France, a glimpse of things to come. *ABA Banking Journal, 89*(3), 57-62.

OECD. (1989). *Electronic Funds Transfer: plastic cards and the consumer.* Paris: OECD.

Okine, N. O., & Shen, L. D. (1995). *Security issues of emerging smart cards fare collection application in mass transit.* Paper presented at the IEEE Conference on Vehicle Navigation and Information Systems.

Parliament of the Commonwealth of Australia. (1988). Feasibility of a National ID Scheme: the Tax File Number: Australian Government Publishing Service, Canberra.

PBS. (1998). Danmoent. from http://www.pbs.dk/pbs_uk/www.danmoent.dk/

Perkins, K. (1987, 18 September). ID Card- What you say. *The Sun,* p. 16.

Plastag. (1998). Products. from http://www.plastag.com/products.html

Polding, L. (1996). Credit card fraud- the good news. *Credit Control, 17*(5), 23-25.

Pope, N. G. (1990). The cashless services system. *British Telecommunications Engineering, 9*(July), 112-117.

Privacy Commissioner. (1997). *Information papers no. 3: community attitudes to privacy.*

Privacy Committee of NSW. (1995). Smart Cards: Big Brother's Little Helpers. *66*(August).

Proton. (1999). Proton Word. from http://www.protonworld.com

Radu, C. (2002). *Implementing Electronic Card Payment Systems*. New York: Artech House.

Ramo, J. C. (1998, 27 April). The big bank theory and what it says about the future of money. *Time,* 46-55.

Ransom, A. (1986, 5 December). The ID card is a fraud on the people. *The Sydney Morning Herald.*

Read, R. J. (1989). EFTPOS: electronic funds transfer at point of sale. *Electronics and Communication Engineering Journal, 1*(6), 263-270.

Reistad, D. L. (1979). Everything with electronic chips: but how close are we to the cashless society? *Asia Finance, 5.*

Revell, J. R. S. (1983). *Banking and Electronic Fund Transfers*. Paris: OECD.

Ross, D. (2003). Back on the cards [ID cards]. *IEE Review, 49*(11), 22-23.

Rothfeder, J. (1995). Invasion of privacy. *PC World, 13*(11), 152-162.

Scott, M. D. (1994). United States. In R. Campbell (Ed.), *Data transmission and privacy* (pp. 491-507). Canada: Martinus Nijhoff Publishers.

Smith, E. (1989). *The Australia Card: the story of its defeat*. Australia: Macmillan.

Smith, M. T. (1998). Smart cards: integrating for portable complexity. *Computer, 31*(8), 110-112, 115

Smith, R. (2002, 17 November). Gang to increase robberies on ATMs. *The Sunday Telegraph*, p. 3.

Smith, S. (1995). Welfare's big brother. *Computer Weekly*, 40-41.

Stewart, C. (1999). *IEE driver information systems*. Paper presented at the Telematics Conference.

Stix, G. (1994). Dr. Big Brother. *Scientific American*(February).

Stroud, J. (1998). Magnetic print foils counterfeiters technology may put halt to credit card theft (pp. 1-2): 1998 Post-Dispatch Archives.

Sun, M. (2002, 18 December). E-tags on slow road to change. *The Daily Telegraph.*

Svigals, J. (1987). *Smart Cards: the new bank cards*. New York: Macmillan Publishing Company.

SWIFT. (2008). Company Information. *SWIFT* Retrieved 28 November 2008, from http://www.swift.com/index.cfm?item_id=68432

Thompson, A. A. (1997). *Big brother in Britain Today*. New York: Joseph.

Todd, K. (1990, 15-16 October). *The introduction and performance of the "Faresaver" smart card electronic bus ticketing system*. Paper presented at the Proceedings of the AIC Conference Smart Card technology: applications for the 1990's, Sydney.

Tren, R. (1995). Trends in the Cards Industry. *Andersen Consulting*, 1-99.

Tucker, G. (1992). *Information Privacy Law in Australia*. Melbourne: Longman Cheshire.

Tyler, G. (1995). The cashless revolution. *Management Services, 39*(6), 26-27.

van Grinsven, L. (1996, 8 October). It's on the cards: Dutch will be first to get smart. *The Australian,* p. 32.

Vartanian, T. P. (1997). A cashless world. *Credit Union Management, 20*(2), 14-15.

Vincent, N. (1995, 26 August). Big brother is selling you. *The Daily Telegraph.*

VISA International. (1995). Australia First in Line for Cashless Society. Sydney: Visa International Press Release.

Wacks, R. (1993). *Privacy* (Vol. vol. 1 & 2). Sydney: Dartmouth.

Wahab, A., Tan, E. C., & Heng, S. M. (1999). Biometrics electronic purse. *IEEE TENCON: Proceedings from the Region 10 Conference, 2,* 958-961.

Walker, F. (1987, 6 September). The Australia card debate: a day in your life with an ID card. *The Sun-Herald,* pp. 10-11.

Wallis, K. (2001, 9 January). Tram fleet to adopt Octopus smart card. *Hong Kong iMail,* p. B5.

Walsh, K.-A. (1987, 24 September). I.D. card out. *The Daily Telegraph,* p. 1.

Washington University in St. Louis. The magnetics and information science center – MISC. Retrieved 4 December 2002, from http://www.misc.ee.wustl.edu/misc_intro.html

Watson, F. (2001). Overcoming global terror. *Biometric Technology Today, 9*(6), 1.

Watson, R. (2002, 8 December 2002). Detectives seize ATM theft device. *The Sunday Telegraph,* p. 2.

Watts, D. (1997, 13 May). Inadequate privacy laws open door to data abuse. *The Australian,* p. 42.

Weinstein, S. B. (1984). Smart credit cards: the answer to cashless shopping. *EEE Spectrum, 21*(2), 43-49.

Wenter, P. (1994). *Automatic fee collection on German autobahns- the ChipTicket system.* Paper presented at the IEE, Seventh International Conference on 'Road Traffic Monitoring and Control'.

Wesley, R., & Wilke, C. (1997). Travel and Entertainment. In C. A. Allen & W. J. Barr (Eds.), *Smart Cards: Seizing Strategic Business Opportunities* (pp. 199-208). New York: McGraw-Hill.

Will, I. (1983). *The Big Brother Society.* London: Harrap Limited.

Woods, W. (1995). Cashless society becomes reality. *Fortune, 131,* 24.

Wright, D., & Burton, R. (1999). Leicester environmental road tolling scheme (LERTS). *EEE Seminar, Electronic Tolling and Congestion Charging,* 4/1-4/3.

Yan, G., Paradi, J. C., & Bhargava, S. (1997). *Banking on the Internet and its applications.* Paper presented at the IEEE Proceedings of the Thirtieth Hawaii International Conference on System Sciences.

Young, J. B. (1978). *Privacy.* Toronto: John Wiley and Sons.

Zimmerman, T. (2001, August 25-29). *Travel card: airport self-check in using a wireless PDA.* Paper presented at the IEEE Intelligent Transportation Systems Conference Proceedings.

Zlatinov, I. (2001). The next generation of transit cards. *Cards Now Asia*(July/August), 35-36.

Zoreda, J. L., & Oton, J. M. (1994). *Smart Cards*. Boston: Artech House.

ENDNOTES

[1] Jones (1987a) writes on the secret Australian government plan to push ID on citizens; Walker (1987) a feature article on the Australia Card debate; Evans (1987) highlights just how invasive the Card would become interlinking all facets of life; Collier & Hill (1987) present the power of the government to introduce the ID card; Walsh (1987) on the demise of the card; Perkins (1987); Fewster (1986) on the potential ID card non-compliance penalties; Cumming (1986) on the declining support for Australia's proposed national ID card; Glynn (1987); Dawes' (1986) letter to the editor discussing how one number would reveal all; Ransom's (1986) letter to the editor alleging that the ID card is a fraud on the people; and Hurry's (1987) advertisement about the hidden clauses of the proposed Australia Card, in the interest of the community. Apart from all the media press, the government also published a number of reports on the topic of an Australia Card, for instance, Commonwealth Department of Health (1987) and Joint Select Committee (1986). A relevant research paper by Graham (1990) is on bureaucratic politics and the Australia Card as well as a NSW Combined Community Legal Centres Group (1988) submission to the Senate on a national identification system for Australia. For a short summary of the bureaucratic issues with the Australia Card see Martin et al. (1997, pp. 27-30) , and see Greenleaf (1988) for lessons from the Australia Card. For an American perspective on the national ID card debate see Eaton (1986). While an Australian citizen card did not make an appearance, a tax file number (TFN) eventually did in its place (Clarke 1991). See Hogarth (1997, p. 4); Parliament of the Commonwealth of Australia (1988) on the feasibility of a national ID scheme (i.e. the TFN); Davies (1992, ch. 3) on the government versus the people; and Clarke (1993) on why people are scared of the public sector. The media added fuel to the debate by reporting on cases that were related to social security fraud and stolen identities which caused some consumer groups to lobby against the idea of a card altogether. Yet what most consumer groups did not realize is that they were really arguing against an identity number and not the card itself. While an Australian citizen card did not make an appearance, a tax file number (TFN) eventually did in its place.

[2] For a variety of definitions on the term 'cashless society', see Hendrickson (1972), Reistad (1979), Bequai (1980), Australian (1981), Bowne (1984), Dean (1984), Lasky (1984), Weinstein (1984), ASTEC (1986), Keir (1986, 1987), Pope (1990), Brooks (1995), Helm (1995), Federal Bureau of Consumer Affairs (1995), Financial (1995), MasterCard International (1995), Tyler (1995), VISA International (1995), Woods (1995), Allard (1995; 1997), Muhammad (1996), Manchester (1997), Vartanian (1997), Computergram (1999).

[3] See Economist (1995) for the notion of "ticketless" air travel using smart card media. It should be noted that articles written before the recent spate of terrorist attacks are a little naïve in terms of how air travel can be made more convenient without the traveler having to go through so many individual checkpoints to board a plane. Compare Economist (1995) with Watson (2001b) who writes: "September's attacks added a new dimension to airline security."

Chapter VII
Smart Cards:
The Next Generation

SMART CARD TECHNOLOGY

Historical Overview

The history of the smart card begins as far back as 1968. By that time magnetic-stripe cards while not widespread, had been introduced into the market (Purdue, 2008). Momentum from these developments, together with advancements in microchip technology made the smart card a logical progression. Two German inventors, Jürgen Dethloff and Helmut Grötrupp applied for a patent to incorporate an integrated circuit into an ID card (Rankl & Effing, 1997, p. 3). This was followed by a similar patent application by Japanese academic, Professor Kunitaka Arimura in 1970. Arimura was interested in incorporating "one or more integrated circuit chips for the generation of distinguishing signals" in a plastic card (Zoreda & Oton, 1994, p. 36). His patent focused on how to embed the actual micro circuitry (Lindley, 1997, p. 13).

Smart Cards in the 1970s

In 1971 Ted Hoff from the Intel Corporation also succeeded in assembling a computer on a tiny piece of silicon (Allen & Kutler, 1997, p. 2). McCrindle (1990, p. 9) made the observation that the evolution of the smart card was made possible through two parallel product developments- the microchip and the magnetic-stripe card- that merged into one product. However, it was not until 1974 that previous chip card discoveries were consolidated. Roland Moreno's smart card patents and vision of an electronic bank manager triggered important advancements, particularly in France. In that year, Moreno successfully demonstrated his electronic payment product by simulating a transaction using an integrated circuit (IC) card. What followed for Moreno, and his company Innovatron, was a batch of patents among which was a stored-value application mounted on a ring which connected to an electronic device.

By the late 1970s the idea of a chip-in-a-card had made a big enough impression that large telecommunications firms were committing research funds towards the development of IC cards. In 1978 Siemens built a memory card around its SIKART chip which could function as an identification and transaction card. Despite early opposition to the new product it did not take long for other big players to make significant contributions to its development. In 1979 Motorola supplied Bull with a microprocessor and memory chip for the CP8 card. In July of that year Bull CP8's two-chip card was publicly demonstrated in New York at American Express. French banks were convinced that the chip card was the way of the future and called a bid for tender by the seven top manufacturers at the time: CII-HB, Dassault, Flonic-Schlumberger, IBM, Philips, Transac and Thomson. Ten French banks with the support of the Posts Ministry created the Memory Card Group in order to launch a new payment system in France. Such was the publicity generated by the group that more banks began to join in 1981, afraid they would be left behind as the new technology was trialed in Blois, Caen and Lyon. Additionally, the US government awarded a tender to Philips to supply them with IC identification cards.

Smart Cards in the 1980s

By 1983 smart cards were being trialed in the health sector to store vaccination records and to grant building access to hemodialysis patients. But it the French who recognized the potential of smart cards in the provision of telephony services. The first card payphones were installed by Flonic Schlumberger for France Telecom and were called Telecarte. By 1984 Norway had launched Telebank, Italy the Tellcard, and Germany the Eurocheque. A number of friendly alliances began between the large manufacturers who realized they could not achieve their goals in isolation. Bull signed an agreement with Motorola and Philips signed and agreement with Thomson. Meanwhile, MasterCard International and Visa International made their own plans for launching experimental applications in the United States. In 1986 Visa published the results of its collaborative trials with the Bank of America, the Royal Bank of Canada and the French CB group. The "...study show[ed] that the memory card [could] increase security and lower the costs of transactions" (Cardshow, 1996, p. 1). Visa quickly decided that the General Instrument Corporation Microelectronics Division would manufacture their smart cards. The two super smart card prototypes were supplied by Smart Card International and named Ulticard. In 1987 MasterCard decided to spend more time reviewing the card's potential and continued to conduct market research activities. Issues to do with chip card standardization between North America and Europe became increasingly important as more widespread diffusion occurred.

Smart Cards in the 1990s

The 1990s was a period characterized by the 'microprocessor explosion'. Smart cards became a part of that new interest in wearable computing- computer power that was not only cheap and small, but was always with you (Cook, 1997, p. xi). The progress toward the idea of ubiquitous computing is quite difficult to fathom when one considers that the credit-card sized smart card possesses more computing power than the 1945 ENIAC computer which: *"...weighed 30 tones, covered 1500 square feet of floor space, used over 17000 vacuum tubes... 70000 resistors, 10000 capacitors, 1500 relays, and 6000 manual switches, consumed 174000 W of power, and cost about $500000"* (Martin, 1995, p. 3f). Today's smart card user is capable of carrying a 'mental giant' in the palm of their hand. Smart cards can now be used as payment vehicles, access keys, information managers, marketing tools and customized delivery systems (Allen & Kutler, 1997, pp. 10-11).

Many large multinational companies have supported smart card technology because the benefits are manifold over other technologies. It was projected that by the year 2000, an estimated volume of smart-card related transactions would exceed twenty billion annually (Kaplan, 1996, p. 10). Michael Ugon, a founding father of smart card, said in 1989 that the small piece of plastic with an embedded chip was destined to "...invade our everyday life in the coming years, carrying vast economical stakes" (Ugon, 1989, p. 4). McCrindle (1990, p. ii) likewise commented that the smart card "...ha[d] all the qualities to become one of the biggest commercial products in quantity terms this decade". And the French in 1997 were still steadily pursuing their dream of a smart city, "...a vision made real by cards that [could] replace cash and hold personal information (Amdur, 1997, p. 3). Currently, while there is a movement by the market to espouse smart card technology, numerous countries and companies continue to use magnetic-stripe cards. However, the vision for smart card now looks achievable, as some countries have vastly upgraded their payment systems (e.g. Singapore and Hong Kong). For a specific history of smart card in Russia see Travin (2008).

The Smart Card System

When considering which type of smart card technology to implement for a given service, buyers need to think about their requirements. What is paramount is that there must be a logical fit from the cardholder's point of view (Hendry, 2007, p. 219). Major issues which need to be resolved include: card type, interface method, storage capacity, card operating functions, standards compliance, compatibility issues and reader interoperability, security features, chip manufacturers, card reliability and life expectancy, card material and quantity and cost.

Memory, Microprocessor Cards and Super Smart Cards

As Lindley (1997, p. 15f) pointed out there is generally a lack of agreement on how to define smart card. This can probably be attributed to the differences not only in functionality but also in the price of various types of smart cards. According to Rankl and Effing (1997, pp. 12-14) smart cards can be divided into two groups: memory cards and microprocessor cards. In a memory card there is a memory chip, and in a microprocessor card there is a microcontroller chip. Processor cards which are more sophisticated can be further classified into processor cards with or without coprocessors for executing asymmetric cryptographic algorithms such as RSA (Rivest, Shamir and Adleman). There are also 'super smart cards' which have displays and a keypad directly available to the user, many of which were prototyped to market electronic wallets and purses of the future (Rankl, 2007, p. 2). Ferrari et al. (1998), dedicate a whole chapter to the card selection process in their IBM Redbook (ch. 4).

As described by Allen and Kutler (1997, p. 4) memory cards are: "...primarily information storage cards that contain stored value which the user can "spend" in a pay phone, retail, vending, or related transaction." Memory cards are less flexible than microprocessor cards because they possess simpler security logic. Only basic coding can be carried out on the more advanced memory cards. However, what makes them particularly attractive is their low cost per unit to manufacture, hence their widespread use in pre-paid telephone and health insurance cards (M'Chirgui, 2005). According to Hendry (2007, p. 17) an external application views a memory card as a data storage device with a limited range of functions. Today, wired-logic cards are much more common in which access is protected via a security protocol, either using encryption or a password. Memory cards are still highly marketable for mass market applications such as in transport applications (Blythe, 2000). For example NXP's MiFare™ divides memory into sectors and fields, with each sector having separate access permissions (Figure 1).

Figure 1. A commuter boards a bus and pays for her ticket using a MiFare contactless card. NXP have sold over 1 billion MiFare cards and 7 million readers and terminals around the world. Courtesy of NXP Semiconductors.

The other type of smart card, the microprocessor card is defined by the International Standards Organization (ISO) and the International Electronic Commission (IEC), as any card that contains a semiconductor chip and conforms to ISO standards (Hegenbarth, 1990, p. 3). The microprocessor actually contains a central processing unit (CPU) which "...stores and secures information and makes decisions, as required by the card issuer's specific application needs. Because intelligent cards offer a read/write capability, new information can be added and processed" (Allen & Kutler, 1997, p. 4). The CPU is surrounded by four additional functional blocks: read only memory (ROM), electrical erasable programmable ROM (known as EEPROM), random access memory (RAM) and the input/output (I/O) port. The Smart Card Forum Committee (1997, p. 237) outlines that the card is: *"...capable of performing calculations, processing data, executing encryption algorithms, and managing data files. It is really a small computer that requires all aspects of software development. It comes with a Card Operating System (COS) and various card vendors offer Application Programming Interface (API) tools."*

One further variation to note is that microprocessor cards can be contact, contactless (passive or active) or a combination of both (Petri, 1999). Thus users carrying contactless cards need not insert their card in a reader device but simply carry them in their purse or pocket. While the contactless card is not as established as the contact card it has revolutionized the way users carry out their transactions and perceive the technology. Rankl and Effing (1997, pp. 40-60) provide an exhaustive discussion on different types of microcontroller cards.

Card Formats

Smart card dimensions are typically 85.6 mm by 54 mm. The standard format 'ID-1' stipulated in ISO 7810 was first created in 1985 for magnetic-stripe cards. As smart cards became more popular, ISO made allowances for the microchip to be included in the standard. The standard size in the magnetic-stripe and smart cards gave way to the possibility of card migration. Smaller smart cards have been designed for special applications such as GSM handsets; these are ID-000 format known as the 'plug-in' card and ID-00 known as the 'mini-card' (Rankl & Effing, 1997, p. 21). It is important to note, that while smart cards come in numerous formats, the common feature is their thickness which is 0.76 mm. For a discussion on form factors of smart cards see Hendry (2007, pp. 54-56).

More recently mini-cards have been marketed and issued by companies such as VISA. The mini-card is almost half the size of a standard credit card at only 40 mm by 66 mm. It is considered a "companion card" to a normal full sized VISA card. The card contained a perforated hole at the bottom left corner so that it can easily be attached to a key chain, mobile phone, or other carry-along device. When the VISA Mini was launched in Australia during breakfast television programs, it was modeled fastened to a chain around the neck of young adults, who claimed it would increase their mobility. On their web site VISA (2008) have stated: *"[w]hether you are going out for lunch with colleagues or friends, shopping at your neighborhood store, clubbing or dancing, on vacation or even when you are out for a jog! Visa Mini is the answer to your demand for increased convenience and mobility in your everyday life."*

Card Elements

Several different types of materials are used to produce smart cards (Haghiri & Tarantino, 2002). The first well-known material (also used for magnetic-stripe cards) is PVC (polyvinyl chloride). PVC smart cards however, were noticeably non-resistant to extreme temperature changes, so ABS (acrylonitrile-butadiene-styrol) material has been used for smart cards for some time. PVC cards have been known to melt in climates that reach consistent temperature of 30 degrees Celsius. For instance, when the ERP system was launched in Singapore in 1998 a lot of people complained that melting smart cards had destroyed their card readers. Among the group who reported the most complaints to local newspapers were taxi drivers, who were driving for long periods of time. Similarly card errors often occur to mobile handsets that have been left in high temperatures. PET (polyethylene terephthalate) and PC (polycarbonate) are other materials also used in the production of smart cards.

The two most common techniques for mounting a chip on the plastic foil is the TAB technique (tape automated bonding) and the wire bond technique. The former is a more expensive technique but is considered to have a stronger chip connection and a flatter finish; the latter is more economical because it uses similar processes to that of the semiconductor industry for packaging strips but is thicker in appearance. New processes were developed in the mid 1990s that allowed a card to be manufactured in a single process. Rankl and Effing (1997, p. 40) explain, "[a] printed foil, the chip module and a label are inserted automatically into a form, and injected in one go".

Multiapplication and Multifunction Cards

Most smart cards have a single function only. They are issued by a company to a customer for a specific purpose. For example, the first smart card payphone cards were used to make phone calls alone. The customer loaded the card up with money, made a telephone call, and the telephone operator charged the usage amount to the card. Multifunctionality should not be confused with multiapplication cards. Several functions on a smart card might include not only say a function to lend books out from a library, but also stored value for photocopying requirements and proof of identification of the person lending the books. The functions can be card-based (i.e. on board) or server-based via host and database.

Hendry (2007, p. 13) makes the distinction that a multiapplication card is one where several programs have been placed in the card's memory. These applications can share data within the card, although this is not what usually occurs in practice. Often, a specific application is owned by separate entities, and cardholders need to select which application they wish to use during a given transaction, if it is not readily apparent to the terminal.

Operating Systems

Smart card operating systems can be classified into native operating systems (e.g. using machine language) and interpreter-based operating systems (e.g. Java) (Hansmann et al., 2002). The principal task of operating systems is managing files (Rankl, 2007, p. 11). Where there is more than one application present on the smart card, a multi-application operating system is also present. According to Hendry (2007), such an operating system has to perform application protection, memory management, application downloading and updating. Well-known operating systems include Multos (originally developed by Mondex International), IBM's MFC, Advantis (which follows GlobalPlatform's JAVA architecture) and SECCOS (Secure Chip Card Operating System).

Interface, Readers and Terminals

Contact vs. Contactless Cards

In contact smart cards, a power supply requires to have physical contact for data transfer. The tiny gold-plated 6-8 contacts are defined in ISO 7816-2. As a rule, if a contact smart card contains a magnetic-stripe, the contacts and the stripe must never appear on the same side. Each contact plays an important role. Two of the eight contacts have been reserved (C4 and C8) for future functions but the rest serve purposes such as supply voltage (C1), reset (C2), clock (C3), mass (C5), external voltage for programming (C6), and I/O (C7). Contactless smart cards on the other hand work on the same technical principles that animal transponder implants do. For simple solutions the card only needs to be read so that transmission can be carried out by frequency modulation.

Contactless solutions are becoming increasingly popular for ticketing applications due to the convenience factor. Commuters do not have to stop and queue to wait for "contacts" to read the card, they just go about their normal business and payment takes care of itself, after initialization of the ticket type (e.g. one journey, weekly or monthly). The International Standards Organization (ISO) has standardized the technologies used in contactless smart cards. The relevant standards are ISO14443 for proximity cards and ISO15693 for vicinity cards. ISO14443 is divided into four parts defining different aspects of the interface including physical characteristics, radio-frequency power and signal interface, initialization and anticollision, and transmission protocol. In simple terms, the microchip on a contactless card communicates with the card reader through RFID induction technology. Typically the read range needs to be not more than 10 cm to avoid charging other commuters accidentally. They are often used when transactions must be processed quickly or hands-free, such as on mass transit systems, where smart cards can be used without even removing them from a wallet (Trapanier, Tranchant & Chapleau, 2007).

Readers

A device that reads a smart card is known as a card accepting device (CAD) as it does not only read information from the card but also can write to it. Most smart card readers are embedded in larger terminal devices and usually follow application standards such as EMV (JCB Co, MasterCard and VISA), GSM or Calypso (Hendry, 2007, p. 22). Readers can either be insertion readers or motorized readers, the difference being how cardholders interact with the reader and the cost. Insertion readers are more privy to damage while motorized readers usually incorporate a shutter so they cannot be tampered with. Motorized readers slowly draw the card into the reader device, whereas insertion readers expect the cardholder to swipe the card through the contact points manually. This might lead to several read attempts if the cardholder does not know which way to face the card to be read properly etc.

Terminals

Terminals can take on various forms depending on where they are being utilized and for what purpose. For example, you can find smart card terminals at the point of sale (POS), in vending machines, kiosks, PC-connected readers, even personal smart-card readers. In the retail sector, the same terminal can be used to read multiple smart card applications. For example the same device can allow a consumer to purchase goods at the checkout, for an employee to log on to a cash register, even to grant customers loyalty points. The trend increasingly is toward self-service devices that cater for the needs of the individual, such as in the case of home banking applications.

Standards and Security

Similarly to magnetic-stripe technology, the most common method of user identification in smart cards is the personal identification number (PIN). The PIN is usually four digits in length (even though ISO 9564-1 recommends up to twelve characters), and is compared with the reference number in the card. The result of the comparison is then sent to the terminal which triggers a transaction- accept or reject. Additional to the PIN is a password which is stored in a file on the card and is transparently verified by the terminal. While the magnetic-stripe card relies solely on the PIN, smart card security is implemented at numerous hierarchical levels (Ferrari et al., 1998, pp. 11f).

There are technical options for chip hardware (passive and active protective mechanisms), and software and application-specific protective mechanisms. With all these types of protection against a breach of security, logical and physical attacks are said to be almost impossible (Rankl & Effing, 1997, pp. 261-272). The encryption in smart cards is so much more sophisticated than that of the magnetic-stripe. Crypto-algorithms can be built into smart cards that ensure both secrecy of information and authenticity. However, contactless cards are considered more susceptible to the breakage of keys than contact-only cards. External security features that can be added to the card include: signature strip, embossing, watermarks, holograms, biometrics, microscript, multiple laser image (MLI) and lasergravure (Figure 2). While the smart card is a secure auto-ID technology it has been proven in some instances that the device is still susceptible to damage, loss and theft without the reliance on expensive equipment. This has led to biometrics being stored on the smart card for additional security purposes. Thus we can say that while smart-card security is steadily advancing, at the same time "the range of attacks available to the determined attacker grows continuously wider" (Hendry, 2007, p. 230). What seems to be the consensus view is that even if a card is actually penetrated by an attacker, the wider systems the card is used to link to must remain secure.

THE SMART CARD INNOVATION SYSTEM

Social Specialization of Labor

The fundamental difference between the smart card and magnetic-stripe card is the on-board intelligence. Yet while the smart card is a far more sophisticated technology it does not mean it should be

Figure 2. An employee logs onto his company's intranet using his employee ID badge. The badge contains a microchip, some personal details, and a photograph for the purposes of corporate security. The employee logs on by placing his index finger on the biometric reader, and the data gathered from that transaction is compared against the information stored on the smart card. Access is granted if a match is found, and denied if there is no match. Courtesy of NXP Semiconductors.

considered superior *per se*. Chadwick (1999, pp. 142-143) for instance, asserts that smart cards are not always the smart choice. Since the smart card's invention, the microchip has acted to boost the profile of the device. The ultimate vision for the card has been that of a 'PC in your pocket', i.e., a mobile PC. Shogase (1988) coined the term 'plastic pocket bank'. He worked for the Toshiba Corporation while they were developing the VISA SuperSmart Card. Although the card did not achieve expected diffusion rates in places like North America in the mid 1980s, entrepreneurs did not abandon it (especially in Europe). In the late 1980s, Bright (1988, ch. 8) wrote that France and Japan were leading the way followed by the U.S. Today, this geographic concentration still exists but other markets, particularly in Asia are starting to make an impact on the smart card industry, such as Hong Kong, Taiwan, Singapore, and China (McKenna & Ayer, 1997, ch. 3).

The Smart Card Stakeholders

Throughout the 1990s smart card gave rise to a new breed of start-up companies that were eager to exploit opportunities as they arose. The excitement even attracted some traditional magnetic-stripe card manufacturers. This was especially true of the system integration specialists who now had the job to build systems that could "talk" to each other (Ferrari, 1998, ch. 13). Not all auto-ID system integration companies were up to the task however, acquiring smart card knowledge required employee retooling and training (Keenan, 1997, p. 35f). With these new start-up companies came new knowledge and also the delineation of niche areas of expertise. Hendry (1997, p. 250) suggests a T-shaped knowledge base in a smart card organization where there are many people who have a top-level understanding of the technology while a few people need to develop detailed knowledge. These companies included: integrated circuit (IC) manufacturers, smart card manufacturers, terminal manufacturers, smart card integrators, smart card software specialists (operating systems, applications and access) and numerous other third parties.

Gathering Project Requirements

Smart card product development was unlike traditional technologies. Part of the difficulties with smart card, besides the fact that it was a relatively new high-technology is that most often project requirements were ill-defined, and they kept shifting throughout the lifetime of the project. Timeframes for each phase of development were hard to estimate along with costs and exactly what resources were required and when. Coordinating efforts between various suppliers was also problematic. In addition smart cards were privy to high rates of technical change and higher levels of uncertainty than other technologies (Fruin, 1998, pp. 241-249).

With so many individual stakeholders, many of whom were extremely specialized, designing an end-to-end smart card solution was a complicated task (Slawsky & Zahar, 2005; Davis & Mitchell, 1996). Some of the more complex issues are: *"[h]ow can smart cards include multiple brand logos without confusing the consumer? Who is liable for lost and/or stolen cards and how are they replaced? Who provides customer service and how is it made seamless to the consumer? How are applications developed, certified, installed, and upgraded? How are privacy, accuracy, and security insured? How are revenues shared?"* (Allen & Kutler, 1997, p. 12f; Ferrari et al., 1998, ch. 12; Barr et al., 1997, pp. 64-68). Fruin (1998, p. 248) summarizes developing smart card technology as "[h]ighly problematic, fraught with technical, organizational, managerial, and human resource difficulties". Hendry (2007, p. 219) describes the difficulties associated with the implementation of smart card and emphasizes the importance of using a roadmap to help answer questions at each stage.

Utilizing Limited Human Resources

Apart from the few large smart card manufacturers, the other technology providers were usually small in size and had limited resources (Dreifus & Monk, 1998, pp. 305-314). Departments within the company had to be agile and customer-oriented but also forward-looking in terms of building generic hardware and reusable software. It is not always easy to mobilize resources in companies whose core products are applicable to more than just one high technology. For instance, in the case of integrated circuit suppliers, smart cards are only one technology among many that they are supplying. It is the same in the case of ISVs (Independent Software Vendors) who may be developing software for not only smart card players but also Internet-centric applications etc. It can be a dangerous proposition to freeze resources on a product-by-product basis but a fine balance needs to be struck between the two possible extremes.

Partnering

At the same time smart card component suppliers were also dependent on one another, particularly because no one vendor could provide the whole solution without relying on contributions from smaller players (Lindley, 1998, p. 87). In the VISA SuperSmart card development, Fruin (1998, p. 243) observed that "[n]either Toshiba nor Yanagicho boasted the complex and precise component-design, system-development, and product/process capabilities required for the project. A need for these forced Yanagicho to forge alliances with other Toshiba units and outside vendors." In addition, one company may have the capabilities to do a particular part of the design process but the sheer magnitude of the project may not afford the time to complete tasks in-house, or there are other firms that have certain core competencies that would do that particular phase more economically.

When several organizations are working together to ensure that a service is available to a customer, it is important that the organizations are working to a common schedule. So many times the media has reported vendors of technology have let down their customers. Multiple vendors working together may have had four-fifths of a given solution ready but missing a vital component that ensures the ability to 'go-live' on a project. According to Hendry (2007, p. 220) priorities and decision-making processes need to be aligned and the choice of partners should not limiting in any way.

Firm-to-Firm Collaboration

Firm-to-firm collaboration between smart card companies continued to proliferate particularly in Europe (Allen & Kutler, 1997, p. 20; Cagliostro, 1999), even though the North American market was still struggling. Cortese (1997) also reported how the smart card market was poised to grow in the U.S. The establishment of the Smart Card Forum (SCF, 2002) in 1993 was an attempt to bring stakeholders even closer together. Citicorp, Bellcore, and the U.S Treasury Financial Management Services Division were integral to the formation of the Forum attracting business leaders from the public and private sector to share a common smart card vision. By the end of 1997, the Forum boasted 230 corporate and government international entities (Allen & Barr, 1997, pp. 268-273). The common goals of SCF included the:

- Promotion of the interoperability of cards, devices, and systems to assure an open market capable of rapid growth
- Facilitation of information exchange, communications, and relationship development across industries in order to stimulate market trials
- Service as a resource to policy makers, regulatory bodies, and consumer groups on issues impacting smart cards, especially in the areas of social responsibility and privacy (Allen & Barr, 1997, p. 266).

Working groups and cross-industry committees were subsequently set up to brainstorm on issues specific to applications. The results of the studies are routinely published in white papers, standards and delivered at industry presentations. Similar forums have begun to sprout throughout the globe. For example, the Asia Pacific Smart Card Forum (APSCF) based in Australia was established in 1995 and had over fifty members in 2001. APSCF not only brought firms with common interests together but also promoted the interests of members to key policy makers at both the political and bureaucratic level of government (APSCF, 2000). The Forum does not exist in its original form, although there are now a number of smart-card related e-governance forums online. There is also the Asia Pacific Smart Card Association (APSCA, 2008) which is active in China, Singapore, Hong Kong, Taiwan, Japan, Korea, Malaysia and Thailand who may not have a large count of members, but boast memberships from the larger organizations such as Chunghwa Telecom Laboratories, Gemalto, IBM, Sony, Unisys, and Zebra.

Geographic Clustering

A pattern soon began to emerge linking the success of the smart card technology provider to its physical proximity to the customer. Lindley (1997, p. 88) also noted this stating that there was globally "...a strong correlation between the incidence of local suppliers and smart card application users." In an effort to increase their revenues, European and Asian suppliers entered the US market, establishing a local presence in the hope that this would result in sales. Some of these smart card suppliers in the US believe that a smart card manufacturing group should be established in Silicon Valley: "[a] group such as this is needed to provide a road map, if you like, and a vision for the industry over the next decade." Townend believed that the full spectrum of industry should participate in the group (McIntosh, 1997, p. 45) in order for greater collaboration to take place between firms and also as a central location to be able to demonstrate the full potential of smart card to prospective customers.

Private Enterprise and University: Forging New Links

As a result of geographic clustering very useful relationships began to form between private enterprise and local university research institutes. Not only was this a mechanism to perform useful collaborative research and development but it was also a way to attract skilled talent into the industry. Big smart card players like Schlumberger continued to fund and support initiatives particularly during the 1990s. The University of Michigan's Centre for Information Technology Integration (CITI) is just one example. In late 1999 it formed a partnership with Schlumberger to develop the world's smallest web server to run on a smart card (Media, 1999; University of Michigan, 1999). Prior to that CITI was investigating the future possibilities of the U-M card, the university's campus smart card, supplied by Schlumberger. Both groups believed that the partnership would be mutually beneficial in the long term. At the University of Malaga the GISUM group was also researching smart card in 2002 (GISUM). The work was being supported by the European Union (EU) and the Spanish Ministry of Science. Two projects are of interest here- the eTicket project and the electronic forms framework for citizen-to-government (C2G) Internet-based transactions. Some collaboration between universities and enterprises, have resulted in university campus space being dedicated to technology parks/centers. For instance, the Smart Card Design Centre (SMDC, 2002) was operated as a business unit, housed within the City University of Hong Kong. The Smart Card Design Centre was funded by the Innovation and Technology Commission and the Hong Kong Government.

Consortiums and Alliances

The late 1990s saw a trend towards the formation of consortia and strategic alliances. Consortiums in high-tech typically pool together specialist resources from private enterprise, universities and other institutes, usually in anticipation of a new opportunity. As opposed to collaborative research on a specific topic that seeks to satisfy particular outcomes, a consortium's scope is broader and usually more exploratory in response to a government or prospective large customer initiative. An example of this is the VerifiCard project in Europe which had six partners from four different countries, though it is not unusual to find consortiums with twenty partners containing mostly private companies. The VerifiCard project included: the University of Nijmegen (Netherlands), INRIA (France), Technical University of Munich (Germany), University of Kaiserslautern (Germany), Swedish Institute of Computer Science (Sweden) and SchlumbergerSema (France) (Partners, 2002). Most consortia usually have at least one or two big players that influence the direction of the rest of the group. It is also not unusual to find fierce competitors come together in consortiums, although typically this is avoided in overly competitive scenarios whereby separate consortia form.

Traditional players in auto-ID applications have especially sought to form alliances with providers of infrastructure, including banks, financial services, and telecommunications companies (Allen &

Kutler, 1997, p. 16; Keenan, 1997, p. 37; Tam & Ho, 2007). Smart card business developers have identified new creative possibilities, piggybacking on the success of existing applications but in many cases the market response from users and merchants has been uncertain. For instance, there is the possibility for telecommunications operators to be earning revenues from public payphones capable of acting as cashless de facto ATMs or consumers being able to add vending machine purchase charges to their mobile phone bill or even CATV companies making use of set-top boxes to give subscribers online services on-demand. All these ideas sound very useful but in addition to the possibility of very slow take-up rates, deployment can be very tricky as well.

Independent software vendors (ISVs) specializing in smart card can build what look to be cutting-edge applications but without the access infrastructure (fixed or wireless), it is impossible to proceed. Hendry (1997, p. 250) makes the important observation that while individual applications can be built in a very short time frame (especially for closed systems), it can take two to three years for a national infrastructure to support the application to emerge and even five to ten years for a global one. Hendry's analysis is precise: "[g]etting the infrastructure right, and making it easy to upgrade and add applications, should… be a top priority for any scheme." In the same way telecommunication operators may wish to deploy state-of-the-art applications but how to collect revenues from subscribers (i.e. billing issues) and how to share profits between the players in the value chain may be fuzzy.

Alliances also act to curb the threats from non-traditional new entrants that may know little about the smart card business but have the venture capital to invest. With the rise of the dot.coms, non-traditional players especially entered the banking and telecommunication sectors hoping to make a lot of money from online applications. Many of these companies were attracted by the inflated revenue forecasts that were being predicted by analysts so the whole business case was built on shaky foundations from the outset. There was little in the form of user surveys granting valuable feedback, and unfortunately millions of dollars have been wasted during this time on 'get rich quick' schemes. Kaplan (1996, ch. 4) has identified successes and failures in the smart card industry pre-1996. He provides a good example in the Smart Card International experience (Kaplan, 1996, p. 22). The company assembled worldwide licensing rights but it was unable to distribute its product because it had no strategic alliances with other companies to assist with reselling locally, e.g. the Global Chipcard Alliance.

Communicating Information

With smart card development innately encouraging so many interactions between stakeholders it is no surprise that so much literature has been published on the topic. The distribution of information has acted to continually educate all the various stakeholders, including users, about smart cards and their applications. Today users are a lot more technically astute than they used to be. The PC, cable television, game play-stations, Internet and mobile phone, and more recently the personal digital assistant (PDA) and internet POD (iPOD) have all contributed to a more technology-savvy society. In some ways the permeation of so much information may have been one reason why some users have resisted the change (Lindley, 1998, pp. 144-145; Keenan, 1997, pp. 26-34). The Internet has played an important role in granting people access to information that was otherwise in hard-copy form in limited locations, such as public libraries.

Today there are daily reports on worldwide smart card activities. Apart from the numerous web sites like SCN (1999) there are a number of industry magazines dedicated to smart cards is indicative of the general growth of the auto-ID industry over the years. Some of the more prominent journals include:

Card Technology, Cards&Payments, Card Technology Today (now CTT), *Report on Smart Cards, Smart Card and Systems Weekly, Smart Card Monthly, Smart Card News* and *Smart Cards and Comments.* There is an explicit knowledge infrastructure that has grown with the industry.

Industry associations are also contributing to smart card growth, like the Smart Card Industry Association (SCIA) that was established in 1989. SCIA acts as a resource centre and is also involved in organizing conferences and other industry events. SCIA's primary purpose is educational in nature. SCIA represents smart card technology providers. Other institutions include the SmartCard Developers Association, the International Card Manufacturers Association (ICMA) and the Smart Card Club, Card Europe. The latter association which tries to promote user confidence in smart cards believe (Kaplan, 1996, p. 318): *"...that only by achieving consensus across both industry and country borders, [they]... will be able to achieve a true representative set of products and standards leading to full interoperability with a multi-service capability..."*

The Importance of ISO

According to ISO, "[s]tandards are documented agreements containing technical specifications or other precise criteria to be used consistently as rules, guidelines, or definitions of characteristics, to ensure that materials, products, processes and services are fit for their purpose" (Dreifus & Monk, 1998, p. 29). It is not difficult to see why standards play such an important role in smart card development. Without them there would be no common point of reference for any of the stakeholders to follow. ISO is a worldwide federation of national standards bodies which has worked towards ways of making cards and equipment interoperable (ISO, 2008). Adherence to ISO standards is not compulsory but it is advisable.

Unlike magnetic-stripe cards where proprietary schemes could possibly increase the security of applications in particular scenarios, smart cards have in-built security features and standardization is almost always desirable (Mayes & Markantonakis, 2008). In the case of magnetic-stripe card technology, it was no coincidence that ISO 7810 was composed, "rather [it was] the close cooperation among major providers that established global standards and specifications" (Kaplan, 1996, p. 210). Early smart card developers adopted existing magnetic-stripe standards initially in order to allow a smooth migration from magnetic-stripe. Today all three technologies can be utilized on the same card- "the information... can be accessed by reading the chip, swiping the magnetic stripe, or making an imprint from the embossing" (Dreifus & Monk, 1998, p. 31).

Other important ISO standards that influenced the rise of smart cards were ISO 7816 which defines ICCs (Integrated Circuit Cards) with contacts and ISO 10536 which defines contactless ICCs (Jacquinot Consulting, 2008). ISO 7816 contains seven parts stipulating guides to physical characteristics, dimensions and locations of the contacts, electrical signals and transmission protocols, inter-industry commands, application identifiers and data elements for interchange. Suppliers should be ISO 7816 or ISO 10536 compliant even though adhering to ISO standards does not ensure that interoperability is achieved between cards and terminal equipment. ISO leaves room for industry-level specifications but when none exist mismatches can happen (McKenna & Ayer, 1997, p. 48). Hendry (1997, pp. 253-258) provides a complete list and description of ISO standards as related to smart cards. Ferrari et al. (1998, ch. 3) also discusses standards and specifications, especially ISO 7816, CEN726 (the ETSI version), GSM, EMV (MULTOS), PC/SC, the OpenCard framework, IATA Resolution 791, SEIS (Secured Electronic Information in Society), Cryptoki, CDSA (Common Data Security Architecture), PC/SC Workgroup, and MASSC a generic architecture for multiapplication smart cards.

Specifications

As has already been mentioned ISO ICC standards are not so constraining that there is no room for industry-specific standards. Thus in some cases additional specifications need to be drawn. In late 1993, Europay, MasterCard and Visa took the initiative to join forces as EMV to formulate ICC Specifications for Payment Services. As Kaplan (1996, p. 214) explains, the EMV cooperation was the pooling of expertise for a common goal. The objective was, *"to eventually permit interoperability among chip-based payment cards for credit and debit applications [Figure 3]. Without common technical standards, an array of incompatible systems would proliferate- building serious barriers to both consumer and merchant acceptance" (Allen & Kutler, 1997, p. 8).* Dreifus and Monk (1998, p. 42) notice that the development of the EMV specification followed a series of evolutionary steps. The EMV specifications were delivered in three parts each focusing on a different set of issues. EMV-1 described the smart card and its environment, EMV-2 described the terminal environment and EMV-3 described how data would be exchanged between the card and the terminal.

EMVCo was established by the EMV alliance in 1999 to administer EMV standards for debit/credit cards. The newer CEC (Chip Electronic Commerce) and the existing SET (Secure Electronic Transaction) was combined in the EMV specification (Jones, 2000; EMVCo, 2003; SET, 2000). It also should be noted that e-purse standards emerged (not in competition to EMV but at another layer of detail) called CEPS (Common Electronic Purse Specifications) and TAPA (Terminal Architecture for PSAM Applications), i.e. PSAM standing for Purchase Secure Application Modules. "The PSAM is a device that performs security functions during an electronic purse purchase transaction. TAPA provides a structure for terminals that can process single or multiple applications" (Jones, 2000). In 2002, MasterCard acquired Europay and in 2004, JCB International joined EMVCo alongside MasterCard and VISA. An important lesson learnt from the development of the EMV specification is (Allen & Kutler, 1997, p. 12): "that progress... requires collective discussion, and action. No one company can optimize smart cards unilaterally, and even industry-wide coordination through, say, a banking or retailing association, will fall short of the mark."

Figure 3. A customer pays for her meal using a MasterCard contact smart-card. MasterCard is one of the three companies responsible for the EMV specification. Courtesy of NXP Semiconductors.

Just like EMV, ETSI (European Telecommunications Standard Institute) decided to formulate an industry specification in the 1980s for its proposed Global Systems for Mobile (GSM) network. The specification, known as SIM (Subscriber Identity Module) is predominantly used in Europe and Asia. The SIM has the functionality to perform authentication and offer a personalized service to subscribers. GSM offers international compatibility and allows for the subscriber to roam in any country where there is GSM coverage. GSM specifications include: security aspects (02.09), SIM (02.17), network functions (03.20) and SIM interface (11.11). When designing smart card solutions different levels of standards need to be adhered to dependent on the application. These levels may pertain to the physical card itself, the contact pads, the card reader, the interface, the Application Programming Interface (API), the application itself, even card management. Standards and specifications can change and/ or evolve. According to Dreifus and Monk (1998, p. 46) changes in standards are "…a result of the natural evolution and the maturation of the technology".

Legal, Regulatory and Policy Issues

Regulation E and Stored Value Cards (SVCs)

In 1987 Svigals (p. xviii) noticed that the national governments of Japan and France were beginning to implement government policies and actions relating to smart cards. Twenty years later the rise of smart card schemes in operation has brought the question of regulation into the spotlight. This is not necessarily a bad thing for the industry; some experts see it as an evolutionary step in the life-cycle of smart cards. Barr et al. (1997, p. 69) believe that a technology such as smart card is becoming commercially significant when lawyers and regulators begin to study the legal, regulatory and policy implications. From about the late 1990s discussion about Regulation E has increased. "Regulation E was promulgated by the Federal Reserve Board as the implementing regulation for the Electronic Fund Transfer Act of 1978. It is designed to protect consumers and defines the right and obligations of consumers and 'financial institutions' with respect to electronic transaction affecting consumer accounts" (Barr et al., 1997, p. 70). In the past it has been easier to identify smart card applications that require financial transactions to be performed and need appropriate regulations, but with the introduction of multiapplication smart cards this defining line has blurred. According to Barr et al. (1997, p. 78), the following issues need to be considered: *"is the issuer of a SVC going to be treated as a bank for federal or state purposes; will there be export control restrictions because of the encryption used in the smart cards; and how will general commercial law principles which have evolved in connection with old-style payment systems apply to smart card."*

Financial institutions are no longer banks, building societies and credit unions; they can be anything from telecommunications companies to airlines, it all depends on the services being offered. The Federal Reserve board believes "that if cards are used to access an account" they are subject to Regulation E (Noe, 1995, p. 44). Thus, the Board has issued proposed changes to Regulation E and how it should be applied to stored value cards (SVCs). Owens and Onyshko (1996) provide a comprehensive discussion on regulations, legal and privacy issues as they relate to credit cards, debit cards and SVCs. One industry spokesman, the president of Cash Station Incorporated, James Hayes, does not think that Regulation E should be imposed on SVCs. Hayes rather compares SVCs to cash equivalents rather than customer transaction accounts. He believes that smart card "development will be impeded by regulation imposed before the purpose, risks and benefits can be clearly assessed... [he] cautioned that smart card regulation is in its infancy and that it will continue to evolve" (Noe, 1995, p. 45).

In 1997, the US Federal Reserve issued a clarification and simplification of Regulation E, finally providing protection to credit cardholders (Grupe, Kuechler & Sweeney, 2003). "Maintaining consumer confidence, managing technology and preventing fraud are among the most often cited reasons for applying regulation E to smart card transactions" (Puri, 1997, p. 138). One of the biggest problems of Regulation E is that it requires a receipt to be kept for every transaction, and in the case of smart cards, this is very difficult given the breadth of applications a single card could support (e.g. parking meters, vending machines etc) (Figure 4). In 1998 O'Connor wrote about the *de minimis exemption* for stored value cards in proposed changes to Regulation E. He pointed out that removing SVC protections would make cardholders easy targets for either unscrupulous vendors or fraudulent issuers who disburse defective cards. He called this an "open invitation to fraud". To make things even more complicated it is no longer the point of sale (POS) in which companies focus on but the point of interaction. Furletti (2004b) believes the whole area of payment cards and Regulation E is very "unsettled" which has led to a great deal of consumer confusion. There has been a clear call for uniform standards to be introduced (Furletti, 2004a).

Who Has Access to Information and Where?

In 1997, Puri (p. 134) stated that on average 80 more times of data can be stored on a smart card than a magnetic-stripe card; today about 10 megabytes of data can be stored on a smart card. No matter how one looks at future possibilities, the smart card is set to play a major role in remote banking services. Tarbox (1997, p. 262) believes that smart card issuers must therefore disclose to application developers and consumers, how and who will have access to information, and how it will be distributed. For a thorough discussion on privacy see Branscomb (1994). On the topic of smart cards (p. 70) she provocatively questions: *"[b]ut are we willing to have so much medical information about ourselves contained in so little electronic space, with possible access not only to us and the doctors treating us, but as well to our insurance companies, our employers, and the FBI, not to mention that bizarre world of computers voyeurs?"* Cuddy (1999), Brin (1998), and Davies (1996, ch. 7; 1992, ch. 4) offer groundbreaking insights into this area. When considering the rise of multiapplication cards, the problem of 'who owns information' is even more complex. At least a single application card can undergo some sort of assessment with visible limits.

Figure 4. Single journey electronic ticket issuing machines at Hong Kong's Central Station to be utilized on the Mass Transit Railway (MTR). Photo taken in 2001.

Another question mark that surrounds world-wide interoperability of smart cards is how they will be regulated when they are used in different countries. For example, does a regulation applied in the U.S. have any legal bearing in Australia or Japan? Some have suggested the enactment of a number of privacy torts related to smart card, others are encouraging the use of electronic contracts between issuers and consumers since new laws are not about to appear overnight. The contract should give the consumer confidence that they will have full control of personal information on the card (i.e., in case of error); why this personal information is required, who will use it and for how long; how the consumer's privacy is protected to ensure non-disclosure and if a particular application is covered by existing statutes; and reference to the issuer's privacy policy (Cavazos & Morin, 1995, pp. 34-45; Barr et al., 1997, p. 76).

Sources on Consumer Acceptance of Smart Card

Svigals (1987, ch. 16) was one of the first authors to discuss the potential societal impacts of smart card as was C. P. Smith (1990, ch. 9). For key strategies and considerations for user acceptance of smart cards refer to Lindley (1994) and Cooper, Gencturk & Lindley (1996). Consumer acceptance of the smart card in some geographic regions is very low, even in some cases where adoption of other high-technologies such as mobile phones has been high (Bright, 1988, pp. 145-149; Card World, 1990, pp. 42-45; Radigan, 1995; Smart Card Alliance, 2006). Specifically it was user privacy concerns that initially hampered smart card diffusion in many parts of the world (Lindley, 1997, pp. 132-142; Barr et al., 1997, pp. 73-78; Vincent, 1995). A number of links can be found on Ontario's Smart Card Project created by the Information Policy Research Program (2002). The site contains useful press clippings and articles on public policy and smart card. Included in this site are links to Roger Clarke's articles on public policy issues related to identification (Clarke, 1997). Other useful reports include: Privacy Committee of NSW (1995) and the Privacy Commissioner (1995).

The Social Implications of Mass Market Chip Cards

Many citizens across the globe have vehemently protested the use of smart cards for citizen identification. However in some countries citizens are powerless to voice their concerns, while in other countries governments have already introduced unique lifetime identifiers (ULI) linked to an 'everything' card (Drudge, 1998) without much public discourse or consultation. It is not the technology itself that most people fear but what it represents and how the capability of unique ID can be used by anyone who has access to the information, particularly potential totalitarian governments or regimes. For a comparison between Australian and UK national ID proposals, see Jackson and Ligertwood (2006, pp. 45-55) and for an indepth review of Australia's identity card proposals see Jordan (2008).

While there are many advantages gained by the use of multiapplication smart cards for government and non-government applications, more research needs to go into what these advantages mean in real terms. Almost always, the economics behind large schemes such as national ID cards are unjustified, costing the taxpayer more in the long-term (M.G. Michael & K. Michael, 2006, pp. 359-364). The notion of many 'little brothers' versus one Big Brother has been put forward in opposition to multiapplication cards. While the intent of the issuer may be noble, i.e. to offer a better service to its customers, no one can guarantee that the information will not be used 'against' an individual. These are not conspiracy theories but lessons from history (K. Michael & M.G. Michael, 2006).

One of the most infamous uses of dossiers against a people was that of the Nazis against the Jews (Black, 2001). Evans (1987) writes with reference to the proposition of an ID card in Australia: "I can understand why many people- particularly those who have lived under totalitarian regimes or fled from Nazism- oppose the Australia card". In 2006, the Australian government proposed the Human Services Access Card which was to replace 17 different cards issued by 4 government agencies (Australian Privacy Foundation, 2007; Greenleaf, 2007). In the end the proposal did not gain support (Clark, 2008, pp. 156-166). This is contrast to country-specific mass market cards in Hong Kong (Octopus, 2008) and Britain (e.g. Oyster Card). There seem to be cultural differences in the adoption of new mass technologies. Due to their multiapplication capabilities, smart cards are renowned for function creep.

Function creep is defined by Clarke (1996) as "the commencement of a scheme with a small number of uses, but with accretion of additional uses (and often intrinsically more invasive ones) at a later stage." For example, the Octopus Card was never meant to be a government ID card, but specific applications were deployed after the card was introduced as a solution for transit (Figure 5). Observers suspect that the British Oyster Card may be going down the same roadmap. Each Oyster smart card has a unique ID number which is linked to the registered owner's name. Every time the card is used a transaction is recorded of where and when it occurred. Commuters have been told that the data is retained for planning purposes to help in the provisioning of services, but it is well-known that the data could also be released to law enforcement agencies (Turban & Brahm, 2000; Mustafa, Giannopoulos & Pitsiava-Latinopoulou, 1995; Teal, 1994). Mark Littlewood of the civil rights group Liberty in the UK reflects: "[a]ll too often we have seen data collected for one apparent purpose, only for it to end up being used for something entirely different" (Scullion, 2003).

SMART CARDS APPLICATIONS

Overview

Like the magnetic-stripe card and bar code card before it, the smart card can be applied to many different applications (Datamonitor, 1996, ch. 3). The question is whether or not the smart card is the best-fit

Figure 5. The turnstiles at Kowloon Station enabling a commuter to present their electronic ticket in order to board the Airport Express train on one of the lines of the Mass Transit Railway (MTR) serving Hong Kong. The terminals installed in 1998 could read magnetic-stripe cards and later were upgraded to read Hong Kong's ubiquitous Octopus Card. Photo taken in 2000.

solution to the problem at hand (Carr, 2002). For example, "[i]n France, virtually all bank cards have been converted from magnetic stripe technology to chip technology to cut down on fraud" (Lever, 1997, p. 18); yet the same level of migration cannot be assumed in all parts of the world. It is therefore not surprising that it was also in France that one of the first multiapplication city smart cards was trialed in Vitrolles in 1990 (Sola, 1990). The UK also announced a similar CityCard project in 1998. Smart cards are also being used more and more for travel and to reduce traffic congestion. The Electronic Road Pricing (ERP) system in Singapore, officially launched in March of 1998, collects two forms of road revenue: using a particular stretch of road and for entering the CBD (Central Business District) during designated busy hour traffic periods. Inserted in the reader of each vehicle is a Cash Card which is debited each time the vehicle crosses an ERP area. Parking is yet another application for smart cards used for charging drivers for the time they occupy a space and/or given access to a car park (Figure 6). Prepaid smart cards have even been used for consumer electricity payment (Raad, Sheltami & Sallout, 2007).

Health cards using smart card technology have also become common. The main motivators for the use of smart cards in health care from the patient, service provider and payer perspectives can be found in Brainerd and Tarbox (1997, p. 155). Smart cards can store patient information making the processing of transactions particularly in hospitals easier. In some countries like Germany, the health care smart card has been implemented successfully but for the greater part controversy surrounds privacy aspects of the card. There is a fear that if health data is stored centrally then it may be at risk of being misused by independent entities. Errors in patient records can also be damaging to an individual if they go unnoticed. However fully networked and integrated health care systems that incorporate end-to-end health provision are still lacking. It is envisaged that in the future, a patient will be able to visit his/her doctor, receive a diagnosis from the doctor and store this information on the smart card. If the patient requires drugs, prescriptions could be made electronically to ensure non-conflicting medications were given. Visits to specialists and test results could also be stored on the card.

The largest application of smart cards however is for public telephones. Figures released by Datamonitor indicated that in 1996 around 66 countries had adopted smart card payphones and smart cards for

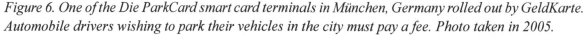

Figure 6. One of the Die ParkCard smart card terminals in München, Germany rolled out by GeldKarte. Automobile drivers wishing to park their vehicles in the city must pay a fee. Photo taken in 2005.

payphones accounted for approximately 75% of all smart cards sold globally. While the benefits offered by smart payphone cards over magnetic-stripe payphone cards are negligible, telephone operators are strategically positioning themselves for tomorrow's mass market consumer mobile payment applications. If the smart card infrastructure in payphones is ready to be used, it is only a matter of additional software to be written for other applications such as banking. Imagine using a payphone or a mobile device that could act as an ATM (Figure 7). The development of the Global Standard for Mobile Telecommunications (GSM) required a subscriber identity module (SIM) to be inserted into the mobile handset. The SIM is the mechanism that allows a subscriber to connect to the network and is essentially a smart card made to ISO specifications (Moorhead, 1994). Smart cards are also being used for satellite and cable television (CATV) to prevent unauthorized viewing of programs and for metering of household energy use. Security algorithms decode the signal via a set-top box. Monnin (1992, pp. 418-421) writes of the exclusive advantages in pay-TV. University campus smart cards are also widely used.

Many governments are also looking into smart cards for social welfare and more generally for citizen identification (e.g. for voting). The Malaysian Government multiapplication smart card known as MyKad began being issued by the National Registration Department in 2001. The ID card is now issued to all citizens and permanent residents over the age of 12 years old and there are now about 20 million active MyKads with more to follow as citizens continue to migrate from the older ID card. MyKad card holds drivers license details, passport data, and other information. In some countries such national cards have been launched without adequate data protection and privacy legislation. In 2002, there is the well-known case of the Japanese government who launched JukiNet effectively linking national, regional and local government databases together, without adequate privacy protections. Within 24 hours, local authorities had disconnected from the network citing privacy problems. A privacy law was then rushed through Japan's judicial system. According to Hendry (2007, p. 199) the Diet and Juki Cards which are now commonplace in Japan, contain the name, address, civil status, and a link to the holder's records in JukiNet.

Figure 7. A consumer pays for her groceries using her mobile phone at the point of sale (POS). Courtesy of NXP Semiconductors.

Case 1: Smart Cards in Telecommunications

Pre-Paid Telephones Cards

Without a doubt, prepaid smart cards for public payphones account for the largest segment of the smart card market (Crotch-Harvey, 1996), and this continues to hold true today. In 1995, telecommunication-specific smart cards accounted for 80 per cent of the market. More recent market share forecasts are available. They indicate that the market share has shifted by application type (Freedonia, 2003; Frost & Sullivan, 2004; IMS, 2008). The future for broadband services continues to flourish which forced traditional telecommunications companies in the 1990s to form alliances or even merge with CATV companies, Internet Service Providers (ISPs), Web software businesses and media corporations in a bid to share their risks and make sure they are not left out of the race (Wilson, 2001). All these applications require smart cards for subscriber access authorization with capabilities to bill customers for services used and information content downloaded (Hadeed, 2000).

The first recognized trial of smart cards for prepaid telephone cards was by the French Post Telephone and Telegraph (PTT) in 1982-83. The French justified the move from coin operated payphones to smart card payphones by highlighting that about 15 per cent of phone call tariffs were lost as a direct result of telephone charging frauds and coin theft (Svigals, 1987, p. 97). The French trials were so successful that in 1984 ten thousand smart card payphones were installed in France with 400,000 smart cards issued to consumers. By 1995 there were a reported 1.5 billion prepaid telephone cards sold- "four hundred million of these were smart cards that can be accepted in one of every five payphones in more than 70 countries" (Lutz, 1997, p. 131). The smart cards used by French Telecom were made by Gemplus (now Gemalto). Gemplus is the leading maker of smart phonecards with 40 per cent of the market share. It supplies smart cards to 50 national telephone operators in about 50 countries worldwide. Gemplus sold 120 millions smart cards in 1994 alone.

In 1994 US WEST marketed the Telecard smart card in conjunction with the Nortel Millennium payphone. In 1995, Québec Telephone became the first company in North America to modernize its entire payphone system. In 1996, BellSouth chose to team up with Nortel at the Atlanta Olympic Games. BellSouth deployed 200 smart card-compatible Nortel Millennium intelligent payphones which were able to handle VISA Cash. Nortel was the first to bring smart card capable payphones to North America and in 2003 they had more than 100000 Millennium terminals installed throughout the region. It was a way for BellSouth to differentiate itself from the other 866 payphone providers in Georgia. The Millennium payphone was multi-pay, multi-card capable, accepting "VISA Cash as well as magnetic-striped, commercial credit and calling cards, and coins" (Scarlett & Manley, 1996, p. 3). By 1997, the smart cards had become so popular that Mondex International decided to use the Nortel Millennium payphone and Nortel PowerTouch 360 (also known as the Vista in Canada) to offer electronic banking and home banking services. Customers now have the additional ability to 'reload' their prepaid cards by transferring funds from their personal accounts. In essence, the intelligent telephone has now become a remote ATM.

Subscriber Identity Modules in Mobile Phones

Another use of smart cards in telecommunications since 1992 is as a SIM card, also known as the User Identity Module (UIM), for mobile handsets. As Kaplan describes (1996, p. 162): *"SIM cards contain non-volatile information embedded by the manufacturer related to security and identity, and a program-mable memory (electrically erasable) to provide for optional and dynamically changeable information."* It is the microchip in the SIM card that authorizes the subscriber's connection to the network. This way the subscriber can place and receive calls. The card is personalized in such a way that the subscriber's account information is stored on the microchip. Other data includes card ID, PIN, service features, access class and memory configuration. Subscribers can remove the SIM card and put it into any other GSM handset and all the subscriber-customized features will work, provided they are the same standard size (e.g. standard ISO SIM card). Another excellent feature of the SIM is that it allows for global roaming. Global roaming provides the subscriber access worldwide at the operating frequency or technology used in a particular country (e.g. GSM, DCS 1800, PCS 1900, DECT, UMTS or satellite systems). The most important function of the SIM card is that of billing (pre-paid or post paid). A subscriber can take their card with them anywhere and have total control of who uses it- the PIN enabling the SIM is always a safe practice for any subscriber just in case they lose their phone or have it stolen.

Mobile Payment Systems

Reports which herald the SIM as a vital piece of tomorrow's wireless personal digital assistants (PDA) do so for good reason (Ince, 1997, pp. 26-30). Japan's NTT DoCoMo launched i-Mode at the end of 2000, to trial a packet-switched mode of transmission over the 2G mobile environment. By 2003, about 3000 companies were offering transaction capabilities over i-Mode officially linked to DoCoMo's mobile commerce billing system. The results speak for themselves; in 2003, more than 50 per cent of mobile subscribers use i-Mode and about 40,000 new subscribers were joining the network each day. The first generation of i-Mode applications allowed the user to do anything that the 'fixed' Internet offered, such as book airline tickets, buy and sell shares on the stock market, play games, check the latest weather forecasts, shop and browse for products, play government-approved lotteries, download images and even use a company's intranet. DoCoMo's c-Mode, marketed in 2004 was also set to challenge the way in which consumers spent their money. Using their wireless handset, consumers were able to purchase items from vending machines and be billed accordingly on their i-Mode bill. Today, i-Mode in Japan boasts 48 million subscribers and currently more than 95,000 Internet sites are providing a variety of content (NTT-DOCOMO, 2008).

In Singapore consumers can pay for their taxi fare via their mobile phone as well as purchase coke from a vending machine. In the Australian market, Vodafone and 3 were eager to follow the Japanese example, although the readiness of the market was debatable in 2003. In 2002, Telstra began running trials in Bronte, Sydney: "[c]ashless parking meters activated by mobile phones and smart cards..." (R. Smith, 2002, p. 11). But it is not inconceivable that the wireless personal digital assistant (PDA) or e-wallet will become the future mechanism by which all purchases, even government transactions will be made. Coupled with mobility will be the ability to use the same smart card in the home. In the case of such cable television applications like video-on-demand (VoD) or home shopping, smart cards have the ability to not only grant the customer access to subscription channels but also to charge the individual for content viewed and items purchased (Hendry, 1997, p. 153). Lutz adds (1997, p. 141) that "[s]mart cards can add substantial value to th[e] growing industry by providing payment options, access authorizations, personalized services, and security".

Smart vs. "Dumb" Cards

PhoneCards

In 1990, Telecom Australia introduced the Phonecard- a prepaid telephone card system. The technology supplied by the Anritsu Corporation had been used in Japan for some years successfully. Cook (1994, p. 1) an executive of Telecom's payphone services business unit described the technology choice in conference proceedings. *"The technology revolves around an encoded magnetic stripe which is credited with a series of dollar values ($5, $10, $20 and $50) that are decremented according to the call type when inserted in the payphone..."* Telecom saw many benefits to the widespread roll-out of magnetic-stripe technology. They believed that it would increase profitability of their payphone business, reduce vandalism and theft of public payphones and be more convenient for the consumer. Telecom produced in excess of 10 million cards per year and over 75 per cent of payphones accepted PhoneCard. However, Telecom did reveal that the costs of producing and distributing the cards were expensive when counted with the costs of upgrades to payphones (Cook, 1994, p. 5). The Telecom experience is quite typical of many telephone operators' experience in the United States. The company was aware of smart card technology being used in France at the time of making the magnetic-stripe decision but opted for the 'safer' option. Perhaps this was a strategic decision, for Telecom Australia (now Telstra), to gauge consumer reaction to the PhoneCard before moving towards the more expensive smart card solution. Still, this was either an expensive strategic move or an expensive loss.

Smart PhoneCards

In 1997, Telstra launched 'Smart Phonecards' in Perth. Within a six-month transition period all magnetic-stripe cards were phased out and new payphone terminals were installed (developed by Spanish manufacturer Amper) (Figure 8). Telstra have made it obvious that the new Telstra Smart Phonecard

Figure 8. The Telstra Smart Phonecard and coin payphone machine on the University of Wollongong campus, in Wollongong, NSW, Australia. The gold smart card symbol can be seen on the top right. Photo taken in 2001.

would also facilitate cashless payment for a variety of goods. The Phonecard experience seems to be a recurring pattern in other countries worldwide. In Pakistan for example, where 100 million people had access to only 2000 payphones in Islamabad and Lahore in 2002, competing operators implemented different auto-ID solutions. In Britain, BT (British Telecom) replaced their optical card payphones with smart card. Even in the United Arab Emirates, old coin and magnetic-stripe payphone terminals were replaced with smart-card capable ones (Fromentin & Traisnel, 1995, p. 82). Yet in the mid 1990s, the U.S. smart card payphone situation was still *"very much in its infancy, with only a few payphones equipped with readers capable of handling credit cards or telephone chargecards. There are signs of change, however, with several operators conducting trials with magnetic stripe cards"* (*Communications, 1995, p. 58).*

Plain Old Calling Cards

Telecom's pre-paid PhoneCard should be differentiated from other services that are presently being offered by telephone operators. For instance, using the AT&T Direct Service requires a consumer only to be in possession of a recognized credit card such as American Express, MasterCard, Diners Club or an AT&T corporate card. The service offered by AT&T does not require the use of the magnetic-stripe technology to make a call internationally. The process only requires the use of a touchtone telephone. The cardholder enters the special AT&T Access Number (dependent on where the call is being originated), dials the international telephone number and then enters the AT&T Calling Card number plus the credit card number followed by the four digit expiration date to complete the call. All calls are then billed to the cardholder's credit card. If the process of dialing all these numbers seems prone to error, that is because it is. Telephone operators have a host of calling card services some of which only require the cardholder of an access card to dial an operator which then places a call on behalf of the caller. Newer more innovative secure network access can be achieved using biometrics (Messmer, 1998, pp. 1-2).

Case 2: Smart Cards for Health Care

Almost every patient in a more developed country (MDC) possesses a health care card of some type, whether he or she is covered by either private health insurance or a government medicare scheme or both. While in Europe and Canada smart cards have been prevalent in the health care sector other countries such as the U.S. and Australia have lagged behind. In the U.S. several attempts have been made to introduce a health care card (Hausen & Bruening, 1994, pp. 24-32), especially by the Clinton administration but these failed; the same as in the Australian case. In Clinton's proposal the smart card would carry an ID number, and the information to be stored on the card was very comprehensive including blood type, allergies, health insurance details, treatment programmes and major illnesses (Stix, 1994).

In Europe and Canada

France

In contrast, in France the Sesame Vitale scheme has been in place since 1986. The smart card scheme used to assist the French Social Security boasted of approximately 10 million French citizens and over 100000 doctors and other health professionals in the late 1990s. Ultimately the scheme will cover the entire French population for the primary purpose of proving the identification of the cardholder and conveying prescriptions to pharmacists. The scheme is not directly concerned with individual patient medical records- this is the task of another card called Santal. Other projects that have been piloted in France include the Biocarte system and the Transvie card.

Germany

In 1989 the German Health Insurance Card, Versichertenkarte, was distributed to citizens by government, enforceable by law. In the case of Germany where a national health care card was introduced, Kaplan (1996, pp. 158-161) describes the advantages to patients, insurers and health care providers noting however, that there are privacy risks associated with the scheme. Also, Hendry (1997, ch. 13) discusses medical records, prescriptions and patient monitoring and Gogou et al. (2000, pp. 559-561) a smart card network for health services. The Versichertenkarte card was used to provide individuals with access to medical treatment and to assist with billing of services and the reduction of administration costs. Schaefer (1997, p. 1) reported that by October 1994, 63.4 million cards had been distributed to insured persons and about 135,000 readers had been installed at medical institutions. The card was accepted by about 93 per cent of health insured persons and about 45 per cent of all doctors. By the end of 1994 the card was issued to about 79 million persons. The content on the patient card included: title, given name, surname, date of birth, address, name of health fund, insurance company identification number, patient health insurance number, status of the insured and the card expiration date. The magnitude of this project cannot be underestimated.

Canada

The Québec health card developed by the Laval University Medical center and the Québec Health Insurance board was piloted in May 1993. About 7,000 cards were issued to potential participants and about 300 doctors, pharmacists and nurses were targeted. The information on the health card was grouped in five separate zones: identification, emergency, vaccination, medications and medical history. In Ontario, in the same year the Encounter smart card was also piloted. Cards were issued to about 2,200 volunteers and 80 health care providers. The card contained three separate sections: biographical, health status data and encounter (patient visiting) data. However what was different about this card was that it contained not only numbers relevant to health but also the unique lifetime identifier (ULI) of the patient represented in the registered persons official database. According to Lindley (1997, p. 97) there were over 30 health card trials between 1985-1990, some were implemented widely while others were not. For an overview of a smart health care service case study see Kaplan (1996, pp. 104-109). McCrindle (1990 ch. 9) provides a generic overview of medical applications with some international examples.

Europe-Wide

Since the Schengen Agreement, European-wide smart card health schemes have also been promoted by specific programs like the Advanced Informatics Medicine (AIM). It is envisaged that cross-border national medical sectors in Europe will be integrated in a shared system. One of the functions of the Eurocard will be to reduce health administrative costs. The Diabcard is also making headways in Germany, Austria, Italy and Spain. The Diabcard "...provides the specification for a chip card-based medical information system (CCMIS) for the treatment of patients with chronic diseases" (Engelbrecht et al., 1996; Schaefer, 1997, p. 4). In 2004, the European Health Insurance Card was introduced as a proof of national health insurance valid in all countries of the EU (Hendry, 2007, p. 187). The Card allows a cardholder or their family to receive necessary healthcare in a public system of any European Union country or in

Switzerland, if they become ill or injured while on a temporary stay in that country. According to the European Commission (2004), "the health insurance card represents an essential stage in the possible development of new services or functions using information technologies, such as storing medical data on a smart card or secure access to the medical file through the insured's identifier." Under the eEurope 2002 charter of *Smart Card Initiatives*, the card is seen as paving the way forward to responding to the needs of citizens and the business community.

Privacy Concerns over the Smart Card

The Medicare card distributed to all Australian citizens entitles the cardholder to receive government-funded medical services and benefits. For example, the card can be used to subsidize patient visits to general practitioners (GPs). The card contains a magnetic-stripe, an embossed number, an expiry date and the name(s) of the cardholder(s). Before a cardholder can see a doctor, he/she must present the card which is carbon-copied and forwarded to the Health Insurance Commission (HIC) for processing. Due to earlier privacy concerns regarding pseudo national ID cards, attempts to introduce a smart card were extinguished. The Minister of Health in 1991 promised the public that a smart card would never replace the existing system (Davies, 1992, pp. 52-55). However, the Warren Center still believed that a smart card would "improve the administration of PBS, and reduce fraud and errors... a smart chip could also be added to the Medicare card, storing the history of the drugs issued and for which benefits had been paid" (Privacy Committee of NSW, 1995, p. 32). The process proposed by the Warren Center was not only seen as efficient to administration but possibly life-saving for the patient. Despite the on-board security of smart cards, a great number of Australians still view the smart card with some distrust, primarily because of its storage capacity.

Private health care funds in Australia are also beginning to roll-out magnetic-stripe cards. MBF (Medical Benefits Fund) distributed cards to their customers in 1998 and NIB in 1999. The MBF card unlike the Medicare Card is not embossed but does display the cardholder's signature. When patients claim rebates on health services that are not covered by Medicare, they must now present their private health insurance card as a way for the health fund to track expenses. Previously, the system was confusing for patients and health institutions wishing to claim money owed to them- several different medical bills for health services made reconciliation difficult. The MBF cardholder is also entitled to discounts at certain health-related companies like Rebel sports store and entertainment venues (MBF, 1999).

The Potential for Biometrics and RFID

Other auto-ID devices being used in health care include biometrics and RFID (Fulcher, 2003). For a person in a critical condition who requires urgent medical attention, and who is unconscious, biometric identification in the form of hand or fingerprint scanning could end up preventing further damage or death (Takac, 1990, p. 19). Many people have died unnecessarily because of injections they are either allergic to or have received too high a dosage. Even as early as 1999, SJB reported that there were over 70 live installations of biometrics in health care. Menendez (1999) also writes about biometrics for health care. In 1992, Kaufman and Woodward (1992, pp. 165-167) who pioneered a medical record system called Plustag-Magic, also demonstrated the use of alternative technology for health care.

Today, RFID tags and transponders are being adopted, mainly for the precise identification of new-born babies, mentally-ill patients or those suffering from allergies. While there are many tags or bracelets that do not possess any intelligence (like bar code), RFID is a technology that is predicted to change everything from physical access control in hospitals to drug delivery using biochips to treat illnesses like diabetes. During the Severe Acute Respiratory Syndrome (SARS) epidemic, Ling (2003) described the use of the Contact Track & Trace system, and the Hospital Movement Tracking System, based on RFID technology used to monitor visitors, patients and hospital staff. The system worked as follows. Every individual given physical access to the hospital was issued with a RFID sensor card to be worn around the neck. As people walked around the hospital, data was captured via RFID readers and stored in the central computer's database. Information about an individual's contact in the hospital was stored for 21 days after each new contact point.

Medical Implantable Devices

RFID transponders which store a unique ID can now also be implanted for emergency response applications (Michael, Michael & Ip, 2007). It is estimated there are over two thousand recipients of these tiny identification devices, most of which are sourced back to the Food and Drug Administration approved products of the VeriChip Corporation, based in the United States. The premier implantable VeriChip is used for the VeriMed application, namely patient identification. There are over 900 registered medical facilities that are now equipped with VeriChip readers. The VeriMed system claims to overcome the problems often associated with 'at-risk' individuals. For example, to aid patients in times of crisis- if they have collapsed, suffered memory loss, are unable to communicate, or have a complex medical history they cannot recollect. Corporate marketing identifies the following benefits of the VeriMed system: rapid identification in the emergency response (ER) room, instant medical record access, and improved emergency response (VeriMed, 2007). The chip simply stores a unique identification number, and associated medical records are stored in a secure global Verichip subscriber (GVS) registry database. The chip is inserted through a basic medical procedure, in the subdermal layer of the skin in the left or right upper arm, much as in the case of a dog or cat implant. VeriChip's other non-implantable applications are related to infant protection, wander prevention, and emergency management among others. An alternate approach to the medical implantable device is the wireless monitoring technology called Digital Plaster (Toumaz, 2008; BBC News, 2005).

Smart Cards Today

The smart card as an auto-ID technique came up against a number of barriers which hampered its success early on (Kaplan, 1996, pp. 22-24; Hill, 1996, p. 1). Mitchell (1995) believed that one of the primary reasons that smart cards had not reached their anticipated potential in the U.S. was because merchants did not accept the card to begin with. The merchant indifference towards smart card meant that consumers could not offer the payment method to purchase goods and services because the likelihood of their being an available device to read the card was very low. A Gartner study in 1998 also reported that smart cards were a push technology and until new developments established their business value, that the technology would continue not to meet wild expectations (Essick, 1998, p. 1). For instance, Dataquest's (1999) worldwide chip market forecast for 1997-2002 was off the mark. Schiffer (2000) provides an insight into why the smart card encountered such obstacles, giving the analogy of the electric automobile, and the way that social behavior stifled its development process. Part of the blame should also be shared with the system developers who overlooked the fact that customers have a mind of their own and they cannot be manipulated to act in a certain way (Rankl, 2007, p. xi).

The period post the dot.com crash saw smart card giants endure some turmoil as expectant smart card demand projections were not reached. Smart card companies like Schlumberger and Gemplus shed a sizeable chunk of their workforce at this time. It must be stressed that this is not to set a pessimistic undertone about the future of the smart card, only to underscore that other types of cards such as bar code and magnetic-stripe, have maintained their place in the auto-ID industry. Today, smart cards have proliferated in a variety of countries and for stable mass market applications like national ID cards. Countries like China and Hong Kong have rolled out citizen identification cards that are truly multiapplication in nature. The Octopus Card in Hong Kong for instance, is not only a national ID card, but it is used for passenger transport and as an e-payment mechanism (Chau & Poon, 2003; Poon & Chau, 2001). While it is indisputable that the Octopus Card has suffered function creep, its citizens do not seem to feel that their privacy is encroached but much rather that the card is highly convenient in their busy lives. Hendry (2007, p. 219) has written that the scope of multi-application smart card projects has a strong tendency toward 'function creep' as has been discussed already in this chapter.

Rankl (2007) believes that today, the smart card has reached a turning point in its lifecycle, a type of paradigm shift. He believes that the driver for smart card has little to do with technology being pushed onto consumers, and that today, it has more to do with the needs of users preoccupying developers. He writes: "[t]his is quite a normal cycle in the course of technology development, as has been seen repeatedly in this form and in similar forms" (Rankl, 2007, p. xi). The authors agree with Rankl, that it was quite a 'normal' path for smart card to go through on the product lifecycle curve but it came with associated tangible and intangible costs to the industry at large as well.

CONCLUSION

Multiapplication smart cards have the potential to herald in a pure cashless society. Attempts in the 1990s by private enterprises like Mondex, toward the acceptance of a smart card wallet were only mildly successful. Some critics would go as far as stating that these ventures were a dismal failure. ePayment solutions beyond anything such as petty cash transactions, seem to be a stumbling block for smart card city-based schemes. The promise of smart card seems more practicable in a government-mandated solution whereby an ID card has multiple applications and multiple functionalities onboard. While these sorts of schemes seem to be popular in Asia and some parts of Europe, the United States, Canada, Australia and lesser developed countries have chosen other routes for personal ID, such as tax file numbers and the like. Time will tell if even these countries will adopt smart ID solutions, especially given the seemingly increased sense of nations requiring better border security. Contact smart cards have been widely adopted in health care for patient tracking and also by the steady telecommunications industry, particularly for mobile telephony. Contactless smart cards on the other hand, remain popular as access control solutions and in electronic road pricing as vehicle solutions. It is true to say that for the time being, the full force of smart cards have yet to be unleashed, although as in the case of bar code and magnetic stripe card, the infrastructure that is growing around the technology, takes time to build. We may well be entering a new decade where the capacity for smart card as an epayment solution will explode, coupled with broadband Internet, cable television, high definition television (HDTV), and the like.

REFERENCES

Allen, C. A., & Barr, W. J. (Eds.). (1997). *Smart Cards: Seizing Strategic Business Opportunities.* New York: McGraw-Hill.

Allen, C. A., & Kutler, J. (1997). Overview of smart cards and the industry', in Smart Cards: seizing strategic business opportunities. In C. A. Allen & W. J. Barr (Eds.), (pp. 2-20). New York: McGraw-Hill.

Amdur, D. (1997). *France moves toward chip card future- Internet seen as opportunity in the United States.*

APSCA. (2008). Members. *Asia Pacific Smart Card Association.* Retrieved 1 December 2008, from http://www.apsca.org/members/member.php

APSCF. (2000). *Australian Smart Card Capabilities.* Paper presented at the Asia Pacific Smart Card Forum, The Warren Centre for Advanced Engineering, the University of Sydney.

Argy, P., & Bollen, R. (1999). Australia: raising the e-commerce comfort level. *IT Pro*(November-December), 56-58.

Australian Privacy Foundation. (2007). The Federal government calls it a 'Human Services Access Card'. Retrieved 3 December 2008, from http://www.privacy.org.au/Campaigns/ID_cards/HSAC-FAQ3.html

Barr, W. J. (1997). Shifting boundaries. In C. A. Allen & W. J. Barr (Eds.), *Smart Cards: Seizing Strategic Business Opportunities* (pp. 57-78). New York,: McGraw-Hill.

BBC News. (2005). 'Digital plaster' monitors health. *BBC News.* Retrieved 5 December 2008, from http://news.bbc.co.uk/1/hi/health/4617633.stm

Black, E. (2001). *IBM and the Holocaust.* UK: Little, Brown and Company.

Blythe, P. (2000). Transforming Access to and Payment for Transport Services through the Use of Smart Cards. *Journal of Intelligent Transportation Systems, 6*(1), 45 - 68.

Brainerd, L., & Tarbox, J. D. (1997). Healthcare and smart card technology. In C. A. Allen & W. J. Barr (Eds.), *Smart Cards: Seizing Strategic Business Opportunities* (pp. 151-168). New York: McGraw-Hill.

Branscomb, A. W. (1994). *Who Owns Information?* New York: Basic Books.

Bright, R. (1988). *Smart Cards: principles, practice, applications.* New York: John Wiley & Sons.

Brin, D. (1998). *The Transparent Society: will technology force us to choose between privacy and freedom?* Massachusetts: Perseus Books.

Browne, F. X., & Cronin, D. (1996). Payment technologies, financial innovation, and laissez-faire banking. *Cato Journal, 15*(1), 101-116.

Cagliostro, C. (1999). Rosy outlook predicted for US smart card market. *Card Forum International*(November/December), 45-47.

Card World (Ed.). (1990). *ITALY- Slowed by cultural resistance.* Surrey.

Cardshow. (1996). The birth of smart cards: 1974-1989. *The Smart Card Cybershow- Smart Card Museum*, from http://www.cardshow.com/museum/ex70.html

Carr, M. R. (2002, 20-24 October). *Smart card technology with case studies.* Paper presented at the 36th Annual 2002 International Carnahan Conference on Security Technology.

Cavazos, E. A., & Morin, G. (1995). *Cyberspace and the Law: Your rights and duties in the on-line world.* Massachusetts: The MIT Press, Massachusetts.

Chadwick, D. (1999). Smart cards aren't always the smart choice. *IEEE Computer*(December), 142-143.

Chau, P. Y. K., & Poon, S. (2003). Octopus: An E-Cash Payment System Success Story. *Communications of the ACM, 46*(9), 129-133.

CITI. (2002). Center for Information Technology Integration. Retrieved 6 December 2002, from http://www.citi.umich.edu/

Clark, S. R. (2008). Privacy and National Identity Cards: A legal and technical study. In K. Michael & M. G. Michael (Eds.), *Australia and the New Technologies: Evidence Based Policy in Public Administration.* Wollongong: University of Wollongong.

Clarke, R. (1996). Privacy Issues in Smart Card Application in the Retail Financial Sector *XamaX Consultancy.* Retrieved 3 December 2008, from http://www.anu.edu.au/people/Roger.Clarke/DV/ACFF.html

Clarke, R. (1997). Roger Clarke's main publications on data surveillance and information privacy. *Xamax Consultancy.* Retrieved 15 September 1997, from http://www.anu.edu.au/people/Roger.Clarke/DV/RogersDVBibl.html

Communications. (1995). The word on the street... *Communications International, 22*(4), 56-58.

Cook, J. (1994, 15-16 October). *Lessons from the Phonecard: "Watch this space" advertising.* Paper presented at the AIC Conference.

Cook, S. (1997). Foreword. In C. A. Allen & W. J. Barr (Eds.), *Smart Cards: Seizing Strategic Business Opportunities* (pp. xi-xiv). New York: McGraw-Hill.

Cooper, J., Gencturk, N., & Lindley, R. A. (1996). A sociotechnical approach to smart card systems design: an Australian case study. *Behaviour & Information Technology, 15*(1), 3 - 13.

Cortese, A. (1997). The ultimate plastic. *Business Week,* 119-122.

Crotch-Harvey, T. (1996). Smart cards in telecoms. *Smart Card News*, from http://www.smartcard.co.uk/telecoms.htm

Crowley, M. J. (1996). *Stored value: an analysis of its institutional and economic implications.* Melbourne: Monash University.

Cuddy, D. L. (1999). *Secret Records Revealed: the men, the money & the methods behind the new world order.* Oklahoma City: Hearthstone Publishing.

Datamonitor. (1996). *Global Smart Cards*. London: Datamonitor.

Dataquest. (1999). Smart card research. from http://www.smartcardcentral.com/research/

Davies, S. (1992). *Big Brother: Australia's growing web of surveillance*. Australia: Simon and Schuster.

Davies, S. (1996). *Monitor: extinguishing privacy on the information superhighway*. Sydney: PAN Macmillan.

Davis, R. H., & Mitchell, H. (1996). Smart cards: a design for the future. *Journal of Information Technology, 11*(1), 79 - 97.

Devargas, M. (1992). *Smart Cards and Memory Cards*. New York: Blackwell Publishing.

Dreifus, H. N., & Monk, J. T. (1997). *Smart Cards: a guide to building and managing smart card applications*. New York: John Wiley and Sons.

Drudge, M. (1998). ID number to track medical history. from http://www.warroom.com/natid.html

EMVCo. (2003). Europay, MasterCard and Visa Co. from http://www.emvco.com/

Engelbrecht, R., Hildebrand, C., Bruguas, E., De Leiva, A., & Corcoy, R. (1996). DIABCARD an application of a portable medical record for persons with diabetes. *Informatics for Health and Social Care, 21*(4), 273 - 282.

European Commission. (2004). European health card for 1 June 2004. *Employment, Social Affairs and Equal Opportunities*. Retrieved 3 December 2008, from http://ec.europa.eu/employment_social/news/2003/feb/hicard_en.html

Eurosmart. Eurosmart: the voice of the smart card industry. from http://www.eurosmart.com/

Evans, D. (1987, 12 August). Everything you wanted to know about the Australia Card… but were afraid to ask. *The Daily Mirror*.

Ferrari, J., Mackinnon, R., Poh, S., & Yatawara, L. (1998). *Smart Cards: a case study*: Research Triangle Park.

Freedonia Group. (2003). World Smart Cards to 2006 - Demand and Sales Forecasts, Market Share, Market Size, Market Leaders. Retrieved 3 December 2008, from http://www.freedoniagroup.com/World-Smart-Cards.html

Fromentin, J.-R., & Traisnel, J. (1995). Smart payphone services. *Telecommunications, 29*(7), 82-83.

Frost and Sullivan. (2004). World Contactless Smart Card Market and Market Share Study. Retrieved 3 December 2008, from http://www.researchandmarkets.com/reports/365434

Fruin, W. M. (1998). Smart cards and product-development strategies in the electronics industry in Japan. *IEEE Transactions on Engineering Management, 45*(3), 241-249.

Fulcher, J. (2003). *The use of smart devices in eHealth*. Paper presented at the Proceedings of the 1st international symposium on Information and communication technologies Dublin.

Fünfrocken, S. (1999). Protecting mobile web-commerce agents with smartcards. *First International Symposium on Agent Systems and Applications*, 90-102.

Furletti, M. (2004a). Payment System Regulation and How It Causes Consumer Confusion. Retrieved 1 December 2008, from http://www.philadelphiafed.org/payment-cards-center/publications/discussion-papers/2004/PaymentSystemRegulation_112004.pdf

Furletti, M. (2004b). Prepaid Card Markets & Regulation. Retrieved 1 December 2008, from http://papers.ssrn.com/sol3/papers.cfm?abstract_id=927077

GISUM. (2002). GISUM research group. Retrieved 6 December 2002, from http://www.lcc.uma.es/~gisum

Gogou, V. (2000, July 23-28). *A smart card network in health care services.* Paper presented at the Proceedings of the 22nd Annual EMBS International Conference, Chicago, Illinois.

Greenleaf, G. (2007). Australia's Proposed ID Card: Still Quacking Like a Duck *Computer Law & Security Report, 23.*

Grupe, F. H., Kuechler, W., & Sweeney, S. (2003). Dealing with Data Privacy Protection: An Issue for the 21st Century. *Information Security Journal: A Global Perspective, 11*(6), 45 - 56.

Hadeed, A. (2000). *Using Smart Cards to Gain Market Share.* New York: Gower Publishing Company.

Haghiri, Y., & Tarantino, T. (2002). *Smart Card Manufacturing: A Practical Guide.* London: Wiley.

Hansmann, U., Nicklous, M. S., Schäck, T., & Schneider, A. (2002). *Smart Card Application Development Using Java.* Germany: Springer.

Hausen, T., & Bruening, P. (1994). Hidden costs and benefits of government card technologies, *IEEE Technology and Society Magazine* (Vol. 13, pp. 24-32).

Hayes, S. (2002). SIMple device for coke online. *The Australian,* p. 8.

Hegenbarth, M. (1990, 15-16 October). *The latest status in standardisation of smart card technology.* Paper presented at the in proceedings of the AIC Conference, Smart Card technology: applications for the 1990's, Sydney.

Hendry, M. (1997). *Smart Card Security and Applications (Artech House Telecommunications Library).* Boston: Artech House.

Hill, M. J. (1996). Contact and contactless cards. from http://mot2.mot-sps.com/csic/smartcrd/library/cc_simple.html

IMS. (2008). The Worldwide Market for Smart Cards and Semiconductors in Smart Cards. *IMS Research Group.* Retrieved 3 December 2008, from http://www.electronics.ca/reports/ic/smart_cards.html

Ince, J. (1997). Simplicity & standards. *Cellular Business, 14*(2), 26-30.

Information Policy Research Program. (2002). Ontario smart card project. from http://www.fis.utoronto.ca/research/iprp/sc/

ISO. (1999). 35.240.15 Identification cards and related devices. *International Standards Organisation*, 1-3.

ISO. (2008). ISO/IEC 7816-15:2004. *International Organization for Standardization*. Retrieved 5 December 2008, from http://www.iso.org/iso/iso_catalogue/catalogue_tc/catalogue_detail.htm?csnumber=35168

Jackson, M., & Ligertwood, J. (2006). Identity management: is an identity card the solution for Australia? In K. Michael & M. G. Michael (Eds.), *The Social Implications of Information Security Measures on Citizens and Business* (pp. 45-55). Wollongong: Wollongong University.

Jacquinot Consulting. (2008). The ISO 7816 Smart Card Standard: Overview *CardWerk: Smart Card Solutions*. Retrieved 5 December 2008, from http://www.cardwerk.com/smartcards/smartcard_standard_ISO7816.aspx

Johnston, M. (1997, 19 May). The ultimate plastic. *Business Week*, 62-33.

Jones, D. (2000). Europay and Visa issue new e-purse standards. *Ctt, 11*(6), 5-6.

Jordan, R. (2008). Identity Cards and the Access Card. *Australian Government: Parliamentary Library* Retrieved 5 December 2006, from http://www.aph.gov.au/library/intguide/LAW/IdentityCards.htm

Jouet, J. (Ed.). (1991). *European Telematics: the emerging economy of words*. Holland: North-Elsevier Science.

Kaplan, J. M. (1996). *Smart Cards: the global information passport- managing a successful smart card program*. London: International Thomson Computer Press.

Kaufman, A., & Woodward, L. H. (1992). PlusTag-Magic medical record system. *Computing Applications to Assist Persons with Disabilities*, 165-167.

Keenan, W. (1997). Components of the business proposition: the consumer demand proposition:the consumer demand proposition. In C. A. Allen & W. J. Barr (Eds.), *Smart Cards: Seizing Strategic Business Opportunities* (pp. 21-43). New York: McGraw-Hill.

Lever, R. (1997). Smart cards: the next generation of money. *Europe, 365*, 16-18.

Lindley, R. A. (1997). *Smart Card Innovation*. Australia: Saim.

Ling, T. C. (2003). Contact track and trace. *Electronics Review, 16*(2).

Lokan, C. J. (1991). The design and applications of smart cards. *he Australian Computer Journal, 23*(4), 159-164.

Lopez, J. (2002). The role of smart cards in practical information security. *ERCIM News*, from http://www.ercim.org/publication/Ercim_News/enw49/merino.html

Lutz, K. (1997). Telecommunications and information services. In C. A. Allen & W. J. Barr (Eds.), *Smart Cards: seizing strategic business opportunities* (pp. 128-150). New York: McGraw-Hill.

M'Chirgui, Z. (2005). The economics of the smart card industry: Towards coopetitive strategies. *Economics of Innovation and New Technology, 14*(6), 455-477.

Macaire, A. (2000). *An open secure terminal infrastructure for hosting personal services*. Paper presented at the IEEE International Conference on Technology of Object-Oriented Languages.

Marron, K. (2000, 9 June). Incubators nurture e-com ventures. *The Globe and Mail*, p. E5.

Martin, C. D. (1993). The myth of the awesome thinking machine. *Communications of the ACM, 36*(4), 120-133.

Mayes, K., & Markantonakis, K. (Eds.). (2008). *Smart Cards, Tokens, Security and Applications*. Germany: Springer.

MBF. (1999). 'Member privileges', Living Well (MBF), pp. 22-23.

McCrindle, J. (1990). *Smart Cards*. London: Springer-Verlag.

McIntosh, T. (1997, 29 April). Curly questions for smart cards. *The Australian*, p. 45.

McKenna, J., & Ayer, K. (1997). Worldwide developments and player motivations. In C. A. Allen & W. J. Barr (Eds.), *Smart Cards: Seizing Strategic Business Opportunities* (pp. 44-56). New York: McGraw-Hill.

Media. (1999, 19 November). University of Michigan develops the world's smallest web server in partnership with Schlumberger. *ScreamingMedia*, from http://industry.java.sun.com/javanews/stories/print/0,1797,20667,00.html

Messmer, E. (1998). Using 'body language' to secure networks. *NetworkWorldFusion*, 1-2.

Michael, K., Michael, M., & Ip, R. (2007). *Microchip Implants for Humans as Unique Identifiers: a Case Study on VeriChip*. Paper presented at the 3TU: Ethics, Identity and Technology, The Hague, The Netherlands.

Michael, K., & Michael, M. G. (2006). Historical Lessons on ID Technology and the Consequences of an Unchecked Trajectory. *Prometheus, 24*(4), 365 - 377.

Michael, M. G., & Michael, K. (2006). National Security: The Social Implications of the Politics of Transparency. *Prometheus, 24*(4), 359-364.

Mitchell, R. (1995). Sorry we don't take smart cards. *Credit Card Management, 8*(5), 16, 18.

Monnin, G. (1992). *Smart cards exclusive advantages in pay-TV*. Paper presented at the IBC 1992.

Moorhead, S. (1994). *Personalisation of GSM telephones*, AIC Conferences.

Mustafa, M. A. S., Giannopoulos, G. A., & Pitsiava-Latinopoulou, M. (1995). The Electronic Road Tolling and Enforcement Experiment of Thessaloniki. *Journal of Intelligent Transportation Systems, 2*(4), 327 - 340.

Noe, J. (1995). The dawn of smart card regulation. *America's Community Banker, 4*(11), 44-45.

NTT-DOCOMO. (2008). i-mode. Retrieved 3 December 2008, from http://www.nttdocomo.com/services/imode/index.html

O'Connor, S. M. (1998). The De Minimis Exemption of Stored Value Cards From Regulation E: An Invitation to Fraud? *The Richmond Journal of Law and Technology, 5*(2).

Octupus. (2008). Welcome to Octupus. Retrieved 3 December 2008, from http://www.octopuscards. com/consumer/en/index.jsp

Owens, R. C., & Onyshko, T. S. (1996). Legal regulations and privacy concerns relating to credit cards, debit cards and stored-value cards. Retrieved 21 January 1999, from http://www.smythlyons.ca/it/credit/ index.htm

Partners, V. (2002). VerifiCard Project. from http://www.cs.kun.nl/VerifiCard/files/partners.html

Petri, S. (1999). An Introduction to Smart Cards. *Messaging Magazine.* Retrieved 5 December 2008, from http://www.opengroup.org/comm/the_message/magazine/mmv5n5/SmartCards.htm

Poon, S., & Chau, P. Y. K. (2001). Octopus: The Growing E-payment System in Hong Kong. *Electronic Markets, 11*(2), 97 - 106.

Privacy Commissioner. (1995). Smart Cards: implications for privacy: Commonwealth of Australia, Canberra.

Privacy Committee of NSW. (1995). Smart Cards: Big Brother's Little Helpers. *66*(August).

Purdue. (2008). Magnetic Stripe. *Material Handling and Industrial Distribution Lab: School of Industrial Engineering at Purdue University.* Retrieved 5 December 2008, from http://cobweb.ecn.purdue. edu/~tanchoco/MHE/ADC-is/Magnetic/main.shtml

Puri, V. (1997). Smart cards – the smart way for the banks to go? *International Journal of Bank Marketing, 15*(4), 134–139.

Raad, M. W., Sheltami, T., & Sallout, M. (2007, 26-27 July). *A Smart Card Based Prepaid Electricity System.* Paper presented at the 2nd International Conference on Pervasive Computing and Applications.

Radigan, J. (1995). Consumers are lukewarm on smart cards. *US Banker,* 105(9), 24.

Rankl, W. (2007). *Smart Card Applications: Design Models for using and Programming Smart Cards.* West Sussex: John Wiley and Sons.

Rankl, W., & Effing, W. (1997). *Smart Card Handbook.* New York: John Wiley and Sons.

Rijn, F. V. (1988, 24-27 June 1987). *Concerning home telematics.* Paper presented at the proceedings of the IFIP TC 9 conference on social implications of home interactive telematics, Amsterdam.

RUN. (12 March 2008). Dismantling contactless smartcards. *Radboud University Nijmegen.* Retrieved 25 November 2008, from http://www2.ru.nl/media/pressrelease.pdf

Scarlett, D., & Manley, T. Smart cards brighten Atlanta this summer. *Northern Telecom, Enterprise: Millennium- SmartCard,* from http://www.nortel.com/home/about/articles/smartcard/

SCF. (2002). Smart Card Forum. from http://www.smcardforum.org

Schaefer, O. P. (1994). Introduction of chip technology to healthcare in Germany. *Smart Card News,* from http://www.smartcard.co.uk/health.htm

Schiffer, M. B. (2000). Looking back: why the electric automobile lost market share: How social behaviour can affect product technology. *IEEE Potentials,* 40-43.

SCIA. SCIA...Your link to a smart future. Retrieved 20 January 1999, from http://cardtech.faulknergray.com/scia.htm

Scullion, A. (2003). Smart cards track commuters. *BBC News | Technology*. Retrieved 3 December 2008, from http://news.bbc.co.uk/2/hi/technology/3121652.stm

SET. (2000). Secure Electronic Transaction. from http://www.setco.org/

Shogase, H. (1988). The very smart card: a plastic pocket bank. *IEEE Spectrum, 25*(10), 35-39.

SJB. (1999). Biometrics are hot in health care. *smartcard&biometrics Research News*(July), 2.

Slawsky, J. H., & Zafar, S. (2005). *Developing And Managing a Successful Payment Cards Business*. London: Ashgate Publishing.

Smart Card Alliance. (2006). Contactless Payments: Consumer Attitudes and Acceptance in the United States. *Smart Card Talk*. Retrieved 5 December 2008, from http://www.smartcardalliance.org/newsletter/december_2006/feature_1206.html

Smart Cards. (2002). SchlumbergerSema smart cards, terminals, consulting and system integration. Retrieved 6 December 2002, from http://www.smartcards.net/

SMDC. Centre information. from http://www.smartcard.com.hk/layout.htm

Smith, C. P. (1990). Smart Cards- the user's view. In P. L. Hawkes (Ed.), *Integrated Circuit Cards, Tags and Tokens: New Technology and Applications* (pp. 165-176). Oxford: BSP Professional Books.

Smith, R. (2002, 28 July). Motorists dial up to pay parking fees. *The Sunday Telegraph*, p. 11.

Sola, R. (1990, 15-16 October 1990). *Case study: City card implementation in Vitrolles, France- from concept to reality*. Paper presented at the AIC Conferences.

Stix, G. (1994). Dr. Big Brother. *Scientific American, February*, 79.

Sun-Herald. (2002, 29 December). Multimedia phones put friends in frame. *The Sun-Herald*, p. 27.

Svigals, J. (1987). *Smart Cards: the new bank cards*. New York: Macmillan Publishing Company.

Takac, P. F. (1990, 15-16 October). *An analysis of the issue of smartcard applications within the health services sector*. Paper presented at the AIC Conference.

Tam, K. Y., & Ho, S. Y. (2007). A Smart Card Based Internet Micropayment Infrastructure: Technical Development and User Adoption. *Journal of Organizational Computing and Electronic Commerce, 17*(2), 145 - 173.

Tarbox, A. (1997). Security, privacy, and smart cards. In C. A. Allen & W. J. Barr (Eds.), *Smart Cards: seizing strategic business opportunities* (pp. 248-264). New York: McGraw-Hill.

Teal, R. F. (1994). Using Smart Technologies to Revitalize Demand Responsive Transit. *Journal of Intelligent Transportation Systems, 1*(3), 275 - 293.

The Australian. (2002, 7 May). Pay your taxi fare by mobile phone. *The Australian*, p. 2.

Toumaz. (2008). Connected Freedom. *Toumaz Technology.* Retrieved 5 December 2008, from http://www.toumaz.com/public/page.php?page=sensium_intro

Trapanier, M., Tranchant, N., & Chapleau, R. (2007). Individual Trip Destination Estimation in a Transit Smart Card Automated Fare Collection System. *Journal of Intelligent Transportation Systems, 11*(1), 1 - 14.

Travin, V. (2008). The history of smart-cards and their place in modern Russia *St.Petersburg State University: Faculty of Economics.* Retrieved 5 December 2008, from http://works.tarefer.ru/29/100312/index.html

Tual, J.-P. (1999). MASCC: a generic architecture for multiapplication smart cards. *IEEE Micro*(September-October).

Turban, E., & Brahm, J. (2000). Smart Card-Based Electronic Card Payment Systems in the Transportation Industry. *Journal of Organizational Computing and Electronic Commerce, 10*(4), 281 - 293.

Ugon, M. (1989). Smart card- present and future. In D. Chaum (Ed.), *Smart Card 2000: the future of IC cards.* New York: North-Holland.

University of Michigan. (1999). Joint investigation of enhancements to smart card technology. from http://www.umich.edu/~newsinfo/Releases/1999/Feb99/r020999c.html

VeriMed. (2007). Solutions: VeriMed. *VeriChip Corporation.* Retrieved 7 December 2007, from http://www.verichipcorp.com/content/solutions/verimed

Vincent, N. (1995, 26 August). Big brother is selling you. *The Daily Telegraph.*

VISA. (2008). VISA Mini: A breakthrough in Card Design. *VISA-ASIA.* Retrieved 24 November 2008, from http://www.visa-asia.com/ap/au/cardholders/cardsservices/visa_mini.shtml

Website, S. C. I. A. SCIA home. Retrieved 27 November 2001, from http://www.scia.org

Wilson, C. (2001). *Get Smart: The Emergence of Smart Cards in the United States and their Pivotal Role in Internet Commerce.* New York: Artech House.

Zoreda, J. L., & Oton, J. M. (1994). *Smart Cards.* Boston: Artech House.

Chapter VIII
Biometrics:
In Search of a Foolproof Solution

BIOMETRIC TECHNOLOGY

Historical Overview

Manual Biometrics

Biometrics is not only considered a more secure way to identify an individual but also a more convenient technique whereby the individual does not necessarily have to carry an additional device, such as an ID card. As defined by the Association for Biometrics (AFB) a biometric is "...a measurable, unique physical characteristic or personal trait to recognize the identity, or verify the claimed identity, of an enrollee." The technique is not a recent discovery. There is evidence to suggest that fingerprinting was used by the ancient Assyrians and Chinese at least since 7000 to 6000 BC (O'Gorman, 1999, p. 44). Over a thousand years ago, potters in East Asia, placed their fingerprints on their wares as an early form of brand identity and in Egypt's Nile Valley, merchants were identified by their physical characteristics (Raina, Woodward & Orlans, 2002, p. 25). The practice of using fingerprints in place of signatures for legal contracts is hundreds of years old (Shen & Khanna, 1997 p. 1364). It is believed that the first scientific studies investigating fingerprints were conducted some time in the late sixteenth century (Lee & Gaensslen, 1994).

In the nineteenth century Alphonse Bertillon in France developed anthropometrics as well as noting peculiar marks on a person such as scars or tattoos. It was as early as 1901 that Scotland Yard introduced the Galton-Henry system of fingerprint classification (Halici, L.C. Jain, Erol, 1999, p. 4; Fuller et al. 1995, p. 14). Since that time fingerprints have traditionally been used in law enforcement. As early as 1960, the FBI Home Office in the UK and the Paris Police Department began auto-ID fingerprint studies (Halici, L.C. Jain, Erol, 1999, p. 5). Until then limitations in computing power and storage had prevented automated biometric checking systems from reaching their potential. Yet it was not until the late 1980s when personal computers and optical scanners became more affordable that automated biometric checking had an opportunity to establish itself as an alternative to smart card or magnetic-stripe auto-ID technology.

Background

According to Parks (1990, p. 99), the personal traits that can be used for identification include: facial features, full face and profile, fingerprints, palmprints, footprints, hand geometry, ear (pinna) shape, retinal blood vessels, striation of the iris, surface blood vessels (e.g., in the wrist), electrocardiac waveforms. Withers (2002), Jain, A. et al. (1999), Lockie (2000), Ferrari et al. (1998, p. 23) and Hawkes (1992, p. 6/4) provide good overviews of various biometric types. Keeping in mind that the aforementioned list is not exhaustive, it is impressive to consider that a human being or animal can be uniquely identified in so many different ways. Unique identification, as Zoreda and Oton (1994, p. 165) point out, is only a matter of measuring a permanent biological trait whose variability exceeds the population size where it will be applied. As a rule however, human physiological or behavioral characteristics must satisfy the following requirements as outlined by Jain et al. (1997, pp. 1365f):

- **Universality:** Every person should possess that characteristic
- **Uniqueness:** No two persons should have the same pattern in terms of that characteristic
- **Permanence:** The characteristics should not change over time (i.e. invariance)
- **Collectability:** The characteristic should be quantifiably measurable.

The four most commonly used physiological biometrics include, face, fingerprint, hand geometry and iris while the two most common behavioral biometrics are signature and voice recognition. Other examples of biometric types include DNA (deoxyribonucleic acid), ear shape, odor, retina, skin reflectance, thermogram, gait, keystroke, and lip motion (Bolle et al., 2007, p. 7; Greening, Kumar, Leedham, 1995, pp. 272-278). Even the Electroencephalogram (EEG) can be used as a biometric as proven by Paranjape et al. (2001, pp. 1363-1366). Most of these techniques satisfy the following practical requirements (Jain et al., 1997, p. 1366):

- **Performance:** Refers to whether or not the identifier is accurate, there are technical resources able to capture and process that identifier, and whether there are environmental factors which impact negatively on the decision policy outcome
- **Acceptability:** Addresses whether or not people are willing to use the system
- **Circumvention:** Refers to how easily a system may be duped.

The Biometric System

Independent of which biometric identifier is under consideration for a given application, they are all viewed as automated pattern recognition systems. Typically a biometric system includes a biometric reader, feature extractor and feature matcher. Biometric readers act as sensors, feature extractors take the input signals and compute those special attributes that are unique, and feature matchers compare biometric features attempting to find a match. Typically a biometric authentication system consists of an enrollment subsystem, an authentication subsystem, and database.

Figure 1. The iris recognition enrolment wizard process in the Cornerstone product developed by bio-metrics company Argus Solutions. Cornerstone allows a user to manage the identity profile of a person and their access and rights privileges, all from a single point. The biometric enrolment is a very fast and easy process, while the addition of personal data is very straight forward. All data can be recorded from a central point and managed from a central point. Courtesy of www.argus-solutions.com.

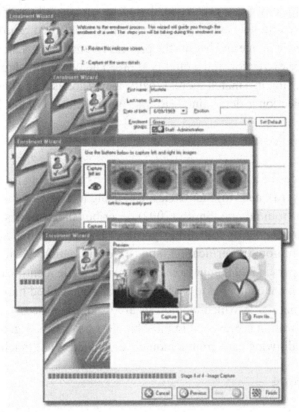

Components and Subsystems

In order for a biometric system to work, an individual must be enrolled, at which point the person's basic measurements of one or more biometrics are taken by the feature extractor and stored in the database (Figure 1). Relevant associated details may be stored alongside the biometric such as the enrollee's name and unique ID. If the method of authentication uses verification then typically a type of card is also linked to a person's biometric feature. A subject provides an identifier like an ATM card and places their biometric on a reader. The reader senses the biometric measurements, extracts the features, and compares the input features with what is stored on the database. The system either accepts or rejects the subject from the given application. In the case of straightforward identification during authentication, a biometric sample from the subject is taken and the entire database is searched for matches (Bolle et al., 2007, p. 7). In practice, two separate steps occur: first an authentication mechanism will verify the identity of the subject, and second an authorization mechanism ties the appropriate actions to someone's identity (Smith, 2002).

There are four steps that typically take place when using a biometric system. First data is acquired from the subject. The digital image captured of the biometric is transferred to the signal processing function (also known as image processing). Usually the data acquisition apparatus is collocated with the signal processor, but if it is not, the image is encrypted prior to transmission taking place. Second the transmission channel which acts as the link between the primary components will transfer the data. It can transfer internal to the device, or over a distributed system, usually over a private network. On occasion data may be acquired remotely at branch locations and data stored centrally. Third the signal processor takes the raw biometric image and begins the process for matching. The process of segmentation occurs resulting in a feature extraction and a quality score. The matching algorithm attempts to find a record that is identical resulting in a match score. Finally, a decision is made based on the resultant scores, and an acceptance or rejection is determined (Raina, Woodward & Orlans, 2002, p. 29-30).

Authentication vs. Verification

There are three modes of authentication: (i) possessions (e.g. using a smart card), (ii) knowledge (e.g. recollecting a password), and (iii) biometrics (e.g. using a physiological characteristic of an individual to distinguish them from others). Smith (2002) describes these modes as (i) something you have, (ii) something you know, and (iii) something you are. During automated authentication in biometrics, two methods are common: (i) verification, and (ii) identification. Verification is based on a unique ID which singles out a person and that person's biometrics, while identification is based only on biometric measurements which are compared to a whole database of enrolled individuals (Bolle et al. 2004, p. 5). Depending on the manner in which biometrics are used, the process of authentication differs. Today, multi-factor authentication is prevalent in most biometric systems (e.g. the use of PINs, ATM cards and a biometric for withdrawing cash from a biometric-enabled ATM machine).

Biometric Identifiers

Since there are several popular biometric identifiers, some space must be dedicated to each. While some techniques are further developed than others, there is not one single identifier that fits all applications. "Rather, some biometric techniques may be more suitable for certain environments, depending on among other factors, the desired security level and the number of users... [and] the required amount of memory needed to store the biometric data" (Zoreda & Oton, 1994, p. 167f). Dr J. Campbell, a National Security Agency (NSA) researcher and chairman of the Biometrics Consortium agrees that no one biometric technology has emerged as the perfect technique suitable for all applications (McManus, 1996).

The brief technical description offered for each major biometric identifier only takes into consideration the basic manner in which the biometric transaction and verification works, i.e., what criteria are used to recognize the individual which eventuates in the acceptance or rejection of an enrollee (Bigun et al., 1997). For each technique verification is dependent upon the person's biological or behavioral characteristic being previously stored as a reference value. This value takes the form of a template, a data set representing the biometric measurement of an enrollee, which is used to compare against stored samples. In summary, fingerprint systems work with the Galton-defined features and ridge information; hand geometry works with measurements of the distances associated between fingers and joints; iris systems work with the orientation of patterns of the eye; and voice recognition uses voice patterns (IEEE, 1997, p. 1343).

Fingerprint Recognition

Fingerprints are classified upon a number of fingerprint characteristics or unique pattern types, which include arches, loops and whorls (Cohen 1994, p. 228). If one inspects the epidermis layer of the fingertips closely, one can see that it is made up of ridge and valley structures forming a unique geometric pattern. The ridge endings are given a special name called minutiae. Identifying an individual using the relative position of minutiae and the number of ridges between minutiae is the traditional algorithm used to compare pattern matches (Jain, L. C. et al., 1999; Meenen & Adhami, 2001, pp. 33-38). The alternative to the traditional approach is using correlation matching (O'Gorman, 1999, pp. 53-54) or the pores of the hand. Pores have the characteristic of having a higher density on the finger than the minutiae which may increase even more the accuracy of identifying an individual.

The four main components of an automatic fingerprint authentication system are acquisition, representation (template), feature extraction, and matching (Jain et al., 1997, p. 1369). To enroll a user types in a PIN and then places their finger on a glass to be scanned by a charge-coupled device (CCD). The image is then digitized, analyzed and compressed into a storable size. In 1994, Miller (p. 26) stated that the mathematical characterization of the fingerprint did not exceed one kilobyte of storage space; and that the enrolment process took about thirty seconds and verification took about one second. Today these figures have been significantly reduced. For instance, the template size for a fingerprint in 2002 was 256 Bytes. For major fingerprint and hand geometry biometric developments refer to Higgins (2002, pp. 45-68).

Hand Recognition

Hand recognition differs from fingerprint recognition as a three dimensional shape is being captured, including the "[f]inger length, width, thickness, curvatures and relative location of these features..." (Zunkel, 1999, p. 89). The scanner capturing the images is not concerned with fingerprints or other surface details but rather comparing geometries by gathering data about the shape of the hand, both from the top and side perspectives. The hand, i.e. palm facing downward, is position on the faceplate and a capacitive switch senses the hand is present and initiates a scan. The measurements gathered are then compared to the stored data for matching (McCrindle 1990, p. 101). A set of matrices helps to identify plausible correlations between different parts of the hand. Some equipment vendors use five pegs to help position and stabilize the hand on the faceplate. These pegs act as control points. Typically more than one digital image of the hand is taken- from the view of the faceplate, and also a side view.

The hand geometric pattern requires less storage space than the fingerprint (between 9 Bytes and 20 Bytes depending on the manufacturer) and it takes less time to verify someone's identity. Quality enrolment is very important in hand recognition systems due to potential errors. Some systems require the enrollee to have their hand scanned three times, so that readings of the resultant vectors are averaged out and users are not rejected accidentally (Ashbourn, 1994, p. 5/5).

Face Recognition

While fingerprinting and hand recognition require a part of the body to make contact with a scanning device, face recognition does not. It is for this very reason that facial recognition systems have been used widely for surveillance and monitoring applications (Figure 2). For example, they are able to scan faces in public places and compare them to watch list databases. Facial recognition usually refers to "...static, controlled full-frontal portrait recognition" (Hong & Jain, 1998, p. 1297). In fact, recognizing someone by their appearance is quite natural and something humans have done since time began

Figure 2. A facial recognition system developed by Argus Solutions in St Leonards, NSW, Australia. Increasingly facial recognition systems are being used in surveillance roles and usually based on video technology. Digital images captured from video or still photographs are compared with other pre-captured images. Recognition is based on geometric or statistical features derived from face images. The biggest emerging market for such biometrics is in law enforcement. Courtesy of www.argus-solutions.com.

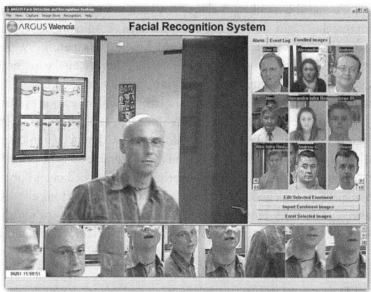

(Sutherland, Rengham & Denyer, 1992, p. 29; Weng & Swets, 1999, p. 66; Howell, 1999, p. 225; and Sirohey, Wilson & Chellappa, 1995, pp. 705-740).

Identifying people by the way they look is not as simple as it might sound (Pentland, 2000, pp. 109-111). People change over time, either through the natural aging process or by changes in fashion (including hair cuts, facial hair, make-up, clothing and accessories) or other external conditions (Miller, 1994, p. 28). If humans have trouble recognizing each other in certain circumstances, one can only begin to imagine how much more the problem is magnified through a computer which possesses very little intelligence especially across a sizable population.

What may seem like an ordinarily simple algorithm is not; to a computer a picture of a human face is an image like any other that is later transformed into a map-like object. Paramount in facial biometrics is that the subject must be wholly within the image frame being investigated. This is especially tricky when looking at applications like crowd control where there are dense pockets of people and with variation in seating or stance. The camera's location, field of view, and background setting need to be tested in extreme situations, to enable faces to be viewed and non-face images to be removed. In facial recognition systems, the segmentation phase is complex, removing background noise. This feature vector is compared against the discriminating power, the variance tolerance, and the data reduction efficiency. Shen and Khanna describe these variables (1997, p. 1422): *"[t]he discriminating power is the degree of dissimilarity of the feature vectors representing a pair of different faces. The variance tolerance is the degree of similarity of the feature vectors representing different images of the same individual's face. The data-reduction efficiency is the compactness of the representation."*

Engineers use one of three approaches to automate face recognition. These are eigen-face, elastic matching, and neural nets (IEEE, 1997, p. 1344). Once the face image has been captured, dependent on the environment, some pre-processing may take place. The image is first turned into grayscale and then normalized before being stored or tested. Then the major components are identified and matching against a template begins (Bigun et al., 1997, pp. 127f). A typical facial pattern can be stored in a template of between 86 Bytes and 100 Bytes. Facial recognition systems work best within controlled environments, and performance depends on this and other environmental factors.

Iris Recognition
The spatial patterns of the iris are highly distinctive. According to Williams (1997, p. 24) the possibility that two irises would be identical by random chance is approximately 1 in 10^{52}. Each iris is unique (like the retina). Some have reckoned automated iris recognition as only second to fingerprints, while others claim that it is the most accurate biometric identifier available today (Daugman, 2006). According to Wildes (1997, p. 1349) these claims can be substantiated from clinical observations and developmental biology. While some manufacturers claim to be able to capture a digital iris image at even 10 meters, commercial systems have a focal distance typical not more than an arm-length away (e.g. ATMs based on iris recognition).

The iris is "a thin diaphragm stretching across the anterior portion of the eye and supported by the lens" (IEEE, 1997, p. 1344). While it was ophthalmologists who were awarded the patent of describing methods and patterns for iris recognition in 1987, it was an academic from Cambridge University who developed the fundamental algorithms to encode an iris pattern (Daugman, 2008). While still involved in academia, Daugman has commercialized most of his research.

The first step in the process of iris identification is to capture the image (Figure 3). This can be done using a normal digital camera with a resolution of 512 dpi (dots per inch). The user must be a predetermined distance from the camera (Jain, A. et al., 1999, p. 9). Second, the image must be cropped to contain only the localized iris, discarding any excess. Third, the iris pattern must be matched, either with the image stored on the candidate's card or the candidate's image stored in a database. Between the second and third step processing occurs to develop an iris feature vector. This feature vector is so

Figure 3. The process of capturing an iris for automated recognition systems. Step 1: a digital image of the iris is captured. Step 2: The digital image is prepared for analysis. Step 3: A pattern of the iris is coded and stored on 512 Bytes of memory. Step 4: The stored template is used for authentication. The IrisCode product was developed by LG and used by Argus Solutions. Courtesy of www.argus-solutions. com.

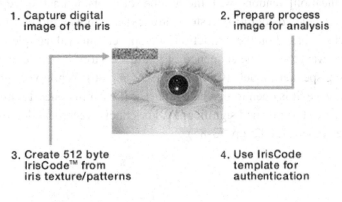

rich that it contains more than 400 degrees of freedom, or measurable variables. Most algorithms only need to use half of these variables and searching an entire database can take only milliseconds with an incredible degree of accuracy (Williams, 1997, p. 23). Matching algorithms are applied to produce scale, shift, rotation and distance measurements to determine exact matches (Camus et al., 1998, pp. 254-255 and Daugman, 1999, pp. 103-121).

Since iris recognition systems are non-invasive/ non-contact, some extra protections have been invented to combat the instance that a still image is used to fool the system. For this reason, scientists have developed a method to monitor the constant oscillation of the diameter of the pupil, thus declaring a live specimen is being captured (Wildes, 1997, p. 1349). A transaction time of between 4 and 10 seconds is required for iris recognition, although most of that time is spent aligning the subject for the digital image capture.

Voice Recognition

The majority of research and development dollars for biometrics has gone into voice recognition systems, also known as voice verification systems. Due to its attractive characteristics, telecommunications manufacturers and operators in the 1990s like Nortel and AT&T, along with a number of universities allocated large amounts of funds to research in this domain. Since there are literally billions of telephones in operation globally, voice recognition can be used as a means to increase operator revenues and decrease costs (Miller, 1994, p. 30). Among one of the most well-known voice recognition implementations was Sprint's Voice FONCARD which ran on the Texas Instruments voice verification engine (Boves and Os, 1998, pp. 203-208).

There are two main types of identification in voice recognition, unconstrained and constrained modes of speech. Unconstrained verification is when someone talks as normal, using a diverse lexicon familiar to them, and answering questions naturally without being prompted. This form of verification while still relatively successful is dependent on the application. Depending on the individual's accent and proficiency in a given language, sometimes this kind of verification is plagued by errors. It can almost be likened to recording an interview on a digital recorder, and running the recorded speech through an automated recognition system- the results are often quite poor. Constrained verification achieves considerably lower errors rates. This is because constrained verification relies on predetermined single words or phrases, often prompted by the system. Australia's Centrelink call centre is now for the greater part based on voice recognition. A question is posed to the caller and then an answer is captured by the system, and then replayed to callers for confirmation.

Out of all the variety of biometric technologies, consumers consider voice recognition as the most friendly. Markowitz (2001) wrote that "[d]espite the dot.com crash, 2001 [was] ... a very good year for [speaker verification] vendors, with the number of pilots and actual deployments increasing". The two major types of voice recognition systems are text-dependent and text-independent. The way voice recognition works is based on the extraction of a speech interval sample typically spanning 10 to 30 ms of the speech waveform. The sequence of feature vectors is then compared and pattern matched back into existing speaker models (Campbell, 1999, p. 166). While voice recognition is not the most secure technology, i.e. it is open to playback attacks, if used in concert with a PIN or smart card, false acceptance rates are strengthened significantly. For concise technical details on how voice recognition systems work see Orlans (2002, pp. 83-85).

System Accuracy

While biometric techniques are considered to be among the most secure and accurate automatic identification methods available today, they are by no means perfect systems. False accept rates (FAR) and false reject rates (FRR) for each type of biometric are measures that can be used to determine the applicability of a particular technique to a given application (Ruggles, 1996b). Some biometric techniques may also act to exclude persons with disabilities by their very nature, for instance in the case of fingerprint and hand recognition for those who do not possess fingers or hands. In the case of face recognition systems, one shortcoming is that humans can disguise themselves and gain the ability to assume a different identity (Jain, A. et al., 1999, p. 34). Other systems may be duped by false images or objects pertaining to be hands or iris images of the actual enrollee (Miller, 1994, p. 25). Carter and Nixon (1990, p. 8/4) call this act forgery. Putte (2001) discusses the challenge for a fingerprint scanner to recognize the difference between the epidermis of the finger and dummy material (like silicone rubber) (BBC, 2002).

In the case of the ultimate unique code, DNA, identical twins are excluded because they share an identical pattern (Jain, A. et al., 1999, p. 11). Even voice recognition systems are error-prone. Some problems that Campbell (1997, p. 1438) identifies include: "misspoken or misread prompted phrases, extreme emotional states, time varying microphone placement, poor or inconsistent room acoustics, channel mismatch, sickness, aging." Another issue with voice recognition systems is languages. Some countries like Canada have populations that speak several languages, i.e., English and French. Finally the environment in which biometric recognition systems can work must be controlled to a certain degree to ensure low rates of FAR and FRR. To overcome some of these shortcomings in highly critical applications, multimodal biometric systems have been suggested. Multimodal systems use more than one biometric to increase fault tolerance, reduce uncertainty and reduce noise (Hong & Jain, 1999, pp. 327-344). Automated biometric checking systems have acted to dramatically change the face of automatic identification. It is believed that in the future, esoteric biometric systems, including things like brain wave patterns, will prevail. It is possible that the driver's license of the future may not only be able to identify a driver using traditional physiological biometric, but also detect if someone should be driving or otherwise under the influence of alcohol or drugs using esoteric biometrics (Woodward, Orlans & Gatune, pp. 135-136).

THE BIOMETRIC INNOVATION SYSTEM

An Emerging Technology

At the turn of the 21st century, the biometrics industry was considered "young" and "emerging" (Kroeker, 2000, p. 57; Tilton, 2000, p. 130; A. Jain, 2004). Today, propelled forward by changes to traditional travel documents due to a turbulent global environment, biometrics are rapidly being deployed worldwide. As Burnell (1998, p. 2) accurately stated, "[f]our years ago, if you talked about a biometric, it was new to just about everybody... That's just not the case anymore. Resellers are seeing the benefits of biometrics for certain applications". In 2001, the biometrics industry was made up of about 150 separate hardware and software vendors (Liu & Silverman, 2001, p. 30). The number has oscillated in the last few years, as some biometrics hardware vendors have converged and new software-related vendors have emerged. Estimates in 1990 (Parks, p. 98) indicated that there were over one hundred firms, institutions and government agencies that had substantial activity in the area of Automatic Personal Identification (API). Biometrics companies are usually small in size when compared to the rest of the computer industry. For this reason they are dependent on resellers and systems integrators to get their product to market (Burnell, 1998, p. 2).

Given the nature of the technology it can be a difficult task finding the right integrators in the right place at the right time to implement a particular type of solution. While integrators and support technology providers play an important role in biometric implementation, the actual service provider is equally responsible for the longer-term operational success of the application (M2SYS, 2008). Realizing this, the Department of Social Services in Connecticut made extensive use of cross divisional workgroup teams to ensure a buy-in of the new process by DSS staff first. The work group teams focused primarily on process integration (Connecticut Dept., 1998, p. 1).

A fair degree of customizability and niche expertise is required in biometric applications- it is not a case of one size fits all. For example, an integrator specializing in fingerprint recognition systems usually does not have the same level of competency to do a voice recognition implementation. Thus, each new customer contract is not only an opportunity to gain more revenue but also exposure to a different set of problems that will equip all the stakeholders with valuable tacit insights for the longer-term.

Over the last ten years, integrated solutions for biometrics have seen the formation of a number of alliances that have led to a greater acceptability of the auto-ID technique. For instance, in 1999, biometrics provider Sensar had seven high profile partners including: Citibank, OKI, Siemens Nixdorf, Fujitsu, NCR, LG Electronics and WANG Global (Sensar, 1999). In most cases the hardware suppliers are teaming with software companies, while some other companies have enjoyed such synergy within an alliance that they have sought to form completely new companies together. Investors have generally been wary of sponsoring technologies like biometrics that have not proved completely roadworthy in certain situations; and in these instances "banks [especially] tend to err on the side of caution" (Jacobs, 1998, p. 1). Even government departments are said to stay away from bleeding edge technology that are not on the evaluated list of products (EPL). They need to undergo thorough testing before they are adopted (Withers, 2002, p. 78).

In recent times however, the major computing, networking, security and Original Equipment Manufacturers (OEM) have begun to play a more visible role in the support and development of biometric technology as they have seen its potential bolster, particularly through government adoption for mass market applications. An example of an OEM agreement in smart card is between Australian company Intellect and NCR. Some of Intellect's smart card system components are NCR-badged (Bell, 1997, p. 37). The NCR brand name is more well-known than that of Intellect and NCR like to promote a uniform brand image to their customers so it looks like they can provide an end-to-end smart card solution. As end-to-end solution providers start to surface and the infrastructure to support biometrics is put in place the technology will inevitably stabilize.

From Proprietary to Open Standards

The Increasing Need for Interoperability

One problem that so many small players in biometrics causes is in the fragmented and non-standard manner in which vendors develop their products, in isolation from one another. For instance, Vendor A may have developed a robust biometric technology that solves a particular part of an overall solution, and Vendor B may have a supplementary piece of technology, but the two products from each vendor cannot be integrated for a particular solution without some expensive and arduous programming. As has often been stated, "[t]his makes it difficult to link biometric technologies from different vendors, freely substitute biometric technologies, or use a single technology across multiple applications" (Lawton, 1998, p. 18). This has deterred customers from choosing biometric solutions and in the opinion of many players has held back the industry.

Like most new technologies, biometrics companies have been slow to embrace a set of standards. "The existence of a single industry standard will settle the confusion caused by competing specifications and hasten the adoption of biometric technology for a wide range of commercial applications" (Tilton, 2000, p. 132). Standards play a strategic role in deregulating the industry and making it a more competitive field, granting customers a greater variety of choice. Lazar (1997, p. 3) believes that biometric technology is not different to any other new technology. Initially, there are few standards and most systems are proprietary contributing to a lack of standard infrastructure for storing and transferring data captured. The important features organizations seeking to adopt biometric technology should look for are outlined by Liu and Silverman (2001, p. 32). These include: "the biometric's stability, including maturity of the technology, degree of standardization, level of vendor and government support, market share, and other support factors. Mature and standardized technologies usually have stronger stability."

The Development of Standards for Law Enforcement

Traditionally biometric technology was used for government and law enforcement applications where a high degree of custom integration was required. Manual standards for instance existed since the 1920s when the FBI (Federal Bureau of Investigation) in the U.S. started processing fingerprint cards. These standards ensured completeness, quality and permanency. In the 1980s another standard was devised to herald in the new live-scan fingerprint devices; the Minimum Image Quality Requirements (MIQR) was born. Eventually the FBI allowed virtual fingerprint cards to be submitted electronically and a new set of standards had to be introduced including "comprehensive guidelines on the required message formats and image quality standards" (Higgins, 1995, p. 2). Finally the FBI transitioned to the Integrated Automated Identification System (IAFIS). Higgins observed that many of the existing standards had corollaries in the electronic world- they did not just disappear, but were carried over. For example, ANSI/NIST-CSL 1-1993 describes the record types associated with digital fingerprint transmission. Today what is needed is off-the-shelf type biometrics for rapid deployment and this is currently what is being evolved.

BioAPI

With so many small companies, and so many different types of biometric techniques and components one can only imagine the number of proprietary interfaces, algorithms and data structures that were introduced by the biometrics community. As the small industry began to grow, vendors started to offer software development kits (SDKs) with proprietary APIs. While this was a step in the right direction the standards were still proprietary. According to Burnell (p. 1) 1998 was a defining stage in biometrics history as suppliers began to reach out to the wider computing community. Several specifications were published by ANSI, the International Computer Security Association (ICSA) certified biometrics products for the first time, and AIM USA began undertaking biometrics efforts along with the formation of the International Biometrics Industry Association (IBIA). The standards issue gathered momentum as large players like the Microsoft Corporation saw the technology's potential and the BioAPI Consortium was born.

The creation of a standard application programming interface (API) was championed by the Consortium. *"BioAPI is an open-systems standard developed by a consortium of more than 60 vendors and government agencies. Written in C, it consists of a set of function calls to perform basic actions common to all biometric technologies, such as enroll user, verify asserted identity (authentication), and discover identity" (Liu & Silverman, 2001, p. 30).* The importance of the BioAPI standard is highlighted in Dunstone (2001, pp. 351-354). BioAPI is based on an architecture model which contains two to four layers, depending on the design. The highest level contains the fundamental biometric functions. The lowest level is where the control of interfaces with devices occurs (Tilton, 2000, p. 131). An example of a draft level standard is the Biometric Exchange File Format which defines how to store and exchange data from a variety of biometric devices (Liu & Silverman, 2001, p. 30). Subsequent to the fine work of the BioAPI Consortium has been that of the Information Technology Laboratory (ITL).

After the tragic events of the September 11th attacks, biometric standards activities were accelerated in response to newly formed U.S. security legislation. ITL spearheaded this development in collaboration with Federal Agencies, end-users, biometric vendors and the IT industry at large. In 2003, the standards activities were extensive and gaining a great deal of attention. Some of these standards activities included the INCITS M1-Biometrics Technical Committee, Common Biometric Exchange File Format, ANSI INCITS 358-2002 Information Technology- BioAPI Specification (Version 1.1), Human Recognition Services Module (HRS) of the Open Group's Common Data Security Architecture, ASNI X9.84-2000 Biometrics Management and Security for the Financial Services Industry, ANSI/NIST-ITL 1-2000 Fingerprint Standard Revision, AAMVA Fingerprint Minutiae Format/National Standards for the Driver License/Identification Card DL/ID-2000, Part 11 of the ISO/IEC 7816 standards, and NIST Biometric Interoperability Performance and Assurance Working Group (NIST, 2002; INCTIS, 2002).

Formal ISO Standards

It is without a doubt that the BioAPI Consortium activities placed pressure on the International Standards Organization (ISO) to develop "formalized" biometric standards to assist with the proliferation of biometric applications worldwide (Stapleton, 2003). Without a common language, the implementation of automated recognition systems would have been severely inhibited. In 2002, Subcommittee 2 of the ISO Technical Committee 68 (TC68/SC2) was tasked with developing standards directly related to the security management and general banking operations audience in the financial industry. At that time ISO also established a Joint Technical Committee (JTC) with the International Electrotechnical Commission (IEC) to address information technology standards relevant to biometric technology. Since that time, a great deal of change has occurred and a number of new standards have emerged (ISO, 2008). Some of these include:

- JTC 1/SC 37 (focused on information technology and biometrics)
    - ISO/IEC TR 24741:2007 Information technology -- Biometrics tutorial
    - ISO/IEC 24713-2:2008 Information technology -- Biometric profiles for interoperability and data interchange -- Part 2: Physical access control for employees at airports
    - ISO/IEC TR 24714-1:2008 Information technology -- Biometrics -- Jurisdictional and societal considerations for commercial applications -- Part 1: General guidance
    - ISO/IEC TR 24722:2007 Information technology -- Biometrics-- Multimodal and other multibiometric fusion

- JTC 1/SC 17 (focus on identification)
  - ○ ISO/IEC 11694-6:2006 Identification cards -- Optical memory cards -- Linear recording method -- Part 6: Use of biometrics on an optical memory card
  - ○ ISO/IEC 18013-1:2005 Information technology -- Personal identification -- ISO-compliant driving licence -- Part 1: Physical characteristics and basic data set
- TC 68/SC 2 (focus on security and management in financial services)
  - ○ ISO 19092:2008 Financial services -- Biometrics -- Security framework

Of particular interest is the more recent activity in 2007/08 in the formation and further enhancement of standards to meet a need in the industry at large, not to mention changes to legislation especially in the United States.

Consortiums and Associations

Apart from the BioAPI Consortium, a number of other working groups have formed to support biometric technology. These consortiums differ somewhat from the smart card consortiums. They have been established for the purpose of instilling stakeholder confidence in the technology and to bring together key representatives who have a common interest. Among the list of consortiums and associations active at the turn of the century, was the European Biometrics Forum (EBF), International Biometric Association (IBIA), the Commercial Biometrics Developer's Consortium (CBDC), the Biometric Testing Services (BIOTEST), the Association for Biometrics (AfB), the Financial Services Technology Consortium, the International Association for Identification (IAI), and the National Centre for Identification Technology. It is standard practice for government tenders to be channeled through consortia. The tender responses are usually championed by integrators such as TRW, Unisys, Siemens, IBM and include traditional biometrics manufacturers like Motorola, NEC, Sagem and Cogent, and card manufacturers like Gemalto (Didier, 2004).

The EBF (2008) is one of the more active forums in Europe and has the aim of "addressing barriers to adoption and fragmentation in the marketplace. The forum also acts as the driving force for coordination, support and strengthening of the national bodies." IBIA which is based in the United States, mainly "focuses on educating lawmakers and regulators about how biometrics can deter identity theft and increase personal security" (Kroeker, 2000, p. 57). The IBIA has established a strong code of ethics for members to follow. BIOTEST is a European project aimed at developing standard metrics for measuring/comparing the performance of biometric devices. The AfB want to be considered an international authority on biometrics. Whereas *"...other industry organizations are mainly designed for biometric industry companies, the AfB's membership will continue to be a broad church comprising biometric suppliers, end users, government agencies, academics and consultants"* (Lockie, 2001).

The Biometric Consortium

Perhaps the most influential of them all however is the Biometric Consortium (Alyea & Campbell, 1996). The Biometric Consortium can be likened to the Smart Card Forum in aim and purpose, except that it is working on behalf of the U.S. Government and represented by officials from six executive government departments and each of the military services. Lawton (1998, p. 18) makes an interesting observation about biometric technologies, stating that "[s]ecurity technologies start with the government, and work their way down to industrial and then finally to personal applications" (Lawton, 1998, p. 18). The Biometric Consortium was established in 1992 (its charter formally approved in 1995) and meets to promote biometrics, create standards and relevant protocols, provide a forum for information exchange between stakeholders, to encourage government and commercial interaction, to run workshops linking academia and private industry and address ethical issues surrounding the technology among other things (Alyea & Campbell, 1996, p. 2). By establishing one central body for the research, development, testing and evaluation of biometrics, the National Security Agency (NSA) formed the Consortium as part of its Information Systems Security mission and invested personnel resources and funds to provide support to the Consortium. The NSA considered biometrics to have excellent potential for DOD (Department of Defense) applications and other Federal agencies and wanted the independent technical capability to make decisions for government needs.

The U.S. government became especially interested in biometrics in the 1970s. They commissioned the Scandia Labs to compare various biometric identifiers. The report concluded that this technique was more accurate than the others. So influential were the findings of the government-commissioned report, that "[t]he impact of the study was to shift focus on fingerprint technology. Because of this early emphasis on fingerprint technology, the years since 1970 have produced a large body of research and development in fingerprint identification algorithms and integrated systems" (Ruggles, 1996a, p. 8). Thus it is not surprising that the U.S. government, more than twenty years later, invested time and money into the establishment of the Biometrics Consortium. The Consortium however, is also concerned with the exchange of information between the government, private industry and academia. For now, it serves as the U.S. government's testing ground for the future of biometrics in public administration.

Government and Industry Links with Academia

Biometrics research centers have sprouted up all over the globe (BC, 2009). This is one technology where there is a lot of scope for government and industry linkages with academia for the development of potential biometric applications. In 2001, for instance, DOD became a member of the Centre for Identification Technology Research (CITeR) at West Virginia University (WVU). WVU has one of the world's leading forensics degree programs (CITeR, 2008). CITeR was developed in collaboration with Marshall University, Michigan State University and San Jose State University to serve as one of the first academic biometric centers. The latter was awarded a 400,000 U.S. dollar contract in 1995 to "study and develop standards for biometric identifiers for use with commercial truck drivers' licenses" (Woodward, 1997, p. 1482). Research on biometrics at San Jose University began in 1994.

In 1997 the Biometric Consortium established the National Biometric Test Centre at the university. San Jose is also the only university to participate as a member in the Biometric Consortium. In Asia, the Hong Kong Polytechnic University has some impressive ties with industry and other academic institutions including the National Tsing Hua University in Taiwan, University of Sinica and University of South Florida. The Lab in Hong Kong specializes in transferring multiple biometric technologies to industry and is currently exploring integrated biometric solutions. It is continually building up its knowledge base as it sees local opportunities for biometrics arising. Other universities involved in biometric research include: MIT Lincoln Labs, Purdue University, Nagoya University (Japan) and Rutgers University. Some of the European universities researching biometrics include: the University of Bologna (Biometric Systems Laboratory in Italy), the University of Neuchatel (Pattern Recognition Group- IMT in Switzerland), and the University of Cambridge (Speech Vision and Robotics Group).

Legislation and New Technologies

Laws almost always lag behind new innovations. In the case of biometrics, this is not any different (Walden, 2000, pp. 2/1-2/11). Kralingen, Prins and Grijpink (1997, p. 2) believe that "[w]hen a new technology is introduced, its applicability and the adequacy of existing laws needs to be examined." Yet opinions are divided whether present laws are sufficient to handle privacy issues or new protections for privacy need to be introduced specifically for biometrics (van der Ploeg, 2003). Woodward (2002b, pp. 220-231) discusses the right to privacy with respect to biometrics using three paradigms referencing the work of Robert Ellis Smith, editor of the *Privacy Journal*: physical privacy, decisional privacy and informational privacy. Physical privacy has to do with freedom from contact with others including those who are tasked with monitoring. Decisional privacy is the freedom of the individual to make choices, such as whether they may opt-in or opt-out of a service, without coercion or pressure by the government. And informational privacy is the right of the individual to limit information about him or herself. For information privacy as related to the law, the works of Solove should be studied extensively (Solove, 2004, 2008a, 2008b; Solove, Rotenberg & Schwartz, 2005, 2006).

Biometric Laws, Regulations or Codes of Conduct?

Despite their increasing deployment due to the falling cost of biometrics and government policy, for courts the technology is still new- there is no law governing biometrics in the United States. Woodward (1997, p. 1487) argues that "[w]e do not need a new "Law of Biometrics" paradigm; the old bottles will hold the new wine of biometrics quite well." The best service providers can do is to develop their own Code of Fair Information Practice (CFIP) to gain the confidence of the consumer, even if these are not enforceable by law (Woodward, 1997, p. 1484). It follows from this that there is a growing need for policy makers to understand biometric technology and how unique human features stored digitally can be misused.

In Australia, the Biometrics Institute (2006) introduced a Privacy Code which was approved by the Privacy Commissioner in 2006 as related to Section 18BB(2) of the *Privacy Act 1988* (Cth). According to the Biometrics Institute, the Privacy Code sought to build on Australia's national privacy principles (NPPs) in *"a manner that provides the community with the assurance needed to encourage informed and voluntary participation in biometrics programs. Biometrics Institute members understand that only by adopting and promoting ethical practices, openness and transparency can these technologies gain widespread acceptance."* As is the case with all "codes" the level of enforceability is questionable. Yes, members promise to adopt ethical practices, but generally the stakeholders developing the technology are not the ones who are tasked with ensuring the end-user's private information remains private in the long term. Still, at least the Australian Government has attempted to address the matter rather than ignoring it altogether (DCITA, 2004).

Government Biometric Applications and Legislation

Kralingen, Prins and Grijpink (1997, p. 1) prefer the proactive approach rather than "simply waiting until problems arise and then think[ing] up an ad hoc legal solution" later. By the time a new innovation is introduced and adopted by the mass market, some analysis of the legal implications of those applications can be conducted. At the present, the reverse can be said to be taking place, as governments especially, throughout the world implement citizen mass market biometric applications for voting and social security welfare without a great deal of public discourse. In 1998 Mexico and Brazil followed several other countries when its national parliaments officially decided to use biometric technology to secure the voting process (Bunney, 1998, pp. 2-3). This is not to say that governments are ignoring legislative impacts of the technologies they are using to facilitate citizen services. Rather, it seems that government choices in technology are driving legislation in some states to enable the deployment to be fast-tracked. Wayman (2000, p. 76) supports this argument: "[e]ncouraged or mandated by federal legislation, governmental agencies at all levels have turned to technology in an attempt to meet... requirements."

One of the most contentious issues in biometrics today is whether enrolment in particular applications is obligatory as opposed to voluntary. Wayman's (2000, pp. 76-80) study on federal biometric technology legislation covers drivers licensing, immigration, employment eligibility, welfare and airport security and uncovers some interesting findings. The former has statutory implications (Kralingen, Prins and Grijpink, 1997, p. 2) because a biometric can be considered a type of personal data, owned by the individual. Perhaps the fundamental question is whether or not a government requirement to record a particular biometric is in breach of a citizen's legitimate right to privacy. However, what court cases in the U.S. have consistently ruled on, is that certain biometrics do not violate federal laws like the Fourth Amendment.

O'Connor (1998, p. 9) determined that the "...real test for constitutionality of biometrics... appears to be based on the degree of physical intrusiveness of the biometric procedure. Those that do not break the skin are probably not searches, while those that do are". Incidentally, O'Connor's legal consideration is not in contradiction with a critical theological interpretation of the "mark" of the beast (Revelation 13:17). In the original Koine Greek (*New Testament*), the "mark" is described as a *charagma*, which literally means an incision into the skin, not just a mere surface mark such as a tattoo (M.G. Michael, 1998, p. 278, ft. 3). Yet, even scars and tattoos are being collected by the Federal Bureau of Investigation (FBI) so that several pieces of biometric information can be used to positively identify a suspect (Arena & Cratty, 2008).

In purely rational terms it is also a difficult case to argue against a technology that could save governments (and subsequently taxpayers) millions of dollars in areas like Social Security by reducing fraud. For example, in the U.S. changes to Regulation E in 1994 granted citizens, limited liability to EBT (Electronic Benefits Transfer) at the federal, state and local government level. "The Government Office of Accounting (GAO) projected fraud losses as a result of the Regulation E amendment, in the vicinity of 164 million and 986 million dollars" (Fuller et al., 1995, p. 8). In another example in the U.K. the National Audit Office (NAO) reported that one in ten welfare claims are fraudulent. In 1995 NAO estimated that 561,000 people made fraudulent Social Security claims at a cost to the government of 1.4 billion U.K. pounds (SJB ed., 1996a, p. 1). The fear is however, that biometrics gathered for one purpose could be submitted as admissible proof, in a court of law, for a completely different purpose. Among the most versatile biometrics used to show criminal activity are fingerprints and DNA (Brinton & Lieberman, 1994).

The Terrorism Threat

O'Connor (1998) has suggested that guidelines be set-up for biometric records such as in the case where an arrest does not lead to a conviction. Consider the national DNA database established by the FBI (Herald Tribune, 1998, p. 7) and its subsequent implications. The database is similar to that launched in the U.K. in 1995 that has matched 28,000 people to crime scenes and made 6,000 links between crime scenes. The debate over access to biometrics has taken on another perspective since the recent terrorist attacks on the U.S. World Trade Centre in 2001 and the Bali bombing in 2002. As a result of the September 11th attacks, the U.S. moved quickly to create several Public Laws. Relevant to biometrics are Public L No 107-56 (US Government, 2001), 107-71 and 107-173 (USA Government, 2002). Public L No 107-65 describes the appropriate tools required to intercept and obstruct terrorism, Public L No 107-71 focuses on introducing emerging technologies like biometrics for airport security for personnel, and Public L No 107-173 is about enhanced border security and visa entry reforms (NIST, 2002; Snyderwine & Murray, 1999).

O'Connor (1998, p. 9) prophetically stated years before the events of September 11th, that "[t]he government [would] still be able to show compelling state interests in combating terrorism, defending national security, or reducing benefits fraud sufficient to preserve the program's constitutionality." In these extreme circumstances (i.e. terrorism attacks) the case for mandatory biometric identification seems a great deal stronger. When comparing the mandatory recording of a biometric feature against the innocent loss of lives in a terrorist attack, biometrics as a human rights violation diminishes in importance. However, "[w]hile some people have revised their opinions about the invasiveness of various biometric techniques in light of the September 11th tragedy, the privacy debate continues throughout the US. If this hurdle is to be overcome, accurate information and education will still be required" (Watson, 2001). Having said that, government applications that use biometrics should be considered carefully (O'Neil, 2005).

A current case (S. AND MARPER v. THE UNITED KINGDOM) which was fought out in the European Court of Human Rights unanimously ruled that the storage of fingerprints and DNA in Britain of all criminal suspects, even individuals who turned out to be innocent, was a violation of the human right to privacy (European Court of Human Rights, 2008). More than any other in modern times, this court case has shown the conflict between technological progress and jurisdictional and societal issues pertaining to biometrics (Freeman, 2003; Lyall, 2008). While the outcome of this court case has far-reaching implications in Britain and more broadly in the European Union, it remains to be seen what kind of power the ruling has in non-member states internationally. Will the government of the United States, for instance, ever consider ceasing to collect fingerprint records of all aliens traveling to its shores? We will not be able to go back to an era of purely paper-based documentation without microchips in passports and the like. Layers of infrastructure built-up are almost impossible to tear down.

Kralingen, Prins and Grijpink (1997, p. 3) stipulate that the government has a role to play in ensuring that an adequate framework is in place for a given context, that special attention be placed on user acceptance, and the quality of critical social processes is to be guaranteed. The legislative process to get a bill through parliament can take a long time. In the case of the Connecticut DSS (Department of Social Security) it took three years for welfare recipients (those on general assistance (GA) and Aid to Families with Dependent Children (ADFC)) to be digitally fingerprinted. Jeanne Garvey who worked on the legislation said the process was unexpectedly difficult. She is quoted as saying "I didn't know the process or the key people, but I know one thing- if you want to get something done you go to the top" (Storms, 1998, p. 2). The article by Storms on Garvey shows the complexity of human relationships in these types of projects. One is left to ponder on whether Garvey's endeavor to reduce DSS fraud turns out to be a self-seeking journey to topple her opponents. Garvey says: "[i]f you want something badly enough, you have to be in people's faces a little bit harder". Perhaps however, it is not about wanting something badly enough, it is about doing the right thing by citizens, since as a senator you are acting on behalf of your constituents. Garvey continues: "I had to baby-sit this thing like a hawk... the thing

I learned through this whole experience was never, never, never give up... these are once-in-a-lifetime type things" (Storms, 1998, pp. 3-4).

Biometrics and Privacy: Friend or Foe?

There are two schools of thought when it comes to biometrics: either these devices are privacy safeguards or they are privacy's foe (Woodcock, 2005). Woodward (1997, pp. 1485-1489) explains the notion of "privacy foe" and "privacy friend" in his landmark paper on biometrics and elaborates further in a book chapter (2002a, pp. 197-215). Woodward summarizes the case of biometrics being privacy's foe by discussing the loss of anonymity and autonomy, the "Big Brother" scenario, function creep and the degradation of the individual's right to privacy. Of "privacy's friend" Woodward discusses biometrics with respect to safeguarding identity and integrity, limiting access to private information, serving as a privacy enhancing technology, as well as providing benefits of convenience.

Dunstone (2001) describes the opposing thoughts in another way, those users who believe that there is no downside to privacy by using biometric technology and those who would only use biometrics in extremely limited circumstances (if at all). He writes: "[b]oth sides have salient points to back up their views. However there is significant middle ground which deals with the responsible and pragmatic use of biometrics". The positions have been summarized by Clarke (1994):

1. *Biometrics do help to protect an individual's right to privacy because identification is ensured and access to information is limited;*
2. *Biometrics is "a threat to civil liberties, because it represents the basis for a ubiquitous identification scheme, and such a scheme provides enormous power over the populace (Clarke, 1994).*

For Clarke and others like him, any high-integrity identifier such as biometrics represents a threat to civil liberties, potentially providing the State with enormous power over the populace.

Citizen Fears

Those who belong to privacy's foe hold numerous fears about biometrics and related technologies (Computing, 1999; Moskowitz, 1999, p. 85). McMurchie (1999, p. 11) writes of the risks associated with biometrics. First, some users do not like the idea that they must give up a biometric identifier which is unique. Second, some people believe that an underground market will form around biometric data. Third, people believe that before too long, biometric data may be used for law-enforcement purposes. Fourth, some biometric data may be linked to centralized databases containing medical history (Woodward, 1997, p. 1484). Fifth, data gathered for one purpose may be used for another depending on who has power over it. This is the very real possibility of function creep. Davies is adamant, *"[w] e would go for outright prohibition on the transfer of biometric data for anybody, for any purpose. If I give my biometric data for a specific purpose then it is locked-in, for all time, for that purpose. I cannot give my consent for its transfer and no one can force, or request for access to that information"* (Roethenbaugh, 1998, p. 2). The U.S. social security number (SSN) introduced in 1936 is an excellent example of function creep (Hibbert, 1996, p. 686). It ended up being used by the banking sector, among numerous other uses. "The risks to privacy therefore do not lie in data by themselves, but in the way in which they are concatenated- or, more, generally, 'processed' or 'handled'- for some specific purpose" (Sieghart, 1982, p. 103).

Sixth, biometrics technology discriminates some persons with disabilities. Jim Wayman, head of the National Biometrics Test Centre at San Jose State University, says that biometric systems are not perfect. He notes that 2% to 3% of the population cannot use them at any given time: "[e]ither they don't have the (body) part or the part doesn't look and work like everyone else's, or something is just off" (Weise, 1998, p. 2). It is to this end that widespread consumer acceptance of the technology has been hampered. Service providers are aware of people's privacy concerns and are conducting trials before implementing fully operational biometric systems to gauge the amount of end-user resistance. For example, when Nationwide considered using iris identification, a spokesman said: "[i]t's a very unknown area, and we want to see what the reaction is like and whether or not it is commercially viable" (Craig, 1997, p. 3). What trials have discovered is that in general, "[t]he less intrusive the biometric, the more readily it is accepted" (Liu & Silverman, 2001, p. 32).

Government Tracking Citizens without Individual's Consent

Agre (2001) argues that "[f]ace recognition systems in public places... are a matter for serious concern. The issue came to broad public attention when it emerged that fans attending the 2001 Super Bowl had unknowingly been matched against a database of alleged criminals..." In his case study on this event, Woodward (2001, p. 7) writes of the potential for "super surveillance" and refers to the ability of a tracker (in this case authorities) to follow a person and monitor their individual actions in real time or over a period of time. Agre's concerns about facial recognition are similarly voiced by Rosenweig (2000).

In Hong Kong, Mathewson (1998) reported how hair testing helped detect drugs in school students. In this case, if a sample of hair was retained for DNA records it would be unethical. Increasingly, civil-libertarians are rejecting the implementation of any biometric technology: *"Imagine an America in which every citizen is required to carry a biometrically-encoded identification card as a precondition for conducting business. Imagine having your retina scanned every time you need to prove your identification. Imagine carrying a card containing your entire medical, academic, social, and financial history. Now, imagine that bureaucrats, police officers, and social workers have access under certain circumstances to the information on your card. Finally, imagine an America in which it is illegal to seek any employment without approval from the United States government"* (Williams, 1996, p. 1). Woodward (1997, pp. 1489-1490) differentiates between the notion of biometric centralization versus balkanization.

According to Wayman (2000, p. 76), the privacy fear is very much related to how governments could use biometric records in the future to track individuals in real-time. Wayman states that those people who propose, design and implement biometric solutions for government applications are sympathetic to citizen concerns about potential breaches in privacy. This is likely to be true but as vigilant as the technology providers may be there are defining limits to the number of hours and the number of resources any one company can dedicate to a project. In a perfect world, a perfect biometric solution could operate without any qualms but the world we live in is not perfect, and no one can categorically state that a system is foolproof even if the teams working on the solutions do their very best. Dale (2001) writes that privacy concerns are an issue for biometrics used, especially those for the purposes of law enforcement. The challenge is in the sharing of sensitive data between the relevant agencies. In an interview Davies states: "[w]e can conceivably end up with a multiple purpose national/international system from which people can't escape" (Roethenbaugh, 1998, p. 2).

Perhaps the most controversial of all biometrics is DNA and its potential future applications. According to the Privacy Committee of Canada (1992, pp. 16-25), current and potential uses of genetic testing (i.e. acquiring a DNA sample) include: workplace testing, screening associated with human reproduction, screening as part of basic medical care, genetic screening to determine the right of access to services or benefits, forensic DNA analysis in criminal investigations and testing for research. For example: *"[e]mployers (both public and private sector) may wish to identify "defective" (less productive) or potentially defective employees or applicants through genetic screening"* (p. 16); and *"Governments may one day wish to test persons to see if they are genetically suited to have access to certain services (advanced schooling, immigration or adoption)... or benefits (disability payments)"* (p. 20). While the Privacy Committee of Canada offer a number of recommendations, one can only begin to ponder on the potential privacy issues linked with such widespread use of DNA. An incorrect record entry could affect an individual's life indefinitely. An opposing argument however could lay claim that neglecting to use DNA evidence in a court of law may mean that innocent persons are not exonerated for crimes they have not committed.

End-User Resistance

Biometrics has also differed to any other auto-ID device before it, in terms of its level of invasiveness. According to the Sandia report, retinal scan had the most negative client reaction when compared to other biometric techniques. The "users have... concerns about retina identification, which involves shining an infrared beam through the pupil of the eye" (Ruggles, 1996a, p. 7). Lazar (1997, p. 4) has noted that *"[f]ears of 'Big Brother'- combined with intrusive measuring devices such as bright lights and ink pads- have had even technophiles dragging their feet on occasion. As the systems have become less intrusive however, user resistance has dwindled, but the suspicion is still there, vendors said, and agencies should not underestimate the importance of a user feeling comfortable with a technology."* According to Gunnerson (1999) people were used to remembering PINs and carrying cards but they were definitely not used to using body parts to grant them access to funds etc.

Biometrics has forced an ideological and cultural shift to take place (Ng-Kruelle, Swatman, Hampe, & Rebne, 2006, p. 16). The human body almost becomes an extension of the machine for that one moment that the physical trait is being verified or authenticated (Solove, 2004). The body becomes analogous to a token, i.e., *something we have* but at the same time, it is *something we are.* Davies (1996, pp. 236-239) describes something similar to this in his book on the section entitled the *Future of Fusion*. This is what could be considered intimate human-computer interaction (HCI). And biometrics designers have had to pay attention to consumer requirements when building biometric systems to minimize resistance. For example, the stigma that biometrics is for law enforcement has some users opposed to being fingerprinted even for physical access control applications (Lazar, 1997, p. 2). When biometrics for social security services was first proposed in the state of Connecticut to say it was controversial "... would be an understatement... Public perception and the association of fingerprinting with the criminal element was pervasive" (Connecticut Dept., 1998, p. 1). But this in itself did not stop its implementation (Heckle, Patrick, Ozok, 2007).

The Right to Opt Out of Any System for Any Personal Reason

While designers can respond to making biometric systems more user friendly, they really cannot cater for the needs of those people who hold religious beliefs about how biometric technology may lead to the fulfillment of prophecy, particularly in the widely quoted Book of Revelation (Michael, 1999). Short of calling this group of people fundamentalists, as Woodward (1997, p. 1488) does of one prominent leader,

Davies is more circumspect in his appraisals: *"I think they're legitimate [claims]. People have always rejected certain information practices for a variety of reasons: personal, cultural, ethical, religious and legal. And I think it has to be said that if a person feels bad for whatever reason, about the use of a body part then that's entirely legitimate and has to be respected"* (Roethenbaugh, 1998, p. 3).

Dunstone (2001), the executive director at the Biometrics Institute also adds *"[p]ublic concerns over biometric use should be taken seriously. It is particularly important that these issues are openly recognized as valid, both by the biometric vendors and by system implementers, if they are to reduce the risk of adverse public sentiment, particularly for those systems that are intended for wide scale deployment."* Opponents to the DSS Connecticut fingerprint imaging scheme for instance, mostly argued that fingerprinting was invasive and dehumanizing. These opponents cannot be considered fundamentalists just because they do not agree with the State. The naive response of the DSS was to "narrow [public] perception" by making the states chief executive the first to be fingerprinted (Connecticut Dept., 1998, p. 2). Of course, if it was that easy to change public perception, it would be equally easy to change people with all sorts of cultural, religious and philosophical objections against biometrics. This kind of intolerance to diverse attitudes however is dangerous. The Australian Federal Privacy Commissioner and the president of the Australian Council of Liberties have expressed concerns over privacy implications for an Australian passport based on face recognition. The response has been "whether we like it or not, it's going to happen" (Withers, 2002, p. 79).

Towards Multi-Modal Biometrics

One of the least discussed topics in biometrics which is related to privacy is ethics. Davies stated in 1998 that "[t]he biometrics industry need[ed] to develop an ethical backbone" (Roethenbaugh, 1998, p. 3). This was with specific reference to the targeted use of biometric technology on minority groups such as prisoners, uniformed personnel and the military. Davies is quoted as saying: "I've heard it said that captive groups are a good target market and that the biometrics industry can work outwards from there… The idea of target captive populations is offensive and sneaky" (Roethenbaugh, 1998, p. 3). In the same token, multimodal biometrics present more ethical dilemmas. "Sandia envisage multiple biometrics being used for ultra-secure physical access control applications in the future. They are working on a system that simultaneously applies facial, voice and hand geometry checks" (SJB ed., 1996, p. 1).

The legitimacy of one or two biometrics being used for a variety of applications may be warranted but the use of numerous biometrics could be considered somewhat intrusive and dangerous. Multimodal biometrics may be convenient but there still seems to be a fair degree of privacy issues that have not been considered. It is regularly expressed that "[c]ivil libertarians worry that we're moving toward a world where our privacy is the price of convenience" (Weise, 1998, p. 1). However, multimodal biometrics vendors pronounce that several modalities "…achieves much greater accuracy than single-feature systems" (Frischholz & Dieckmann, 2000, p. 64). In the final analysis, "[d]espite 20 years of predictions that biometrics devices will become the next big thing, proliferation has been slow because of technical, economic, human-factor, legal, ethical, and sociological considerations" (San Jose, 2002, p. 1). Before the announcement by U.S. President George W. Bush, that the U.S. government was going to utilize advanced technologies for administrative purposes, biometrics deployments seemed to be only steadily increasing. It was during the Bush administration's reign that the future of biometrics was solidified forever (Bain, 2008).

BIOMETRIC APPLICATIONS

Overview

First-Mover Biometric Deployments for Government Applications

At the turn of the century, Unisys was just one of about twenty well-known companies that promoted biometric technology to be used with respect to the following applications: social services, driver's licensing, voter registration, inmate verification, national identity, immigration control, patient verification and banking (Figure 4). In 2003, several U.S. states had biometric identification programs already for the distribution of social welfare including in Arizona, California, Connecticut, Illinois, Massachusetts, New York, New Jersey and Texas. Today that number is closer to about thirty U.S. states and many more with plans to implement biometrics in the future (Motorola, 2005).

Prior to the September 11 attacks, very few U.S. airports were equipped with biometric technology for the purpose of immigration control. At Newark and JFK airports, the Immigration and Naturalization Service Passenger Accelerated Service System (INSPASS) used hand recognition terminals. In the U.S., Charlotte/Douglas, Orlando, Reagan, Washington Dulles, Boston Logan and Chicago O'Hare international airports also had biometric systems, all but the former using fingerprints. Andreotta (1996) provides detailed information on what INSPASS was and how it worked and Bernier (1993) gives a

Figure 4. A sample screenshot of a prototype biometric-centric application developed for the Queensland Police in Australia. The database stores personal details including a digital photograph, name, date of birth, height, build, hair, complexion and other distinguishing features. Arrest details also feature including an arrest ID, date of arrest, location of arrest, and reason for arrest. Courtesy of www.argus-solutions.com.

brief overview. The feature article on immigration and biometrics by Atkins (2001) raises some very important issues. For one of the most in depth case studies on biometric ID see Schulman (2002) on the US/Mexico border crossing card (BCC). The study looks at the differences in personal identification requirements before and after the September 11th attacks and documents some of the changes that have taken place between the US/Mexico border check-point.

The Federal Bureau of Investigation (FBI) is another user of biometric equipment. One of the pioneers of fingerprint technology was Identicator Technology. Since the early 1970s they have specialized in inkless fingerprint products. Some of Identicator's commercial partners in the late 1990s included S.W.I.F.T. and MasterCard. Identicator customers included the National Security Agency (NSA), U.S. Secret Service and the Social Security Administration (SSA) (Identicator, 1999). Before IAFIS (Integrated Automated Fingerprint Identification System) was developed, the FBI manually processed fingerprint cards, since about the 1920s. By 1997, the projected growth of automated fingerprint live-scans was estimated at 20,000 per work day (Higgins, 1995, p. 409), although this figure is more precisely 20,000 per month (T. Jones, 2006).

The United Kingdom (UK) National AFIS (NAFIS) involving the Police Information Technology Organization (PITO) is another system that shares similar characteristics to IAFIS. As Roethenbaugh reported (1998, p. 2): "By the year 2000, it is expected that NAFIS will support a database of over six million ten-print sets (60 million images) and up to one hundred thousand scenes of crime latents. Between eight and nine million ten-print sets are expected in the database by 2010." This projection was surpassed in 2004 when 8.2 million ten-print images were stored on the database along with 1.2 million scene-of-crime marks (NG, 2004). Northrop Grumman Mission Systems was the prime contractor and system integrator for the design, development, installation, integration, test, operation, and maintenance of NAFIS in the UK.

In Columbia, voters must have an official voter identification card complete with photograph and digitized fingerprints before they can legally participate in the election process (O'Connor, 1998, p. 4). Jamaica is also experimenting with fingerprint minutiae data for a register of eligible voters (Woodward, 1997, p. 1483). BallotMaster is a biometrics-based voting system that ensures one vote per citizen. It was developed jointly by Neurodynamics and Surveys International. The system uses a bar code card for pre-registered voters and takes advantage of fingerprint biometric technology. Inmate verification is another application of biometrics. Since 1990, Cook County (Illinois) Sheriff's Department has been using retinal scanning to process prisoners (Ritter, 1995). The Department processes between 300 and 500 people per day, mostly in the morning and has compiled a database of 350,000 individuals (Brakeman, 1998, pp. 1-3). According to Tom Miller of the U.S. Department of Justice, inmates, prison staff and visitors will be required to enroll in the biometric system at all Federal prisons in a bid to reduce inmate escapes (Figure 5). *"A major use of biometric-based security systems is not so much designed to keep people out, as to keep them in. Prisons have begun using fingerprint and hand geometry readers to track prisoners. Such systems have also been employed to monitor parolees..." (O'Connor, 1998, p. 5).* The Australian Government invested in speech recognition and natural language software developed by ScanSoft in 2003 in a bid to cut personnel costs in Centrelink's high volume contact center.

Biometrics for Private Enterprise

Biometrics systems once considered for law enforcement purposes are now being used in private enterprises (Woodward et al., 2001). Products such as the AFIM (Automated Fingerprint Recogni-

Figure 5. The Cornerstone product by Argus Solutions also has a built in True Identity Manager which allows individual user paths to be visualized in a GUI. The user paths functionality is useful for high risk environments such as prisons and detention centers which have unique security requirements in terms of prisoner, visitor and employee management. Iris recognition is used to provide human authentication. By establishing a series of 'logical gates' which can only be progressed through in sequence, users have complete control over visitor movements. Additionally, real time reports can be generated showing exactly who is in the facility and where they are. Courtesy of www.argus-solutions.com.

tion Machine) Time Security System by International Automated Systems (IAS) are being marketed to employers who would like additional payroll accuracy. Among the advantages IAS outlined are cost effectiveness, improvement in manager's effectiveness, and employee morale. Australia's largest supermarket chain, Woolworths Ltd has been using Identix fingerprint scanners for almost a decade to monitor employee attendance: "[i]nstead of punching time cards, about 100,000 employees check into PCs located in 500 stores. Each store has one or two PCs running time and attendance software" (Aragon, 1998, p. 5). The Coca-Cola Company uses hand scanning for time and attendance for some of its employees (Chandrasekaran, 1997) as do many medical facilities such as hospitals (Woodward et al., 2001, pp. 93-99).

At universities, biometric systems have been introduced for meal allowances, entrance into examinations and tutorial attendance. At the University of Georgia for example, hand geometry has been in place since 1972 for payment of meals (Weise, 1998, p. 3). In banking several trials have been conducted using fingerprint identification for ATM cardholder verification in order to do away with the traditional PIN. Since the mid-1990s the prospect of iris ATMs have been given attention in the popular press (Fernandez, 1997, p. 10). Sensar's prototype, IrisIdent was one of the first iris recognition systems proposed for the banking sector. Coventry, Angeli and Johnson (2003) have conducted usability studies that reinforce the promise of biometrics at the ATM interface. Still, it will be some time before this kind of authentication enters the market commercially in the banking sector.

One of the most challenging to design and yet the most acceptable form of biometrics is voice recognition. Nortel Networks has been a world leader in offering total solutions for public and private operators. In Canada and the U.S. people were able to use spoken commands to access information as far back as the late 1980s. In Canada, for instance, a subscriber who wished to access directory assistance or dial a number could do so by speaking the digits into the handset (Cameron, 1996, p. 32): *"ADAS Plus used speech recognition to discern the caller's language preference, the city for which a telephone number was requested, and whether the listing is residential or non-residential. The system displayed the information on a monitor, and a human operator provided the actual listing."* The business case for high-volume call centers like hotels, airlines or car reservation companies to incorporate voice recognition is becoming more and more viable (Datamonitor, 1998). More innovative uses of biometrics is for animal ID, particularly for monitoring whales as they migrate in the ocean, and even mice (Nilsson et al., 2003). Exceptionally novel is the Argus Solution developed especially for patience recovering from drug addictions etc (Figure 6).

Case 1: Biometrics in Government Applications

Social Services and Citizen ID

In the U.S. biometrics systems have been used for electronic benefits transfer (EBT) and other social services since July 1991 (Campbell et al., 1996). In a bid to stop fraud, the Los Angeles County in Cali-

Figure 6: A screenshot of the Methadose product developed by Argus Solutions. Methadose is an integrated system for the monitoring and administering of Methadone and other controlled substances using iris identification. Eliminating the inefficient manual processes associated with Methadone dispensing, Methadose completes all statutory reporting requirements automatically. The accuracy offered by iris recognition removes the margin for error in patient identification, virtually eliminating the possibility of human error. Courtesy of www.argus-solutions.com.

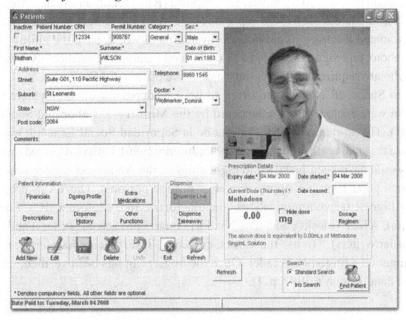

fornia introduced AFIRM (Automated Fingerprint Image Reporting and Match) for the administration of its General Relief (GR) program in the Department of Public Social Services (DPSS). The following extract is from the Hewlett-Packard (HP) case study on the Los Angeles deployment (HP, 1995, p. 3). *"Using the AFIRM system, a GR applicant places his or her index finger on a live-scan camera which displays the image on a workstation in the district office. The prints are scanned... The image is then analyzed by the workstation to ensure acceptable quality and correct positioning. If necessary, the system prompts the clerk to re-attempt image capture. If the image is satisfactory, it is transmitted over a dedicated phone line, along with the demographic data, to the central site where it is compared against all other prints in the database..."* GR is for people who are not eligible for financial assistance from both the federal and state governments.

In 1994, National Registry Incorporated (NRI) supplied finger-image identification systems to the Department of Social Services (DSS) in Suffolk County and Nassau County, New York. The New Jersey Department of Human Services and DSS of Connecticut were also later clients of NRI- all requiring finger-image systems to eliminate fraudulent activities. David Mintie, the project coordinator of Digital Imaging for the state of Connecticut, reported that this electronic personal ID system (1996, p.1):

- *Conveniently and accurately enrolls qualified General Assistance (GA) and Aid to Families with Dependent Children (AFDC) clients into a statewide database*
- *Issues tamper-resistant identification cards that incorporate finger-image 'identifiers' stored in two-dimensional bar codes*
- *Uses finger-image identification to verify that enrolled clients are eligible to receive benefits.*

In 1995 the San Diego Department of Social Services (DSS) announced that it was implementing a pilot project for a fingerprint identification solution to ensure that public funds were being distributed to the correct recipients. Among the problems of the legacy system outlined by the county supervisor were the falsification of photos, signatures and social security numbers which were encouraging applicants to sustain multiple identities, commonly referred to as double-dipping. In November of 1996 the Pennsylvania DPW issued a Request for Proposal (RFP) for an automated fingerprint identification system (AFIS). As Mateer of BHSUG reported (1996, p. 2), the system was referred to as PARIS (Pennsylvania Automated Recipient Identification System) and would have the ability to "capture digitized fingerprint, photo, and signature images of cash, food stamp, and medical assistance 'payment name' recipients, who are required to visit county assistance offices (CAOs)."

In 1996 in Spain, all citizens requiring to be considered for unemployment benefits or worker's compensation were issued with a smart card by the Ministry of Labor and Social Security (Kaplan, 1996, pp. 31f). The so-named TASS (Tarjeta de la Seguridad Social Espanola) initiative required the fingerprints of the smart card holder (Pepe, 1996; Jurado, 1996). Unisys reported that by early 1997 about 633 kiosks would have been installed in eight cities of the Andalucia region, covering about one fifth of Spain's total population (i.e. approximately 7 million persons). The TASS project brought together some of the biggest telecommunications manufacturers, like Motorola (IC), Fujitsu-Eritel (network infrastructure), AT&T (kiosks), Siemens Nixdorf (smart card reader/writers) and Telefonica Sistemas (portable reader/writers). "To use the kiosks, citizens... insert their smartcards and then are prompted to place a finger on a fingerprint reader. Once the fingerprint has been verified, citizens are... granted access to the data" (Unisys, 1997, p. 1).

Similarly the Dutch National ChipCard Platform (NCP) requires the cardholder's personal and biometric data to be stored on a smart card "...and be readable across a wide variety of terminals- for instance at libraries, banks, insurance companies, theatres, municipal authorities and mass transit undertakings" (D. Jones ed., 1996, p. 6). Cambodia's national identification card also stores biometrics (fingerprints) but on a 2-D bar code instead of an integrated circuit. The cards have a 2D bar code that contains the citizen's name, photograph, a digital fingerprint and demographic information. Initially the cards are to be used as identification for travel, voting and employment; but other applications to be added later have not been discounted (Automatic ID, 1998, p. 20).

Customs and Immigration Control

INSPASS was once envisioned to grow to include other airports at Miami, Chicago, Honolulu, Houston, Los Angeles and San Francisco, until the introduction of the ePassport. Prior to September 11th old sites at JFK, Newark, Toronto and Vancouver were upgraded with the latest technology. The strategy was to replace hand geometric devices with fingerprint devices in the long-term to ensure standardization. In 1996, the German federal government was seeking to implement hand geometry at Frankfurt's Main Airport. The preferred German biometric technology was hand geometry which differed to that biometric used in the INSPASS project at Newark, JFK and Toronto airports.

The U.S. and Canada are not the only nations that are working on automated inspection systems for immigration purposes. In 1996, others countries included Australia, Singapore, Hong Kong, Holland, Germany, and the United Kingdom, Bermuda. Travelers who preferred to be identified using biometrics had to undergo a profile security check by authorities. In the case of North America, this included checking whether the traveler was a permanent resident or citizen of the U.S., Canada, Bermuda or part of the Visa Waiver Pilot Program (VWPP), had a criminal history or any previous customs infringements. If the traveler was deemed to be of low risk, they were enrolled to use the system for one year- the pass renewed annually. *"At enrolment demographic details are captured and stored, along with a photograph and signature as well as the templates and images of prints from their two index fingers... Arriving travelers go to the CANPASS immigration lane and insert their card in a terminal for their fingerprints to be verified. The card is automatically checked against a database to ensure that it is valid... Travelers with goods to declare just put the relevant form in a slot and the correct amount of duty is charged to their credit card"* (SJB, 1996c, p. 1). Only PortPASS holders were required to pay a small fee to enroll. When INSPASS began there were 2000 frequent fliers, in early 2003, there were over 100000.

Today, the rollout of the ePassport has had a major impact in the way travelers are authenticated, especially upon arrival. In Australia, several trials were begun and the first deployment of the SmartGate Automated Border Processing was in August of 2007 at Brisbane's International Airport (Department of Immigration and Citizenship, 2008). The SmartGate solution was part of a broader strategy by the Australian Government to employ biometrics towards the improvement of border security techniques. The SmartGate solution works using a two step process. At the kiosk the traveler checks if they are eligible to self-process by placing their ePassport into the reader and answering standard declarations via a touch-screen. If the traveler is eligible to proceed a ticket is printed for them, and they carry this to the 'smart' gate where a live identity check and clearance is performed. By inserting their ticket into the reader, a photo of the traveler's face is taken and compared with the image in their ePassport. If the two images match, the traveler is allowed entry. If the images do not match, the ticket is retained and the traveler is directed to go via a manual process (i.e. a Customs officer check).

Towards Biometrics as a Hub for Integrated Auto-ID Systems

In the past, governments worldwide have been criticized for their inefficiencies regarding the distribution of social services. Reports of persons who have been able to collect over ten times what they are lawfully owed by declaring several different identities (and postal addresses) have increased. Other reports indicate that persons who have the greatest need for social concessions are not the ones who are necessarily receiving them because of incorrect information that has been supplied about their eligibility to authorities. There are still many developed countries around the world which use paper-based methods in the form of vouchers, coupons, ration cards, concession cards to operate large-scale federal and state programs. As recent as 1994, even the Department of Agriculture in the U.S. issued paper coupons for food stamp programs, although it was not long before they moved to an electronic system (Hausen & Bruening, 1994, p. 26).

Since that time, the U.S. also introduced 'food card' applications using magnetic-stripe (Pennsylvania- since 1984) and smart cards (Ohio since 1992). Some states used magnetic-stripe cards to help verify that the patient is indeed eligible for 'free' consultations to the doctor. The magnetic-stripe card first replaced paper based records that were prone to error. Smart cards are also being increasingly promoted by government agencies, many of them set to store citizen biometrics for additional security purpose. The latest trend in Federal and State government systems is program centralization (Marshall, 1997, pp. 10-15). Using database matching principles and smart card technology, one card can be used to store all the citizen's personal information as well as their eligibility status to various State programs. Data-matching has been defined as "the comparison of two or more sets of data to identify similarities and dissimilarities... the term is used to denote the use of computer techniques to compare data found in two or more computer files to identify cases where there is a risk of incorrect payment of personal financial assistance or of tax evasion" (Privacy Commissioner, 1990, p. 1).

In England a similar model has been implemented (D. Jones, 2000): "the Department of Social Security (DSS) announced details of its new Generalized Matching Service (GMS)... It is hailed as the first system of its kind in Europe and will cross-match data across a number of benefit areas" (Smith, 1995, p. 40). The system has provided the foundations for national ID smart cards in the U.K. According to the UK Home Office (2008): *"[t]he National Identity Scheme is an easy-to-use and extremely secure system of personal identification for adults living in the UK. Its cornerstone is the introduction of national ID cards for UK and EEA residents over the age of 16... Each ID card will be unique and will combine the cardholder's biometric data with their checked and confirmed identity details, called a 'biographical footprint'. These identity details and the biometrics will be stored on the National Identity Register (NIR). Basic identity information will also be held in a chip on the ID card itself."*

Gold (1996) estimated that the highly organized fraud racket in the U.K. was costing the government about 2 billion pounds a year. This was obviously an over-inflated figure with more recent statistics from the Home Office showing that identity fraud has cost the UK over 1.7 billion pounds in sum total. The UK's Fraud Prevention Service also recorded 67,406 victims of identity fraud in 2006, over 10,000 fake passport applications annually and 430,000 illegal migrants residing in the UK. Identity-related benefit fraud was costing the taxpayer between twenty to fifty million per annum.

The single card approach is not only purported to greatly reduce operational costs but is equipped to catch out persons who have deliberately set out to mislead the government. In the U.S. for instance, there was a new Electronic Benefits Transfer (EBT) paradigm which called for a single card that could deliver benefits from multiple government programs across all states. The hope was that the system would be in place by 1999 (Robins, 1995, p. 58). The initial focus was on food stamps and AFDC but other benefits such as old-age pension, veteran survivors, and unemployment would eventually be integrated into the system (Jackson, 1996a, pp. 1-2).

Singapore, Spain, Germany and the Czech Republic were some of the first countries to introduce national ID smart cards. Proposed national ID schemes in other countries like Greece have fuelled much debate since the mid-1990s. In Greece, the preliminary decision to record a person's religion on the national ID card was not surprisingly met with opposition, particularly by religious minority groups. One of the largest-scale smart card government projects is in China, led by China Citizen Card Consortium. The plan was to have one integrated card for citizen identification, health care and financial purposes. "The smart card is set to store the bearer's ID number, health care code, address, birthdate, parents' names, spouse's name and a fingerprint" (Valles, 1998, p.7). The Taiwan government also considered following the Chinese initiative as their own paper-based identification card (as of 1998) was extremely ineffective- it did not carry a magnetic-stripe, nor did it have embossed numbers and it was very flimsy. The Philippines government was also embarking on a national ID card project which would have included biometric data as were the South Africans with the Home Affairs National ID System (Woodward, 1997, p. 1483).

Malaysia and Thailand are also following in the footsteps of Singapore. Malaysia's MultiPurpose Card project, Mykad, is a flagship of the Multimedia Super Corridor (MSC). "The plastic card... has an embedded chip... that can perform a variety of functions... designed to combine national ID, driver's license, immigration information, health information, e-cash, debit card and ATM card applications" (Creed, 2000, p. 1). In 1998 in South America, there were smart card trials in Brazil (Curitiba) where 30000 city employees were issued with smart cards that acted as a government ID and allowed monetary transactions. In 1999, the program was extended to families of municipal employees, and then to the city's entire 1.5 million urban population" (Automatic ID, 1998, p. 1). This ID card has an RF interface, i.e. it is contactless. More recently, Saudi Arabia has embarked on a national ID scheme. Post Sept 11, there was a series of attempts to introduce national ID card schemes in numerous countries as documented by Privacy International (PI, 2002). One of the main findings from an investigation into national ID cards was that they do not in any way curb the threat of terrorism.

The U.S. Department of Defense (DOD) instituted a multiapplication smart card to replace the various military paper records, tags and other cards. The MARC program (Multi-Technology Automated Reader Card) was a targeted pilot in the Asia Pacific with 50000 soldiers. According to authorities, it was so successful that the card was distributed to all 1.4 million active duty armed forces personnel. Many believe that MARC was a large-scale trial necessary to prove-in a national ID for all citizens in the U.S., incorporating numerous government programs. Coordinator, Michael Noll said that the ultimate goal of MARC was: *"'[a] single standard, multiple-use card that [could] be used across the government'... for applications such as payroll, employee records, health care and personnel assignments" (Jackson, 1996b, p. 41).* MARC was first used during the Gulf War crisis. The card contains a magnetic-stripe and integrated circuit, as well as a photograph and embossed letters and numbers and it can handle up to 25 applications. Today all military personnel use the Common Access Card (CAC) for a number of different applications (Kozaryn, 2000). After the September 11th attacks on the U.S., Oracle's CEO Larry Ellison offered to provide free software for a mandatory national ID smart card which would contain at minimum a photograph and fingerprint (Levy, 2001, p. 1). Sun's CEO Scott McNealy also advocated a national ID (Scholtz & Johnson, 2002, p. 564).

Like the U.S., Singapore also tested a military ID card in 2002. The Clinton Administration also wanted to adopt smart card technology to track the expenses of federal government staff, responsible for 8.5 billion US dollars of annual expenditure. The card would be used to log travel expenses, make small purchases and allow for building access (D. Jones ed., 1998, p. 16). Also, smart cards were touted to be the driving force behind digital signatures allowing for encrypted messages between government agencies and citizens when Internet ecommerce applications like online taxation become mainstream applications. An exhaustive list of U.S. government applications using card technologies can be found in the U.S. Financial Management Service (1990). This study, though dated now, is a very comprehensive investigation into all the card programs in the U.S. at the federal and state level. Federal applications include: agriculture, commerce, energy, justice, NASA, transportation, treasury and veteran affairs. Defense was a topic that was treated as a special government application. The military takes advantage of numerous types of auto-ID technologies. In Bosnia in 1997 the military provided the most modern logistics system, featuring long-range RFID, smart card and bar code working in concert (Seidman, 1997, p. 37).

Case 2: Entertainment

Expo '92 was held in Seville, Spain. There, season ticket holders had to carry a smart card and use a biometric fingerprint reader to have access to the various sites and exhibits. The biometric fingerprint system was produced by the Bull subsidiary, Telesincro (M. Chadwick, 1992, p. 253). The aim at this event was to prevent ticket holders from giving their passes to their friends and family members to use (Zoreda & Oton, 1994, p. 172). This was quite an innovative solution for its time. Similarly visitors wishing to have seasonal or annual passes into Walt Disney's theme parks in Florida U.S.A., also have to use a fingerprint biometric system (Chandrasekaran, 1997; Higgins, 67-68). Magic Kingdom, Epcot and Disney MGM are all involved in the biometric trial. The system uses fingerprint recognition and the measurement is useable at each of the three theme parks (SJB, 1996b, p. 1). Today, Walt Disney World is the largest single commercial application of biometrics in the U.S., with tens of millions of people using biometric readers to gain access to four theme parks in Orlando (Harmel, 2006). It is no secret that the U.S. Government have consulted Walt Disney toward large-scale civilian implementations of biometrics (Hopkins, 1999).

Face recognition systems have even made their debut in ten Nevada casinos. The joint venture between Mr. Payroll and Wells Fargo & Company uses the Miros TrueFace engine and Atreva machines. Gaming patrons can only cash their checks after agreeing for their picture to be taken. Once enrolled the patrons have their image stored for future identification. In 2001, Identix installed fingerprint recognition systems for patrons in two Las Vegas casinos. Biometrics systems are also used at global sporting events like the Olympic Games. Since Barcelona (Spain) in 1992 the level of security biometrics offers was recognized more widely. Access to the air traffic control tower at the airport in Barcelona was limited to fewer than 200 persons using signature recognition in case of terrorist attacks. At the 1996 Atlanta Olympic Games over 40000 athletes, staff and volunteers used a biometric system which measured hand geometry. Those wishing to have access to the Olympic Village required to have their hand characteristics verified. There were 125 verification devices installed at entry points into high security areas. Despite these security measures an attacker was still able to plant a bomb that went off in the village. At the 1998 Nagano Winter Olympics a biometric system was used to track biathletes.

An Australian company Nightkey is changing the way patrons gain entry to nightclubs across several states. Among the clubs to have adopted the Nightkey biometric system is Liquid NiteClub, Sultan's Nightclub, Meche, Alma, Amplifier, Metropolis Fremantle, Capitol, The Highlander, and the Gate Bar and Bistro. Nightkey works using a four step process. First a manual ID check is conducted by the club's authorized personnel, and then scanned using typical OCR software. The image taken is stored on the venues database. Secondly, the right index finger of the patron is then scanned to create a unique ID. As soon as this is done, the original image is deleted and only a value is stored. Step three requires a photo to be taken of the patron and linked to the fingerprint image. Finally, step four takes all the information collected and stores it on a remote co-located server using a secure link. This ensures that patron information does not find its way into terminals or somewhere where it is easily accessible. The benefits of such a scheme are considered to be deterrence from attracting patrons who may engage in some form of anti-social behavior.

Card Technologies Welcome

Companies who are still promoting magnetic-stripe cards for instance, find that entertainment applications are a steady market. Access Control Technologies (ACT) Incorporated specializes in entertainment solutions using prepaid card systems for cashless vending. Like ACT Incorporated, the Plastag Corporation is also a supplier of magnetic-stripe cards to entertainment companies. Plastag is one of the largest manufacturers of casino cards, servicing many states in the U.S. like Naivete, New Jersey, Michigan, Indiana and Missouri.

Smart cards are being used more and more in the entertainment business. Casinos, clubs and bars, sports complexes, cinemas, arcades, fun parks and conferences are using card technologies to encourage loyalty and to verify the user's ID. McCrindle (1990, pp. 163-170) describes some of the earliest international examples:

- ***Pathe Cinema in France:*** *The smart card is pre-loaded with ten tickets. Used as a loyalty card by offering discounts on bulk ticket purchases*
- ***Club Mediterranee in France:*** *Guests can use the smart card as a payment card. All their transactions are billed to the one card and can be checked at any time using terminals around the club facilities*
- ***Dallington Country Club:*** *The smart card grants users access to sporting facilities, bars, restaurants, and other shops. The card also has an electronic purse function- users are charged accordingly. The system... [is also used for] monitoring membership control, subscription collection and other statistics.*

As already mentioned Olympic and Commonwealth Games venues are always promoting the use of cash cards and other auto-ID technologies. An estimated 100000 disposable smart cards and 2000 reloadable smart cards were used at Kuala Lumpur at the Commonwealth Games in 1998. The cards were a showcase for the proposed identification card in Malaysia. It was also more convenient for visitors to use electronic cash for buying goods and services. Athletes can also attach RFID transponders to their shoelaces to ensure fair play and accuracy in times recorded (Finkenzeller, 1999, pp. 261-263). One of the first manufacturers of RFID transponders for marathons was Texas Instruments with their ChampionChip product. Marathon runners also wear placards to the front and rear which usually have bar codes (LaMoreaux, 1995, p. 12).

Beyond things one can carry, or one can posses, there are now clubs such as the Baja Beach Club in Barcelona, Spain, where RFID implants grant a patron access to a VIP zone that offers a host of exclusive services (V. Jones, 2004). The cost of getting the implant injection is about $153 USD. Patrons who visit the club regularly believe it is a solution which is about convenience, fashion and safety. There is no longer a need to carry a wallet or ID cards, which can often be stolen or misplaced in crowded spaces. The implant also signifies a fashion statement, and places a patron in an elite group of chipped persons, among who is the director of the Club, Mr Conrad Chase. The Baja Beach Club web site claims that it is the first discotheque in the world to offer the VIP VeriChip (Chase, 2009).

Biometrics Today

Post September 11th biometrics has proliferated for government-to-citizen applications. While the United States was a pioneer in the use of biometrics for border control, the new national security climate spurred on by frequent terrorist attacks has changed state-to-state dynamics (Petermann, Sauter & Scherz, 2006). Anyone entering the United States for instance must now have their fingerprints taken or risk being refused entry. Biometric systems by default do not have an opt-out clause because opting-out usually means being excluded from participation altogether. In this sense, government applications that rely on biometric identification may be considered mandatory. Individuals wishing to be eligible for social security payments need either accept a plastic card with their biometrics on-board or live with the consequences of not being recognized as a valid recipient of services. When biometrics were first introduced as potential solutions for companies (e.g. payroll and access control), the systems were considered clunky, highly proprietary and prohibitively expensive. Today, the systems are lightweight in terms of hardware, the software user-friendly for registration and administration purposes, and the technology scalable making it affordable to even the smallest organization (Osadciw, Varshney & Veera-machaneni, 2002). The technology has also become more pervasive, used to earn patrons reward points at casinos and even granting families entry into fun parks (Xiao, 2007). In addition, guidelines have also now been introduced to conduct payments wirelessly using a biometric (Grabensek & Divjak, 2006). Multimodal biometrics is also on the rise, used to minimize errors and ensure that modality equates to eligibility for all potential registrants. Despite its increased adoption, privacy fears remain, and the issue with who really owns ones biometrics continues to be highly controversial.

CONCLUSION

Biometrics are the first auto-ID technique that required users to place a body part directly onto a digital reader (e.g. fingerprint and handprint). First instituted for law enforcement purposes, biometrics was once considered to be a technology specifically used for convicted criminals. Later it became utilized in closed systems such as prisons, or university campuses. Today, interactive voice recognition systems (IVRS) rely heavily on voice recognition in the absence of call center personnel. Biometrics have also become popular as an additional security feature on the bar code and magnetic-stripe, particularly on government-to-citizen card-based applications. The biometric stored on a 2D bar code for instance, has acted to reignite interest in the bar code as an identification technique. Hybrid cards are now very common. Despite the roll-out of mass market applications however, biometrics are clouded with very real privacy concerns. Stories abound of large databases on external storage media that have accidentally gone missing at airports or have been stolen. The sensitivity of biometric details, such as fingerprint minutae in digital format is of much higher value than ID numbers. Of the most sensitive biometric is an individual's DNA, which if disclosed, has the potential to reveal very private details (e.g. predisposition to disease). The proliferation of biometric systems presently, are as a result of sweeping changes to legislation which many would argue have been rushed through the political process without adequate thought and safeguards in place.

REFERENCES

Agre, P. (2001 14 November). Your Face is not a bar code: Arguments Against Automatic Face Recognition in Public Places. Retrieved from http://dlis.gseis.ucla.edu/people/pagre/bar-code.html

Alyea, L. A., & Campbell Jr, J. P. (1996). Update on the US government's biometric consortium. *Biometric Consortium.* Retrieved 4 August 1998, from http://www.vitro.bloomington.in.us:8080/~BC/REPORTS/CTSTG96

Andreotta, T. (1996). INSPASS update. *Biometric Consortium.* Retrieved 4 August 1998, from http://www.biometrics.org/REPORTS/INSPASS2.html

Aragon, L. (1998). Show me some ID: Biometrics is leaving its Fingerprints on the Market with Low-cost Devices. *PC Week.*

Arena, K., & Cratty, C. (4 February 2008). FBI wants palm prints, eye scans, tattoo mapping. *CNN.com: Technology.* Retrieved 2 January 2009, from http://www.cnn.com/2008/TECH/02/04/fbi.biometrics/index.html#cnnSTCText

Ashbourn, J. (1994). Practical implementation of biometrics based on hand geometry. *IEE Colloquium on Image Processing for Biometric Measurement*, 5/1-5/6.

Atkins, W. (2001). 'Immigration issues. *Biometric Technology Today, 9*(5), 8-11.

Automatic ID. (1998). Progress made on Cambodian ID. *Automatic I.D. News Asia*(October/November), 20.

Bain, B. (6 June 2008). Bush pushes biometrics for national security. *FCW.COM.* Retrieved 3 January 2008, from http://www.fcw.com/online/news/152750-1.html

BBC. (2002, 17 May). Doubt cast on fingerprint security. *BBC News*, from http://news.bbc.co.uk/1/hi/sci/tech/1991517.stm

BC. (2009). Biometric Consortium: Research Database. *Biometric Consortium* Retrieved 2 January 2009, from http://www.biometrics.org/research-resources.php

Bell, J. (1997, 16 December). Intellect sets smart standard. *The Australian,* p. 37.

Bernier, N. (1993). Your hand is your passport: technology cuts the time spent in line. *Airport,* 68.

Bigun, J., & Smeraldi, F. (Eds.). (1997). *Audio- and Video-based Biometric Person Authentication.* Crans-Montana, Switzerland: Springer, Berlin.

Biometrics Institute. (2006). Biometrics Institute Privacy Code. *Australian Government: Office of the Privacy Commissioner.* Retrieved 20 December 2008, from http://www.comlaw.gov.au/ComLaw/Legislation/LegislativeInstrument1.nsf/0/B85ED08C656C8E0ECA2571B80005D36F/$file/2006-07+Biometrics+Institute+Privacy+Code+approval+determi.pdf

Bolle, R., Connell, J., Pankanti, S., & Ratha, N. (2003). *Guide to Biometrics (Springer Professional Computing).* Berlin: Springer.

Boves, L., & Os, E. (1998). Speaker recognition in telecom applications. *IEEE Interactive Voice Technology for Telecommunications Applications,* 203-208.

Brakeman, L. (1998). Retinal scans always get their man. *Automatic I.D. News,* pp. 1-4.

Brinton, K., & Lieberman, K. (1994). Basics of DNA fingerprinting. *University of Washington.*

Bunney, C. (1998). Two more legislatures go biometric. *btt, 6*(5), 2.

Burnell, J. (1998). Identifying the biometric opportunity. *Automatic I.D. News,* 1-5.

Cameron, H. (1996). Speech recognition- from the lab to the real world, *Telesis- Northern Telecom* (pp. 28-41).

Campbell, J. P. (1996). Biometric security: government applications and operations. *Biometric Consortium,* from http://www.vitro.bloomington.in.us:8080/~BC/REPORTS/CTSTG96/

Campbell, J. P. (1999). Speaker Recognition. In A. K. Jain (Ed.), *Biometrics: personal identification in networked society* (pp. 87-101). Boston: Kluwer Academic Publishers.

Carter, J., & Nixon, M. (1990). An integrated biometric database. *IEE Colloquium on Electronic Images and Image Processing in Security and Forensic Science,* 8/1-8/6.

Chadwick, M. (1992). The hottest technology under the sun Expo '92. *IEE Review, 38*(7-8), 251-253.

Chandrasekaran, R. (1997, March 30). Brave new whorl: ID systems using human body are ere, but privacy issues persist. *Washington Post.*

Chase, C. (2009). Baja Beach Club. Retrieved 4 January 2009, from http://www.bajabeach.es/

CITeR. (2008). The Center for Identification Technology Research. *West Virginia Univerisity* Retrieved 20 December 2008, from http://www.citer.wvu.edu/

Clarke, R. (1991). The Tax File Number scheme: a Case study of Political assurances and Function Creep. *Xamax Consultancy,* from http://www.anu.edu.au/people/Roger.Clarke/DV/PaperTFN.html

Clarke, R. (1994). Human identification in information systems: management challenges and public policy issues. *Information Technology & People, 7*(4), 6-37.

Computing. (1999). Why the fear of biometrics? *Computing Canada, 25*(15), 8.

Connecticut Department of Social Services. (1998a). Biometrics and privacy issues. from http://www.dss.state.ct.us/digital/privacy.htm

Connecticut Department of Social Services. (1998b). Legislation authorising Connecticut's digital imaging project. Retrieved from http://www.dss.state.ct.us/digital/faq/dilegis.htm

Connecticut Dept. (1998). Understanding public perception. *Connecticut Department of Social Services*, from http://www.dss.state.ct.us/faq/disuppt.htm

Coventry, L., Angeli, A. D., & Johnson, G. (2003). *Usability and biometric verification at the ATM interface*. Paper presented at the Proceedings of the SIGCHI conference on Human factors in computing systems

Craig, A. (1997). Eye-scanning ATMs ready to face the public. *TechWeb*, from http://www.techweb.com/wire/story/TWB19971202S0001

Creed, A. (2000). Malaysian Government smart card project gets under way. *Newsbytes*, from http://www.fis.utoronto.ca/research/iprp/sc/malaysia06062000.html

Datamonitor. (1998). *Customer Care in Financial Services*. London: Datamonitor.

Daugman, J. (2006). Probing the uniqueness and randomness of IrisCodes: Results from 200 billion iris pair comparisons. *Proceedings of the IEEE, 94*(11), 1927-1935.

Daugman, J. (2008). Webpage for JOHN DAUGMAN. *University of Cambridge: Computer Laboratory* Retrieved 20 December 2008, from http://www.cl.cam.ac.uk/~jgd1000/

Davies, S. (1996). *Monitor: extinguishing privacy on the information superhighway*. Sydney: PAN Macmillan.

DCITA. (2004). Biometrics: An Australian Government Perspective. *Department of Communications, Information Technology and the Arts*. Retrieved 20 December 2008, from http://www.dbcde.gov.au/__data/assets/pdf_file/0004/23467/Biometrics_-_An_Australian_Government_perspective.pdf

Department of Immigration and Citizenship. (2008). Fact Sheet 71 - SmartGate Automated Border Processing. *Australian Government* Retrieved 29 December 2008, from http://www.immi.gov.au/media/fact-sheets/71smartgate.htm

Didier, B. (2004). Biometrics. In B. Stevens (Ed.), *The Security Economy* (pp. 35-54): OECD.

Dunstone, T. (2001). Getting to grips with public policy. *Biometric Technology Today, 9*(6), 7-8.

EBF. (2008). About the European Biometrics Forum. Retrieved 20 December 2008, from http://www.eubiometricsforum.com/index.php?option=content&task=view&id=2&Itemid=28

European Court of Human Rights. (4 December 2008). *CASE OF S. AND MARPER v. THE UNITED KINGDOM (Applications nos. 30562/04 and 30566/04)*. Strasbourg.

Fernandez, B. (1997, 15 April). Bank keeps eye on iris technology. *The Australian*.

Ferrari, J., Mackinnon, R., Poh, S., & Yatawara, L. (1998). *Smart Cards: a case study*: Research Triangle Park.

Finkenzeller, K., & Waddington, R. (2001). *RFID Handbook: radio-frequency identification fundamentals and applications*. New York: John Wiley & Son.

Freeman, E. H. (2003). Biometrics, Evidence, and Personal Privacy. *Information Security Journal: A Global Perspective, 12*(3), 4-8.

Frischholz, R. W., & Dieckmann, U. (2000). BioID: A multimodal biometric identification system. *IEEE Computer*, 64-68.

Fuller, H. R. (1995). *Use of biometrics in proposed EBT program*: GAO/OSI-95-20.

Furui, S. (2001). *Toward flexible speech recognition- recent progress at Tokyo Institute of Technology.* Paper presented at the Canadian Conference on Electrical and Computer Engineering.

Gold, S. (1996, 20 May). UK govt plans social security benefit smart cards. *Newsbytes*.

Greening, C. M., Kumar, S. V., & Leedham, G. (1995, 16-18 May). *Handwriting identification using global and local features for forensic purpose.* Paper presented at the European Convention on Security and Detection.

Gunnerson, G. (1999). Are you ready for biometrics?, *PC Magazine* (pp. 160).

Halici, U., Jain, L. C., & Erol, A. (1999). Introduction to Fingerprint Recognition. In L. C. Jain (Ed.), *Intelligent Biometric Techniques in Fingerprint and Face Recognition* (pp. 4-34): CRC Press.

Harmel, K. (2006). Walt Disney World: The Government's Tomorrowland? *News21: A Journalism Initiative of the Carnegie and Knight Foundations* Retrieved 30 December 2008, from http://newsinitiative. org/story/2006/09/01/walt_disney_world_the_governments

Hausen, T., & Bruening, P. (1994). Hidden costs and benefits of government card technologies. *IEEE Technology and Society Magazine, 13*(2), 24-32.

Hawkes, P. (1992). Automatic user authentication & access control. *IEE Colloquium on Designing Secure Systems*, 6/1-6/4.

Heckle, R. R., Patrick, A. S., & Ozok, A. (2007). *Perception and acceptance of fingerprint biometric technology* Paper presented at the Proceedings of the 3rd symposium on Usable privacy and security.

Herald Tribune. (1998). FBI gets national DNA database. *The Straits Times*, p. 7.

Hibbert, C. (1996). What to do when they ask for your social security number. In R. Kling (Ed.), *Computerisation and Controversy: value conflicts and social choices* (pp. 686-696). New York: Academic Press.

Higgins, P. T. (1995). Standards for the electronic submission of fingerprint cards to the FBI. *Journal of Forensic Identification, 45*(4), 409-418.

Higgins, P. T. (2002). Fingerprint and Hand Geometry. In J. D. Woodward, N. M. Orlans & P. T. Higgins (Eds.), *Biometrics* (pp. 45-70). London: John Wiley and Sons.

Hong, L., & Jain, A. (1998). Integrating faces and fingerprints for personal identification. *IEEE Transactions on Pattern Analysis and Machine Intelligence, 20*(12), 1295-1298.

Hong, L., & Jain, A. (1999). Multimodal Biometrics. In A. K. Jain (Ed.), *Biometrics: personal identification in networked society* (pp. 327-344). Boston: Kluwer Academic Publishers.

Hopkins, R. (1999). An Introduction to Biometrics and Large Scale Civilian Identification. *International Review of Law, Computers & Technology, 13*(3), 337 363.

Howell, A. J. (1999). Introduction to Face Recognition. In L. C. Jain (Ed.), *Intelligent Biometric Techniques in Fingerprint and Face Recognition*. London: CRC Press.

HP. (1995). State, provincial and local government industry: Los Angeles county stops fraud with automated fingerprint matching system. *HP Business and Technical Computing*, 1-3.

Identicator. (1999). About Identicator Technology. from http://www.identicator.com/about/index.html

IEEE. (1997). Special issue on automated biometrics. *Proceedings of the IEEE, 85*(9), 1343-1345.

INCITS. (2002). M1-biometrics. *International Committee for Information Technology Standards (INCITS)*, from http://www.ncits.org/tc_home/m1.htm

ISO. (2008). Biometric Standards. *International Standards Organization* Retrieved 20 December 2008, from http://www.iso.org/iso/search.htm?qt=biometrics&sort=rel&type=simple&published=on

Jackson, W. (1996a). EBT cards for food programs get smarter. *Government Computer News, 15*(2), 1-3.

Jackson, W. (1996b). The MARC card gets smarter. *Government Computer News, 15*(1), 41-43.

Jacobs, A. (1998). Fingerprint security promises convenience. *Computerworld*, 1-2.

Jain, A. K. (2000). Filterbank-based fingerprint matching. *IEEE Transactions on Image Processing, 9*(5), 846-859.

Jain, A. K. (2004, 28-30 April). *Biometric recognition: how do I know who you are?* Paper presented at the Proceedings of the IEEE 12th Signal Processing and Communications Applications Conference.

Jain, A. K., Bolle, R., & Pankanti, S. (Eds.). (1999). *Biometrics: personal identification in networked society*. Boston: Kluwer Academic Publishers.

Jain, A. K., Hong, L., Pankati, S., & Bolle, R. (1997). An identity-authentication system using fingerprints. *Proceedings of the IEEE, 85*(9), 1365-1387.

Jain, L. C., Halici, U., Hayashi, I., Lee, S. B., & Tsutsui, S. (Eds.). (1999). *Intelligent Biometric Techniques in Fingerprint and Face Recognition*. London: CRC Press.

Jones, D. (1996). Dutch Model for Universal Smart Card. *Card Technology Today, 10*(2), 6.

Jones, D. (1998). Electronic Commerce in Government. *Card Technology Today, 10*(2), 13-16.

Jones, D. (2000). UK government launches smart card strategy. *Card Technology Today, 11*(6), 2.

Jones, T. (2006). i3 First to Submit Type 14 Fingerprint Live Scans to FBI. *FindBiometrics*. Retrieved 20 July 2007, from http://www.findbiometrics.com/press-release/3451

Jones, V. (7 April 2004). Baja Beach Club in Barcelona, Spain Launches Microchip Implantation for VIP Members. *InfoWars.Com* Retrieved 3 January 2009, from http://www.prisonplanet.com/articles/april2004/040704bajabeachclub.htm

Jurado, P. (1996). Spain connects with citizens on-line. *Dialogue- Andersen Consulting, 6*(2), 11.

Kaplan, J. M. (1996). *Smart Cards: the global information passport- managing a successful smart card program*. London: International Thomson Computer Press.

Kozaryn, L. D. (2000). DoD Issues Time-saving Common Access Cards. *About.Com: US Military*. Retrieved 30 December 2008, from http://usmilitary.about.com/od/theorderlyroom/l/blsmartcards.htm

Kroeker, K. L. (2000). Biometric organisations. *IEEE Computer, 33*(2), 57.

LaMoreaux, R. D. (1998). *Barcodes and Other Automatic Identification Systems*. New York: Pira International.

Lawton, G. (1998). Biometrics: a new era in security. *Computer,* 16-18.

Lazar, G. (1997). Agencies scan biometrics for potential applications. *Tech Briefing*, from http://www.few.com/pubs/few/1997/0120/feature.htm

Lee, H. C., & Gaensslen, R. E. (Eds.). (1994). *Advances in Fingerprint Technology (CRC Series in Forensic and Police Science)*. New York: CRC Press.

Levy, S. (2001, 8 October). A high-tech home front. *Newsweek*, from http://www.mnbc.com/news/635417.asp?cp1=1

Liu, S., & Silverman, M. (2001). A practical guide to biometric security technology, *IT Professional* (January/February ed., Vol. 3, pp. 27-32).

Lockie, M. (2000). Ear, eye, gait, keystroke, lip and nailbed biometrics, *Btt* (February ed., Vol. 7, pp. 8-11).

Lyall, S. (4 December 2008). European Court Rules Against Britain's Policy of Keeping DNA Database of Suspects. *New York Times*. Retrieved 20 December 2008, from http://www.nytimes.com/2008/12/05/world/europe/05britain.html

M2SYS. (2008). Challenges of Biometric Integration. *M2SYS Technology* Retrieved 2 January 2009, from http://www.m2sys.com/sales/whitepapers/Integration.pdf

Markowitz, J. (2001). Speaker verification. *Biometric Technology Today, 9*(1), 9-11.

Marshall, W. T. (1997). EBT: Keeping the benefits in proper balance. *America's Community Banker, 6*(5), 10-15.

Mateer, S. (1996). Pennsylvania Automated Recipient Identification System (PARIS). *Biometrics in Human Services User Group, 1*(2), 2.

Mathewson, R. (1998). Testing times as school launches new drug checks. *Sunday Morning Post*, p. 3.

McCrindle, J. (1990). *Smart Cards*. London: Springer-Verlag.

McManus, K. (1996, May 6). At banks of future, and eye for an ID. *The Washington Post*.

McMurchie, L. L. (1999). Identifying risks in biometric use. *Computing Canada, 25*(6), 11.

Meenen, P., & Adhami, R. (2001). Fingerprinting for security. *IEEE Potentials*(August-September), 33-38.

Michael, M. G. (1998). *The Number of the Beast, 666 (Revelation 13:16-18): Background, Sources and Interpretation.* Macquarie University, Sydney, Australia.

Michael, M. G. (1999). The Genre of the Apocalypse: What are they saying now? *Bulletin of Biblical Studies, 18,* 115-126.

Michels, S. (2002, 25 February). National ID. *Online NewsHour,* from http://www.pbs.org/newshour/bb/fedagencies/jan-june02/id_2-26.html

Miller, B. (1994). Vital signs of identity. *IEEE Spectrum*(February), 22-30.

Mintie, D. (1996). Digital imaging FAQ's: Implementing a statewide biometric identification system. from http://www.dss.state.ct.us/faq/diplan.htm

Moskowitz, R. (1999). Are biometrics too good? *Network Computing,* 85.

Motorola. (2005). Motorola's a global leader in biometric identification. *Motorola: Fact Sheet* Retrieved 24 December 2008, from http://www.motorola.com/staticfiles/Business/Solutions/Business%20Solutions/Biometrics/Biometrics%20Identification/_Documents/Static%20Files/Motorola_History_of_Biometrics_New.pdf

Ng-Kruelle, G., Swatman, P. A., Hampe, J. F., & Rebne, D. S. (2006). Biometrics and e-Identity (e-Passport) in the European Union: End-user perspectives on the adoption of a controversial innovation *Journal of Theoretical and Applied Electronic Commerce Research, 1*(2), 12-35.

NG. (2004). National Automated Fingerprint Fingerprint Identification System. *Northrop Grumman: Mission Systems* Retrieved 24 December 2008, from http://www.northropgrumman.co.uk/utils/downloads/NAFIS.pdf

NightKey. (2008). Nightkey Explained: A Four Part Process. *Nightkey* Retrieved 3 December 2008, from http://www.nightkey.com.au/nightkey-explained/

Nilsson, K., Rognvaldsson, T., Cameron, J., & Jacobson, C. (2006). *Biometric Identification of Mice.* Paper presented at the 18th International Conference on Pattern Recognition.

NIST. (2002). Legislation- biometrics. *The Biometrics Resource Center Website (Information Technology Laboratory),* from http://www.itl.nist.gov/div895/biometrics/legislation.html

O'Neil, P. H. (2005). Complexity and Counterterrorism: Thinking about Biometrics. *Studies in Conflict & Terrorism, 28*(6), 547-566.

O'Connor, S. (1998). Collected, tagged, and archived: legal issues in the burgeoning use of biometrics for personal identification. *Stanford Technology Law Review* Retrieved 20 December 2008, from http://www.jus.unitn.it/USERS/pascuzzi/privcomp99-00/topics/6/firma/connor.txt

O'Gorman, L. (Ed.). (1999). *Fingerprint Verification in Biometrics: personal identification in networked society.* Boston: Kluwer Academic Publishers.

Orlans, N. M. (2002). Facial and Voice Recognition. In J. D. Woodward, N. M. Orlans & P. T. Higgins (Eds.), *Biometrics* (pp. 71-88). London: John Wiley and Sons.

Osadciw, L., Varshney, P., & Veeramachaneni, K. (2002, 8-11 July). *Improving personal identification accuracy using multisensor fusion for building access control applications.* Paper presented at the Proceedings of the Fifth International Conference on Information Fusion.

Paranjape, R. B. (2001). *The electroencephalogram as a biometric.* Paper presented at the Canadian Conference on Electrical and Computer Engineering.

Parks, J. R. (1990). Automated personal identification methods for use with smart cards. In P. L. Hawkes (Ed.), *Integrated Circuit Cards, Tags and Tokens: new technology and applications* (pp. 92-135). Oxford: BSP Professional Books.

Pentland, A. (2000). Looking at people: sensing for ubiquitous and wearable computing. *IEEE Transactions on Pattern Analysis and Machine Intelligence, 22*(1), 107-119.

Pepe, M. (1996). Kiosks: Unisys is the name in Spain. *Computer Reseller News, 674*(11), 107-108.

Petermann, T., Sauter, A., & Scherz, C. (2006). Biometrics at the borders: the challenges of a political technology. *International Review of Law, Computers & Technology, 20*(1), 149-166.

PI. (2002). National ID Cards. *Privacy International* Retrieved 30 December 2008, from http://www.privacyinternational.org/issues/idcard/_index.html

Privacy Commissioner. (1994). Data-matching guidelines. *Privacy Commissioner Human Rights Australia,* from http://www.austlii.edu.au/au/other/hreoc/privacy/dmguide.htm

Raina, K., Woodward, J. D., & Orlans, N. (2002). How Biometrics Work. In J. D. Woodward, N. M. Orlans & P. T. Higgins (Eds.), *Biometrics* (pp. 25-44). London: John Wiley and Sons.

Ritter, J. (1995, June 22). Eye scans help sheriff keep suspects in sight. *Chicago Sun-Times.*

Robins, G. (1995). Reinventing electronic benefits transfer. *Stores, 77*(6), 58-59.

Roethenbaugh, G. (1998). Simon Davies- Is this the most dangerous man in Europe? *Biometrics in Human Services User Group, 2*(5), 2-5.

Roethenbaugh, G. (1998a). Police and thieves. *Biometrics in Human Services User Group, 2*(4), 2-3.

Rosenweig, B. (2000, 12 July). The new face of law and order. *The Globe and Mail.*

Ruggles, T. (1996a). The California statewide fingerprint imaging system (CA SFIS) project. *Biometrics in Human Services, 1*(2), 5-6.

Ruggles, T. (1996b). Comparison of biometric techniques. *The Biometric Consulting Group* Retrieved 2 January 2002, from http://biometric-consulting.com/bio.htm

San Jose University. (2000). Biometric identification. *Research at San Jose University* Retrieved 12 December 2002, from http://www.engr.sjsu.edu/biometrics/

Scholtz, J., & Johnson, J. (2002). Identification technologies: can they make us more secure? *SIGCHI Bulletin*(July/August), 9.

Scholtz, J., & Johnson, J. (2002, 20-25 April). *Interacting with identification technology: Can it make us more secure?* Paper presented at the CHI 2002: changing the world, changing ourselves, Minnesota, USA.

Schulman, A. (2002). The US/Mexico border crossing card (BCC): A case study in biometric, machine-readable ID. *Proceedings of the 12th Annual Conference on Computers, Freedom and Privacy.* Retrieved 20 August 2003, from http://www.undoc.com

Seidman, S. (1990). Wallet-size solutions. In R. Ames (Ed.), *Perspectives on Radio Frequency Identification: What is it, Where is it going, Should I be Involved?* (pp. 1-19- 11-27). New York: Van Nostrand Reinhold.

Sensar. (1999). Sensar partners. *Sensar* Retrieved 2 June 1999, from http://www.sensar.com/partners/partners.stm

Shen, W. (1997). Evaluation of automated biometrics-based identification and verification systems. *Proceedings of the IEEE, 85*(9), 1464-1478.

Sieghart, P. (Ed.). (1982). *Microchips with Everything: the consequences of information technology.* London: Comedia Publishing Group.

Sirohey, S., Wilson, C., & Chellappa, R. (1995). Human and machine recognition of faces: a survey. *Proceedings of IEEE, 83*(5), 705-740.

SJB. (1996a). Biometrics could prevent fraudulent welfare claims. *Biometric Technology Today*(26 February 1998).

SJB. (1996b). Finger geometry is passport to Disney theme parks. Retrieved 26 February 1998, from http://www.sjb.co.uk/pr/18069603.txt

SJB. (1996c). Hi-tech biometric 'passports' speed immigration checks. Retrieved 26 February 1998, from http://www.sjb.co.uk/pr/23029603.txt

Smith, R. E. (2002). How Authentication Technologies Work. In J. D. Woodward, N. M. Orlans & P. T. Higgins (Eds.), *Biometrics* (pp. 3-23). London: John Wiley and Sons.

Smith, S. (1995). Welfare's big brother. *Computer Weekly*, 40-41.

Snyderwine, M., & Murray, D. (1999). *O'Hare International Airport's air cargo security access system.* Paper presented at the IEEE 33rd Annual International Carnahan Conference on Security Technology.

Solove, D. J. (2004). *The Digital Person: Technology and Privacy in the Digital Age.* New York: New York University Press.

Solove, D. J. (2008a). *The Future of Reputation: Gossip, Rumor, and Privacy on the Internet.* New York: Yale University Press.

Solove, D. J. (2008b). *Understanding Privacy.* Harvard: Harvard University Press.

Solove, D. J., Rotenberg, M., & Schwartz, P. M. (2005). *Information Privacy Law* (2nd ed.). New York: Aspen Publishers.

Solove, D. J., Rotenberg, M., & Schwartz, P. M. (2006). *Privacy, Information And Technology*. New York: Aspen Publishers.

Stapleton, J. (2003). State of Biometric Standards. *Biometritechexpo 2003* Retrieved 20 December 2008, from http://publicaa.ansi.org/sites/apdl/Documents/News%20and%20Publications/Links%20Within%20Stories/DI-4%20Standards%20Stapleton-%20Jeff%20Stapleton.ppt

Storms, J. (1998). *Legislative background: Never give up*. Retrieved 23 November 1998. from http://www.dss.state.ct.us/digital/faq/digarvey.htm.

Sutherland, K., Rengham, D., & Denyer, P. B. (1992). Automatic face recognition. *First International Conference on Intelligent Systems Engineering*(360), 29-34.

Tilton, C. J. (2000). An emerging biometric API industry standard. *IEEE Computer, 33*(2), 130-132.

U.S. Financial Management Service. (1990). *Applications of computer card technology*. Hyattsville: Government Printing Office.

Unisys. (1997). Spain plays it smart with smartcard (pp. 1-2): Personal ID Solutions.

USA Government. (2001). Uniting and Strengthening America by Providing Appropriate Tools Required to Intercept and Obstruct Terrorism (USA Patriot Act) Act of 2001. Retrieved 20 December 2008, from http://frwebgate.access.gpo.gov/cgi-bin/getdoc.cgi?dbname=107_cong_public_laws&docid=f:publ056.107

USA Government. (2002). Enhanced Border Security and Visa Entry Reform Act of 2002. Retrieved 20 December 2008, from http://frwebgate.access.gpo.gov/cgi-bin/getdoc.cgi?dbname=107_cong_public_laws&docid=f:publ173.107

Valles, E. (1998, 7 October). Smart ID cards to guarantee privacy: National card plans get underway amid anxieties. *China News*, p. 7.

van der Ploeg, I. (2003). Biometrics and Privacy: A note on the politics of theorizing technology. *Information, Communication & Society, 6*(1), 85-104.

van der Putte, T. (2001). Forging ahead. *Biometric Technology Today, 9*(6), 9-11.

van Kralingen, R., Prins, C., & Grijpink, J. (1997). Using your body as a key; legal aspects of biometrics. Retrieved 20 August 1998, from http://cwis.kub.nl/~frw/people/kraling/content/biomet.htm

Walden, I. (2000). The legal implications of biometrics data. *IEE Colloquium on Visual Biometrics*, 2/1-2/11.

Watson, F. (2001). Overcoming global terror. *Biometric Technology Today, 9*(6), 1.

Wayman, J. L. (2000). Federal biometric technology legislation. *IEEE Computer*, 76-80.

Weise, E. (1998). Body may be key to foolproof ID. *USA Today*, from http://www.usatoday.com/life/cyber/tech/ctc447.htm

Weng, J. J., & Swets, D. L. (1999). Face Recognition. In A. K. Jain (Ed.), *Biometrics: personal identification in networked society* (pp. 65-101). Boston: Kluwer Academic Publishers.

Wildes, R. P. (1997). Iris recognition: an emerging biometric technology. *Proceedings of the IEEE, 85*(9), 1348-1363.

Williams, G. O. (1997, April). Iris recognition technology. *IEEE AES Systems Magazine,* 23-29.

Withers, S. (2002). Who are you? *Technology and Business*(July), 72-79.

Woodcock, A. (2005). Biometric cards: privacy invaders vs. a safer America. *ACM SIGCAS Computers and Society, 35*(1), 3.

Woodward, J. D. (1997). Biometrics: privacy's foe or privacy's friend? *Proceedings of the IEEE, 85*(9), 1480-1492.

Woodward, J. D. (2001). Super Bowl Surveillance: Facing Up to Biometrics. *RAND.* Retrieved 21 December 2008, from http://www.rand.org/pubs/issue_papers/2005/IP209.pdf

Woodward, J. D. (2002a). Biometrics and Privacy. In J. D. Woodward, N. M. Orlans & P. T. Higgins (Eds.), *Biometrics* (pp. 197-216). London: John Wiley and Sons.

Woodward, J. D. (2002b). Case Study: Super Bowl Surveillance. In J. D. Woodward, N. M. Orlans & P. T. Higgins (Eds.), *Biometrics* (pp. 247-258). London: John Wiley and Sons.

Woodward, J. D. (2002c). Legal Considerations of Government Use of Biometrics. In J. D. Woodward, N. M. Orlans & P. T. Higgins (Eds.), *Biometrics* (pp. 217-246). London: John Wiley and Sons.

Woodward, J. D., Orlans, N. M., & Gatune, J. (2002). Esoteric Biometrics. In J. D. Woodward, N. M. Orlans & P. T. Higgins (Eds.), *Biometrics* (pp. 115-138). London: John Wiley and Sons.

Woodward, J. D., Orlans, N. M., & Higgins, P. T. (2002). *Biometrics.* London: John Wiley and Sons.

Woodward, J. D., Webb, K. W., Newton, E. M., Bradley, M. A., Rubenson, D., Larson, K., et al. (2001). Army Biometric Applications: Identifying and Addressing Sociocultural Concerns. Retrieved 3 January 2009, from http://www.rand.org/pubs/monograph_reports/MR1237/

Xiao, Q. (2007). Technology review - Biometrics-Technology, Application, Challenge, and Computational Intelligence Solutions. *IEEE Computational Intelligence Magazine, 2*(2), 5-25.

Zoreda, J. L., & Oton, J. M. (1994). *Smart Cards.* Boston: Artech House.

Zunkel, R. L. (1999). Hand Geometry Based Verification. In A. K. Jain (Ed.), *Biometrics: personal identification in networked society* (pp. 87-101). Boston: Kluwer Academic Publishers.

Chapter IX
RFID Tags and Transponders:
The New Kid on the Block

RADIO-FREQUENCY IDENTIFICATION TECHNOLOGY

Historical Overview

Radio frequency identification (RFID) in the form of tags or transponders is a means of auto-ID that can be used for tracking and monitoring objects, both *living* and *non-living*. One of the first applications of RFID was in the 1940s within the US Defense Force (Hodges & McFarlane, 2004, p. 59). Transponders were used to differentiate between friendly and enemy aircraft (Ollivier, 1995, p. 234; Scharfeld (1998, p. 9). Since that time, transponders continued mainly to be used by the aerospace industry (or in other niche applications) until the late 1980s when the Dutch government voiced their requirement for a live-stock tracking system. The commercial direction of RFID changed at this time and the uses for RFID grew manifold as manufacturers realized the enormous potential of the technology.

Before RFID, processes requiring the check-in and distribution of items were mostly done manually. Gerdeman (1995, p. 3) highlights this by the following real-life example: "[e]ighty thousand times a day, a long shoreman takes a dull pencil and writes on a soggy piece of paper the ID of a container to be key entered later... This process is fraught with opportunity for error." Bar code systems in the 1970s helped to alleviate some of the manual processing, but it was not until RFID became more widespread in the late 1990s that even greater increases in productivity were experienced. RFID was even more effective than bar code because it did not require items that were being checked to be in a stationary state or in a particular set orientation. As Finkenzeller (2001, p. 1) rightly underlines, *"[t]he omnipresent barcode labels that triggered a revolution in identification systems some considerable time ago, are being found to be inadequate in an increasing number of cases. Barcodes may be extremely cheap, but their stumbling block is their low storage capacity and the fact that they cannot be reprogrammed".* RFID limits the amount of human intervention required to a minimum, and in some cases eliminates it altogether (Hind, 1994, p. 215).

The fundamental electromagnetic principles that make RFID possible were discovered by Michael Faraday, Nikola Tesla and Heinrich R. Hertz prior to 1900. *"From them we know that when a group of electrons or current flows through a conductor, a magnetic field is formed surrounding the conductor.*

The field strength diminishes as the distance from the wire increases. We also know that when there is a relative motion between a conductor and a magnetic field a current is induced in that conductor. These two basic phenomena are used in all low frequency RFID systems on the market today" (Ames, 1990, p. 3-2). Finkenzeller (2001, pp. 25-110) provides a detailed explanation of fundamental RF operating and physical principles. Ames (1990, p. 3-3) points out that RFID works differently to normal radio transmission. RFID uses the near field effect rather than plane wave transmission. This is why distance plays such an important role in RFID. The shorter the range between the reader and the RF device the greater the precision for identification. The two most common RFID devices today are tags and transponders but since 1973 (Ames, 1990, p. 5-2) other designs have included contactless smart cards, wedges (plastic housing), disks and coins, glass transponders (that look like tubes), keys and key fobs, tool and gas bottle identification transponders, even clocks (Finkenzeller, 2001, pp. 13-20). The size and shapes of tags and transponders vary. Some more common shapes include: glass cylinders typically used for animal tracking (the size of a grain of rice), wedges for insertion into cars, circular pills, ISO cards with or without magnetic stripes, polystyrene and epoxy discs, bare tags ready for integration into other packaging (ID Systems, 1997, p. 4). RFID espouses different principles to smart cards but the two are closely related according to Finkenzeller (2001, p. 6). RFID systems can take advantage of contactless smart cards transmitting information by the use of radio waves.

The RFID System

RFID can be defined as an electronic tagging technology that allows objects to be automatically identified at a distance without direct line of sight, using an electromagnetic challenge/response exchange (Want, 2004). An RFID system primarily consists of RFID tags or transponders and RFID readers, but can be extended to include antennas, radio characteristics and the computer network used to connect RFID readers (Finkenzeller, 2003). Figure 1 illustrates the configuration, components and interactions present in an RFID system (Hamilton, Michael & Wamba, 2009). RFID readers contain radio frequency modules that emit pulses of radio energy that are detected by tags and responded to with information, such as the tag's serial number. RFID tags are the labels that are attached to the object to be identified. RFID tags consist of an antenna, a small silicon chip that contains a radio receiver, a radio modulator, control logic, memory and a power system (Garfinkel & Rosenberg, 2005). RFID tags are classified as

Figure 1. Components of an RFID system

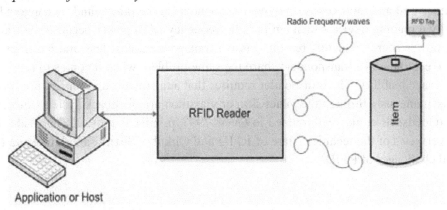

being passive, semi-passive or active based on their composition. Passive tags are the most common tags, solely powered by the radio frequency signal that is used to transport information, whereas active tags are equipped with on-board batteries (Nemeth, Toth, & Hartvanyi, 2006). Semi-passive tags are passive tags that have had a battery added to boost signal range (Angeles, 2005).

Active vs. Passive Tags and Transponders

An RFID system has several separate components. It contains a re-usable programmable tag which is placed on the object to be tracked, a reader that captures information contained within the tag, an antenna that transmits information, and a computer which interprets or manipulates the information (Gerdeman, 1995, pp. 11-25; Schwind 1990, p. 1-27). Gold (1990, p. 1-5) describes RF tags as: *"[t]iny computers embedded in a small container sealed against contamination and damage. Some contain batteries to power their transmission; others rely on the signal generated by the receiver for the power necessary to respond to the receiver's inquiry for information. The receiver is a computer-controlled radio device that captures the tag's data and forwards it to a host computer."* The RFID tag has one major advantage over bar codes, magnetic-stripe cards, contact smart cards and biometrics- the wearer of the tag need only pass by a reading station and a transaction will take place, even if the wearer attempts to hide the badge (Sharp, 1990, p. 1-15). Unlike light, low-frequency (or medium-to-high) radio waves can penetrate all solid objects except those made of metal. Thus the wearer does not have to have direct physical contact with a reader.

Transponders, unlike tags, are not worn on the exterior of the body or part. On humans or animals they are injected into the subcutaneous tissue. Depending on their power source, transponders can be classified as active or passive. Whether a system uses an active or passive transponder depends entirely on the application. Geers et al. (1997, p. 20f) suggests the following to be taken into consideration when deciding what type of transponder to use. *"When it is sufficient to establish communication between the implant and the external world on a short-range basis, and it is geometrically feasible to bring the external circuitry a very close distance from the implant, the passive device is suitable... On the other hand choosing for an active system is recommended when continuous monitoring, independent transmission or wider transmission ranges are required. In particular for applications where powering is of vital importance (e.g. pacemakers), only the active approach yields a reliable solution."*

Active transponders are usually powered by a battery that operates the internal electronics (Finkenzeller, 2001, p. 13). Some obvious disadvantages of active transponders include: the replacement of batteries after they have been utilized for a period of time, the additional weight batteries add to the transponder unit and their cost. A passive transponder on the other hand, is triggered by being interrogated by a reading device which emits radiofrequency (RF) power because the transponder has no internal power source. For this reason, passive transponders cost less and can literally last forever. Both active and passive transponders share the same problem when it comes to repair and adjustment which is inaccessibility. The transponder requires that adjustments and repairs are "operated remotely and transcutaneously through the intact skin or via automatic feedback systems incorporated into the design" (Goedseels et al., 1990, quoted in Geers 1997, p. xiii). Paret (2005) provides one of the most recent overviews of the technical state of RFID and Ohkubo, Suzuki and Kinoshita (2005) cover the technical challenges of RFID.

RFID Components Working Together

Electronic tags and transponders are remotely activated using a short range and pulsed echo principle at around 150 kHz. Once a tag or transponder moves within a given distance of the power transmitter coil (antenna), it is usually requested to transmit information by activating the transponder circuit. The transponder may be read only, one-time programmable (OTP) or read/write. Regardless the type, each contains a binary ID code which after encoding modulates the echo so that information is transmitted to a receiver using the power of an antenna (Curtis, 1992, p. 2/1). The whole procedure is managed by a central controller in the transmitter. Read only tags contain a unique code between 32 and 64 bits in length. Read/write tags support a few hundred bits, typically 1 kbit, although larger memories are possible. The ID field is usually transmitted from a tag with a header and check sum fields for validation, just in case data is corrupted during transmission. Transmission is also a vital part of any RFID system. When information is transmitted by radio waves it must be transformed into an electromagnetic radiation form. According to Geers et al. (1997, p. 8), *"[e]lectromagnetic radiation is defined by four parameters: the frequency, the amplitude of the electric field, the direction of the electric field vector (polarization) and the phase of the wave. Three of these, namely amplitude, frequency and phase, are used to code the transmitted information, which is called modulation."*

Two types of modulation are used- analogue or digital. Common encoding techniques for the former include pulse amplitude modulation (PAM) and pulse width modulation (PWM); for the latter pulse coded modulation (PCM) is common. According to Finkenzeller (2001, pp. 44f) digital data is transferred using bits as modulation patterns in the form of ASK (amplitude shift keying) or FSK (frequency shift keying) or PSK (phase shift keying). A bit rate can be determined by the bandwidth available and the time taken for transfer. Error detection algorithms like parity or cyclic redundancy checks (CRC) are vital since radio communication, is susceptible to interference. It can never be taken for granted that the message transmitted has not been distorted during the transmission process but with error detection implemented into the design, "accuracy approaches 100 percent" (Gold, 1990, p. 1-5).

THE RFID INNOVATION SYSTEM

The essence of innovation is the blending of ideas with the science and practice of engineering. Nowhere is this process more active than in the area of identification technologies. (Schuster, Allen & Brock, 2008, p. 3)

A Time to Grow, a Time to Nurture

In the mid-to-late 1990s there were relatively a small number of manufacturers in RFID. Coupled with this was the lack of standardized equipment. Service providers therefore had a limited range of systems to choose from. In 1997 Geers et al. (p. 90) identified only "ten manufacturers of passive electronic identification transponders for animals (subcutaneously injectable, bolus, eartag)." Some of the companies on this list included AVID, DataMars, Destron/ID and Euro-ID/Trovan. Within a space of one to two years, this figure more than tripled to include companies that specialized in something other than just the implantation of animals. Some of these companies include: Amtech Corporation, Checkpoint Systems, Cochlear, Electronic Identification Devices, Elmo-Tech, HID Corporations, Identichip, LipoMatrix,

Tagmaster, and Trolley Scan. More recently, the potential of RFID has drawn many new companies to the technology, especially for supply chain automation and the tracking of humans and livestock. "At the end of 1988 there were approaching 500 companies which either manufacture or supply auto ID technologies and which were members of an AIM association somewhere in the world" (Smith, 1990, p. 49). This figure of 500 includes companies involved not just in RFID tags and transponders but other auto-ID devices as well, i.e., the whole auto-ID industry. As of February 2009, AIM Global had 50 gold members with chapters in thirteen countries (AIM, 2009).

Early Interoperability Problems

According to Kitsz (1990, p. 3-41) the issue of interoperability in RFID has hardly been addressed in the 1980s. Users could not pick and choose different equipment from several vendors based on price or capability (or any other differentiating factor) with the assurance that everything would work together. As Gerdeman had precisely captured, *"[s]tandards have been a cornerstone to the computer revolution and the identification community. Without standards the user community would have significant troubles in communicating with their constituents, gaining significant productivity from common capabilities, or having a point of comparison reflecting the views of the experts"* (Gerdeman, 1995, p. 45). In fact, the likelihood even at the turn of the century was that equipment would not work together seamlessly: "systems of one vendor must be compatible with those of another, and must additionally operate under both foreign and domestic regulations. Efforts to develop standards for RFID and various applications are continuing" (Scharfeld, 2001, p. 9). For instance, tags purchased from one vendor would not be read by a device from another vendor.

The conflict in RFID equipment was particularly prevalent in the microchipping of domesticated animals. One politician in Taipei called the microchipping of animals the "joke of the century". Shu-ling (2001, pp.1f) explained that "…electronically tagged dogs haven't been reunited with their owners because of the poor quality of some ID chips or conflicting scanner and tag systems… competing tag and scanner systems available on the market make it difficult to facilitate reunions, as public shelters are unlikely to be equipped with a collection of different scanners that could decode every chip in existence." An American Pet Association (APA) press release in 2001 also discussed the shortcomings of animal chip implants (APA, 2001). These shortcomings could be overcome with standard equipment. This is not to say that RFID implants for pets have not been successful. There are now over 15 million pets that have been implanted worldwide, and increasingly pets are now being reunited with their owners. It is now compulsory to chip implant your pet (cat or dog) in the state of New South Wales in Australia, and to register it with the local council. Simpson (2002, p. 5), provides the following example in the article, 'Microchip saves trauma for Benson'. "Mrs Stewart said she feared for the worst when her dog went missing. But council rangers were able to identify Benson because he had been microchipped and obtained a lifetime registration."

According to (Automatic ID News, 1998a, pp. 2f): *"[t]he goal of standardization is to create a generic tag and reader that ideally could be purchased from several vendors, resulting in lower costs and multiple ready sources of supply. While standardization makes specifying easier, standards pose a problem in that the tag-to-reader communication is typically proprietary to each manufacturer. The problem is compounded by the fact that tags come in many differing forms and information capacities, and are used in different environments"*. This has surely deterred some users from choosing RFID over other auto-ID technologies. Consider the service provider who needs to make a large investment in RFID and only has a choice between vendors and not between equipment components such as tags, transponders, readers, software, etc. In this instance, a proprietary solution from one vendor alone has major implications. For instance, will the vendor support products sold for the lifetime of the business? Will the vendor maintain the system for a substantial period of time? Will future product changes mean that the user will have to make future mandatory investments? Will future expansion cost too much to implement?

To offset this predicament, advocates of RFID point to the ever-increasing investment in new start-up companies focused on RFID technology and applications. These new companies are vital to the technology's accelerated growth. As users, present and potential, see more and more players entering the market they become more comfortable with the technology and are more likely to purchase RFID systems for long-term solutions. Ames (1990, p. 6-10) uses the words "legitimacy" and "credibility" to describe the effects that new companies have on users and the industry worldwide. More recently however, users are becoming more critical of new start-up companies in most areas of IT&T. Citizens are even more cautious today to buy shares in any company that has not proven itself over time. As one industry analyst put it, the technology needs to be "cooked not eaten raw and today's businesses have products that haven't even thawed".

Standardization: Opposing Forces at Hand

The fact that some RFID manufacturers see standardization as a threat to their survival (Ames, 1990, p. 5-6) does not comfort potential users at all. RFID veteran, Gerdeman, (1995, p. 45) stated that "[g]enerally, politics surround the formation of a standard. There is also a significant amount of technical engineering support" that is required. Some manufacturers believe their core business is based on remaining a closed system supplier so they are not concerned about contributing to a global standards process. The reality is that conforming to a set of open standards will inevitably lead to a reduction in competition based on proprietary interfaces and protocols. However there have been some major trials and industry movements, especially in supply chain management (SCM) demonstrating the value of common standards. Other differentiating factors will subsequently become the basis for competitive advantage.

As RFID begins to find applicability in open systems, vendors have a lot to lose if they are not willing to conform to a set of standards. The potential for the technology is incredible but as long as "[n]obody's system is ever compatible with anybody else's" the technology will fall short of its mark (Kitsz, 1990, p. 3-41). Back in 1990 Ames (1990, p. 5-8) predicted that interoperability would become a critical issue after the year 2000, particularly for applications with a global purpose, and this was found to have been true. In the example of herd management, tags are still utilized in proprietary environments. However, worldwide, governments have started to impose regulations which will affect farmers, particularly in Europe and the U.S (Trevarthen, 2006). As traceability of individual animals, literally from the farm onto the kitchen table, becomes a directive rather than a proposal, "[i]nteroperability is essential, and any animal identification system that is not compatible with the larger system will lose its value" (Look, 1998, p. 3). Technology providers will be forced to weigh up the benefits and costs of standardization, the latter of which are likely to be short-term.

From Industry-Specific to Global Standards

"According to industry experts, the growth of RFID, despite its potential, has been stymied by the inability of RFID systems to communicate with each other" (Tuttle, 1997, p. 7). The problem is very much related to the manner in which RFID technology was applied historically. As new applications for RFID were conceived, lead manufacturers with the greatest expertise in that area funneled their resources towards getting that application to market. Over time, standards were developed sporadically and in almost every case prior to 2000, those standards (if any) were industry-specific, for instance for trucking, rail, etc. *"All major RFID vendors offer proprietary systems, with the result that various applications and industries have standardized on different vendors' competing frequencies and protocols. The lack of open systems' interchangeability has hindered RFID industry growth as a whole, and has resulted in slower technology price reductions that often come with broad-based interindustry use"* (AIM Global, 1999, p. 2).

Tuttle (1997, p. 7) is in agreement that "[s]ingle source supplying creates monopoly, which drives prices up- and deters customers." To solve this problem, manufacturers started working towards a RFID global open standard for communications. Several industry-specific and global organizations have progressed towards addressing RFID standardization, bringing about some commonality in systems. Common items of concern listed by Gerdeman (1995, p. 46) that should be considered as part of the standardization process included: reliability, accuracy, tag life, speed, temperature, frequency, tag position, data content and distance. Since 2000, new RFID ventures like the Electronic Product Code (EPC) initiative of the Auto-ID Centre have been working towards standardization. Part of the vision of EPC is to create a "Smart World" where there is intelligent infrastructure linking between objects, information and people, through a computer network. This infrastructure would be based on "...open standards, protocols and languages to facilitate worldwide adoption of this network" (Brock, 2001, p. 5). Before launching any type of commercial product the Auto-ID Center focused on a standardized architecture model.

The Electronic Product Code

EPCglobal has aided the prospects of RFID throughout the globe (Zeisel & Sabella, 2006, p.145-151). While it has been around for almost a decade now, it is leading the development of industry-driven standards for the electronic product code (EPC). Consider a world where all things are interconnected to support trade. The basic premise of the EPC is that it is globally unique (GS1, 2009). In actual fact, a pallet could be given a unique number, so could a carton within that pallet, and an item within that carton. The usefulness of such an approach is that independent of where a tag is in the supply chain, it can be found and an acknowledgment returned revealing its whereabouts. The EPCglobal network will allow organisations to share information about the data gathered via the RFID tags using secure infrastructure. During the early stages of development, authorities of the EPCglobal network saw an urgent need to apply the network to track and trace within the entire supply chain, theft detection (Huber & Michael, 2007) (Figure 2), inventory management, product obsolescence and the management of production within military supply chains. Today, there are still some teething problems to overcome with how the EPCglobal standard synchronizes with other established systems like GS1's Global Standards Management Process (GSMP) (GS1, 2008).

Figure 2. An RFID reader placed in a customer exit point at a retail hardware store for theft prevention. Courtesy of Mr Dane Hamilton, 2007.

Organizations Supporting Change

The most influential standards-support group that helped to get RFID off the ground in the early days was AIM. "AIM brings together products with one common capability... [and] has been liberal in including products in the definition of automatic identification" (Ames, 1990, p. 5-19). Byfield (2002, p. 1) concurs with Ames that the term "Auto ID" is an umbrella word to represent all technologies which automatically identify coded items. AIM differs from other organizations in that its purpose is industry-wide. With such a massive potential in auto-ID there was a need "for a specialist non-commercial association to coordinate national and international education. AIM has now firmly established itself as such an association" (Smith, 1990, p. 49) and with global coverage. In 2006, they even had a RFID expert group (REG) working on 7 different projects besides ISO standards: regulatory, privacy, effects of RFID radiation health & safety (public policy), technology selection, and RFID emblem revision and maintenance (AIM, 2006).

First set up in the United States as the Automatic Identification Manufacturers (AIM) association, similar associations are now in operation in Argentina, Belgium, Brazil, China, Denmark, Germany, India, Italy, Korea, The Netherlands, Russia and the UK, although historically they had even been established in New Zealand, Australia, and France.. "These associations have been licensed to operate as AIM affiliates by AIM International, the overall governing body..." (Smith, 1990, p. 49. AIM member companies are located in all these countries and they are mostly technology providers, inventors, developers and suppliers of auto-ID technologies. For a list of AIM contacts and locations see AIM Global (1999, p. 13). It offers a host of services including a library of technical literature, an online web site www.aimglobal.org, educational videos, comprehensive exhibitions and conferences on auto-ID (e.g. SCAN-TECH), it publishes *Auto ID Today* and it is a cosponsor of the Auto-ID User Association among other things (Smith, 1990, p. 50). ISO has also realized the importance of RFID standards and together with the International Electrotechnical Commission (IEC) has sponsored a Joint Technical Committee (JTC) to accomplish some milestones. Two committees that are addressing the critical issues of standardization include: Sub-committee 31 (SC31) Automatic ID and Data Capture and Sub-Committee 17 (SC17) Contactless Card Working Group. There are ways to bypass particular steps in the ISO process but one should be aware that there are potential pitfalls to fast-tracking (Halliday, 1999, p. 1). See also the more recent but peripheral work of AIM such as: the guideline on RFID-enabled labels submitted to ISO/IEC JTC 1/SC 31/WG 4/SG 5 as ISO/IEC TR 24729-1; the guidelines on recycling submitted to ISO/IECJTC 1/SC 31/WG 4/SG 5 as ISO/IEC TR 24729-2, and the guideline on RFID tag and transponder quality incorporated into ISO 17367.

Abiding by Regulations

Frequency Ranges and Radio Licensing Regulations

Manufacturers may voluntarily respect standards but they must abide by regulations. RFID requires the use of radio spectrum "[b]ecause RFID systems generate and radiate electromagnetic waves" (Finkenzeller, 2001, p. 111). It is important that radio services of any kind do not impact one another negatively. To this end, RFID systems are allotted a special frequency range within which they may suitably operate. RFID systems designers need to comply with these regulations. It should also be noted that the spectrum available for RFID is a limited national resource which is managed independently by each country. For example, in Japan there was no spectrum available for RFID as it had been taken up by other radio services. It was only midway through 2003 that the Japanese government announced that it would allocate a portion of the ultra high frequency (UHF) spectrum for use by RFID systems. "The move paved the way for the global use of UHF tags to track goods in the supply chain" (RFID, 2003).

Back in 1998, Marsh wrote: *"[i]n order to bring a measure of uniformity the world has recently been divided into three regulatory areas with a view to trying to get some uniformity within the areas. Uniformity will however only be achieved towards the year 2010 as it requires each country to implement the plans for that region. The regions are: (1) Europe and Africa, (2) North and South Africa, (3) Far East and Australasia."* And this indeed is increasingly coming to fruition. Related to the issue of regulation, Geers et al. (1997, p. 4) see the major problems of RFID as being *"the availability of sufficient radiofrequencies with adequate bandwidths, the complexity of governmental regulations and, extremely important, the interference of other users. Another aspect regarding implant applications is the potential damage of the high-frequency waves to the living tissue."* Particular applications will be allotted particular frequency bands, according to the bandwidth required for an application to be successful. For example, injectable transponders require a frequency band of less than 125 kHz whereas an EAS (Electronic Articles Surveillance) transponder systems in retail stores require between 1.95 mHz and 8.2 mHz. Thus RFID regulation can be broken down into four levels- international, national, local and application-specific.

Application-Specific Regulations

The tracking of farm animals is beginning to be stringently regulated in some countries such as Australia (Trevarthen, 2006). Among the most regulated markets for the identification and recording of animals is within the European Union. The Council Directive 92/102/EC of 27 November 1992 made it mandatory for certain types of livestock to be marked. In the U.S. AIM and the National Livestock Trust are playing a coordinating role with regard to farm animals. "However, there is no consensus on whether or not one system has to be used for all species, and whether or not there should be only one central database" (Geers et al., 1997, p. 29). In the U.K. farmers ear tag their animals and record them in a central database 36 hours after birth. Farm animals in the Netherlands have been uniquely identified since 1975 for animal health and breeding support. Farmers have the choice of plastic or electronic ear tags or injectable transponders. In the future the animal's DNA code may be used as a unique identifier. Farmers in the Netherlands use ISO protocol (ISO/DIS 11788-1) to exchange information with central registers. In Belgium a system called SANITEL is in operation which was developed by the Ministry of Agriculture for disease surveillance and premium control (Geers et al., 1997, pp. 29-32). Ever since major outbreaks of bovine spongiform encephalopathy (BSE) in Europe, the most recent of which was in 2001, and even greater number of regulations have been introduced by government bodies. In the case of the mad cow disease the European Union implemented new rules as of January 2001 "...requiring all cattle over 30 months old to be tested for the disease. The EU has set aside about $1 billion for the tests, which cost about $100 per animal... The European Commission estimates the cost of incinerating slaughtered animals at $3.3 billion" (PBS, 2001). With such losses, countries are looking to safeguard themselves from future disasters by using RFID tags and transponders.

The Importance of Collaboration

Collaboration within the Firm

RFID systems are nowhere near as straightforward as bar code systems. With developing standards, enforced regulations, and technical rules to follow, open internal collaboration within RFID companies themselves is paramount. Both as an entrepreneur and employee, working for a new high-tech company is a challenge. Resources are limited and employees are most likely to be juggling more than one job role. When RFID companies were initially established, interaction between firms was still premature with few competitors willing to share any part of their intellectual property. Thus entrepreneurs of new start-ups have to be focused- on employing the right people with the necessary skills and experience, to be motivated to achieving company goals, to attract investors, to have sufficient capital to continue the development of products and to be able to pay for on-going expenses (Ames, 1990, p. 6-12). Without products, customers cannot buy any equipment from a company, and without frequent incoming sales revenue a business will eventually discontinue operating. This is another reason why companies start small and build up over time.

RFID companies have traditionally begun with a size of 5-10 employees and reached levels of 80-100 persons as customer demand increased. Some larger companies that manufacture contactless smart cards have very large global staff counts however due to multiple downturns in the economy, first around the dotcom crash, and then during the financial crisis beginning in late 2008, companies have begun to lay off thousands of employees. The initial team usually comprises of experts that are technical and have general application knowledge. The most valuable employee in the formative years of an RFID company is one that can deliver solutions to meet the customer's requirements. The employee will typically have good communication skills to complement their sound technical know-how.

Biomark's "Our People" description on its web site stated that the company employed people with a wide range of expertise and experience. Drawing these individual resources together to work as a team is paramount. "The team concept used in developing a system ensures the customer of a well thought out, tried and tested solution..." The "Company Philosophy" description supports this: "[d]evelopment and innovation emerge from Biomark's strongest resource- its employees. Employees are actively encouraged to pursue new theories and ideas in an environment created to foster intellectual growth and development. A team philosophy is utilized in creating new systems for clients; a solution is built upon a solid platform of unified individual strengths" (Biomark, 1999).

The employer is usually the one that builds up the reputation of the firm and makes the initial customer contacts, as well as keeping abreast with what everybody else in the industry is doing. In a great number of countries, particularly in Asia, entrepreneurs realize that it is not solely about 'who has the best product at the least cost' but about developing business relationships. As the start-up company becomes involved in the bidding process and wins contracts, a new interactive process begins between the firm and the customer. Ames (1990, p. 5-21) describes this creative process of product innovation in RFID: *"[t]he products either come into existence primarily in two ways. First, a company goes outside the 'business or industry they are in' to combine existing technologies in a new way, or second potential customers describe problems facing them and the attributes of various products that are needed to solve the problem and this description becomes the blue print for a totally new product. In either case, confusion about what exists, stimulate creative thought and results in a new product- as in the hypothetical example- or a new way to apply existing ones, resulting in a higher quality solution for users."* Compare Ames with Schuster, Allen and Brock (2008, p. 8) who state: "[t]he development of the EPCglobal Network and RFID technology will undoubtedly take many turns in practice. It is seldom that new technology finds application without a great deal of experimentation and a number of failures."

Private Enterprise and University Collaboration

As firms grow in confidence and stature new relationships begin to take shape outside the company. The least threatening relations a technology provider can form are those with public institutions such as universities. Not only is this a positive public relations (PR) strategy but the research conducted can bear some good fruit. For example as of 2003, Symbol Technologies had established an affiliation with Nankai University of Tianjin in China to support technology-based research. Symbol had strategically chosen a China-based university as a way to show local business partners in commerce and government that it is committed to solutions for the Chinese market. In addition, "Symbol Technologies has always placed a great emphasis on training and education. Some of the most important technological breakthroughs that Symbol has developed have been achieved by working closely with universities" (Picker, 1999, p. 1). A number of university-based research projects had also been funded by the Defense Advanced Research Projects Agency (DARPA) involving RFID including investigations into the miniaturization of RFID tags (i.e. the PENI tag) and landmine detection equipping bees with RFID "backpacks".

Undoubtedly the most proactive university-based RFID initiative was the establishment of the Auto-ID Centre which was based at MIT (Hodges & McFarlane, 2004, p. 60). "The Auto-ID Centre is an industry sponsored research centre charged with investigating automated identification technologies and their use with disparate technologies such as the Internet" (Engels et al., 2001, p. 76). Almost from the beginning of its charter, the Center had the support of bar code associations like the Uniform Code Council and EAN International. It was also funded by major companies like Proctor and Gamble, Gillette International Paper, Sun Microsystems and Invensys who were all keen to profit by EPC. The Auto-ID Centre Research Labs are located within Massachusetts Institute of Technology (MIT), University of Cambridge, and the University of Adelaide (Australia). The labs undertook research in three domains including: infrastructure, application and synthesis. Each laboratory was complementary to the other, drawing on individual established strengths. Case in point, the new RFID chair at the University of Adelaide is backed by Gemplus Tag Australia, a company that was originally Integrated Silicon Design (ISD) formed to commercialize technology developed by the university in the 1980s. This company has more than 15 years experience in their respective specialization (Denby, 2001, p. 1). Cambridge, for instance, had a plethora of experience within its Institute for Manufacturing. Initially the research programme was linked to the Automation and Control Group although eventually it was hoped that there would be multidisciplinary participation from groups across the University. The Auto-ID Centre was also the host of the 15th Automatic Identification and Data Capture Institute (AIDC) in 2001. This Institute brings educators together from all over the world to share material on various topics to enable the suitable realignment of undergraduate and postgraduate auto-ID programs being offered by universities worldwide. Other prominent universities who have RFID laboratories include: UCLA, University of Arkansas, Michigan State University, University of Wollongong. University of Wisconsin-Madison, Villanova University, McMaster University, University of Houston.

Patent Explosion

Patents are generally a good measure of the activity within an industry. The greater the number of RFID-related patents filed each month, the greater the likelihood that the technology is growing in importance. Patents also become a source of formal knowledge for firms. By keeping abreast of official patents (using publicly available databases), firms can learn about the latest developments of other companies and their core business focus well in advance of a product launch. According to RFID inventor Mike Marsh who had about 200 international patent applications and was editor of Transponder News (Marsh, 1998, p. 1f): *"[t]he time to publication seems typically to be three years, therefore the patents effectively document the state of technology to within three years of the leading edge inventions. This is generally much shorter than one will find in either technical books or even commercial products on the shelves."* A visit to the Transponder News (1998) web site is extremely informative for manufacturers, customers, regulators, academics and other organizations. By 2004, there were over 4000 patents related to RFID. So important was the matter of intellectual property, that 70 lawyers met to discuss ways to overcome obstacles for the industry at large. One point that was focused on was "on just how many patents were covered by EPCglobal's IP policy and what that meant for vendors building products based on the EPC Gen 2 specification."

Necessary Product Improvements Before 2000

In 1990 Ames (p. 5-4) believed there was room for cross-the-board improvement in RFID systems, particularly in capacity and cost. He also believed that the lack of LAN connectivity on the factory floor and the availability of application software were stifling RFID growth. By 1997 Geers et al. (p. 4) described all the major problems of RFID to being related to regulations. In the seven years between these observations, many incremental improvements were made to RFID. The problem-focus shifted as the technology started to show signs of wider applicability, yet the design goals remained relatively unchanged throughout the same period. In 1990 Ames (p. 6-9) stated that the efficiency of the use of power had to be improved, at the same time reducing the feature size of the tag (as soon as was practical) and incorporating the use of superconductive on-chip interconnection. In 1997 Geers et al. (p. 15) wrote that the main design goal was to develop optimum performance systems, the ability to manufacture items cheaply in large quantities by putting a micro-electronic or integrated circuit (IC) in the transponder, and producing as small a transponder as possible.

Product improvements specific to transponders that are injected into animals was a topic that received attention in the late 1990s. The design of the new transponder itself was highly miniaturized- about the size of a grain of rice. At the same time the implant must have had the ability to transmit information on the ID and body temperature suitable for both animals and humans (Geers et al., 1997, p. 106). Along with miniaturization, low power consumption is seen as a continual mandatory improvement to the transponder. Additionally, chip movement and migration within the body of the animal or human must be eliminated. It is not without significance that *"[t]here have also been reports of the chip moving or migrating from its initial injection location over the shoulder. This is very rare in the cat, and slightly more common in dogs with very loose skin... New designs, including the use of special coatings now used in human implants, will make migration less likely"* (Vetinfonet, 1998, p. 2).

The Destron Fearing Corporation developed Bio-Pond (a porous polypropylene polymer sheath) which fits snugly on transponders, so that implants stay at the original implant location (Park & Weiser et al., 2001, pp. 1-4). An additional improvement (which was more of a safeguard than a technical advancement) was the ability for the transponder to resist high temperatures within the body of the animal or human. Passive radiofrequency tags should be used in this case but if active transponders are needed, safety must be implemented so that the batteries do not explode or lose power when exposed to high temperatures (Geers et al., 1997, p. 62). Surgical implantation also needed to be improved. "Surgery... has been shown to create some degree of stress, and 4-7 days may be required for the animal to return to equilibrium" (Geers et al., 1997, p. 77). The degree of animal discomfort in the microchip implant procedure has often been misrepresented. Canada's national pet registry, PETNET, publicized in 1999 that the implant procedure was "quick, safe and painless" (Anitech, 1999, p.1). This is in direct contrast to Geers (1997). While this may be sufficient for animals, it is not for humans. Some of these improvements have come through major technical breakthroughs discovered by university research.

Consumer Fears

The implanting of a foreign object into an animal brings with it some health issues. First, what type of object is being implanted and does it have the capacity to cause harm to the animal? Second, if the animal is being raised for human consumption is the final produce free from contamination? Both these issues may appear hyper-sensitive but they all have their basis in regulations. For example, a transponder's signal strength must comply with the Postal and Telecommunications Service (PTT) regulations. It was limited to 150 kHz in 2003 but more recently, the European Committee for Electrotechnical Standardization (CENELEC) has proposed higher strengths. Tests are being conducted to see how animals react to this higher signal strength. Active transponders that contain batteries may also pose health risks particularly if there is breakage. Similarly larger devices housed in glass may also be more prone to the risk of breakage. As Geers et al. comments (1997, p. 68): *"[i]ntroducing foreign material into animals intended for human consumption inevitably leads to questions about the toxicity hazard for the animal itself, and the risk of contaminating the food chain. The choice of a suitable material encapsulating the electronic circuit is crucial, since it determines the level of biocompatibility as well as other mechanical and physical aspects (e.g. breakage resistance, radiowave transparency)."* Even products such as readers must comply with government agency requirements. For instance, Destron's readers are tested for compliance with the Federal Communications Commission (FCC) Part 15 Regulation for Electromagnetic Emissions. It should be well noted that the question of chip implants for humans brings with it an even greater number of issues, vastly more complex as well (Rahmoeller, 1988, p. 1).

Once Labeled Conspiracy Theories

While consumers recognize other auto-ID devices like bar codes and magnetic-stripe cards, RFID technologies are more discrete and have traditionally been used for industrial supply automation. Communications about the technology have been mostly between technology and service providers- the average consumer still lacking an elementary understanding of RFID capabilities and its potential uses (Renegar & Michael, 2009; Eckfeldt, 2005). One area that has however caught the attention of some members of the community is prospective humancentric applications for transponder implants (Witt, 1999, p. 89). Conspiracy theorists believe that the ultimate security device, to be enforced by government, will be microchip implants that contain a Universal Lifetime Identifier (ULI). According to conspirators, these implants will be linked to databases that store personal information for each individual that is born. They will be capable of releasing signals into the body that stimulate certain behavior. Ultimately GPS technology and RFID will be used together to track citizens (Michael & Michael, 2009). The ethical and legal implications of such an application have not yet been discussed widely enough, at least not in targeted forums (Michael & Michael, 2005). Once labeled conspiracy theories, scientists and private enterprise have proven that human implants for monitoring and access purposes are not only possible but commercially viable innovations (Masters & Michael, 2007). Consider two examples cases where RFID implants are being marketed for patient IDentification (VeriChip Corporation) and for other bio-sensing related applications (Digital Angel Corporation). The message on the homepage the latter company reads: *"Digital Angel: GPS and RFID products are utilized around the world to save lives, ensure the safety of our food supply, reunite loved ones and improve the quality of life. We are a leading developer of technologies that enable the rapid and accurate identification, location tracking, and condition monitoring of what is important to people. Applications of our products include identification and monitoring of pets and fish with our implantable RFID microchips, identification of livestock with our ear tags, GPS based search and rescue beacons for aircraft, ships, boats, and individuals"* (Digital Angel, 2009).

Nowadays, however, it is a little rash to label "techno-observers" as conspiracy theorists or even worse "fundamentalists" of one kind or another. Founded in 1999 by Katherine Albrecht, CASPIAN (Consumers Against Supermarket Privacy Invasion and Numbering) has been among the most vocal organizations speaking out against RFID on retail items and human implants. The current protests on CASPIAN's home page have to do with the application of RFID in retail product by Gillette, Duracell, Braun appliances, and Oral B products. Albrecht (2003) who is a Harvard University PhD graduate summarized the mission of The Auto-ID Center in 2003 as follows. *"The ultimate goal is for RFID to create a "physically linked world" in which every item on the planet is numbered, identified, catalogued, and tracked. And the technology exists to make this a reality. Described as "a political rather than a technological problem," creating a global system "would involve negotiation between, and consensus among, different countries." Supporters are aiming for worldwide acceptance of the technologies needed to build the infrastructure within the next few years."* It is also worth noting that Albrecht has written several books on the matter including Albrecht and McIntyre (2005; 2006).

According to Mechanic (1996), Israeli-born Daniel Man, a practicing plastic surgeon, first patented a homing device implant designed for humans in 1987. A fuller list of patents can be found in Michael (2003) and Masters (2003). Predictions of human implant trials in the 1990s were not that far-fetched after all. At its face value, the idea seems harmless enough- an implant the size of a point on a ballpoint pen is inserted into the subdermal layer of the skin, and only used for identification purposes. A remote database that stores more specific information about the individual is then queried once identification has been determined. The invention has the potential to be a life-saving device and could be used as a complementary component in any location-based system. Yet a greater amount of discussion at all levels of the community is required before the application becomes widely adopted. For an article surrounding privacy concerns posted by VeriChip on their very own web site, see Lade (2007). Interestingly PETNET in Canada promoted the idea of the "microchip as a guardian angel" (Anitech, 1999).

As RFID companies jostle for market share, strategic mergers and acquisitions between key players in complementary technologies continue to take place. For example, Applied Digital Solutions (ADS) acquired the Destron Fearing company in 2000 for 130 million US dollars. Applied Digital Solutions' main product is the Digital Angel. By acquiring Destron Fearing, ADS now own patents on implanted transmitter technology given Destron Fearing specialized in implanted animal tracking systems (Cochrane, N., 2001, pp. 1-4). While ADS originally denied it was going to use similar technology on humans, within two years of acquiring Destron Fearing it launched a human-centric RFID system. Some organizations like Trovan had dealer agreements that "...prohibited placing a chip under human skin" (Lange, 1997, p. 1) but for the greater part today, most companies have abandoned such statements.

Applied Digital Solutions was just one company that pioneered efforts focused on providing human chip implant services as far back as 2002/03. ADS market their VeriChip solution to people who would like to use it for emergency situations. Shortly after ADS announced the Digital Angel product, Gossett (2002) reported that the Verichip manufacturer was plagued by multiple law suits. The controversy surrounding the Verichip was manifold. First, the FDA launched an investigation into whether the product had been misrepresented; four class-action lawsuits were filed on behalf of shareholders. Second, the company was plagued by auditors, the NASDAQ threatening to de-list the Florida-based company. ADS also announced prematurely certain technical solutions instead of reporting on the real news. Following the premature announcement shares of Digital Angel and ADS rose by 10 percent. Yet the company continues to operate and attract attention. To some degree the organization has now seemingly stabilized, although news breaking of a cancer-related health risk to rats that trialed the original device, sent VeriChip shares plummeting (Morrissey, 2008).

Before microchip implants for humans became commercially viable, wristbands were introduced that contained RFID tags. Among the first companies to launch these wristbands for human monitoring purposes was Sensormatic (Figure 3). They launched a child safety marketing service called SafeKids™, targeting childcare centers especially (Saad & Ahamed, 2007). *"The anti-theft tags are embedded in wristbands placed on children upon entering the childcare centre. Security cameras also beam images to monitors located throughout the store"* (Sensormatic, 1999). *At about the same time that Sensormatic released its product Olivetti marketed the "tot tracker".* Olivetti's technology was a device placed in

Figure 3. Sensormatic gates on entry and exit at the Kmart store in Shellharbour Stocklands, New South Wales, Australia. Photo taken in 2007.

the child's backpack instead of a wristband device (WISC, 1998). Other niche companies getting on board include ParentNet and Simplex Knowledge Company (Time Digital, 1997, p. 5). Many observers tracking the evolution of microchip applications believe that the wristbands were really de facto trials for the chip implants which were launched at the turn of the century. Comparing Olivetti's Active Badge product solution for health (Puchner, 1994, p. 26) with the "tot tracker" gives an indication of the RFID trajectory.

In 2003, DARPA awarded Eagle Eye Technologies "…a contract to build a bracelet-sized mobile terminal designed for compatibility with existing satellite communication systems. The contract is overseen by the U.S. Army Space and Strategic Defense Command at Hunstville, Alabama. Suggested uses, according to Eagle Eye, include "tracking Alzheimer's patients, children, executives, probationers and parolees, and military personnel- a market that could conceivably encompass the world's entire populace in just a few decades" (Lange 1997, p. 2). Compare the idea of "electronic jails" (Goldsmith, 1996, p. 32) with "future smart homes" and how they will be advantageous to the elderly and young children (OOMO 2002, pp. 2-5; ISTSEC, 2003). With RFID devices or company names like Biomark, BioWare, BRANDERS, MARC, Soul Catcher, Digital Angel, Therion Corporation, it is not surprising that some religious groups and civil libertarians among others are very concerned and not at all amused with such metaphors.

Advantages and Disadvantages of RFID

The characteristics of RFID technology aforedescribed differentiate them from other automatic identification technologies (Hamilton, Michael & Wamba, 2009). One of the main physical advantages of RFID technology is that tags, unlike barcodes do not require line of sight to be read and multiple tags can be read simultaneously (Jones, Clarke-Hill, Shears, Comfort, & Hillier, 2004). A field test carried out by UK retailer Marks and Spencer tagged 3.5 million bins and recorded that it took just 3 minutes to read 25 trays when it used to take 17.4 minutes using barcodes, an 83% reduction in reading time for each bin. RFID systems are unaffected by dust, moisture, oils, coolants, cuttings, gases. In addition to this RFID tags can operate in extreme temperatures and last for longer periods, in some cases longer than the items they are attached to (Michael & McCathie, 2005). RFID tags and systems are also characterized by having a greater data density and data quantity than traditional automatic identification technologies in the form of barcodes. This allows RFID tags to carry unique serial numbers more easily than a barcode, which would require a long symbol or a two-dimensional variant, which is difficult to scan and fit into available space. A final major advantage of RFID systems is that they capture data in real time. Capturing data in real time allows organizations to improve data quality, as the information captured is more timely and accurate. All these advantages detailed have the potential to improve operations within organizations.

Studies and literature reveal that due to RFID's novelty in commercial and manufacturing applications, a number of challenges have created concerns about the feasibility of its implementation. The majority of problems that have been encountered when implementing RFID are technical and hardware issues (Albano & Engels, 2002). Issues have been raised such as the reliability of RFID tag reads. It has been discovered that when a tag is oriented perpendicular to a reader it is difficult to read it. Michael and McCathie (2005) state that radio waves can be absorbed by moisture in the immediate environment. Radio waves can be hidden, distorted or reflected by metal and the noise from electric motors and that fluorescent lights can also interfere with RFID communications.

In the past the cost of RFID technology has had an impact on its uptake as tags were considered to be too expensive, especially for item-level tagging. However the cost per tag continues to fall. The absence of global standards is another major problem of RFID as they are still developing through the formation of the EPC global network. To date systems have utilized multiple standards restricting interoperability (Lefebvre, Lefebvre, Bendavid, et. al., 2006). Organizations that implement RFID systems must also review the information technology infrastructure they have in place, as a copious amount of real-time data is captured by these systems. The final challenge of RFID relates to privacy concerns. As RFID is used to track items, privacy activists are concerned about the use of technology on retail items such as clothes which could allow retailers to send and receive information after items have been purchased (Albrecht & McIntyre, 2005). Privacy concerns, like all the other issues identified in this section, require more attention for RFID to become widespread in the commercial and manufacturing industries.

RFID APPLICATIONS

Overview

RFID tags and transponders can be used for a variety of applications (Micron, 1999). Micron Communications has the ability to apply RFID to a plethora of applications including: retail automated fuelling, fleet management, container tracking, access control, laundry automation, beef/cattle tracking and government/ military asset tracking. Its RFID products come in a range of tags, badges and transponders. Texas Instruments is another RFID vendor (TI, 1998) that has applied RFID even to vehicle tracking (Ollivier, 1993, pp. 8/1-8/8) and hazardous materials (Hind, 1994, pp. 215-227). RFID can be used to identify humans, animals, places and things. For an introduction into the use of RFID for humancentric applications see Amelia Masters (2003) undergraduate honors thesis. The principal conclusion of Masters' (2003, p. 97) research is that *"humancentric applications of RFID are incrementally being built on the foundations of non-humancentric commercial and animal applications. In the current state of humancentric development, stand-alone applications exist for control, convenience and care purposes, but with control being the dominant context."* For a discussion on the security and privacy of RFID with relation to biomedical applications see a detailed study by Stuart, Moh and Moh (2008).

Some of the humancentric applications considered in this work include personal identification, location based services (Moen & Jelle, 2007), enforcement, banking, medical and monitoring (Wu, Kuo & Liu, 2005). Perhaps what brought a great deal of attention to RFID early on was its use for identifying pets. A local Australian council pamphlet for the municipality of Kiama, NSW, stated: "[a]fter 1 July 1999 we must permanently identify and register any puppy or new dog. We have three years to transfer older dogs from annual registration to the new lifetime system... Also from 1 July 1999 all cat owners must identify their cat either by collar and tag or by microchip" (Local Government, 1998, p. 3). In most major cities it is now a requirement to implant pets with microchip. In the City of Toronto, there are microchip by-laws for pets like dogs and cats (Anitech, 1999). License fees vary depending on the length of the license (annual versus lifetime). In some cities penalties apply for non-compliance (e.g. Indianapolic, Ind., Albuquerque, N.M., and Dade County, Florida). In terms of "things", retail products have now begun to be tagged (Roussos, 2006), mostly high-value items which warrant the cost of the tag so that they are not subject to theft (Huber & Michael, 2007). RFID proof of concepts based on the electronic product code, are also being considered for application throughout the retail supply chain (Wamba, Lefebvre & Lefebvre, 2006; Bendavid, Wamba & Lefebvre, 2006; Neiderman et al., 2007).

In summary, consider the following RFID product innovations outlined by Schwind (1990, pp. 1-20), which are still representative of the vast opportunities for RFID today:

- *People, livestock, laboratory animals, fish, and many other live species fit the animal category...*
- *Livestock can be coded with a collar and code tag that could be used to record their movements and allot feed or access to it...*
- *Laboratory mice all look alike but an injectable code transponder serializes each to permit sorting... and to accurately record experiments*
- *Place or positions are important to many operations. Guided vehicles can use RFID to locate pick-up and drop-off points*
- *Place or position can be identified as a check, demarcation, action or identification point.*

Of course the applications are not limited to these alone. 'Electronic jails', pet microchipping, studies in animal migration, monitoring postal system efficiency, car immobilizers, electronic article surveillance (EAS), electronic asset tracking (Min et al., 2007), information management (Erkayhan, 2007), gun control, tracking athletes during marathons and triathlons, paging doctors and other hospital staff, visitor guidance, patient retinal and cochlear implants, toll tagging (Kovavisaruch & Suntharasaj, 2007) and lot access (Pala & Inanc, 2007), automatic phone re-direction, lighting and climate quality control, alarms and safety can all be implemented using RFID tags and transponders. The greatest impact RFID transponders have made is in industrial automation.

Case 1: Animal Tracking and Monitoring

Transponders are excellent mechanisms to identify and keep track of animals especially in closed systems (Finkenzeller, 1999, pp. 245-253). Among the key attributes of RFID are permanency, inexpensiveness, ease of application and legibility at a distance (Geers et al., 1997, p. 25). Traditional animal ID techniques *"[f]or mammals are: eartagging, ear notching, tattoos, freeze branding, horn branding and the use of natural marks. For identification of birds also leg banding, patagial tags, flipper bands and underwing tattooing have been used. Snakes, lizards and other reptiles often carry individually distinctive scale patterns, which can be photographed or sketched for permanent record"* (Geers et al., 1997, p. 70). Traditional methods of identifying animals are considered inefficient when compared to transponder implant technology. *"First, tags can be damaged, lost or tampered with which means data integrity is limited. Second, the information from the tag must be manually entered into the information system, leaving the barn door open for errors. Tattooing horse, cow and dog lips provides positive identification but it requires manual inspection and verification"* (Scan Journal, 1990, pp. 4-9).

An example of a transponder that has been developed for the purpose of identifying animals is the Destron electronic ID (Electronic ID, 1997; Destron, 1998). The electronic ID can be injected into an animal and the device remains embedded in the animal for life. Anytime the microchip is scanned by the correct reader, it provides the animal's unique ID code. Other transponder systems include: TRO-VAN, TIRIS, AVID, Biomark and TX1400L (Hughes Identification Devices). Such transponders are being used to positively identify animals in field research, pet theft and loss, zoological parks (Zulich, 1998, p. 1) monitoring endangered species, tracking wild animal numbers (Stonehouse, 1978), breeding programs, quarantine (Scan Journal, 1990, pp. 4-10), livestock management schemes and industrial husbandry systems (Geers et al., 1997, p. xiv). Thus far most commonly implanted animals include the common household pets (dogs, cats and birds), common livestock (cows, sheep and pigs), animals used for experimental research (mice and monkeys), and pests (rabbits) that need to be continually tracked to control numbers (Figure 4).

The use of tags and transponders in livestock farm management has revolutionized the way farmers work (Trevarthen & Michael, 2007). The farm database has become an integral part of successful farm management practice. While it was once difficult for the farmer to monitor his/her livestock because of the sheer number of animals kept, transponders have made tracking livestock easier. It is not uncommon for farmers to use their computers to: *"...follow-up of premiums, milk-record control, tracing back of transit and disease prevention, progeny testing and herdbook administration, electronic feeding stations, automatic gating in group housing facilities, accountability to markets and slaughterhouses, animal health control, public health control, animal welfare surveillance, prevention of fraud, tracing back of stolen stock, facilitating trade, central database facilities"* (Geers et al., 1997, p. 39).

Figure 4. Australian dairy farm showing cow bearing a National Livestock Identification System (NLIS) tag on its ear.

Allflex (Cumbria, United Kingdom), together with Oxley Systems (Grange over Sands, United Kingdom) are just two companies that have been promoting RFID tags as a management tool for agribusiness co-use. The farmer has the ability to centralize all his operations whether it be in the prevention of disease in herds, feed-control or in meeting production goals. The new generation of transponders will be even more powerful with specific sensors to monitor the physiological status of the each animal, "... early warning of diseases, monitoring of oestrus, welfare and all aspects related to integrated quality control" (Geers et al., 1997, p. 39). Regulations have also meant the mandatory identification of animals, especially in Europe, has acted to increase the adoption of RFID tags and transponders.

In the U.S. in 1996, the FDA's Center for Veterinary Medicine (CVM) revised its regulatory policy regarding electronic IDs for animals, stipulating in its definition that electronic identification equated to RFID transponders. In the CVM Update (17/01/96), the importance of removing the RFID transponder in the slaughter process of animals was highlighted and that adequate precautions should be taken for trimmed parts (that may contain the device) not be given to animals as feed (Kryo, 1996). Geers et al. (1997, p. 37) explain the potential problems more precisely with respect to the recovery of the transponders in the slaughter process. *"Transponders injected in the head of the animal do not follow the carcass through the slaughterline when the head is cut off... All transponders should be recovered in the slaughterhouse before the carcasses are released for further processing. Recovery procedures should not damage the carcass... and this can be avoided when transponders have been injected properly."*

The 1992 EU Council Directive 92/102/EC stated: "[a]nimals for intra-Union trade must be identified in accordance with the requirements of the Community rules and be registered in such a way that the original or transit holding, center or organization can be traced" (quoted in Geers 1996, p. 29f). One of the earliest animal tracking major trials in Europe, was known as IDEA (Identification Electronique des Animaux). The trial consists of approximately 500000 cattle from six European countries including France and Germany. In the future, breakthroughs in DNA may allow the tracking of meat even to the kitchen table (Unger, 1994). Look (1998, p. 8) also believes that "the full history of every piece of beef will appear on the package label for consumers to read" in the future. *"Ever since the possibility was raised of a link between the cattle disease BSE and a new variant of a similar disorder in humans (Creutzfeld-Jakob disease), the word "traceability" has become a mantra of the meat industry. A statement last year from the European Parliament put it this way: "The necessary security for consumers requires both the identification and registration of bovine animals and labeling of beef... To achieve this, the [European] Commission has outlined a standard format for the national databases to follow. The format includes an alphanumeric code, the first two letters being the alpha-2 country code (as set out in Decision 93/317/EEC), followed by a numeric code of not more than 12 characters, thus making it possible to identify each animal individually..."* (Look, 1998, pp. 1-2). Refer also to Harrop and Napier (2006) who discuss food and livestock traceability.

Traditional Manual Identification for Animals

Leather or nylon collars with metal tags (upon which contact details can be engraved) are still very popular methods of identification for pets such as dogs and cats. The Ventura County Animal Regulation (Ventura, 2001) still encourages traditional methods of pet identification to RFID implants: "[t]his is a great supplement to identification tags, but it is not a substitute! If someone without an Infopet scanner finds your animal, they will not be able to trace it back to you unless it has current ID tags." The Veterinary Information Network and Pet Care Forum suggest that the tag includes as much information as possible. The downside of this type of tag is that it can be removed by anybody, be uncomfortable for the pet or be damaged. A more innovative idea that has received some attention is the "Lost and Finder Owner Notification System" which makes use of ID tags and a dedicated voicemail box. The Internet has become another medium of communication to post messages about lost pets, however this is fairly inefficient.

For farm animals, the Destron Fearing Corporation has introduced the Fearing Duflex brand of ear tags, for visible identification only. The ear tags are made out of polyurethane and can withstand environmental conditions over long periods of time. Hot-stamped numbers on metal tags and ink jet bar code labels can also be produced. Kryo Kinetics Associates, Incorporated specialize in horse identification and offer a number of different solutions other than microchipping. One example of this is freeze marks using the International Angle System, developed by Dr Keith Farrell in Washington University in the 1960s. Freeze marks are recognized internationally and can be used in a court of law. This technique shows a visible mark rather than the microchipping technique and may be more of a deterrent to thieves. Every animal is marked with symbols that are protected by international copyright and a matching laminated ID card for each horse is given to the owner. "The marking site, always on the neck, is clipped and cleaned and... the mark is applied with a cold iron, the horse feels little more than pressure". Ownership brands are another technique but this presupposes that the brand is unique and has passed the registration process with the appropriate authorities. It can turn out to be an expensive practice though, as registrations have to be entered for different states.

Like brands, tattoos can also be applied by almost anyone. As opposed to freeze marks, tattoos can be altered, they are often hard to read and there is no single registry. Having said that tattoos have shortcomings the American Pet Association (APA) was still supportive of the manual technique in 1998 considering it to be the *"best form of permanent identification... The micro chip implant, although an interesting, high tech idea, is not a pet identification solution... The American Pet Association's answer... is simple, effective and reliable. All pets registered through the APA's VIP program are tagged and tattooed with an ID number that begins with the trademarked letters "APA". It is a simple solution for shelters; if a pet is tattooed with the "APA" letter, they need only to call the APA's 800 number"* (APA, 1998; Mieszkowski, 2000).

Vetinfonet (1998) also agree with APA that "...the most reliable form of identification still remains a collar and ID tag". In Australia, Pawprint Pet ID Tags by Silver Roo have also made their debut working on the same principles as the APA VIP program but instead of a numbered tag, Silver Roo manufacture a choice of 12 types of tags. Animals, especially small insects like bees, can also be bar coded (LaMoreaux, 1995, pp. 48-49). Kryo also highlights blood typing and DNA (deoxyribonucleic acid) testing. Two companies that specialize in DNA-based profiles for animals are Therion Corporation and Zoogen Incorporated. The latter was founded by Dr Joy Halverson, a veterinarian. "DNA pawprints" are taken of the animal's genotype (genetic pattern) and it is digitally analyzed by a computer. The method is so accurate that it can virtually identify any dog in the world with a zero error rate. The company which began in 1989 prides itself on not only being able to identify a dog but offer more information to owners about the parentage and pedigree of the animal, bloodline uniformity etc.

A more recent initiative was launched in the UK with the aim of "barcoding" every species on Earth. Scientists are attempting to establish a giant catalogue of life. The initiative was launched in London at the International Conference for the Barcoding of Life. The aim is to establish a short DNA sequence for every form of life on the planet, some 10 - 30 million species on Earth, beginning with birds and fish (Amos, 2005).

Figure 5. The Wherifone by Wherify Wireless can now be used by organizations to help them locate their employees. The Wherifone fits into the palm of your hand. Courtesy of Wherify Wireless.

Case 2: Human Security and Monitoring

Some employers require their staff to wear RFID tags in a visible location for identification purposes and for access control (Kitsz, 1990, pp. 3-37). A company's security policy may stipulate that staff badges be secured onto clothing or employees must wear tags that are woven into their uniforms. This type of integration of computers into clothing (i.e. unobtrusive wearable computers) is a design philosophy that Steve Mann (1987) has named 'eudemonic computing', after a group of physicists known as the Eudemons. There are a wide variety of wearable tags available today. The rugged smart label developed by Gemplus called the GemWave Stamp and Olivetti's "active badge" are two examples (Pountain, 1993, p. 58; Want et al., 1992, pp. 91-102). The Olivetti tag is able to "localize each staff member as he or she moves through the premises... It is possible to automatically re-route telephone calls to the extension nearest an individual" (Puchner, 1994, p. 26) (Figure 5). *"Recent developments in hardware are allowing us to capture automatically events in our working lives. For example the Olivetti active badge, a small 'wearable' device, allows us to record which room of a building we are in. If our colleagues wear badges too, it is possible to record who we were with, and if badges are attached to equipment it is possible to record what equipment we are close to"* (Brown, 1995, p. 6/1). Martin (1995, pp. 306-309) describes another identification, location and tracking system that he has called WatchIt™ that uses IR/ RF (infrared/ radio-frequency) principles.

Whereas employers want to know who is inside their premises, there are some applications that want to know who has trespassed outside a certain zone. The concept of "electronic jails" for low-risk offenders is starting to be considered more seriously. Sweden and Australia have implemented this concept and there are trials taking place in the U.K., U.S., Netherlands and Canada. Whilst tagging low-risk offenders is not popular in many countries it is far more economical than the conventional jail. Since 1994 in Sweden: *"...certain offenders in six districts have opted out of serving time, choosing instead to be tagged by an electronic anklet and follow a strict timetable set by the probation service... about 700 people have taken part in the Swedish scheme, open to people sentenced to two months or less"* (Goldsmith, 1996, p. 32). Signals are transmitted from the tag of the offender to the host computer several times a minute. All tagged prisoners set off an alarm in a nearby monitoring center if they deviate from their daily routine (Perusco & Michael, 2007).

Numerous applications have been developed to assist individuals who depend on carers for support. This group of persons may consist of newly-born babies, sufferers of mental illness and Alzheimer's disease, persons with disabilities and the elderly. For example, Project Lifesaver, a non-profit organization is dedicated to assisting and responding to challenges that caregivers face related to illnesses and conditions like Alzheimer's disease, autism, and special needs. Project Lifesaver works on the basis that clients are registered and wear a personalized bracelet that emits a unique automatic tracking signal every second, twenty-four hours a day. There are also those like Martin Swerdlow, who as a U.K. member of the government's Foresight Science and Technology Group stated that there would come a time when certain groups in the population would have tags implanted at birth (Woodford, 1993). He believed the idea of a national identity system based on implants was not impossible and highlighted that babies were already electronically tagged at present and nobody was objecting. It is worthwhile then to spend some time looking at a tagging system that prevents babies from being switched at birth or being kidnapped. The South Tyneside Healthcare Trust Trial in the U.K. is an excellent case. Early in 1995, Eagle Tracer installed an electronic tagging system at the hospital using their TIRIS electronic tags and readers from Texas Instruments. Detection aerials were hidden at exit points so that in the event a baby was taken away without authorization, its identity would be checked and the alarm would be raised immediately. The alarm could potentially lock doors, alert the maternity ward staff and security guards. Automatic-ID News (1997) reported: *"The TIRIS tags, passive and batteryless transponders, carry a unique security code and are securely attached to even the smallest newborn babies without causing harm or discomfort. The carrier material has been developed in such a way as to prevent the removal by anyone other than a specialist..."*

The trial was so successful that the hospital was considering expanding the system to include the children's ward. The clinical director of obstetrics and gynecology told Automatic-ID News that, "[t]he system ha[d] been very enthusiastically received by the midwives as well as the mums." Mr Trevor Dean, the 1993 chairman of the Bar Code Committee of Standards Australia said "...it was technologically possible for a baby's bottom to be tattooed with a bar code... One of the most obvious advantages would be to lessen the likelihood of two babies being swapped accidentally at birth." The response from the Privacy Commission was to liken this proposition to when the Nazis tattooed people. They noted that going down that kind of path would be dangerous. Weinstein is quoted here as saying: "There will be a short window where the bad guys aren't aware of the technology, but then it will be routine for them to dig around in their victims to see if they're wearing GPS receivers... The overriding issue is do you create a bigger danger to the person than existed in the first place?" (Scheeres, 2002). Recently Olivetti has also marketed its 'tot tracker' product which works by placing a tag on your child or in his/her backpack to allow for global tracking via a global positioning system (GPS) (High Tech, 1998, p. 1).

The idea of placing transponders in the human body or implanting microchips in selected body parts like the hand or head are not new. The study of medicine is always pushing technological developments to new frontiers. As it has been well described, *"[c]ommercially available implantable telemetry devices can have sensors on board for measuring the following physiological variables: temperature, body activity, heart rate, electrocardiogram, electromyogram, electroencephalogram, blood pressure and different biopotentials. The dimensions of these devices are a few cubic centimeters, and have to be implanted under general anesthesia. In most cases the sensors are wire-connected to the implantable module. The transmission range is dependent on the frequency band selected, and on the available power source. It can vary from a few centimeters to a few kilometers. The operational life time is usually a few months, depending on the battery specifications"* (Geers et al., 1997, p. 22). Implantable devices such as pacemakers have been used in humans with heart conditions for years (Banbury, 1997; Ryan et al., 1989, pp. 7.6.1-7.6.4). Once thought radical the device is now commonplace. For a discussion on somatic surveillance see Monahan and Wall (2007).

Scientists have been conducting experiments involving microchips and humans for decades. It is through such research that scientists hope to discover ways to combat blindness, deafness and other disabilities. "A chip implanted on the optic nerve, for example, could correct defective images or simply transmit entire images to the nerve. The notion of putting computers inside the body may be more realistic than it sounds" (Harrison, 1994, p. 13). Examples of these types of studies include the nerve chip research at Stanford University by doctors Kovacs, Hentz and Rosen and the silicon retinal implant research by Edell, Rizzo, Raffel and Wyatt which will be discussed in the following chapter. It is now becoming increasingly public knowledge that there is a concerted effort to fuse the flesh with technology (Davies, 1994). Initially a medical solution, transponder implants are now being considered for emergency services and potentially even a way to reduce fraud. Hewkin was one of the first people to suggest officially, in a respected academic IEE journal, that 'subminiature read-only tags' would be injected under human skin using a syringe to reduce problems such as fraud (1989, p. 205). This was probably in response to Dr Daniel Man's, October 1987 patent regarding a homing device implant designed for humans called 'Man's Implanted'. Mechanic (1996, p. 2) reported: *"...[t]he human device runs on long-lasting lithium batteries and periodically transmits a signal that would allow authorities to pinpoint a person's exact location... the batteries... could be replenished twice a year..."*

Man's invention has not been marketed because the U.S. Food and Drug Administration (FDA) have yet to approve the device. For this he will require a substantial amount of cash for miniaturization and regulatory approval (Wells, 1998). But the inventor has received several inquiries from U.S. government agencies and interested companies. The device is perceived by some as being a future 911 advancement, locating kidnapped children or older persons who may become disoriented, useful for soldier tracking and even criminal tracking. The Daily Mail (1997, p. 13) reported that "[s]cientists are testing a revolutionary watch which can be implanted beneath the skin of the wrist... Researchers believe the same technology could be used to create a range of electronic tags for criminals. It could also be adapted to record... blood pressure." For implantable health applications refer to Eng (2002), Streitfeld (2002) and Murray (2002). Man believes this human tracking device would be voluntary only and that nobody would be forced to use it if they did not want to for reasons of culture, philosophy or religion. In fact, "the surgeon is taken aback by all this talk of Armageddon and by the conspiracy buffs who say the invention could ultimately be used by the government to monitor its citizens" (Mechanic, 1996, p. 5). Man is quoted as saying that he's only looking at the positive aspects of the implanted device. See also Nortel World (1998, p. 28) in contrast to Kindgom (2003).

In 1994 Bertrand Cambou, director of technology for Motorola's Semiconductor Products in Phoenix, predicted that by 2004 all persons would have a microchip implanted in their body to monitor and perhaps even control blood pressure, their heart rate, and cholesterol levels. Harrison reported (1994, p. 13) that: *"Cambou has been a part of the miniaturization of microprocessors and the development of wireless communication technologies. Both would have central roles in putting computers inside the human body."* When questioned by Harrison about the effects the technology would have in the body Cambou responded (1994, p. 13): *"We are not aware of any current obstacles to the encapsulation and implanting of electronic devices within the body, and the transmission characteristics [of radio frequencies] through the body are well known."*

In 1998, Professor Kevin Warwick (2002) of the University of Reading became the first official person to embed a silicon transponder (23 by 3 millimeter) into his body (arm). The manufacturer of the chip remained anonymous. The surgical procedure only took ten minutes while he was under a local anesthetic (Sanchez-Klein, 1998). The ten-day trial was confined to the boundaries of his university department. Sensors around the department were triggered every time Professor Warwick was in range of a reader, where Warwick is shown holding the transponder in his fingertips and a map of the ground floor of the Cybernetics department with his location information. The chip was limited to acting as a location device but its potential is left to a visionary's discretion. Professor Warwick reported to *Newsbytes* (Dennis, 1998): *"In five years' time, we will be able to do chips with all sorts of information on them. They could be used for money transfers, medical records, passports, driving licenses, and loyalty cards. And if they are implanted they are impossible to steal. The potential is enormous."* Angell and Kietzmann (2006) write of the very real possibility that RFID will replace cash altogether.

In a CNN interview with Sanchez-Klein (1998, p. 2) Warwick reflected: *"I'm feeling more at one with the computer. It's as though part of me is missing when I'm not in the building... In my house, I have to open doors and turn on lights. I don't feel lonely, but I don't feel complete."* Warwick believes the ultimate goal of the transponder technology is to connect humans more closely with computers and perhaps have a direct connection from the brain to the computer. He told CNN that it was an excellent device to track employees while they were at work, prevent mass murders my keeping track of gun owners and tagging pedophiles to keep them away from schools or child centers. However, it should be noted that Warwick is aware of the big brother issues, negative and sinister side of the technology. In the fight against the SARS outbreak, countries like Singapore were proposing the electronic tagging of citizens using RFID (Michael and Masters, 2006a; 2006b). The tagging is primarily to help stop the spread of the virus and to aid health authorities to locate the root cause of the problem, thus cordoning off infected areas. Logistically it is proving too difficult to track frequent travelers and to gather data manually. One individual who has introduced another dimension to the implant research is RFID implantee, Mr Amal Graafstra (2007). For the opportunities and challenges related to identifying people who bear an implant see Rotter, Daskala and Compano (2008), Foster and Jaegar (2007, 2008), and Perakslis and Wolk (2006).

The Importance of the ID Number

Common technologies that are used for human monitoring as opposed primarily to human security include bar code, magnetic-stripe, smart cards and biometrics. For example, in *The Roanoke Times*, Hammack reported that 'Bracelets and bar codes track jail inmates.' Card technologies have been traditionally linked to an ID number (normally 8-15 alphanumeric characters in length); the type of card technology employed is a secondary matter. In the example of government schemes such as social security, taxation and health care a fair amount of off-line monitoring occurs to ensure that citizens are actually being taxed accordingly and receiving the right amount of social benefits. In 1999, Japan began to debate a national ID number scheme, not a national ID card type. Williams (1999) reported: "[a] ten-digit number would enable officials to identify a person's name, address, sex and date of birth and be used by local and national government agencies in place of differing identification methods used now."

An interesting pattern emerges when one studies the person number (PN) systems of countries in the world (Lunde et al. ed., 1980, pp. 39-47). They were either developed during WWII or after 1970. The former were created for the purpose of census registers; the latter mainly for the computerization of citizen records. Thus one will find that only the ID numbers instituted after 1970 are truly unique (based on database principles such as a primary key), the other numbers are composed of date of birth, sex and place of birth, with sometimes zero or only one or two check digits. Enter the urgent need for a more sophisticated way of monitoring human activity and governments around the world have done one of two things; either they have issued new ID numbers to all citizens and implemented smart card schemes, or they have kept existing ID numbers and implemented an integrated system- smart cards for transactions and biometrics to verify the cardholder's identification. Still there are many government schemes around the world that have more than one citizen with exactly the same ID number.

The prospect of human monitoring entering a new level altogether has been made possible by numerous developments in telecommunications. Mobile telephone users can be pinpointed to the coverage area of the mobile base station (BS) that was used to connect their telephone call. Network triangulation can pinpoint an individual's location to 50-150 meters in accuracy. And if a handset is GPS-enabled, then it can be located up to 15 meters of the recipient. Piece this information together over a period of time and someone could know an awful lot about your movements (K. Michael et al, 2006). Whether somebody cares to do this or not is perhaps not the issue, the information is still available. In the not-to-distant future however GPS devices will become so small and affordable that monitoring and tracking of humans in real-time would be feasible (Werb, 1999, p. 52).

GPS was developed by the U.S. military and has both defense and commercial application. If one is to contemplate the unlimited commercial union between GPS and auto-ID systems, a myriad of location-based applications could be born (Recagno et al., 2001). For example, GPS systems for cars that would enable manual street directories to become obsolete and track car thieves as they make their escape, in addition to safety and security services including emergency response, crash detection, roadside assistance (Figure 6) and diagnostics monitoring (Brennan, 1995; CarCom, 2000; Wheatley, 1993). For two Australian studies where people or vehicles were overtly tracked see Iqbal and Lim (2007) and Michael, McNamee, Michael and Tootell (2006) (Figure 7). And also there is the ability to track children so that

Figure 6. An NRMA roadside assistance vehicle fitted with a Global Positioning Systems (GPS) receiver in Parramatta, New South Wales. Photo taken in 2007

Figure 7. The Magellan Sports Global Positioning Systems (GPS) navigator, allowing for the storage of way-points, and other data. In route mode, the longitude and latitude coordinate is stored every 3 seconds. The device has the ability to store speed, distance, time, and altitude data. Photo taken in 2005.

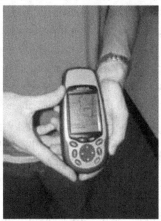

Figure 8. The Wherifone technology that can be used by children to call home, to call an operator, or call for emergency assistance. The Wherifone is small enough to put in a child's pocket, or even to be worn on a belt buckle. The phone is rugged and cannot be easily damaged. It is increasingly becoming common today for parents to provide their children with a mobile phone or other PDA-like devices for peace of mind. Photo courtesy of Wherify Wireless.

in the case they are kidnapped police know their exact whereabouts; track mentally ill patients who may become lost; monitor criminals who are released and have a long record of crime (Pottorf, 1998) (Figure 8). The GIS (geographic information system) makes the visual real-time tracking of people and objects possible. One need only spend some time looking at Google Maps. Distributed systems could display the movement at various levels of details on a map. Large ships and large trucking companies already use this type of technology (Sky Eye Company, 2003).

RFID Today

While RF principles were well-established partway through the 20th century, the modern application of RF for identification and tracking purposes is a recent phenomenon. RFID has promised much and delivered only a fraction. This is not to say that it does not have a bright future ahead of it- the technology itself can be applied in a number of very advanced ways, with the potential to supersede previous auto-ID technologies in stealth and capability. However, the obstacles that plague it will not go away overnight. Of the academic literature that has been written about RFID the most recent has been on how to reconcile privacy and security issues, especially in the retail sector where RFID could act to revolutionize how people shop and how companies purchase and sell their products. Alfonsi (2004), Lee and Kim (2006), Rieback, Crispo and Tanenbaum (2006) and Perusco, Michael and Michael (2006) have all written on the RFID privacy debate pertaining especially to consumers. Perakslis & Wolk (2006) have gone one step further to concentrate on the use of RFID transponders for national security reasons such as national ID. These papers all point to the current sticking point of RFID- the technology may have a great number of benefits and a convincing business value proposition but it is clouded with too many privacy issues corresponding to end-user resistance in adoption.

By far the biggest proposed application of RFID is in the retail sector in the implementation of the electronic product code, across entire supply chains. *"Sometime between now and 2010, the internet is poised to reach beyond virtual space and take root in the physical world. According to many futurist thinkers, almost every object you can see around you carries the possibility of being connected to the internet. This means that your domestic appliances, your clothes, your books and your car may one day be assigned a unique IP address, just as both computers and web pages are assigned them today, to enable them to talk to each other"* (Dodson, 2009). While these supply chains may be beneficial for large players like the United States Department of Defense (DoD), they may be less useful for local supermarket chains, despite the fact that companies like WalMart and Proctor and Gamble have begun extensive RFID trials (Coltman, Gadh, Michael, 2008). The sticking point seems to be one surrounding control- who has it, who can apply it, and what are the consequences. More to the point, RFID tags and transponders have yet to reach economies of scale, and cost is a major deterrent at the present time. Who will pay for the new infrastructure across the entire supply chain, and who will receive the greatest benefit from its introduction. There may well be a cost-benefit stakeholder mismatch which has not encouraged individual players to become involved for fear of bearing the majority of the start-up costs with little return on investment.

CONCLUSION

RFID has been responsible for a great leap in mindset. While previous auto-ID technologies have been wearable or contactless in nature, RFID is the only auto-ID technology to also be "implantable". In addition, the implants are not just for animals but for people as well. At the heart of any system are people. People have direct links to the world around them- whether they be living or nonliving things. People have relationships- to other people, to animals, to items. The Auto-ID Center's conceptualization of an "Internet of Things", are just these meshed and complex links and relationships taking full life in IP address space – version 6 (IPv6). RFID can personalize all these links in permutations of personal area networks (PANs) and local area networks (LANs), dependent on the context. The question is whether or not people wish to take this seemingly next great leap forward, and what this leap will mean in "real" terms. While purchasing goods which have an RFID tag on them can be considered relatively harmless (beyond the potential for data to be mined by third parties etc), what of the implanting of people with RFID transponders for health applications? There is a stark difference here- technology with which a transaction is facilitated versus technology with which we intimately interact with which is an extension of the human body. For now, standards bodies like GS1 and EAN are investing a lot of resources into seeing the RFID-retail dream become a reality but at the same time the number of niche RFID applications being introduced into the market are rising exponentially- each more radical than the one before.

REFERENCES

ADS. (2002). Applied Digital Solutions. from http://www.adsx.com/

AIM. (2006). AIM Global: Annual Report. *AIM Global* Retrieved 4 February 2009, from http://www.aimglobal.org/aboutaim/content/pdfs/2006annual_report.pdf

AIM. (2009). AIM Organization. Retrieved 4 February 2009, from http://www.aimglobal.org/aboutaim/CurrentMembers.asp

AIM Global. (1999). Radio frequency identification RFID: A basic primer. *AIM International WP-98/002R*, from http://www.aimglobal.org/techinfo/rfid/aimrfidbasics.html

AIM Global. (2000). *Bar code badge guidelines*: AIM Global Inc.

Albano, S., & Engels, D. (2002). Auto-ID Center field trial: phase I summary. *Auto-ID Labs at MIT* Retrieved 10 October 2008, from http://autoid.mit.edu/whitepapers/MIT-AUTOID-TR006.PDF

Albrecht, K. (2003). Consumers Against Supermarket Privacy Invasion and Numbering. *CASPIAN*, from http://www.nocards.org/AutoID/overview.shtml

Albrecht, K. (2009). Consumers Against Supermarket Privacy Invasion and Numbering. *CASPIAN*, from http://www.nocards.org/AutoID/overview.shtml

Albrecht, K., & McIntyre, L. (2005). *SPYCHIPS: How Major Corporations and Government Plan to Track your Every Move with RFID*. United States: Nelson

Albrecht, K., & McIntyre, L. (2006). *The Spychips Threat: Why Christians Should Resist RFID and Electronic Surveillance*. United States: Nelson

Alfonsi, B. J. (2004). Privacy debate centers on radio frequency identification. *IEEE Security & Privacy Magazine, 2*(2), 12.

Ames, R. (Ed.). (1990). *Perspectives on Radio Frequency Identification: what is it, where is it going, should I be involved?* New York: Van Nostrand Reinhold.

Amos, J. (2005). *Science intends to tag all life,* BBC News, from http://news.bbc.co.uk/1/hi/sci/tech/4251309.stm

Angell, I., & Kietzmann, J. (2006). RFID and the end of cash? *Communications of the ACM, 49*(12).

Anitech. (1999). PETNET: Canada's national pet registry. *Anitech Enterprises Inc.*

APA. (1998, 5 April). APA offers Final Solution to the Lost and Stolen Pet Problem. *American Pet Association*, from http://www.apapets.com/pro1.htm

Automatic ID. (1998). Everything you ever wanted to know about RF/ID... Examining the technology's benefits, future. *Automatic I.D. News*, from http://www.autoidnews.com/technologies/concepts/need.htm

Banbury, C. M. (1997). *Surviving Technological Innovation in the Pacemaker Industry 1959-1990.* New York: Garland Publishing.

Bendavid, Y., Wamba, S. F., & Lefebvre, L. A. (2006). *Proof of concept of an RFID-enabled supply chain in a B2B e-commerce environment.* Paper presented at the Proceedings of the 8th international conference on Electronic commerce: The new e-commerce: innovations for conquering current barriers, obstacles and limitations to conducting successful business on the internet.

Biomark. (1999). About Biomark, Inc. *Biomark: Specialists in Electronic Identification*, from http://www.biomark.com/aboutus.html

Biomark. (2009). Biomark. Retrieved 4 February 2009, from http://www.biomark.com/

Brennan, W. (1995, 20 August). Smart card way to stop car theft. *The Sunday Telegraph.*

Brewin, B. (1999, 19 July). Army awards 2nd piece for logistics redo. *Federal Computer Week, 13*, 1-2.

Brock, D. L. (2001). *The Electronic Product Code (EPC): A naming scheme for physical objects.* Massachusetts: Auto-ID Center.

Byfield, I. (2002). What do you mean, auto ID? *www.logisticsit.com*, from http://www.logisticsit.com/artman/publish/printer_10.shtml

CarCom. (2000). Retrieved from http://www.carcom.com.au

China Post. (1998, 6 November). Global mobile phone network. *The China Post*, p. 12.

Cochrane, N. (2001). More on Digital Angel, chip implants, and human tracking. *Declan McCullagh's Politech*, from http://www.politechbot.com/p-02154.html

Coltman, T., Gadh, R., & Michael, K. (2008). Special Issue on RFID and Supply Chains. *Journal of Theoretical and Applied Electronic Commerce Research, 3*(1).

Curtis, S. P. (1992). Transponder technologies, applications and benefits. *IEE Colloquium on the Use of Electronic Transponders in Automation*, 2/1-2/8.

Daily Mail. (1997, 29 March). The body clock you can't forget will remain with you for life. *Daily Mail*, p. p. 13.

Davies, S. G. (1994). Touching Big Brother: how biometric technology will fuse flesh and machine. *Information Technology & People, 7*(4), 1-9.

Denby, M. (2001). University establishes chair in RF/ID systems. *Dialinfolinkelectronics*, from http://www.dialelectronics.com.au/articles/00/0c002100.asp

Dennis, S. (1998). UK professor implants chip, turns himself into Cyborg. *Newsbytes*, from http://www.newsbytes.com/pubNews/110782.html

Destron. (1998). Electronic ID- applications. *Destron Fearing*, from http://www.destronfearing.com/elect/compan.html

Digital Angel. (2009). Digital Angel. Retrieved 1 February 2009, from http://www.digitalangel.com/

Digital, T. (1997). Mommy, can you see me? *Time Magazine*, 5.

Dodson, S. (2009). Lives tangled in growing net. Retrieved 15 February 2009, from http://www.smh.com.au/news/digital-life/articles/lives-tangled-in-growing-net/2009/01/24/1232471647772.html?page=fullpage#contentSwap1

Eckfeldt, B. (2005). What does RFID do for the consumer? *Communications of the ACM, 48*(9).

Electronic ID Inc. (1997). Destron-fearing electronic ID: Background. *Electronic ID Incorporated*, from http://www.dfw.net/~tqg/electronicid/eidback.html

Eng, P. (2002, 25 February). I, Chip? Technology to meld chips into humans draws closer. *ABCNEWS.com*, from http://abcnews.go.com/sections/scitech/DailyNews/chipimplant020225.html

Engels, D. W. (2001). The networked physical world: an automated identification architecture. *The Second IEEE Workshop on Internet Applications*, 76-77.

Erkayhan, S. (2007, 5-6 September). *The Use of RFID enables a holistic Information Management within Product lifecycle Management (PLM)*. Paper presented at the RFID Eurasia, Istanbul, Turkey.

Finkenzeller, K. (2003). *RFID Handbook: Fundamentals and Applications in Contactless Smart Cards and Identification*. West Sussex: John Wiley and Sons.

Finkenzeller, K., & Waddington, R. (2001). *RFID Handbook: radio-frequency identification fundamentals and applications*. New York: John Wiley & Son.

Fordyce, S. W., & Wu, W. W. (1994). The myth and reality of mobile satellite communications. *IEEE Singapore ICCS*, 393-399.

Foster, K. R., & Jaegar, J. (2007). RFID Inside. *IEEE Spectrum, 44*(3), 20-25.

Foster, K.R. and Jaeger, J. (2008). Ethical Implications of Implantable Radiofrequency Identification (RFID) Tags in Humans, *The American Journal of Bioethics*, 8(8), pp. 44-48.

Franciosi, F. (2001). EAN.UCC white paper on radio frequency identification. Retrieved 21 November 2001, from http://www.ean-int.org

Garfinkel, S., & Rosenberg, B. (Eds.). (2005). *RFID: Applications, Security, and Privacy*. Upper Saddle River: Addison-Wesley.

Geers, R., Puers, B., Goedseels, V., & Wouters, P. (1997). *Electronic Identification, Monitoring and Tracking of Animals*. Oxon: CAB International.

Gerdeman, J. D. (1995). *Radio Frequency Identification Application 2000: a guide to understanding and using radio frequency identification*. North Carolina: Research Triangle Consultants.

Goedseels, V. (1990). A concept for animal monitoring and identification. *Agrarinformatik, 20*, 63-66.

Gold, A. E. (1990). An overview of automatic identification technologies. In R. Ames (Ed.), *Perspectives on Radio Frequency Identification: what is it, where is it going, should I be involved?* (pp. 1-2- 1-8). New York: Van Nostrand Reinhold.

Goldsmith, B. (1996, 8 October). Homing in on electronic jail. *The Australian,* p. p. 32.

Gossett, S. (2002). Lawsuits plague chip-implant company: Digital Angel, VeriChip manufacturer mired in controversy. *WorldNetDaily*, from http://www.worldnetdaily.com/news/printer-friendly. asp?ARTICLE_ID=27917

Graafstra, A. (2007). Hans On. *IEEE Spectrum, 44*(3), 14-19.

GS1. (3 April 2008). Alignment of EPCglobal Standards with the GS1 System. *GSMP: Process Change Notification* Retrieved 4 February 2009, from http://www.gs1.org/docs/gsmp/PCN/PCN_08-002_EP-Cglobal_%20and_GS1%20_System_02-Apr_08.pdf

GS1. (2009). What is EPCglobal? Retrieved 3 Feburary 2009, from http://www.gsluk.org/RFID/EPC-global.asp

Halliday, S. (1999). Shortcuts to the standardisation process. *ADC News & Solutions Online*, from http:// www.manufacturing.net/magazine/adc/standards/standard.htm

Hamilton, D., Michael, K., & Wamba, S. F. (2009). Overcoming Visibility Issues in a Small-to-Medium Retailer Using Automatic Identification and Data Capture Technology: An Evolutionary Approach. *International Journal of Electronic Business, in press*.

Hammack, L. n. d. Bracelets and bar codes track jail inmates. *The Roanoke Times*.

Harrison, P. L. (1994). The body binary. *Popular Science*, 1-2.

Harrop, P., & Napier, E. (2006). *Food and Livestock Traceability*. London: IDTechEx.

Hendry, M. (1997). *Smart Card Security and Applications (Artech House Telecommunications Library)*. Boston: Artech House.

Hewkin, P. F. (1989). Future automatic identification technologies. *Colloquium on the Use of Electronic Transponders in the Automation*, 6/1-6/10.

Hind, D. J. (1994). *Radio frequency identification and tracking systems in hazardous areas*. Paper presented at the Fifth International Conference on Electrical Safety in Hazardous Environments.

Hodges, S., & McFarlane, D. (2004). RFID: The Concept and the Impact. In B. Stevens (Ed.), *The Security Economy* (pp. 55-75): OECD.

Huber, N., & Michael, K. (2007, 9-11 July). *Minimizing Product Shrinkage across the Supply Chain using Radio Frequency Identification: a Case Study on a Major Australian Retailer*. Paper presented at the The Sixth International Conference on Mobile Business, Toronto, Canada.

Iqbal, M. U., & Lim, S. (2007). Privacy implications of automated GPS tracking and monitoring. In K. Michael & M. G. Michael (Eds.), *From Dataveillance to Überveillance and the Realpolitik of the Transparent Society* (pp. 225-240). Wollongong: University of Wollongong.

ISTSEC. (2003). Vivago. from http://www.istsec.fi/eng/Etuotteet.htm

Jones, P., Clarke-Hill, C., Shears, P., Comfort, D., & Hillier, D. (2004). Radio frequency identification in the UK: opportunities and challenges. *International Journal of Retail & Distribution Management, 32*(3), 164-171.

Kingdom. (2003). KingdomBaptist. from http://www.kingdombaptist.org/article658.cfm

Kitsz, D. B. (1990). Promises and problems of RF identification. In R. Ames (Ed.), *Perspectives on Radio Frequency Identification: What is it, Where is it going, Should I be Involved?* (pp. 1-19- 11-27.). New York: Van Nostrand Reinhold.

Kovavisaruch, L., & Suntharasaj, P. (2007, 5-9 August). *Converging Technology in Society: Opportunity for Radio Frequency Identification (RFID) in Thailand's Transportation System.* Paper presented at the Portland International Center for Management of Engineering and Technology.

Kryo. (1996). Regulation of animal electronic identification products. *Kryo Kinetics Associates*, from http://www.horseweb.com/client/kka/cvm.htm

Lade, D. C. (17 September 2007). Privacy concerns surround microchip implants with medical info. *South Florida South-Sentinel.* Retrieved 4 Feburary 2009, from http://www.verichipcorp.com/news/1190041745

LaMoreaux, R. D. (1998). *Barcodes and Other Automatic Identification Systems.* New York: Pira International.

Lange, L. (1997). Biometry: human-tracking system goes global. *EETimes*, from http://www.techweb.com/se/directlink.cgi?EET19970203S0090

Lange, L. (1997). Engineering, medical worlds coalesce on chip-implant experiments -- A heady proposition-- First two parts. (939), 1-5.

Lee, H., & Kim, J. (2006, 20-22 April). *Privacy threats and issues in mobile RFID.* Paper presented at the The First International Conference on Availability, Reliability and Security.

Lefebvre, L., Lefebvre, E., Bendavid, Y., Wamba, S. F., & Boeck, H. (2006). *RFID as an enabler of B-to-B e-Commerce and its impact on business processes: a pilot study of a supply chain in the retail industry.* Paper presented at the 39th Annual Hawaii International Conference on System Sciences, Hawaii.

Lifesaver (2009). *How Does It Work?*, Project Lifesaver Ontario. from http://www.projectlifesaver.ca/

Local Government. (1998). Companion Animals Act. Australia: Department of Local Government.

Look, G. (1998). Auto ID makes tracks in livestock traceability. *ID Systems - The European source for auto ID*, from http://www.idsyseuro.com/cow0498.htm

Lunde, A. S., Lundeborg, S., Lettenstrom, G. S., Thygesen, L., & Huebner, J. (1980). *The Person-Number Systems of Sweden, Norway, Denmark, and Israel*. Maryland: DHSS.

Lynch, A. (1999, 3 August). Smart-card system faces global scrutiny. *The Australian*, p. 3.

Mann, S. (1997). Eudaemonic computing ('underwearables'). *IEEE First International Symposium on Wearable Computers*, 177-178.

Marsh, M. (1998a). Recently granted patents in the USA - September-November. *Transponder News*, from http://rapidttp.co.za/transponder/cpat98no.html

Marsh, M. (1998b). Standards relating to transponders. *Transponder News*, from http://rapidttp.co.za/transponder/standard.html

Martin, B. W. (1995). *WatchIt™- A fully supervised identification, location and tracking system*. Paper presented at the Institute of Electrical and Electronics Engineers 29th Annual 1995 International Carnahan Conference on Security Technology.

Masters, A. (2003). *Humancentric applications of RFID: the current state of development*. University of Wollongong, Wollongong.

Masters, A., & Michael, K. (2007). Lend Me Your Arms: the Use and Implications of Humancentric RFID. *Electronic Commerce Research and Applications, 6*(1), 29-39.

Mechanic, M. (1996). Beastly implants. *MetroActive*, from http://www.metroactive.com/papers/metro/12.12.96/implants-9650.html

Michael, K. (2003). *The Auto-ID Trajectory*. University of Wollongong, Wollongong.

Michael, K., & Masters, A. (2006a). The Advancement of Positioning Technologies in Defense Intelligence. In H. Abbass & D. Essam (Eds.), *Applications of Information Systems to Homeland Security and Defense* (pp. 196-220). Hershey, USA: Idea Group Publishing.

Michael, K., & Masters, A. (2006b). Realised Applications of Positioning Technologies in Defense Intelligence. In H. Abbass & D. Essam (Eds.), *Applications of Information Systems to Homeland Security and Defense* (pp. 167-195). Hershey, USA: Idea Group Publishing Press.

Michael, K., & McCathie, L. (2005). The pros and cons of RFID in supply chain management. In E. Lawrence (Ed.), *International Conference on Mobile Business* (pp. 623-629). Sydney: IEEE.

Michael, K., McNamee, A., Michael, M. G., & Tootell, H. I. (2006). *Location-based Intelligence- Modeling Behavior in Humans using GPS*. Paper presented at the International Symposium on Technology and Society, Piscataway, NJ, USA.

Michael, K., & Michael, M. G. (2005). Microchipping People: The Rise of the Electrophorus. *Quadrant, 414*(3), 22-33.

Michael, M. G., & Michael, K. (2009). Microchipping People and the Assault on Privacy. *Quadrant, in press*.

Micron Communications. (1999). RFID overview. from http://www.microncommunications.com/rfid/overview.htm

Mieszkowski, K. (2000). Put that silicon where the sun don't shine. *Salon*, from http://www.salon.com/tech/feature/2000/09/07/chips/

Min, Z., Wenfeng, L., Zhongyun, W., Bin, L., & Xia, R. (2007, 18-21). *A RFID-based Material Tracking Information System.* Paper presented at the IEEE International Conference on Automation and Logistics.

Moen, H. L., & Jelle, T. (2007, 17-19 October). *The Potential for Location-Based Services with Wi-Fi RFID Tags in Citywide Wireless Networks.* Paper presented at the 4th International Symposium on Wireless Communication Systems.

Monahan, T., & Wall, T. (2007). Somatic Surveillance: Corporeal Control through Information Networks. *Surveillance and Society Journal, 4*(3), 154-173.

Morrissey, S. (18 October 2008). Are Microchips Tags Safe? *Time* Retrieved 18 October 2008, from http://www.time.com/time/health/article/0,8599,1672865,00.html?xid=feed-cnn-topics

Murray, C. J. (2002). Prodigy ready to receive chip implant. *The Work Circuit*, from http://www.theworkcircuit.com/story/OEG20020220S0060

Nemeth, P., Toth, L., & Hartvanyi, T. (2006). *Adopting RFID in supply chains.* Paper presented at the IEEE International Conference on Mechatronics.

Niederman, F., Mathieu, R. G., Morley, R., & Kwon, I.-W. (2007). Examining RFID applications in supply chain management. *Communications of the ACM, 50*(7).

Nortel World. (1998). Silicon implant, *Nortel World* (Vol. 4, pp. 28).

Ohkubo, M., Suzuki, K., & Kinoshita, S. (2005). RFID privacy issues and technical challenges. *Communications of the ACM, 48*(9).

Ollivier, M. M. (1993). *TIRIS: a vehicle tracking system using passive radio transponders.* Paper presented at the IEEE Colloquium on Vehicle Location and Fleet Management Systems.

OOMO. (2002). A 'smart' home, to avoid the nursing home. from http://senrs.com/future_homes.htm

Pala, Z., & Inanc, N. (2007). *Smart Parking Applications Using RFID Technology.* Paper presented at the RFID Eurasia, Istanbul, Turkey.

Paret, D. (2005). *Technical state of art of "Radio Frequency Identification -- RFID" and implications regarding standardization, regulations, human exposure, privacy.* Paper presented at the Proceedings of the 2005 joint conference on Smart objects and ambient intelligence: innovative context-aware services: usages and technologies.

Park, D., & Wieser, J. (2001). Summary of field studies evaluating the efficacy of Bio-pond®, a porous polymer sheath, on radio frequency identification (RFID) transponders to prevent migration from a known implant site. *Life-Chip- RFID Report*, from http://www.animal-id.com.au/report.html

PBS. (2001). Mad cow disease: an online NewsHour special report. *Online NewsHour*, from http://www.pbs.org/newshour/bb/health/mad_cow.html

Perakslis, C., & Wolk, R. (2006). Social Acceptance of RFID as a Biometric Security Method. *IEEE Technology and Society Magazine, 25*(3), 32-42.

Perusco, L., & Michael, K. (2007). Control, Trust, Privacy, and Security: Evaluating Location-Based Services. *IEEE Technology and Society, 26*(1), 4-16.

Perusco, L., Michael, K., & Michael, M. G. (2006). *Location-based Services and the Privacy-Security Dichotomy.* Paper presented at the The Third International Conference on Mobile Computing and Ubiquitous Networking (ICMU 2006), London, UK.

Picker, D. (1999). Symbol technologies establishes affiliation with leading chinese university, to advance technology education. *Symbol: News* Retrieved 19 December 2002, from http://www.symbol.com/news/pressreleases/press_releases_wirelesslans_45.html

Pottorf, C. (1998). Location-based services: applications beyond E-911. *IDC*(September), 1-12.

Pountain, D. (1993, December). The active badge system. *BYTE,* 56-58, 62, 64.

Puchner, P. (1994, 8 July). Badges can track staffing needs. *Pacific Computer Weekly.*

Rahmoeller, G. A. (1988). *Industry concerns with the regulatory process.* Paper presented at the Special Symposium on Maturing Technologies and Emerging Horizons.

Raza, N. (1999). Applications of RFID Technology. *IEE Colloquium on RFID Technology,* 1/1-1/5.

Recagno, V. (2001). MOCONT: a new system for automatic identification and location of containers. *IEEE-VTC,* 2609-2613.

Renegar, B. D., & Michael, K. (2009). The privacy-value-control harmonization for RFID adoption in retail. *IBM Systems Journal, 48*(1).

RFID. (30 June 2003). Japan Opens Up UHF for RFID Use. *RFID Journal* Retrieved 4 Feburary 2009, from http://www.rfidjournal.com/article/view/477/1/1

Rieback, M. R., Crispo, B., & Tanenbaum, A. S. (2006, 13-17 March). *Is your cat infected with a computer virus?* Paper presented at the Fourth Annual IEEE International Conference on Pervasive Computing and Communications.

Roberti, M. (2004). Navigating the RFID Patent Landscape. *RFID Journal* Retrieved 4 February 2009, from http://www.rfidjournal.com/article/view/1187/1/1

Rotter, P., Daskala, B., & Compano, R. (2008). RFID Implants: Opportunities and Challenges for Identifying People. *2, 27*(2), 24-32.

Roussos, G. (2006). Enabling RFID in retail. *Computer, 39*(3), 25-30.

Ryan, J. G. (1989). *A four chip implantable defibrillator/pacemaker chipset.* Paper presented at the IEEE Custom Integrated Circuits Conference.

Saad, M. K., & Ahamed, S. V. (2007). Vulnerabilities of RFID systems in infant abduction protection and patient wander prevention. *ACM SIGCSE Bulletin, 39*(2).

Sanchez-Klein, J. (1998). Cyberfuturist plants chip in arm to test human-computer interaction. from http://cnn.com/TECH/c...ng/9808/28/armchip.idg/index.html

Scan Journal. (1990). Sorry, I thought you were someone else... *Perspectives on Radio Frequency Identification: What is it, Where is it going, Should I be Involved?*, 4-9- 4-10.

Scharfeld, T. A. (2001). *An Analysis of the Fundamental Constraints on Low Cost Passive Radio-Frequency Identification System Design.* Massachusetts Institute of Technology, Massachusetts.

Scheeres, J. (2 May 2002). A Satellite Baby-Sitting Service. *Wired* Retrieved 4 February 2009, from http://www.wired.com/science/discoveries/news/2002/05/52253

Schwind, G. (1987). Electronic codes for automatic identification. In R. Ames (Ed.), *Perspectives on Radio Frequency Identification: What is it, Where is it going, Should I be Involved?* (pp. 1-19- 11-27). New York: Van Nostrand Reinhold.

Sensormatic. (1999). SafeKids™. Retrieved 3 June 1999, from http://www.sensormatic.com/html/safekids/index.htm

Sharp, K. R. (1987). Automatic identification improves the bottom line. In R. Ames (Ed.), *Perspectives on Radio Frequency Identification: What is it, Where is it going, Should I be Involved?* (pp. 1-9- 1-18). New York: Van Nostrand Reinhold.

Shu-ling, K. (2001). Councilor barks over dog tag system. *Taipei Times,* pp. 1-2.

Simpson, N. (2002, 6 March). Microchip save trauma for Benson. *The Advertiser,* p. 5.

Sky Eye Company. (2003). Welcome: where on earth...? Anywhere you want to be, with Sky Eye. Retrieved 5 January 2003, from http://www.sky-eye.com/en/index.html

Smith, I. G. (1990). AIM- an industry activity group for automatic identification. *Computing & Control Engineering Journal, 11,* 49-52.

Stonehouse, B. (1978). *Animal Marking- Recognition Marking of Animals in Research.* London: Macmillan Press.

Streitfeld. (2002). from http://www.10meters.com/verichip_fda.html

Stuart, E., Moh, M., & Moh, T.-S. (2008). Security and Privacy of RFID for Biomedical Applications: A Survey. In S. Ahson & M. Ilyas (Eds.), *RFID Handbook: Applications, Technology, Security, and Privacy* (pp. 657-674). London: CRC Press.

TI. (1998). Texas Instruments. from http://www.ti.com/mc/docs/tiris/docs/

Transponder. (1998). Transponder News. from http://rapidttp.co.za/transponder/

Trevarthen, A. (2006). The National Livestock Identification System: The Importance of Traceability in E-Business. *Journal of Theoretical and Applied Electronic Commerce Research, 2*(1), 49-62.

Trevarthen, A., & Michael, K. (2006, 9-11 July). *Beyond Mere Compliance of RFID Regulations by the Farming Community: A Case Study of the Cochrane Dairy Farm.* Paper presented at the The Sixth International Conference on Mobile Business, Toronto, Canada.

Tuttle, J. R. (1997). Traditional and emerging technologies and applications in the radio frequency identification (RFID) industry'. *IEEE Radio Frequency Integrated Circuits Symposium*, 5-8.

Unger, T. (1994). *Advances in biological identification: applications for the livestock industry.* Bowling Green: Livestock Conservation Institute.

Ventura. (2001). Microchip implants. *Ventura County Animal Regulation* Retrieved 20 November 2001, from http://www.ventura.org/animreg/infopet.html

Vetinfonet. (1998). Identifying your pet. from http://www.vetinfonet.com/id.htm

Wamba, S. F., Lefebvre, L. A., & Lefebvre, E. (2006). *Enabling intelligent B-to-B eCommerce supply chain management using RFID and the EPC network: a case study in the retail industry.* Paper presented at the Proceedings of the 8th international conference on Electronic commerce: The new e-commerce: innovations for conquering current barriers, obstacles and limitations to conducting successful business on the internet.

Want, R. (2004). The magic of RFID. *Queue, 2*(7), 40-48.

Want, R., Hopper, A., Falcao, V., & Gibbons, J. (1992). The active badge location system. *ACM Transactions on Information Systems, 10*(1), 91-102.

Warwick, K. (1998). Professor Kevin Warwick. from http://cyber.reading.ac.uk/K.Warwick/

Warwick, K. (2002). Professor of Cybernetics: University of Reading. *Professor Kevin Warwick*, from http://www.rdg.ac.uk/KevinWarwick/

Warwick, K. (2002). Project Cyborg 2.0. *Kevin Warwick* Retrieved 4 January 2003, from http://www.rdg.ac.uk/KevinWarwick/html/project_cyborg_2_0.html

Wells, W. (1998). The chips are coming. *Biotech Applied*, from http://www.accessexcellence.com/AB/BA/biochip.html

Werb, J. (1999). H-m-m-m-m... where is it? *Communications News, 36*(3), 52.

Wheatley, S. E. (1993). Tracker- stolen vehicle recovery system. *IEE Colloquium on Vehicle Security Systems*, 1/3-1/3.

Williams, M. (1999, April 13). Japan begins debating national ID number scheme. *Newsbytes*.

Wired. (2002). *Wired*, from http://www.wired.com/news/technology/0,1282,52253,00.html

WISC. (1998). High-Tech surveillance equipment for rent. *Wisc Edu*, from http://whyfiles.news.wisc.edu/056spy/other.html

Witt, S. (1999). Professor Warwick chips in. *Computerworld*, 89.

Woodford, J. (1993, 2 September). Bar code bottoms smacked down. *The Sydney Morning Herald*.

Wu, F., Kuo, F., & Liu, L.-W. (2005). *The application of RFID on drug safety of inpatient nursing healthcare.* Paper presented at the Proceedings of the 7th international conference on Electronic commerce.

Zeisel, E., & Sabella, R. (2006). *RFID+*. USA: Que Certification.

Zulich, A. (1998). Use of implanted transponders for permanent identification of reptiles and amphibians'. *Reptile & Amphibian Magazine*, from http://www.pythons.com/trovan.html

Chapter X
The Auto–ID Technology System

INTRODUCTION

This chapter analyses the findings from the case studies on bar codes, magnetic-stripe cards, smart cards, biometrics and RFID tags and transponders. Its main aim is to describe the auto-ID innovation process, especially the prevalence of patterns of migration, integration and convergence in auto-ID techniques and devices. Migration will be shown to have occurred in the transition between magnetic-stripe cards and smart cards, and the transition between bar codes and RFID transponders. Integration will be demonstrated through the example of auto-ID hybridization, especially on multi-technology cards, and the use of biometric minutiae on 2D bar codes. The third pattern to be described is that of convergence, as in the case of radio-frequency capable smart cards. The auto-ID selection environment will also be discussed from the perspective of the service provider who is increasingly facing pressure to choose the right auto-ID technique for a given application context.

WHO ARE THE AUTO-ID STAKEHOLDERS?

Having studied the cases of five auto-ID technologies and their respective networks, it can be seen that the interactions of stakeholders in the industry are paramount to the overall success of the innovation process. Indeed, auto-ID innovation is highly complex. The sheer number of stakeholders including private enterprise (technology and service providers), universities and consortia, government agencies (regulators and legislators), standards bodies, committees and other institutions (industry associations and forums), and end-users (consumers and employees) means that feedback to and from each stakeholder becomes integral in progressing an auto-ID application from conception to diffusion. It does therefore make sense to study auto-ID as a single technology system (TS). While Braco (1997, pp. 116-119) and Elliot and Loebbecke (1998) define lists of stakeholders for single auto-ID innovations, there definitions do not encapsulate all the stakeholders that are required to get a technique from invention to diffusion.

The stakeholders presented in the case studies can broadly be categorized into two groups, including those involved:

i.   In the invention, innovation and supply of auto-ID technological system components such as manufacturers, universities and government research bodies; and

ii.   In the provision of services that require customers to use auto-ID technological system components such as issuers, merchants and consumers.

The customer stakeholders include consumers, issuers and merchants; the technology provider stakeholders include manufacturers, system integrators and value-added resellers; and finally the service provider stakeholders, the owners of the operation, act to bring the two former groups together. Both the customers and technology providers have an infrastructure within which to operate. Customers use a physical infrastructure in the way of information technology and telecommunications (IT&T) to carry out transactions, and technology providers use a knowledge infrastructure that includes standards committees, university researchers, regulators and others. Essentially organizations are those entities that are consciously formed with an explicit purpose and institutions are those that are formed spontaneously to regulate interaction between people. The economic relationships that exist between organizations and institutions can be described as physical and knowledge infrastructures. The interplay between all these different stakeholders forms the technology system specific to auto-ID.

Noticeable in Figure 1 are the feedback loops inherent in the auto-ID innovation process. Without collaboration a given product innovation will not reach its potential and probably fade away to find a resting place in the mass of great ideas that were never realized. For example, if standards committees do not work with manufacturers to understand their requirements and learning experiences, then a default standard will most likely not be adhered. With each new major invention, a system is formed giving it the support and momentum it requires to follow a particular path. For instance, firms did not just happen to invent bar codes and then make commodity suppliers use them. There had to be some

Figure 1. Stakeholders in the auto-ID technology system. Innovation as a process of interactive learning.

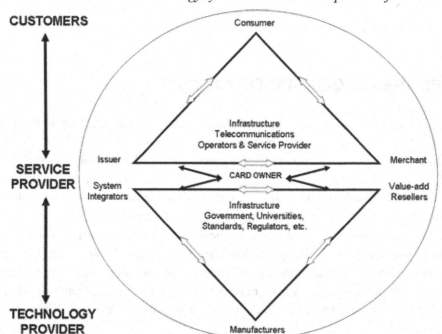

Table 1. The auto-ID innovation process

Generic Steps that Occur in the Auto-ID Innovation Process
1. A new idea for an auto-ID technology is conceived. A brief description of the idea is recorded.
2. The inventor, usually an employee of a manufacturing firm, develops a prototype from his/her discoveries. Meanwhile he/she searches for any existing patents that are related to the idea and have already been issued.
3. The manufacturer attempts to protect their new developments by filing for a national or international patent.
4. A patent is accepted and a patent number issued to the manufacturer.
5. The manufacturer promotes the auto-ID technology as a solution to a business problem and usually concentrates its efforts in targeting only one or two market segments specific to an industry.
6. Academic and government research grants are geared towards supporting the new technology.
7. Initial trials are conducted by the manufacturer and other affiliates, usually in closed systems such as university campuses or the military.
8. Service providers or customers purchase the auto-ID technology because it is a suitable solution for their application(s) needs.
9. By this stage resistance to the technology may have been felt internal to the business/ vertical industry; or end-user acceptance may have been overestimated. Relevant stakeholders meet to work through initial teething problems.
10. The media usually get involved at this point highlighting how the new technology may be used in the future.
11. Meanwhile, other new or existing manufacturing companies perhaps specialising in complementary technologies continually scour through registered patents and industry trade publications attempting to develop similar or add-on products.
12. Potential service providers and customers are confronted with several manufacturers who can produce very similar auto-ID technology components. Choosing between manufacturers becomes difficult but is based on differentiation. Proprietary standards are still being used by companies.
13. Physical infrastructure to support the technology quickly begins to permeate. This most likely includes physical networks, terminals such as browsers, kiosks and ATMs and other equipment.
14. New associations, forums, conferences, industry magazines come into existence to support the growth of the technology. A knowledge infrastructure begins to form.
15. By this stage the technology has either impacted consumers or business employees and advocate groups are in full swing on either side of the debate.
16. Auto-ID technology providers launch marketing campaigns targeted not only at customers but at end-users also. They attempt to clarify any misconceptions that may have eventuated during the process of diffusion.
17. As the market continues to grow for the new technology, the small number of manufacturers, realise that standards are vital if the technology is going to succeed being implemented regionally or nationally or even internationally. Large customers like the government, who usually have a vested interest in security devices, try to influence this process.
18. All suppliers are "forced" to adhere to the one standard which differs to most (if not all) current proprietary solutions. Standards bodies like ISO are usually involved in this process, which takes some years to officially complete. Industry-specific standards for particular applications like banking or telecommunications are also devised.
19. There is a growth in firms and skill sets in the industry. However, there are more customers, and technology providers have a relative bigger piece of the pie. Firms begin to collaborate with one another to promote the technology through the formation of alliances and consortiums.
20. Customers are able to purchase from any number of suppliers and know that the products are interoperable, even if some custom systems integration is required.
21. Specifications are written for particular industry applications.
22. Regulatory and legislative issues arise which require urgent attention. These are often difficult to solve because they are usually "after-the-fact". By this time there are usually several cases and precedence on particular situations. Some laws are amended, or newly introduced but mostly at the local and state level. This is a long-winded process as most laws were enacted when computer technology was not pervasive. Substitute Acts and Statutes attempt to protect end-users from such things as breaches in privacy or liability.
23. Social issues receive widespread media attention lead by advocacy groups who may hold philosophical, cultural or religious objections to the technology's permeance to everyday applications. There are also the economic repercussions in job losses etc.
24. Incremental technical improvements are made to the product over time. The auto-ID technology gets smaller, increases in capacity and processing power, has more security and is more reliable in an open systems environment.
25. The technology is most likely involved in a process of migration, integration or convergence. Creative symbiosis is likely to take place between other auto-ID technologies thus starting the whole innovation process again.

degree of interaction between the relevant actors and more importantly some mutual agreement on how to go forward. For example, suppliers of the technology had to make attempts to engage merchants, but via their commodity suppliers first.

THE AUTO-ID INNOVATION PROCESS

At discrete points in the innovation process (Table 1), stakeholders may find their level of active participation and contribution to oscillate between intensive and non-intensive. The innovation process is not linear, it is meshed and iterative. To that end, the feedback and interaction between the various stakeholders is also dependent on the dominant dimension(s) at any given point in time in the process. For instance, physical infrastructure problems may plague an auto-ID application early on and then the need for interoperability may become a dominant consideration. Indeed, several simultaneous interactions may be taking place, and this dynamic exchange may be incurring multiple changes throughout the development process.

Figure 2 highlights some of the more probable events that may occur as a result of stakeholder interactions. The events are mapped against six categories that depict separate stages in the innovation process life cycle. The stage titled 'Inhibitors' indicates the concerns and barriers of introducing a new auto-ID technology into the market. For the greater part these inhibiting factors affect the organization, those firms that are involved with manufacturing the new technology. The 'Evolution' stage is characterized by a need for technology providers to come together to share their experiences and knowledge.

Figure 2. Stakeholders in the auto-ID technology system. Innovation as a process of interactive learning.

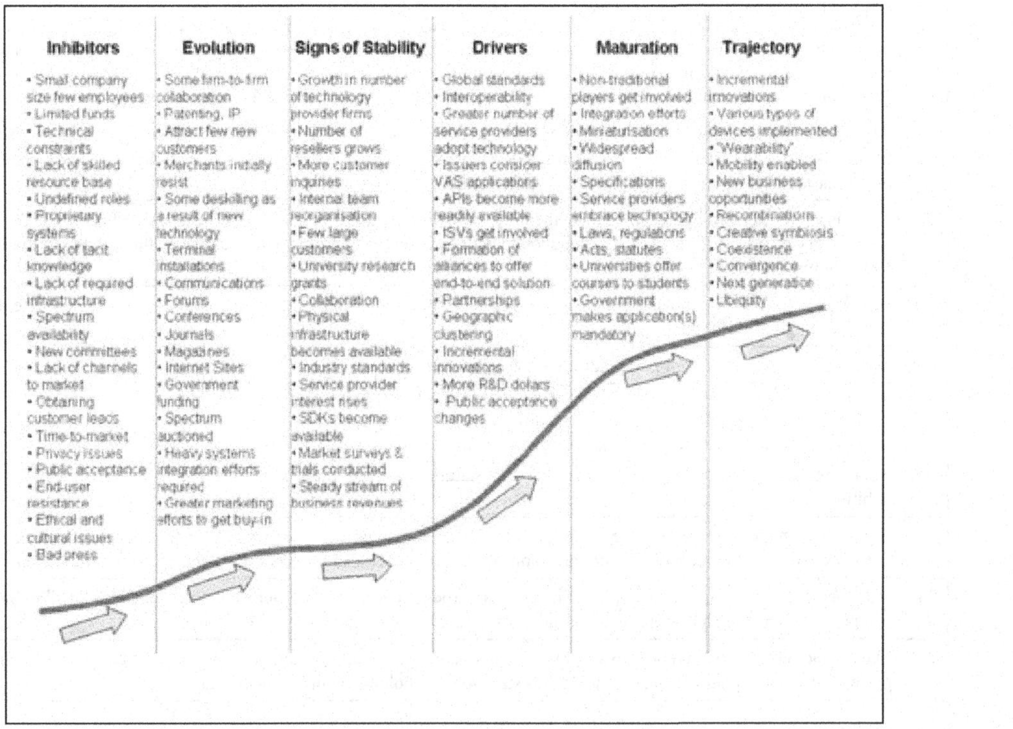

An economic infrastructure, both tacit and physical begins to form providing the way forward for the patenting of new inventions and the establishment of committees. Firm-to-firm collaboration also occurs as organizations realize they are unable to offer end-to-end solutions on their own; not only are system components manufactured by different vendors but software for systems integration, and networks for communication, are required. The new auto-ID innovation is still in a state of flux as institutions scramble to introduce a common standard which can be adopted. The formation and adoption of these global standards is a 'Sign of Stability'. The number of customers by this stage has grown, providing for a steady stream of revenue, particularly for manufacturers. Auto-ID technology providers begin to increase their headcount as the demand for their services increases and specialist skills are required.

The 'Drivers' stage of the innovation process is the period where technology providers and service providers partner together to introduce the auto-ID application to a mass market audience. Interoperability has now been achieved, firms have begun clustering together in geographic locations close to customers, and citizens have accepted the new technology realizing its convenience offerings. There is a healthy growth in peripheral companies linked to the technology, specializing in niche complementary and supplementary innovations. The 'Maturation' stage of the innovation process finds non-traditional players become involved in offering new services based on auto-ID. Specifications by this stage are well-defined and linked to vertical sectors such as banking, telecommunications and transportation. Laws, acts, and statutes are a topic of debate as the new auto-ID technology is used or misused in ways that legislation does not know how to address. It is during the maturation stage that many governments also introduce mandatory auto-ID technologies linked to social service applications. Universities continue to be involved in the incremental development of existing auto-ID devices as newer auto-ID technologies are introduced into the market. Funds are dedicated to research and development to continue to push the barrier of innovation. The 'Trajectory' stage is where coexistence of several auto-ID technologies is experienced but also where opportunities for integration and convergence can materialize. At the height of its proliferation, the auto-ID technology begins to be used in ways for which it was not originally intended becoming even more powerful in functionality when combined with one or more existing information technologies.

AUTO-ID TRENDS AND PATTERNS

Patterns of migration and integration were prevalent in the examples found in the embedded case studies in the preceding chapters. Dependent on the application in question, some customers and service providers migrated from one auto-ID device to another, seeking better security, greater functionality, a reduction in fraud and counterfeit, even a smaller device that was more convenient for the end-user to carry. Convergence was also identified but predominantly at the application-level rather than at the device level. For instance, the ability to have more than one application on a smart card is quite different to 'true' technological convergence, where one device seamlessly coalesces with another. Integration is also all too often confused with convergence, although both can be considered forms of creative symbiosis (i.e. recombinations). Integration is the ability to use two or more auto-ID techniques on the same device. Integration has proven quite popular as legacy card technology systems have changed with the times- from embossed numbers, to bar codes, to magnetic-stripe and microprocessor functionality all on the same card device.

Many predictions have been made about particular auto-ID technologies becoming obsolete, however, one need only to look at the widespread diffusion of devices in the market today to consider this an unlikelihood (for the conceivable future anyway). Bar codes will for a long time yet serve their purpose, albeit in developing countries which cannot afford RFID devices; and magnetic-stripe cards will maintain their niche, perhaps not in banking but in other applications such as electronic ticketing. In addition, there are continual improvements being made to all auto-ID devices, of course in differing frequencies, but nevertheless the breakthroughs enable certain weaknesses in each technology to be overcome. The diversity in auto-ID techniques also allow for an end-to-end capability such as in the case of military applications.

Table 2 identifies the relationship between different auto-ID techniques. The abbreviations used include 'M' for migration, 'I' for integration, and 'C' for convergence. The matrix is to be read from left to right. For instance, taking the case of bar code, one can see that both migration and integration (MI) trends occurred between it and RFID transponders. The asterisk depicts a redundant flow. Dependent on a given application scenario, some customers and service providers may choose to migrate from one auto-ID device to another, seeking better security, more storage capacity, greater functionality, a reduction in fraud and counterfeit, even a smaller device that would be more convenient for the end-user to carry. Integration of various auto-ID techniques has also proven popular and this is particularly obvious with respect to card technologies. Service provider legacy identification systems have evolved as the techniques have become available- from embossed numbers, to bar codes, to magnetic-stripe and microprocessor functionality all on the same device. Auto-ID technologies have even converged, as can be seen from the example of the contactless smart card, a recombination that brought together a RFID tag with an on-board IC.

Migration from Magnetic-Stripe to Smart Cards

Joseph Sheppard (1999) CEO of Xico Incorporated, a magnetic-stripe equipment manufacturing company, summed up the situation well: "[i]n short, the smart card industry assertion 10 years ago that magnetic stripes were dead was premature by at least half a century." This is graphically illustrated by the cover of the October 1997 issue of *Card Technology*, which tracks the trends in both magstripe and smartcard technologies and applications... "[w]hile smart card makers tout their benefits, mag-stripe card usage continues to proliferate. Don't expect that to change anytime soon." In 1997 "...less than 5% of smart cards worldwide [we]re issued by banks... Mass rollout of smart cards is years away because of the cost to convert magnetic-strip credit, debit and ATM card systems to chip technology" (Bank Systems, 1997, p. 21). From this it can be seen that auto-ID migration is not as simple as choosing to invest in a new card technology, the decision also has implications for existing infrastructure and investment.

Table 2. Migration (M), Integration (I), and Convergence (C) Patterns occurring in the auto-ID industry

Auto-ID Technique	Bar Code	Magnetic-Stripe	Smart Card	Biometrics	RFID Tags
Bar Code	*	MI	MI	MI	MI
Magnetic-Stripe	I	*	MI	MI	MI
Smart Card		I	*	MI	MIC
Biometrics	IC	IC	IC	*	M
RFID Tags		I	C		*

While most banks and financial institutions still utilize magnetic-stripe on their customer FTCs, particularly in the U.S., all of the banks in France are reaping the benefits of smart card. "All bankcards in France have a chip imbedded in them... When a French cardholder makes a purchase, the transaction is processed at the point of service using the chip and not the magnetic stripe" (Ayer & McKenna, 1997, p. 44). Each of the French chip cards carry a payment application known as B0'. Smart cards have always been a dormant threat to magnetic-stripe but in most countries it has taken until the year 2000 for noticeable migration from the magnetic-stripe card to the smart card to happen. It took almost 40 years to distribute plastic payment cards widely; it will probably take another 10-15 years before consumers worldwide are comfortable with the multiapplication smart card.

Many banks have conducted feasibility studies on smart cards, either by doing secondary research or conducting pilot studies. It is not an uncommon practice today for banks to issue customers with hybrid technology cards until the migration from magnetic-stripe to smart cards is complete. Major banks across the world have begun marketing the smart card concept to consumers. In *The Australian* in 1997 (pp. 6-7) for instance, the ANZ bank advertised the change from magnetic-stripe to smart card in full-page advertisements. One of these announcements is worth noting in full- a magnetic-stripe bankcard appears on the left page and a VISA card (with IC) on the right: *"October 1974. There it was in your letterbox. Whether you wanted it or not. A Bankcard. They all looked the same and their new owners likewise, were all treated the same. You were told where to use it and how much you could spend. All that changed. At ANZ it changed faster than most. To the point where you can now enjoy ANZ cards that not only provide credit... Cards that are aligned to your telecommunications company, your airline, and many other major companies you do business with on a daily basis. What next? Well, we're currently at the forefront of smart card technology. Cards that use a microchip to record details of transactions and the balance on the card. Now won't that be a nice change?"*

In France there are even migrations occurring from smart bank cards developed in the 1980s to newer smart cards that adhere to the EMV standard and are based on the MULTOS operating system. Clearly this has been an unsettling period for banks and merchants as the costs to upgrade or replace existing ATM, EFTPOS, electronic cash registers, self-service fuel dispensers and other such terminals to make them smart card-ready are very high.

Murphy (1996, p. 80) also asserts that, "smart cards are the talk of the card manufacturing industry, but the magnetic stripe will be the bread and butter of card makers for the near term." Yet, one cannot ignore the gravitational pull that is obviously occurring from magnetic-stripe to the chip card. "Visa, MasterCard and other players in the smart card business contend that an 'evolution' or a 'migration' to smart card technology is under way. The pace of that evolution, though, is anybody's guess" (Nixon, 1995, p. 22). The magnetic-stripe card was more of an enabler, a convenience card; something that would accustom people to a particular behavioral style. The smart card is being heralded as the grand solution to personalization, tailored to the specific needs of the individual. Hybrid cards may well end up facilitating the evolution and be phased out gradually as they are not required. Already the widespread use of magnetic-stripe has ensured that the size of smart cards must maintain the same ISO standard dimensions. Hybrid cards now have a physical location for microchips, magnetic-stripes, bar codes, embossed characters, holograms and photographs. Read/write equipment is even starting to become multi-technology capable (Hendry, 1997, pp. 45f).

In 1987 Svigals was undecided whether the pattern taking place was "magnetic stripe evolution or smart card migration". Perhaps what can be said, in the case of magnetic stripe and smart card, is that the "migration" phase is part of a larger evolutionary process. What Svigals observed in the card technologies was equally applicable to tag technology over a decade later. Many ATM machines have already been upgraded to accept both magnetic-stripe and smart cards. Some smart cards have even been developed to emulate magnetic-stripe or bar code cards so that very costly card readers do not have to be entirely replaced, at least in the short term. This has posed a special challenge to card issuers who are attempting a seamless migration. McCrindle (1990, p. 72) stated: "[e]xisting equipment, such as ATMs, are not going to be discarded overnight. A smart card must, therefore, be capable of being used in the current generation of machines as well as in smart card based equipment... the two types of technology must coexist." Murphy (1996, p. 83) also agrees that "...cards will be issued for many years with both mag stripes and computer chips." Jerome Svigals attributed this trend to a global evolution from cash to electronic currency but admitted he could not predict how long the evolution would take to complete (Nixon 1995, p. 27). What is of interest to note however, is that the longer the migration phase continues, the more it will become ingrained into applications as a de-facto standard.

Migration from Bar Codes to RFID Transponders

RFID manufacturers are starting to make inroads into the bar code market (McCathie & K. Michael, 2005). While some predict RFID will replace bar codes, it is more realistic to say (as has Phil Calderbank, general manager of Sensormatic's RFID group) that RFID will have a market for high-cost items rather than low-cost items (Gurin, 1999). The trend is towards combining RF with EAS (electronic article surveillance), as have Sensormatic Electronics and Checkpoint Systems. Bar codes have poor readability rates in applications that are exposed to harsh environments whether it is indoors or outdoors. RFID can capitalize on this and other weaknesses, particularly where material handling and tracking of components is of the utmost importance. RF tags have many advantages over bar code (K. Michael & McCathie, 2005). First, they can be placed anywhere and can store a lot of information, whereas the bar code is limited by its own label size. Second, RFID does not require LoS (line-of-sight) and cannot be erased by strong magnetic fields. Third, the systems have almost 100 per cent accuracy. Fourth, the tag is not affected by substances such as dirt or paint which may cover the tag from time to time. Fifth, tagged objects can be mobile, without the need to stop to be identified which speeds up the process significantly. And finally, non-metallic objects can come between the tag and the reader without interfering with the system (Automatic ID, 1998, p. 2). Marsh (1998, p. 2) believes that bar codes have played an incredible role in reaching widespread productivity benefits in industry but that there time is now coming to an end: "[t]he RFID tag to replace barcodes is about to arrive from a number of different suppliers who are all working towards this goal." There are however, numerous counter arguments for why bar code will not be replaced altogether by RFID. For the time being at least, it seems impossible that every single bar coded item in existence today will have a RFID tag or transponder attached to it. Well-known proponents of RFID such as Wal-Mart, Gillette, and Proctor & Gamble have already conducted trials for item-level tracking using the EPCglobal standard.

Integration – The Rise of Multi-Technology Cards

It is difficult to say whether "integration" was a consequence of an attempt at "migration" in some applications areas or an independent phenomenon. Initially integration of auto-ID techniques on the same device was born from the idea that each technique could serve its own function for different applications (this was particularly true of closed systems). In addition, as a consequence of migration patterns, multi-technology cards served as a way to transition from auto-ID legacy systems to future modes of operation. The requirement to include more than one technique on the card was a result of roll-out phases of the new technologies (i.e. different geographic regions transitioning at different times). New cardholders receive the latest cards while existing cardholders are transitioned prior to card expiration. This interim period usually requires hybrid cards to be used. Hodgson (1995, p. 19) described this incidence of multi-technology cards as an evolutionary process. *"When multi-technology cards first came on the scene, many saw them as a potential solution to a sticky problem- how to eliminate the need for numerous cards or keys without going to a lot of expense to integrate whole systems. Beginning with dual technology, the cards then evolved to true multi-tech capabilities, incorporating functions such as lending items (bar code), time and attendance (magstrip) and photo ID. Now they are much more than just a temporary solution to a non-integrated system. Their evolution is just beginning, and will include not only new applications, but also new technology- specifically the smart card."*

Multi-technology cards form a strong argument and present us with a compelling reason of why individual auto-ID techniques will continue to co-exist independent of a declining adoption rate. In Portugal for instance, the SIBS (Sociedade Interbancaria de Servicos) have introduced the Multibanco electronic purse, yet another hybrid card incorporating a microprocessor for purse applications and magnetic-stripe for credit facilities. Close to 7000 smart card terminals have been introduced, the majority are off-line and about one-third can read both magnetic-stripe and smart card technology.

Converging Auto-ID Technologies

The convergence of auto-ID technologies is now starting to become evident at different levels such as standards, regulations, infrastructure and applications. True convergence however at the auto-ID device level is not as common as it is often portrayed. It all depends on the definition one uses to describe what they mean by convergence. Greenstein and Khanna (1997, p. 203) identify two types of industry convergence: convergence in substitutes and convergence in complements. *"Two products converge in substitutes when users consider either product interchangeable with the other. Convergence in substitutes occurs when different firms develop products with features that become increasingly similar to the features of certain other products... Two products converge in complements when the products work better together than separately or when they work better together now than they worked together formerly. Convergence in complements occurs when different firms develop products or subsystems within a standard bundle that can increasingly work together to form a larger system..."*

Depending on the perspective taken, the selection environment of automatic identification can be considered to fit into either classification. The most authentic example in auto-ID of convergence in complements at the present is that between the contact smart card and RFID card capabilities (i.e. contactless). Smart cards once required to make contact with a reader, today a RF smart card can either be utilized by inserting it in a reader or by presenting it close to a RF field. Companies like AT&T and GEC have demonstrated smart cards which communicate using radio frequency signals (Monk & Dreifus, 1997). The ability to store biometric templates on a bar code or magnetic-stripe is another example of convergence in complements. In the case of the bar code, the biometric replaces the need for a unique ID number to be stored, with an ID derived from a fingerprint or other unique human characteristic. Biometric techniques can be used seamlessly in just about any type of card or transponder-based technology making it highly versatile. Multimodal biometrics also encourages the use of more than one type of biometric match for authentication. Biometrics has been responsible for revitalizing the prospects of stand-alone magnetic-stripe cards given the additional security embedded in the technique itself

AUTO-ID TECHNOLOGIES SHARE IN THE SAME TRAJECTORY

Upon their introduction, individual auto-ID technologies underwent a process of continual refinement until a dominant design materialized in each case. Once a dominant design emerged, widespread diffusion was experienced by each of the technologies, initially through niche industry applications and later through respective mass market applications. Auto-ID innovation was traditionally understood as consisting of separate life cycle curves, one for each device. This pattern resembled a number of continuous waves, depicting that each technology was a likely successor to the one before it (Figure 3). Auto-ID technologies however are much more complex and do not fit the traditional product life cycle curve (compare with Figure 4). Roughly a five to ten year period has separated the diffusion of the auto-ID techniques studied in this investigation, starting with bar code and ending with RFID transponder implants. With each successive window (i.e. the period of time between one technology's diffusion and the next), companies considered new opportunities that would leverage upon their existing knowledge. Apart from incremental innovation that continued on frontline products to match market requirements, cross-pollenization began to occur between companies specializing in different auto-ID techniques.

Figure 3. Traditional understanding of auto-ID innovation- separate life cycle curves for each technology

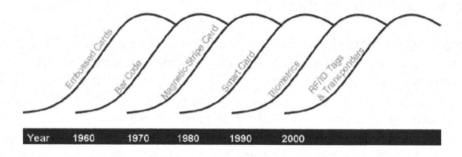

Figure 4. Contemporary understanding of auto-ID innovation- sharing in the same trajectory

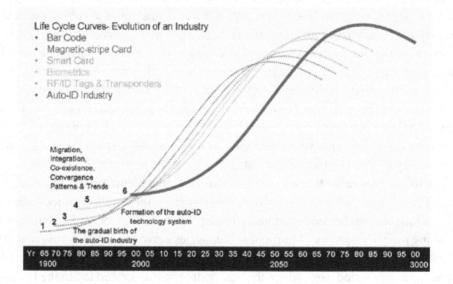

For instance, bar codes appeared on magnetic-stripe cards, and biometrics was used in smart cards for added security, among many other examples. This recombination of existing knowledge is what sparked collaborative relationships and began a whole new set of interactions between various actors- the auto-ID technology system was born. With the phenomenon of integration and convergence of technologies comes one common shared auto-ID industry life cycle curve (figure 4).

While recombinations and mutations of auto-ID technologies are continually being invented, it does not mean that existing markets for particular techniques will suddenly disappear. On the contrary meeting requirements to new business problems increases the range and depth of auto-ID innovations and should be understood as an evolutionary step in the development of the industry at large. It is through this interaction and feedback- between service providers that require EC applications and auto-ID technology providers that assist in designing solutions for them- that end-user needs are met and on-going innovation is assured. In this manner, coexistence can be put forward as a plausible model of the future for the auto-ID industry (Figure 5). Examples of coexistence can be found especially in peripheral devices like readers and printers. Some readers are able to read both magnetic-stripe cards and smart cards, and some printers can print dual-mode bar codes and RFID labels. *"Today, many of us see Auto ID technologies as "complementary," with each filling a space in the market defined by the fit between its strengths and weaknesses, and the requirements of target applications. And looking forward, I believe we'll evolve from a "coexistence" model to one that leverages the many converging opportunities around the intersections and in the gaps between those technologies"* (Swartz, 1999, p. 22).

In open systems especially, it is highly unlikely that a single auto-ID device could ever cater for the needs of a complete end-to-end application, rather auto-ID technologies usually work in concert to fulfill large-scale initiatives. And while some have a vision that every single non-living thing will eventually be 'smart' or 'intelligent', as put forward by the development of the Electronic Product Code (EPC), consumers will probably insist that certain items remain 'dumb'. In understanding the auto-ID

Figure 5. An RFID/bar code label printer, pointing towards a model of coexistence in the identification of cartons and pallets.

selection environment, the paradigm has shifted from an economy that seeks the domination of one auto-ID device, towards an economy that accepts (if not welcomes) the coexistence of numerous auto-ID devices. While the relative shares of production for each auto-ID device may vary over time, and some devices will address particular market needs better than others, overall several technologies will continue to coexist.

EVOLUTION OR REVOLUTION?

When auto-ID technologies first made their presence felt in retail and banking they were considered revolutionary innovations. They made sweeping changes to the way people worked, lived, and interacted with each other. Before their inception, both living and nonliving things were identified manually; auto-ID devices automated the identification process, allowing for an increase in the level of accuracy and reliability. Supermarket employees could check-out non-perishable items just by swiping a bar code over a scanner, and suppliers could distribute their goods using unique codes. Consumers could withdraw cash without walking into a bank branch and purchase goods at the point-of-sale (POS). And subsequently banks no longer required the same number of staff to serve customers directly. Auto-ID enacted radical change. This cluster of related innovations differed considerably from any others. Though most auto-ID technologies had their foundations in the early 1900s, all of these required other breakthroughs in system components to take place first before they could proliferate.

Up until the 1970s, consumers were largely disconnected from computer equipment. About the most sophisticated household item was the television set. While ordinary people knew computers were changing the face of business, their first-hand experience of these technologies was limited. Mainframe computers at the time were large, occupying considerable floor space and there was a great mystique surrounding the capabilities of these machines. One must remember that the personal computer did not officially arrive until 1984. Meanwhile, bar codes and scanner equipment were being deployed to supermarket chains and credit card companies were distributing magnetic-stripe cards in mass mail-outs. Consumers were encouraged to visit automatic teller machines (ATMs), and for many this was their first encounter with some form of computer. No matter how elementary it may seem to us today typing a PIN and selecting the "withdraw", "amount", and "enter" buttons was an experience for first-time users who had most likely never touched a terminal keypad before. By the time the 1990s had arrived, so had other technologies like the laptop, mobile phone and personal digital assistants (PDAs). The range of available auto-ID devices had now grown in quantity, shape and sophistication including the use of smart cards that could store more information, biometric techniques that ensured an even greater level of security, and wireless methods such as radio-frequency identification tags and transponders that required little human intervention. By this time, consumers were also more experienced users. Auto-ID had reached ubiquitous proportions in a period of just over thirty years.

The changes brought about by auto-ID were not only widespread but propelling in nature. No sooner had one technology become established than another was seeking entry into the market. The technical drawbacks of magnetic-stripe cards for instance led to the idea that smart cards may be more suitable for particular applications (Shelfer & Procaccino, 2002). A pattern of migration from one technology to the other seemed logical until biometric techniques increased security not only in magnetic-stripe cards but bar code cards as well. There was also the movement from contact cards to contactless cards and bar codes to RFID but by no means were the technologies making one another obsolete but spurring on even more research and development and an even greater number of new applications and uses (Michael, 2002, pp. 135-152). Diagram 5 shows the different types of changes that occurred between auto-ID devices. The three main flows that are depicted in the diagram are migration, integration and convergence.

The recombination of existing auto-ID techniques flourished in the 1990s with integrated cards and combinatory reader technologies (e.g. 4p-Mobile, 1999). These new product innovations indicated that coexistence of auto-ID devices was not only possible but important for the success of the industry at large. A few techniques even converged as was the case of contactless smart cards and RFID systems. Auto-ID had proven it maintained a driving force of its own while still piggybacking on the breakthroughs in microchip processing speeds, storage capacity, software programs, encryption techniques, networks and other peripheral requirements that are generally considered auto-ID system enablers. The State of Connecticut ID card uses biometric data stored in a bar code, some student cards carry both a microchip and bar code as well as a photograph for identification, some tickets use both bar codes and RFID transponders, and some applications using biometrics take advantage of magnetic-stripe technology for verification purposes.

Now having said that auto-ID belonged to that cluster of IT&T innovations that can be considered revolutionary, the process of innovation was in fact evolutionary. There is no doubt that auto-ID techniques were influenced by manual methods of identification, whether it was labels that were stuck onto objects, plain or embossed cards, comparing signatures or methods for fingerprint pattern matching. Early breakthroughs in mechanical calculators, infrared, electro-magnetic principles, magnetic tape encoding and integrated circuits also aided the advancement of auto-ID technologies. Allen and Kutler (1997, p. 11) called this the "evolving computing" phenomenon. McCrindle (1990, ch. 2) even discussed the "evolution of the smart card", tracing the historical route all the way back from French philosopher Blaise Pascal (1623-1662).

The development of auto-ID followed an evolutionary path, yet the technologies themselves were revolutionary when considered as part of that cluster known as information technologies. From devices that one could carry to devices one could implant in themselves. The advancement of auto-ID technology, since its inception, has been so great that even the earliest pioneers would have found the changes that have taken place since the 1970s inconceivable. For the first time, service providers could put in place mechanisms to identify their customer base and also to collect data on patterns of customer behavior and product/services traffic. Mass market applications once affected or 'infected' by auto-ID continue to push the bounds of what this technology can or cannot do. Technology has progressed from purely manual techniques to automatic identification techniques. Furthermore auto-ID continues to grow in sophistication towards full-proof ways for identification. The aforementioned auto-ID cases show that major development efforts continue both for traditional and newer technologies. Even the humble bar code has been resurrected as a means of secure ID, revamped with the aid of biometric templates stored using a 2D symbology.

In addition, the lessons learned from the widespread introduction of each distinct technique are shaping the trajectory of the whole industry. For instance, the smart card has not neglected to take advantage of other auto-ID techniques such as biometrics and RFID. Thus, new combinations of auto-ID technologies are being introduced as a result of a cross-pollenization process in the industry at large. These new innovations (that could be classified as either mutations or recombinations) are acting to thrust the whole industry forward. The importance of this chapter is that it has established that auto-ID is more than just bar code and magnetic-stripe card and that coexistence and convergence of auto-ID technologies is occurring.

Figure 6. It is quite ironic that at the RFID Australasia 2005 Exhibition (17-18th August), barcodes were used for delegate registration. The first step in the process required delegates to pre-register online. After the pre-register stage the delegate received an automated email with a barcode. And on day of the exhibition, the delegate could self-scan their invitation and print out their badge at a collection station before entering the Exhibition Centre in Sydney.

MAJOR FINDINGS

The auto-ID case studies have uncovered a number of significant evolving trends and patterns related to auto-ID innovation. First, that auto-ID devices independent of type, share a similar generic innovation process. Their journey from invention to diffusion is one that traverses like themes involving like stakeholders and infrastructures. This stands as the foundation premise for an auto-ID technology system (TS). It is therefore correct to refer to an "auto-ID industry" which collectively espouses auto-ID techniques from bar codes to biometrics. Second, that the selection environment for auto-ID is one where alternate or substitute technologies are available, specific to an application. A customer interested in card technologies for instance, can choose from a range of auto-ID card types as is the case with tag devices. Third, that over time a pattern of migration, integration and convergence has occurred between devices in the auto-ID industry- these trends are apparent in some devices more than others. When considered together these interactive forces point to a common auto-ID trajectory. Fourth, that despite the creative symbiosis taking place, the individual auto-ID technologies will continue to co-exist serving a variety of needs. The hypothesis that one super-device will render all other devices obsolete is highly unlikely given the diverse requirements of customers and their applications throughout the world. Fifth, the pervasiveness of auto-ID has acted to result in changes to mass market applications that have continued to evolve since the 1970s especially. Sixth, that the ultimate trajectory of auto-ID is *electrophoresis*. In the future it is likely that humans will be bearers of automatic technology for a variety of applications such as drug delivery and emergency services.

The Auto-ID Industry as a Technology System (TS)

The auto-ID industry is a technology system (TS) that is bringing diverse stakeholders together to innovate by enabling interaction and sharing resources. Whether it is in the establishment of new research centers that embrace multiple auto-ID techniques, the use of common network infrastructure, system integrators that are increasingly conversant with generic auto-ID topologies or the formation of associations that encourage joint collaboration, the notion of an auto-ID industry is beginning to prevail.

Previous studies have mainly focused on one auto-ID technology and to this end it has been difficult to identify patterns or trends common to all techniques. Rather than seeing auto-ID as one larger structure embodying numerous technologies, usually one auto-ID device was highlighted by authors at the neglect of others. But auto-ID is more than just bar code or RFID. The case studies in this study present an unbiased and balanced view of numerous technologies from the innovation perspective, and how each plays an important role in the overall success of the auto-ID TS.

The Auto-ID Selection Environment

The embedded case studies have acted to show the diverse applicability of auto-ID technologies in their many shapes and forms. What came through these cases is just how pervasive the technologies have become, important in almost every facet of life, independent of jurisdiction. Comparisons between technologies applied to the same application also showed that some techniques were more suitable in particular situations. This however, does not mean that all service providers or customers opt for one type of solution in a given scenario. It is entirely a decision that is based on factors that go beyond the need for 'the most secure device' or the one device that is considered by most to be the "optimum" choice or that 'which is the most cost-effective'. A selection environment is just that, an environment from which people can "make a selection" based on a number of criteria that are personalized to a specific problem in a specific market. In all the case studies that were conducted, it was shown that auto-ID devices can be used interchangeably with one another in any given scenario. For instance, auto-ID card solutions were in abundance, as were combinations of devices on the same card (i.e. hybrid cards).

Numerous auto-ID vendor solutions were also presented, showing the subtlety of differentiation between supplier products. The market for auto-ID continues to grow replacing manual ways of performing transactions. Traditionally it has been business-to-business (B2B) and business-to-consumer (B2C) transactions that have made use of auto-ID, but more recently, governments worldwide are beginning to realize the vast benefits auto-ID have over legacy methods in servicing an entire population (i.e. G2C). Proposals for national ID schemes using multiapplication smart cards are now commonplace (K. Michael, 1997). Some stakeholders are predicting the elimination of several government-centric cards for one "everything" card that is focused on social security applications and has other peripheral functions. Commercial applications are set to remain separate to national ID cards however. It also looks inevitable that the banking sector will undergo major changes in the provision of services as telecommunication providers attempt to enter the same market space. It does seem probable that numerous commercial organizations will begin to form alliances with one another so that they are able to build super-brand images using smart transaction cards. Multi-purpose smart card systems, for instance, are becoming widespread, especially at the campus level. Affiliations between major players are already starting to surface as the potential returns get higher and higher (Michael, 2003, pp. 135-152)..

The Need to Forecast Auto-ID Innovation

Forecasting and determining potential patterns and rates of change offer important insights for the future. Even if predictions turn out to be short-lived or blatantly wrong, they are still a vehicle for considering all the possibilities. It provides a stimulus for discussion and debate. In some situations forecasting may be said to be pre-emptive of actual events in the future. In other instances, the forecast depicted is considered unfavorable, and events that would have led to an expected outcome are redirected in scope and focus. Given that evolutionary theory underpins the SI framework, the forecasting or predictive nature of this study has been based almost solely on current research and development (i.e. history). Incremental changes in innovations have pointed to a path dependency. The shorter term the predictions are, the higher the likelihood that they will eventuate as they are based on "known" factors and not on wild assumptions. For instance, it is easier to forecast what will happen in the next year or two, rather than what will happen in twenty, fifty or one hundred years. Having said that, longer-term visions are equally important; science fiction has provided much in the way of future possibilities. Many do not acknowledge these contributions as important however few would dispute that predictions made by Arthur C. Clarke years in advance of their happening were unimportant or entirely coincidental.

CONCLUSION

The auto-ID industry is a technology system (TS) that is bringing diverse stakeholders together to innovate by enabling interaction and sharing resources. Whether it is in the establishment of new research centers that embrace multiple auto-ID techniques, the use of common network infrastructure, system integrators that are increasingly conversant with generic auto-ID topologies or the formation of associations that encourage joint collaboration, the notion of an auto-ID industry is beginning to prevail. Previous studies have mainly focused on one auto-ID technology and to this end it has been difficult to identify patterns or trends common to all techniques. Rather than seeing auto-ID as one larger system embodying numerous technologies, usually one auto-ID device was highlighted by authors at the neglect of others. But auto-ID is more than just bar code or RFID. The case studies in this study present an unbiased and balanced view of numerous technologies from the innovation perspective, and how each plays an important role in the overall success of the auto-ID technology system. Auto-ID technologies thus share in the one common trajectory, which is, to be implemented in a ubiquitous way, on almost every tangible item, living and non-living.

REFERENCES

4p-Mobile. (1999, 28 May 1999). Dat500: The All-in-one Palmtop System. *4p-Mobile-Dp*, from http://www.4p-mobile-dp.com/4p/dat500.html

Allen, C. A., & Kutler, J. (1997). Overview of smart cards and the industry', in Smart Cards: seizing strategic business opportunities. In C. A. Allen & W. J. Barr (Eds.), (pp. 2-20). New York: McGraw-Hill.

Anonymous. (1997). ANZ Bank Smart Card. *The Australian,* pp. 6-7.

Automatic ID. (1998). Radio frequency identification (RFID). *Automatic I.D. News*, from http://www.autoidenews.com/technologies/concepts/rfdcintro.htm

Ayer, K., & McKenna, J. (1997). Worldwide developments and player motivations. In C. A. Allen & W. J. Barr (Eds.), *Smart Cards: Seizing Strategic Business Opportunities* (pp. 44-56). New York: McGraw-Hill.

Bank Systems. (1997). Move to chip technology still a ways off. *Bank Systems & Technology, 34*(6), 21.

Braco, R. (1997). Financial services. In C. A. Allen & W. J. Barr (Eds.), *Financial services in Smart Cards: seizing strategic business opportunities* (pp. 112-127). New York: McGraw-Hill.

Elliot, S., & Loebbecke, C. (1998). *Smart-card based electronic commerce: characteristics and roles.* Paper presented at the IEEE Proceeding from the Thirty-First Hawaii International Conference, Hawaii.

Greenstein, S., & Khanna, T. (1997). What does industry convergence mean? In D. B. Yoffie (Ed.), *Competing in the Age of Digital Convergence* (pp. 201-226). Massachusetts,: Harvard Business School.

Gurin, R. (1999). Scanning technologies adapt to changing times: As hand-held, fixed- position scanners become commodity items, wireless connectivity, 2D bar code support will be key product differentiators. *Automatic I.D. News, 15,* 28.

Hendry, M. (1997). *Smart Card Security and Applications (Artech House Telecommunications Library).* Boston: Artech House.

Hodgson, K. (1995). Multi-tech cards: just the beginning. *Security, 32*(10), 19-20.

Marsh, M. (1998). Editorial: can RFID tags replace barcodes cost-effectively? *Transponder News*, from http://rapidttp.co.za/transponder/editori1.html

McCathie, L., & Michael, K. (2005, 3-5 October). *Is it the end of barcodes in supply chain management?* Paper presented at the Collaborative Electronic Commerce, Talca, Chile.

McCrindle, J. (1990). *Smart Cards*. London: Springer-Verlag.

Michael, K. (1997, 20-21 September). *Federal government adoption of multiapplication smart cards.* Paper presented at the Science and Technologies Studies Today: Forging New Links.

Michael, K. (2002). The automatic identification trajectory: from the ENIAC to chip implants. In E. Lawrence (Ed.), *Internet Commerce: digital models for business* (pp. 131-134, 136). Queensland: John Wiley and Sons.

Michael, K., & McCathie, L. (2005). *The pros and cons of RFID in supply chain management.* Paper presented at the International Conference on Mobile Business Sydney.

Murphy, P. A. (1996). Does plastic still have a great future? *Credit Card Management, 9*(3), 80-90.

Nixon, B. (1995). The smart card evolution. *America's Community Banker, 4*(5), 21-27.

Shelfer, K. M., & Procaccino, J. D. (2002). Smart card evolution. *Communications of the ACM, 45*(7), 83-88.

Sheppard, J. J. (1999). It's in the cards: basic of magnetic stripe card technology. from http://site117044.primehost.com/inf1.html

Svigals, J. (1987). *Smart Cards: the new bank cards*. New York: Macmillan Publishing Company.

Swartz, J. (1999). The growing 'MAGIC' of automatic identification, *IEEE Robotics & Automation Magazine* (pp. 20-22, 56).

Chapter XI
Geographic Information Systems & Location–Based Services

INTRODUCTION

This chapter is about geographic information systems (GIS) and its relevance to the location-based services industry. One might initially ask how relevant GIS is to a book that is predominantly about automatic identification and its future trajectory. The answer becomes apparent quickly as the reader is introduced to the importance of geocoding information, i.e., geographically linking data such as personal details using a unique ID number. In the past data matching programs have received a great deal of attention from privacy advocates, especially those used for the administration of government procedures. Till now, automatic identification has facilitated electronic services (e-services), allowing an individual to be matched to a fixed address, usually their place of residence. But it is one thing to tag and another to track. Today, we are moving towards a model of tracking and monitoring people as they go about their daily business, in real time. We are no longer satisfied with knowing where an individual lives but we want to know their every move- so that we can estimate traffic congestion on a busy road, design 3G mobile networks that have enough capacity during busy hours, and to ensure someone's safety when adequate supervision is not available.

GEOGRAPHIC INFORMATION SYSTEMS

Geographic information systems (GIS) are playing a crucial role in the success of location-based services (LBS). GIS is defined by Burroughs (1986) as a "set of tools for collecting, storing, retrieving at will, transforming, and displaying spatial data from the real world for a particular set of purposes" (Taylor & Blewitt, 2006, p. 9). Dransch (2005, p. 32) classifies LBS as a subset of mobile geoservices. A location-based service is the ability for an information system to denote the position of a user, based on a device they are carrying or their position in a given context (Gartner & Uhlirz, 2005, p. 159). LBSs have the ability to provide specific, relevant information according to a given "spatial location associated with a physical point or region relative to the surface of the earth (Dawson et al., 2006, p. xv). While a great deal is written about the network technologies that allow for the tracking and monitoring of objects and subjects, GIS is usually considered the add-on feature. However, without GIS, most location-based services would not be plausible as commercial offerings. According to Lopez (2004, p. 171) "LBS consist[s] of a broad range of services that incorporate location information with contextual data to provide a value-added experience to users on the Web or wireless device." It then follows that GIS is integral to the success of LBS (Brimicombe & Li, 2007). Motivations for using GIS in LBS include: cost-effectiveness, service provisioning, system performance, competitive advantage, and database creation, access, and use (Shiode et al., 2004, p. 363).

What is the Difference between GIS and LBS?

Lopez (2004) is extensive in his book chapter on the differences between GIS and LBS. He stipulates that GIS is about mapping, spatial indexing, spatial operators, geocoding and routing technology. LBS on the other hand, is different to GIS because it makes use of information technology and wireless technology. GIS is about maps, people, places, buildings, points of interest, while LBS is about using that basic knowledge to provide some kind of meaningful application such as "find the nearest Automatic Teller Machine" or "help me, I'm lost". Performance, scalability and interoperability are three other differentiators of LBS and GIS. LBS requires numerous components to work together to provide an end-to-end solution while GIS is quite localized in that it manages and stores information using proprietary data structures and models. Consider the location service for WAP phone users in shopping centers, such as the Colombo Centre located in the Iberian Peninsula (Câmara & Dia, 2004). GIS provides the spatial background usually in the form of a map form with georeferenced points of interest while the LBS provides the awareness, the reality of the user's position in a given context.

The Importance of Geocontent to LBS

In his classic text, *Location-Based Services: fundamentals and operation*, Axel Küpper (2005, p. 35) stipulates that while spatial databases and geographic information systems cover a broad range of applications such as surveying and transportation, it is in the context of LBS that "they are important for indicating the positions of one or several targets with respect to geographical content like borders of cities and countries, road networks, or buildings. They are used for mapping spatial location onto meaningful descriptive location information and vice versa, which is referred to as *geocoding* or *reverse geocoding* respectively, as well as for creating digital maps and routing information, or for finding nearby points of interest." Here Küpper is referring to geocontent. Jensen (2004, p. 117) has written that geocontent is *essential* to LBS, citing the metaphor that "[u]sers think of the real content as being located in a transportation infrastructure and access the content via the infrastructure." Jensen uses the example of a point of interest (POI) location which is typically given in terms of a civic address (i.e. containing a street name), and the routing directions for how to reach that destination are given in terms of the transportation infrastructure. However, it is important to note that while LBS uses *location* as a "context parameter to which the presented information is referred", it is about "the complete situation in which a user acts and requires spatial information" that is becoming increasingly important (Dransch, 2005, p. 32). It is not only about *where they are* or *where it is*, but in the context of the time, the temperature, the lighting, the humidity, the precipitation level, the elevation, the sugar level in the bloodstream, the proximity of the user to a shopping mall, to a friend, to family, to normal patterns of behavior including speed and spending patterns. Shiode (2004, p. 352) predicts that this kind of capability- referring specifically to the ability to analyze objects with respect to a particular location in terms of relationships to each other- will have a transforming effect on "average" LBS solutions in the future.

LOCATION-BASED SERVICES

In location-based services, GIS is used to help end-users visually determine where an object or subject has been (i.e. provide a track or breadcrumb of a subject) or to do an instantaneous locate of that subject (i.e. to pinpoint their location). At the same time, the location headquarters requires a visualization of an object or subject every time a device is triggered putting through a request (e.g. an emergency request for urgent assistance). In this instance, using the GIS to see the "locate" information visually is more beneficial than just receiving a longitude and latitude coordinate (Figure 1). Emergency services prefer a civic address or "nearest to" this address than coordinates. The GIS also grants the end-user the ability to check on multiple mobile devices at once with the ability to analyze their spatial relationship. Many industry analysts see GIS as forming the foundation for many LBS developments as a core area in managing, processing and delivering spatial information (Shiode et al., 2004, p. 351). Commercial location-based services that use GIS software include fleet management companies that specialize in all forms of transit, personal locate devices for humans for care, convenience and control purposes, and asset tracking companies which focus on supply chain management and other e-business applications (Michael, 2004). Elliot and Phillips (2004, pp. 14-15) categorize location based services into five groups: product retailing, information, maps, purchasing, and access.

The LBS Value Network

The best way to view GIS with respect to LBS is in the context of a well-functioning value chain or value network. Jensen (2004, p. 116) believes that at a high level of abstraction, the LBS value network "begins with *content providers* that supply various types of content that can be georeferenced to a content

Figure 1. Simplified view of how location based services work

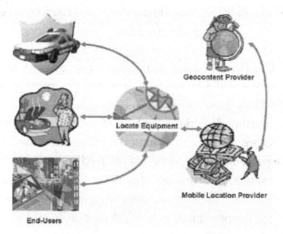

integrator". According to Paavilainen (2001) however, the LBS value chain includes mobile networks, software development, application development, content and online service providers, branded portals, and end-user devices. Here again, Lopez (2004, p. 172f) makes the distinction between the value chain of GIS which is generally limited to the providers of a desktop or client-server solution versus the complex value network of LBS. "Another major difference is that LBSs impose significant technology and service capabilities that exceed the general requirements of static GIS uses." There is now a burgeoning list of stakeholders that are involved in the delivery of a sophisticated LBS application using technologies and techniques that are converging such as telecommunications infrastructure (mobile network), positioning methods, mobile in- and output devices and multimedia cartographic information systems (Gartner & Uhlirz, 2005, p. 159). These are the main prerequisites for the development of applications which use position information as a variable in a system (Figure 2).

The Rise of IP Location-Based Services

Currently, end-users are able to view the results of their requests in an offline mode or an online mode. Offline modes are not very popular but are useful for non-critical applications or where post-mortem analysis is conducted. On-line modes of response are popular because they can reach end users in a relatively short period of time (from 2-3 minutes to a couple of seconds), depending on the network access type (Figure 3). The most popular vehicle for the response to be fulfilled continues to be the Internet, even though the telephone is heavily relied upon in emergency situations. The current state of development is focused on delivering LBS solutions to any access method independent of device type, such as Personal Digital Assistants (PDAs) and cellular phones. The current limitations include device screen sizes and bandwidth availability, although the latter is changing with broadband techniques and third generation networks.

Karimi (2004, p. 7f) emphasizes the impact that wireless networks and Internet-based GISs have had in meeting the requirements of telegeoinformatics, in particular the rising use of mobile location-aware devices. "Wireless networks are the fundamental enabling technology for emerging Internet-based GISs providing access and solutions to both desktop and mobile users." Meng and Reichenbacher (2005,

Figure 2. LBS as a catalyst for information and communication technology (ICT) convergence.

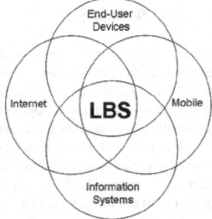

Figure 3. Future Access Types for IP Location (Dawson, Winterbottom & Thomson, 2006). Reproduced with permission from McGraw-Hill.

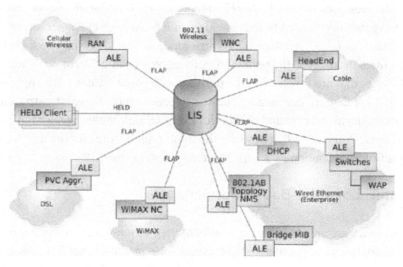

p. 6) identify map-based mobile services as a special type of value-added LBS that "...afford[s] both descriptive information and procedural knowledge." Edwardes et al. (2005, p. 11) discuss the extreme demands that mobile mapping has had on GIS. There is an obvious trade-off between the highly flexible *all you can have and eat* view of GIS (i.e. the endless possibilities one might have through the use of detailed satellite imagery and other rich GIS media) versus the crippling constraints in end-user device screen resolution, limited processing power and irregular patterns of network connectivity. Clearly there is a chasm between the *what is possible in GIS* and the realities in the current state of development in mobile. Gartner and Uhlirz (2005, p. 160) agree that "[t]he possibilities of transmitting spatial information in the context of a determined position by various presentation forms is primarily restricted by the limitations of the used mobile device". This is not to say however, that fixed Internet GISs are not hindered by any limitations with respect to mapping or location-based services but the problems in that environment are different and are mainly preoccupied with licensing issues, royalties and suitable subscriber billing models.

Precision vs. Proximity Location Technologies

The visual precision of a map displaying someone's location is intrinsically linked to the level of detail and preciseness that can be extrapolated from the location determination technology being used in the network. For example, indoor and outdoor applications have differing levels of capability. In some instances, precise location information can be obtained, in others proximity information can be obtained down to a couple of meters, and still in others showing that a subject is within a post code may be the level of refined searching that can be done and subsequently displayed. While precise and proximity polling is available today, it comes at a price. Beyond the cost factor, which will inevitably drop over time, there is the obvious limitation that some technologies work well outdoors (like GPS), while other technologies like wireless fidelity (wi-fi) can be used within a building or campus.

Precision versus proximity can also be determined by how a *locate* of a handset takes place, i.e., is it via a network-based solution by a mobile operator or is it via a handset-based solution (Paavilainen, 2001, p. 169). Handset-based solutions which allow for highly accurate locates, are becoming increasingly popular with mobile handset manufacturers, as prices for GPS receivers fall and innovative software solutions can be built into software on a SIM card. Increasingly humancentric LBS applications are relying on integrated network infrastructures to be able to poll a device out in the field. For example, the Global Positioning System (GPS) is now being used with cellular networks to offer a precise locate using Assisted-GPS (A-GPS) techniques (Taylor & Blewitt, 2006, ch. 4-5). When the device carrying the receiver is out of a cellular footprint range, the service only then reverts to GPS. In this instance, the location headquarters needs GIS beyond that of the purpose of network management.

According to leading researchers in the field, the main research questions in the context of cartographic LBS include: integrative positioning, route information systems, information presentation and visualization (e.g. e-maps and virtual reality). The complementarity between outdoor and indoor positioning will offer powerful surveillance possibilities to governments, employers, and citizens never before seen. Pervasive computing is set to revolutionize the way we live and work and is closely allied to LBS. Jensen (2004, p. 118) also believes that the dynamic union between what he calls *geocontent* and *real content* will offer giant leaps in LBS VAS. In actual fact, he is referring to live geocoding practices which will likely be at the centre of true fourth generation intelligent mobile applications (Timpf, 2006). He writes "[i]n LBS, the special-purpose GIS world and the general-purpose relational data management world need to be integrated."

Case 1: Mobile Location Tracking Applications

The data for the following cases was collected between 2002 and 2004 from three company web sites. The cases stand as a historical snapshot of three early deployments of LBS. Some of the more representative LBS applications on the market in 2004 included: iMode by NTT DoComo, mMode by AT&T Wireless, the Personal Locator by WherifyWireless (Figure 4), and the VeriChip by Applied Digital Solutions. Five years later, in 2009, the capabilities of LBS throughout the world have grown in sophistication and functionality. In 2004, iMode and mMode offered consumers and business users a diverse range of mobile commerce applications, including LBS functions to find people nearby, find facilities nearby, and get directions, weather and traffic reports. The Personal Locator used a GPS wristwatch and additionally took advantage of the wireless operator's footprint within the coverage area to identify an individual's latitude and longitude coordinates (figure 5). The VeriChip device on the other hand allowed for identification of a user in a building and could be used for offender monitoring and patient-supplied healthcare-related information. VeriChip's VeriTrack application offering was marketed as the "who, what and where of your company... VeriTrack is designed to track, monitor and protect all assets within an organization or company, including people." Other niche LBS are those such as the DestronFearing Corporation offering for animal ID, Skye-Eye for asset tracking, SnapTrack for fleet tracking, Starmax's Startrax monitoring system, and CarCom as a locator for cars.

mMode

AT&T Wireless was the first mobile carrier to launch m-Commerce applications in the US in July 2001. Following the success of NTT Docomo's i-mode and c-mode in Japan, mMode provided a value-added

Figure 4. The January 2009 homepage of Wherify which clearly identifies the location-based services opportunities as being focused on "family finder," "social networking," "fleet management," "mobile search and advertising," "asset tracking" and more. Courtesy of Wherify Wireless Location Services.

data-centric package to AT&T's voice and SMS basic plans. Subscribers to mMode could use numerous devices to communicate including IP-enabled phones, PDAs, handhelds and even vertical devices such as the Panasonic Toughbook and Microslate Sidearm. The service was carrier-grade and based on a GSM network architecture that used new network elements, namely the Gateway Mobile Location Centre (GMLC), Serving Mobile Location Centre (SMLC), and the Location Measurement Unit (LMU). The accuracy of the specific location-based applications was dependent upon the general location of the mobile transmission tower most recently contacted by the customer's device. For example, the IP device could be right next to a tower or some fifteen kilometers away. In metropolitan areas the accuracy is greater given the number of base transceiver stations is higher than in less urbanized areas.

"My mMode: This time it's Personal"

mMode is heavily oriented towards the consumer market, although AT&T Wireless also offered package deals to business users specifically for the purposes of email (plus attachments), web access, and remote access. mMode was marketed as the beginning of mLife, next generation services that 'one could not live without' (McDonough, 2002). Among its mCommerce suite that includes news, music and finance services are a number of LBS solutions. mMode's LBS applications were diverse- everything from a mobile traffic report to directions 'to the nearest' and find people nearby (AT&T, 2003). Some of the more creative LBS applications were featured in chat and date, and travel and dining. There were four plans subscribers could choose from including: mini, mega, max and ultra. The plans were charged monthly ranging from $2.99 to $19.99 USD and included a limited megabytes (MB) download. Additional usage fees were charged at between 2c and 0.6c per extra kilobyte (KB) received or sent, dependent on the plan. These fees did not include voice calls and SMS. The mMode service was bundled allowing the subscriber maximum personalization to choose from any application they required. The myMode web site allowed the subscriber to customize their preferences and settings.

WherifyWireless

mMode's location identification was not pin-point such as in the Wherify Personal Locator solution that was based on a combination of GPS satellites and code division multiple access (CDMA) PCS network triangulation methods (Figure 6). The Personal Locator wrist-worn device was accurate within 30 meters of the wearer, possibly even as close as a meter. The GPS device could be controlled by both the subscriber and individual wearer, allowing the parent subscriber to track the wearer, and for the wearer to alert the parent subscriber and/or location centre headquarters in case of an emergency. Coverage was available throughout the US given the GPS capability but was dependent on the PCS network coverage footprint. The Wherify (2004) frequently-asked-questions (FAQs) page stated: *"[i]f a GPS signal is received, but the Locator is outside the digital wireless coverage area or does not receive a digital wireless signal, no location report will be provided. If the Locator receives a digital wireless signal, but no GPS signal is available, a CDMA tower-based location report will be available for emergencies."* On December 30th 2003, Wherify unveiled its new GPS Universal Locator Phone which was targeted at all age groups of both the consumer and business market. After its initial market testing phase, Wherify is now marketing the WheriPhone which has the same functionality, and is small and compact.

Personal Locator "Just For Kids"
In contrast to AT&T Wireless, Wherify strategically chose to enter the market with a niche LBS application for a Personal Locator Just For Kids, specifically targeted at parents of children between the age of four and twelve (Figure 7). The device previously cost $399 USD but was slashed in 2004 for

Figure 5. The prototype GPS Locator for Children with a built-in pager, a request for 911, GPS technology and a key fob to manually lock and unlock the locator. This technology is not currently sold. It is interesting to see purely from a product development perspective, how Wherfy returned to a mobile looking device which could fit in the palm of your hand with a wide range of trendy handset colors to choose from to appeal to the youth market. Courtesy of Wherify Wireless Location Services, 2003.

Figure 6. A five step overview of how the Wherify location based services work. Courtesy of Wherify Wireless Location Services, 2009.

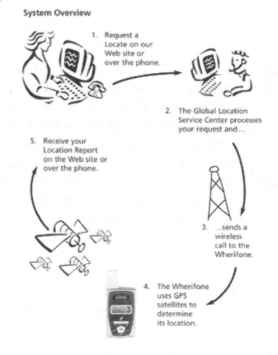

Figure 7. The GPS Locator for Children web page. The slogan reads: "Peace of mind for parents. Cool for kids." Courtesy of Wherify Wireless Location Services, 2003.

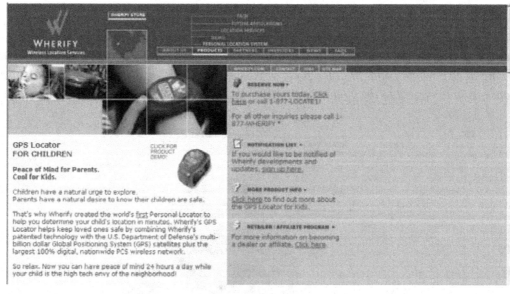

a "back to school special" of $199. Monthly plans for the LBS application ranged from an average of $19.95 to $44.95 dependent on the plan chosen (liberty, independence or freedom). There was a one-time activation fee of $35 USD plus usage fees related to additional page requests above the included locates, additional operator assistance calls and subsequent emergency calls. Wherify (2003) made it clear that it was looking to diversify to other niche applications including Alzheimer's and law enforcement, even though the Locator for Kids was the only marketable application demoed on the web site at the time. In 2009, Wherify was marketing the following location-based applications: family finder, social networking, fleet management, mobile search and advertising and asset tracking, among others.

Wherify's location service centre (LSC) was at the heart of its product innovations. A carrier-class server and software hub, the LSC manages and presents location-based information. Unlike mMode, Wherify utilizes wireless data and aGPS. Consider the following scenario where a parent wants to be reassured that their child made it to school alright after missing the bus. The parent requests a location report via the Internet using a Microsoft IE browser (or ringing the toll-free telephone number). The LSC contacts the child's Personal Locator via the PCS network (if within the footprint), and then downloads the current GPS data and requests a location. Using the data from the LSC, the device that is identified by an electronic serial number (ESN), finds the closest satellite and then computes the longitude and latitude coordinates of the child's location. The Personal Locator then communicates location information to the LSC and the LSC generates a location report for the parent via the Internet. The whole process from request to report takes about sixty seconds. The parent is able to look at the report visually on a scalable map which shows streets and other feature points in a vector or aerial view, using geographic information systems (GIS) capabilities (Figure 8). Each report requested by the parent is logged in the customer's event file database for billing and subscriber profiling. The location database included a time

Figure 8. An online demonstration of the web page that a user might see when they request an aerial map of the location history of a minor. Today it would even be possible to view the locations as a follow up from a Google Street View perspective. Courtesy of Wherify Wireless Location Services, 2003. Google Latitude will have a major impact on the commercial social networking "location-services" offerings.

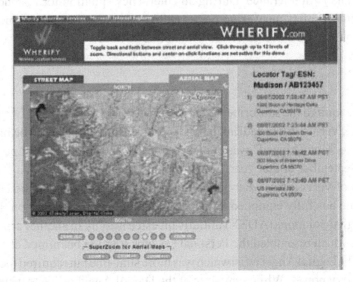

Figure 9. An online demonstration of the web page that a user might see when they request a location history of a minor. The page shows each location, listing a time and date stamp, latitude and longitude location, nearest street address and location type. Courtesy of Wherify Wireless Location Services, 2003.

stamp along with the longitude/ latitude coordinates (Figure 9). The wearer's profile was also stored including: age, gender, height, weight and features.

In 2004, Wherify made no secret of their technology partners. They included an impressive list of companies: SiRF who provide the GPS chipset that is integrated into the Personal Locator based on a-GPS; Qualcomm for the CDMA chipset; Baldwin Hackett & Meeks who are applications developers, Conexant who provide the RF board; Advanced Micro Systems who specialize in flash memory; Compaq for the server technology; Intrado for emergency communications; and GlobeXplorer Online for the component of aerial photography. Security firewalls are paramount in the Personal Locator system as is redundancy and fault tolerance. During an emergency situation for instance, the LSC is even able to interact with public safety answering points (PSAP) through Wherify's emergency operation service. There are customer care representatives available 24x7x365.

VeriChip

While mMode required the subscriber to carry a device, and the Personal Locator required an individual to wear a device, VeriChip was radical in that it required the subscriber to be implanted with a microchip. The campaign to "Get Chipped" was launched in early 2003, and the first person to do so formally was implanted in September of that year. The chipping procedure only lasts a few minutes. In 2003, there were a number of Veri centers where the procedure could take place in the US. There was even a high-tech ChipMobile bus fully equipped to perform the implant procedure, 'on the road'.

Applied Digital Solutions (ADSX) initially invested heavily in another product they called the Digital Angel in 2002, which resembled the Personal Locator solution but aimed at a broader market base than just children. The Digital Angel wristwatch was more slim-line but required the user to carry an additional wallet with battery power. While remnants of the Digital Angel web site were still operational in 2004, it was VeriChip which had become the flagship product of the VeriChip Corporation (a subsidiary of ADSX). About the size of a grain of rice, the VeriChip was the world's first subdermal radio-frequency identification (RFID) microchip. According to an ADSX (2003) press release: "[t]he standard location of the microchip is in the triceps area between the elbow and the shoulder of the right arm."

In theory an implantee could be identified in a wi-fi network, such as in a workplace or university campus. Whereas GPS has limitations in-building locations due to construction materials used, RFID thrives in a local area network (LAN) setting, allowing walkways and door entries to act as scanners. RF energy from the scanner triggers the dormant VeriChip and in turn sends out a signal containing the unique verification number. The exchange of data is transparent and seamless in the case of RFID, there is no need to physically stop to verify a biometric feature- the network is ubiquitous. In another scenario, an individual could be identified by the RFID implant, giving emergency services access to the implantee's medical data and history that could be potentially life-saving. Unlike other fixed services, m-Commerce applications grant the subscriber access to services twenty-four hours a day, seven days a week. In the case of the VeriChip it is not only "always on" but "ever-present" inside the body of the subscriber. Unlike physical biometric attributes, the VeriChip is inconspicuous to the naked eye.

In a recent comment provided by a VeriChip spokesperson, Ms Allison Tomek said to Channel 9 News in New South Wales, Australia, that VeriChip was not pursuing "an implantable microchip with GPS technology" (Asher, 2009). While this statement is in fact probably true, one need only look at the service mix of today's Digital Angel (2009) Corporation which has suddenly made a resurgence back into the global market, after selling its stakes in the VeriChip Corporation late last year (RFID News, 2008). It is hard to see what went wrong in just a little over a year since the two organizations agreed to develop an "implantable glucose-sensing microchip, negating the need for diabetics to draw blood to monitor their blood glucose levels" (Sensors, 2008). According to the homepage of the Digital Angel Corporation (2009), the company currently specializes in "GPS and RFID products... utilized around the world to save lives, ensure the safety of food supply, reunite loved ones and improve the quality of life." For Digital Angel it is clear that accurate identification, location tracking and condition monitoring are important humancentric applications that will converge.

"Get Chipped" with VeriChip: "Technology that Cares"

There was little information on the ADSX web site about the pricing of the VeriChip, however it was stated that the global VeriChip subscriber (GVS) registry subscription fee is $9.95 USD monthly. There was a cost for the implant medical procedure as well, although this was not provided. In 2002 the first one hundred pre-registered persons were granted a $50 USD discount on the chipping procedure (ASDX, 2003). The pricing for the new VeriPay and VeriGuard services had yet to be published on the WWW. The "Trusted Traveler" and residential security programs (i.e., prisoners serving their sentence from home) are two examples of VeriGuard LBS applications. One desirable feature of VeriGuard was that it could operate in conjunction with other auto-ID technologies like smart cards and biometrics, rendering customer legacy systems reusable.

VeriChip was based on RFID. RFID networks are usually small in scale when compared to nation-wide or global networks. They include the following components: the RFID transponder, a reader that captures information, an antenna that transmits information, and a computer which interprets or manipulates the information gathered. In the case of VeriChip, there was a requirement that each subscriber registers their personal details (and other relevant information they desire) on the GVS database. In 2004, all the transponders issued by VeriChip were passive but it is likely that active transponders will be issued in the future, despite the fact that they require on-board battery power to operate internal electronics. When an individual passes an associated scanner, information is read and sent to the computer via an antenna. Dependent on the application, a log may be retained or the implantee's location updated a predefined number of times in a set period.

GEOCODING FOR BUSINESS APPLICATIONS

Geocoding with the intent of conducting geodemographic analysis for business applications is the process of linking intelligence data (e.g. customer counts) to longitude and latitude (*x* and *y*) co-ordinates based on a spatial reference (Harris et al., 2005). This reference may be a street address, a post code or state. Geographic coding is like placing a pin on a map for each record in a database thus linking each pin to the corresponding data (Kennedy, 2006; MapInfo, 1998). Geocoding has become synonymous with converting street addresses to longitude and latitude coordinate positions (Schiller & Voisard, 2004, p. 32). Geocoding methods include: the direct survey and property of boundaries, simple database queries, and other specialized geocoding options (Cowen, 1997). Motivations for geocoding for business applications may include for strategy, logistics support, operational support, marketing, and service (Keenan, 2005, ch. 1; Pick, 2005).

One can geocode against almost any level of detail whether it be linked to region, line or point objects. Almost all data has a geographic unit it belongs to, even data that seemingly looks unstructured at first glance. Commonly defined boundaries include: administrative, political, telecommunications, social and land-use. Data linked to line objects include: roads, rivers, contours, flight paths, teletraffic and transport routes, fiber links. Data linked to points include: landmarks, buildings/ dwellings, points of interest, civil services, and utility points. In human geography, analysts often use geocoding as a way to link spatial information with a new set of data they have generated or manipulated. This can then be used in the process of thematic mapping or districting.

The Process of Geocoding

On the process of geocoding, Cowen (1997) writes that a feature "must have a field which can be linked to a geographic base file with known geographic coordinates". For instance, a database of information can be used to join the geographic coordinates of the base map with address details. The *geocode table* is that foreign table the end user wants to import into the GIS. It can take the form of a text file (comma separated value .csv, or .txt), spreadsheet or database. The user must specify which column is being used to geocode (if there are several keys defined or various location data). The boundary column is a column that allows the user to run a geocode on a partial set of data, for example, statistical local areas (SLA) within a given statistical division (SD). The *search table* is that table which is already native to the GIS. It consists of a base map that has associated data stored in a table. When geocoding the user also has the option to signify which regions, lines or objects have been successfully geocoded by displaying a designated symbol on the centroid of the object after the parse has been completed.

Geocoding can be done in a manual, interactive or automatic fashion. When a user is not confident about the quality of the data they are trying to attach to a spatial reference they will probably select the *manual* geocoding process. This requires the user to hand select an item from the search table to match the base map. This is a detailed process and while accurate is unfeasible for large batches of geocoding.

Automatic geocoding occurs when the unique keys of each table are compared and only those records with an exact match are processed. Those records that remain ungeocoded remain unlinked. *Interactive* geocoding works to bring to the attention of the user, only those records that the software has not been able to automatically link. The user is then required to manually intervene to link each record in an external dataset and match it correctly to a record on the base map. Geocoding requires that at least one field in each table is defined as the unique key. In the base map, it then follows that the unique key must have a geographic context. Simple geocode results will often stipulate how many records were geocoded, how many remain ungeocoded and how many have been previously geocoded.

Geocoding Software

Geocoding is a fundamental feature of all geospatial applications. Most GIS software has built-in geocoding functionality and in addition some offer add-on specialized geocoding engines built for larger tasks. The add-on geocode modules allow for the conversion of the geocode files into a database format, then software records are parsed and geocoded. An output file is also generated indicating the geocode status of all records, and subsequently map points are created (MapInfo, 1998, p. 2). More advanced geocoding software can help users match individual credit information down to an individual in a dwelling. By locating individuals to their home, a bank can use a Marking Customer Information File (MCIF) to determine for instance, which branches are running efficiently and which may be closed (Reider, 2003, p. 44). Retailers or election campaigns can also target market direct mail based on the results of geocoding (Harris et al., 2005, pp. 63f).

Schiller and Voisard (2004, p. 164) believe that a geocoder service should support the following features: (a) given an address, the address-matching geocoding algorithm should be able to determine the x and y position, (b) handle more than one address in a single geocode request, (c) fuzzy address matching where an incomplete address is given and data returned after normalization, (d) count the number of exact matches as a subset of the total number of records parsed, (e) provide information on the quality of the result using a special pre-defined match code (e.g. where an exact match was not found,

Table 1. Sample geocode output table structure

Field Name	Data Type	Size	Description	Sample content
Street	Character	Up to 512	Street number, name, and type	Level 4, 67a Smith Street
Suburb	Character	Up to 37	Suburb name	Wollongong
Post Code	Character	4	Post code number	2500
State	Character	3	State	NSW
X_Coord	Decimal	11,0	Longitude of geocoded point	Blank for output
Y_Coord	Decimal	11,0	Latitude of geocoded point	Blank for output
Result_code	Small integer		Geocode result code (i.e. match)	Blank for output
Parsed address	Character	40	Parsed street address	Blank for output
Parsed suburb	Character	40	Parsed suburb	Blank for output
Boundary Tag	Character	11	ID of independent boundary	Blank for output

indicate whether the record has been locked to the centroid of a street or a post code or other). Table 1 shows the table structure of a file that is about to be geocoded and the field names of where the results post geocoding will be stored. Specialized geocode software like MI's MapMarker Pro allow the user to save settings within configuration files, so as to ensure options have remain unaltered when future geocodes are performed.

Limitations of Geocoding
The process of geocoding is dependent on the number of records in each table. It takes longer to geo-code databases that contain millions of records than smaller databases with only a couple of hundred records. Central processing speed, the amount of random access memory (RAM), and storage space are all important factors in geocoding large amounts of data. Processing can occur in batch mode or single file mode, and different batches compared based on a pre-defined configuration. Different geo-coders have different thresholds for processing based on the way they work but a rule of thumb is not to geocode in excess of 1,000,000 records at a time. Commercial off-the-shelf data is also limited in how much assistance it can grant the user who tries to reconcile the "ungeocoded" records with actual physical locations. Newly erected dwellings and new estates are just some of the issues users encounter when dealing with movements of people and business locations.

Old, Dirty, Incomplete, Incorrect, Unstructured or Foreign Data

The success of geocoding all depends on how clean the data sets are. "It is not uncommon to have a geocoding hit rate of under 50% on your first attempt" MapInfo, 2002, p. 140). Consider variations in the way names, companies, dates, phone numbers are recorded and the resultant issues that would arise in a custom GIS (SearchSoftware 1997, pp. 7-8). The old adage, Garbage In/ Garbage Out (GIGO) could not be more appropriate than in the context of geocoding. Dirty data can have a large impact on the number of geocoded records and on the length of time the user spends debugging. This is true in particular of street-level data (see Table 2). Are records incomplete or incorrect? Have certain keywords been omitted or abbreviated in data entry? Is data free of spelling errors? What happens in the case of street corners, or post office boxes, or floors and suites, shopping malls, or roads that are so long they are differentiated by the words East or West, North or South? What happens if the same postcode has multiple streets or roads with the same name? Some conventions and standards do exist but they are hardly followed. The problem with geocoding is that the user is seldom in charge of the data they are given to geocode. The data has either come from a third party organization, a department who has kept records on an ad-hoc basis, a piece of telecommunications equipment whose database is almost impossible to decode, or a customer who is willing to divulge only so much of their intellectual property.

Even when the data is clean, how to join it to spatial references that were created before or after the data set is a complex problem on its own. Trying to match records from different vintages almost al-ways affects the overall number of successful hits obtained (Sears, 2004). For example, census-defined boundaries like statistical local areas (SLAs) may change names from one census to the next or grow to encompass more collection districts (CDs) within their bounds. Any change in numerical values or alphabetical content in the unique key also means that a match does not occur. Consider post codes in the United Kingdom. Harris et al. (2005, p. 114) make the point that even post codes do not stay constant. And with that inconstancy, almost always comes changes to postal geography. Consider another scenario also, where the creation of industry-specific boundaries have been created for historical reasons, such as telecommunication exchanges. One might be able to geocode the number of telephone lines for each

Table 2. Errors in geocoding (e.g. Address Data Entry)

Errors that occur in Geocoding:
1. spelling errors
2. incorrect address number
3. incompatible abbreviations
4. ambiguous address

Examples:
- Smith Street, Wollongong
- Smith St, Wollongong
- Sith St, Wollongong
- Smith Street, 2500
- Smith Road, 2500
- Smith Lane, 2500
- Smith Place, 2500
- 67a Smith St, Wollongong
- Level 4, 67a Smith Street, Wollongong
- Level 4, 67a Smith Street East, Wollongong
- Level 4, 67a Smith East Street, Wollongong
- Fourth Floor, 67a Smith Street, Wollongong
- 67a, Fourth Floor Smith Street, Wollongong
- 67a/4 Smith Street, Wollongong
- 4(67A) Smith st, Woll
- Crnr Smith and Johnson Lane, Wollongong
- 1 Johnson Lane, Wollongong
- 1 Johnson Ln, Wollongong
- 1 Johnston Lane, Wollongong
- 1 Jonson Ln, Wollongong
- 1 Jensen Ln, Wollongong

exchange, but as soon as one attempts to geocode post code-level information to exchanges a problem arises in an irregular spatial fit.

Many companies are now trying to tap into unstructured data sets as a form of rich intelligence. Mapping this data into a physical space is an admirable aim of any organization but is a long process. One does not always know what they are looking for when they start out, so one way to narrow the possibilities down is to consider the question of one's digital map granularity. Data in a language other than English (particularly non-character based languages) may also present a stumbling block for users, despite the fact that the process of geocoding remains unchanged in this context. One can always revert to using ASCII or Unicode during the pre-geocode stage of data trimming, cleaning, concatenation and searching, and then reapply the appropriate font style post-geocode. A precautionary measure in this situation would be to hire a local planner who has the language skills to check the results of the analysis in the event that errors have crept through without notice. Anthes (2005, p. 61) goes one step further and calls the process of geocoding from external and internal sources "tricky" and emphasizes that "[t]here is a limit to what you can do with GIS technology and how much you want to trust maps" (Anthes, 2005, p. 61).

The success of geocoding accuracy is also about the type of application requirement one has- if it is a critical application it must be precise- but if it is not, then interpolating based on dwelling frontage or floor space, is an equally valid approach. For example, a user could begin by gathering the start and end coordinates of a street segment, identify the address ranges for that street, and then approximate a "fix" for a given address based on the range divided by the number of households (Schiller & Voisard, 2004, p. 60). Interpolation is a good approach for estimating demand in a given area, but it would not be useful for precision planning such as in the case of local councils who need to be able to overlay geocode map points with cadastre plots and perhaps other raster imagery.

BUSINESS INTELLIGENCE SOURCES

Geocoding becomes extremely powerful when multiple sources of intelligence are brought together telling the story of a bigger picture (figure 4). In private enterprise internal intelligence is used alongside external intelligence (Michael, 2003, p. 496). In this instance, customer address detail records may be geocoded and used in tandem with government statistical information. By using this approach, one can make certain aggregate assumptions on household income, household size, and telecommunications needs.

From Postal Codes to Pinpointing Households

McCurley (2001, p. 223) writes that although the standardization of mail addresses is a fairly well studied problem, it is complicated by the fact that each country has its own set of rules. Each postal address is typically made up of several fields- the street number and street name, the post code ID, and the post code name with any number of variations on format and content. Compare for instance post codes in the United Kingdom, with post codes in the United States, China, Australia, and Greece. Even when a successful geocode has occurred it does not imply accuracy. University campuses in Australia are renowned for being spread over many kilometers, each with their own local mail facilities. Mapping data to a centroid of the campus cadastre is not good enough for most applications.

Enter the global street databases which are usually maintained through government bodies bestowed with the authority. In Australia, G-NAF is the Geocoded National Address File which brings together the resources of thirteen government agencies. G-NAF is considered the ultimate solution to a problem that has been plaguing large organizations like telecommunications operators who have spent in some cases hundreds of thousands of dollars on this problem. In the past, wrongly embedded data in the base search map subsequently meant that wrong data was being geocoded. The Postal Service in the United States distributes a similar product to G-NAF called Tiger/Zip+4 containing 35 million records, and the United Kingdom has the Ordinance Survey that has 25 million address points. In addition, the U.K. have a product called Code-Point that "gives coordinates for the 1.6 million different postal codes within England, Scotland, and Wales. Each postal code contains an average of fifteen adjoining addresses. The resolution of this data is 1 meter" (McCurley, 2001, p. 224). Much of the trend toward geocoding at the address level was borne out of the federal census (Brassel et al., 1977, p. 79). Data is also being resold in packages like BusinessMap Pro that show customer lead information by size and type of business based on the Standard Industry Classification (SIC) code. Data also typically found in Dun & Bradstreet MarketFind sources exists within a GIS. For example, BusinessTracker provides a list of more than 10 million businesses that you can search and display by company name, location, SIC code, size by sales volume or employees, or classification" (Hollander, 1998, p. 78). TeleAtlas and Navtek are two more companies that have a global focus on the collection of location information.

The Risks of Geocoding in Mission Critical Systems

In his book *Geographic Information Science: mastering the legal issues*, Cho (2005, pp. 356-358) masterfully discusses the importance of quality and liability. Schiller and Voisard (2004, p. 32) echo these sentiments- accuracy is critical to the quality of the results. Unfortunately the first indication that there are problems with geocoded information is when something goes wrong- either mail is sent to the wrong address, or even worse, a major accident takes place (Cho, 2005, pp. 357f). Embedded data is becoming more and more invisible to the user and error detection harder and harder. Take for example the 1999 bombing of the Chinese Embassy in Belgrade by United States military forces. The target had previously, and wrongly, been identified as the head office for the Yugoslav Federal Directorate for Supply and Procurement (FDSP). Instead, what actually stood in the target location was the Chinese Embassy. The bombs, all GPS-guided missiles reached their geographic target successfully, killing three Chinese journalists and injuring twenty embassy staff. In later press releases and formal statements of apology, the U.S. government admitted that the bombing was both an error and an accident. The positioning technology had functioned correctly but the knowledge systems supporting it had failed (Michael & Masters, 2006, p. 211).

THEMATIC MAPPING IN THE TELECOMMUNICATIONS INDUSTRY

Thematic mapping is that part of cartography that deals with mapping data on a particular theme (Carter & Icove, 1976, p. 164). The word *thematic* refers to the theme of the map, that value which is chosen

Table 3. Sample table for thematic mapping (target market- residential)

Collection District Zone	Homes Passed	Cable TV Subscribers	Cable Internet Subscribers	ADSL Internet Subscribers
Osborne St	100	30	20	30
Armstrong St	250	75	50	75
Wilson St	75	12	8	2
Fern St	600	220	180	190
Pacific Ave	400	100	70	85
Geering St	150	20	10	45

Table 4. Sample table for thematic mapping (target market- business)

City Building Address	Number of Floors	Number of Large Businesses	Number of Small-to-Medium Businesses	Estimated Total Number of Desktops
57 George St	45	1	70	1500
101 Collins St	67	3	102	2200
1500 Pitt St	20	0	48	770
99 Castlereagh St	55	1	99	2000
540 Macquarie St	69	2	144	2555
2 Grosvenor Plc	9	0	12	320

for a given location, illustrated by a selected color or pattern (Reider 2003, p. 43). Thematic maps link a data element to an underlying geographic unit, such as a building location, major road, a cadastre parcel, census district, post code, region or province (see Table 3 and 4). Items that may be mapped in telecommunications range from an operator's market share for data services, the number of potential customers by market segment by census district, and the types of assets owned by a bandwidth provider across regions. A selling point of most geographic information systems (GIS) software today is that they allow for fast manipulation of tables and maps, granting even novice users the ability to analyze and visualize their data using thematic mapping. The technique does more than just graphically show you your data however, it lets you see it mapped to a real world context, revealing patterns and trends that are almost impossible to detect in lists (MapInfo 2002, p. 209).

In 1977, Brassel et al. (pp. 84f) defined twelve types of thematic maps including: choropleth mapping, graduated circle maps, ring diagrams, graduated rectangle maps, frame diagrams, graduated segmented circle maps (pie charts), point symbol mapping, contour mapping, 3-D mapping, fence maps, dot maps, and cartograms. It is important to note, that just one year prior to that, Carter and Icove indicated there were only three main types: dot (e.g. density in terms of dots per area), choropleth (e.g. based on a fixed area unit of data collection such as a census tract) and isarithmic maps (e.g. smooth continuous surface maps such as elevation or population density). Advancements in the cathode rode tube (CRT), terminals, printers, and plotters have revolutionized what can be achieved with thematic maps. Users today have the capability to plot detailed ISO A0 formatted paper maps in a matter of minutes. Yet in the late 1970s, papers were being published about resolving screens into a "matrix of 25 rows by 80 columns with colored characters on colored backgrounds" and describing the limitations of terminals "in terms of the selection and brightness of the eight colors, the dimensions of the cells and the ability to mix colors in small cells" (Carter and Icove, 1976, p. 163).

Different Types of Thematic Maps

Malerba et al. (2001, p. 291) distinguish between thematic maps and composite maps, the former being concerned with one geographic feature and the latter with several separate thematic maps (one for each layer). Today's GIS software allows for thematic maps to take the following form- district maps, dot density maps, graduated maps, grid maps and graphic maps such as pie charts and bar charts (Table 5). The MapInfo GIS, for example, allows for a variety of *ranged value* thematic maps including: equal count, equal ranges, natural break, quantiling, and standard deviation. Depending on the type of data being analyzed, or the desired resultant effect, the user will choose accordingly. It should be stated however, that choosing the wrong ranged value technique will result in a misleading visual result, even if a cartographic legend accompanies the map. Fotheringham et al. (2000, pp. 72-92) describe some of the varying techniques used in exploratory spatial data analysis and emphasize the need to produce maps that do not misrepresent reality. For the greater part it is about understanding your dataset well enough to know how it should be displayed as well. MapInfo (2002, p. 250) also describe the use of bivariate thematic mapping which "uses point or line objects to represent two thematic variables." For example, a star can represent one variable, such as the number of mobile phone users, while a gold fill for the star represents their annual number of SMS messages.

Data Sources for Thematic Maps

Data for thematic maps can come from (a) the same table, (b) different tables such as in the case of bivariate maps, (c) by joining different tables together based on a unique key, or (d) by creating expressions which change the values in your table for a meaningful way. Sources of data for thematic maps can come

Table 5. Thematic mapping in telecommunications by business function

Sales and Marketing
- Show operator and service provider market share by region
- Highlight the operator's coverage area of service offerings (e.g. ADSL)
- Show the monthly expenditure for telecommunications services per household for a census district
- Understand the business target market by standard industry code (SIC) and size of business
- Highlight specific subscriber calling patterns, and communities-of-interest for on-selling value-added services
- Help aid in the definition of sales territory districting and sales force automation of field personnel
- Define different geographic types like metropolitan, urban, suburban and rural areas based on demographic data like population density
- Define different types of target markets based on demographic values
- Identify the number of business by road or the number of computer terminals by building
- Estimate the bandwidth requirements of businesses for customer leads
- Represent operator market shares for different regions of nations
- Look at the spread of main offices to branch offices of major companies

Engineering
- Show regulatory communication boundaries as defined by the government
- Estimate the auction price of spectrum allocation lots (e.g. 3G mobile strategy for contiguous/non-contiguous purchases of lots)
- Show numbering plans in a given country with respect to incumbent switch exchanges
- Show different *rights-of-way* that exist for backbone networks such as sewage routes, electricity grids, highways, or other
- Consider varying roll-out options for a new technology (e.g. fast roll-out, slow roll-out, or cascaded roll-out)
- Show different types of network equipment elements for a proposed network plan, based on their capacity and coverage constraints
- Show the spread of wireless service penetration versus wireline service penetration for a new network proposal
- Define high-level coverage areas for base stations catering for the busy hour of traffic and indicate the number required before exporting the information into a more specialised engineering program like plaNET
- Engineer elements in the network properly by homing equipment to the nearest neighbour node, based on a distance or other variable
- Show transmission routes in terms of their capacity
- Show the provisioning of services by type (present and future)
- Traffic engineering estimates for voice and data services showing demand in the busiest hours of the day
- Show the costs for delivering a call in different zones in terms of interconnect fees and other charges

Managing Resources
- Display the different types of assets that an operator has currently deployed and highlight legacy equipment and those due for decommissioning
- Characterise low-grade and high-grade copper twisted pair and other physical characteristics and show these for upgrade and maintenance purposes
- Indicate potential optimal location centres to house telecommunications equipment
- Show the building infrastructure owned or leased by a given operator
- An ISP's points of presence (PoPs)
- Indicate what equipment or infrastructure is leased and what is wholly owned

Business Planning
- Highlight areas of high customer spend per annum per census district
- Indicate the share of customers that use different types of services such as Internet or cable television for the prospect of bundling services
- Help aid investment decisions for strategic planning purposes (e.g. compare introducing new services in India as opposed to Hong Kong)
- Forecast demand over a period of time for a given service set
- Determine financial payback of new services based on customer density and expected adoption rates

from in-house business intelligence systems such as customer datawarehouses, or external intelligence such as free public data, or even commercially available data. The better the source of information in terms of vintage, data detail at the smallest object or region level, the better the value of the thematic maps. Network planners for instance find it useful to create thematic maps at varying layers of detail- by region, census tract, administrative boundary, clutter type, road, cadastre, building, longitude/latitude coordinate. Brassel et al. (1977, p. 83) make the point that users are restricted in creating particular types of thematic maps based on the data they have in their dataset. "For instance, specific thematic data (aggregated-disaggregated) require particular spatial-referencing information, whereas geometric data (centroids-segments-area outlines) govern the kinds of thematic display possible."

When to Use Thematic Maps

Thematic maps are ideal for executive strategic level presentations when the fine details are not a requirement, but an overall big picture view needs to be gained. Many planners and designers rely on the results of thematic mapping for timely decision making (Table 5). For example, thematic mapping can assist with the decision of where to place a base station tower- in terms of its proximity to human (e.g. schools) and natural features (e.g. crown land). Sales people also require thematic maps for identifying new customer leads and for market segmentation purposes. Telecommunications companies also have a large base of assets in terms of equipment and other pieces of infrastructure that age over time. Asset managers are beginning to rely more and more on thematic mapping, especially for managing customer installations for contractual or compliance purposes. In an informal survey of a global telecommunications switching vendor in 2001, it was identified that out of the 80,000 employees hired by the company, about 2,000 employees were "developer" users of geographic information systems software, and even more were recipients of the information produced by the GIS.

Steps in Producing a Thematic Map

Some software programs offer automated features that allow users to create thematic maps using wizard-like procedures. Initial steps require the user to choose from a template of options, including size, color, type, and effect. The next step requires the user to indicate which table and attribute is to be used for the thematic mapping. At this stage the user has the option of creating an "on the fly" join between a base map and an imported table or using the expression function to do some limited additional calculations on specific data. The user may also choose whether to ignore null values or blank fields from the overall dataset, especially if what they are trying to limit options to a few choices and there are too many zero values. The final step requires the user to check whether the settings they chose in step one are still suitable for the display of their map. For example, if the symbol size chosen in the template is too big or tool small, this can be changed at this final stage. The legend also allows for titles, subtitles and custom labels to be recorded and to determine the label ordering in ascending or descending order. Some GIS software even grants the user the option to save templates that they have custom created. For an overview of how to map geodemographic information with GIS with commercial examples, see Harris et al. (2005, pp. 88-102).

CONCLUSION

Consider the possibility of a *Google Street View* 'in motion'. Imagine not only being able to view your house or that of your neighbor's but with the potential of subscribing to a service that let's you 'watch' breadcrumbs of people's behavior. While the ability to geocode large numbers of records has been around a long time, the telecommunications infrastructure to support real-time location based services is only just beginning to sprout. The problem with too much data, e.g. location information being captured every three seconds, is that the margin for error is great dependent on the measuring instrument in question. Not only is there the possibility of errors creeping into geocoded data due to the data matching principles employed but also we cannot be certain that because an individual is located somewhere during the day, that they are/are not engaged in a particular act. For example, my location profile may show that I am at the university library but in no way does that mean that I am actually studying or researching.

The problem with constant location tracking is that commercial entities and the government (e.g. law enforcement agencies) will inevitably use the advanced capabilities to generate minute by minute thematic reports either for the conduct of social sorting (Lyon, 2004) or for evidence in a court of law. The danger with the creation of thematic maps based on pre-defined categories is that assumptions about a given individual will be based on data pertaining to speed, distance, time and altitude. Even worse still will be the co-location of persons in a questionable zone of activity that may have absolutely nothing in common and never met previously, adding new meaning to words like "suspect" or "alleged" or "possibility". The scenarios in this context are endless. Today the mobile phone has become an extension of the person, just like one's DNA or ID number. Increasingly, people are taking notice of the potential for surveillance and some are even opting out altogether, preferring to have their mobile phones permanently switched off, save for emergencies (Renegar & Michael, 2009).

REFERENCES

ADSX. (2003). Implantable Personal Verification Systems. *Applied Digital Solutions*. Retrieved 15 April 2004, from http://www.adsx.com/prodservpart/verichip.html

Anthes, G. H. (2005). Beyond ZIP codes. Computerworld. 39(38), 56, 58, 61.

Asher, J. (30 January 2009). Humans 'will be implanted with microchips'. *ninemsn.com.au*. Retrieved 1 February 2009, from http://news.ninemsn.com.au/technology/735519/humans-will-be-implanted-with-microchips

AT&T. (2003). Feature and Services User Guide. *AT&T Wireless*. Retrieved 15 April 2004, from http://www.attwireless.com/personal/features/mmode/mmode_guide.jhtml

Berkin, M., Clarke, G., Clarke, M. & Wilson, A. (1996). Intelligent GIS: location decisions and strategic planning. Cambridge: GeoInformation International.

Brassel, K. E., Utano, J. J. & Hanson, P. O. (1977). The Buffalo crime mapping system: a design strategy for the display and analysis of spatially referenced crime data. ACM Siggraph, Proceedings of the Fourth Annual Conference on Computer Graphics and Interactive Techniques, 78-85.

Brimicombe A.J. & Li. C. (2007). Location-Based Services and Geo-Information Engineering. Chichester: Wiley.

Bureau of the Census. (1970). Census use study. The Dime Geocoding System, 4, 1-38.

Câmara, A.S. & Dia, A.E. (2004). Location-based services for WAP phone users in a shopping centre in J. Stillwell & G. Clarke (eds) Applied GIS and Spatial Analysis, West Sussex: John Wiley & Sons, 55-70.

Carter, J. R. & Icove, D. J. (1976). The application of the Intercolor 8000 terminal to thematic cartography. ACM Siggraph Computer Graphics, Proceedings of the Third Annual Conference on Computer Graphics and Interactive Techniques SIGGRAPH '76, 10(2) 163-166.

Cho, G. (2005). Geographic Information Science: mastering the legal issues. Australia: John Wiley & Sons.

Cowen, D.J. (1997). Unit 016 - Discrete Georeferencing. URL: http://www.ncgia.ucsb.edu/education/curricula/giscc/units/u016/u016_f.html, Australia.

Dawson, M., Winterbottom, J. & Thomson, M. (2006). IP Location: Geographic Location Measurement, Delivery and Conveyance. New York: McGraw-Hill Communications.

Digital Angel. (2009). Digital Angel. Retrieved 1 February 2009, from http://www.digitalangel.com/

Dransch, D. (2005). Activity and context- a conceptual framework for mobile geoservices in L. Meng, A. Zipf & T. Reichenbacher (eds) Map-based Mobile Services: Theories, Methods and Implementations, Munich: Springer, 31-42.

Edwardes, A., Burghardt, D. & Weibel, R. (2005). Portrayal and generalisation of point maps for mobile information services in L. Meng, A. Zipf & T. Reichenbacher (eds) Map-based Mobile Services: Theories, Methods and Implementations, Munich: Springer, 11-30.

Elliot, G. & Philips, N. (2004). Mobile Commerce and Wireless Computing Systems. England: Addison Wesley.

Foody, G. M. (2000). Image classification with a neural networks in P.M. Atkinson & N.J. Tate Advances in Remote Sensing and GIS Analysis, New York: John Wiley & Sons, 17-38.

Fotheringham, A.S., Brunsdon, C. & Charlton, M. (2000). Quantitative Geography: Perspectives on Spatial Data Analysis. London: Sage Publications.

Gartner, G. & Uhlirz, S. (2005). Cartographic location-based services in L. Meng, A. Zipf & T. Reichenbacher (eds) Map-based Mobile Services: Theories, Methods and Implementations, Munich: Springer, 159-171.

Harris, R., Sleight, P. & Webber, R. (2005). Geodemographics, GIS and neighbourhood targeting. West Sussex: John Wiley and Sons.

Hollander, G. (1998). BusinessMap Pro turns information into clear images. InfoWorld. 20 52(1), 78.

Jensen, C. S. (2004). Database aspects of location-based services in J. Schiller & A. Voisard Location-Based Services. Amsterdam: Elsevier, 115-147.

Jones, K. & Hernandez, T. (2004). Retail application of spatial modelling in J. Stillwell & G. Clarke (eds) Applied GIS and Spatial Analysis. West Sussex: John Wiley and Sons, pp. 11-53.

Karimi, H.A. (2004). Telegeoinformatics: current trends and future directions in H.A. Karimi & A. Hammad (eds) Telegeoinformatics: Location-Based Computing and Services, London: CRC Press, 5-25.

Keenan, P. (2005). Concepts and theories of GIS in business in J.B. Pick (ed) Geographic Information Systems in Business. Hershey: Idea Group Publishing, pp. 1-19.

Kennedy, M. (2006). Introducing Geographic Information Systems with ArcGIS: featuring GIS software from Environmental Systems Research Institute. New Jersey: John Wiley.

Küpper, A. (2005). Location-Based Services: fundamentals and operation. England: John Wiley & Sons.

Laserna, R., Landis, J. & Strategic Mapping. (1989). Desktop Mapping for Planning and Strategic Decision-Making. New York: Strategic Mapping.

Lopez, X. R. (2004). Location-based services in H.A. Karimi & A. Hammad (eds) Telegeoinformatics: Location-Based Computing and Services, London: CRC Press, 171-188.

Lyon, D. (2004). Surveillance Technologies: Trends and Social Implications. In OECD (Ed.), *The Security Economy* (pp. 127-148): OECD.

Malerba, D., Esposito, F., Lanza, A. & Lisi, F.A. (2001). Machine learning for information extraction from topographic maps in H. Miller & J. Han (eds), Geographic Data Mining and Knowledge Discovery, London: Taylor and Frances, 291-314.

MapInfo. (1998). GeoLoc. Australia: MapInfo Australia.

MapInfo. (2002). MapInfo Professional: User's Guide v7.0. New York: MapInfo Corporation.

MapInfo. (2004). MapInfo MapMarker UK 2.0 takes address cleaning & geocoding to new levels of accuracy and consistency. M2 Presswire. 16 November 2004, 1.

McCurley, K. S. (2001). Geospatial mapping and navigation on the web. *ACM*, WWW10, 221-229.

McDonough, B. (17 April 2002). AT&T Wireless Pushes mLife with mMode. *CIO Today*. Retrieved 6 April 2004, from http://cio-today.newsfactor.com/perl/story/17307.html

Mendez-Wilson, D. (2001). Plotting the location points. Wireless Week. 7(7), 28.

Meng, L. & Reichenbacher, T. (2005). Map-based mobile services in L. Meng, A. Zipf & T. Reichenbacher (eds) Map-based Mobile Services: Theories, Methods and Implementations, Munich: Springer, 1-10.

Michael, K. & Masters, A. (2006). The advancement of positioning technologies in defense intelligence in H. Abbass & D. Essam (eds), Applications of Information Systems to Homeland Security and Defense, IDG Press, 211.

Michael, K. (2003). The importance of conducting geodemographic market analysis on coastal areas: a pilot study using Kiama Council, in C. D. Woodroffe & R. A. Furness (eds.), Coastal GIS 2003: an integrated approach to Australian coastal issues, Wollongong: Centre for Maritime Policy, 481-496.

Michael, K. (2004). Location-based services: a vehicle for IT&T convergence in K. Cheng et al. (eds), Advances in e-Engineering and Digital Enterprise Technology, London: Professional Engineering Publishing, 467-477.

Paavilainen, J. (2001). Mobile Business Strategies: Understanding the Technologies and Opportunities. London: Wireless Press.

Pick, J.B. (2005). Geographic Information Systems in Business. Hershey: Idea Group Publishing.

PSMA (2006). G-NAF. URL: http://www.g-naf.com.au/about.htm, Australia.

Reider, S. (2003). Map your market with GIS. ABA Bank Marketing. (35)7, 42-46.

Renegar, B.D. & Michael, K. (2009), Privacy-value-control harmonization for RFID adoption in retail, IBM Systems Journal, 48(1), in press.

Robinson, A.H. (1982). Early Thematic Mapping in the History of Cartography. Chicago: University Of Chicago Press.

RFID News. (13 November 2008). Digital Angel sells stake in VeriChip. *RFID News* Retrieved 1 February 2009, from http://www.rfidnews.org/2008/11/13/digital-angel-sells-stake-in-verichip

Schiller, J. & Voisard, A. (2004). Location-Based Services. Amsterdam: Elsevier.

SearchSoftware (1997). The Math, Myth and Magic of Name Search and Matching: see how to improve your business applications. Connecticut: SearchSoftware America.

Sears, B. (2004). Geocoding challenges: why accuracy matters. Directions Magazine. URL: http://www.directionsmag.com/article.php?article_id=558&trv=1, 20 April.

Sensors. (24 May 2007). Digital Angel, Verichip to Design Implantable Microchip. *Sensors Magazine*. Retrieved 1 February 2009, from http://www.sensorsmag.com/sensors/article/articleDetail.jsp?id=429191

Shiode, N., Li, C., Batty, M. et al. (2004). The impact and penetration of location-based services in H.A. Karimi & A. Hammad (eds) Telegeoinformatics: Location-Based Computing and Services, London: CRC Press, 349-366.

Stolz, P. (2000). Voice a 'killer app' for E911. Wireless Week. 6(50), 73.

Taylor, G. & Blewitt, G. (2006). Intelligent Positioning: GIS-GPS Unification. West Sussex: John Wiley & Sons.

Timpf, S. (2006). Wayfinding with mobile devices: decision support for the mobile citizen in S. Rana, & J. Sharma (eds) Frontiers of Geographic Information Technology. Heidelberg: Springer, 209-228.

Wherify. (2003). Wherify Wireless GPS Locator For Kids. *Wherify Wireless*. Retrieved 15 April 2004, from http://www.wherifywireless.com/prod_watches.htm

Wherify Wireless. (2004). Frequently Asked Questions. Retrieved 15 April 2004, from http://www.wherifywireless.com/faq.asp

KEY TERMS

3D Maps: Using a process of rendering, three dimensional shapes are projected in two dimensions in computer graphics. 3D thematic maps are becoming increasingly popular with large companies who are even utilising "fly-bys" over terrain.

Automatic Geocoding: Automatic geocoding occurs when the unique keys of each table are compared and only those records with an exact match are processed.

Bivariate Thematic Maps: Allows comparisons to be made between records and to draw conclusions about variables in the entire dataset.

Cadastral Map: Maps defined by local councils indicating land ownership of a given area.

Context-Aware Systems: These are systems that support location-based services that rely on the dissemination of contextual information such as temperature.

Data Cleaning: Data sets to be used for geocoding may contain embedded characters that affect the geocoding process, even if they cannot be seen by the user. Cleaning prepares data for geocoding by applying standards, trimming, concatenation or separation of some content in the table.

District Maps: Displays common data elements in the same symbol, line or region colour. For example, shading for regions that are managed by the same salesperson is color-coded identically.

Dot Density Maps: Displays the data in your table as dots on a map. Each dot has a corresponding value. When the number of dots is multiplied with that value, the total value for that region is obtained. This is usually used to show the number of consumers or employees in a given area.

Exact Match: Occurs in geocoding when the source and target information are exactly the same-word for word, letter to letter.

Geocode: The process of assigning X and Y coordinates to records in a table so that the records can be shown on a map.

Geocontent Provider: A geocontent provider is a type of content provider who specialises in the management, storage and distribution of spatial content at multiple levels of detail- including topographic information, points of interest, and postal information. Content providers need to ensure their databases are up-to-date especially when distributing information to mission-critical systems in the government sector.

Geodemographics: Geodemographics is the analysis of people by where they live and work.

Geoparsing: Geoparsing is the recognition of geographic context, whereas geocoding is the process of assigning geographic coordinates (McCurley, 2001, p. 222).

Geosorting: Once data has been geocoded then the GIS can perform a number of spatial queries allowing users to conduct geosorting (Birkin et al., 1996, p. 31).

Graduated Symbol Maps: Displays a symbol (such as a person, or dollar sign) for each record in the table. The size of each symbol is directly proportional to the data value.

Interactive Geocoding: When you geocode interactively you are not changing the data record, you are redirecting the software to look for different information.

Interpolation: A simple method of geocoding which constructs a set of new data points from a discrete set of known data points.

Joining Tables: When data is stored in two separate tables and required for the one thematic map, a join must occur to bring the data together. The join feature adds a temporary column of information to the data set.

LBS Value-Chain/Network: Various stakeholders (including geographic content providers, handset manufacturers and network access providers) work together to offer an end-to-end LBS solution. The value chain of LBS is considered complex and meshed.

Localisation: Localization (noun), locate (verb), is the determination of the locality (position) of an object or subject.

Location-Based Services: Typical LBS consumer applications include roadside assistance, who is nearest, where is, and personal navigation. LBS business applications differ in their focus and many are linked to core business challenges such as optimising supply chain management (SCM) and enhancing customer relationship management (CRM). Some of the more prominent LBS business applications include: fleet management (incorporating vehicle navigation), property asset tracking (via air, ship and road) and field service personnel management (i.e. people monitoring).

Longitude and Latitude Coordinates. A coordinate system for representing geographic objects on a map.

Parsing: Parsing is the recognition of geographic context.

Pervasive Computing: Pervasive computing is a term that is being used to describe future LBS applications in 4G mobile networks. These services will be rich in location-based information, in context awareness, and will depend on intelligent agents and intelligent devices with unobtrusive access, anywhere, anytime.

Pull Services: A type of on-the-spot location-based service. These are generally considered easier to implement than LBS push applications because a polling request only occurs when the services are needed, i.e. the network does not have to track the user continuously. For example, locate your friends or family, emergency services, yellow pages inquiry services, Go2Systems.

Push Services: A type of location-based service based on real-time monitoring. For example, LBS applications such as retail alerts based on the position of the subscriber, cell advertising, traffic reporting.

Ranged Maps: Display data values across different types of objects. For example, the annual telecommunications household expenditure by collection district.

Telematics: Global Positioning System (GPS) chipsets are being increasingly installed in computers and mobile communication technology to allow them to be tracked and monitored. The word telematics is synonymous with vehicles and intelligent road systems, but is beginning to be used in the context of people tracking.

Thematic Templates: Thematic templates allow users to reuse the same values and settings (e.g. colors) when they create new thematic maps. They can be considered thematic defaults which users can alter at any time.

Thematic Values: Any value (string, number or other) that is used in a thematic map to represent something meaningful.

Theme Legends: Legends are integral to thematic maps. They contain textual descriptions of what is being represented in the map including headings, names of attribute columns, symbols used, and other optional information such as counts and the number of objects. The metadata aspect of legends is paramount.

Ungeocoding: Ungeocoding is the process of removing objects that have been attached to data records either because the relationship is no longer valid, or an error in attachment has occurred. Users have the option of ungeocoding the whole table or selected records (MapInfo 2002, p. 162).

Workspace: A workspace saves an instance of a user's "work" at a given point in time. It means that any previously opened tables and windows can be automatically reopened at the same location, with one menu selection only.

Interview 11.1
The Geographer

Professor Brimicombe, London, England
Interview conducted by Katina Michael on 12 October 2006.

INTERVIEW

Katina Michael: What are the main areas that the Centre of Geo-Information Studies is involved in, in the UK?

Professor Brimicombe: We concentrate on three areas; one is GIS coupled with numerical simulation modeling which could be related to the physical or social environment (Figure 1). The second is related to data mining that is knowledge extraction from large databases such as crime databases, health databases or business transaction databases where a key kind of explanatory dimension is where things happen so it is spatial. And the third area is location based services.

Figure 1. An aerial raster image that can be registered in a geographic information system. Additional attributes can be combined to individual map objects to show street names, points of interest (POI), and other custom information.

Katina Michael: Given the Centre has three arms I was very intrigued by the geo-information studies title. Could you tell me the history about how that was established?

Professor Brimicombe: Going back to the early 1990s when I was establishing a department in the Hong Kong Polytechnic University from scratch which would focus on land surveying and GIS. And an issue was what to call the department so I called it 'Land Surveying and Geo-Informatics'. Because GIS is a technology and we need a word which reflects a discipline rather than a specific technology. So I chose the word "Geo-informatics" and it was hyphenated. Then University of New South Wales wrote a paper in an Australian surveying journal saying since Hong Kong had chosen this word 'geo-informatics' they were quite keen to have a word like "Geo-matics" for their department, so there was competition for students. When we came to this research, I didn't want to call it "Geo-information Systems", people don't really understand what Geo-Information Engineering is at the moment, which is kind of engineered solutions that are reliable and trusted that use spatial technologies and so on, and the word geographical would get muddled up with geography departments and then people in the UK despise "Geo-studies". Hence we got Geo-Information Studies.

Katina Michael: I'd like to focus on geo-information engineering, as it is not well understood in the literature. You identified location based services, could you talk to me about what your description of geo-information engineering is?

Professor Brimicombe: I can use an analogy here, when you get in a lift and press a button for the 5th floor you don't really want to know how lifts are designed. Nor do you really want to know what an electrical, structural and manufacturing engineer needs to know in order to produce a lift. All you need to know is when you press the button it will take you to the 5th floor, it will take you there safely, and reliably. And you'll get out and think nothing of it. This is the goal of Geo-information Engineering. In the past there has been too much sanctity about GIS as being something complicated for gurus to do for other people. As long as we have that attitude of GIS we'll never get anywhere. The things that are really successful are what we might call invisible technologies. We want to put on the air conditioner so we point a remote device at it, click, and it comes on. You don't need to be an Einstein to do it, a kid can do it. But when we get to the stage where the types of products we create around spatial data and technologies are that easy to use that they can be integrated into daily life so we don't have to think about whether or not they exist or how they work in their complexity, I think we have achieved a kind of integration into mainstream. Which is where GIS needs to go...

So GIE is about getting spatial technology into the mainstream, so in effect they are invisible and can be used by ordinary folk that have no knowledge of GIS whatsoever. So it might be a way-finding application on a mobile phone. Where you don't need to know how GIS works or how you are positioned and how the databases are working behind- you just get the information from a fairly simple interface by using a device. When you send a text message you don't need to know the word processing behind it you just write it and send it.

Katina Michael: In that context, I guess you are aware of the quite innovative applications of companies like WherifyWireless where they have care applications and wander alerts based on GPS devices such as wristwatches and so forth. Do you describe those kinds of applications as GIE applications?

Professor Brimicombe: I'm not familiar with the specific services of that company but you're your description, yes, I would call that a GIE solution. The individual doesn't really need to know how the device works. If the device works reliably then they are achieving their goal, I just wonder what these wristwatches do when you go into a building. For example on my mobile phone which is run by Vodafone in the UK. It's got a kind of 'where am I' type of function, it doesn't have GPS in the phone but on the network triangulation, on the network side it is very "iffy". On different days, I can stand in the same place and it will tell me I am in a different place each time. These places can be quite distant from where I am so it is not really in that respect a trusted technology yet, because it will not even be an invariant solution to the problem; and directions it might give me to my nearest ATM/Cinema might assume I am starting in a different place than where I am and therefore not be very useful. It is kind of moving in that direction.

Katina Michael: Professor, do you think these types of applications will ever be "trusted" applications?

Professor Brimicombe: I'm sure they will, it is a matter that many of these applications that are being put onto mobile phones that are location aware, quite often don't really involve people with a spatial background with respect to how they are designed and implemented. I'm not really knocking computer scientists here but there are different ways into solutions, but where we effectively have a spatial problem there should really be someone like a spatial scientist involved in working out adequate solutions. I'm not sure it will come because although there is a huge research agenda, it is only on the way, and we have just scratched the surface. There is some way to go yet.

Katina Michael: I guess you've been in the area quite a while now and you've seen the type of data resolution that was around in the 1980s and the type of data resolution we have available to us today. Could you comment on that?

Professor Brimicombe: Ok, for good location based services we have to consider both the spatial and temporal granularity of the data we are using. Sure in the late 1990s we saw the kind of bursting of the data bottleneck, we were always hampered before then either by the ability to process large amounts of data or the availability of large amounts of data… now that is all gone. I can do millions of records on my laptop quite quickly so really there is no problem there so databases grow on a daily basis. But at the moment, in the UK for example, the amount of detail we have at address level is still quite poor. There is something called "address point" which is a co-ordinate per address but I mean what is happening at that address is really not there in a structured way at the moment (Figure 2). So the temporal granularity needs to be increased, to almost real time. So we are still some way in terms of data collection technology, in order to achieve this. We need to work at the integration of many sources of data whether it is electronic yellow pages or company web pages. *There needs to be a view that is not going to be collecting data just by satellite imagery or GPS from the tops of cars, we need to have web crawlers that go out and check spatial databases for information that is already out there waiting to be harvested and used. So we need to have a step change on what it is, to collect spatial and attribute data but it will mean potentially we will have huge databases, therefore I don't think we will have single repositories of very large datasets, we are going to have distributed networks of databases which will need sharing protocols and purchase protocols. And I think it will all be agent driven, so from your mobile phone you will activate an agent which then goes out and finds the information you require and there may be a number of different business models to do that.*

Figure 2. The MapMarker® Australia product allows for intelligent address matching. In this pilot study, residential records were geocoded to street address locations in a suburb of the Australian Capital Territory. Left: pinpoint address matching using the household owner or occupier surname. Right: pinpoint address label showing street number and street.

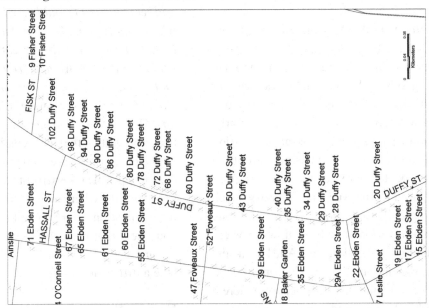

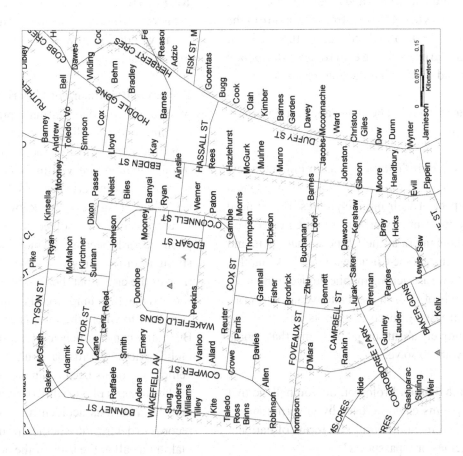

Katina Michael: Could you perhaps provide us with some examples of the more innovative Location Based Service applications you have been involved in or have heard of.

Professor Brimicombe: Well there are beginning to be "buddy systems", let's say for example a group of individuals who are going out for a day on a cycling spree who may not stick together rigidly and therefore you may want at any one time to know where your buddies are. Similarly, on your mobile phone you can use an application where you can have your buddies marked out to know which of them are nearby at a particular moment to find them. And that is pretty much like tracking children. Another interesting one is mobile gaming which involves knowing where individuals are as part of the game. And I think, the most extraordinary one I've seen is from Finland in the North of Lapland, an application where a dog is fitted with a GPS and mobile phone device so that the owner of the dog from the nature of the dog's bark can know whether or not the dog is out of range and by speaking to the dog via the mobile device and direct what the dog has to do.

Katina Michael: The latter application is certainly very innovative!

Professor Brimicombe: I was in Finland a few weeks ago, in Helsinki, and Nokia showed me a new aspect of their mobile phones. If you have a menu in front of you, written in Chinese, you point the camera at the Chinese characters and it will translate the Chinese for you… What this means is we are getting mobile devices with multiple kinds of tools in them and we need to work with harnessing these new tools and thinking imaginatively about spatial problems that people might want to solve.

Katina Michael: Professor, do you believe that LBS systems could be used by governments to track citizens in the future, in terms of national ID schemes or e-passports?

Professor Brimicombe: *I'm living in the UK, where on your daily activities you on average end up on 300 CCTV cameras anyway. I think there has to be the trade-off between privacy and security and I wouldn't want to second guess where that is going but a mobile phone company knows where you are at certain times anyway. So I think in the UK we are pretty used to the fact that we are being observed and tracked at the moment. For example, we have something called an "Oyster Card" in London.* If you regularly use a route, then they will email you to say when engineering works are going to take place (figure 3). Some people take affront when somebody has been tracking where they go but on the other hand, the application offers you a kindly service to let you know that next week your usual journey is going to be hell-on-earth, "can we suggest you take a different route".

Katina Michael: I noted that one of the research areas was crime analysis in your department and I was wondering how GIS was currently being used to track crime?

Professor Brimicombe: The crime analysis that we do is largely a data mining application through to numerical modeling of crime patterns, both from the perspective of the location of crimes through to modeling victims of crime. So we can do repeat victimization etc. We have a whole series of tools (Figure 4). I do know of one instance where a crime was solved through the mobile phone records because the individual had a fairly strong alibi for being in a particular town at the time of the crime but their mobile phone records showed that they made a call from a cell that was very near to where the serious crime took place. But police can routinely ask for mobile traffic and mobile phone records particularly in the case of vehicle accidents because in the UK it is against the law to use a phone whilst driving. Every time there is a serious accident they will check the records to determine whether the driver had been making a call at the time of the accident.

Figure 3. In Australia Google Maps now has the capability to provide a street view of the physical environment. The end-user simply types in an address and a photograph of the location is displayed. 'Spying' on one's neighbor has never been easier. Permission to reproduce this photo in this book was granted by the owner of 56 Barden St, Tempe, NSW, Australia 2044.

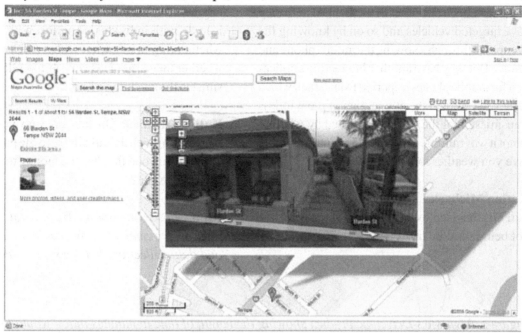

Figure 4. The same house depicted in figure 3 from an aerial perspective. Google Earth can now be used to 'see into' what once used to be a private backyard.

But as for tracking criminals from their mobile phones, yes, there are incidents and we know from the news, for example, the Israelis track people they want to target using mobile devices because there have been a number of incidents where they have targeted vehicles and so on by knowing the occupants through knowing the mobile phone and things. But they have another interesting application for mobile phones, reported from Israel, which is they have noted the attenuation of the wireless transmission of the cell was affected by whether or not it was raining. Therefore they could actually give you weather forecasts cell-by-cell.

Katina Michael: I guess on the flip side of that will GIS be used by professional thieves, if it is not being used by them now?

Professor Brimicombe: I don't know to what extent GIS is used by professional thieves now, thieves may well use in-car mapping navigation systems, which is a kind of form of geo-information engineering. I think a lot of petty criminalization is to do with individuals comfort with maps and whether they are familiar with an area or not. But whether they organize crime or use GIS for more sinister things, I don't know.

Katina Michael: On that note do you believe there is too much data available to the public today basically anyone that has the money to pay for it, can purchase it?

Professor Brimicombe: *Well, a lot of people react to the amount of mechanical observation and data collection that goes on virtually every*

Figure 5. MapInfo's Drivetime product showing the length of time in minutes that it would take to traverse particular streets.

transaction that we do in our lives as the Big Brother Syndrome. I think the only kind of counter to the BB syndrome is whether anybody can find out anything about anybody else, you counteract the BB effect. So if the government wants to know about me, then I can equally well know about the government. Or if my neighbor wants to know about me, I can equally well know about my neighbor (figure 4). The BB effect is neutralized by in effect, access by all to all.

Katina Michael: That is a very interesting perspective. In terms of national security, like in the UK we've had a couple of terrorist attempts that have happened very recently. Do you think the authorities, will use GIS for national security purposes?

Professor Brimicombe: GIS is reused routinely by the police and security agencies in the UK they are not strangers to that. The type of work that we have done, has allowed geographical fixing of routinely recorded data to be increased (table 1). A typical match of a crime database against addresses only results in a 40% match of geocoding (table 2). We've provided tools that will increase that to over 90%. We've also produced tools that will allow repeats to be easily identified whether they are victims, individuals or locations. So the technologies are there to analyze, that's no problem; to match whether individual analysts are going to use the newer aspects of GIS to dig deeply or whether GIS is going to be used in a very simple way.

Let me explain that further, a lot of the analogies that we do are not done in GIS. GIS is used to organize data, to integrate on small geography, to visualize what is being geo-coded. But then if we need to do text or data mining these are all done outside GIS because GIS really does not have the capability. Really then, we get into a geo-computational environment where we are bringing together all sorts of tools, adaptive

learning, neural nets, or just spreadsheet macros written on Excel or in Access, but then to do the analysis work we can just put it back into GIS so we can visualize what the results are. So it is a matter of whether these agencies are using the kind of computational analytical tools and are passing data backwards and forwards between tools and then passing them back into GIS. I know GIS is routinely used, but whether it is used for more than a hot spot map, I can't say.

Katina Michael: Professor, could you tell us a little bit about the projects you are working on specifically related to environmental applications and location-based services.

Professor Brimicombe: One of my colleagues is developing agent based driven tools for really testing the fitness of use of environmental modeling. If I explain that, when you go and collect a data set you should be able to get meta-data about how it is collected, what its level of accuracy is etc. What meta-data cannot tell you is the fitness for use of that dataset in a particular application when combined with other data sets. So you have to go through geo-analysis using a form of simulation tools etc in order to work out where the combinations of data sets are fit for use after you have run a numerical simulation model. This can be done manually but it would be smarter to use agents that have different kinds of functions to allow you to build various tests that can tell you whether or not you are going to get sufficient fitness for use at the end.

On the same tack I have a PhD student that is working on a variogram agent, as one of the key problems in geo-graphical data is spatial dependence. One of the key ways of looking at this is through the variogram, but the variogram is highly dependant on individual skill. So by developing an agent that can learn from people building variograms, it has various components going and collecting data in analyzing the internal structure of the data and then deciding what kind of steps and lags or models would be appropriate and so on. I've also got another student working on the LBS aspect- on automated updating of route networks. In other words, when you are on a new road that is not in the in car navigation system, the navigation system just says 'turn back'. *Instead of doing that if it went into data collection mode, we are looking at using neural nets to decide where that individual has gone, whether they have really left the road and are wondering around a pasture side or whether they might really be on a new road that hasn't been mapped. If there are sufficient indicators to add the track of that vehicle as a new road on probation, and if the track is used a sufficient number of times by different vehicles then it can correspond say, for example, to a picture that appears on satellite imagery as a road with a particular geometry, then we can add to the database without having to wander around wondering where new roads are.*

Katina Michael: Thank you for accepting to be interviewed for our forthcoming book. It will be a book full of different perspectives across disciplines.

Professor Brimicombe: I think this will be a valuable contribution to the literature.

Katina Michael: Thank you.

Professor Brimicombe: So I wish you all fortitude with that.

Katina Michael: Thank you.

KEY TERMS

Address Point: A coordinate per address. In Australia G-NAF provides this functionality.

Big Brother Syndrome: The invasion of privacy through the use of surveillance techniques. A metaphor based on George Orwell's novel *1984*. Personal privacy is eroded as Big Brother exercises power through 24x7 surveillance leading to the elimination of private thoughts.

Coordinate: Any of the magnitudes which define the position of a point, line, or the like, by reference to a fixed figure, system of lines, etc. For example an x,y coordinate in a Cartesian coordinate system, or a latitude or longitude location in an earth coordinate system.

Database: An organized collection of data in the form of text, numbers, maps, graphics or other. A database typically has fields and records.

Data Mining: The process of sorting through large amounts of data and picking out relevant information.

Geoanalysis: Any type of analysis that is based on a geographic unit of detail often displayed in the form of a thematic map.

Geocode: The process of assigning X and Y coordinates to records in a table so that the records can be shown on a map.

Geocomputational: Computation that requires knowledge of a geographic component on which to base processing to derive a solution.

Geographical Information Systems (GIS): An organized collection of computer hardware and software designed to efficiently create, manipulate, analyze, and display all types of spatially referenced data.

Geo-Information Engineering (GIE): Simplifying the act of retrieving location-related data by constructing applications that do not require previous technical knowledge by the end-user. GIE is about encapsulating the level of complexity of GIS applications so that location services become more accessible.

Localisation: Localization (noun), locate (verb), is the determination of the locality (position) of an object or subject.

Location Aware: These are systems that support location services that rely on the dissemination of location information such as a civic address.

Location-Based Services (LBS): LBSs are services that use the location of the target for adding value to the service, where the target is the "entity" to be located.

Map: A representation, on a flat surface, of a part or the whole of the earth's surface, the heavens, or a heavenly body.

Numerical Simulation Model: A mathematical model which attempts to find analytical solutions to problems which enables the prediction of the behavior of a particular system from a set of parameters and initial conditions.

Organized Crime: Crime in which the acts of wrongdoing are part of the operation of a criminal organization.

Oyster Card: The Oyster card, a blue credit-card sized stored value card which can hold a variety of tickets, is a form of electronic ticketing used on public transport services within the Greater London area of the United Kingdom.

Physical Environment: Of or relating to material things. Environmental geography combines physical and human geography and looks at the interactions between the environment and humans.

Spatial: Of or relating to space; existing or occurring in space; having extension in space.

Telematics: Global Positioning System (GPS) chipsets are being increasingly installed in computers and mobile communication technology to allow them to be tracked and monitored. The word telematics is synonymous with vehicles and intelligent road systems.

Variogram: A function used in geostatistics for describing the spatial or the temporal correlation of observations.

Section III
The Social Implications of Auto-ID and LBS Technology

Chapter XII
The Auto–ID Trajectory

INTRODUCTION

This chapter considers the automatic identification (auto-ID) trajectory within the context of converging disciplines to predict the realm of likely possibilities in the short-term future of the technology. The chapter relies heavily on presenting a cross-section of research conducted primarily up until 2003 when the first commercial chip implant occurred, as a window to forecasting what kinds of technologies may become widely diffused by 2020. After showing the evolutionary development from first generation to third generation wearable computing, medical breakthroughs using implantable devices are documented. The findings of the chapter suggest that before too long, implantable devices will become commonplace for control, convenience and care-related applications. The paradigm shift is exemplified in the use of auto-ID, from its original purpose in identifying humans and objects to its ultimate trajectory with multifunctional capabilities buried within the body.

THE RISE OF WEARABLE COMPUTING

According to Siewiorek (1999, p. 82) the first wearable device was prototyped in 1961 at MIT (Massachusetts Institute of Technology) by Edward Thorp and Claude Shannon. The idea for the device came in 1955 in an attempt to be able to predict roulette. However, the term "wearable computer" was first used by a research group at Carnegie Mellon University in 1991, coinciding with the rise of the laptop computer (early models of which were known as "luggables"). Wearable computing can be defined as: "anything that can be put on and adds to the user's awareness of his or her environment... mostly this means wearing electronics which have some computational power" (Sydänheimo et al., 1999, p. 2012). While the term "wearables" is generally used to describe wearable displays and custom computers in the form of necklaces, tie-pins and eyeglasses, it is the opinion of the researchers that the definition should be broadened to incorporate PDAs (personal digital assistants), e-wallets, and other mobile accessories such as cellular phones and smart cards that require the use of belt buckles or satchels attached to conventional clothing.

Before the widespread diffusion of personal computers (PCs) and laptops it was auto-ID devices in the form of bar code cards, magnetic-stripe cards and smart cards that were 'luggable' and to some degree wearable with the aid of an external clip or fastener. In the case of contactless smart cards they could even be carried in a wallet or purse or in a trouser or shirt pocket. While they did not have the same processing power as PCs or laptops, auto-ID devices did point to a practical ideal, in terms of their size. IBM and other computer manufacturers have quickly caught onto the notion of wearable computing- their vision of a portable computer that could be worn instead of carried has been well-documented. According to Phil Hester of IBM's Personal Systems Group, the wearable PC, a hybrid device, would allow a user to freely walk around a building connected to a wireless network and perform all the day-to-day functions like send emails but with the added option of voice navigation/recognition (Wilcox, 1999, p. 1).

Wearable computing is about to reinvent the way we work and go about our day-to-day business, just like auto-ID devices did in the 1970s and 1980s. It is predicted that highly mobile professionals will soon take advantage of smart devices that will be built into their clothing so that they will be able to "…check messages, finish a presentation, or browse the Web while sitting on the subway or waiting in line at a bank" (Schiele et al., 2001, p. 44). And not just professionals but society at large is taking advantage of the latest gadgetry. MIT's "Group-Media" are creating socially intelligent wearables for the following projects: The Jerk-O-Meter, MoodPhones / VibePhones, Elevator Rater, Human Interest-Meter, Speed Dating v2, Negotiations, and Movie Audience Reactions (Pentland, 2009).

1G WEARABLES: MOBILE DEVICES, PDAS AND PAGERS

Early prototypes of wearable computers throughout the 1980s and 1990s could have been described as outlandish, bizarre, abnormal-looking or even weird. For the greater part, wearable computing efforts have focused on head-mounted displays (a visual approach) that unnaturally interfered with human vision and made proximity to others cumbersome (Sawhney & Schmandt, 1997, p. 171). But the long-term aim of research groups is to make wearable computing inconspicuous as soon as technical improvements allow for it (Figures 1 and 2). The end user should look as 'normal' as possible (Mann, 1997, p. 177). One need only consider the size of the first mobile phones in the early 1990s; they weighed the size of a small

Figure 1. Self-portraits of Mann with wearable-computing gear from the 1980s to the 1990s. Professor Mann started working on his WearComp invention as far back as his high school days in the 1970s. Courtesy of Professor Steve Mann.

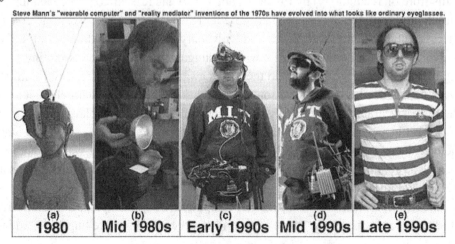

Figure 2. Steve Mann is featured here with the 1981 wearable computer (wearcomp) combined with a 1970s lightspacer apparatus for wearable computational photography. Courtesy of Professor Steve Mann and John Wiley and Sons (Mann, 2001).

brick, were expensive, and very few people thought that widespread diffusion would be achieved. Yet today, numerous countries have reached in excess of 80 per cent penetration, which equates to a mobile phone for almost every adult in that country. As Cochrane (1999, p. 1) observed, "[t]oday, mobiles are smaller than a chocolate bar and cost nothing, and we can all afford them. And they are not bolted into vehicles as was originally conceived, but kept in pockets and hung on trouser belts."

Today it is commonplace to find professionals and younger technology-savvy students not only carrying mobile phones but 3G-enabled notebooks, GPS-enabled PDAs and even miniature secondary storage units that can hold hundreds of gigabytes worth of data. To this list Starner (2001a, p. 46) adds a pager, electronic translator and calculator wristwatch. Starner even made the observation that "[s]ome people wear too many computers." He noted that these separate computers have similar components such as a microprocessor and memory. In other words, there is a fair amount of redundancy in the separate devices. Wearable computers of the future will integrate all these functions into the one unit. The hope of wearable device developers is that the capabilities will converge to such an extent that the user will not consider the mobile phone as separate from a PDA or a PDA separate from a notebook. Nokia's 6260 classic series is an example of this integration- it has a 5 megapixel camera with Carl Zeiss optics and flash, both HSUPA and HSDPA support, WiFi, aGPS, Bluetooth, web browser, music player and more. Global positioning systems devices especially are becoming increasingly powerful. The Trackstick Pro (2009) is also another example of powerful computing one can carry to geotag photos or create logs of routes taken. Trackstick Pro is now being marketed to a whole range of segments including: fleets, contractors, emergency services, commercial equipment, personal and business, sporting activities, government and national security. At just a little over $350 Australian dollars there is technology that can now be used for covert surveillance.

Case 1: Industrial Application

Wearable computers should not just be considered solely for personal electronics but suitable for industrial purposes as well. Several companies like Symbol Technologies (now Motorola), Honeywell and Xerox have researched industrial wearable devices for over a decade, along with names completely focused to this cause including Xybernaut and ViA (Figure 3-5). Perhaps one of the most well-known industrial uses

Figure 3. The wearable computer for the professional. The left eye is free to roam the physical world while the right eye looks into a small monitor- a window into the virtual world. Courtesy of Xybernaut Corporation, 2002.

Figure 4. The wearable computer targeted at the socialite market. The lady depicted in the picture looks hip. With battery pack in pocket, mouse in hand, and crown on head, she is ready to make her presence known in the City. Courtesy of Xybernaut Corporation, 2002.

Figure 5. The wearable computer for the paramedic, as a first responder to a trauma victim. The paramedic follows the appropriate instructions via the headset view, and acts accordingly. Courtesy Xybernaut Corporation.

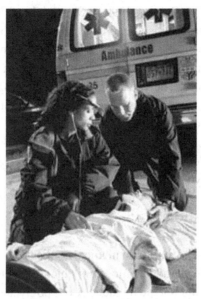

of wearable computing is the United Parcel Service (UPS) case study. In 1995, UPS challenged Symbol Technologies "…to create a Wearable Data Collection device for their package loaders" (Stein et al., 1998, p. 18). Symbol's goal "was to create a wearable system that increased efficiency and productivity through mobility and hands-free computing and scanning" (Stein et al., 1998, p. 19). After considerable feedback between users at UPS and Symbol and evaluations for possible disease transmission given the wearable computer would assume skin contact, the Wrist Computer was released in 1996. At one point Symbol was shipping about seventeen thousand units per month to UPS, such was the success of the product. What is interesting to note is that Stein et al. (1998, p. 24) report that the "[t]he initial response from users who had been using hand-held computers was to not want to give up the wearable once they tried it." Perhaps the same can be said for other wearable devices. How many individuals can do without their mobile phones today, or PDAs, or camera phones or recorders?

2G WEARABLES: E-WALLETS AND WRISTWATCHES

As wearable computing devices get smaller and smaller there has been a conscious effort to create an electronic wallet that combines the traditional wallet, the computer and communication technology. For some time many believed that the Mondex smart card system would act to revolutionize the way people exchanged money. AT&T was so convinced that it invested in developing an electronic wallet. The "Mondex Wallet allows users to perform on-line transactions and view balance and transaction information stored on their card" (Cooper, 1999, p. 87). The Mondex Wallet has not reached its potential diffusion rates but this has more to do with market maturity than anything else. While the Wallet is not the sophisticated type of wearable device that Mann and others envision, it was an incremental step towards that vision. Swatch had also introduced an electronic wallet in the form of a wristwatch, known as Swatch Access. The wristwatch featured a "miniature antenna and a computer chip, similar to those used in conventional smart card payment systems. This allowed users to perform transactions using money stored on the chip" (Cooper, 1999, p. 87). Trials of the watch have taken place in Finland's transport system. Another more sophisticated wristwatch solution known as, Digital Angel, "offered a unique combination of GPS, wireless Internet and sensor technologies" (ADS, 2002b). The all-in-one unit which looks like a conventional watch can monitor temperature, contains a boundary alert function and has panic button feature. The versatility of the technology is seen in its wide range of formats and configurations such as a pager-like device, necklace, pendant, bracelet, and even belt buckle (ADS, 2002b). In 2008, Williams reported that NTT DoCoMo was very close to prototyping a bio-sensing cell phone which carried a DNA chip. One main obstacle remained- how to get molecules from the user's body to the cell phone. The idea of molecular communication was raised and preliminary testing took place at the University of Tokyo.

Case 2: Medical Application

Wearables have also found a niche market in medical applications. Hinkers et al. (1995, p. 470) describes a small wearable device that continuously monitors glucose levels so that the right amount of insulin is calculated for the individual reducing the incidence of hypoglycaemic episodes. Hinkers once predicted the use of automated insulin delivery systems as well which are currently under development. Medical wearables even have the capability to check and monitor 26 different products in one's blood (Ferrero, 1998, p. 88). Today medical wearable device applications include: "…monitoring of myocardial ischemia, epileptic seizure detection, drowsiness detection… physical therapy feedback, such as for stroke victim rehabilitation, sleep apnea monitoring, long-term monitoring for circadian rhythm analysis of heart rate variability (HRV) (Martin et al. 2000, pp. 44)." Some of the current shortcomings of medical wearables are similar to those of conventional wearables, namely the size and the weight of the device is too heavy. In addition wearing the devices for long periods of time can be irritating due to the number of sensors that may be required to be worn for monitoring. The gel applied for contact resistance between the electrode and the skin can also dry up causing nuisance. Other obstacles to the widespread diffusion of medical wearables include government regulations and the manufacturers' requirement for limited liability in the event that an incorrect diagnosis is made by their equipment (Martin et al., 2000, p. 44). More recently the issue of privacy has been raised especially for medical wearable devices that are applied within shared hospital facilities where access to results could be abused (Kargl, Lawrence, Fischer, & Lim, 2008).

Of worthy note here is how much we have come in just a little under 10 years. Wearable devices are usually no longer clunky. In fact, consider Toumaz Technology's Digital Plaster prototype or a current product the Sensium Life Pebble TZ203002 (Toumaz, 2009). The Life Pebble has the ability to enable continuous, auditable acquisition of physiological data without interfering with the patient's activities. The device can continuously monitor ECG, heart rate, physical activity and skin temperature.

3G WEARABLES: SMART CLOTHES AND ACCESSORIES

There are two things we carry with us everywhere we go, that is, clothes (such as undergarments, shirts, pants and accessories) and our actual bodies (composed of skin, muscles, nerves, water). Wearable computing experts have always sought a seamless and transparent way to introduce their high-tech devices. Many wearable computing developers believe the answer lies in distributing the equipment evenly throughout the body so that it does not feel excessively heavy for the end-user or look cumbersome. Known as "smart clothes" or "underwearables", they will do more than keep you warm:- "[w]ith the help of computers and special high-tech fabrics, smart clothes could send and receive information and adjust to give you what you need at any moment" (Kastor, 2000, p. 1). A research group in Belgium had been developing the "i-Wear" range (i.e. Intelligent Wear). Siddle (2000, p. 1) reported that the clothes: "will perform many of the current functions of mobile phones, computers and even hospital monitoring equipment… The company [i-Wear] says the range of tasks that the clothes will be able to perform is vast, from taking phone calls to keeping a check on the health of the wearer."

While mass-scale commercial production of such clothes is probably two decades away, shirts with simple memory functions have been developed and tested. Sensors will play a big part in the functionality of the smartware helping to determine the environmental context, and undergarments closest to the body will be used for body functions such as the measurement of temperature, blood pressure, heart and pulse rates. For now however, the aim is to develop ergonomically-astute wearable computing that is actually useful to the end-user. Head-mounted displays attached to the head with a headband may have acted to prototype the capabilities of wearable computing but it was not practical and definitely not attractive. Displays of the next generation will be mounted or concealed within eyeglasses themselves (Spitzer et al., 1997, p. 48). See here especially the incredibly imaginative work of Professor Steve Mann of the University of Toronto (Mann, 2009). Accessories like ear-rings, cuff-links, tie-pins and pendants are also considered wearables if they contain intelligence. The Gesture Pendant, for instance, can be used in an Aware Home granting occupants the ability to be recognized and their activities interpreted to improve the quality of their life. The wearer has the ability to control different house elements like lights, the television, radio, telephone via simple hand gestures that are detected and interpreted by the smart pendant. The target audience for the Gesture Pendant is the elderly or disabled who suffer from particular ailments but who would still want to maintain their independence by living in their own homes. The device could be also used for medical monitoring over time. Georgia Tech's aware home research initiative is an incredible introduction providing scenarios for the possibilities today (GVU, 2009).

Case 3: Military Application

The military is paying particular attention to wearable computing developments. Combatants of the future may look like something/someone out of a film like "Universal Soldier". This should not be surprising since as far back as the 1960s there were attempts to make a "Man Amplifier"; to grant a soldier the added help of an exoskeleton, a sort of first line of defense in protection of the mortal flesh. While the Man Amplifier was unsuccessful due to obvious technological limitations of the time, today systems like FREFLEX (Force Reflecting Exoskeleton) are being trialed to augment human strength characteristics (Repperger et al., 1996, pp. 28-31). The US Army for instance, has been involved in trying to build a military uniform that utilize wearable computing components. They are seeking a uniform that can make: *"…soldiers nearly invisible, grant superhuman strength and provide instant medical care… All this would be achieved by developing particle-sized materials and devices- called "nanotechnology"- nestled into the uniform's fabric… Supercharged shoes could release energy when soldiers jump… Microreactors could detect bleeding and apply pressure… Light-deflecting material could make the suit blend in with surroundings"* (LoBaido, 2001, p. 1).

Figure 6. Courtesy of Steve Mann (1998). In his landmark paper on humanistic intelligence, Mann presented this figure showing simple examples of cloth which have been rendered conductive. He explained: "(a) Cords on early headsets, telephones, etc., often felt more like rope than wire. (b) A recent generation of conductive clothing made from bridged-conductor two-waymannhistorical (BC2) fabric. Although manufactured to address the growing concerns regarding exposure to electromagnetic radiation a, such conductive fabric may be used to shield signal processing circuits from interference. Signal processing circuits worn underneath such garments were found to function much better due to this shielding. This outerwear functions as a faraday cage for the underwearable computing.

 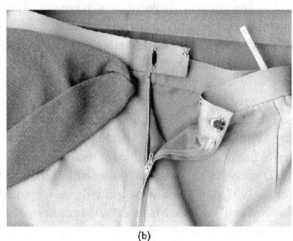

(a)   (b)

This may sound highly exaggerated or Hollywood-esque but it is not. A British company that has called itself the Electronic Shoe Company have developed a pair of walking boots that can be used to power electrical equipment such as a mobile phone. Footwear could also be used to help orientate the soldier, leading them to specific targets through the safest possible route, with the capability of even detecting landmines. In the event of injury to a soldier it is hoped that smart shirts like the Sensate Liner (in which is woven optical fiber) can even aid to localize life-threatening wounds to the upper torso (Gorlick, 1999, p. 121). According to Kellan (2000, p. 1) each soldier would be equipped with a wearable computer, GPS locator and wireless connections to the military network. This would grant individuals the ability to send signals back to base camp in times of trouble or for base camp to send new instructions to the soldier based on more up-to-date intelligence reports. It is not inconceivable for whole divisions to be redirected to areas of safety, minimizing the loss of life (for one side of the combatants at least). It is no surprise that the U.S. Army have major interests in areas like nanotechnology (Samuel, 2002). It is well-publicized that nanotechnology will play a major role in defense (Carstairs, 2008).

FROM WEARABLE DEVICES TO IMPLANTABLE DEVICES

A new line of "wearables" is now emerging that does not quite fit the definition of the traditional wearable that makes an assumption about a device being worn on the outside the human body. Implantable devices such as RFID transponders cannot correctly be referred to as "wearables" because the component is not worn, rather it is ingrained, embedded, entrenched in the human body. The implant device is more than an extension; it becomes one with the body, a seamless fusion between flesh and foreign object. Years ago, automated biometric recognition techniques were heralded as a coming together of humans and machines but today we have something beyond a meeting point, we have the potential for a union of biological proportions on an evolutionary scale. The term "cyborg" seems to have been hijacked by science fiction novels and movies to mean "part machine, part human". *"Saffo, director of the Institute for the Future, does not doubt that people may become a race of cyborgs- "part man and part machine"... "We put all sorts of implants in [our bodies] today," says Saffo. "If we have metal hips, it only makes sense to have chips in, too"* (Eng, 2002). But the definition of cyborg would be more relevant to bionics than to implantable devices.

The human who has been implanted with a microchip is an *Electrophorus*, a bearer of electric/electromagnetic technology. One who "bears" (i.e. a *phorus*) is in some way intrinsically or spiritually connected to that which they are bearing, in the same way an expecting mother is to the child in her womb. The root "electro" comes from the Greek word meaning "amber" and "phorus" means to "wear, to put on, to get into". To electronize something is "to furnish it with electronic equipment" and electrotechnology is "the science that deals with practical applications of electricity". The *Macquarie Dictionary* definition of electrophorus is "an instrument for generating static electricity by means of induction." The term "electrophoresis" has been borrowed here, to describe the act that an electrophorus is involved in. McLuhan and Zingrone (1995, p. 94) believed that "...electricity is in effect an extension of the nervous system as a kind of global membrane." The term electrophorus seems increasingly more suitable today than that of any other term, including "cyborg".

So why the requirement for implantable devices when the same devices could apparently be worn? Two opposing arguments have come from the same institution. Chief futurologist, Ian Pearson, of British Telecom (BT) is not convinced that implants will take the place of wearable components, whereas x-BT researcher, Peter Cochrane is convinced otherwise. Pearson's argument is that "[t]here is nothing you can do with embedded chips that you can't do with wearable ones" (LoBaido, 2001, part 1, pp. 2f). Pearson however, does believe in the pervasive nature of the chips predicting that by 2006 wearable identity chips will be implemented. And yes, they were, a whole two years earlier than what he had originally predicted. Only one year prior to this interview, Peter Cochrane told McGinity (2000, p. 17) that there *"...will come a day when chips are not just worn around the neck, but are actually implanted under a human's skin." When I [McGinity] scoffed at such an idea as merely science fiction, Cochrane offered up that he himself would be testing out such a human chip and looked forward to the opportunity."*

And who could ever doubt such a possibility after Professor Kevin Warwick's 1998 Cyborg 1.0 trial? After the microchip implant Warwick was able to walk around his rigged up building in the Cybernetics department at the University of Reading and be recognized as being "Kevin Warwick." As he walked through the doorways, the radio signal energized the coil in the chip, produced current, and gave the chip the ability to send out an identifying signal (Witt, 1999, p. 2). Warwick and Cochrane are not alone in their efforts. Mieszkowski (2000, part 1, p. 2) writes: *"[m]any theorists see people carrying embedded technology as mobile computing's next "killer application"... Instead of just implanting machines into humans to reconstruct joints or regulate heartbeats, they imagine the addition of sensors and chips in bodies which will make people better, stronger and faster."* For those like Mr Amal Graafstra, however, they may not be so interested in the "better, stronger and faster" scenario, but just enjoy tinkering on their computer, looking at how they can go further each time they dabble with "fun-stuff," and just make life that little bit easier. What of the divide between the motivations of the three types of stakeholders: researcher, hobbyist and commercial organization

The Role of Auto-ID

Shortly after the excitement of the Warwick implant (1998) wore off and Cochrane launched his *Tips for Time Travelers* (1999), Applied Digital Solutions (ADSX) was founded. The company first announced its VeriChip solution on December 19, 2001. RFID, traditionally used in contactless smart cards, tags and keys, and transponders interwoven into clothing, was now being marketed as a suitable identity verification chip for a variety of security, financial, emergency service and healthcare applications for humans. In a press release the company announced that the VeriChip would be "…available in several formats, some of which [could] be inserted under the skin" (ADS, 2002a, p. 2). The Chief Technology Officer (CTO) of ADSX told Scheeres (2002, p. 1) that "[t]he chip… is injected into the subject's forearm or shoulder under local anesthesia during an outpatient procedure and leaves no mark." Furthermore VeriChip is expected to sell at a low two hundred US dollars with the Digital Angel service packaged at a monthly $29.95 US dollars with a one year minimum contract (Associated Press, 2002; Farrell, 2002). Scanners that could identify the VeriChip, very similar to those used to identify pet implants would cost between one thousand and three thousand US dollars. More recently ADSX have begun to aggressively market their products, attracting a lot of publicity as both young and old have opted for the chip implant. The "Get Chipped™" promotion and the ChipMobile™ that roams the US have increased the awareness level of the general public. ADSX had scheduled visits to "recreation and stadium events, health clinics, nursing homes" among other locations (ADS, 2002c).

The Impact of Mobility

The added function of networking to wearable computing components and implantable devices has acted to create an extremely powerful platform for monitoring and tracking humans "anywhere, anytime". Starner (2001b, p. 54) identified three network communication levels: (i) off the body to a fixed network (e.g. wireless-enabled wristwatch); (ii) between different wearable devices on the body (e.g. between intelligent eyeglasses and belt buckle); and (iii) near the body between the user and objects (e.g. between a gesture pendant and a television set). Location has always been an important attribute in people-centric applications but it is only now that the capability exists to query this data in real-time (Michael, 2004). Krikelis (1999, p. 13) calls this "context information" and this is exactly what is set to revolutionize daily consumer and business activities. Future fourth generation (4G) mobile services base their core value proposition around being able to retrieve this type of data.

A typical 4G service example could be as follows (Michael, 2002, p. 293): *"An employee who works for a multinational company is traveling from Sydney to China and making a stopover in Singapore. While on his way to Sydney airport, the employee encounters a major traffic accident on the Harbour Bridge. Traffic stops to a standstill, while police and ambulance treat people at the scene. A camera on the bridge tracks all delays, alerting the roads and traffic authority (RTA). The RTA estimates that the delay will be in excess of two hours and sends this information to the central information bureau. The employee is alerted by the wireless service provider that they will most likely miss his flight and will have to stay at Sydney's Airport Hilton overnight waiting for the next available flight which is scheduled to depart in the morning. The employee replies to the message and updates are made to his itinerary*

Figure 7. Singaporean taxi fleet which is managed using location-based services. The LCD provides the job number, the pick up address, and the drop off address as well as a date and time stamp. No more vying for which taxi will pick up the customer who is waiting. If you are in the vicinity you can bid for the job, but if you are outside the predefined boundary you have to wait for a job that is closer to you. Photo taken in 2005.

as detailed on his reply message. The panic of having to reorganize everything is removed from the traveler. Though he will end up missing the first meeting in Singapore, he is relieved with the almost instantaneous knowledge that he will be leaving Sydney in time for subsequent meetings."

Throughout this scenario a number of smart devices are being used to execute operations seamlessly. These may include a RFID device in the car of the employee traveling to the Airport, a wireless mobile phone carried by the individual to be able to send and receive information (either by voice or data), a smart wristwatch which contains itinerary information about flights, hotels and forthcoming meetings. Somewhere in amidst all this would be a GPS-enabled trigger that lets the respective service providers know where the individual is located and grants them the ability to calculate estimated times of arrival (Figure 6). This kind of service however would require the cooperation of numerous stakeholders, via web services that rely on workflow business process management standards and tools.

Global Positioning System (GPS) Tracking

Having established the importance of network communications to wearable and implantable devices let us consider the role of the Global Positioning System (GPS). Ferrero (1998, p. 87) ponders: "[i]magine GPS in your wallet, cell phone, or watch to tell you where you are." Well, one does not have to imagine that any longer, there are services being offered right now, beyond the smart car navigation systems. Companies like Wherify, ChildLocate, StarMax, SnapTrack, Gen-Etics, Pro-Tech, Sky-Eye and Digital Angel/ADSX are taking advantage of what GPS and other 2G wireless technologies have to offer and using it to track living and non-living things. In terms of people tracking, this is done for a variety of reasons including: child safety, reducing the incidence of kidnapping of high profile persons, for those suffering from Alzheimer's disease who may become disorientated, for those suffering from mental illness, for parolees, for prison inmates, for military personnel, for emergency services, or just for peace of mind (K. Michael & Masters, 2004). Wherify's (2003) "GPS Locator for Children" for instance, states that: *"[c]hildren have a natural urge to explore. Parents have a natural desire to know their children are safe. That's why Wherify created the world's first Personal Locator to help you determine your child's location in minutes. Wherify's GPS Locator technology helps keep loved ones safe by combining Wherify's patented technology with the U.S. Department of Defence's multi-billion dollar Global Positioning System (GPS) satellite plus the largest 100% digital, nationwide PCS wireless network. So relax. Now you can have peace of mind 24 hours a day while your child is the high tech envy of the neighborhood!"*

The watch worn by Wherify users contains a built-in pager, an atomic synchronized clock, an emergency 911 button, a lock button and an on-board GPS. One pitfall of the Wherify technology is that it can be seen, thus alerting a perpetrator to the possibility that their location will be found out. The evolutionary vision therefore is a technology that is fully implantable and cannot be seen by an attacker or anyone else for that matter. "Enter the Digital Angel: according to CEO Richard Sullivan, the solution combines GPS wireless communications with biosensors, powered by body heat in the form of a dime-sized chip, which can be embedded in a watch, bracelet or medallion, even under your flesh" (Mieszkowski, 2000, part 2, p. 2). Now given GPS only works outdoors, other wireless systems must cater for in-building/in-container solutions, most of which take advantage of RFID tags and transponders, video cameras, sensors or infrared signals.

Towards a Unique ID for Universal Personal Telecommunications

There are two developments that are enabling this capability: the first is the blurring between what is wireline and wireless, the second is that the new IP-based networks have turned the traditional notion of voice and data up-side-down. These two changes are setting the stage for a global platform that requires that an individual have a unique lifetime identifier (from the time of birth), either in the form of a number or email address. Some of the early protocols such as SIP (Session Initiation Protocol) and H.323 rely on such an identifier. In 2000, Bell Canada launched the "Find-Me Number Service" which allowed phone calls to follow an individual (Bell, 2000). With time this service will extend to incorporate emails and other forms of messaging. We seem to be moving towards a course dictated by the notion of a "universal" Personal Communications Service (PCS) model that is hybrid in approach, utilizing the best of both worlds (both GPS and PCS) when it is required. The critical question is how interlinked will this scheme be to a potential *unique lifetime identifier* chip implant? I.e., a unique identifier for communications could be just as suitable for personal user authentication. Farrell (2001) predicts, "[o]ther uses could be to replace keys and ATM cards with implanted chips, making it possible for a single implant to unlock your house, start your car and give you money from a cash point."

Case 4: Medical–Related Implants

Auto-ID devices, in particular implantable devices like smart microchips and passive and active RFID transponders, have found themselves being utilized in medical applications for completely different purposes to what they were originally invented. Apart from serving their designated purpose as an automatic identification device they have somehow found themselves to be integral components of life-saving devices, in some instances either to the prevention or cure of particular disabilities, ailments or diseases. The devices have of course been further developed and adapted to match the requirements of the specific medical application. The evolutionary path indicates that due to developments in auto-ID and microcircuitry in general, today's medical implantable devices have much overtaken the "humble" pacemaker. In Banbury's (1997) historical account of technological innovation in the pacemaker industry (1959-1990), there is a chapter dedicated to the incremental changes that have taken place on pacemaker technology since 1963. Her findings are useful in considering the future use of RFID for health-related applications (p. 54).

Many technological innovations that occurred in the pacemaker industry during the incremental era changed some aspect of the product and how it was used. These changes resulted from innovations in pacing technology or from innovations in input technologies, where the research and development could have been conducted by pacemaker firms or firms and research institutions external to the pacemaker industry. Innovations in semiconductor technology and in surgical procedures used to implant pacers are examples of external innovations that were later adapted to pacing technology. Innovations in electrode and lead technologies are examples of innovations developed by firms both inside and outside of the industry. However, developments in the pacing mode, the core technology, were introduced by pacing firms. The following innovation cases point to a future path for auto-ID as something more than an identification technology, a new electrophorus paradigm (with all of the ensuing social, religious, and political rejoinders) that is set to revolutionize the way humans consider technology- no longer as a separate entity but as a life-enhancing artifact carried within the body.

Biochips for Diagnosis and Smart Pills for Drug Delivery

It is not unlikely that biochips will be implanted at birth in the not-too-distant future. "They will be able to diagnose disease with precision, pre-determine a patient's response to treatment and make individual patients aware of any pre-disposition to susceptibility" (Wales, 2001). With response to treatment for illness, drug delivery will not require patients to swallow pills or take routine injections; instead chemicals will be stored on a microprocessor and released as prescribed. The idea is known as "pharmacy-on-a-chip" and was founded by scientists at the Massachusetts Institute of Technology (MIT) in 1999 (LoBaido, 2001, part 2, p. 2). The following extract is from The Lab (1999): "Doctors prescribing complicated courses of drugs may soon be able to implant microchips into patients to deliver timed drug doses directly into their bodies."

Microchips being developed at Ohio State University (OSU) can be swathed with a chemical substance like pain medication, insulin, different treatments for heart disease, or gene therapies, allowing physicians to work at a more detailed level (Swissler, 2000, p. 1). The breakthroughs have major implications for diabetics especially who require insulin at regular intervals throughout the day. Researchers at the University of Delaware are working on "smart" implantable insulin pumps that may relieve people with Type I diabetes (Bailey, 1999, p. 1). The delivery would be based on a mathematical model stored on a microchip and working in connection with glucose sensors that would instruct the chip when to release the insulin. The goal is for the model to be able to simulate the activity of the pancreas so that the right dosage is delivered at the right time. The implantable chips are also being considered as a possible solution to clinical depression and/or for patients who are incapable of committing to a prescribed regime. Gasson (1998, p. 1) first named this capability as "cyberdrugs"/ "cybernarcotics" with a well-meaning intent. Professor John Santini of MIT, knowing the possible implications of such an innovation, however, has repeatedly outlined that the focus is strictly "therapeutic", a better way to treat diseases (LoBaido, 2001, part 2, p. 2). Scientists at universities are not the only ones researching biochips or smart pills

Figure 8. Seven years in the making, Cochlear's Nucleus Freedom implant with Contour Advance™ electrode, features a sophisticated electronics platform with a powerful new microchip. Nucleus Freedom is safe for MRI scans up to 1.5 Tesla without the need to remove the magnet. The remarkably small size of the implant is suited to infants and adults. It's designed to enable short surgery and fast recovery. The silicone enclosure allows the implant to bend, fitting snugly and securely. The unique 22-channel electrode is designed to deliver a finer representation of sound when stimulating the hearing nerves, which is important for optimizing sound clarity. Courtesy of Cochlear Australia.

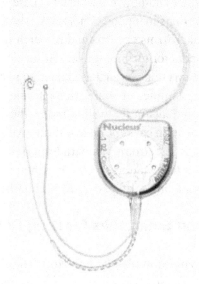

according to Wales (2001) production is quickly becoming a big business as genomic-based medicine is the next buzz-word. Some of the more well-known players include: Affymetrix, Motorola Life Sciences Codelink Division, Packard BioScience, Agilent, and Hitachi.

Cochlear Implants – Helping the Deaf to Hear

In 2000, more than thirty-two thousand people worldwide already had cochlear implants (Manning, 2000, p. 7D). In 2006, that number had grown to about 77,500 for the Nucleus implant alone which had about 70 per cent of the market share (Patrick, Busby, & Gibson, 2006) (Figure 7). Cochlear implants can restore hearing to people who have severe hearing loss, a form of diagnosed deafness. Unlike a standard hearing aid that works like an amplifier, the cochlear implant acts like a microphone to change sound into electronic signals. Signals are sent to the microchip implant via RF stimulating nerve fibers in the inner ear. The brain then interprets the signals that are transmitted via the nerves to be sound. For a closer look at the cochlear implant see the Clarion and Nucleus product innovations. Another company, Canadian-based Epic Biosonics, teamed up with Professor Christofer Toumazou of Imperial College in 1999. Toumazou had made significant inroads to cutting the costs of cochlear implants and making them more comfortable for the individual. Most cochlear implants today require power packs worn on belts with connecting wires generated by battery power that generally do not look aesthetically good, Toumazou has made major leaps in changing this impracticality (Imperial College, 1999, p. 2).

For now, cochlear implants are being used to overcome deafness, tomorrow however they may be open to the wider public as a performance-enhancing technique (Cooper, 2008, pp. 10-11). Audiologist, Steve Otto of the Auditory Brainstem Implant Project at the House Ear Institute in Los Angeles predicts that some day "implantable devices [will] interface microscopically with parts of the normal system that are still physiologically functional" (Stewart, 2000, p. 2). He is quoted as saying that this may equate to "ESP for everyone." Otto's prediction that implants will one day be used by persons who do not require them for remedial purposes has been supported by numerous other high profile scientists. The major question is whether this is the ultimate trajectory of these technologies.

Retina Implants - On a Mission to Help the Blind to See

The hope is that retina implants will be as successful as cochlear implants in the future. Like cochlear implants cannot be used for persons suffering from complete deafness, retina implants are not a solution for totally blind persons but rather those suffering from aged macular degeneration (AMD) and retinitis pigmentosa (RP). Retina implants have brought together medical researchers, electronic specialists and software designers to develop a system that can be implanted inside the eye (Ahlstrom, 2000, p. 1). A typical retina implant procedure is as follows:

"[s]urgeons make a pinpoint opening in the retina to inject fluid in order to lift a portion of the retina from the back of the eye, creating a pocket to accommodate the chip. The retina is resealed over the chip, and doctors inject air into the middle of the eye to force the retina back over the device and close the incisions" (Datamaster, 2001, p. 1).

Brothers Alan Chow and Vincent Chow, one an engineer the other an ophthalmologist, developed the artificial silicon retina (ASR) and began the company Optobionics Corp in 1990. This was a marriage between biology and engineering, first conceived of over a Thanksgiving dinner. "In landmark surgeries at the University of Illinois at Chicago Medical Centre on June 28, the first artificial retinas made from silicon chips were implanted in the eyes of two blind patients who have lost almost all of their vision because of retinal disease." In 1993 Branwyn (p. 3) reported that a team at the National Institute of Health (NIH) led by Dr. Hambrecht, implanted a 38-electrode array into a blind female's brain. It was reported that she saw simple light patterns and was able to make out crude letters. The following year the same procedure was conducted by another group on a blind male resulting in the man seeing a black dot with a yellow ring around it. Joseph Rizzo of Harvard Medical School's, Massachusetts Eye and Ear Infirmary has cautioned that it is better to talk down the possibilities of the retina implant so as not to give false hopes. The professor himself had expressed that they are dealing with "science fiction stuff" and that there are no long-term guarantees that the technology will ever fully restore sight, although significant progress is being made by a number of research institutes (Wells, 1998, p. 5). Among these pioneers are researchers at The John Hopkins University Medical Centre in Baltimore, Maryland. Brooks (2001, pp. 4f) describes how the retina chip developed by the medical centre will work: *"...a kind of miniature digital camera... is placed on the surface of the retina. The camera relays information about the light that hits it to a microchip implanted nearby. This chip then delivers a signal that is fed back to the retina, giving it a big kick that stimulates it into action. Then, as normal, a signal goes down the optic nerve and sight is at least partially restored."*

Tapping into the Heart and Brain

If it was possible as far back as 1958, to successfully implant two transistors the size of an ice hockey puck in the heart of a 43 year old man (Nairne, 2000, p. 1), what will become possible by 2058 is constrained by the imagination alone. Heart pacemakers are still being further developed today, but for the greater part, researchers are turning their attention to the possibilities of brain pacemakers. In the foreseeable future brain implants may help sufferers of Parkinson's, paralysis, nervous system problems, speech-impaired persons and even cancer patients. While the research is still in its formative years and the obstacles so great because of the complexity of the brain, scientists are hopeful of major breakthroughs in the next twenty to fifty years.

The brain pacemaker endeavors are bringing together even more people from different disciplines headed mainly by neurosurgeons. By using brain implants electrical pulses can be sent directly to nerves via electrodes. The signals can be used to interrupt incoherent messages to nerves that cause uncontrollable movements or tremors. By tapping into the right nerves in the brain, particular reactions can be achieved. Using a technique that was first founded, almost accidentally in France in 1987, the following extract describes the procedure of "tapping into" the brain: *"Rezai and a team of functional neurosurgeons, neurologists and nurses at the Cleveland Clinic Foundation in Ohio had spent the next few hours electronically eavesdropping on single cells in Joan's brain attempting to pinpoint the precise trouble spot that caused a persistent, uncontrollable tremor in her right hand. Once confident they had found the spot, the doctors had guided the electrode itself deep into her brain, into a small duchy of nerve cells within the thalamus. The hope was that when sent an electrical current to the electrode, in a technique known as deep-brain stimulation, her tremor would diminish, and perhaps disappear altogether (Hall, 2001, p. 2)."* There are companies that have formed like Medtronic Incorporated (Minneapolis, Minnesota) that specialize in brain pacemakers (Med, 2009). Medtronic's Activa implant has been designed specifically for sufferers of Parkinson's disease (Wells, 1998, p. 3).

Attempting to Overcome Paralysis

In more speculative research surgeons believe that brain implants may be a solution for persons who are suffering from paralysis such as spinal cord damage. In these instances the nerves in the legs are still theoretically "working", it is just that they cannot make contact with the brain which controls their movement. If somehow signals could be sent to the brain, bypassing the lesion point, it could conceivably mean that paralyzed persons regain at least part of their capability to move (Dobson, 2001, p. 2). In 2000 Reuters (pp. 1f) reported that a paralyzed Frenchman [Marc Merger] "took his first steps in 10 years after a revolutionary operation to restore nerve functions using a microchip implant... Merger walks by pressing buttons on a walking frame which acts as a remote control for the chip, sending impulses through fine wires to stimulate legs muscles..." It should be noted, however, that the system only works for paraplegics whose muscles remain alive despite damage to the nerves. Yet there are promising devices like the Bion that may one day be able to control muscle movement using RF commands (Smith, 2002, p. 2). Brooks (2001, p. 3) reports that researchers at the University of Illinois in Chicago have: *"... invented a microcomputer system that sends pulses to a patient's legs, causing the muscles to contract. Using a walker for balance, people paralyzed from the waist down can stand up from a sitting position and walk short distances... Another team, based in Europe... enabled a paraplegic to walk using a chip connected to fine wires in his legs."* These techniques are known as functional neuromuscular stimulation systems (Case Western Reserve University, 2007).

Granting a Voice to the Speech-Impaired

Speech-impairment microchip implants work differently to that of the cochlear and retina implant. Whereas in the latter two, hearing and sight is restored, in implants for speech-impairment the voice is not restored, but an outlet for communication is created, possibly with the aid of a voice synthesizer. At The Emory University, neurosurgeon Roy E. Bakay and neuroscientist Phillip R. Kennedy were responsible for critical breakthroughs early in the research. In 1998, Versweyveld (p. 1) reported two successful implants of a neurotrophic electrode into the brain of a woman and man who were suffering from Amyotrophic Lateral Sclerosis (ALS) and brainstem stroke, respectively. In an incredible process, Bakay and Kennedy have somehow replicated the ability to explicitly capture the patient's thoughts to a computer screen by the movement of a cursor. "The computer chip is directly connected with the cortical nerve cells... The neural signals are transmitted to a receiver and connected to the computer in order to drive the cursor" (Versweyveld, 1998, p. 1). This procedure has major implications for brain-computer interaction (BCI), especially bionics. Bakay predicts that by 2010 prosthetic devices will grant patients that are immobile the ability to turn on the TV just by thinking about it and by 2030 to grant severely disabled persons the ability to walk independently (Dominguez, 2000, p. 2; Adee, 2009, pp. 37-40). Despite the early signs that these procedures may offer long term solutions for hundreds of thousands of people, some research scientists believe that tapping into the human brain is a long-shot. The brain is commonly understood to be "wetware" and plugging in hardware into this "wetware" would seem to be a type mismatch according to Steve Potter, a senior research fellow in biology working at the California Institute of Technology's Biological Imaging Centre in Pasadena. Instead Potter is pursuing the cranial route as a "digital gateway to the brain" (Stewart, 2000, p. 1). Others believe that it is impossible to figure out exactly what all the millions of neurons in the brain actually do- but it should be reminded that this is the exact same argument that was presented when there were initial discussions about the Human Genome Project.

Up until now this chapter has focused on implants that are attempts at "orthopaedic replacements", corrective in nature, required to repair a function that is either lying dormant or has failed altogether. Implants of the future however, will attempt to add new "functionality" to native human capabilities, either through extensions or additions. Globally acclaimed scientists have pondered on the ultimate trajectory of microchip implants. The literature is admittedly assorted in its viewpoints of what will and will not be possible in the future; but one of the lessons that history has taught us is that if a concept has been conceived the probability that it will come into material fruition is high. Warwick's Cyborg 2.0 project for instance, intended to prove that two persons with respective implants could communicate sensation and movement by thoughts alone (Dobson, 2001, p. 1). The prediction is that terminals like telephones would eventually become obsolete if thought-to-thought communication became possible. Warwick describes this as "putting a plug into the nervous system" (Dobson, 2001, p. 1) to be able to allow thoughts to be transferred not only to another person but to the Internet and other mediums. While Warwick's Cyborg 2.0 may not have achieved its desired outcomes, it did show that a form of primitive Morse-code-style nervous-system-to-nervous-system communication is realizable (Green, 2002, p. 3). Warwick is bound to keep trying to achieve his project goals given his philosophical perspective. And if Warwick does not succeed, he will have at least left behind a legacy and enough stimuli for someone else to succeed in his place, even if, as Berry (1996) says, the prediction will come true 500 years from now.

CONCLUSION

It has been shown that auto-ID devices have a trajectory that is, in part, radically different from the intent of the inventors. Initially attached to non-living things and later adopted to be carried by humans, it now seems inevitable that the devices will become one with humans. Converging disciplines are making the realm of the "impossible", potentially "possible". For the first time, the attribute of mobility is being linked to automatic identification and wearable computing components, and being applied to completely non-traditional areas of electronic commerce. Of course some resistance will be experienced initially but as society continues to change becoming more and more techno-centric, it will decide what auto-ID will be used for, even if it has little to do with what it was originally designed (Branwyn, 1993, p. 6). Society continues to be increasingly dependent on the promise of technology and it is difficult to see who and how many will resist the ultimate hope of "living for ever". It is important to note here that the accomplishment is not in the rise of the computer/information age, it is as Grier (2000, p. 83) puts it, in "the vision, it has maintained" (Grier, 2000, p. 83).

When the ENIAC was publicly announced in 1946, no one could predict its ultimate impact. The founder of IBM famously forecasted a worldwide market of five computers (Coughlin, 2000, p. 1)! The same could be said for brain implants today but we should at least pay some respect to the instructive lessons of history. Perhaps what we really need to do is start afresh considering the implications that such developments may have without discounting them outright as an improbable science fiction or even at the other extreme, as a possible universal remedy. One reason this chapter depended so heavily on quoting research at the turn of the century was to actually dispel the myth that any type of dialogue is premature. It clearly is not. 2010 is literally just around the corner; and much of what took place in the laboratories of universities and private enterprise almost a decade ago is well on its way to being commercialized. The force of the momentum is such that continual attempts will be made to go beyond that which has been achieved. It is not enough to begin discussing possible implications when the technology reaches the early adoption stage- by then the technology would have taken root- as it seems to have done already to some degree. Ultimately humanity will have a choice, and as Warwick has openly stated, hopefully it will be an individual choice- for those who would like to remain mere human and those who would like to continue to evolve.

REFERENCES

Adee, S. (2009). The Revolution will be Prosthetized: DARPA's Prosthetic Arm Gives Amputees New Hope. *IEEE Spectrum, 46*(1), 37-40.

ADS. (2002a, 3 October). Digital Angel Corporation is awarded United States Patent for Next-generation, Enhanced-performance Implantable Microchip. *Applied Digital Solutions*, from http://www.adsx.com/news/DA2002/100302.html

ADS. (2002b, 15 August). Responding to Growing Customer Inquiries and Media Interest, Applied Digital Solutions Highlights Anti-kidnapping Potential of Its "Personal Safeguard" Technologies. *Applied Digital Solutions*, from http://www.adsx.com/news/2002/081602.html

ADS. (2002c, 7 October). VeriChip Corporation will Benefit from New United States Patent (#6,400,338) Awarded to Digital Angel Corporation- Manufacturer of VeriChip. *Applied Digital Solutions*, from http://www.adsx.com/news/2002/100702.html

ADSX. (2003). Implantable Personal Verification Systems. *Applied Digital Solutions*. Retrieved 15 April 2004, from http://www.adsx.com/prodservpart/verichip.html

Ahlstrom, D. (2000, 20 November). Microchip implant could offer new kind of vision. *The Irish Times*, from http://www.ireland.com/newspaper/science/2000/1109/sci1.htm

Associated Press. (2002). Company gets okay to sell ID-only computer chip implant. *The Detroit News* Retrieved 5 April, from http://www.detnews.com/2002/technology/0204/05/technology-457686.htm

AT&T. (2003). Feature and Services User Guide. *AT&T Wireless*. Retrieved 15 April 2004, from http://www.attwireless.com/personal/features/mmode/mmode_guide.jhtml

Bailey, R. (1999). Implantable insulin pumps. *Biology About.com*, from http://biology.about.com/library/weekly/aa061099.htm

Banbury, C. M. (1997). *Surviving Technological Innovation in the Pacemaker Industry 1959-1990*. New York: Garland Publishing.

Bell. (2000). Bell Canada consumer services: Find-Me Number Service. *Bell Canada*.

Berry, A. (1996). *The Next 500 Years: life in the coming millennium*. New York: Gramercy Books.

Branwyn, G. (1993). The desire to be wired. *Wired, September/October*, 65.

Brooks, M. (2001, 14 November). The Cyborg cometh. *Worldlink: The Magazine of the World Economic Forum*, from http://www.worldlink.co.uk/stories/storyReader$844

Burak, A., & Sharon, T. (2003, 5-10 April). *Analysing Usage of Location Based Services*. Paper presented at the CHI 2003: New Horizons, Florida, USA.

Case Western Reserve University. (2007). Study of an Implantable Functional Neuromuscular Stimulation System for Patients With Spinal Cord Injuries. *Clinical Trials. gov*. Retrieved 4 February 2009, from http://clinicaltrials.gov/ct2/show/NCT00004445?recr=Open&cond=%22Rare+Diseases%22&rank=38

Cochrane, P. (1999). *Tips For Time Travellers: visionary insights into new technology, life, and the future on the edge of technology*. New York: McGraw-Hill.

Cooper, L. (1999). *A run on Sterling- personal finance on the move*. Paper presented at the The Third International Symposium on Wearable Computers.

Cooper, R. A. (2008). Quality of Life Technology: A Human-Centered and Holistic Design. *IEEE Engineering in Medicine and Biology, 27*(2), 10-11.

Coughlin, K. (2000, 4 January). The melding of man and machine. *The Star-Ledger: The Newspaper for New Jersey*, from http://www.nj.com/page1/ledger/e1576d.html

Datamaster. (2001). More tests of eye implants planned. *BrainLand: The Neuroscience Information Centre*, 1-2.

Dobson, R. (2001, 5th June). Professor to try to 'control' wife via chip implant. *Rense.com*, from http://www.rense.com/general10/professortotry.htm

Dominguez, A. (2000). The brain as a remote control. *CBS News*, from http://www.cbsnews.com/now/story/0,1597,249757-412,00.shtml

Eng, P. (2002, 25 February). I, Chip? Technology to meld chips into humans draws closer. *ABCNEWS.com*, from http://abcnews.go.com/sections/scitech/DailyNews/chipimplant020225.html

Farrell, N. (2002, 30 July). Kids to be served up with chips. *IT Week*, from http://www.itweek.co.uk/News/1133990

Ferrero, J. L. (1998). Wearable computing: one man's mission. *IEEE Micro, 18*(5), 87-88.

Gasson, M. (1998). Implants and bioengineering. *Research- Implant*, from http://www.madlab.rdg.ac.uk/madlab/research/implant.htm

Gorlick, M. M. (1999). Electric suspenders: a fabric power bus and data network for wearable digital devices. *The Third International Symposium on Wearable Computers*, 114-121.

Green, D. (2002, 2 August 2002). Why I am not impressed with Professor Cyborg. *BBC News*, from http://news.bbc.co.uk/2/hi/uk/2163947.stm

Grier, D. A. (2000). Anecdotes. *IEEE Annals of the History of Computing*, 82-85.

GVU. (2009). Aware Home - Homepage. *A Residential Laboratory at Georgia Institute of Technology* Retrieved 4 February 2009, from http://awarehome.imtc.gatech.edu/

Hall, S. S. (2001, September 2001). Brain pacemakers. *An MIT Enterprise Technology Review*, from http://www.technologyreview.com/magazine/sep01/hall.asp

Hinkers, X. (1995, June 25-29). *Microdialysis system for continuous glucose monitoring.* Paper presented at the The 8th International Conference on Solid-State Sensors and Actuators, and Eurosensors IX, Stockholm, Sweden.

Imperial College. (1999). Micro-electronics behind novel bionic ear. *Imperial College News*, from http://www.ic.ac.uk/templates/text_3.asp?P=2570

Kargl, F., Lawrence, E., Fischer, M., & Lim, Y. Y. (2008). *Security, Privacy and Legal Issues in Pervasive eHealth Monitoring Systems.* Paper presented at the 7th International Conference on Mobile Business, Barcelona, Spain.

Kastor, E. (2000, 28 December). Smarty-Pants pants… and shirts. *Washington Post*, from http://www.washingtonpost.com/ac2/

Kellan, A. (2000, 19 October). Wearable gadgets offer modern look for military. *CNN.com*, from http://www.cnn.com/2000/TECH/computing/10/19/wear.gadgets.t_t/index.html

Krikelis, A. (1999). Location-dependent multimedia computing. *IEEE Concurrency*(April-June), 13-15.

LoBaido, A. C. (2001). Soldiers with microchips: British troops experiment with implanted, electronic dog tag. *WorldNetDaily.com*, from http://www.fivedoves.com/letters/oct2001/chrissa102.htm

Mann, S. (1997). Eudaemonic computing ('underwearables'). *IEEE First International Symposium on Wearable Computers*, 177-178.

Mann, S. (1998). Humanistic Intelligence: `WearComp' as a new framework and application for intelligent signal processing, *Proceedings of the IEEE, 86*(11), 2123-2151. Available from http://wearcam.org/hi/index.html

Mann, S. (2001). *Intelligent Image Processing.* John Wiley and Sons, New York, p. 384.

Mann, S. (2009). Prof. Steve Mann. *University of Toronto* Retrieved 30 January 2009, from http://www.eecg.toronto.edu/~mann/

Manning, A. (2000, 2 May). Implants sounding better: smaller, faster units overcome 'nerve deafness'. *USA Today,* p. 7D.

Martin, T. (2000). Issues in wearable computing for medical monitoring applications: a case study of a wearable ECG monitoring device. *IEEE The Fourth International Symposium on Wearable Computers*, 43-49.

McDonough, B. (17 April 2002). AT&T Wireless Pushes mLife with mMode. *CIO Today* Retrieved 6 April 2004, from http://cio-today.newsfactor.com/perl/story/17307.html

McGinity, M. (2000). Body of the technology: It's just a matter of time before a chip gets under your skin. *Communications of the ACM, 43*(9), 17-19.

McLuhan, E., & Zingrone, F. (1995). *Essential McLuhan.* USA: BasicBooks.

Med. (2009). Deep Brain Stimulation. *Medtronic* Retrieved 4 February 2009, from http://professional.medtronic.com/interventions/deep-brain-stimulation/overview/index.htm

Michael, K. (2002). The rise of the wireless Internet. In E. Lawrence (Ed.), *Internet Commerce: digital models for business* (pp. 291-294, 296). Queensland: John Wiley and Sons.

Michael, K. (2004). *Location-based Services - a Vehicle for IT&T Convergence.* Paper presented at the Advances in E-Engineering and Digital Enterprises Technology - 1: Proceedings of the Fourth International Conference on e-Engineering and Digital Enterprise Technology (e-ENGDET), Leeds, United Kingdom.

Michael, K., & Masters, A. (2004, 18-21 July). *Applications of human transponder implants in mobile commerce.* Paper presented at the The 8th World Multiconference on Systemics, Cybernetics and Informatics, Orlando, Florida.

Mieszkowski, K. (2000). Put that silicon where the sun don't shine. *Salon*, from http://www.salon.com/tech/feature/2000/09/07/chips/

Nairne, D. (2000). Building better people with chips and sensors. *scmp.com*, from http://special.scmp.com/mobilecomputing/article/FullText_asp_ArticleID-20001009174

Patrick, J. F., Busby, P. A., & Gibson, P. J. (2006). The Development of the Nucleus® FreedomTM Cochlear Implant System. *Sage Publications, 10*(4), 175-200.

Pentland, S. (2009). Wearable Computing. *MIT Media Lab* Retrieved 4 February 2009, from http://www.media.mit.edu/wearables/themes.html

Rao, B., & Minakakis, L. (2003). EVOLUTION of Mobile Location-Based Services. *Communications of the ACM, 46*(12), 61-65.

Repperger, D. W. (1996). *Human tracking studies involving an actively powered, augmented exoskeleton.* Paper presented at the IEEE Proceedings of the 1996 Fifteenth Southern Biomedical Engineering Conference.

Sawhney, N., & Schmandt, C. (1997). *Nomadic Radio: A spatialized audio environment for wearable computing.* Paper presented at the IEEE First International Symposium on Wearable Computers.

Scheeres, J. (2002, 15 February). Politician wants to 'get chipped'. *Wired News*, from http://www.wired.com/news/technology/0,1282,50435,00.html

Schiele, B. (2001). Sensory-augmented computing: wearing the museum's guide. *IEEE Micro*, 44-52.

Siddle, J. (2000, 30 December). Clothes that do the thinking. from http://news.bbc.co.uk/hi/english/sci/tech/newsid_1092000/1092422.stm

Siewiorek, D. P. (1999). Wearable computing comes of age. *IEEE Computer*, 82-83.

Smith, D. (2002, 16 February). Chip implant signals a new kind of man. *The Age*, from http://www.theage.com.au/news/national/2002/02/16/FFX9B13VOXC.html

Spitzer, M. B. (1997). Eyeglass-based systems for wearable computing. *IEEE First International Symposium on Wearable Computers*, 48-51.

Starner, T. (2001a). The challenges of wearable computing: part 1. *IEEE Micro*(July-August), 44-52.

Starner, T. (2001b). The challenges of wearable computing: part 2. *IEEE Micro*(July-August), 54-67.

Stein, R. (1998). Development of a commercially successful wearable data collection system. *IEEE Second International Symposium on Wearable Computers*, 18-24.

Stewart, S. (2000). Neuromaster. *Wired 8.02*. February. from http://www.wired.com/archive/8.02/potter.html

Swissler, M. A. (2000, 8 September). Microchips to monitor meds. *Wired*. Retrieved from http://www.wired.com/news/technology/0,1282,39070,00.html

Sydänheimo, L. (1999). *Wearable and ubiquitous computer aided service, maintenance and overhaul.* Paper presented at the IEEE International Conference on Communications.

The Lab. (1999, 28 January). Microchip implants for drug delivery. *ABC: News in Science*, from http://www.abc.net.au/science/news/stories/s18502.htm

Toumaz. (2009). Sensium Life Pebble. *Toumaz Technology*. Retrieved 4 February 2009, from http://www.toumaz.com/public/page.php?page=sensium_pebble

Trackstick. (2009). Get a Trackstick. Retrieved 4 February 2009, from http://www.trackstick.com/store/index.html

Versweyveld, L. (1998). Chip implants allow paralysed patients to communicate via the computer. *Virtual Medical Worlds Monthly*. Retrieved 13 October, from http://www.hoise.com/vmw/articles/LV-VM-12-98-13.html

Wales, E. (2001, 20 November). It's a living chip. *The Australian*, p. 4.

Warwick, K. (1998). Professor Kevin Warwick. from http://cyber.reading.ac.uk/K.Warwick/

Wells, W. (1998). The chips are coming. *Biotech Applied*, from http://www.accessexcellence.com/AB/BA/biochip.html

Wherify. (2003, 5 January 2003). GPS Locator for children: Peace of mind for parents, cool for kids. *Wherify Wireless Location Services*, from http://www.wherifywireless.com/prod_watches.htm

Wherify. (2004). Frequently Asked Questions: Wherify Wireless. Retrieved 15 April 2004, from http://www.wherifywireless.com/faq.asp

Wilcox, J. (1999, 20 December). More details emerge on IBM's wearable PC. *CNet.com*. Retrieved from http://news/cnet.com/news/0-1006-200-1501451.html

Williams, M. (29 March 2008). NTT DoCoMo Close to Bio-Sensing Cell Phones. *PC World*. Retrieved 4 Feburary 2009, from http://www.pcworld.com/article/143933/ntt_docomo_close_to_biosensing_cell_phones.html

Witt, S. (1999, 14 January). Is human chip implant wave of the future? *CNN.com*. Retrieved from http://www.cnn.com/TECH/computing/9901/14/chipman.idg/

Zeimpekis, V., Giaglis, G., & Lekakos, G. (2003). A Taxonomy of Indoor and Outdoor Positioning Techniques for Mobile Location Services. *Journal of ACM SIGecom Exchanges, 3*(4), 19-27.

Interview 12.1
The Biomedical Pioneer

Professor Christofer Toumazou, London, England
Interview conducted by MG Michael on 18 October 2006.

INTERVIEW

M.G. Michael: I'm here with Professor Chris Toumazou in London at Imperial College and he has been most generous in affording this time to me. Professor Toumazou will go through and answer some of the questions which I have prepared for him, as he sees fit.

Christofer Toumazou: Okay, my research interest in biomedical and what has inspired this. I guess the inspiration has really been that from an early age I've been especially interested in semiconductor technology and I was part of the evolution of what we call radio frequency technology, things like silicon chips that go into mobile phones and other devices. And it just became very apparent to me that if you applied a fraction of the sort of technologies in this space to health care you could make major innovations but the issue is always that the medics and the engineers weren't working together. Advances were taking place in isolation. So I was very keen on finding a way of taking technologies that are very well versed in that particular field to an application base that

would actually make an impact. And the reasons that my technology was very relevant to implants, is that I've worked in a field of analogue and not digital electronics. Analogue is more speech, sound, voice, touching, smelling, they are all analogue. Whereas for years we graduated engineers with flat fingers and ones and zeros- the digital revolution. And people then started ignoring the physics of semiconductors, so trying to make very precise machines out of ones and zeros and that's the digital domain.

Now in the human space we don't need very high precision, because we don't see with 20 bits, we don't hear with high precision. So there was a very interesting concept here. *Let's say, well why don't we use the area between the one and zero of the digital device to actually create functions that replicate biology out of silica, rather than using ones and zeros to try and mimic biological systems which are quite inefficient.* Because ones and zeros are very precise if you want number crunching, mathematical calculations but the trade off is power, power consumption. And it struck me when a company approached me, a medical device company about four to five years ago and they developed an electrode array. An electrode array that behaves like the proboscis of a butterfly, it's a spiral array with 16 taps of electrodes and the idea was that the surgeon could implant it by inserting a pin in the array, pressing it into the ear, pulling the pin out, and it would spiral around and make physical contact to the nervous tissue. Now this was great because it meant that unlike other cochlear devices this device didn't rely on the conductivity of the fluid in the ear to make the electrical connection, so the power consumption in the electrodes was very, very low. And now they needed something to model the biology behind the cochlear, or the inner ear, and they could do it in a digital fashion with all the ones and zeros, all the filtering, everything that takes place. So that way they would have this electrode implanted in the ear with wires, and a big digital chip hanging outside. So my technology was one where I could replace all that digital electronics by mimicking the traveling wave properties, pressure wave properties of the cochlear but in added filters, added electronic filters that you would find in a radio. And by doing that we were able to integrate the electronics onto the electrode and have the whole thing totally implantable because the brain does all the rest. You see the beauty of the cochlear implant, is that if you were to try to replace it exactly out of the silicon chip, you would have to replace something like twenty-four thousand hair cells, which are the things that go from- the neural transmitters that connect from the optic to auditory nerve- now that would mean twenty-four thousand electrodes and twenty-four thousand filters. We did this implant with only sixteen electrodes because the brain does all the regenerative work, it does all the encoding and decoding. From just a simple array of electrodes a deaf person can hear because then the brain takes over. So you don't need that high precision in the technology, because biology is personalized and can then take over. So this inspired this whole area of effectively looking at cochlear implants that would make two things, the surgical procedure very efficient, because of the surgical implant, secondly because the power consumption is very small, then these sort of devices could be powered up with things like tooth brush, inductive loops, with little implantable lithium batteries which

means they wouldn't have to be replaced so often. So again not so much surgery. Now where the real costs are, are not in the semiconductors and the chip, the costs have always been in the surgical procedure, so by reducing the cost of the surgical procedure then we've reduced the cost of the overall implant. So we've gone from thousands, about $20,000 as it used to be, down to a few thousand dollars and that's the sort of approach we've taken.

M.G. Michael: And from cochlear prosthetics? Where to from there?

Christofer Toumazou: Obviously we've sort of moved along from cochlear prosthetics to use the same idea for retina prosthetics and with the retina, we had similar issues. That if you try and replace all the intelligence of the ganglions in the inner eye of the retina, because the retina has something like a hundred million photo receptors which then stimulate ganglion cells which then connect to the optic nerve… so our idea was to take the behavior of those photo receptors and make an array of photo diodes. Now this is where the beauty of the technology comes in, because what we're doing is rather then do things globally- if you take a camera like a CCD (charge-coupled device) camera you do things globally and you get over exposure and every pixel doesn't actually do something, it will do something across the whole array of pixels- whereas with the retina, on every single pixel you have got local intelligence because the retina is the only part of the brain that is visible. So what we do is on every pixel we put gain control, quantization, filtering. *You can understand then, that we are creating local intelligent sensor devices that effectively mimic the exact behavior of the biology. Because that's what the biology is doing there is lots of local intelligence in biology, and again we would not be able to achieve that in a power efficient way using digital electronics.* So the semi-conductor technology was very interesting, and the other thing to say about the technology behind this is the fact that as you, if you think of the transistor, its like saying... okay imagine an egg timer you've either got all the sand on one side and then it falls to the other side so after a couple of minutes it's either all or nothing, that's the digital clock. Now the analogue clock is when its in-between, it's between the one and the zero so it's continuous, and it's the in-between that's really efficient. So effectively what is happening with the semiconductor industry now is that people are trying to put billions of transistors onto silicon chips and these transistors are being switched on digitally. Fortunately for us, one of the biggest problems for the semiconductor industry is the leakage currents, and it's that leakage between the one and zero that we have been exploiting to do this analogue work. So effectively we've been looking at the weakness of the digital electronics to make some very efficient, very low power analogue. We're talking nano-watts of power consumption. A nano-watt is a billionth of the power of a light bulb to do all this sort of intelligence.

Now if we move through because there's a lot here about implants, and technology and issues along those lines. One of the things that I was able to do was, okay, I got very much involved initially in the telecom space and you've seen the migration into the biomedical world because of the work on cochlear and retina, but what also became very apparent is that I used to run a large group in electrical engineering and I was then asked to run the department of bioengineering here at the college and I found that the engineers were really the innovators in the medical space. I had rocket scientists working with me that were the best designers of heart pumps, left ventricular devices, the best designers, aeronautical engineers...

M.G. Michael: Is this something you are especially promoting? I mean the cross-disciplinary involvement?

Christofer Toumazou: *Yes. The whole cross disciplinary area is something that I tried to promote at the department of engineering. So I tried to break down this traditional silo that we have in academic institutions. Each department is a good ingredient, so electrical is an ingredient, mechanical is an ingredient and the clinicians have their ingredient.* So the idea of the department for me was to try and get these ingredients to make a mixture and it was this large scale mixture. Without that mixture the cochlear implant would have been very difficult to achieve. And the icing on the cake are obviously the medical devices. Now it was very hard even in the department, because a department in an institution like this is in competition to other departments. So I decided to create something a level higher then departments, and this new institute that we've got, the Institute of Biomedical Engineering, it's the largest institute in Europe. I raised about thirty million pounds actually, over the past two and a half years to build this. This used to be the Royal School of Mines, so we have gone from mining to biomedical engineering! So it shows you the sort of differences that happen with time.

M.G. Michael: Yes, I would reckon there is a metaphor...

Christofer Toumazou: Yes, absolutely. But the motivation for this institute that we've created is to effectively graduate very wealthy noble laureates because the next generation graduate is quite entrepreneurial so there is a very big mix.

But coming back to the technology so we have to think, I come from a background which is very much consumer-oriented, the mobile phone and that sector being an electrical engineer, so how do we leverage on the economies of scale in the sort of health care arena. That's where all the new paradigms are being set up. You'll find in a number of big companies, even Intel, have set up digital health, and what is it that's attracting them? Well first of all we're seeing people living longer, you're seeing in some places now the demographics, you get more people living over sixty-five than under sixty. So people need better quality of life, they are living longer. Obesity, problems like that, we need early detection to avoid Type 2 diabetes and Type 1 diabetes. Chronic disease management is costing the National Health Service (NHS) over here and the Medicare in Australia, and others, its costing huge amounts of money. So I needed to set this institute up around a technology base which was disrupted enough to break into the economies that would allow the medical device out of the hospital and into the home. Much more oriented towards the consumer rather than the hospital. So we created a division in this institute around the field that we call personalized health care. And personalized health care is both diagnostics and therapeutics in a combination. The diagnostics are really around this whole idea of 24/7 monitoring.

M.G. Michael: Is that the much talked about idea of prediction and prevention?

Christofer Toumazou: Yes. It's also managing chronic disease. I mean, I can say this and you can put it on the interview or not, for the last three years my son has been on dialysis, kidney dialysis, and he has had a transplant about two months ago, a kidney transplant. And I saw first hand during that period of time the stress of going to the hospital, of going to have a blood test, going to have a blood pressure test. All those things are very, very stressful, when most of the time it would have been okay, because his blood pressure would have been okay. Whereas these monitors and this whole technology base is about having the ability to measure these parameters in a way which is non-invasive, and that's effectively transparent. But also in a way that allows freedom of the individual just to go on with their daily life, they don't know that they are being monitored and only if a particular vital sign is detected will it indicate an

alarm. That alarm then gets compared with their patient database information, which then will only activate them to go to the hospital if that trend was so evident in the past two or three hours. So that sort of technology which is an application of the radio work, combined with the sensors, combined with the intelligence locally, which means you're doing a lot of the intelligent work on the sensor, measuring blood pressure, measuring heart rate, measuring heart rate variability in a continuous way. I think that this point of care, out of the hospital and in the home, for early detection for chronic disease management is critical. But the only way that is going to break through is that if the economies are there, it's a matter of the hospitals and the NHS saving money by us using these technologies. So that private insurance companies are taking them on board.

M.G. Michael: So the nuts and bolts of the technological infrastructure are already in place?

Christofer Toumazou: The end-to-end infrastructure is there now and the end to end infrastructure is basically going from the patient right through to the hospital database. But the provider of this technology which is the end-to-end infrastructure is only economically viable if the technology that is being used has two important factors. One, it has to be continuous 24/7 monitoring. If it's an accelerometer for the elderly, if they fall over you know they've fallen over and it sends a signal off to the medic, to the health care worker if its heart its 24/7 monitoring. *And also that its 24/7 monitoring but also cheap and disposable. So that's how we leverage on the semiconductor industry. Now that's why the semiconductor industry is pushing that not for just therapeutics with cochlear and retina but they're pushing for things that are actually much more part of the consumer world in a sense that makes the medical device much more of a gadget, so your medical device interfaces with your personal digital assistant (PDA). You could* imagine somebody who is obese so there needs to be conformity that they go to the gym, now they don't need to go to the gym, but they have a digital plaster which is a heart monitor, and this heart monitor connects to their PDA so if they do go to the gym then the information will be compared to their database and they might get a reward via the phone… say we're going to download you a free tune for your iPod. That is why mobile phone network operators are now getting involved, why the Oracles are providing the databases for these systems, and why the sensor manufacturers want a piece of the pie. They are all getting very much involved in bringing this whole space together and this is great because it means now that we are not inventing new technologies, but we are applying well-known technologies to this human space.

M.G. Michael: So as human beings you see us as being part of an extensive and evolving network?

Christofer Toumazou: That's right.

M.G. Michael: So we are part of that network right now?

Christofer Toumazou: We are part of it, but we are mobile, we are free. We are not wired- this is the wireless world now.

M.G. Michael: Have we moved beyond the wired network?

Christofer Toumazou: Yes, that's right we've moved beyond the wired network.

M.G. Michael: So mobility is the key here?

Christofer Toumazou: That's the whole idea.

M.G. Michael: Ubiquitous computing-

Christofer Toumazou: Ubiquitous computing and pervasive monitoring and the whole sensor network. But that's only feasible now because people have been designing these devices for many years. But there are three important things that have changed. First of all is the technology has become basically almost disposable, so it has become very, very cheap. Secondly-

M.G. Michael: And accessible…

Christofer Toumazou: And accessible… Secondly peoples' understanding of their own health and well being, they're a lot more educated. People are living longer and they're accepting that. And thirdly we're creating these end-to-end infrastructures that weren't available before, you couldn't go out there with a medical device on its own, you know it wouldn't- it has to fit into something. And in fact in the States they've got these networks now where they are trying to create standards around the whole medical infrastructure.

M.G. Michael: Are these the protocols in engineering?

Christofer Toumazou: Protocols in engineering, yes. So the company I launched called *Toumaz Technology*, about five years ago now, when we kicked off we were making radios, digital audio broadcasting chips basically, and then we demonstrated that we could make a processor for these radios that consumes something like a thousand times less power then a digital processing chip. That's when my migration to the health care and the cochlear work took place so all I decided to do with *Toumaz Technology* as a business was I would focus *Toumaz* just on the medical space and apply this technology, this sort of low power analogue digital technology to the health care arena, spin out the radio work to much more of a consumer radio arena. And we set up a company called *Future Waves* which makes these products which are digital radios, and digital TV into chips and mobile phones and laptops. Now all along this work is to do with things like... you know, there are the non-invasive technologies, that we can look at and there are things like the technologies for senile dementia and medical illness. *And again, if we can monitor people we can monitor their behavior by using wireless non-obtrusive technologies. It makes it applicable and then it saves the costs... the bottom line is saving costs and helping the individual.*

M.G. Michael: And it's also important to make these things as non-visible as possible?

Christofer Toumazou: Absolutely, unobtrusive.

M.G. Michael: That's what the market's demanding?

Christofer Toumazou: Absolutely, and the product of *Toumaz*, by the way it is called a *Digital Plaster*, and its actually a chip smaller than the one you can see here... smaller then this silicon chip and it sits behind a band-aid so effectively its disposable because it's powered up by power paper so it sticks and measures your ECG 24/7 (Figure 1). It's wirelessly connected to your modem or your PDA it sends the information 24/7 to the patient. Now we've applied these technologies to two other types of diseases. The more mature is for epilepsy control because again what we are realizing is that there are ways of remotely monitoring and then providing stimulation as well as recording. Lots of people do that separately, you diagnose and then you come up with a therapy. So we have been looking at the vegas nerve (the nerve that connects from the central nervous system throughout the body)

And the idea is we are using cup electrodes but we are not using electrical recording- we have this patent here around the idea of using chemi-

Figure 1. Professor Christofer Toumazou with a patient wearing the "digital plaster"; a tiny electronic device meant to be embedded in ordinary plaster that includes sensors for monitoring health-related metadata such as blood pressure, temperature and glucose levels. The "digital plaster" contains a Sensium silicon chip, powered by a tiny battery, which sends data via a cellphone or PDA to a central computer database. The device was developed by Toumaz Technology in the UK. Courtesy of Christofer Toumazou, 2008.

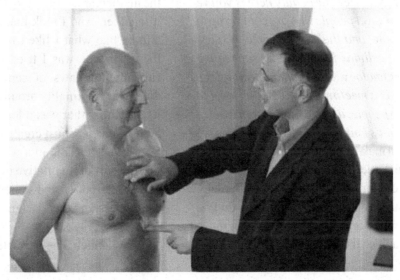

cal recording. Because the brain is made up of electrical and chemical behavior and so what we're very keen on is looking at reaction monitoring and looking at the reaction, the chemical reaction due to sodium and potassium ionic changes as a result of say an epileptic seizure or as a consequence of a depression. From the chemical response we can then predict the onset of either a depressive fit or an epileptic fit; and then once predicted the nerve can be stimulated to counter the seizure. And that is truly personalized health care.

M.G. Michael: What is making these new technologies increasingly possible?

Christofer Toumazou: It's possible to have because we are moving away from the huge technological devices, these big halter monitors for measuring heart, these big electrodes for measuring neural disorders to very, very low power biomedical, electrical, lab-on-a-chip technologies. This institute for example is pulling together. I've got biochemists working with aeronautical engineers with electrical engineers, and we're putting everything on a chip. So you've got the sampling the micro fluidics, you've got the mechanical silicon structures (MSS), and you've got the electronics all on a chip and its possible now because we've miniaturized right down to the nanotechnology space. *The beauty here is you've got the cellular level people who are coming up to the micro people, and the micro people who are coming to the cellular level, and we're meeting at the nanotechnology. So what nanotechnology means to me, is a meeting of the cellular level to the microchip people, it's that integration level of the two and that's fantastic.* And by doing that we can then sort of make things like carbon nanotubes, we can make diode scaffolds and we've got work going on here where we are using our technology to monitor stem cell growth. Again how do you know if a stem cell is growing into a lung or into a heart or into a liver, the whole idea is that we grow

these things initially in bio-reactors. But then if we could monitor their expansion properties we can look at growth properties and then we can provide the correct mixtures and we can monitor how they are going remotely, then if it's not doing the right thing we correct it. So monitoring and diagnostics are really where this technology is really, really headed.

I think we are going to move away from using things like silicon implants to replace biology and we're going to be using tissue engineering, stem cell engineering to replace biology, but what we are going to be doing is using the electronics to monitor the biology. So that's where the therapy will be replaced by actually growing new organs, but the actual diagnostics will be taking place with all the low powered engineering that we are looking at. And I think that the whole point is that the digital revolution has been a good revolution for the telecoms, for the computer world, but for the medical arena and for the human space we need to go back to the physics of our semiconductors. Some of the early work I did was at Caltech, and what they were doing- this is where Kevin Warwick's group and others come in- was to look at the physics of the semiconductor and try to fit it to the biology. Say, you know, this has got a mathematical function and this is exactly the mathematical function of the cochlear, let's fit it together. And I took that whole approach, it's almost like what I like to call creating a silica, the difference was I tried to give it also some fundamental laws of semiconductors so that there was a formality around it. I wanted to give it something that was a lot more formal, then it being well "let's just create this and create that". So it's very artistic in a way. I'm trying to give it some sort of qualitative design, giving it some sort of instruction and some language so that you can understand that design.

M.G. Michael: The variables-

Christofer Toumazou: The variables, exactly- You know, I've written a book called *Trade Offs* in this design context and the whole idea is, to understand those tradeoffs, because its understanding "trade offs". Because the whole biology is full of trade offs and there's a couple of students with me now, I've got a couple of Greek-Cypriots... one of those is working on an artificial pancreas for diabetes and what we've done here is it's actually got some sensors for measuring in real time the glucose levels that are coming out of either, into the tissue or fluid or the blood. Now what happens is once you take, once you measure the glucose levels then how much insulin do you need to secrete? There is this organ that we use called the beta cell, that's part of the pancreas and it is quite an intelligent cell, it actually works out from the glucose the exact amount of insulin. Now you could be hyperglycemic or you could be hypoglycemic and the regulation of that is by the beta cell and that's personalized to each individual so your glucose levels will change or your diet or insulin secretion will change. What he has done here, is taken the mathematics of the beta cell, the neural mathematics and he has created or replicated that mathematics in silicon and he has integrated that onto the sensor. So now what's coming out of the sensor is a 24/7 indication of exactly the amount of insulin that needs to be secreted in a diabetic rather then the just take a spot measure. So you take your spot measurement, this is the amount of glucose you need, you go and have dinner and it has completely changed.

Now there are companies which are actually making implantable insulin pumps that fit under the peritoneal cavity. They are basically open loop, there is no way of closing it. The intelligence to close that loop based upon this beta cell does not exist as far as we know, so what we're looking at is using this as a wireless closed loop system so it's automatic. For instance, we've successfully made an artificial pancreas using this local intelligence idea. And why now? Because we can make it with a few microns of silicon, very, very low power using this sort of mixed signal analogue and digital electronics, but not just pure digital electronics.

M.G. Michael: If I could ask a question here... this is all fascinating, truly extraordinary... Katina and I have proposed a few new concepts to help describe this new environment and one of them is, the Electrophorus. I would like you to correct our thinking on this if you think we are off course. In our papers we speak of the Electrophorus in the context that we are now becoming the bearers and couriers of electricity, "Electro-phorus." So one of our key terms, and what we speak of is the rise of the *Electrophorus*, that we are going to be the literal and manifest bearers of electricity. So the first thing I would like to ask is how do you see that? Are we onto something here as a concept, as a metaphor of this potentially new state of *being*? And the second thing is we are also thinking, to try and understand where we are going as humans and we thought of the *Homo Electricus* as a generic term to denote this perceived evolution. So we are speaking of Electrophorus and Homo Electricus (with a big nod to Marshall McLuhan) to try and explain where we are heading as people, as humans, because of the "new connection" to technology. How do you see these concepts? Are they indicative, are they strong enough concepts to describe a reality which for some thinkers is just around the corner.

Christofer Toumazou: *I think you're onto something very important here because I think the human now will actually be an integral part to the actual device itself.* The biology of the human itself will interact very much with the sensors that we are developing and it's that information that we're wirelessly going to send. You can't have something, you can't integrate a sensor without having the human biology as part of that sort of media. So I think that is a very interesting way that you put it, I am definitely for that. And that is why we call it the sort of the "human space." I mean my terminology is the *human space*. And we've become almost a part of this integrated network, and we are all personalized. You know, so you have your personal ID, and you have your personalized health care. The thing that's also quite interesting is that there are technologies being developed where we can practically, not as a metaphor, we are actually practically using the body to generate that electricity, so there's work going on here where we are using the beating of the heart, to create capacitive effects which will then generate the power that we need to actually give us all unique capabilities. That's much more than a metaphoric sort of example.

M.G. Michael: How is this electricity generated?

Christofer Toumazou: We're actually physically generating electricity from MSS devices and I think you know, there was some very early work which I did sort of follow and I tried to get involved with but unfortunately my colleague passed away, a man called Jack Beledis who was a French physicist who was very interested in this idea that the body is electrical information and from that electrical information being emitted we could actually diagnose things or we can almost you known transfer from one ear to another, almost going back to tele-presence. But there was a lot of that and there was some very good physical fundamental theory around Froehlich a very famous physicist, and Einstein of course. We're almost a magnet, the human has become a magnet, and where we are moving away from is the mobile technologies the PDA from being a fashion accessory but much more now for the good of mankind you know that's where this is being put. So we are becoming part of it in a human sort of diagnostic sense. So I totally agree with your point there.

M.G. Michael: What I'd like to ask you before we move on and conclude here are a couple of important points that I want to know if you have an interest in. What I'd like to ask is, first question, how do you understand ethics in all of this? Is there a role for ethics? Do you consider it in your work? Do you think it's important? There are a lot of questions but basically the question is how do you understand ethics in what you are doing? You spoke about cross disciplinary work, would you include ethics in that, would you be interested in what an ethicist or a theologian has to say, when you speak of cross disciplinary work? Should ethics be involved in the conversation, should there be ethical discourse?

Christofer Toumazou: *Yes, I think that in fact the ethics is extremely important and I would include it. In fact I'm very keen that we have an ethics course here in the Institute for these medical scientists.* You know what stimulated this thinking was that I gave a lecture in the UK to school kids, you know some of them 13 or 14 and most of their questions were around the ethics of the technology and not the technology, and it was very interesting. So from the point of view of understanding the ethical issues, I think it is mandatory. Ethics have to be a part of the procedure that we need to go through to validate the medical device and hence my interest in, for example, the area of stem cell research. It's important for me to show that okay, we can develop technologies that can actually measure what is happening with stem cells so that you can then make the decision on whether or not this thing can be feasible. *There was a very interesting question that one of the school kids asked me. He said now that you can make retinal implants, you can make super cameras, does that mean you could give people better sight than they ever had? Can you make Superman although that-*

M.G. Michael: And should you?

Christofer Toumazou: Well. And that's where I come to a halt, because effectively I think that a deaf person that has heard and lost their hearing and they can get their hearing regained is fine. But actually trying to give someone that can hear, *super* hearing is not fine.

M.G. Michael: There is then a discernible line at human engineering?

Christofer Toumazou: Exactly, that's the term.

M.G. Michael: So, in an ethical construct you would say, and I'm going to be only general and not specific here, you want to repair the human, not recreate the human. So that's basically the ethical paradigm.

Christofer Toumazou: Absolutely.

M.G. Michael: Simple as that?

Christofer Toumazou: That was very well said.

M.G. Michael: I feel very pleased that you would think so.

Christofer Toumazou: It's exactly that.

M.G. Michael: It's really good to know that. It answers many other questions I would have had.

Christofer Toumazou: And I'm really just looking at ways that we could you know, repair, you say repair biology to give the function that we had. Also I think that the sooner we get the technologies around early detection of disease, I believe that will solve a lot of problems because to me that's where the major innovation has to be. *We are going to have to move away from the repairing to the early diagnostic so we can control and manage rather than repair and I think that's very, you know very interesting.* There is a quote from General Electric, saying that you know "doctors look at your medical history, wouldn't it be great if they could look at your medical future" and that is actually what this whole DNA work that we are involved in is doing, looking at predisposition. And I don't know if there is another ethical question around predisposition.

M.G. Michael: Professor Toumazou, thank you very much. It was a great privilege, indeed, to have met you and spoken with you.

Christofer Toumazou: Michael, thank you.

KEY TERMS

Analog: Any device which represents a variable by a continuously moving or varying entity as a clock, the hands of which move to represent time.

Bio-Engineering: The application of engineering principles to the design and manufacture of such medical aids as artificial limbs.

Biological Systems: Denotes a group of organs that work together in concert to perform a task. The human body is composed of a group of systems, for example, the nervous system.

Biomedical: Denotes the biological sciences which relate directly to medicine, as histology, embryology.

Bionic (Wo)man: Combining both biological and electronic elements in a man or woman that allow prosthetic limbs to be controlled by on-board computers.

Bioreactor: An apparatus used industrially for biochemical reactions, such as fermentation, or for processing biological materials.

Cochlear Implant (CI): A surgically implanted electronic device that provides a sense of sound to a person who is profoundly deaf or severely hard of hearing. Unlike hearing aids, the cochlear implant does not amplify sound, but works by directly stimulating any functioning auditory nerves inside the cochlea with electric field stimulated through electric impulses.

Diabetes: A disease in which the ability of the body to use sugar is impaired and sugar appears abnormally in the urine.

Diagnostics: The art or science of diagnosis; the process of determining, by examination of the patient, the nature and identity of a diseased condition.

Digital: Describes electronic technology that generates, stores, and processes data in terms of two states: positive and non-positive.

Deoxyribonucleic Acid (DNA): A nucleic acid that contains the genetic instructions used in the development and functioning of all known living organisms and some viruses. The main role of DNA molecules is the long-term storage of information.

Electrocardiogram (ECG/EKG): Is a non-invasive transthoracic graphic produced by an electrocardiograph, which records the electrical activity of the heart over time.

Electrode: A device that emits, controls or receives electricity. An electrode array is a configuration of electrodes.

Electrophorus: A human bearer of electricity. The root electro comes from the Greek word meaning "amber," and phorus means to "wear, to put on, to get into." When an electrophorus passes through an electromagnetic zone, he or she is detected, and data can be passed from an implanted microchip (or in the future directly from the brain) to a computer device.

Epilepsy: A neurological disease usually characterized by convulsions and almost always by loss of consciousness.

Ethics: A system of moral principles, by which human actions and proposals may be judged good or bad or right or wrong.

Lithium Batteries: Lithium batteries are disposable batteries that have lithium metal or lithium compounds as an anode. Depending on the design and chemical compounds used, lithium cells can produce voltages from 1.5V to about 3.0V, twice the voltage of an ordinary zinc-carbon battery or alkaline cell. Lithium batteries are widely used in products such as portable consumer electronic devices.

Nanotubes: A hollow cylindrical molecule made of carbon. Nanotubes are being investigated as semiconductors and for uses in nanotechnology.

Nano-Watt (nW): One thousand millionth (10^{-9}) of a watt.

Neural Disorders: A disorder (or disease) that usually results in the loss of dopamine-producing brain cells. Dopamine is a chemical messenger responsible for transmitting signals within the brain. In the case of Parkinson's disease the loss of dopamine causes the nerve cells to fire out of control, leaving patients unable to direct or control their movement in a normal manner.

Pervasive Monitoring: Are systems that are used for personalized healthcare services for the electronic data capture of patient information. For example, at-risk heart patients may be monitored remotely using devices that transmit blood pressure to a central database.

Prosthesis: The addition of an artificial part to supply a defect of the body; such a part, as an artificial limb.

Semiconductor: A substance like silicon whose electrical conductivity is intermediate between that of a metal and an insulator.

Sensors: A device that measures or detects a real-world condition, such as motion, heat or light and converts the condition into an analog or digital representation.

Superman: A man of more than human powers.

Therapeutics: The branch of medicine concerned with the remedial treatment of disease.

Transistor: A small electronic device containing a semiconductor with at least three contact points that regulates voltage flow and acts as a gate for electronic signals.

Transplant: The transplanting of tissue from one patient to another, also known as allogenic transplantation, as in the case of transplanting a donor kidney into a recipient.

Ubiquitous Computing (UC): The ability to access one's personal computer data via the Internet from anywhere in the world, indoors or out, by using, for example, a handheld computer and a mobile phone.

Chapter XIII
The Socio–Ethical Implications of Automatic Identification and Location Services

INTRODUCTION

The number of automatic identification (auto-ID) technologies being utilized in eBusiness applications is growing rapidly. With an increasing trend toward miniaturization and wireless capabilities, auto-ID and LBS technologies are becoming more and more pervasive. The pace at which new product innovations are being introduced far outweighs the ability for citizens to absorb what these changes actually mean, and what their likely impact will be upon future generations. This chapter attempts to cover a broad spectrum of issues ranging from the social, cultural, religious and ethical implications of auto-ID with an emphasis on human transponder implants. Previous work is brought together and presented in a way that offers a holistic view of the current state of proceedings on the topic.

BACKGROUND

The relative ease of performing electronic transactions by using auto-ID has raised a number of social, cultural, religious and ethical issues. Among others, civil libertarians, religious advocates and conspiracy theorists have long cast doubts on ID technology and the ultimate use of the information gathered by it. Claims that auto-ID technology impinges on human rights, the right to privacy, and that eventually it will lead to totalitarian control of the populace have been put forward since at least the 1970s. This chapter aims to explore these themes with a particular emphasis on emerging human transponder implant technology. At present, several US companies are marketing e-business services that allow for the tracking and monitoring of individuals using RFID implants in the subcutaneous layer of the skin or Global Positioning System (GPS) wristwatches worn by enrollees. Until 2003, literature had not consistently addressed philosophical issues related to chip implants for humans in the context of e-business. We can point to some of the works of Roger Clarke, (1994), Simon Davies (1996), and Steve Mann (2001) who touched upon the idea of implants but it was popular online news sources like CNN (Sanchez-Klein,

1998) and the BBC (Jones, 2000) that were among the few mainline publishers discussing the topic with genuine and continued interest, albeit in a fragmented manner. The credible articles on implanting humans are mostly interviews conducted with proponents of the technology, such as Applied Digital Solutions (ADS, 2002) representatives who are makers of the VeriChip system solution (ADSX, 2004); Professor Kevin Warwick of the University of Reading who is known for his Cyborg 1.0 and 2.0 projects (Warwick, 2002); and implantees like the Jacobs family in the US who bear RFID transponder implants (Goldman, 2002). Block passages from these interviews are quoted throughout this chapter to bring some of the major issues to the fore using a holistic approach.

More recently academic papers on human transponder implants covering various perspectives have surfaced on the following topics: legal and privacy (Ramesh, 2004; Unatin, 2002], ethics and culture (Gotterbarn, 2002), technological problems and health concerns (Covacio, 2003), technological progress (Warwick, 2003), trajectories (Norman, 2001, Bell & Gray, 2001). Since 2005, over 40 refereed journal papers have been published on the topic of the socio-ethical implications of microchip implants and most of these can be found listed in Michael, Fusco and Michael (2008) and Michael (2007). While there is a considerable amount of other popular material available especially on the Internet related to human chip implants, much of it is subjective and not properly sourced. One major criticism of these reports is that the reader is left pondering as to the authenticity of the accounts provided with little evidence to support respective claims and conclusions. Authorship of this literature is another problem. Often these articles are contributed anonymously, and when they do cite an author's name, the level of technical understanding conveyed by the individual is severely lacking to the detriment of what he/she is trying to convey, even if there is a case to be argued. Thus, the gap this chapter seeks to fill is to provide a sober presentation of cross-disciplinary perspectives on topical auto-ID issues with an emphasis on human transponder implants, and second to document some of the more thought-provoking discussion which has already taken place on the topic, complemented by a comprehensive introductory bibliography.

TOWARDS UBIQUITOUS COMPUTING

From personal computers (PCs) to laptops to personal digital assistants (PDAs) and from landline phones to cellular phones to wireless wristwatches, miniaturization and mobility have acted to shift the way in which computing is perceived by humans (Figure 1). Lemonick (1995) captures this pace of change well in the following excerpt: *"[i]t took humanity more than 2 million years to invent wheels but only about 5,000 years more to drive those wheels with a steam engine. The first computers filled entire rooms, and it took 35 years to make the machines fit on a desk- but the leap from desktop to laptop took less than a decade... What will the next decade bring, as we move into a new millennium? That's getting harder and harder to predict."* Once a stationary medium, computers are now portable, they go wherever humans go (McGinity, 2000). This can be described as technology becoming more human-centric, "where products are designed to work for us, and not us for them" (Stephan, 2001). Thus, the paradigm shift is from desktop computing to wearable computing (Sheridan, 2000).

Quite remarkably in the pursuit of miniaturization, little has been lost in terms of processing power. "The enormous progress in electronic miniaturization make it possible to fit many components and complex interconnection structures into an extremely small area using high-density printed circuit and multichip substrates" (Lukowicz, 2001). We now have so-named Matchbox PCs that are no larger than a box of matches with the ability to house fully functional operating systems (DeFouw & Pratt, 1999).

Figure 1. We have seen GPS-enabled watches, now here come RFID hand watches. Coming in several different trendy colors, your ID badge never looked brighter and more like another fashionable accessory than now.

"The development of wearable computer systems has been rapid. Salonen (1997), among others (Mann, 1997) are of the belief that "quite soon we will see a wide range of unobtrusive wearable and ubiquitous computing equipment integrated into our everyday wear". The next ten years will see wearable computing devices become an integral part of our daily lives, especially as the price for devices keeps falling. Whether noticeable or not by users, the change has already begun.

Technology is increasingly becoming an extension of the human body, whether it is by carrying smart cards or electronic tags (Millanvoye, 2001) or even PDAs and mobile phones. Furui (2000) predicts that "[p]eople will actually walk through their day-to-day lives wearing several computers at a time." Cochrane described this phenomenon as technology being an omnipresent part of our lives. Not only will devices become small and compact but they will be embedded in our bodies, invisible to anyone else (Pickering, 1999). For the time being however, we are witnessing the transition period in which auto-ID devices especially are being trialed upon those who either i) desperately require their use for medical purposes or ii) who cannot challenge their application, such as in the case of armed forces or prison inmates. Eventually, the new technology will be opened to the wider market in a voluntary nature but will most likely become a de facto compulsory standard (i.e. such as in the case of the mobile phone today), and inevitably mandatory as it is linked to some kind of requirement for survival. Upon reflection, this is the pattern that most successful high-tech innovations throughout history have followed.

Mark Weiser first conceived the term "ubiquitous computing" to espouse all those small information systems (IS) devices, including calculators, electronic calendars and communicators that users would carry with them every day (Sydänheimo, 1999). It is important to make the distinction between ubiquitous and wearable computing. They "have been posed as polar opposites even though they are often applied in very similar applications" (Rhodes, 1999). Kaku (1998) stated that ubiquitous computing, is the time "when computers are all connected to each other and the ratio of computers to people flips the other way, with as many as one hundred computers for every person." This latter definition implies a ubiquitous environment that allows the user to seamlessly interface with computer systems around them. Environments of the future are predicted to be context-aware so that users are not disturbed in every context, save for when it is suitable (van Laerhoven & Cakmacki, 2000). Kortuem (1998) stated that "[s]uch environments might be found at the home, at the office, at factory floors, or even vehicles."

There is some debate however of where to place sensors in these environments. For example, should they be located around the room or should they be located on the individual. Locating sensors around the room enforces certain conditions on an individual, while locating sensors on an individual means that that person is actually in control of their context (i.e. sousveillance, Mann, Nolan and Wellman, 2003). The latter case also requires less localized infrastructure and a greater degree of freedom. Rhodes et al. (1999) argue that by "properly combining wearable computing and ubiquitous computing, a system can have the advantages of both."

SOCIAL ISSUES

Privacy Concerns and Big Brother Fears

Starner (2001) makes the distinction between privacy and security concerns. "Security involves the protection of information from unauthorized users; privacy is the individual's right to control the collection and use of personal information." Mills (1997) is of the opinion that some technology, like communications, is not non-neutral but totalitarian in nature and that it can make citizens passive. *"These glamorous technologies extend and integrate cradle-to-grave surveillance, annihilating all concept of a right to personal privacy, and help consolidate the power of the national security state... every technology, being a form of power, has implicit values and politics..."* Over the years terms like Big Brother (Davies, 1992; Davies, 1996) and function creep (Hibbert, 1996) have proliferated to correspond to the all-seeing eyes of government and to the misuse and abuse of data. In most western countries data matching programs were constructed, linked to a unique citizen ID, to cross-check details provided by citizens, claims made, and benefits distributed (Kusserow, 1996; Privacy Commissioner, 1990). More recently however, the trend has tended towards information centralization between government agencies based around the auspices of a national ID to reduce fraud (Jones, 2000) and to combat terrorism (Michels, 2002). Currently computers allow for the storage and searching of data gathered like never before (Rosenberg, 2004). The range of automated data collection devices continues to increase to include systems such as bar codes (with RF capabilities), magnetic-stripe card, smart card and a variety of biometric techniques, increasing the rapidity and ease at which information is gathered. RFID transponders especially have added a greater granularity of precision in in-building and campus-wide solutions, given the wireless edge, allowing information to be gathered within a closed environment, anywhere/ anytime, transparent to the individual carrying the RFID badge or tag.

Now, while auto-ID itself is supposed to ensure privacy, it is the ease with which data can be collected that has some advocates concerned about the ultimate use of personal information. While the devices are secure, breaches in privacy can happen at any level- especially at the database level where information is ultimately stored after it is collected (Brin, 1998). How this information is used, how it is matched with other data, who has access to it, is what has caused many citizens to be cautious about auto-ID in general (Branscomb, 1994). Data mining also has altered how data is filtered, sifted and utilized all in the name of customer relationship management (CRM). It is not difficult to obtain telemarketing lists, census information aggregated to a granular level, and mapping tools to represent market segments visually. Rothfeder (1995) states: "[m]edical files, financial and personnel records, Social Security numbers, and telephone call histories- as well as information about our lifestyle preferences, where we shop, and even what car we drive- are available quickly and cheaply."

Looking forward, the potential for privacy issues linked to chip implants is something that has been considered but mostly granted attention by the media. Privacy advocates warn that such a chip would impact civil liberties in a disastrous way (Newton, 1995). Even Warwick, himself, is aware that chip implants do not promote an air of assurance: *"Looking back, Warwick admits that the whole experiment [Cyborg 1.0] "smacked of Big Brother." He insists, however, that it's important to raise awareness of what's already technically possible so that we can remain in the driver's seat. "I have a sneaking suspicion," he says, "that as long as we're gaining things, we'll yell 'Let's have Big Brother now!' It's when we're locked in and the lights start going off- then Big Brother is a problem"* (Masterson, 2001). In this instance, Warwick has made an important observation. So long as individuals are "gaining" they generally will voluntarily part with a little more information. It is when they stop gaining and blatantly start being taken advantage of that the idea of Big Brother is raised. On that point, chip implants promise the convenience of not having to carry a multitude of auto-ID devices, perhaps not even a wallet or purse.

According to McGinity (2000) "[e]xperts say it [the chip] could carry all your personal information, medical background, insurance, banking information, passport information, address, phone number, social security number, birth certificate, marriage license." This kind of data collection is considered by civil libertarians to be "crypto-fascism or high-tech slavery" (Associated Press, 2002a). The potential for abuse cannot be overstated (Mieszkowski, 2000). Salkowski (2000) agrees pointing to the ADSX VeriChip system, stating that police, parents and ADSX employees could abuse their power. "It might even be possible for estranged spouses, employers and anyone else with a grudge to get their hands on tracking data through a civil subpoena". Hackers too, could try their hand at collecting data without the knowledge of the individual, given that wireless transmission is susceptible to interception (Figure 2). At the same time, the chip implant may become a prerequisite to health insurance and other services. "You could have a scenario where insurance companies refuse to insure you unless you agree to have a chip implant to monitor the level of physical activity you do" says Pearson of British Telecom (LoBaido, 2001). This should not be surprising given that insurance companies already ask individuals for a medical

Figure 2. Singaporean employees on their lunch break at a McDonald's store at a Mall which has a wi-fi hotspot. Using today's IP location capabilities, special queries can be done to locate your position based on the fact that you have simply turned on your laptop which has a wireless access card. Photo taken in 2002.

history of illnesses upon joining a new plan. Proponents say the chip would just contain this information more accurately (Goldman, 2002). Furthermore, "[c]ost-conscious insurance companies are sure to be impressed, because the portability of biomems [i.e., a type of medical chip implant] would allow even a seriously ill patient to be monitored after surgery or treatment on an outpatient basis" (Swissler, 2000). Now a chip storing personal information is quite different to one used to monitor health 24x7x365 and then to relay diagnoses to relevant stakeholders. As Chris Hoofnagle, an attorney for the Electronic Privacy Information Centre in Washington, D.C., pointed out, "[y]ou always have to think about what the device will be used for tomorrow" (Black, 2002). In its essential aspect, this is exactly the void this paper has tried to fill.

Mandatory Proof of Identification

In the US in 2001 several bills were passed in Congress to allow for the creation of three new Acts related to biometric identification of citizens and aliens, including the Patriot Act, Aviation and Transport Security Act, and the Enhanced Border Security and Visa Entry Reform Act. If terrorism attacks continue to increase in frequency, there is a growing prospect in the use of chip implants for identification purposes and GPS for tracking and monitoring. It is not an impossible scenario to consider that one day these devices may be incorporated into national identification schemes. During the SARS (severe acute respiratory syndrome) outbreak, Singapore (RFID, 2003) and Taiwan (Editor, 2003) considered going as far as tagging their whole population with RFID devices to monitor automatically the spread of the virus. Yet, independent of such random and sporadic events, governments worldwide are already moving toward the introduction of a single unique ID to cater for a diversity of citizen applications. Opinions on the possibility of widespread chip implants in humans range from "it would be a good idea," to "it would be a good idea, but only for commercial applications not government applications," to "this should never be allowed to happen".

Leslie Jacobs, who was one of the first to receive a VeriChip told Scheeres (2002d), *"[t]he world would be a safer place if authorities had a tamper-proof way of identifying people... I have nothing to hide, so I wouldn't mind having the chip for verification... I already have an ID card, so why not have a chip?"* It should be noted that some tracking and monitoring systems can be turned off and on by the wearer, making monitoring theoretically voluntary (Wherify, 2004). Sullivan a spokesperson for ADSX, said: *"[i]t will not intrude on personal privacy except in applications applied to the tracking of criminals"* (Mieszkowski, 2000). *ADSX have claimed on a number of occasions that it has received more than two thousand emails from teenagers volunteering to be the next to be "chipped"* (Scheeres, 2002a). There are others like McClimans (1998) that believe that everyone should get chipped. Cunha Lima, a Brazilian politician who also has a chip implant is not ignorant of the potential for invasion of privacy but believes the benefits outweigh the costs and that so long as the new technology is voluntary and not mandatory there is nothing to worry about. He has said, "[i]f one chooses to 'be chipped,' then one has considered the consequences of that action" (Scheeres, 2002c). Lima argues that he feels more secure with an implant given the number of kidnappings in South America of high profile people each year- at least this way his location is always known.

Professor Brad Meyers of the Computer Science Department at Carnegie Mellon University believes that the chip implant technology has a place but should not be used by governments. Yet the overriding sentiment is that chip implants will be used by government before too long. Salkowski (2000) has said, "[i]f you doubt there are governments that would force at least some of their citizens to carry tracking implants, you need to start reading the news a little more often." Black (2002) echoes these sentiments: *"Strictly voluntary? So far so good. But now imagine that same chip being used by a totalitarian government to keep track of or round up political activists or others who are considered enemies of the state. In the wrong hands, the VeriChip could empower the wrong people."* In a report written by Ramesh for the Franklin Pierce Law Centre the prediction is made that (Horn, 2000): *"[a] national identification system via microchip implants could be achieved in two stages: Upon introduction as a voluntary system, the microchip implantation will appear to be palatable. After there is a familiarity with the procedure and a knowledge of its benefits, implantation would be mandatory."* Bob Gellman, a Washington privacy consultant, likens this to "a sort of modern version of tattooing people, something that for obvious reasons- the Nazis tattooed numbers of people- no one proposes" (Mieszkowski, 2000; Levi, 1998; Lifton, 1986). Compare Gellman's position with Zivotofsky, Zivotofsky, and Jotkowitz (2008) who state that RFID tags are not tattoos. The real issue at hand as Gellman sees it is "who will be able to demand that a chip be implanted in another person." Mieszkowski supports Gray by observing how quickly a new technological "option" can become a requirement. Resistance after the voluntary adoption stage can be rather futile if momentum is leading the device towards a mandatory role.

McMurchie (1999) reveals the subtle progression toward embedded devices: *"[a]s we look at wearable computers, it's not a big jump to say, 'OK, you have a wearable, why not just embed the device?'... And no one can rule out the possibility that employees might one day be asked to sport embedded chips for ultimate access control and security..."* Professor Chris Hables Gray uses the example of prospective military chip implant applications. How can a marine, for instance, resist implantation? Timothy McVeigh, convicted Oklahoma bomber, claimed that during the Gulf War, he was implanted with a microchip against his will. The claims have been denied by the U.S. military (Nairne, 2000), however the British Army is supposedly considering projects such as APRIL (Army Personnel Rationalization Individual Listings) (LoBaido, 2001). Some cyberpunks have attempted to counteract the possibility of enforced implantation. One punk known by the name of "Z.L" is an avid reader of MIT specialist publications like open|DOOR MIT magazine on bioengineering and beyond. Z.L.'s research has indicated that: *[i]t is only a matter of time... before technology is integrated within the body. Anticipating the revolution, he has already taught himself how to do surgical implants and other operations. "The state uses technology to strengthen its control over us,"* he says. *"By opposing this control, I remain a punk. When the first electronic tags are implanted in the bodies of criminals, maybe in the next five years, I'll know how to remove them, deactivate them and spread viruses to roll over Big Brother"* (Millanvoye, 2001).

Health Risks

Public concern about electromagnetic fields from cellular phones was a contentious issue in the late 1990s. Now it seems that the majority of people in More Developed Countries (MDCs) have become so dependent on mobile phones that they are disregarding the potential health risks associated with the technology (NRPB, 2004). Though very little has been proven concretely, most terminal manufacturers do include a warning with their packaging, encouraging users not to touch the antenna of the phone during transmission (ACA, 2000). Covacio (2003) is among the few authors to discuss the potential technological problems associated with microchips for human ID from a health perspective. In her paper she provides evidence why implants may impact humans adversely, categorizing these into thermal (i.e. whole/partial rise in body heating), stimulation (i.e. excitation of nerves and muscles) and other effects most of which are currently unknown. She states that research into RFID and mobile telephone technology: *"...has revealed a growing concern with the effects of radio frequency and non-ionizing radiation on organic matter. It has been revealed a number of low-level, and possible high-level risks are associated with the use of radio-frequency technology. Effects of X-rays and gamma rays have been well documented in medical and electronic journals..."*

In considering future wearable devices, Salonen (1997) puts forward the idea of directing antenna away from the head where "there may be either a thermal insult produced by power deposition in tissue (acute effects) or other (long-term) effects" to midway between the shoulder and elbow where radiation can be pushed outward from the body. Yet chip implants may also pose problems, particularly if they are active implants that contain batteries and are prone to leakage if transponders are accidentally broken. Geers et al. (1997) write the following regarding animal implants.

Another important aspect is the potential toxic effect of the battery when using active transponders. Although it should be clear that pieces of glass or copper from passive tags are not allowed to enter the food chain. When using electronic monitoring with the current available technology, a battery is necessary to guarantee correct functioning of sensors when the transponder is outside the antenna field. If the transponder should break in the animal's body, battery fluid may escape, and the question of toxological effects has to be answered. In fact, we need only consider the very real problems that women with failed silicon breast implants have had to suffer. Will individuals with chip implants, twenty years down the track, be tied up in similar court battles and with severe medical problems? Surgical implantation, it must also be stated, causes some degree of stress in an animal and it takes between four to seven days for the animal to return to equilibrium (Geers et al., 1997). Most certainly some discomfort must be felt by humans as well.

In the Cyborg 1.0 project, Warwick was advised to leave the implant under his skin for only ten days. According to Trull (1998), Warwick was taking antibiotics to fight the possibility of infection. Warwick also reportedly told his son while playing squash during Cyborg 1.0: "Whatever you do, don't hit my arm. The implant could just shatter, and you'll have ruined your father's arm for life" (Witt, 1999). It is also worthwhile noting Warwick's appearance after the Cyborg 2.0 experiment. He looked pale and weary in press release photographs, like someone who had undergone a major operation. Covacio (2003) believes ultimately that widespread implantation of microchips in humans will lead to detrimental effects to them and the environment at large. Satellite technology (i.e. the use of GPS to locate individuals), microwave RF and related technological gadgetry will ultimately "increase health problems and consequentially increase pressure on health services already under economic duress."

CULTURAL ISSUES

The Net Generation

When the ENIAC was first made known to the public in February of 1946 reporters used "anthropomorphic" and "awesome characterizations" to describe the computer. The news was received with skepticism by citizens who feared the unknown. In an article titled "The Myth of the Awesome Thinking Machine", Martin (1995) stated that the ENIAC was referred to in headlines as "a child, a Frankenstein, a whiz kid, a predictor and controller of weather, and a wizard". Photographs of the ENIAC used in publications usually depicted the computer to completely fill a small room, from wall-to-wall and floor-to-ceiling. People are usually shown interacting with the machine, feeding it with instructions, waiting for results and monitoring its behavior. One could almost imagine that the persons in the photographs are 'inside the body' of the ENIAC (Michael, 2002). Sweeping changes have taken place since that time, particularly since the mid 1980s. Consumers now own personal computers (PCs) in their homes- these are increasingly being networked- they carry laptop computers and mobile phones and chip cards, and closely interact with public automated kiosks. Relatively speaking, it has not taken long for people to adapt to the changes that this new technology has heralded. Today we speak of a Net Generation (N-Geners) who never knew a world without computers or the Internet (Tapscott, 1998); for them the digital world is as ubiquitous as the air that they breathe (Figure 3). What is important to N-Geners is not how they got to where they are today but what digital prospects the future holds: *"[O]ur increasing cultural acceptance of high-tech gadgetry has led to a new way of thinking: robotic implants could be so advantageous that people might actually want to become cybernetic organisms, by choice. The popularization of the cyberpunk genre has demonstrated that it can be hip to have a chip in your head" (Trull, 1998).*

Science Fiction Genre

The predictions of science fiction writers have often been promoted through the use of print, sound and visual mediums. To follow is a list of sci-fi novels, films and television series that undoubtedly have influenced and are still influencing the trajectory of auto-ID. Chris Hables Gray (2001) tells his students "…that a lot of the best cyborgology has been done in the mass media and in fiction by science fiction writers, and science fiction movie producers, because they're thinking through these things" (Walker, 2001). The popular 1970s series of *Six Million Dollar Man*, for instance, began as follows: "We can rebuild him. We have the technology. We have the capability to make the world's first Bionic man." Today bionic limbs are a reality and no longer science fiction (Wallace, 2009). More recently AT&T's Wireless mMode magazine alluded to Start Trek (Goldberg, 2004): "They also talked about their expectations- one media executive summed it up best, saying, "Remember that little box that Mr. Spock had on Star Trek? The one that did everything? That's what I'd like my phone to be…"

Figure 3. It's hip to think barcode; the trendy "barcode" shoe store at Darling Harbour, Sydney, Australia. Photo taken in 1997.

Beyond auto-ID we find a continuing legacy in sci-fi genre toward the electrification of humans- from Frankenstein to Davros in *Dr Who*, and from *Total Recall* to *Johnny Mnemonic*. While all this is indeed 'merely' sci-fi, it is giving some form to the word, allowing the imagination to be captured in powerful images, sounds and models. What next? A vision of a mechanized misery (Wilmington, 2004) as portrayed in Fritz Lang's 1927 cult film classic *Metropolis*? Only this time instead of being at the mercy of the Machine, we have are apparently going one step further and are inviting the Machine to reside inside the body. As several commentators have noted, "[w]e live in an era that… itself often seems like science fiction, and Metropolis has contributed powerfully to that seeming" (McRoy, 2001).

Some of the more notable predictions and social critiques are contained within the following works: *Frankenstein* (Mary Shelley 1818), *Paris in the 20th Century* (Jules Verne 1863), *Looking Backward* (Edward Bellamy 1888), *The Time Machine* (H.G. Wells 1895), *Rossum's Universal Robots* (Karel Čapek, 1921), *We* (Yevgeny Zamyatin 1921), *Brave New World* (Aldous Huxley 1932), *1984* (George Orwell 1949), *I, Robot* (Isaac Asimov 1950), *Foundation* (Asimov 1951-53, 1982), *2001: A Space Odyssey* (Arthur C. Clarke 1968), *Do Androids Dream of Electric Sheep* (Philip K. Dick 1968), *The Sprawl Trilogy* (William Gibson 1984), *The Marked Man* (Charles Ingrid 1989), *The Silicon Man* (Platt 1991), *Bridge trilogy* (William Gibson 1993-1999), *Silicon Karma* (Thomas A. Easton 1997), *Oryx and Crake* (Margaret Atwood 2003), *The Traveler* (John T. Hawks 2005), *Never Let Me Go* (Kazuo Ishiguro 2005), *Next* (Michael Crichton 2006). The effects of film have been even more substantial and dramatic on the individual as they have put form and dynamism to the predictions. These include: *Metropolis* (Fritz Lang 1927), *Forbidden Planet* (Fred Wilcox 1956), *Fail Safe* (Sidney Lumet 1964), *THX-1138* (George Lucas 1971), *2001: A Space Odyssey* (Stanley Kubrick 1968), *The Terminal Man* (George Lucas 1974), *Zardoz* (John Boorman 1974), *Star Wars* (George Lucas 1977), *Moonraker* (Lewis Gilbert II 1979), *Star Trek* (Robert Wise 1979), *For Your Eyes Only* (John Glen II 1981), *Blade Runner* (Ridley Scott 1982), *War Games* (John Badham 1983), *2010: The Year We Make Contact* (Peter Hyams 1984), *RoboCop* (Paul Verhoeven, 1987), *Total Recall* (Paul Verhoeven 1990), *The Terminator Series, Sneakers* (Phil Alden Robinson 1992), *Patriot Games* (Phillip Noyce 1992), *The Lawnmower Man* (Brett Leonard 1992), *Demolition Man* (Marco Brambilla 1993), *Jurassic Park* (Steven Speilberg 1993), *Hackers* (Iain Softley 1995), *Johnny Mnemonic* (Robert Longo 1995), *The NET* (Irwin Winkler 1995), *Gattaca* (Andrew Niccol 1997) *Enemy of the State* (Tony Scott 1998), *Fortress 2* (Geoff Murphy 1999), *The Matrix* (L. Wachowski & A. Wachowski 1999), *Mission Impossible 2* (John Woo 2000), *The 6th Day* (Roger Spottiswoode 2000), *A.I. Artificial Intelligence* (Steven Spielberg 2001), *Minority Report* (Steven Spielberg 2002), *I, Robot*, (Alex Proyas 2004), *Untraceable* (Gregory Hoblit 2008).

Shifting Cultural Values

Auto-ID and more generally computer and network systems have influenced changes in language, art (King, 2001), music and film. An article by Branwyn (1993) summarizes these changes well.

- **Language:** "Computer network and hacker slang is filled with references to "being wired" or "jacking in" (to a computer network), "wetware" (the brain), and "meat" the body".
- **Music:** "Recent albums by digital artists Brian Eno, Clock DVA, and Frontline Assembly sport names like Nerve Net, Man Amplified and Tactical Neural Implant." See also the 1978 album by Kraftwerk titled "The Man Machine".

- **Film:** "Science fiction films, from Robocop to the recent Japanese cult film Tetsuo: The Iron Man, imprint our imaginations with images of the new."

Apart from the plethora of new terms that have been born from the widespread use of IT&T and more specifically from extropians (much of which have religious connotations or allusions (Dery, 1996), it is art, especially body art that is being heavily influenced by chip implant technology. Mieszkowski (2000) believes that "chipification" will be the next big wave in place of tattoos, piercing and scarification. In the U.S. it was estimated in 2001 that about two hundred Americans had permanently changed their bodies at around nine hundred dollars per implant, following a method developed by Steve Hayworth and Jon Cobb (Millanvoye, 2001).

Canadian artist Nancy Nisbet has implanted microchips in her hands to better understand how implant technology may affect the human identity. The artist told Scheeres (2002b), "I am expecting the merger between human and machines to proceed whether we want it to or not…"

As far back as 1997, Eduardo Kac "inserted a chip into his ankle during a live performance in Sao Paulo, then registered himself in an online pet database as both owner and animal" (Tysome, 2001). Perhaps the actual implant ceremony was not Kac's main contribution but the subsequent registration onto a pet database. Other artists like Natasha Vita More and Stelarc have ventured beyond localized chip implants. Their vision is of a complete prosthetic body that will comprise of nanotechnology, artificial intelligence, robotics, cloning, and even nanobots (Walker, 2001). More calls her future body design Primo 3M Plus. Stelarc's live performances however, have been heralded as the closest thing there is to imagining a world where the human body will become obsolete (Tysome, 2001). *"A Stelarc performance… usually involves a disturbing mix of amplified sounds of human organs and techno beats, an internal camera projecting images of his innards, perhaps a set of robotic legs or an extra arm, or maybe tubes and wires connecting the performer's body to the internet with people in another country manipulating the sensors, jerking him into a spastic dance. It's a dark vision, but it definitely makes you think"* (Walker, 2001). Warwick (2002) believes that the new technologies "will dramatically change [art], but not destroy it."

Medical Marvels or Human Evolution

As Sacleman wrote in 1967 "…the impact of automation on the individual involve[d] a reconstruction of his values, his outlook and his way of life". Marshall McLuhan (1964, 1989) was one of the first explorers to probe how the psycho-social complex was influenced by electricity. "Electricity continually transforms everything, especially the way people think, and confirms the power of uncertainty in the quest for absolute knowledge" (E. McLuhan & Zingrone, 1995). Numerous examples can be given to illustrate these major cultural changes- from the use of electricity for household warmth, to wide area networks (WAN) enabling voice and data communications across long distances, to magnetic-stripe cards used for credit transactions (Ellul, 1964; Toffler, 1981; Gates, 1995; Negroponte, 1995. But what of the direct unification of humans and technology, i.e., the fusion between flesh and electronic circuitry (Moravec, 1988, 1999; Paul & Cox, 1996)?

Consider for a moment the impact that chip implants have had on cochlear recipients. A medical marvel perhaps but it too, not without controversy. There are potentially 500,000 hearing impaired persons that could benefit from cochlear implants (Sorkin & McClanahan) but not every deaf person wants one. *"Some deaf activists… are critical of parents who subject children to such surgery [cochlear implants] because, as one charged, the prosthesis imparts "the nonhealthy self-concept of having had something wrong with one's body" rather than the "healthy self-concept of [being] a proud Deaf"* (Weber, 2000). Assistant Professor Scott Bally of Audiology at Gallaudet University has said: *"Many deaf people feel as though deafness is not a handicap. They are culturally deaf individuals who have successfully adapted themselves to being deaf and feel as though things like cochlear implants would take them out of their deaf culture, a culture which provides a significant degree of support"* (Branwyn, 1993).

Putting this delicate debate aside it is here that some delineation can be made between implants that are used to treat an ailment or disability (i.e. giving sight to the blind and hearing to the deaf), and implants that may be used for enhancing human function (i.e. memory). Some citizens are concerned about the direction of the human species as future predictions of fully functional neural implants are being made by credible scientists. "[Q]uestions are raised as to how society as a whole will relate to people walking around with plugs and wires sprouting out of their heads. And who will decide which segments of the society become the wire-heads" (Branwyn, 1993)? Those who can afford the procedures perhaps? And what of the possibility of brain viruses that could be fatal and technological obsolescence that may require people to undergo frequent operations? Maybury (1990) believes that humans are already beginning to suffer from a type of "mental atrophy" worse than that that occurred during the industrial revolution and that the only way to fight it is to hang on to those essential skills that are required for human survival. The question remains whether indeed it is society that shapes technology (Bijker & Law, 1992) or technology that shapes society (Pool, 1997). Inevitably it is a dynamic process of push and pull that causes cultural transformations over time.

RELIGIOUS ISSUES

The Mark of the Beast

Ever since the bar code symbology UPC (Universal Product Code) became widespread some Christian groups have linked auto-ID to the "mark" in the Book of Revelation (13:18): "the number of the beast… is 666" (Relfe, 1982). Coincidentally, the left (101), centre (01010) and right (101) border codes of the UPC bars are encoded 6, 6, 6. As it is now an established standard for every non-perishable item to be bar coded there was a close association with the prophecy: "so that no one could buy or sell unless he had the mark" (Rev 13:17). In full, verses 16-18 of chapter 13 of Revelation read as follows: *"Also it causes all, both small and great, both rich and poor, both free and slave, to be marked on the right hand or the forehead, so that no one can buy or sell unless he has the mark, that is, the name of the beast or the number of its name. This calls for wisdom: let him who has understanding reckon the number of the beast, for it is a human number, its number is six hundred and sixty-six (Rev 13:16-18)."*

According to some Christians, this reference would appear to be alluding to a mark on or in the human body, the prediction being made that the UPC would eventually end up on or under human skin (Watkins, 1996). As the selection environment of auto-ID devices grew, the interpretation of the prophecy further developed as to the actual guise of the mark. It was no longer interpreted to be 'just' the bar code. Some of the more prominent religious web sites that discussed auto-ID and the number of the beast, when RFID implants for animals became popular included: http://www.666soon.com (2003), http://www.greaterthings.com (2003), http://www.countdown.com.org (2003), http://www.raidersnews-update.com (2003), http://www.light1998.com (2003) and http://www.av1611.org (1996). At first the sites focused on bar code technology, now they have grown to encompass a plethora of auto-ID technologies, especially biometrics and looming chip implants. For a thorough analysis of the background, sources and interpretation of the "number of the beast" see M.G. Michael's thesis (1998).

Card technology such as magnetic-stripe and smart cards became the next focus as devices that would gradually pave the way for a permanent ID for all citizens globally: "He also forced everyone, small and great, rich and poor, free and slave, to receive a mark…" (Rev 13:16). Biometrics was then introduced and immediately the association was made that the "mark" [charagma] would appear on the "right hand" (i.e. palmprint or fingerprint) or on the "forehead" (facial/ iris recognition) as was apparently prophesied (Rev. 13:16). For the uses of *charagma* [mark] in the literature of antiquity (a *mark* or *stamp* engraved, etched, branded, cut, or imprinted) see Arndt and Gingrich (1979, p. 876). Short of calling this group of people "fundamentalists", as Woodward (1997) refers to one prominent leader, Simon Davies is more circumspect (Roethenbaugh, 1998): *"I think they're legitimate [claims]. People have always rejected certain information practices for a variety of reasons: personal, cultural, ethical, religious and legal. And I think it has to be said that if a person feels bad for whatever reason, about the use of a body part then that's entirely legitimate and has to be respected".*

Finally RFID transponders made their way into pets and livestock for identification, and that is when some Christian groups announced that the 'authentic' mark was now possible, and that it was only a matter of time before it would find its way into citizen applications (Decker, 2002). Terry Cook (1999), for instance, an outspoken religious commentator and popular author, "worries the identification chip could be the 'mark of the beast', an identifying mark that all people will be forced to wear just before the end times, according to the Bible" (Newton, 2002) (Figure 4). The description of an implant

Figure 4. A parishioner in attendance at the Saint John the Baptist Serbian Orthodox Church in Dapto, New South Wales, Australia is greeted by a sign that reads "24 hour video surveillance." In the apocalyptic context of uberveillance, God himself, is the only entity, who alone possesses both omniscience and omnipresence. It is important to note that omnipresence will not always equate with omniscience in the world of uberveillance.

procedure for sows that Geers et al. (1997) gives, especially the section about an incision being made on the skin, is what some religious advocates fear may happen to humans as well in the future. "*When the thermistor was implanted the sows were restrained with a lasso. The implantation site was locally anaesthetized with a procaine (2%) injection, shaved and disinfected. After making a small incision in the skin, the thermistor was implanted subcutaneously, and the incision was closed by sewing. The position of the thermistor (accuracy 0.1C) was wire-connected to a data acquisition system linked to a personal computer.*"

"Religious advocates say it [i.e. transponder implants] represents 'the mark of the Beast', or the anti-Christ" (Associates Press, 2002). Christians who take this mark, for whatever reason, are said to be denouncing the seal of baptism, and accepting the Antichrist in place of Christ (M.G. Michael, 2002a, 2002b; Baukham, 1993). Horn (2000) explains: "*[m]any Christians believe that, before long, an antichrist system will appear. It will be a New World Order, under which national boundaries dissolve, and ethnic groups, ideologies, religions, and economics from around the world, orchestrate a single and dominant sovereignty... According to popular Biblical interpretation, a single personality will surface at the head of the utopian administration... With imperious decree the Antichrist will facilitate a one-world government, universal religion, and globally monitored socialism. Those who refuse his New World Order will inevitably be imprisoned or destroyed.*" Barnet and Cavanagh (1994) describe the New World Order from an economic viewpoint.

Companies that specialize in the manufacture of chip implant solutions, whether for animals or for humans, have been targeted by some religious advocates. The bad publicity has not been welcomed by these companies- some have even notably "toned down" the graphic visuals on their web sites so that they do not attract the wrong 'type' of web surfers. While they are trying to promote an image of safety and security, some advocates have associated company brands and products with apocalyptic labels. Some of the company and product names include: Biomark, BioWare, BRANDERS, MARC, Soul Catcher, Digital Angel and Therion Corporation. Perhaps the interesting thing to note is that religious advocates and civil libertarians agree that ultimately the chip implant technology will be used by governments to control citizens.

ADSX is one of the companies that have publicly stated that they do not want adverse publicity after pouring hundreds of thousands of dollars into research and development and the multi-million dollar purchase of the Destron Fearing company. So concerned were they that they even appeared on the Christian talk show The 700 Club, emphasizing that the device would create a lot of benefits and was not meant to fulfill prophecy (Scheeres, 2002c). A spokesperson for ADSX said: "[w]e don't want the adverse publicity. There are a number of privacy concerns and religious implications- fundamentalist Christian groups regard [i.e., implanting computer chips] as the Devil's work" (LoBaido, 2000). According to Gary Wohlscheid, the president of The Last Day Ministries, the VeriChip could well be the mark. Wohlscheid believes that out of all the auto-ID technologies with the potential to be the mark, the VeriChip is the closest. About the VeriChip he says however, "[i]t's definitely not the final product, but it's a step toward it. Within three to four years, people will be required to use it. Those that reject it will be put to death" (Scheeres, 2002c). These are, of course, the positions of those who have entered the debate from the so-called fundamentalist literalist perspective and represent the more vocal and visible spectrum of contemporary "apocalyptic" Christianity. In this context the idea of fundamentalism seems to be a common label today, for anyone within the Christian community who questions the trajectory of technological advancement.

However, the top quality work of Katherine Albrecht for instance, founder and director of CASPIAN (Consumers Against Supermarket Privacy Invasion and Numbering), has clearly shown that a credible and educated response from a Christian apologetic narrative is certainly possible.

With respect to the potential of brain chips in the perceived quest for "immortality" (Norman, 2001; Bell & Gray, 2001), many Christians across the denominational confession see this as an attempt to usurp the Eternal Life promised by God, in Jesus Christ, through the Holy Spirit. This is similar to the case of human cloning, where specialist geneticists are accused of trying to play God by usurping the Creator's role. However, the area is notoriously grey here; when for instance, do implants for medical breakthroughs become acceptable versus those required for purposes of clear identification? In the future the technology in question could end up merging the two functions onto the single device. This is a real and very possible outcome, when all factors, both market and ethical, are taken on board by the relevant stakeholders. Ultimately, for most members of a believing religious community, this subject revolves around the most important question of individual freedom and the right to choose (Stahl, 1999; Noble, 1999).

ETHICAL ISSUES

In an attempt to make our world a safer place we have 'inadvertently' infringed on our privacy and our freedom through the use of surveillance cameras and all of the other Big Brother ancillary. We equip our children with mobile phones, attach tracking devices to them or make them carry them (Sensormatic, 1999) in their bags and soon we might even be implanting them with microchips (Raimundo, 1999). This all comes at a price- yet it seems more and more people are willing to pay this price as heinous crimes become common events in a society that has not ethically kept pace with its technological advancements. Take the example of 11-year old Danielle Duval who is about to have an active chip (i.e. containing a rechargeable battery) implanted in her. Her mother believes that it is no different to tracking a stolen car, simply that it is being used for another more important application. Mrs Duvall is considering implanting her younger daughter age 7 as well but will wait until the child is a bit older: "so that she fully understands what's happening" (Wilson, 2002). One could be excused for asking whether Danielle at the age of 11 actually can fully comprehend the implications of the procedure she is about to undergo. It seems that the age of consent would be a more appropriate age.

Kevin Warwick has said that an urgent debate is required on this matter (i.e. whether every child should be implanted by law), and whether or not signals from the chips should be emitted on a 24x7 basis or just triggered during emergencies. Warwick holds the position that "we cannot prejudge ethics" (Warwick, 2002). He believes that ethics can only be debated and conclusions reached only after people become aware of the technical possibilities when they have been demonstrated. He admits that ethics may differ between countries and cultures (Ermann, 1997). The main ethical problem related to chip implants seems to be that they are under the skin (Trull, 1998) and cannot just be removed by the user at their convenience. In fact there is nothing to stop anyone from getting multiple implants all over their body rendering some applications useless. Tien of the Electronic Frontier Foundation (EFF) is convinced that if a technology is there to be abused, whether it is chip implants or national ID cards, then it will because that is just human nature (Eng, 2002). Similarly, Kidscape, a charity that is aimed at reducing the incidence of sexual abuse in children believe that implants will not act to curb crime. Kidscape hold the position that rather than giving children a false sense of security because they are implanted with a tracking device that could be tampered with by an offender, they should be educated on the possible dangers. Implanted tracking devices may sound entirely full-proof but deployment of emergency personnel, whether police or ambulance, cannot just magically appear at the scene of a crime in time to stop an offender from committing violence against a hostage.

Whenever ethical issues are involved in any given area of our lives, normally it will involve making some very difficult decisions from a range of possibilities set out before us. Given that this "range of possibilities" has grown at a super rate in the context of the *information age* we seem to have made things much more problematical and confusing to resolve. The authors are not going to pretend to "solve" the ethics issues in *IT* in this book. That is an awesome and complex subject that demands an entirely new study and specialists to attack it who are uniquely trained in the field (there are such people, Michael J. Quinn, Sara Base, and Herman T. Tavani, for instance, and they have written some marvelous works on the subject). One of the issues, however, which the authors of this present work wish to emphasize, is that we need *not* completely abandon the "old" approach in considering some of these topics. That is, we can still apply some "litmus tests" in the context of *human rights* for example or on questions of *privacy* for instance , in determining the morality and consequences of our decisions.

The Prospect of International ID Implants

There are numerous arguments for why implanting a chip in a person is outright unconstitutional. But perhaps the under-explored area as Gellman puts it are the legal and social issues of who would have power over the chip and the information gathered by its means (Mieszkowski, 2000). Gellman is correct in his summation of the problem but science has a proven way of going into uncharted territory first, then asking the questions about implications later. ADSX, for instance, have already launched the VeriChip solution. Sullivan, a spokesperson for the company told Salkowski (2000): "I'm certainly not a believer in the abuse of power," he offered, suggesting that Congress could always ban export of his company's device. Of course, he admits he wouldn't exactly lobby for that law. "I'm a businessman," he said.

Figure 5. e-TAG on top of rear vision mirror for toll collection for use on Sydney motorways. Photo taken in 2006. Courtesy of Jason Paul Sargent

Black (2002) makes the observation that the US government might well indeed place constraints on international sales of the VeriChip if it felt it could be used against them by an enemy. Consider the governance issues surrounding GPS technology that has been in operation a lot longer than human RFID implants. *"Good, neutral, or perhaps undesirable outcomes are now possible... Tension arises between some of the civil/commercial applications and the desire to preclude an adversary's use of GPS. It is extremely difficult (technically, institutionally, politically, and economically) to combine the nonmilitary benefits of the system that require universality of access, ease of use, and low cost with military requirements for denial of the system to adversaries. Practical considerations require civil/commercial applications to have relatively easy access"* (Pace, 1996).

From a different angle, Rummler (2001) points out that the monitoring and tracking of individuals raises serious legal implications regarding the individual's capacity to maintain their right to freedom. He wrote: "[o]nce implanted with bio-implant electronic devices, humans might become highly dependent on the creators of these devices for their repair, recharge, and maintenance. It could be possible to modify the person technologically... thus placing them under the absolute control of the designers of the technology." The Food and Drug Administration's (FDA) Dr. David Feigal has been vocal about the need for such devices as the VeriChip not to take medical applications lightly and that companies wishing to specialize in health-related implants need to be in close consultation with the FDA (Associated Press, 2002b; 2002c). There is also the possibility that such developments, i.e. regulating chip implants, may ultimately be used against an individual. The Freedom of Information Act for instance, already allows U.S. authorities to access automatic vehicle toll-passes to provide evidence in court (Sanchez-Klein, 1998); there is nothing to suggest this will not happen with RFID transponder implants as well, despite the myriad of promises made by ADSX (Figure 5). Professor Gray is adamant that there is no stopping technological evolution no matter how sinister some technologies may appear, and that we need to become accustomed to the fact that new technologies will continually infringe upon the constitution (Mieszkowski, 2000).

Figure 6. Girl on a mobile phone- a GPS-enabled Wherifone. Courtesy of Wherify Wireless, 2008

Beyond Chip Implants

Luggables, like mobile phones, do create a sense of attachment between the user and the device but the devices are still physically separate; they can accidentally be left behind. Wearable computers on the other hand are a part of the user, they are worn, and they "create an intimate human-computer-symbiosis in which respective strengths combine" (Billinghurst & Starner, 1999). Mann calls this human-computer-symbiosis, "human interaction" (HI) as opposed to HCI (human-computer interaction). *"[W]e prefer not to think of the wearer and the computer with its associated I/O apparatus as separate entities. Instead, we regard the computer as a second brain and its sensory modalities as additional senses, which synthetic synesthesia merges with the wearer's senses* (Mann, 2001)."

Human-computer electrification is set to make this bond irrevocable. Once on that path there is no turning back. If at the present all this seems impossible, a myth, unlikely, a prediction far gone, due to end-user resistance and other similar obstacles facing the industry today, history should teach us otherwise. This year alone, millions of babies will be born into a world where there are companies on the New York Stock Exchange specializing in chip implant devices for humans. "They" will grow up believing that these technologies are not only "normal" but also quite useful, just like other high-tech technologies before them such as the Internet, PCs, smart cards etc. Consider the case of Cynthia Tam, aged two, who is an avid computer user:*"[i]t took a couple of days for her to understand the connection between the mouse in her hand and the cursor on the screen and then she was off... The biggest problem for Cynthia's parents is how to get her to stop... for Cynthia, the computer is already a part of her environment... Cynthia's generation will not think twice about buying things on the Internet, just like most people today don't think twice when paying credit card, or using cash points for withdrawals and deposits"* (Chan, 2001) (Figure 5 and 6).

But you do not have to be a newborn baby to adapt to technological change. Even grandmothers and grandfathers surf the web these days and send emails as a cheaper alternative to post or telephone (Tapscott, 1998). And migrants struggling with a foreign language will even memorize key combinations to withdraw money even if they do not actually fully perceive the actions they are commanding throughout the process. Schiele (2001) believes that our personal habits are shaped by technological change and that over time new technologies that seem only appropriate for technophiles eventually find themselves being used by the average person. "[O]ver time our culture will adjust to incorporate the devices." Gotterbarn is in agreement (2003). We enthusiastically adopt the latest gadget for one use, but then we start to realize that it gives us power for another use. Then there is the inevitable realization that we have overlooked the way it impacts other people, giving rise to professional and ethical issues. What is apparent regardless of how far electrophoresis is taken is that the once irreconcilable gap between human and machine is closing.

Beyond chip implants for tracking there are the possibilities associated with neural prosthetics and the potential to directly link computers to humans (Kurzweil, 1999; 2005). Warwick is also well aware that one of the major obstacles of cyber-humans are the associated moral issues (Irwin, 1998; Warwick, 2003)- who gives anyone the right to be conducting complex procedures on a perfectly healthy person, and who will take responsibility for any complications that present themselves? Rummler (2001) asks whether it is ethical to be linking computers to humans in the first place and whether or not limitations should be placed on what procedures can be conducted even if they are possible. For instance, could this be considered a violation of human rights? And more to the point what will it mean in the future to call oneself "human". McGrath (2001) asks "how human"? "As technology fills you up with synthetic parts, at what point do you cease to be fully human? One quarter? One third?... At bottom lies one critical issue for a technological age: are some kinds of knowledge so terrible they simply should not be pursued? If there can be such a thing as a philosophical crisis, this will be it. These questions, says Rushworth Kidder, president of the Institute for Global Ethics in Camden, Maine, are especially vexing because they lie at "the convergence of three domains- technology, politics and ethics- that are so far hardly on speaking terms."

At the point of becoming an electrophorus (i.e. a bearer of electricity), "[y]ou are not just a human linked with technology; you are something different and your values and judgment will change" (Salon, 1999). Some suspect that it will even become possible to alter behavior in people with brain implants (LoBaido, 2001), whether they will it or not. Maybury (1990) believes that *"[t]he advent of machine intelligence raises social and ethical issues that may ultimately challenge human existence on earth."* Gotterbarn (2003) argues precisely that our view of computer technologies generally progresses through several stages: *"1) naïve innocence and technological wonder, 2) power and control, and 3) finally, sometimes because of disasters during the second stage, an understanding of the essential relationship between technologies and values."*

Bill Joy, the chief technologist of Sun Microsystems, feels a sense of unease about such predictions made by Ray Kurzweil in *The Age of Spiritual Machines* (1999). Not only because Kurzweil has proven technically competent in the past but because of his ultimate vision for humanity- "a near immortality by becoming one with robotic technology" (Joy, 2000). Joy was severely criticized for being narrow-sighted, even a fundamentalist of sorts, after publishing his paper in Wired, but all he did was dare to ask the questions- 'do we know what we are doing? Has anyone really carefully thought about this?' Joy believes (Joy, 2000): *"[w]e are being propelled into this new century with no plan, no control, no brakes. Have we already gone too far down the path to alter course? I don't believe so, but we aren't trying yet, and the last chance to assert control- the fail-safe point- is rapidly approaching."* Surely there is a pressing need for ethical dialogue (Masey, 1998) on auto-ID innovation, location-based services and more generally information and communication technology. If there has ever been a time when engineers have had to act socially responsibly (Wenk, 1989), it is *now* as we are at defining crossroads. The new era of biomedical and genetic research merges the worlds of engineering, computer and information technology with traditional medical research. Some of the most significant and far-reaching discoveries are being made at the interface of these disciplines (Boehringer, 2001).

CONCLUSION

The principal objective of this chapter was to encourage critical discussion on the exigent topic of human implants in e-business applications by documenting some of the central social, cultural, religious and ethical issues. The evidence provided indicates that technology-push has been the driving force behind many of the new RFID transponder implant applications instead of market-pull. What is most alarming is the rate of change in technological capabilities without the commensurate response from an informed community involvement or ethical discourse on what these changes actually "mean", not only for the present but also for the future 'shock'. It seems that the normal standard now is to introduce a technology, stand back to see its general effects on society, and then act to rectify problems as they might arise. The concluding point of this chapter is that the long-term side effects of a technology should be considered at the outset and *not* after the event. One need only bring to mind the Atomic Bomb and the Chernobyl disaster for what is possible, if not inevitable once a technology is set on its ultimate trajectory (Pool, 1997). As citizens it is our duty to remain knowledgeable about scientific developments and to discuss the possible ethical implications over and again (Gotterbarn, 2003). In the end we can point the finger at the Mad Scientists (Walker, 2001) but we too must be socially responsible, save we become our own worst enemy (Ebert, 1998). It is certainly a case of *caveat emptor*, let the buyer beware. A truism well worth repeating.

REFERENCES

ACA. (2000). *Human exposure to radiofrequency electromagnetic energy: information for manufacturers, importers, agents, licensees or operators of radio communications transmitters, Australian regulations*. Melbourne.

ADS. (2002). Applied Digital Solutions. Retrieved from http://www.adsx.com/

ADSX. (2004). VeriChip Corporation. *Applied Digital Solutions*. Retrieved 1 April 2004, from http://www.4verichip.com/

Anonymous. (2001). Will a chip every day keep the doctor away? *PhysicsWeb*. Retrieved 29 November, from http://physicsweb.org/article/world/14/7/11

Arndt, W. F., & Gingrich, F. W. (1979). *A Greek-English Lexicon of the New Testament and Other Early Christian Literature*. Chicago: The University of Chicago Press.

Associated Press. (2002a, 15 October 2002). Chip in your shoulder? Family wants info device. *USA Today: Tech*, from http://www.usatoday.com/life/cyber/tech/2002/04/01/verichip-family.htm

Associated Press. (2002b). Company gets okay to sell ID-only computer chip implant. *The Detroit News* Retrieved 5 April, from http://www.detnews.com/2002/technology/0204/05/technology-457686.htm

Associated Press. (2002c). ID chip ready for implant. *USA Today: Tech*. Retrieved 4 April, from http://www.usatoday.com/life/cyber/tech/2002/04/04/implant-chip.htm

Asturias, C. (2003). Implanted for Life: Help! There's a chip in my body and I can't get it out, Metro: Silicon Valley's Weekly Newspaper, January 9-15.

Baase, S. (2008). *A Gift of Fire: Social, Legal, Ethical Issues for Computing and the Internet* (3rd ed.). Upper Saddle River: Prentice Hall.

Barnet, R. J., & Cavanagh, J. (1994). *Global Dreams: imperial corporations and the new world order*. New York: Simon and Schuster.

Bauckham, R. (1993). *The Climax of Prophecy: Studies on the Book of Revelation*. Edinburgh: T & T Clark.

Bell, G., & Gray, J. (2001). Futuristic forecasts of tools and technologies: digital immortality. *Communications of the ACM, 44*(3), 29-31.

Bijker, W. E., & Law, J. (Eds.). (1992). *Shaping Technology/Building Society: studies in sociotechnical change*. Massachusetts: The MIT Press.

Billinghurst, M., & Starner, T. (1999). Wearable devices: new ways to manage information. *IEEE Computer, 32*(1), 57-64.

Black, J. (2002). Roll up your sleeve – for a chip implant. *Illuminati Conspiracy*, from http://www.conspiracyarchive.com/NWO/chip_implant.htm

Boehringer, B. (2001, 23 October). Benefits of the OHSU/OGI merger. *The Oregon Opportunity: A New Era of Medical Breakthroughs*, from http://www.ohsu.edu/about/opportunity/ohsu_ogi.htm

Branscomb, A. W. (1994). *Who Owns Information?* New York: Basic Books.

Branwyn, G. (1993). The desire to be wired. *Wired 1.4*, from http://www.eff.org/Net_culture/Cyborg_anthropology/cyber_modification.article

Brin, D. (1998). *The Transparent Society: will technology force us to choose between privacy and freedom?* Massachusetts: Perseus Books.

Chan, T. (2001). Welcome to the Internet, baby! *Telecom Asia, 38.*

Clarke, R. (1994). Human Identification in Information Systems: Management Challenges and Public Policy Issues. *Information Technology & People, 7*(4), pp. 6-37.

Cook, T. L. (1999). *The Mark of the New World Order*. USA: ASIN.

Covacio, S. (2003). Technological Problems Associated with the Subcutaneous Microchips for Human Identification (SMHId). *InSITE-Where Parallels Intersect, June*, 843-853.

Davies, S. (1992). *Big Brother: Australia's growing web of surveillance*. Australia: Simon and Schuster.

Davies, S. (1996). *Monitor: extinguishing privacy on the information superhighway*. Sydney: PAN Macmillan, pp. 75-95

Decker, S. (2002). Technology raises concerns: Pros and cons of scientific advances weighed as Christians discuss issue. *The Falcon Online Edition* Retrieved 1 April 2003, from http://www.thefalcononline.com//story/2270

DeFouw, G., & Pratt, V. (1999). *The matchbox PC: a small wearable platform*: IEEE.

Dery, M. (1996). *Escape Velocity: cyberculture at the end of the century*. London: Hodder and Stoughton.

Ebert, R. (1998, 20 November). Enemy of the State. *Chicago Sun Times*, from http://www.suntimes.com/ebert/ebert_reviews/1998/11/112006.html

Ellul, J. (1964). *The Technological Society*. New York: Vintage Books.

Eng, P. (2002). I, Chip? Technology to meld chips into humans draws closer. *ABCNEWS.com*. Retrieved 15 October 2002, from http://abcnews.go.com/sections/scitech/DailyNews/chipimplant020225.html

Ermann, M. D. (1997). *Computers, Ethics, and Society.* New York: Oxford University Press.

Furui, S. (2000). *Speech recognition technology in the ubiquitous/wearable computing environment.* Paper presented at the IEEE International Conference on Acoustics, Speech, and Signal Processing.

Gates, B. (1995). *The Road Ahead.* New York: The Penguin Group.

Geers, R., Puers, B., Goedseels, V., & Wouters, P. (1997). *Electronic Identification, Monitoring and Tracking of Animals.* Oxon: CAB International.

Goldberg, H. (2004). Building a better mMode. *mMode Magazine* Retrieved 1 April 2004, from http://www.mmodemagazine.com/features/bettermmode.asp

Goldman, J. (2002). Meet 'The Chipsons': ID chips implanted successfully in Florida family. *ABC News: techtv.* Retrieved 13 November 2003, from http://abcnews.go.com/sections/scitech/TechTV/techtv_chipfamily020510.html

Gotterbarn, D. (2003). Injectable computers: once more into the breach! The life cycle of computer ethics awareness. *inroads- The SIGCSE Bulletin, 35*(4), 10-12.

Gray, C. H. (2001). *Cyborg Citizen: politics in the posthuman age.* USA: Routledge.

Hibbert, C. (1996). What to do when they ask for your social security number. In R. Kling (Ed.), *Computerisation and Controversy: Value conflicts and social choices* (pp. 686-696). New York: Academic Press.

Horn, T. (2000, 19 February). Opinionet contributed commentary. *Opinionet,* from http://www.opinionet.com/commentary/contributors/ccth/ccth13.htm

Irwin, A. (1998, 15 October). Brain implant lets man control computer by thought. *Telegraph.co.uk* 1238. Retrieved from http://www.telegraph.co.uk/et?ac=000118613908976

Jones, C. (2000, 16 December 2000). Kevin Warwick: Saviour of humankind? *BBC News,* from http://news.bbc.co.uk/2/hi/in_depth/uk/2000/newsmakers/1069029.stm

Jones, D. (2000). UK government launches smart card strategy. *Card Technology Today, 11*(6), 2.

Joy, B. (2000, April 2000). Why the future doesn't need us. *Wired, 8.04,* from http://www.wired.com/wired/archive/8.04/joy_pr.html

Kaku, M. (1998). *Visions: how science will revolutionise the 21st century and beyond.* Oxford Oxford University Press.

King, B. (2001). Robots: It's an art thing. Retrieved 4 January 2003, from http://www.wired.com/news/print/0,1294,48253,00.html

Kortuem, G. (1998). Context-aware, adaptive wearable computers as remote interfaces to 'intelligent' environments. *Second International Symposium on Wearable Computers,* 58-65.

Kurzweil, R. (1999). *The Age of Spiritual Machines.* New York: Penguin Books.

Kurzweil, R. (2005). *The Singularity is Near.* New York: Penguin.

Kusserow, R. P. (1996). The government needs computer matching to root out waste and fraud. In Rob Kling (Ed.), *Computerisation and Controversy: value conflicts and social choices* (Vol. part 6 section E, pp. 653f). New York: Academic Press.

Lemonick, M. D. (1995, 17 July). Future tech is now. *Time Australia, 44-79*.

Levi, P. (1988). *The Drowned and the Saved, trans. Raymond Rosenthal*. London: Summit Books.

Lifton, R. J. (1986). *The Nazi Doctors: medical killing and the psychology of genocide*. New York: Basic Books.

LoBaido, A. C. (2001). Soldiers with microchips: British troops experiment with implanted, electronic dog tag. *WorldNetDaily.com*, from http://www.fivedoves.com/letters/oct2001/chrissa102.htm

Lukowicz, P. (2001). The wearARM modular low-power computing core. *IEEE Micro*(May-June).

Mann, S. (1997). Wearable computing: a first step toward personal imaging. *IEEE Computer, 1*(1), 25-32.

Mann, S. (2001). Can Humans Being Clerks make Clerks be Human? - Exploring the Fundamental Difference between UbiComp and WearComp. Informationstechnik und Technische Informatik, *Oldenbourg Electronic Journals 2*(43), pp. 97-106.

Mann, S. (2001). Wearable computing: toward humanistic intelligence. *IEEE Intelligent Systems*(May/June), 10-15.

Mann, S., Nolan, J., & Wellman, B. (2003). Sousveillance: Inventing and Using Wearable Computing Devices for Data Collection in Surveillance Environments. *Surveillance and Society, 1*(3), 331-355.

Martin, C. D. (1995). ENIAC: Press conference that shook the world. *IEEE Technology and Society Magazine*, 3-10.

Masey, S. (1998). Can we talk? The need for ethical dialogue. *IEE*, 4/1.

Masterson, U. O. (2000, 1 May). A day with 'Professor Cyborg'. *MSNBC*, from http://www.msnbc.com/news/394441.asp

Maybury, M. T. (1990). The mind matters: artificial intelligence and its societal implications. *IEEE Technology and Society Magazine*, 7-15.

McClimans, F. (1998, 2 September). Is that a chip in your shoulder, or are you just happy to see me? *CNN.com*, from http://www.cnn.com/TECH/computing/9809/02/chippotent.idg/index.html

McGinity, M. (2000). Body of the technology: It's just a matter of time before a chip gets under your skin. *Communications of the ACM, 43*(9), 17-19.

McGrath, P. (2001). Technology: Building better humans. *Newsweek*, from http://egweb.mines.edu/eggn482/admin/Technology.htm

McLuhan, E., & Zingrone, F. (1995). *Essential McLuhan*. USA: BasicBooks.

McLuhan, M. (1964). *Understanding Media: The extensions of man*. Cambridge: MIT Press.

McLuhan, M., & Powers, B. R. (1989). *The Global Village*. Oxford: Oxford University Press.

McMurchie, L. L. (1999). Identifying risks in biometric use. *Computing Canada, 25*(6), 11.

McRoy, J. (2001). Science fiction studies. *DePauw University, 28*(3).

Michael, K. (2002). The automatic identification trajectory: from the ENIAC to chip implants. In E. Lawrence (Ed.), *Internet Commerce: digital models for business* (pp. 131-134, 136). Queensland: John Wiley and Sons.

Michael, K. (2007). Selected Works of Dr. Katina Michael. *University of Wollongong*. Retrieved 5 October, 2007, from http://ro.uow.edu.au/kmichael/

Michael, M. G. (1998). *The Number of the Beast, 666 (Revelation 13:16-18): Background, Sources and Interpretation*. Macquarie University, Sydney, Australia.

Michael, M. G. (2000a). For it is the number of a man. *Bulletin of Biblical Studies, 19*(January-June), 79-89.

Michael, M. G. (2000b). 666 or 616 (Rev 13:18): Arguments for the authentic reading of the Seer's conundrum. *Bulletin of Biblical Studies, 19*(, July-December), 77-83.

Michael, M. G., Fusco, S. J., & Michael, K. (2008). A Research Note on Ethics in the Emerging Age of Uberveillance (Überveillance). *Computer Communications, 31*(6), 1192-1199.

Michels, S. (2002, 25 February). National ID. *Online NewsHour*, from http://www.pbs.org/newshour/bb/fedagencies/jan-june02/id_2-26.html

Mieszkowski, K. (2000). Put that silicon where the sun don't shine. *Salon*, from http://www.salon.com/tech/feature/2000/09/07/chips/

Millanvoye, M. (2001). Teflon under my skin. *UNESCO.org*, from http://www.unesco.org/courier/2001_07/uk/doss41.htm

Mills, S. (Ed.). (1997). *Turning Away From Technology: A new vision for the 21st century*. San Francisco: Sierra Club Books.

Moravec, H. (1988). *Mind Children: the future of robot and human intelligence*. Cambridge: Harvard University Press.

Moravec, H. (1999). *Robot: mere machine to transcendent mind*. Oxford: Oxford University Press.

Nairne, D. (2000). Building better people with chips and sensors. *scmp.com*, from http://special.scmp.com/mobilecomputing/article/FullText_asp_ArticleID-20001009174

Negroponte, N. (1995). *Being Digital*. Australia: Hodder and Stoughton.

Newton, C. (2002, 27 February). U.S. to weigh computer chip implant. *Netscape: Daily News*, from http://dailynews.netscape.com/mynsnews/story.tmpl?table=n&cat=51180&id=200202261956000188605

Newton, J. (1995). Reducing 'plastic' counterfeiting. *European Convention on Security and Detection, 408*, 198-201.

Noble, D. F. (1999). *The Religion of Technology: the divinity of man and the spirit of invention*. New York: Penguin Books.

Norman, D. A. (2001). Cyborgs. *Communications of the ACM, 44*(3), 36-37.

NRPB. (2004). Understanding radiation: ionizing radiation and how we are exposed to it. *National Radiological Protection Board* Retrieved 1 May 2004, from http://www.nrpb.org/radiation_topics/risks/index.htm

Pace, S. (Ed.). (1996). *The Global Positioning System: assessing national policies*. New York: Rand Corporation.

Paul, G. S., & Cox, E. D. (1996). *Beyond Humanity: cyberevolution and future minds*. Massachusetts: Charles River Media.

Pickering, C. (1999). *Silicon man lives*. Retrieved from http://www.cochrane.org.uk/opinion/interviews/forbes.htm

Pool, R. (1997). *Beyond Engineering: how society shapes technology*. New York: Oxford University Press.

Privacy Commissioner. (1990). *Selected Extracts from the Program Protocol Data-Matching Program (Assistance and Tax)*. Sydney.

Quinn, M. J. (2006). *Ethics for the Information Age* (2nd ed.). Sydney: Pearson International.

Raimundo, N. (2002). Digital angel or big brother? Retrieved from http://cseserv.engr.scu.edu/StudentWebPages/NRaimundo/ResearchPaper.htm

Ramesh, E. M. (2004). Time Enough: consequences of the human microchip implantation. *Franklin Pierce Law Centre*. Retrieved 1 March 2004, from http://www.fplc.edu/risk/vol8/fall/ramesh.htm

Relfe, M. S. (1982). *The New Money System*. Alabama: Ministries Inc.

RFID. (4 June 2003). Singapore Fights SARS with RFID. *RFID Journal*. Retrieved 10 August, 2005, from http://www.rfidjournal.com/article/articleprint/446/-1/1/

RFID. (2003). Taiwan uses RFID to combat SARS. *RFID Journal*. Retrieved 1 May 2004, from http://216.121.131.129/article/articleprint/520/-1/1/

Rhodes, B. J. (1999). *Wearable computing meets ubiquitous computing: reaping the best of both worlds*. Paper presented at the The Third International Symposium on Wearable Computers.

Roethenbaugh, G. (1998). Simon Davies- Is this the most dangerous man in Europe? *Biometrics in Human Services User Group, 2*(5), 2-5.

Rosenberg, R. S. (2004). *The Social Impact of Computers*. Sydney: Elsevier.

Rothfeder, J. (1995). Invasion of privacy. *PC World, 13*(11), 152-162.

Rummler, D. M. (2001). Societal issues in engineering [Electronic Version], 1-3. Retrieved 6 March.

Sacleman, H. (1967). *Computers, System Science, And Evolving Society: the challenge of man-machine digital systems*. New York: Wiley.

Salkowski, J. (2000). Go track yourself. *StarNet Dispatches*, from http://dispatches.azstarnet.com/joe/2000/0104-946929954.htm

Salon. (1999). Professor Cyborg. *salon.com*, from http://www.salon.com/tech/feature/1999/10/20/cyborg/index1.html

Salonen, P. (1997). *'A small planar inverted-F antenna for wearable applications*. Paper presented at the IEEE Tenth International Conference on Antennas and Propagation.

Sanchez-Klein, J. (1998). Cyberfuturist plants chip in arm to test human-computer interaction. Retrieved from http://cnn.com/TECH/c...ng/9808/28/armchip.idg/index.html

Scheeres, J. (2002a). Kidnapped? GPS to the rescue, *Wired News* (pp. 1-2).

Scheeres, J. (2002b, 15 February). New body art: Chip implants. *Wired News*, from http://www.wired.com/news/culture/0,1284,50769,00.html

Scheeres, J. (2002c, 15 February). Politician wants to 'get chipped'. *Wired News*, from http://www.wired.com/news/technology/0,1282,50435,00.html

Scheeres, J. (2002d, 6 February). They want their id chips now. *Wired News*, from http://www.wired.com/news/privacy/0,1848,50187,00.html

Schiele, B. (2001). Sensory-augmented computing: wearing the museum's guide. *IEEE Micro*, 44-52.

Sensormatic. (1999). SafeKids™. Retrieved 3 June 1999, from http://www.sensormatic.com/html/safekids/index.htm

Sheridan, J. G. (2000). *Spectators at a geek show: an ethnographic inquiry into wearable computing*. Paper presented at the IEEE The Fourth International Symposium on Wearable Computers.

Sorkin, D. L., & McClanahan, J. (2004). Cochlear implant reimbursement cause for concern. *Healthy-Hearing* Retrieved 3 May 2004, from http://www.healthyhearing.com/healthyhearing/newroot/articles/arc_disp.asp?id=147&catid=1055

Stahl, W. A. (1999). *God and the Chip: religion and the culture of technology*. Canada: Canadian Corporation for Studies in Religion.

Starner, T. (2001). The challenges of wearable computing: part 2. *IEEE Micro*(July-August), 54-67.

Stephan, R. (n.d.). The ultrahuman revolution. Retrieved from http://www.moneyzone.com/MTM_features3.28.cfm

Swissler, M. A. (2000, 8 September). Microchips to monitor meds. *Wired*, from http://www.wired.com/news/technology/0,1282,39070,00.html

Sydänheimo, L. (1999). *Wearable and ubiquitous computer aided service, maintenance and overhaul*. Paper presented at the IEEE International Conference on Communications.

Tapscott, D. (1998). *Growing up digital: The rise of the net generation*. New York: McGraw- Hill.

Tavani, H. T. (2007). *Ethics & Technology: Ethical Issues in An Age of Information and Communication Technology*. New York: John Wiley & Sons.

Toffler, A. (1981). *Future Shock*. New York: Bantam Books.

Trull, D. (1998). Simple Cyborg. *Parascope*, from http://www.parascope.com/articles/slips/fs29_2. htm

Tysome, T. (2001). Dance of a cyborg. *The Australian*, p. 35.

Unatin, D. (2002). Progress v. Privacy: the debate over computer chip implants. *JOLT: Notes*. Retrieved 1 March 2004, from http://www.lawtechjournal.com/notes/2002/24_020819_unatin. php

van Laerhoven, K., & Cakmacki, O. (2000). *What shall we teach our pants?* Paper presented at the IEEE The Fourth International Symposium on Wearable Computers.

Walker, I. (2001). Cyborg dreams: Beyond Human: Background Briefing [Electronic Version]. *ABC Radio National*. Retrieved 4 November.

Wallace, G. (2008). *Professor Gordon Wallace at the Intelligence Polymer Research Institute Talks About Nanotechnology*. University of Wollongong, 10 December 2008, from http://www.uow.edu.au/static/GWallaceIPRI_latestReleased_UOW042160.wmv

Warwick, K. (2002). Frequently Asked Questions. from http://www2.cyber.rdg.ac.uk/kevinwarwick/FAQ.html

Warwick, K. (2002). Professor of Cybernetics, University of Reading. Retrieved from http://www.kevinwarwick.com

Warwick, K. (2003). Are chip implants getting under your skin? *Compiler* Retrieved 1 March 2004, from http://www.synopsys.com/news/pubs/compiler/art3_chipimplan-mar03.html

Warwick, K. (2003). *I, Cyborg*. Paper presented at the Joint Lecture: The Royal Society of Edinburgh and The Royal Academy of Engineering, UK.

Watkins, T. (1996). WARNING: 666 IS COMING! *Dial-the-Truth Ministries*, from http://www.secis.com/truth

Weber, D. O. (2000). Me, myself, my implants, my micro-processors and I. *Software Development Magazine* September. from http://www.sdmagazine.com/print/documentID=11149

Wenk, E. (1989). *The design of technological megasystems: new social responsibilities for engineers*. Paper presented at the IEEE Delicate Balance: Technics, Culture and Consequences.

Wherify. (2004). Frequently Asked Questions: Wherify Wireless. Retrieved 15 April 2004, from http://www.wherifywireless.com/faq.asp

Wilmington, M. (2004). Movie review, 'Metropolis (Re-release). *Metromix.com*. Retrieved 3 May 2004, from http://metromix.chicagotribune.com/search/mmx-17922_lgcy.story

Wilson, J. (2002, 3 September). Girl to get tracker implant to ease parents' fears. *The Guardian*, from http://www.guardian.co.uk/Print/0,3858,4493297,00.html

Witt, S. (1999). Professor Warwick chips in. *Computerworld*, 89.

Woodward, J. D. (1997). Biometrics: privacy's foe or privacy's friend? *Proceedings of the IEEE, 85*(9), 1480-1492.

Zivotofsky, A.Z., Zivotofsky, N.T.S. and Jotkowitz, A. (2008). Implantable Radiofrequency Identification (RFID) Tags are not Tattoos, *The American Journal of Bioethics, 8*(8), pp. 52-53.

Interview 13.1
The Economist

Professor Ian Angell, London, England
Interview conducted by MG Michael on 21 October 2006.

INTERVIEW

M.G. Michael: I'm speaking to Professor Ian Angell, who has agreed to answer some of our questions. I'm in London, at the London School of Economics. Thank you so much for the opportunity to speak with you. To begin with, how do you understand homeland security?

Ian Angell: Right. So formal security is just the government trying to tell the population that they are being protected. It's what every politician does. Giving it the name *homeland security*, it is where it all began to go wrong. The population has given the government the right for legitimate violence against them in return for their personal security. The government basically has the monopoly on violence against people.

M.G. Michael: What role do information systems play in national security?

Ian Angell: They are not securing the nation. No nation is secure. It's a fallacy. It's simply offensive securing, and offensive securing is also offensive

controlling of the nation. There are two sides to each story, and here is a practical example: CCTV (Figure 1). We have more TV cameras here in London than anywhere else in the world. You can't

Figure 1. A street sign notifies passer-bys that cameras have been installed in the area for their safety. Sydney's War Memorial at Hyde Park South, Sydney City, NSW, Australia. Photo taken in 2007.

go anywhere without being photographed and of course there are some advantages. They do catch out certain criminals but on the other hand it's not comforting when you find that these images appear on mass media for various materialist purposes. One of the main problems is also to do with the fact is that they, the government, are not controlling it.

M.G. Michael: Could you tell us something about how you understand "singularity".

Ian Angell: That's one of my key thoughts, *singularity. Singularity is something that has occurred for the very first time. It is regarded in any scenario. If something has never happened before, how do you protect against it?* Because you can't see it coming. It's what the IRA said after the "great bombing." They, the government, have to do the overtime, we have to do what we did at once: that's a singularity. You just don't know where the first attack is going to come from. They took as much time to think about getting you, you have to be on your guard every single

moment (Figure 2). This is the problem with every form of security not just national security or organizational security and that's why there are lots of things to do with security.

M.G. Michael: The social implications of what you have said are extensive not only limited to governments, but to private enterprise, and to individuals generally.

Ian Angell: And therefore yes... it's general. And all security fails. It may fail catechismically, catastrophically or it could be just little failures. But little failures damage individuals catastrophically. The nation may be fairly secure but individuals become very damaged.

M.G. Michael: Economics plays a crucial and important role in all of this, doesn't it?

Ian Angell: I would think so. Ultimately you can only do so much before the cost becomes excessive. We are beginning to find now that we have

Figure 2. Singularities. For example, how real is the threat of chemical, biological, radiological (CBR) attacks to global citizens? Photo taken in 2006 at the Safeguarding Australia Conference in Canberra organized by the Australian Homeland Security Research Centre.

become involved with all of these escapades in Iraq and Afghanistan. We just can't afford it.

M.G. Michael: Do you believe tracking terrorist suspects will help to curb terrorism?

Ian Angell: I don't believe we can track terrorists. But I think it's the only way, you've got to use good old fashion black mail, hang traps, not computers (Figure 3). Terrorist is a singularity and computers work statistically. Singularities and statistics don't relate. It steps through the net every time.

M.G. Michael: Are these your own perceptions?

Ian Angell: Yes. How can your model catch something which hasn't been modeled?

M.G. Michael: Surely there are exceptions to the rule?

Ian Angell: It may catch by accident but you can't plan to catch them.

M.G. Michael: So it's self competing?

Ian Angell: Not self competing, it just doesn't work. If it catches somebody it's not because of what you do it's despite of what you do.

M.G. Michael: How should emerging technologies such as RFID be considered?

Ian Angell: *It's a matter of power so the ethics is irrelevant. If the powers want to impose it, they impose it. End of story. Ethics has got nothing to do with it.* And of course they have an economic model in mind they think they are going to save money on-

M.G. Michael: Fraud?

Ian Angell: Fraud, immigration, all of those sorts of things. It's a way of reducing costs (Figure 4). Control freaks.

Figure 3. Singapore's Metropolitan Rapid Transit (SMRT). At Orchard Station commuters are greeted by a digital sign that informs them of a train bound for Jurong East arriving in 7 minutes and a general message encouraging commuters of reporting suspicious behavior to officials. Photo taken in 2002.

Figure 4. Arriving at Sydney Airport to join a one kilometer immigration queue after a long-haul flight. Governments are now moving swiftly to introduce biometric techniques and electronic passports for citizens because they state it will reduce costs and alleviate long queues and enhance an individual's personal security. Photo taken in 2000.

M.G. Michael: Can you make a general comment on the capabilities of RFID?

Ian Angell: It's only just begun and it won't just be the state that will be dealing with RFID cards, everybody will. So whenever you walk down the street people will be able to find out everything that's tagged onto you. So you have a form of RFID voyeur, for instance, going round checking whether your underwear is draws or suspenders or not.

M.G. Michael: So you're forecasting this technology? Is it alarming for you?

Ian Angell: Not really. I'm not alarmed by technology because I don't believe it works the way they tell us it should work. What will happen is it gets so complicated that the whole thing falls over. It implodes.

M.G. Michael: So eventually it's going to be unchecked technologies themselves which will add to the problems which you are citing.

Ian Angell: What you have is all these huge systems in place at vast expense and they actually achieve very little. It's like the drug tsars, huge money is spent on drug barons, they catch hardly anything. It hasn't changed the drug situation one iota.

M.G. Michael: Will the RFID technology as it evolves, will it create an elite?

Ian Angell: It will create an industry.

M.G. Michael: Will it at least meet up with some of its goals?

Ian Angell: It won't achieve any of its aims, but it will be in place and it will keep on going.

M.G. Michael: Will it create a great social divide between the haves and the have-nots? Those that can access the higher echelons of technology, and those that cannot access them? Will that be the case?

Ian Angell: Not really, because those interested in the RFID's are normally the "nobodies." It'll actually be more invasive on the rich rather then on the poor. Because nobody cares about the poor. They're always with us as a great man once said...

M.G. Michael: Are there any applications that you know requiring implantation of transponders into humans?

Ian Angell: This is happening, and it is happening right now.

M.G. Michael: Yes.

Ian Angell: You've got it now in clubs.

M.G. Michael: Oh yes, in London and in Barcelona. It's becoming a fashion statement. Its use for medical purposes is well known.

Ian Angell: It's also for economic purposes. I'm doing it to save money to make *my* society *my* conditions more effective and efficient. I like to save money so I can do the same thing I am doing now, but cheaper. And that's why RFID cards are gaining momentum. Because the technology will take up the slack and do the checks that at the moment is a highly expensive industry.

M.G. Michael: Does it matter if you're rich or if you're not?

Ian Angell: Not necessarily.

M.G. Michael: Why?

Ian Angell: Because technology always increases bureaucracy because it denies the ability to choose, it forces you to operate in very restricted ways.

M.G. Michael: Do you think that eventually RFID technology that we implant in our bodies will become the defacto secure ID?

Ian Angell: Well it depends whether a way is found to bypass it. And then it all becomes irrelevant. You know we will be carrying wallets with aluminium foil inside so that the card money that we are carrying won't be noticeable. And shoplifters will disable the RFID tag and then get out of the store without paying any money. So there have always been ways of beating the system. It is a regular system after all; it's not perfection. And so you can always find a way of beating the system. And if the way is readily available and inexpensive, then the people who push these things are the criminals. It's like the work they did on CD's where they solely put a huge amount of money to stop CD's from being read by computers, and it turned out that if you looked at the back of a CD and drew a black line with a felt tip pen across it you totally bypassed the whole thing. For ninety cents you could actually bypass a multi million-dollar system for protection. So people will come up with something really cheap that will-

M.G. Michael: Bypass?

Ian Angell: *I don't know, I don't try it but people will start thinking about putting magnets next to these things... And then what happens... And then the problem that happens is all technology fails from time to time. What happens when it fails? What backup systems do you have? The engineers who put this in place actually think this stuff is perfectible. And that's one of the problems they believe in a perfectible technology when there is no such thing.*

M.G. Michael: Do they truly subscribe to that thought?

Ian Angell: Yeah, they say it. They say its got to be foolproof.

M.G. Michael: That's quite incomprehensible.

Ian Angell: Yes, totally incomprehensible. But some of these people we are talking about are

not necessarily bright. We're talking about MP's too.

M.G. Michael: So during these final stages of implementation we are seeing policy makers making use of this technology.

Ian Angell: They're not very bright either. And worst of all they talk to the people who are selling the stuff. Now I have no problem with that, if I am selling something well, of course I'm going to push it. I've got no problem with that. Buyer beware. You know *caveat emptor.*

M.G. Michael: What are the most important social implications?

Ian Angell: Well it's going to be privacy and surveillance... that is the big issue, and also compliance. But people are now guilty until proven innocent. And proof of innocence is handing over all information about how much money you've got and where you have been. You could actually prove innocence by having a complete audit trail of your actions.

M.G. Michael: And of course the important thing is *context* because a lot of these things are taken out of context like data mining, that sort of thing.

Ian Angell: Yes.

M.G. Michael: So it's important to make sure the context is accurate and usually we can't do that. Okay- who are the 'shapers' of technology?

Ian Angell: *Does society shape technology, or does technology shape society? I believe in a non-linear world, so both. It's dynamic, there is no opposing relationship there. It is on the go all the time.* Is it the blind leading the blind? Well we're all blind. "All I know is I know nothing." Humanity knows very little, so we are just try-ing things out to see what happens and it works until it fails.

M.G. Michael: It's all a great social experiment?

Ian Angell: It's all an experiment. Life is an experiment.

M.G. Michael: I get the feeling you don't think that there are any solutions per se?

Ian Angell: Well there are no such things as solutions, just temporary results which then start something else. There are no solutions; solutions are a very naive concept. Nothing is over, the journey doesn't end, you just start the next one. So anyone who actually thinks they can solve the problem is a fool. Society goes from one issue to the next one. You think, you start giving injections to get rid of diseases and the diseases mutate, and they become far more dangerous, that's what happens. Think back. Every action has a reaction. It's not that utopian, there is a reaction to every action. There's multiple reactions which then feed back and cause all sorts of trouble.

M.G. Michael: So this technology, let's call it intrusive technology, can it be tested?

Ian Angell: You can't test it. They actually believe-

M.G. Michael: That it's a viable product?

Ian Angell: They believe in the *factory* metaphor. That the world is describable, it's tidy and simple, if you put all your dominos in a line then everything will be wonderful, the trouble is all you need is one of them to trip up and the whole thing goes over line and line. So one of the golden rules of security is not to have perfected security. Localize it. If one part falls over, it doesn't affect the rest. So efficiency is dangerous. If you tried to have an efficient society it is a highly insecure society.

M.G. Michael: Yes, that sounds terribly paradoxical but it makes a lot of sense.

Ian Angell: Security only works when things are going well, when things are going badly then security is an impairment (Figure 5). Efficiency is a problem because it just goes through everything.

M.G. Michael: Do you think that people nowadays are becoming increasingly desensitized to the notion of privacy? Do you think that incrementally we are giving up so much of our privacy that we are ready to comply with almost everything and anything? How do you sense …

Ian Angell: Well, people today you know, in the West, in most of the world, it has never been that way. The way people have been imposed upon-
M.G. Michael: In the West…

Ian Angell: We have been spoilt and what we've got is basically a bunch of fascists who are trying to drag the West in the same direction as everywhere else. That's right? It's power and it's a question of how do… it's the classic problem of the individual versus the collective. A culture is the result of a compromise that occurred in the individual. And different cultures have different compromises. And whenever a technology comes along it almost always destabilizes the relationship, and so now we have to find a new compromise that will link the individual to the collective. You have some societies which will have different solutions to others and so your different cultures, different societies.

M.G. Michael: You notice how some societies depend on religion to define and determine their cultures.

Ian Angell: Religion is just one power base, one way that politicians control the population. See if you forget about religion being true or not true

Figure 5. Going through the immigration queue at Auckland Airport, New Zealand, bound for Sydney, Australia before the September 11, 2001 attacks. The mood, and security procedures seemed very relaxed, and security staff even engaged in small-talk with travelers. No questions were asked of the photographer after taking this photograph in 1998.

and just look at it as a political entity then it's easy to see how it is used for political means by certain groupings.

M.G. Michael: How do you understand-

Ian Angell: I don't understand anything, I just describe it.

M.G. Michael: How do you describe the role of legislation? A lot of the latest legislation coming in quickly to counter balance-

Ian Angell: This is the jerk reaction. It's control freak, and when things don't work out the way they want they just get more freaky, and so they introduce more and more and more. *"When empires are doomed they have many laws," an old Chinese saying. We're going through this vast increase in legislation because it's running out of control.*

M.G. Michael: We were talking before the interview about the people *register*. Can you tell me some more about the British national ID card?

Ian Angell: The register is basically statistical. All the criminals, all the people that it's suppose to target; the ones who have the money who have the investment will be able to bypass everything.

M.G. Michael: What are the alleged benefits of the ID card?

Ian Angell: The actual ID register. With all the confidential information on people. Terrorists will be able to buy false identifications and bypass all the immigration regulations because according to the register they belong here. The only thing registers work on are statistical, that means the vast majority of honest people will be controlled by the registers and its main purpose is going to be taxation. So that's how I see the register. The register enables the government to keep control over a substantial proportion of the population, namely the honest members of society. There will be honest members of society who will have all sorts of grief because of errors in the database. But the perceived benefit is going to be, it will allow the government to tax more people and keep an eye on what they're spending. But as for the criminals or for the malcontents they will be able to find a way behind it all and break into and abuse the system.

M.G. Michael: I know I have caught you at a very busy time and my time with you is just about over. There were many more questions I would have liked to have asked and to have teased out more of the implications of what you have been saying... but thank you once again for meeting with me.

Ian Angell: Thank you, Michael.

KEY TERMS

Caveat Emptor: Let the buyer beware.

Closed Circuit Television (CCTV): Used in monitoring and surveillance. CCTV consists of one or more small video cameras sending images to a receiving monitor, television or video device. Surveillance can be covert or overt.

Confidential Information: Spoken or written in confidence; secret.

Control: To exercise restraint or direction over; dominate; command.

Economics: The science that deals with the production, distribution, and consumption of goods and services, or the material welfare of humankind.

Factory Metaphor: A metaphor used to describe a world where everything is tidy and simple. The problem with this metaphor is that it just takes one false move to have things go wrong one after the other.

Homeland Security: Refers to the broad national effort by all levels of government to protect its territory from hazards, both internal and external, natural and human-made. The term is most often used in the United States; elsewhere, national security has more usage.

Information Systems: Any written, electronic, or graphical method of communicating information. The basis of an information system is the sharing and processing of information and ideas. Computers and telecommunication technologies have become essential information system components.

Irish Republican Army (IRA): The original Irish Republican Army fought a guerrilla war against British rule in Ireland in the Irish War of Independence 1919-1921.

Personal Security: The legal and uninterrupted enjoyment by a human of his life, his body, his health and his reputation.

Register: A book or database in which entries of acts, occurrences, names or the like are made for record.

Religion: Recognition on the part of humans of a controlling superhuman power entitled to obedience, reverence, and worship.

Security: Freedom from risk or danger; safety. Freedom from doubt, anxiety, or fear; confidence.

Singularity: Unexpected events that cannot be predicted. Technology is intrinsically statistical, and that means that it cannot deal with singularities.

Surveillance: Close observation of a person or group, especially one under suspicion.

Terrorism: The use of terrorizing methods, especially the use of violence to achieve political ends.

Chapter XIV
The Rise of the Electrophorus

INTRODUCTION

When Jacques Ellul (1964, p. 432) predicted the use of "electronic banks" in his book, *The Technological Society,* he was not referring to the computerization of financial institutions or the use of Automatic Teller Machines (ATMs). Rather it was in the context of the possibility of the dawn of a new entity- the *coupling of man and machine.* Ellul was predicting that one day knowledge would be accumulated in electronic banks and "transmitted directly to the human nervous system by means of coded electronic messages... [w]hat is needed will pass directly from the machine to the brain without going through consciousness..." As unbelievable as this *man-machine* complex may have sounded at the time, forty years on visionaries are still predicting that such scenarios will be possible by the turn of the twenty-second century. A large proportion of these visionaries are cyberneticists. Cybernetics is the study of nervous system controls in the brain as a basis for developing communications and controls in socio-technical systems.

Michio Kaku (1998, pp. 112-116) observes that scientists are working steadily toward a brain-computer interface. The first step is to show that individual neurons can grow on silicon and then to connect the chip directly to a neuron in an animal. The next step is to mimic this connectivity in a human, the last is to decode millions of neurons which constitute the spinal cord in order to interface directly with the brain. Cyberpunk science fiction writers like William Gibson (1984) refer to this notion as "jacking-in" with the *wetware*; plugging in a computer cable directly with the central nervous system (i.e. with neurons in the brain analogous to software and hardware) (Gates, 1995, p. 133).

In terms of the current state of development we can point to the innovation of miniature wearable media, orthopedic replacements (including pacemakers), bionic prosthetic limbs (Davis, 2006), humanoid robots (i.e. a robot that looks like a human in appearance and is autonomous), and radio-frequency identification implants (Jones, 2006). Traditionally the term *cyborg* has been used to describe humans who have some mechanical parts or extensions. Today however we are on the brink of building a new sentient being, a bearer of electricity, a modern man belonging to a new race, beyond that which can be considered merely *part man part machine.* We refer here to the absolute fusion of man and machine, where the subject itself becomes the object; where the *toolmaker becomes one with his tools* (McLuhan, 1964). The question at this point of coalescence is how human will the new species be (Toffler, 1981);

and what are the related ethical concerns? Does the "evolution" of the human race as recorded in history, come to end when technology can be connected to the body in a wired or wireless form?

FROM PROSTHETICS TO AMPLIFICATION

While orthopedic replacements corrective in nature have been around since the 1950s (Banbury, 1997) and are required to repair a function that is either lying dormant or has failed altogether, implants of the future will attempt to add new functionality to native human capabilities, either through extensions or additions (Figure 1). Kevin Warwick's Cyborg 2.0 project for instance, intended to prove that two persons with respective implants could communicate sensation and movement by thoughts alone. In 2002, the BBC reported that a tiny silicon square with 100 electrodes was connected to the professor's median nerve and linked to a transmitter/receiver in his forearm. Although, "Warwick believe[d] that when he move[d] his own fingers, his brain [would] also be able to move Irena's" (Dobson 2001, p. 1), the outcome of the experiment was described at best as sending "morse-code" messages. Warwick (2002) is still of the belief that a person's brain could be directly linked to a computer network. Commercial players are also intent on keeping ahead, continually funding projects in this area of research. IBM's Personal Area Network (PAN) prototype transmitter, showed the potential to use the human body's natural salinity as a conductor to sending or receiving data electronically. While the devices used were wearable, it showed that as many as four people could exchange electronic messages simply by shaking hands (Scannell, 1996).

THE SOUL CATCHER CHIP

The *Soul Catcher* chip was conceived by former Head of British Telecom Research, Peter Cochrane. Cochrane (1999, p. 2) believes that the human body is merely a *carcass* that serves as a *transport* mechanism just like a vehicle, and that the most important part of our body is our brain (i.e. mind). Similarly Miriam English has said: *"...I like my body, but it's going to die, and it's not a choice really I have. If I want to continue, and I want desperately to see what happens in another 100 years, and another 1000 years... I need to duplicate my brain in order to do that"* (Walker, 2001). Soul Catcher is all about the preservation of a human, way beyond the point of physical debilitation. The Soul Catcher chip would be implanted in the brain, and act as an access point to the external world (Grossman, 1998). Consider being able to download the mind onto computer hardware and then creating a global nervous system via wireless Internet (Fixmer, 1998). By 2050 Cochrane has predicted that downloading thoughts and emotions will be commonplace (LoBaido, 2001). Billinghurst and Starner (1999, p. 64) predict that this kind of arrangement will free up the human intellect to focus on creative rather than computational functions.

Cochrane's beliefs are shared by many others engaged in the *transhumanist* movement (especially Extropians like Alexander Chislenko). Transhumanism is abbreviated as >H or H+ and is an international cultural movement that consists of intellectuals who look at ways to extend life through the application of emerging sciences and technologies. Marvin Minsky believes that this would be the next stage in human evolution; a way to achieve true immortality "replacing flesh with steel and silicon" (Kaku, 1998, p. 94).

Chris Winter of British Telecom has claimed that Soul Catcher will mean "the end of death." Winter predicts that by 2030: "[i]t would be possible to imbue a new-born baby with a lifetime's experiences by giving him or her the Soul Catcher chip of a dead person" (Uhlig, 2001).

THE RISE OF THE ELECTROPHORUS

Microchip implants are integrated circuit devices encased in radio-frequency identification transponders that can be active or passive and are implantable into animals or humans usually in the subcutaneous layer of the skin. The human who has been implanted with a microchip that can send or receive data, is an *Electrophorus*, a bearer of "electric" technology (Michael & Michael, 2005). One who "bears" is in some way intrinsically or spiritually connected to that which they are bearing, in the same way an expecting mother is to the child in her womb (Figure 2). The root *electro* comes from the Greek word meaning "amber," and *phorus* means to "wear, to put on, to get into" (Michael & Michael, 2006, p. 635). When an Electrophorus passes through an electromagnetic zone, he/she is detected and data can be passed from an implanted microchip (or in the future directly from the brain) to a computer device.

To electronize something is "to furnish it with electronic equipment" and electrotechnology is "the science that deals with practical applications of electricity." The *Macquarie Dictionary* definition of electrophorus is "an instrument for generating static electricity by means of induction." The term "electrophoresis" has been borrowed here, to describe the 'electronic' operations that an electrophorus is involved in. E. McLuhan and Zingrone (1995, p. 94) believed that "...electricity is in effect an extension of the nervous system as a kind of global membrane." He argued that "physiologically, man in the normal use of technology (or his variously extended body) is perpetually modified by it and in turn finds ever new ways of modifying his technology" (Dery, 1996, p. 117). McLuhan called this process "auto-amputation", the idea of extending oneself to become the complete person again.

The term electrophorus seems to be much more suitable today than that of any other term, including that of cyborg. It is not surprising then, that these crucial matters of definition raise the metaphysical question of identity, which science fiction writers are now beginning to creatively and in some instances to ontologically address. The Electrophorus belongs to the emerging species of *Homo Electricus*. In its current state the Electrophorus relies on a device being triggered wirelessly when it enters an electromagnetic field. In the future the Electrophorus will act like a network element or node, allowing information to pass through him or her, to be stored locally or remotely, and to send out messages and receive them simultaneously and allow some to be processed actively, and others as background tasks (Figure 3).

At the point of becoming an Electrophorus (i.e. a *bearer* of electricity), Brown (1999), makes the observation that "[y]ou are not just a human linked with technology; you are something different and your values and judgment will change". Some suspect that it will even become possible to alter behavior in people with brain implants, whether they will it or not. Maybury (1990) believes that "[t]he advent of machine intelligence raises social and ethical issues that may ultimately challenge human existence on earth." We know, for example, from the reports of the clinical psychologist Michael Yapko (1998) that a procedure under clinical investigation called *Vagus Nerve Stimulation*, refers to a "pacemaker for the brain" which has been used to treat depression by sending electrical impulses to stimulate those parts of the brain which are considered "the underperforming areas." This, of course, raises the alarmingly obvious questions of the potential for 'mood' and 'mind' control.

THE ETHICAL CONCERNS

Warwick is well aware that one of the major obstacles of *cyber-humans* and bio-electric humans are the associated moral issues- who gives anyone the right to be conducting complex procedures on a perfectly healthy person, and who will take responsibility for any complications that present themselves (Smith, 2002). D.M. Rummler (2001) asks whether it is ethical to be linking computers to humans in the first place and whether or not limitations should be placed on what procedures can be conducted even if they are possible. For instance, could this be considered a violation of human rights? And moreover what will it mean in the future to call oneself "human"? McGrath (2001) asks "how human?" Do we determine our 'humanity' by the number of synthetic or mechanical parts we have willingly invited into our body? The founder of the Institute for Global Ethics, Rushworth M. Kidder (2009) questions the general area of research: "are some kinds of knowledge so terrible they simply should not be pursued?" Kidder believes we are heading for a philosophical crisis and that the root cause lies in the chasm between three domains that are hardly on speaking terms- technology, politics and ethics.

With reference to Kurzweil's prediction of humans merging with robots, Danny Hillis predicts that the change would happen so gradually that we would sooner or later get use to it as if it had been there all along (Joy, 2000). In the wearable computing realm, Steve Mann (1997, p. 31) uses an analogy to express this same idea: "[s]omeday, when we've become accustomed to clothing-based computing, we will no doubt feel naked, confused, and lost without a computer screen hovering in front of our eyes to guide us", just like we would feel our nakedness without conventional clothes today. Warwick too remarked about his Cyborg 1.0 implant, "I don't see it as a separate thing [the implant]… It's like an arm or a leg" (Witt, 1999). There is an underlying theme of control here- the partnership between man and machine will always be disproportionate. The machine in the Electrophorus scenario, though given breath by man, is still the more dominant member. It cannot be held accountable for malfunction, including viruses, and for this reason 'traditional' humanity will always be at the mercy of the machine. *Homo Electricus* is at a greater risk than its predecessors in terms of natural selection, as it cannot exist without a man-made power source. It will also to some degree, rely on the 'have nots' or those who 'opt out' of a virtual existence, as the key to its continuum.

Some of the ethical issues that we have touched upon here and which are connected to this category of scientific research can be discussed in the context of what some modern thinkers have called the *precautionary principle*. The fundamentals of this approach according to Weckert and Moor (2006) can be said to be: "If some action has a possibility of causing harm, then that action should not be undertaken or some measure should be put in its place to minimize or eliminate the potential harm." Of course, the niggling question remains: "who" or "what" will be trusted with the determination of which *action* or *actions* should or should not be undertaken?

WHERE TO NEXT?

We could be forgiven for thinking that the *human-computer* metaphor belongs to science fiction alone, but the empirical evidence is out there that it is certainly not *just* the domain of science fiction (Keiper, 2006; Davis, 2006). When well-known universities in North America and Europe fund brain implant projects and large multinational companies support ideas like the Soul Catcher chip and sponsor cyborg experiments, and government departments like DARPA and NASA discuss future possibilities openly, we can be assured that this is not science fiction but increments of science fact. McGrath (2001) alludes to the German poet Rainer Maria Rilke who makes the observation that the "future enters into us long before it happens."

Science fiction writers and directors, whose predictions are sometimes denigrated or altogether discounted by "professional scientists," have helped to put some form to forecasts by the use of print, sound and visual mediums, especially in novels and motion picture. Some of the more notable predictions and representative examples of the genre: *Frankenstein* (Mary Shelley 1818), *Metropolis* (Fritz Lang 1927), *I, Robot* (Isaac Asimov 1950), *Do Androids Dream of Electric Sleep?* (Dick 1968), *Neuromancer* (William Gibson 1984), *Total Recall* (Paul Verhoeven 1990), *The Silicon Man* (Platt 1991), *The Lawnmower Man* (Brett Leonard, 1992), *Johnny Mnemonic* (Robert Longo 1995), *Otherland* (Tad Williams, 1996-2001), *Gattaca* (Andrew Niccol, 1997), *Forever Peace* (Joe Haldeman, 1997), *Bicentennial Man* (Chris Columbus, 1999), *The Matrix* (Larry Wachowski, 1999), *A.I. Artificial Intelligence* (Steven Spielberg, 2001), *Code 46* (Michael Winterbottom, 2003), *A Scanner Darkly* (Richard Linklater, 2006). Forecasts are important because they "do not state what the future will be... they attempt to glean what it might be" (Braun, 1995, p. 133), and in the same way futuristic-type works help us to understand trends and patterns and to raise challenging issues to do with the impact of technology on society.

Bartholomew (2000) reflects: "PalmPilots. Windows CE. Car phones. Cell phones. Armband computers for warehouse management. Bar-code readers. Pagers. Geophysical positioning devices. Where will it all end?" His compelling question *"where will it all end?"* is noticeably rhetorical. Science holds to the unalterable creed that there is 'no end.' To Bartholomew's list we could add: RFID transponder implants. Cochlear implants. Brain implants. Microchip implants, Soul chips. Bio-sensing implants... This inventory of high-tech innovations bound only by the limits of the imagination. About the Verichip RFID, fourteen year old implant recipient Derek Jacobs commented: "I think it's one more step in the evolution of man and technology... [t]here are endless possibilities for this" (Scheeres, 2002). Kurzweil (1999) believes that we are now entering that explosive part of the technological evolution curve. Kurzweil's *Law of Accelerating Returns* states that "[t]he evolution of biological life and the evolution of technology have both followed the same pattern: they take a long time to get going, but advances build on one another and progress erupts at an increasingly furious pace." In other words, as order exponentially increases the time between salient events grows shorter, i.e. advancements speed up and the returns accelerate at a nonlinear rate. Fixmer (1998) described this plight as humanity's attempt to accelerate its own evolution and Mann calls it a *new kind of paradigm shift* that society has not yet experienced. And Kurzweil (2005) is perhaps the most succinct vision we have of the future in a single volume from this particular genre of writings.

CONCLUSION

The idea of the *Electrophorus* is one that no longer exists *only* in the realm of the imagination. This being true, the requirement for inclusive dialogue is now, not after widespread diffusion. There are many lessons to be learnt from history, especially from such radical developments as the atomic bomb and the resulting arms race. Joy (2000) has raised serious fears about continuing unfettered research into "spiritual machines". Will humans have the foresight to say "no" or "stop" to new innovations that could potentially be a means to a socially destructive scenario. Or will they continue to make the same mistakes? Implants that may prolong life expectancy by hundreds if not thousands of years might sound ideal but they could well create unforeseen devastation in the form of technological viruses, plagues, a different level of crime and violence.

To many scientists of the positivist tradition solely anchored to an empirical world view, the notion of whether something is "right" or "wrong" is redundant and in a way irrelevant. To these individuals a moral stance has little or nothing to do with technological advancement but more with an ideological position. A group of these scientists are driven by an attitude of "let's see how far we can go", not "is what we are doing the best thing for humanity"; and certainly not with the thought of "what are the long-term implications of what we are doing here." One need only consider the maddening race to clone the first animal; though many have long suspected an 'underground' scientific race to clone the first human. In this current climate of innovation, precisely since the proliferation of the desktop computer and birth of new digital knowledge systems, observers believe that engineers and professionals more broadly, lack accountability for the tangible and intangible costs of their actions (O'Connell 1988, p. 288). The dominant belief is that *science* should not be stopped because it will always make things better. The reality is however, that even seemingly small *advancements* into the realm of the Electrophorus if 'unchecked', for anything other than diagnostics and medical prosthesis, will have dire consequences for humanity (Noble, 1999). "Once man has given technique its entry into society, there can be no curbing of its gathering influence, no possible way of forcing it to relinquish its power. Man can only witness and serve as the ironic beneficiary-victim of its power" (Kuhns, 1971, p. 94).

Three key informant interviews follow exploring the usability contexts of control (with Professor Kevin Warwick), convenience (with Mr Amal Graafstra) and care (with Mr Kenneth Lea) as related to humancentric microchip implants and location-based services. The objective of the interviews is to inform the reader of cutting edge developments and future directions in humancentric embedded digital solutions (e.g. for the potential application of microchip implants for citizen IDentification, computer-mediated living, and Alzheimer's disease). The findings of the interviews present a most probable path of the auto-ID and LBS trajectory and emphasize the importance of public discourse and debate on the subject.

REFERENCES

Banbury, C. M. (1997). *Surviving Technological Innovation in the Pacemaker Industry 1959-1990*. New York: Garland Publishing.

Bartholomew, D. (2000). The Ultimate in Mobile Computing. *Industry Weeks: The Value Chain*. Retrieved 10 January, from http://www.iwvaluechain.com/Features/articles.asp?ArticleId=720

Billinghurst, M., & Starner, T. (1999). Wearable devices: new ways to manage information. *IEEE Computer, 32*(1), 57-64.

Braun, E. (1995). *Futile Progress: technology's empty promise*. London: Earthscan Publications Ltd.

Brown, J. (1999, 20 October). Professor Cyborg. *Salon.com*, from http://www.salon.com/tech/feature/1999/10/20/cyborg/index.html

Cochrane, P. (1999). *Tips For Time Travelers: visionary insights into new technology, life, and the future on the edge of technology*. New York: McGraw-Hill.

Davis, R. (2006, 14 September). Meet the $4 million woman. *USA Today*.

Dery, M. (1996). *Escape Velocity: cyberculture at the end of the century*. London: Hodder and Stoughton.

Dobson, R. (2001, 5th June). Professor to try to 'control' wife via chip implant. *Rense.com*, from http://www.rense.com/general10/professortotry.htm

Ellul, J. (1964). *The Technological Society*. New York: Vintage Books.

Fixmer, R. (1998, 11 August). The melding of mind with machine may be the next phase of evolution. *The New York Times*, from http://www.princeton.edu/~complex/board/messages/138.html

Gates, B. (1995). *The Road Ahead*. New York: The Penguin Group.

Gibson, W. (1984). *Neuromancer*. New York: Ace Books.

Grossman, W. (1998, November 1998). Peter Cochrane will microprocess your soul. *Wired 6.11*, from http://www.wired.com/wired/archive/6.11/wired25.html?pg=17

Jones, K. C. (2006). VeriChip wants to test human-implantable RFID on military. *Information Week* Retrieved 23 August, from http://www.informationweek.com/story/shortArticle.jhtml?articleID=192204948

Joy, B. (2000, April 2000). Why the future doesn't need us. *Wired, 8.04*, from http://www.wired.com/wired/archive/8.04/joy_pr.html

Kaku, M. (1998). *Visions: how science will revolutionize the 21st century and beyond*. Oxford Oxford University Press.

Keiper, A. (2006). The age of neuroelectronics [Electronic Version]. *The New Atlantis: A Journal of Technology and Society*, Winter. Retrieved 22 October 2006 from http://www.thenewatlantis.com/archive/11/keiperprint.htm.

Kidder, R. M. (2009). Institute for Global Ethics. Retrieved 1 February 2009, from http://www.globalethics.org/

Kuhns, W. (1971). *The Post-Industrial Prophets: interpretations of technology*. New York: Harper Colophon Books.

Kurzweil, R. (1999). *The Age of Spiritual Machines*. New York: Penguin Books.

LoBaido, A. C. (2001). Soldiers with microchips: British troops experiment with implanted, electronic dog tag. *WorldNetDaily.com*, from http://www.fivedoves.com/letters/oct2001/chrissa102.htm

Mann, S. (1997). Wearable computing: a first step toward personal imaging. *IEEE Computer, 1*(1), 25-32.

Maybury, M. T. (1990). The mind matters: artificial intelligence and its societal implications. *IEEE Technology and Society Magazine*, 7-15.

McGrath, P. (2001). Technology: Building better humans. *Newsweek*, from http://egweb.mines.edu/eggn482/admin/Technology.htm

McLuhan, E., & Zingrone, F. (1995). *Essential McLuhan*. USA: BasicBooks.

McLuhan, M. (1964). *Understanding Media: The extensions of man*. Cambridge: MIT Press.

Michael, K., & Michael, M. G. (2005). Microchipping People: The Rise of the Electrophorus. *Quadrant, 414*(3), 22-33.

Noble, D. F. (1999). *The Religion of Technology: The divinity of man and the spirit of invention*. New York: Penguin Books.

O'Connell, K. J. (1988). Uses and abuses of technology. *IEE Proceedings, A*(5), 286-290.

Rummler, D. M. (2001). Societal issues in engineering [Electronic Version], 1-3. Retrieved 6 March.

Scannell, E. (1996, 25 November). Future technology will wire people up. *Info World News* Retrieved 48, 18, from http://archive.infoworld.com/cgi-bin/displayArchive.pl?/96/48/t22-48.19.htm

Scheeres, J. (2002, 6 February). They want their id chips now. *Wired News*, from http://www.wired.com/news/privacy/0,1848,50187,00.html

Smith, D. (2002, 16 February). Chip implant signals a new kind of man. *The Age*, from http://www.theage.com.au/news/national/2002/02/16/FFX9B13VOXC.html

Toffler, A. (1981). *Future Shock*. New York: Bantam Books.

Uhlig, R. (2001). The end of death: 'Soul Catcher' computer chip due...'. *The Electronic Telegraph*, from http://www.xontek.com/Advanced_Technology/Bio-chips_Implants/The_End_of_Death

Walker, I. (2001). *Cyborg dreams: Beyond Human*: Background Briefing ABC Radio National.

Warwick, K. (2002). Frequently Asked Questions. Retrieved from http://www2.cyber.rdg.ac.uk/kevinwarwick/FAQ.html

Weckert, J., & Moor, J. (2006). The precautionary principle in nanotechnology. *Nanoethics, 20*(2), 191-204.

Witt, S. (1999). Professor Warwick chips in. *Computerworld*, 89.

Yapko, M. D. (1998). *Breaking the Patterns of Depression*. USA: Main Street Books.

Interview 14.1
The Professor who has Touched the Future

Professor Kevin Warwick, Reading, England
Interview conducted by MG Michael on 26 February 2007.

INTERVIEW

Kevin Warwick: Hello.

M.G. Michael: Good morning Professor Warwick.

Kevin Warwick: Greetings.

M.G. Michael: How are you? It's Doctor Michael from Australia. I'm calling from Sydney.

Kevin Warwick: Good morning or afternoon; whatever it may be. I'm fine thanks very much.

M.G. Michael: Kevin, thanks a lot for your time. Katina and I are most appreciative.

Kevin Warwick: It's a shame you couldn't meet us when you were over in the U.K.

M.G. Michael: Yes, I was hoping that we could but that didn't work out, unfortunately. But nev-

ertheless here we are now. Kevin, so we don't repeat the preamble we'll just go through and I'll ask you the questions and you can elaborate. How does that sound?

Kevin Warwick: That's fine.

M.G. Michael: Professor Warwick, can you tell us something about your research group at the University of Reading? Particularly about the type of research you are engaging in right now?

Kevin Warwick: We have a range of research that deals with robotics, artificial intelligence, medical world. Particularly implants. One project involves, growing neural tissue which is originally from rat neural tissue. *That study is used to control robots, we have little robots on wheels, instead of the brain of the robot being a computer or an actual processor, the brain is in fact biological tissue so it's a biological brain for the metallical machine object.* Other projects we have going on at the moment are furthering the implant research that I have been doing. Partly for therapeutic purposes potentially to help people with spinal injuries but also for enhancement in extending the range of human senses and the way we communicate. And I think there is a third area that is slightly important to me at the moment, and that is the next generation of implants for Parkinson's disease. Looking at taking the present stimulators used to overcome the tremor effect associated with Parkinson's disease and make it into a more intelligent stimulation in which we can predict tremors before they occur, and to stop them occurring before they do.

M.G. Michael: This later research does it go back 2 or 3 years? When did you begin to work in this area?

Kevin Warwick: I think I have always been interested and, if you like, informed about Parkinson's disease type stimulator and the problems there with surgeons discussing it for 6 or 7 years and what we could potentially do to improve. But it is only in the last 3 years that we have been studying the signals in the human brain which are prevalent when Parkinson's disease tremors occur and trying to distinguish them from other signals. So only actually about 3 years getting to the gist of the problem.

M.G. Michael: That's fascinating. That reminds me of the sort of work that your friend Professor Toumazou is engaged in with whom I have recently had the pleasure of talking to, who is also concerned with diagnostic work as well.

Kevin Warwick: I think there is an enormous amount that we can do and it frustrates me on many occasions when meeting patients and seeing situations which people are in and knowing technically that we can not now do an awful lot more.

M.G. Michael: We will get to some of the controversial aspects of that in a moment. Many of your papers are being published in medical journals and a lot of your robots are being sold commercially. How do you feel about these two areas converging?

Kevin Warwick: Well for me it's not the areas converging; I am in the middle of it. With things like intelligence and what intelligence is all about and how human brains and machine brains work, it's really one area for me and I think I am sort of in the middle there. One application is in the field of robotics technology and hence our robots are sold and if we can make some money for the University, if we can get it out there in a big way and help kids learn about robots, then great. The *Cybot* robot is being produced and we have sold something like 3 million robots around the world which is a phenomenal number and means an awful lot of kids around the world learn how to build robots and have some idea. But at the same time we can use the robots for medical purposes. It's just another application but a very exciting one.

M.G. Michael: Professor Warwick, what were the primary drivers that led to your research for chip implants in humans?

Kevin Warwick: I think in terms of primary drivers literally we now have the technology to have a look at the possibilities. I think in terms of fundamental pushes when I was a teenager I was excited by various science fiction writers such as Michael Crichton who wrote a book about the *Terminal Man*. About a guy who had an electrode pushed into his brain. I read it very much as a vast possibility and to bring about something like that in later life is pretty fantastic. So, partly science fiction, and partly that the technology is there, partly a drive to very much taking a look at having extra senses and communicating in new ways. Well let's find out, let's see what's there... a scientific curiosity.

M.G. Michael: So, you are also interested in not only repairing but also developing the potential of humans?

Kevin Warwick: Yes. I think in that way I am quite different to other people in the field. I know there are some other people researching in this area but they tend to look more at the therapeutic or repairing. *But it's clear the technology opens up a number of possibilities for upgrading and taking ourselves to the next level. We got the technology, so let's have a look, let's see what's possible, whether we want to do it or not is a sociological question or a commercial question. But at least to find out "can we have extra senses?"... not from a science fiction point of view but from a scientific point of view.* To me this is exciting research but it is important if we can have, say, infrared senses as an extra sense. What does it mean? How does our brain deal with it? Do we want it or not is another thing. We can know if we want it or not when we know what it can do and what it can offer us.

M.G. Michael: So the question of artificial enhancement is something natural to consider?

Kevin Warwick: I see it as a natural thing, it is a technological development. Like technological evolution it is a very much a natural thing. It is something with positives and something with negatives so we definitely need to technically look at what's possible. And also, from an ethical and moral point of view, and how we deal with that. I think realistically it needs to be looked at seriously. Some committees consider the ethics and say while therapy is usually okay, enhancement we are really not sure about. I think it is quite a naive view to separate them like that.

M.G. Michael: Why did you decide to name your first experiment "Cyborg 1.0"? And why did that experiment only last about 10 days? Would you consider embedding an implant in your body for life, even multiple implantable devices?

Kevin Warwick: To answer the last part of that, definitely yes. Looking at the brain as the computer which is the next step, like for me that is 4.0. I think not only consider it, it possibly will be a

necessity. For the brain implant, in the way we are looking at it, if it were to come out again possibly would cause far more trauma than it would be to go in the first place. So definitely the latter one. So Cyborg 1.0 was a radio frequency identification device which I think in 1998 I became the first human to have one of those implanted (Figure 1). Now there are quite a few people who do for different reasons but technically we did what we could in that 9 days and we sorted out what we

Figure 1. On Monday 24th August 1998, at 4:00pm, Professor Kevin Warwick underwent an operation to surgically implant a silicon chip transponder in his forearm. Dr. George Boulous carried out the operation at Tilehurst Surgery, using local anesthetic only. Courtesy of Professor Kevin Warwick.

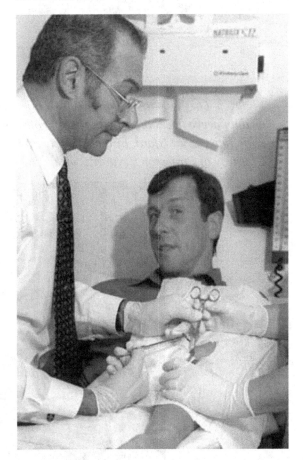

Figure 2. The silicon transponder that was implanted into Professor Kevin Warwick's forearm to allow a computer to monitor him as he moved through halls and offices of the Department of Cybernetics at the University of Reading. The transponder emitted a unique identifying signal so that he could operate doors, lights, heaters and other computers without lifting a finger. Courtesy of Professor Kevin Warwick.

could achieve technically. That is as far as we were looking at and we did it, took it out and it didn't need to stay in any longer. But, that one if it had stayed in could have been a problem because of the nature of that implant, it could have migrated around the body, it wasn't actually designed to be implanted. So, how stable, how robotic it was, it was in a silicon tube, it could have broken in the human body so it wasn't sensible to keep it in for too long, once we had shown what we could do with it (Figure 2).

M.G. Michael: The question of stability and robustness of the implant, are you saying that has been addressed quite adequately right now to your satisfaction?

Kevin Warwick: I think for the Cyborg 2.0 type of implant which involves a link between the nervous system or the brain and the computer is certainly not addressed to my satisfaction (Figure 3). I think it is an enormous question. The implant I have,

Figure 3. On the 14th of March 2002 a one hundred electrode array was surgically implanted into the median nerve fibers of the left arm of Professor Kevin Warwick. The operation was carried out at Radcliffe Infirmary, Oxford, by a medical team headed by the neurosurgeons Amjad Shad and Peter Teddy. Courtesy of Professor Kevin Warwick.

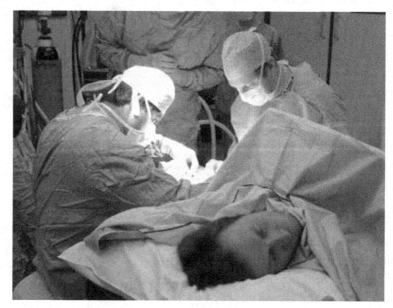

Figure 4. The microelectrode array that was inserted into a guiding tube and placed into a two inch incision made above Kevin Warwick's wrist and then fired into the median nerve fibers below his elbow joint. The procedure took a little over two hours to complete. Courtesy of Professor Kevin Warwick.

the last one, was still only 3 months, I think the longest one in a human has been about 7 months and then from all reports it didn't go too well. So its a problem. On one hand you don't want to put in material that the body will reject, but if you have material like silicon or platinum that the body does link with nicely, then the problem after a few months is that the body can start eating away at it; it starts dissolving, it becomes too close to the material (Figure 4). So, you are trying to find a material in a way of integrating the use for long term stability. The human body will rarely work that closely with foreign material. The technology has moved on quite a lot but there is still some way to go with it.

M.G. Michael: In Cyborg 2.0, in the experiment you and your wife, Irena, were implanted and hoped to receive messages from one another over computer mediation (Figure 5). One of the obvious applications is for disabled persons. Was this one of the sole motivators for the experiment?

Figure 5. Professor Kevin Warwick with his wife Irena who participated in the Cyborg 2.0 experiment. Kevin and his wife both were implanted to investigate how movement, thought or emotion signals could be transmitted from one person to the other, via a computer network. Courtesy of Professor Kevin Warwick.

Kevin Warwick: Yes, I think it was one of the main driving forces. I am historically a communications person having worked for British Telecom for 6 years. For me it was looking at the possibility of opening up a new communications channel for people with Long Tim's Syndrome giving them some way to communicate. It was the bit that I found most exciting, but I am not sure most folk realize what we actually achieved. But, you need to know a lot about telephones and telegraphs in order to appreciate it. *We did communicate, for the first time in the world directly from nervous system to nervous system electronically telegraphically, very simply.*

M.G. Michael: As you said, Kevin, there is a lot of misinformation out there and there is a lot more education that needs to be done for a variety of reasons. What are some of the fundamental, technical, lessons learned from your experiments?

Kevin Warwick: Well, I think in terms of what we can do with extra sensory input, we showed with ultrasonics, it is possible and the human brain adapts to things very quickly. *The human brain is amazingly clever, our brains are obviously not dumb and adapt quite quickly to what's going on and that works to our benefit. And there are enormous possibilities with the technology extra sensory inputs we achieve, extending the human nervous system over the internet, which opens a new way of looking at humans. Our bodies are not restricted to the size and the shape they are, we can send out brain signals in different countries and continents.* Those are things which really opened my mind as to what is going to be possible in the future.

M.G. Michael: Just to add another question Professor Warwick. I am getting a feeling here that questions of metaphysics and ontology do interest you a lot, am I correct?

Kevin Warwick: Yes, they do. But I often come at it from a realistic point of view, which is a bit of a choice.

M.G. Michael: I have been studying your work for some time now. I was especially fascinated to notice that you have a research associate who is from the humanities and that was a wonderful thing to see.

Kevin Warwick: That's Daniela, she's a bit like the devil on my shoulder. It's not like that she comes at it from a negative point of view, but she's more like "what will this mean for society? If we do that, how are people going to take it?" And it's really good to have those questions chipping away at you all the time, you have to think about it in a much broader way.

M.G. Michael: Absolutely. I tell you something that's an entire new interview, isn't it?

Kevin Warwick: Yes. It's not like the case that she is saying "Should you be doing that? This is not good", she's not doing that. She is saying "What does it mean? What are the positives? What are the negatives for society?" It really is a common picture that this is how it is going to be. Even if you're opening up something that is going to have military uses. I think some people say "it's military, it's fine" but how can that be the case, it's the country's staying power and we need the military and in many countries we are dependent on it as a way of life. So it's very prevalent in a lot of the research we do.

M.G. Michael: Are you already looking toward a Cyborg 3.0 or 4.0? And what is coming next?

Kevin Warwick: Yes, well Cyborg 3.0 is what we are working on, with research with Amjad Shad, the neurosurgeon whom we worked on the last one. Cyborg 3.0 is looking at an implant for an individual with a spinal injury and I think it will be a brain implant and it has a number of aspects with it. Which ones will be more successful, we will have to see. What the surgeon wants to do is attempt to bridge over lesions so to literally put implants, as I would put it, to rewire the nervous system where there has been a break. And to see if the person over a period of time, can learn or relearn how to use parts of their body which have become not functional because of the lesion. At the same time we would like to use the signals we can get in order to allow the individual to do things which the patient otherwise wouldn't be able to do. *So, this is someone who is severely paralyzed and what I did in the last experiment, Cyborg 2.0, was for example, to drive the wheel chair around directly from neural signals. What we would like the spinally injured patient to do is drive around a car just by thinking about it, directly by brain signals. Much as a demonstrator to see what is possible and have the person move around for the rest of their life.*

M.G. Michael: There is extraordinary potential there. And my next question is, what do you think is coming next in the foreseeable future, say in the next 5 to 10 years? In your own work specifically.

Kevin Warwick: In my work, we have really been successful in the Parkinson's Disease Project and got quite a lot of money from the Medical Research Council in the UK to take this further. That is, to provide a feedback loop and literally to have an intelligent system, probably the implanted device would be a microprocessor device which will be fully implanted with the Parkinson's tremor stimulator. So, it is the next generation of stimulators. The nice thing is, the microprocessor systems that out-think the human brain. Before tremors occur in Parkinson's Disease, there are signals in the deep brain that say it is going to occur. *The microprocessors pick up on the signals and counteracting the resultant effect so stopping them*

occurring before they do occur. Which is really exciting not just from a Parkinson's Disease point of view, therapeutically, but in a general sense it's looking at a computer sitting in the human brain predicting what the human brain is going to do and then stopping it doing it. So, it has all sorts of applications. How it is going to be used we'll see, but if you take things like slimming, for example, having a piece of electronics in your brain stopping you from eating chocolate cake. Maybe that's a flippant use of that technology but it shows how broadly the technology can be used.

M.G. Michael: I was interested in what you said about the broad uses of the technology once it's introduced. Do you see any problems with that? Do you think there are any risks in the broad use of this technology?

Kevin Warwick: I try when looking at this to be open, rather than to say "I am just developing this for Parkinson's Disease, that's it", that's very naive. We have to look at the potential of other applications. And it can open up what other things can benefit, such as slimming, and it can open up potential negatives, such as remote controlled human beings, which could be misused for military purposes. So we have to be open to what is being developed here. *I think it is important for society to consider the different options rather than in 10 years time be faced with all these people being remote controlled and then saying "Oh what a shock. We didn't know anything about that."* | *"Well, you were told about it 10 years ago and you should have spoken up about it then". I think any progress of this new type of technology is going to have potential positives and potential negatives, it just changes the way humans and technology interact in a very broad range of modes.*

M.G. Michael: That's of course something we could discuss for a long time. Professor Warwick, do you believe that someone who is implanted with a microchip is a "Cyborg"? How do you define "Cyborg"?

Kevin Warwick: Some people say that a person riding a bike is a Cyborg, but that's a bit silly to me. Certainly someone who has technology such as a microchip inside them is a starter and when that allows them to do other things, enhances them, then that's my take on a Cyborg. I think that is has to be integral.

M.G. Michael: It's a qualified sense, isn't it?

Kevin Warwick: Yes, that's right. It's not something like a pair of glasses you put on and off. It is integral and it enhances you. So, just implanting a microchip per se, the answer would be no. If the microchip is actually doing something then it extends the range of your abilities, then yes in that sense.

M.G. Michael: Do you believe we are attempting to evolve as a human species through technology?

Kevin Warwick: I think we can do. Technically we can see possibilities of improving what individuals can do. Evolution tends to imply biologically we will change, which in an individual I think "yes" the brain, the nervous system and the body will change to more closely integrate with technology if that is what the brain wants. The question is whether that biological change is passed onto children and their children. It depends on which theory of evolution you follow. But there are some that follow a strict Darwinian code that say "no that doesn't happen, either you pass on your genes or your genes are fixed. If you do things in your own life that doesn't affect the genes that are passed on". But then you have the Lamarckian theory that say "the habits and things that you do change the genetic make up, to a very small extent, and therefore you pass it on." I am more of the latter school. *So then I would believe that, yes, we can technologically evolve and future offspring, their bodies will be more in tune and more biologically aligned with the technological possibilities.*

M.G. Michael: Is it possible that the group of people that can afford this technology will actually have it and could we be creating a new elitist society, with the haves and have-nots that are actually able to access this technology?

Kevin Warwick: I think very much so. If we look to the evolution answer, I think any technology like this can stretch society, much like an elastic band. It doesn't necessarily pull the bottom end down, in fact, it may actually help the whole way through. But it does stretch society, in terms of people who have more and can influence more. It's a case here though of whether there is so much of an enhancement that the elastic band breaks and we end up with two groups or maybe more. I think, yeah, there is a clear possibility here that those that have could evolve because we are not just looking at physical things you can take off or put on. *We are looking at an intellectual upgrade, your intelligence is improved by having an implant that simply improves how your brain operates.* And then how are humans different from other creatures? Well, I would say it its due to our intelligence, we can out-think other creatures and therefore we, in the evolution sense, we are more dominant than they are. I think there is a distinct possibility we will end up with an upgrade in society.

M.G. Michael: What applications can you see being deployed commercially utilizing human-centric chip implants, say in the next 10 years?

Kevin Warwick: Clearly extra-sensory input, it could be commercially viable. Ultrasonic is useful for people with disabilities. I think most commercial applications in the next 10 years are for helping people with disabilities. To look at upgrading, the communication side of things is enormous but I still think brain to brain communication is pushing that 10 year time frame. *So that will be ultimately the biggest of all, communicating by thought. That's what we want to be able to do in years to come. I reckon most of them are helping people with spinal injuries and helping people who are blind to have a different sensory input, which are not enormous commercial applications.*

M.G. Michael: What would you say to some critics in the field of robotics and artificial intelligence, that may say some of your predictions of the future possibilities are, perhaps, far too speculative?

Kevin Warwick: When I published my book "March of the Machines", one of the original hardbacks, back in 1997, one of the things I was saying "well there are a lot of things that are difficult, having robots walking around on two legs would be 20 years before we see that." Well, of course, before the paperback came out one year later, we had P2 robots and subsequently P3 robots doing exactly what we were saying would take 20 years within one year. So I think a lot of what I say is speculative, sure, but being overly speculative is rarely conservative in many ways. I think one criticism I have, intelligence is a vitally important aspect of what we are and what robots are and there is a clear possibility that humans are developing artificial intelligence that ultimately, could make the big decisions. But once it has an intellectual power that outperforms that of humans, then we're in a very, very dangerous area. But there is nothing, nothing whatsoever, no theory, no equation, no basis that says that cannot happen. If you look at it logically and from any scientific point of view, then it is almost surely going to happen. *And therefore, I think we have to be open, where are we going with it, what are we doing with artificial intelligence? We got to be very, very careful otherwise we're opening*

up Pandora's Box and once we've opened it, once we've switched on machines that are more intelligent than we are, they are not going to let us... they are making the decisions. So it's a one way track, so I think those that say "No, you shouldn't say things like that", I think they are being grossly irresponsible to our society just because they want people to feel nice about them and go to sleep at night with their cocoa and say "that guy's a nice person and that things are not going to be dangerous, I will buy their book, we'll make him a Knight". I think that's grossly irresponsible for science and philosophy towards the general public.

M.G. Michael: And one other thing, the issues that are often raised, being in a capitalist society, there is a rush to patent these things and sometimes in the rush to patent a lot of forethought is not given. So that's an important aspect, isn't it?

Kevin Warwick: I think it is, maybe the commercial reality of it. Money and patents have been detrimental to people in the long term.

M.G. Michael: What do you see as the risks of human beings being implanted with transponders? I know you've touched on some of them but can you tell me more about the risks.

Kevin Warwick: Yes, so you've got medical risks with anything you do like that. I think here we're looking at the human brain adapting in order to improve the overall capabilities. *You don't know how it's going to adapt completely. Ok, we may lose a lot of things if we're taking on board other senses we may lose some of the senses we've got. We simply do not know. It really is something that is out of control but you really don't know which way it is going to go. Positives and negatives as in medical dangers; what we can gain is what we can see, what we can lose or what we will lose is really not clear.* But for sure, we've got to lose something I believe, it's not going to just be gain, gain... I don't think hardly anything in life is like that.

M.G. Michael: Yes, there's always the price to pay for advancements.

Kevin Warwick: In this case, we really don't know what the price is.

M.G. Michael: That's the problem, isn't it? Kevin, what are some of the safeguards that should be introduced to ensure the protection of data for people embedded with transponders? Because we read that a lot of this data can be manipulated, it can be changed, it can be stolen. So what are your thoughts on that?

Kevin Warwick: I think even now with things like credit cards that people use, and particularly with finance it's become purely electronic, you don't actually see money. There is far, far more, than I think any person, even those people in the know can imagine, in terms of data on what a person does; where they live; who they see; where they go. *Now, we are looking at transponder information that shows where a person is more accurately. It is a positive and a negative because in a sense you want the information to be there so the computers do things for you, but at the same time the fact that the information is there, it can be used in other ways. To bring in safeguards, it would be good to do that, but how we do it is not clear.* So, I don't have an immediate answer. I think practically looking at how we can bring in those safeguards is a very difficult picture. Maybe we can stick more to intranet, so the networks and your data which is passed around on it is defined, is restricted. That is one way of limiting the dangers that are there. But it does then limit the practical effectiveness of the data that is there, you really want that data to do something, which is why you got the implant in the first place. But if you don't want the restrictions then you lose the safeguards and privacy.

M.G. Michael: So, is there a bit of trial and error involved here?

Kevin Warwick: I think it is very much trial and error, which is always a risky thing because you don't want to push it too far. You could get something very negative out of it. I think the basis of scientific investigation at the end of the day is the trial and error, you hope that you are not pushing things too far, you hope that you've made a good guess of what is going to happen. That's really all you can do, like "based on the scientific evidence, I think this is going to happen", you hope that you are not going to push this too far. But, you never know what can happen.

M.G. Michael: Do you believe in any way we can prejudge ethics with regards to emerging technologies like RFID?

Kevin Warwick: To a certain extent I think, yes, now that we've been talking about data disappearing and we can see what the technology has to offer. So we can look at it to a certain extent, maybe in the direction it is heading. But in some cases we can't, for example the use of this type of technology for tracking people, it has positives and negatives and it depends ethically which country you are in. In America for example, they are very keen on this technology being developed for things like tracking and monitoring people. They would like a stronger regime that this technology could help in abductions for instance, but if that is then applied in a more general sense across the world it could be extremely restrictive because of the Big Brother issues which seem very dangerous. So I think we can look to a certain extent forwards, but unless something is actually brought in and commercial effects come into play and the sociological effects, whether people want it or not. For example the cell phone, 25 to 30 years ago it was not a practical reality, it was not possible that these things would be able to work, there were all types of practical problems. Going from that, to being something that for many people they couldn't live without- they can't go outside the house without the cell phone is strapped to their ear. So sociologically it's had an enormous impact on how we communicate and interact but to actually predict that in an ethical context, it would be very, very difficult.

M.G. Michael: I can see that. There's a contradiction there, because we can say historical paradigms are critically important but are not always 100% predictive so there's a contradiction there that we have to resolve.

Kevin Warwick: Yes, well taking history and seeing how it's gone can give us some indication. But I think, ethically, we do have to try and look at all the aspects. We need to look at the positives and negatives. We can get some messages from the past but we just can't tell.

M.G. Michael: The trajectory of technology is sometimes unstoppable. Kevin, can you comment on the newly enacted laws such as the chip implant laws in Wisconsin and elsewhere, where it has been moved to make involuntary humancentric implants illegal.

Kevin Warwick: I think there is a discussion there. It raises the attention of people to the fact that "Hey! We do have to look at this seriously in a general way," and what are the results of these discussions because implants are very, very different in nature as to what they do. *So where these discussions go as to what type of implants and what methods can be used. I believe it is important that discussions like this do go on politically, rather than politicians keeping their heads in the sand about the technology moving on.* So, I would welcome it, a discussion whole heartedly. With implants of course you do have therapy enhancement aspects, so to restrict the use of these implants, well, it'd be terrible. You know saying "you've got Parkinson's, you've got

epilepsy. Well, tough; we have the technology but we are not going to let you have any benefits from it". That would be horrible. At the same time, then if you say "yes, we will let you have these implants" then it opens up the possibilities of people enhancing but it is a very, very difficult problem. I hope the politicians don't come up with a silly solution that does not let people have these benefits. But, it's very, very good to have such discussions.

M.G. Michael: Yes, the problem is there, Kevin. Of course "legislation" is usually 4 years according to the term of the party in power. The foresight is usually limited to 4 years, isn't it? And that's one of the problems.

Kevin Warwick: Politicians are often after the short fix. They say "this technology is terrible" to give someone a nice political angle. But in the long term people look and say "well this was terrible for society. We were restricted and everyone else had the technology and we didn't" so yes, it can be problematic in a big way.

M.G. Michael: Do you see the potential for every person to be implanted with a microchip for national security purposes? Especially in the context that we are living in now with the threats of terrorism.

Kevin Warwick: That is a big issue. I think certainly to make it available, thinking of more in terms of passports rather than identity cards. I think certainly making it available for passports so if you wanted to move country to country or you want personally to have a higher level of security, then why not? It's certainly good enough for that now. As to whether it's made for every person, I mean in Britain we still don't have identity cards, I still believe that this is not something against an implant, this is something against, as I would see it, to the freedom of individual too. I believe this is a general identity card attitude that I think a lot of people in Britain, including myself, hold. So I think I am giving an answer that is not anti-implant but is anti-freedom of the individual to impose some sort of identification device on everybody. But of course, as you say, it would very much enhance security on a global scale and therefore there are a lot of positives to it. So, I've successfully not answered that question. *[Laughs]*

M.G. Michael: There are some hints there, there are a few hints there... *[Laughs]* Do you think parents have the right to make their child get an implant for the sake of an emergency situation? Does it promote a false sense of security for the parent? Can it realistically prevent an attack from occurring, for example?

Kevin Warwick: I'll answer the questions in reverse order. I think there is a deterrent factor there. Seriously we hope that a child is never abducted, but realistically it does happen sometimes. Statistics on it are often quite confusing, a situation is only counted as an abduction if nothing else happens. If the child is ultimately murdered, then it is not an abduction it is a murder. So what we are looking at is a lot more prevalent than some people would have you believe. *But I think the deterrent factor is important. And therefore just having an implant is much like having a burglar alarm on your house. But, you actually need a box on the outside that shows you have an alarm on your house.* So it may need something like that, something extra as well as something there. Does it give a false sense of security for the parent? I don't know false sense, but I hope that it does give a sense of security for the parent so they can relax a little bit. I don't think it gives a false sense because there is still a possibility there and I don't think parents take their eye off security aspects. I do get a lot of emails from concerned parents, there are a lot of parents out there concerned about the safety of their child. As for whether it's right, does the parent have the right to give the child

an implant? In your wording there, it is quite interesting. A technical thing here is the right of the child and the decision the child can take. We are not looking at a major thing here like a child getting their leg amputated. We are looking at a little device that is injected under the skin. In terms of injuring the child, it's like having an injection. Parents allow their children to have an injection to prevent cholera, which is good for the child, even in the child says "no, I don't want this" then the parent will say "no, you have to have this injection". So, in a way things like that already go on and if you put it in that context, microchips are there to prevent something from happening. Then it's not too dissimilar to a chemical, this is just having a little bit of electronics injected compared to chemicals. Most chemicals could have a profound effect on the child's brain. The chemicals could have much, much worse an effect. I think putting it in context, it's nowhere near as serious other than if the implant is used in an abusive way. I would see the important thing as: Does the child itself know exactly what is going on? Are they happy with it, knowing they will be protected? Fine. But, if it helps considerably, then I don't see a problem with it. As long as it's not abused, as long as parents don't get access to where their child is 24 hours a day, only actually brought into play if the parents or police are worried and then it is brought to life as it were. So I don't really see there is an issue of it in a big way. Maybe it needs to be taken carefully step by step to ensure it is not used abusively. But, I don't really see it anymore than a kid getting an injection chemically to stop them getting diseases.

M.G. Michael: Kevin, let's just stay a little more in the deep and murky waters of ethics here. Do you think carers of sufferers of Alzheimer's, for instance, have the right to make their loved ones get implants for the sake of an emergency situation, if the patients themselves are not able to make decisions that may affect their well being?

Kevin Warwick: Yes, it's a difficult one. If they are not able themselves, I would say yes. Same question again as giving the patient an injection which can give more profound effects. If they are in a situation where the medical professional or the loved ones can say "yes, this person needs an injection and they'll get an injection", then I would see them in the same place. I cannot see a problem with this because it could save their life, you are looking out for the good of the person. Again, there needs to be some sort of check to ensure it is not abused. But subject to that, I would think, "yes" is the answer, because it could save the person's life.

M.G. Michael: In a similar context, of voluntary versus involuntary, do you think we have the right to embed tracking devices into prisoners or suspected terrorists to ensure we can track and monitor them?

Kevin Warwick: Well, suspected terrorists, is a bit of a contradictory description...

M.G. Michael: Well, let's say "confirmed" terrorists.

Kevin Warwick: I think if a prisoner let's say, they are in prison and they are going to stay in prison for next 2 or 3 years, they could have a little implant if they could be paroled, if it's given as a choice like that. They effectively make the choice, why not? I think the technology is fine, it's not a problem. We are not looking at intrusive technology. The technology we are looking at is far less realistically a bit of body piercing. Pedophiles are a big problem now in the UK. They serve their sentences, they are released into the community, now what do we do? *Do we tell the people they are living there? Or do we not tell people? That could be irresponsible, because you would have little children running around with a convicted pedophile in the community. What can we do? Well, why not let the felon have an implant we*

can monitor where they are and make sure they don't go to certain places. They are not allowed into schools and a remote can sound if they go anywhere near the school. It's using the technology in a sensible way for society. I think there are cases, particularly if the prisoners themselves agree because they benefit from it. Even with "suspected" terrorists... I think the use of the word "suspected"...

M.G. Michael: Yes, it is fuzzy.

Kevin Warwick: Let's put it this way, even if I was "suspected" as a terrorist looking at traveling around, and me being given an implant now allowed everybody to travel around a little more easily, including myself, fine, I'd go for it in a minute. To save an hour at this and that airport, even though I knew then some people knew where I was.

M.G. Michael: My next question may be over simplistic, but in a sense it defines different communities, so I'll ask it. When civil libertarians or privacy advocates or people with particular apocalyptic interpretations, for example those who have studied the Apocalypse of John, "the mark or the name of the beast" in Revelation, chapter 13. When they speak in opposition of humancentric chip implants, how might you respond to these people and groups?

Kevin Warwick: The first thing to say is that I have really been surprised at how little I have had in the way of, if you like, complaints or people speaking against me. Literally maybe a dozen emails, letters, phone calls in a dozen years, which is very, very little.

M.G. Michael: I find that amazing, I find that absolutely amazing, especially given the phenomenal increase of the so-called Christian "end-time" web-sites on the Internet.

Kevin Warwick: It should be more. I would hope it to be more to question what is going on. Whereas there is a lot of emails saying "yeah it's great, that's fantastic". I think if you do have the use of technology to help with people with disabilities and for people to stand against the use of that sort of technology, I think it is terrible. I really feel sad at anybody like that, for the reason that we could be helping an awful lot of people and living with some of those diseases is horrible, if we can use implants to help people. If we are looking though just at the tracking and monitoring type of implants or even there, if it does allow us more security, even the pedophile question being resolved in this way, then let's look at it... I hope we live in such a society that people can voice their opinion and voice their worries. We obviously need to take their worries into account. I am more on the other side, myself, I think there are so many benefits from chip implants that we need to move forward with it.

M.G. Michael: So, what you are saying is religion has a place in this discussion as long as it's informed and contributes to the debate to make this whole issue more clearer to the general population. So, debate is very important here amongst different sectors of the community.

Kevin Warwick: I wish I could have used those words. I think that is exactly it. I think it has an important role to play in this. And no way should we not listen to them as they are vital.

M.G. Michael: Thanks Kevin, that is generous of you. As an implantee how would you feel if data was being collected about you from an un-obtrusive reader?

Kevin Warwick: I guess in a realistic scenario I would suspect that is what is going to happen. Obviously I would not be really happy with it. But, I would suspect it is going to happen because seeing what happens now with credit cards, just where the information turns up and what is known about me that I didn't think was known about me. *But that is me coming at it from a scientific point of view; the obvious answer from someone from the general public view "well this is a terrible thing". But, I think it is something that one has to expect and one has to try and be overly careful about where you go, what you do, and hence prevent the possibility of such information being picked up.*

M.G. Michael: The next question I think we might have already addressed it. But, I'll ask it in case something else has come into your mind. What are some of the other ethical issues that you feel must be addressed before the microchip implant technology can become widespread?

Kevin Warwick: I think ethical issues can often just be used to "how is this going to negatively affect humans?" I think we need to look broadly at commercial opportunities which are important and these are ethical issues as well because commercial opportunities can, for a particular community, open up extra profits and therefore the community can in general be better off because of these new commercial opportunities. So, I think looking at it from a broad ethical sense is important for positive and negative reasons, and making it as broad as possible there will be differences and one has to accept that. But, that is life. So it's more trying to steer that change into a way that we, "we" that's a big "We" there, we would like it to see it go in a broad sense. So I don't know if there is a specific point other than to look broadly at what ethical considerations mean rather than just specifically as to what might normally be considered negative.

M.G. Michael: Kevin, what would you consider to be the most important breakthroughs that you've made in your research to date?

Figure 5. A screenshot of software created for the Cyborg 2.0 experiment which allowed the microelectrode Kevin Warwick had implanted to be configured. The event preview window captures signals emitted from the electrode to the computer interface. Courtesy of Professor Kevin Warwick.

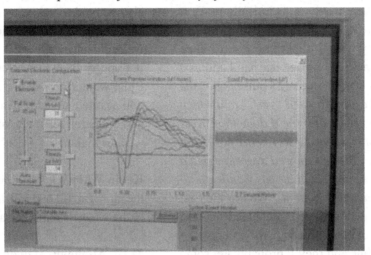

Kevin Warwick: I have no doubt that it goes back, and this is probably not going to be the appropriate answer, but if you put it into context of having an extra sense, an ultrasonic sense and showing that we can do things of that kind, that's really the ultimate communication (Figure 6). *When my brain received neural signals that had come electronically from my wife's brain... that was so exciting that we had achieved that. When you look at some communications, the difference between the telegraph of Morse and then the telephone of Bell, the telephone is not enormously different from the telegraph system as a method of communication. And really we use the same telegraphic methods but really moved on considerably. I mean instead of having to move through pressure waves as we do with the telephone, we went directly from neural signals into the electronics and stayed purely electronic. To me, this is enormous! But, I think the problem is, at the moment, that people don't understand exactly what we did there. To me there is no question the most important breakthrough was the first direct nervous system electronic communication.*

M.G. Michael: To people that only have a basic knowledge of these things, it is extraordinary. I think that people concentrate a lot on the hardware and what they can't see is not considered "real".

Kevin Warwick: I agree.

M.G. Michael: Just on that question, what did it feel like? How did it feel physically when this transmission happened?

Kevin Warwick: Very good question. I did get a surge, it was an electrical current. In terms of how it actually felt, this is going to be a silly answer, but this is how it is- it felt like my wife was communicating with me. It's like you are listening to me on the phone now, how does it feel like to hear me talking? So when I received the first pulse knowing that was from my wife, but my brain knew that it was my wife, the signal that I was looking forward to.

M.G. Michael: So, there was no doubt as to the clarity, the ontology of the sender?

Kevin Warwick: Oh, no, no. How it was set up in the lab, we were on completely different sides of the lab, we both had groups of people around us who were there partly to technically make it happen and partly to check that it was all ok. I couldn't see my wife, I didn't know she'd done anything. She actually moved her hand and as a result of that, my brain received a pulse. *From the other side of the lab I shouted "yes!!" and which the other group knew that she'd done that. It all linked in and only when she moved her hand that I shouted "yes". We just showed it worked and a lot better than we expected. It was wonderful to know we had actually done it.* We are the first in the world whether we get applauded for it in years to come or not. Someone will probably do it in 10 years time and they'll probably get some of the credit. But to know we actually did it, and no one had experienced it before from a scientific point of view, it was terrific.

M.G. Michael: Kevin, I've got to ask you this, so many thoughts are rushing into my mind right now. Did it take a lot of convincing to Irena?

Kevin Warwick: There was a magazine that said I had forced her into it and she was so annoyed with that. She pretty much wanted to be a part of it and we had to get ethical approval for her to be involved. It was a bit of a hassle but she was very much pushing that she wanted to do it. And she knew how important it was that she wanted to be part of it. So far from it, it was more her convincing me "don't stop what you are doing and we are definitely doing this" which was great.

M.G. Michael: Katina and I, in our work, speak of the *Electrophorous* and the *Homo Electricus*; that is we are becoming electric bearers. Does this make sense to you?

Kevin Warwick: Oh yes, I think well the human body is electric.

M.G. Michael: Well, it's very encouraging to hear that because I also asked Professor Toumazou and he was really supportive of our research. I also wanted to ask you, we've had a wonderful conversation here and there are so many points we could have addressed so it's been quite broad, but you've been very clear in your responses… I just wanted to say is there anything final that you wanted to add? Anything you wanted to make clearer for me? Any final comments you wish to make?

Kevin Warwick: I've totally racked my brain at the moment. If I had a little memory chip, I would know what I should be saying here... *[Laughs]*

M.G. Michael: *[Laughs]* Or if I had one? I would have got to ask you questions more in your league…

Kevin Warwick: Things like that we can say jokingly. We don't exactly know how it is going to affect society in the long term. For some people it's worrying but for me it's tremendously exciting. So there we go.

M.G. Michael: Kevin, I would like to thank you for your time. I'm very grateful for your forthrightness and trust. Your unique commentary is critical to our research. I wish you discernment.

Kevin Warwick: Yes. Thanks. I thoroughly enjoyed it. I hope that we do get a chance to meet up in the future.

M.G. Michael: Kevin, I would like very much to meet up with you and so would Katina. There is a lot more to talk about here.

Kevin Warwick: Cheers, well. Send my regards to Katina.

M.G. Michael: Thanks again, Kevin.

KEY TERMS

Artificial Intelligence (AI): The capability of a computer system to learn from its experiences and simulate human intelligence in decision-making.

Convergence: To tend to meet in a point or line; incline towards each other.

Cybernetics: The study of nervous system controls in the brain as a basis for developing communications and controls in socio-technical systems.

Cyborg: The concept of a man-machine combination; a human who adds to or enhances his or her abilities by using technology.

Cyborg 1.0: Phase One of Professor Kevin Warwick's chip implant experiment beginning on the 24th of August 1998. A silicon chip transponder was surgically implanted into the Professor's forearm. This experiment allowed a computer to monitor Warwick as he moved through halls and offices at his workplace using a unique identifying signal emitted by the implanted chip. He could operate doors, lights, heaters and other computers without lifting a finger.

Cyborg 2.0: Phase Two of Professor Kevin Warwick's chip implant experiment beginning on the 14th of March 2002. A one hundred electrode array was surgically implanted into the median nerve fibers of the Professor's left arm. This phase looked at how an implant could send signals back and forth between Warwick's nervous system and a computer. Kevin and his wife Irena, both were implanted to investigate how movement, thought or emotion signals could be transmitted from one person to the other, via a computer network.

Extra-Sensory Input: Beyond the normal range of the sense organs.

Humancentric Monitoring: Is the discrete observation or the continuous real-time observation of a subject, examining, inspecting or scrutinizing their progress or their given state over a period of time for the purposes of systematic review and revision.

Humancentric Tracking: Is the act of following someone or something, in order to find that individual and to understand their pattern of movement over a period of time, or note their course for a particular purpose.

Humanoid: A robot that looks like a human in appearance and is autonomous. The term was derived by Czech playwright Karel Capek in 1920 from the Slav word for worker.

Lamarckian Theory: The theory that characteristics acquired by habits, use, disuse, or adaptations to changes in environment may be inherited.

Mark of the Beast: In the Book of Revelation 13:16f. the mark of the beast is a parody of God's seal, Rev. 7:3. The mark (666) is gained by worshiping the beast and it signifies that the beast is the owner of those who have accepted it.

Microchip Implant: An integrated circuit device encased in radio-frequency identification transponders that can be active or passive and is implantable into animals or humans usually in the subcutaneous layer of the skin.

Misinformation: False or misleading information.

Neurosurgery: The branch of medicine relating to the surgery of the nervous system.

Paralysis: Loss of power of a voluntary muscular contraction.

Parkinson's Disease: A form of paralysis characterised by tremor, muscular rigidity, and weakness of movement.

RFID Implant: A transponder injected into the sub-dermal layer of the skin, or any other part of the body in a human or animal.

Robot: Mechanical self-controlling apparatus designed to carry out a specific task.

Scientific Evidence: Evidence which either supports or refutes a scientific theory. It is usually empirical and follows a set scientific method relevant to a given field of inquiry.

Transponder: Also known as an electronic tag; are remotely activated receiver-transmitters. These devices can be external, injectable tags, or contactless smart cards and are mainly used for identification purposes, transmitting information on-demand.

Trial and Error: Process of experimentation to find the best way of achieving a desired result, in which various methods are tried and eliminated as unsuitable.

Interview 14.2
The Do–It–Yourselfer
RFID Implantee

Mr Amal Graafstra, Bellingham, United States of America
Interview conducted by Katina Michael on 25 May 2007.

INTERVIEW

Katina Michael: Amal, firstly I wanted to begin with asking you about your background- your qualifications, your nationality and your place of residence?

Amal Graafstra: Ok. Well, I am a US citizen. I am currently living in Bellingham, Washington. As for qualifications I really do not have any pieces of paper from any School. I am someone who has followed various technologies since my teens and has built projects and things like that. I had a little bit of College but I actually dropped out to start an Internet access company way back when ISPs were a Mom and Pop type of business. So, I'm just a High School graduate...

Katina Michael: I notice you are the director of a number of mobile companies and was wondering if you were one of these students that may not have been challenged by College perhaps and were more entrepreneurial?

Amal Graafstra: I think that there were plenty of challenging things about College. But a lot of the technical aspects in College were not challenging; basically, they were just so far behind. I did not have the time and finances to be able to go through larger or better schools that were on top of the technology curve. I found the technical parts kind of boring and outdated. So, while I was there I learned as much as I could, but when my friend called me up and said, "Let's start an internet access company," I was like "alright". I left that same day. So that is pretty much me.

Katina Michael: How did you actually get involved with computers and technology?

Amal Graafstra: Ah, that is a fun story. I delved into electronics and wanted to know how they worked. So as a kid I would like to take things apart and put them back together. So, technology and how things work I was interested in at a young age. When I was in third grade actually, I had the privilege of going to a country school which was way out in the sticks. It was a great school because you could stay with the same classmates through each of the grades. It was very small, but oddly enough, it was one of the only schools that had a PET computer. I forget what the acronym stands for, but it was a simple computer with no drives or storage of any kind. You could just turn it on, and type, and that was it.

We actually had a program called R.I.F. which stood for *Reading is Fundamental*. You could go and get a free book, like a "choose your own adventure" book where you would turn the page, read the story and then you would make a selection at the bottom of the page about what you wanted to do next (like, if you want to jump the chasm, turn to page 10). And all of a sudden I found one that was a computer programming "choose-your-own-adventure," you had to type in some IBM BASIC code or Apple 2 code and write programs to move on in the story. *So the problem was the only computer I had access to was the PET, and then PET was slightly different so the code did not work as it was written in the book. I had to figure out how to make the code work and what the differences were. There was no manual so it was just me poking at buttons first, but eventually I figured it out. That shocked me that I could take this thing that was useless, like this thing in the corner that nobody touched, and I could enter information and it would do something useful. That was amazing to me. So my first experience with computers was programming, and things took off from there.*

Katina Michael: Wow! Usually we are all introduced to computers through playing computer games, but you had a different venture into this space. So, can I ask, are you in your early 30's?
Amal Graafstra: I'm actually 30.

Katina Michael: Ok. I'm 31 so I kind of can relate to what you are saying. I had a similar experience but with the Amiga 500.

Amal Graafstra: Oh yeah. All that early stuff was great.

Katina Michael: Do you consider yourself an early adopter of technology?

Amal Graafstra: You know it depends on what type of technology it is. Some things do not interest me at first. When a technology that I think is kind of interesting comes along, I learn about it. Then someone comes up with another piece of technology, and I think hey, if we could marry these two technologies together it would be great and we could solve this problem and do this other thing too. So, I love to do that, find out about technologies and then put them together in a way that solves a different problem or helps someone or is a solution to something.

Katina Michael: For you, is the value proposition the most important factor in the adoption of technology?

Amal Graafstra: Basically it really depends, for me, if it is going to be any fun. There are a lot of things that could be put together but it takes a lot of work and it is not all that enjoyable in the end.

Katina Michael: So for you, it is the novelty that is the most important and best part.

Amal Graafstra: Yes, just being able to look at something and adapt a solution that is not really available. I get really frustrated with the lack of open featured end-user commercial products. For example, there are commercial RFID door readers out there, but none are adapted or marketed to be used with implants. Also, I cannot connect these products with to a microcontroller or my PC unless I am willing to buy some hugely expensive commercial system where these kinds of options are available. Regardless, I have been able to adapt technologies to create a solution that connects these features and technologies together. For example, my RFID door reader is connected to my PC so in addition to a standard RFID reader, I can schedule access only for certain times, or even open the door by sending a text message to the system from my cell phone. This kind of easy

Figure 1. Mr Amal Graafstra demonstrating an RFID-operated door latch application he developed. Over the RFID tag site on his left hand is a single steri-strip that remained after implantation for a few days. His right hand is holding the door latch. Courtesy of Mr Amal Graafstra.

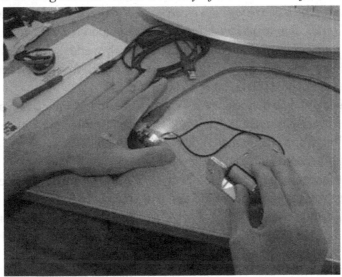

integration is what I look forward to when I am doing these projects (Figure 1).

Katina Michael: Are you interested in patents at all or that does not really interest you?

Amal Graafstra: I looked into that, the patent stuff. The patent process is really interesting, but certain aspects of it are very frustrating of course. That is probably another reason that I'm not super rich, because I have not looked into it as much as I should have. I am coming to realize more and more as I get older that is really what the game is about at this point. To engage in the patent process it has to be really worth it. But for the most part, I am only interested in my own personal use anyway when it comes to building these solutions.

Katina Michael: Do you consider yourself a hobbyist or entrepreneur?

Amal Graafstra: I think on one hand I am an entrepreneur and one the other a hobbyist. There

are a lot of times that I look at a problem and say, "I can put a solution together for that and build it for you," and I'm paid to do that. So, that is kind of entrepreneurial. At other times, I'm only interested in creating a solution for my own purposes, and that is the hobbyist in me. A lot of times what I create just isn't marketable, or not worth trying to market. I like to keep things on the hobby side. Any time you turn a hobby into a job, it usually stops being fun. For example, I like photography a lot, and I take quite a few pictures and I even have got a few magazine covers doing it, but the second that someone says "why don't you do this for a job?" Well, then it would become more stress than fun, and I don't want it to be like that.

Katina Michael: I wanted to ask you how old you were when you first conceived of getting an RFID implant?

Amal Graafstra: When I think back, the reality of it is that I was very young, if I remember correctly only 7 or 8 years old… I was walking around the backyard when I heard my mother, who is very religious, saying that putting a chip into an animal or human aggravated her and disturbed her. *So when the pet chip first came out a long time ago, I remember hearing about it and being convinced that the inventor of this chip would introduce it for pets then move onto babies and tagging babies in hospitals.* The people around me thought it was ominous. I never doubted that point of view because that is what you do when you are a kid. But I thought about it, and considered what would be the purpose of the chip? I thought it could be used by other people to control me, and I believed other common misconceptions of technologies at the time. But there was another part of me that thought "how else could I use that?"

Katina Michael: And later on, what then?

Amal Graafstra: Later in life, around March 2005 to be exact, I found myself moving heavy equipment in and out of my office door almost every day. My office door was one of those latches that locked every time it closed, and I really hated having to carry around and fish for my keys all the time. I started looking at the fact that I had so many keys and what the job of a key was... to identify me as an authorized person and admit access. So, I started looking for a solution and decided to try and come up with an automated access control system that recognized me rather than a key I had to carry around. I started looking into biometrics, things like face recognition cameras and fingerprint readers. The problem I ran into was the fact that these solutions, when done the right way, were very expensive and clunky to implement. There were also concerns over the security and reliability of biometric solutions. Also, because I would need to put the camera or fingerprint reader outside, I was also concerned about vandalism. There weren't many options rated for outdoor use that were available for someone on a budget. On the other hand, I found tons of RFID readers for cheap, and writing my own software to work with them was a

no-brainer. The only down side to RFID was the fact I had to carry around an access card. That got me thinking about the pet implants again, and I realized those were a perfect fit! With RFID, I could create a cheap solution with the best of both worlds... all the benefits of RFID without the need to carry an access keycard!

Katina Michael: So you felt it was a good cheap solution but were there any problems with the pet tags?

Amal Graafstra: There were a few problems with the pet tags. Primarily, I couldn't find any cheap readers that read the pet chips. It turned out there were many different kinds of RFID and they all didn't play well with each other. Another issue was that pet tags had a special anti-migration coating on them that was designed to lock the implant in place, which would make removal or replacement nearly impossible. There was also another option for an RFID implant... VeriChip. I'd already heard of the FDA approving the VeriChip for implantation into humans, but the VeriChip had the same issues that the pet tags had... they also had an anti-migration coating and there were very limited hardware options available. I also found out that you must be entered into the VeriChip database when you receive one of their implants.

So, I figured I would just start with a basic keycard system and find some cheap RFID readers that were easy to hack or designed as OEM hardware I could easily integrate into my project. I found several reader options that read EM4102 based RFID tags, so I started looking around for RFID tags based on the EM4102 chip. What I found just about made me jump out of my seat... I found this one site that sold EM4102 based RFID tags that came in a glass ampoule form factor just like the pet tags! Plus, it didn't have any coating on it. I immediately ordered the reader hardware and a few glass tags (Figure 2).

Figure 2. Graafstra showcasing the HITAG manufactured by Phillips in the palm of his hand. The company markets the RFID tag for livestock tracking, food safety, logistics, waste management, sports timing and casino gaming.

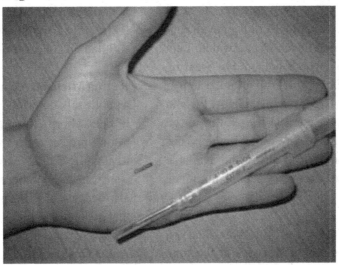

While I waited for them to arrive, I started calling around to find out what all the differences were between the glass tags I ordered and pet and human implantable glass tags. It turns out there were only a few insignificant differences, the first of which was that the tags did not have the anti-migration coating. They also were not sterile. *After several difficult conversations with various manufacturers, I found out the glass used in these industrial glass tags I ordered and medical implant type glass tags was the same stuff. That was good enough for me, so as soon as the tags came in I was already setting up my first implant procedure with a cosmetic surgeon who was a client of mine at the time. Once I confirmed the glass tags worked, I scheduled the implant and started building projects. I was so busy creating an access control project I didn't really tell anyone I was scheduled to get an RFID tag implanted in my left hand. A couple days and a 5 minute procedure later my left hand was RFID enabled and I had a basic access control system built.*

Katina Michael: How did it make you feel? Different in any way?

Amal Graafstra: *Now, of course, I do not feel any different. I even forget they are there until I have to use them. But at first it was kind of weird and when I was bored I would kind of poke at them and feel the implants under the skin. There is kind of this cool factor to it too. I put my hand to the front door and unlock it and people are like "What! Hold on, what just happened?" So that is all kind of fun.* But really over time, I've had it for 3 years or so now, the novelty has kind of worn off, and now it's just the useful tool I always wanted it to be. But I really get into interesting conversations with people about implants and the issues surrounding them like privacy concerns, security issues, and the technology in general… even religious aspects like the "mark of the beast" are interesting to me. The conversation starter aspect of it is much more valuable to me at this point than just being able to open my front door or start my motorcycle.

Katina Michael: Did you ever consider going wearable and perhaps using an RFID watch device?

Amal Graafstra: You know, I did not even consider it because I don't even wear a watch. I am one of those people who is bothered by wearing something on their wrist. If I did wear a watch or wristband with an RFID tag in it, I know I would just take it off and leave it in the shower, or go out for a walk and leave my wallet in the house. I knew that I wanted it to always be available and really hard to lose. So the implants made perfect sense.

Katina Michael: Could I ask you, Amal, had you heard of Professor Kevin Warwick at the time when you got the implant or was it much more of a self discovery?

Amal Graafstra: I remember hearing about it because again, I worked in the medical field doing server management for medical clients. So in '98 or '99 I just started my other company doing that and I heard about the "crazy cyborg guy". But at the time I did not know that it was an RFID implant. I just knew that there was some guy, a professor, who was somehow talking to computers with his body. In that way, I guess that it was kind of a self-discovery thing. Once I got the implants and started using them, I let my friends know what I did. They all wanted to know more, so I put the pictures of the process on *flickr* for a couple of friends. Other people viewed the pictures and spread the word, then some blogs got wind of it and things just exploded. Then a lot of people wanted to get in touch with me and some actually referenced Kevin Warwick as well. So I thought oh yeah, I remember that guy and I looked him up and was like "Oh, look at that, he did it as well". By that time I think he'd already done the Cyborg 2.0 project where he uses a nervous system interface and I found that really interesting. I considered looking into that

but realized it would take a lot more resources and medical contacts to pull that off, plus I wasn't as comfortable actually messing with the nerves in my arm as a DIY type experiment. I figured the RFID implant had been tested on pets for years, so I had no concerns about it.

Katina Michael: A couple of weeks ago, we gave a public talk here and I was just going over some of the Cyborg 2.0 pictures and the background to that project and I thought he was very brave to actually do that experiment. He looked quite weary in the photographs but I am sure it was also because of all the press release commitments that he had.

Amal Graafstra: And that was the other issue, a lot of people had health concerns about this implant, which they called "Cyborg". I really had to remind them that the implant I had, was really not a cybernetic device because it did not interact with my body at all. Both pacemakers and cochlear implants are types of cybernetic devices, but making a skin pocket for an RFID tag is not. That whole process (the nervous system interface), he must've been concerned about it because he did not know at the time if there would be nerve damage. Those kinds of concerns, for me, well... I value my nerves. That was really brave of him and I do not know if I would be able to do that myself.

Katina Michael: In fact, you touch on something interesting; we definitely do not call people with RFID implants "Cyborgs". We have coined a new term "Electrophorus". Electrophorus is a Greek compound word bringing together the word "electro" meaning "amber" and the word "phorus" meaning to "wear, to put on, to get into". Basically, "Electrophorus" means "a bearer of electric technology." We asked Professor Warwick and Professor Toumazou, what they thought about "Electrophorus" as an idea, in place of the commonly used term "Cyborg" and they liked it. What do you think about "Electrophorus"?

Amal Graafstra: Yes, I think that is a really good idea to have a term that separates us. What I am finding is that it really comes down to marketability. Just like people use Kleenex and Xerox as generic terms, people are calling RFID tags *RFIDs*, which if you expand the acronym to Radio Frequency Identifications, it sounds kinda silly. So, I think it is good to have a term to separate cyborgs and RFID implantees. And of course other things like hip replacements, where it does physically enhance your life, but it is a mechanical device, not an electronic device, so what do you call it? Is it a cybernetic device? It's useful to have better terms that describe what we are doing.

Katina Michael: Thanks Amal. All this is very helpful. When you called the doctors and they opted to perform the implant process, were you faced with any barriers or limitations? Did you consider what the Food and Drug Administration would think of it? Or did you think it was your inherent right to do as you chose?

Amal Graafstra: It always comes down to personal responsibility. The problem with some doctors in the medical industry at this point is that when they are dealing with someone who wants to take responsibility for their own actions with their own body, of course they are worried about liability issues; people who say they are going to take responsibility for their own decisions and their own body, and then come back and blame the doctors if things go wrong because of their own decisions.

For me it was not really an issue because I knew the doctors personally, both of them, and they knew me. We had a brief discussion about it, very brief in fact, which was something like "Is it safe?" "Well", I said, "as far as I know, we have 10 or so years of animal testing, so I would assume so." And then she asked "What is it?" So then I started going into the technical details and she was like "I don't care, if you want to put it in, that's fine". So, we did it. *Then the second implant was actually done by my family doctor which was done with an injector similar to the ones used on pets (Figure 3). He is really interested in technology as well, so he asked me "What is it?" and we chatted about that for a while. He had his own concerns about it but they were not health concerns, but other concerns outside the realm of health issues. He asked me about any ethical or moral issues that I might have about it, which I had none. Then he asked me to sign a waiver, a release, and that was it.* The injector came with an animal tag, which I threw away. The doctor put my HITAG in there after disinfecting it with a solution of some kind. I am not sure if it was alcohol or something else, but he was satisfied it was clean enough to be injected. Then it was over in a matter of seconds.

Katina Michael: Amal, did you feel any discomfort during or after the procedure, particularly with the RFID pet implant injector?

Amal Graafstra: No, actually I did not. I think the reason is that I specifically requested on both

Figure 3. The microchip Graafstra chose for his right hand was injected underneath his skin with an instrument manufactured by AVID, much like a hypodermic needle used for straightforward pet vaccinations. The injection was performed by his family doctor. Courtesy of Mr Amal Graafstra.

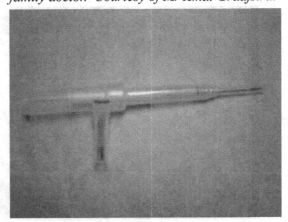

instances to put the implants just below the skin layer. By doing that, you're not diving into more serious flesh- you're not diving into tissue or nerve endings and that kind of thing. The pet implant injector when it is injected into the skin creates a bump, so that bump is a pretty good pocket to put the implant into (Figure 4). In both instances it was a very simple procedure to do and there was very little bruising- actually there was no bruising on either hand and very little bleeding. It was just a very simple procedure to have done. Afterwards, I was told not to use my hand for 24 hours and the other stuff, but being me, I was out there doing things I should not have been doing, but in terms of bruising there was nothing.

Katina Michael: Can you remove the implant by yourself?

Amal Graafstra: Oh yes! Basically because it is just under the skin, I could use an ExactoKnife if I absolutely needed to. I could simply make a small cut and force them out. So you know, in an emergency situation or something like that, because they are not deeply embedded I could

Figure 4. The specific site of RFID implantation in Amal Graafstra's left hand in the webbing between his thumb and index finger. In 2005 he considered tattooing the skin where the RFID tag was inserted after it healed. Courtesy of Mr Amal Graafstra.

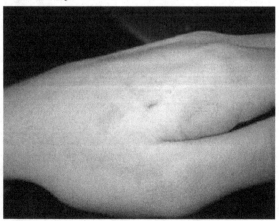

probably remove them myself. A lot of people say, "Well, what if someone cuts off your hand so they can get into your house?" I say, first of all I would hand them the keycard in my wallet. Secondly, if they just were not listening to me and coming at me to cut off my hand, I would just bite it out of my hand myself because it is right there. I'd rather do that than lose my hand.

Katina Michael: I actually read the account of your car window being broken into in Vancouver and you commented something similar like "I would have just gave them the keycard, it was more trouble to get the window replaced".

Amal Graafstra: *Yes, and that comes up as a security aspect of RFID as well. The issue that always comes up security wise is people wondering "well what about security", "what about people cloning the tag?" I have two tags, one is the EM4102 which is a read-only tag, and the other one is the HITAG (Figure 5). It has 40 bit encryption, it's not much but it is just enough to protect me against a basic passer-by type of attack. But the bottom line is that for a personal use scenario, where these tags are used by individuals, a person is going to have to know you and want to attack you personally.* An RFID attack is going to be much more complicated to perform than breaking a window, and unfortunately that is what happened with my car. I would much rather have them use an RFID attack so they could get in there and rummage around because they did not really take much, they just took some change, but they knocked the window out which cost me a lot more in the end.

My point about the RFID security issue is that my usage is much different than business usage. In my case, I've got a system that is a custom built system which was built specifically for my own needs. Someone would have to know me personally and target me specifically to carry out a successful attack. When a business uses RFID, like the Exxon

SpeedPass "pay at the pump" keyfob, there is no need to know who you are attacking because the system is common to everyone using it. I do not know if you have seen rfidanalysis.org but that site shows a couple guys hacking the Texas Instrument DST tag, which is used in many vehicles and the Exxon SpeedPass. In that case, once they hacked the tag's encryption algorithm, they do not need to know the person they are attacking, and they do not need to know where the person lives. All they have to do is attack any random person with a SpeedPass and use their account to go steal gas at any Exxon gas pump. And that really is the difference, the type of scenario and the context that this technology is used in.

Katina Michael: Tell me about the HITAG?

Amal Graafstra: The HITAG is a passive tag. It has 40 bit encryption and 2048 bits of read/write memory.

Katina Michael: Would you ever use an active tag as an implant?

Amal Graafstra: I do not think so, just because I do not like the idea of having to replace them when the battery dies.

Katina Michael: Every two years, is it?

Amal Graafstra: Smaller active tags can last up to two years, larger ISO style tags between three to five years. You can adjust the transmission rate so you can get eight to ten years out of some tags. Basically, I do not like the concept of something that wears out going into my body. I like the fact that these passive tags do not wear out. In terms of memory space on the HITAG though, I do have a limit of 100,000 writes on each bit in the memory block, but I can read those memory bits an infinite number of times without wearing them out. So the chance of something going wrong with either of my RFID tags within my lifetime is very remote.

Katina Michael: If we were to change the scenario a little bit, could I ask you if you would subscribe to any commercial applications, where someone else has the control, and you do not?

Amal Graafstra: That has really been the issue with both RFID and biometrics. The answer to both is really "no". I had an interesting experience at Disney World where they were tying ticket sales to fingerprint biometrics. In this instance, I had already bought the ticket and at the fingerprint gate, either I could choose to accept it and be granted entry or decline it and be declined entry, wasting the money for the tickets and the hotel and all that. It bothered me that when I purchased the tickets there was nothing to alert me that I would be required to give up my biometric information to Disney in order to use the tickets. It really concerned me that I had to trust Disney to not abuse my biometric information once I surrendered it. It's a lot harder to change your fingerprints than remote an RFID tag.

Actually I am sitting at a data centre right now that used to have an iris scanning system and really the issue comes down to who is controlling the data, who is safeguarding the data? The datacenter recently replaced the legacy iris scanning system with a new fingerprint scanner, and I asked someone "so what happens to the old scanner, what happens to my biometric data?" And they're like, "oh well, we don't know exactly, maybe we threw it out"... So, it really concerns me how this data is tossed around, and not really considered to be that important. Like I said before, my concern with biometric systems is that once you opt-in, you cannot really opt-out because you cannot change your biometric data.

But even with implantable RFID, you can opt-out somehow. In some cases it might be painful to do, but you can do it. In my case though, it would be rather easy. Comparatively, once someone has your biometric data, you've lost all control over what's done with it. *The biometric systems being developed now are even more concerning because many of them are passive, which require no action on the part of the user except walking by... there is no consent necessary. There are systems with scent detection that can sniff your unique biochemical mixture. There are systems that analyze gait and how people walk, and facial recognition systems that can tell you which cameras a specific person has shown up on for the last day or month or year depending on how much video footage the system has access to.* There are even iris scanners used in airports that do not require you to press your eye up to anything, you simply look into them... kinda like in the movie, *Minority Report*. I was even reading in a recent medical journal about a researcher who is working on a microchip that has polymer on it with charged ions, and the idea is that you can drop a DNA strand onto it and it would rip apart the strand and identify the person instantly. All of those types of advancements are fascinating and very concerning.

Katina Michael: What do you think about the current state of technology?

Amal Graafstra: My concern is not about the actual technology. I love the technology. I think it is great. I hope it is developed and used for good. My concerns are about the people. A nuclear bomb is no worse than a flower if no one presses the button. You know what I mean? So I have serious doubts about the people that will yield the power of the technology, but as far as the technology goes, I like it and I think that it is fine.

Katina Michael: There is a big debate in the academic space, the question being "is technology neutral or is it not?" There are those that say it is not neutral, and although I believe that technology has inherent functionality and capabilities, it *is* about how you apply it. Like you said, anything can be harmful. A knife we use to spread butter with can be used to kill someone too. That is the point you are trying to make here, that technology itself is not bad; it is potentially how it is used or misused. I think when people like yourself demonstrate the different type of uses of a given technology, basically we can see potential consequences in other areas as well. You have done well, for example, to show in the personal space, how RFID transponder implants can work. Then, you have also, without even realizing I think, opened up this whole new debate about how they may be used if placed in the wrong hands.

Amal Graafstra: *Yes, no pun intended, I am sure! One of the concerns I have about the VeriChip implantation program, the reason I did not get a VeriChip, is that it is a corporate product. It is not designed to be used by hobbyists. To that point, if I implanted a VeriChip, my personal information would have to be enrolled in a VeriChip recipient database, and I did not want that. I also did not like the fact that their implants had an anti-migration coating on them.* By all accounts, their implant is designed to be permanent. I did not like the depth that the implant was put into the arm, which makes removal very very difficult. I also did not like the placement in the arm, which for me would make the implant very difficult to use - I did not want to have to kneel down next to my door to get into my house or office. Putting it in my hand where I did means I can place the implant, which has a very short read range, next to an RFID reader very easily. And the whole point is that this kind of implementation is that it is a consent based system. I pretty much have to put my hand right on the reader to get a read, and that is a consensual process. Being in the hand, I can put it where I need to put it to get a read. All these things are reasons why I did not go with VeriChip, which I had considered for about ten minutes before ordering the other ones. So, there are issues with it.

The major issue I have with VeriChip is that Verichip has built no security into its devices, yet they are tying it to serious information like medical records and payment information. Being a permanent implantable device designed for permanent implantation, you can't easily replace or reprogram it if your ID number is compromised. For example, if you lose a credit card number, you call the issuer and get a new one. If someone scans your arm and gets your unique ID, what are you going to do then? I do not know how they going to secure this piece of technology now? It is obvious they did not take into consideration any of that. I do not know what their plan is, but for business applications, there are serious issues. While this issue was known to many in the RFID community, this was all brought to light when AnnaLee Newitz of *Wired Magazine* got a VeriChip implant, and had that implant cloned successfully by Jonathan Westhues who developed an analog cloning device for basic read-only type RFID transponders.

Katina Michael: Following on from these thoughts, I would like to ask you what your feelings are about microchip implants potentially being used by government to fulfill a mandatory national ID scheme?

Amal Graafstra: I do not think it is going to be the case. I know there are a lot of people pushing for a national ID system and basically we have already got it, it is the social security number in the U.S. And I think in all states now, you cannot get a driver's license without a social security number. In particular this was a problem for my new Canadian wife who is currently going through the immigration process. I am actually urging her not to get a social security number just because she does not really need one right now, so why enroll in the Social Security system when there is no benefit for her to do so. The issue is, if you do not get one, you are pretty much not a member of American society. If there ever was a mark of the beast, I think the Social Security number is probably it. But to answer your question, I do not

see RFID as the technology behind that drive. I definitely see the drive is there to be able to identify everyone nationally, but it will probably utilize something like biometrics.

The concern I have about biometrics is simply, sometimes you do not even know you are opting in to the system as you walk by a camera. I do not see that with RFID because you have to force a foreign object into someone's body to opt them in. It is also so easy to opt-out just by removing the tag. Also, it is very easy to interfere with or confuse the system using typical devices that generate interference. There is also the problem of cloned or emulated tags. All these kind of things do not really provide a good platform for a secure RFID implant based national ID system.

Katina Michael: Since about 2002, I have read a lot of credible accounts, mostly by government officials who have been quoted encouraging the use of RFID devices for immigration control and potential disaster recovery and response. For example in Asia, when SARS hit, business and economics was severely affected in some countries, such as Singapore. Just before SARS was contained, there were proposals to tag everyone that traveled on an airplane between SARS-affected zones. It was going to be a wearable device that would keep track of an individual's location history. I do agree with you, that in the interim, we are not going to have people implanted for national security purposes. But if there is ever a pandemic outbreak like the Spanish Influenza, and there are millions of casualties, ironically there may be a business case for it.

Amal Graafstra: *Yes, well it is like any kind of situation where there is something that induces fear in a populace, they will just about give up anything for the sense of security. It could be real security or the illusion of security, but it is quite often the illusion of security. Fear and hunger are the two great motivators for everyone, so I* *too really hope that is not what it comes down to. But I think honestly, in the very near future as biometrics advances there will probably be a system in place where you probably will not even have to wear a device, it will be like real-time face matching as you are walking. It is kind of a scary proposition, but I do not know what to do about it. I know what to do with respect to RFID I know how to handle that, but biometrics, especially passive biometrics, such as gate analysis, facial recognition and chemical scent and those kinds of things where you just walk through some checkpoint.* I just don't know. Especially in the U.K., where it has become kind of a camera society, the cameras already track individuals without them having to actually opt-in. Just being in a public space is opting in and that is something that is really hard to fight. Even though the monitored society set up in the UK has yet to prove that putting cameras on every corner improves safety and security.

Katina Michael: I think what you are referring to here is the unobtrusive nature of emerging surveillance technologies. It may be okay if the user has opted-in to being tracked for instance, such as in their place of work, but the problems arise when they have not given their consent to be tracked and their location can be revealed in real-time.

Amal Graafstra: Yes.

Katina Michael: I want us now to talk a little about ethical dilemmas, even if in a broad sense. I have studied different types of dependencies and relationships between a parent and a child, a carer and a patient, a parolee officer and a parolee. Can we talk about the different relationships and different ethical dilemmas in these commercial or non-commercial contexts?

Amal Graafstra: I think the parent-child thing, boils down to a basic misconception of how the technology actually works. I am constantly asked,

so now that you have RFID, we can track your every move and know where you are. Obviously, they do not understand how it works with a two inch read range, or even with a twenty-four foot read range, you are not going to get much out of that. The parent-child scenario does not make any sense to me because the only thing that really would be able to be identified is a body part, or something that has been tagged. But a lot of parents are scrambling, they want to be able to track their children to know where they are during the day. A lot of companies are now rushing to fill the void with solutions. For instance, some parents are giving their children cell phones which can actually track their location. So there is kind of an interesting dynamic there. I think anything to do with parents and children is always interesting because the parents want to do the best thing by their child, but the child is its own person. Parents may start to impose things that are irreversible. This sort of goes way off RFID. But things like circumcision, implanting them, tattooing them, enrolling their biometric data in a national ID system, these are things that are pretty much irreversible, with exception of an RFID implant for the most part. So there is always an issue where that fine line is, and whether it is really in the child's best interest to do this or that. Let them make their own decisions as an adult.

Katina Michael: What about medical applications?

Amal Graafstra: In terms of patient care applications, RFID has a lot of commercial potential, especially when it comes to things like operations where you could use RFID labels for identification purposes. Just to double check that the right drugs are being delivered to the right patient, and to fill in the paper work and things like that. I know there are labels that come off and that is fine but as to implanting, it would be someone who wanted it like someone who wanders. I met a guy who has recurrent bouts of amnesia and he wakes up and he does not know where he is. A wearable device in his case would not help him because it could be removed. So he was very interested in implants to solve his dilemma. It is a very niche market, if you are looking at it for a business case. But it is something that he wanted for himself. And that is great. It is like here are your options, and how they are going to know if you have an implant, they will check it in the Verichip systems, what hospitals have it and which do not.

Katina Michael: Do you foresee any ethical issues even for medical applications of RFID implants?

Amal Graafstra: The ethical issues are always coming back. Do the patients really want to adopt the technology, and do they fully understand the ramifications? Whenever you are dealing with a company like Verichip or lobbying a government who wants to use the technology for immigration purposes the issue that comes back to me is much like my Disney Land example. I bought the ticket, I heard nothing about biometric, I get to the gate and after I have spent my money, planned my trip and got all of my stuff... well, now it is like you either do it or you go home. So that I see as a real problem because I did not really have a choice and I had spent a considerable amount of money before I was presented with a choice. So, we all have to deal with that when it is a private industry because people like me, actually there are a lot of us now, Do-It-Yourselfers (DIYers), do understand what is going on.

If we have been caught off guard on occasion, we only have ourselves to blame because we probably did not do the required research beforehand. I know a guy that thought the whole implant thing was cool, went out and got a pet chip and put it in his shoulder and quickly realized, "I cannot really get it out now without doing a lot of cutting," and the only person he could blame was himself. When

you have a marketing strategy saying, "Here's all the great things you can do with it", the negative things are not likely to be raised due to the fact that it is a commercial endeavor. Again, it is the consumer's responsibility and they need to their research carefully. And to a degree, the commercialization of these services and technologies will always try and suppress as much of the negative aspects as possible and that does not do service to the consumers.

Katina Michael: Amal, you mentioned the limitations of RFID to track, for example, you mentioned that if a parent believes they can track their child using an RFID implant, then they are mistaken. Could you comment on the possibilities of convergence with various location tracking devices, not just identification devices, for example, the potential for a GPS-enabled smart phone to work together with an in-built RFID reader?

Amal Graafstra: Sure, actually the term "tracking" is very sensitive to me also. A lot of people use it in a broad way, so tracking to me, says real time, GPS style, you are here right now, we are tracking you, like radars tracking planes as they are flying. Quite often "tracking" is used in place of a logging system. There was actually a system I was reading about recently where kids were wearing an RFID badge and they had readers in different locations, and they had readers set up in various locations in the playgrounds and recess areas. *So, the parent could see their kid was here at this time and there at that time and they are at this location right now. It is a limited technology as far as tracking is concerned. RFID is primarily an identification technology not a tracking technology. I guess convergence is going to play a huge role in being able to do that, but then again for RFID technology to be the main tracking technology, it is going to require a large grid of readers throughout an area. Some suggest that the grid already exists to an extent.*

All it takes is an agreement to share data between retailers, basically having readers at the front door, which a lot of shops already have that. Already there is this ominous grid. As you mention the GPS use of RFID, I think that that might be possible to have a GPS receiver receive location data but a lot of people do not realize that it does not work the other way around. The data comes from satellites down to the receiver, there is no way to get that location data out to the rest of the world, unless you have a cellular technology to relay it. Then you have the convergence of three technologies. I guess, yes you could converge these technologies in some way. A GPS device could track where you have been, then log that information, store it, and as soon as you come in the range of an RFID reader the transponder transmits that data to an outsource. That is a possibility but there are other technologies out there that are more suitable for doing that than RFID.

Katina Michael: Yet RFID has the proximity to the individual, for example, who is wearing the clothing or wearing a device. I think there are lots of people toying with the idea. We are doing some collaborative work with an international company, who primarily deal with location-based services, but they have moved to the IP space now. So they do not really care what device you have, it just has to be IP-enabled.

Amal Graafstra: There are actually some interesting things happening with networking technologies relating to finding and tracking. Microsoft has an IP locator service, meant to be used in place of GPS, in things like mobile devices and laptops as they roam from wi-fi point to wi-fi point. They want to be able to provide mapping services where they do not have access to GPS, but they do have access to hotspots in the city or whatever. So they are creating quite a large database so that they are able to track geographic location to a pretty precise point, given nothing other than an IP address or MAC address. Another interesting innovation is

where companies are turning wifi access points into something like an active RFID system, where these hybrid readers work with middleware to be able to track people and things using nothing but the wi-fi system. A lot of scenarios have the wi-fi network laid out and then right along side it, have the RFID system laid out, whether it is active or passive, it depends on the application. So this company uses wi-fi and RFID in tandem to get a more precise location.

Katina Michael: Yes, I think the next 10 years for wireless networking is going to surprise even some technology experts in the field. And much of it will revolve around location sensitive applications and social networking.

Amal Graafstra: Yes. And you will not even necessarily need an IP address, even a wi-fi device which does not bother with the IP layer is fine, so long as it is attached to a wireless network itself and then it can provide useful information.

Katina Michael: Amal, I want us to return to some ethical issues again. What should younger people consider before going ahead and getting a microchip implant?

Amal Graafstra: Well, actually, there have been quite a number of younger people that have asked about implants. I see a reaction which kind of is the basis for age related interest. Usually people are fearful or doubtful of technology and resist it, whereas young people sort of jump in. The older a person the more they will resist, and the younger they are the more likely they will jump in without carefully researching. So, I would say before getting an implant, seriously consider the health issues, seriously consider the social issues. There are a lot of people who say that implants might pose a danger physically, or consider how people might outwardly disagree with the fact that you have an implant. Be aware of the ethical issues, it is kind of like driving on the road, you might be an excellent driver but you still have to trust that the other person is not going to come over the line and kill you. The same is true with this type of scenario where you are getting an implant to opt into some system. You have to basically trust the system; that they are not going to abuse that power. It is difficult now if you just want to be a member of society. Look at social security cards, for example. Today, the U.S. government even has access to your library records, because of the Patriot Act legislation...

Katina Michael: Yes, they do have the power to do this but then it can be defined as function creep in action.

Amal Graafstra: And that is the thing. I got my library record when all that was not a problem but now things are different. It is not just an issue of trusting *now*, it is an issue of trusting now and into the future. Another issue is that still a lot of people get the EZPass, they get an active type transponder in their car, to be able to just speed through a toll. The issue is that when they got the transponder, and signed the original agreement, the understanding was that the transponder would be solely used for payment. But of course, now people think of additional uses like being able to track traffic and congestion and even speeding. They can now measure how long it takes for an individual car to get from point A to point B? That was a use that people did not sign up for when agreeing to place the transponder on their vehicle. *Then the next thing might be where did they get this guest and for how long did they have access to him, and then someone gets a ticket in the mail for speeding, then what if somebody else is cloning your transponder and you get booked for speeding 200 kilometers per hour.* There are a lot of issues and a lot of people are entering the system without seriously thinking about all the issues. They should be and I cannot believe that people are seriously considering implants for payment without having any security features in

the technology. It is kind of surprising but I guess it should not be.

Katina Michael: I can see, Amal, that the choice aspect is very important to you. You see a need to be able to opt in to an application. You also see a need for an alternative option if you do not want to have your hand scanned. There are clubs now in Spain, which offer their patrons RFID implants so they do not have to carry cash and for access to VIP lounges. There are companies now which are requesting that their employees be implanted. This is very different from the hobbyist or the personal space. Can you prejudge ethics in that you can think about the consequences before actually rolling out and innovating?

Amal Graafstra: *The opt-in and opt-out ethical issues are always at the forefront of my mind and what really brought that to a head for me, was when I really started to realize that I was losing control of my own identity as it relates to society. One big issue for me is what am I going to do about it, and how am I going to deal with it?* For example, I bank at a local bank that has recently been bought out by a national bank chain. When I opened the account, I signed my account card with my signature so they could keep it on file and compare it to checks that I wrote. Later on, I wanted to move my home branch to another branch and move the card as well. So I asked them, "can I go back to the other branch and bring back my signed card?" They said, "No". So I asked them, "why not?" and they replied, "Well, it's because of security... You don't want to let it out of the bank". So I insisted, "Well it's my signature, I signed it. It's my data it's my identifier and now it's in your files, and you are saying now you won't let me take it. What if I just close my account? Can I get my card then?" They are like, "No." So then I said, "So what are you going to do with my card if I close my account and you no longer need it. It's my data, what are you going to do with it?" They did not have an answer for me at the time because

I was at the front desk. Ultimately what happened in this example is that I submitted my signature, they put it on file, and then I lost total control of it. So, that has really raised an issue with me about trusting my bank to release my own identifier to me personally, while the signature continues to be used everywhere, it is universal, it is a global identifier now. That was a major concern to me and has really opened my eyes to the ethical issues as it relates to identification.

So pre-judging things like, how do we make the technology evolve and continue to be developed without getting it shut down based on ethics. I think the issue is always going to be when it comes down to identifying a person there needs to be alternatives to a biometric or implantation system. I think anything that you can opt-out of easily, for example, taking the badge off after work or having a pin code or something that you know, versus something that is more or less permanent, whether that is giving up biometric data or getting an implant that is rather difficult to remove. Having an alternative is always going to be necessary. I do not want to sound like an old-fashioned kind of guy, but there are constant encroaches on my identity in the name of security, in the name of identity theft, and that is a big concern to me because I truly do not have total control over my identity.

Katina Michael: Amal, you mention personal responsibility being very important to you. I want to ask you, whose responsibility is privacy?

Amal Graafstra: That is a good question. I think it is paramount that an individual realizes that it is their own responsibility, and primarily their own. People have to be aware of these things. Secondly, it is the responsibility of proprietors in society at large to enable that individual to make informed decisions about their privacy. For instance, in the United Kingdom they put up cameras to prevent crime and we are told by authorities that they are going to track faces and use certain kinds of analytical methods and yet we are not told what will be done with that data in the long term. So without a certain amount of information, the public cannot make an informed decision about it whether or not they want to be recorded in a public space. Public space is a really big issue because there is no expectation of privacy.

Then we can get into a debate about expectations of privacy in the workplace. I am of the opinion that if you go to work for an employer who says, "We want to have you wear this RFID badge so we can know where you are in the building and at work," I think the employer has the right to do that. I do not think the employer has the right to say, "We want you to implant this thing so we can track you at work" because the implants cannot be removed at the end of the day, that is the bottom line I think. I believe a person in the workplace has the choice of saying, "I do not want to participate in tracking within the workplace" and then they can get a different job. This might be difficult in the future when all employers may require implants. The labor contract is tied to human resources within the company, and if they are going to treat you as a resource, then they kind of have the right to do that. They sign a contract, "I agree to be your resource from 9 till 5" and if that means using them to get a hold of me, and to track me around the building, or whatever the purpose is, that has to be worked out between the employer and employee. Implantation devices or biometric systems where the data and device resides outside the workplace, are usually not opt-out able.

Katina Michael: A question now about the media hype over RFID. We have a lot of people talking about privacy and the Electronic Product Code global standard, Wal-Mart and Benetton etc. I have a research student looking at the journey of barcode in the 60's and the journey of RFID from the late 90's and beyond. What do you think it is about RFID, apart from the line-of-sight capability that evokes such a public response? Is it lack of public education about the technology or is it something else? What do you put it down to? What is the major issue with RFID?

Amal Graafstra: I think the issue of RFID boils down to two essential things. First, when we are conducting a purchase using the bar code, things might take three or more reads to register. That is a pretty conceptual process; I do not see random laser scanners shooting out into the general public. Really it comes down to consent again. RFID is scary because the public is not educated about the technology. But also there is a level of consent that needs to go along with it. The issue with Benetton was that they were embedding these devices into the clothing, and not telling the consumer, and not deactivating the devices when leaving the store. Sure, RFID has its uses within the store and that is the company's right, of course they can manage their own inventory but when the consumer buys an item, it is no longer the store's inventory and they have no right to track that piece of clothing anymore. *So there has to be this debate, and I am glad that it has come to the fore, because it has raised an issue of privacy and RFID. All these growing pains that RFID is going through right now, it is all good. We have people on both sides of the extremes but it means the technology will continue to be developed and the issues will continue to be talked about and hopefully resolved. So extreme arguments on both sides are good, and people like me in the middle are going to benefit from the debate.*

Katina Michael: And the second issue?

Amal Graafstra: The other issue to me is the basic serialization of everything. A barcode does not identify an item- it identifies a class of item. While you could have a serial barcode, that is not how the UPC standard works, it involves a class of items. It could be a particular brand of cereal

or a type of watch. It is not like the exact watch or exact type of serial. People are concerned about the memberization and serialization of everything, of objects, but they are more concerned of the serialization and numberization of life in general, e.g. children, and pets, and living things. There are scary things going on like DNA sequences being patented and life forms being patented, and corn and grains and things that we eat... you can hardly go to a store nowadays and buy anything that has seeds in it anymore, and if you do find something with seeds in it, it is usually not fertile. To get to the point, eventually everything is going to be numbered and tracked, particularly when it comes to compulsory things like food, you are going to have to pay a patent fee when you want to grow your own corn. You know that kind of stuff scares people, it scares me. I think in the general public's mind, RFID serializing every individual object on the face of the earth is a stepping-stone to that horrible nightmare.

Katina Michael: So what is it Amal about RFID when we compare it to say biometrics?

Amal Graafstra: *The public have raised issues about biometrics before but nothing like what they are currently saying about RFID technology. I think it is because with RFID people have an object to place their fears on, whereas with biometric data it is just walking by a camera or just kind of casually putting things on a sensor, and then they forget about it.* A lot of it is intangible and so while there is fear surrounding it, there is nothing to focus on or point the finger at and say, "this is the devil, this is the enemy". Whereas RFID you've got a tag, for example if you buy a piece of clothing and you find the tag that is meant to identify you and track you in and out of the store, you look at that and associate your fear and anger with that object. So RFID is really taking a battering because people have something tangible in their hand. Like you said, Benetton is crossing the line with their products. Like "okay we are going to sell these items but then we are going to get the added benefits of tracking people in and out of the store." And of course they are not thinking ahead or having any concerns about other retailers starting to read the data from Benetton. What happens if other retailers start sharing data like "Oh this person was in this store, then they went here, and then there".

Let me give you another example that is also relevant here. My sister actually got a loyalty card for a supermarket which for a long time used an individual's phone number as their identifier. The phone number is not used anymore but I still remember it. They have gas stations now linked to the loyalty scheme, so that when I am driving all over the country I will head for that brand, and I will use the number, and get a message saying "Hello Ms Graafstra, thank you for buying the gas". Now, anyone in the country could be that person buying the gas and there are certain cases where police have used loyalty card transaction histories to track down individuals suspected of committing a crime. So I always wondered if something happened in the vicinity, would my sister be blamed for that because I used her phone number to make that purchase. Likewise, if somebody borrows my sweater with an RFID tag in it and murders someone, am I going to get the blame for that? So there are all these issues kind of swimming around but I think there is animosity towards the RFID because there is tangible evidence there.

Katina Michael: You mentioned that your Mother is very spiritual. Also that young people should consider the social consequences of RFID. For some people transponders are considered the mark of the beast and many people refer to the Book of Revelation, and they will mention Chapter 13 as the fulfillment of prophecy or looking towards fulfillment. I have downloaded quite a few You-Tube clips from particular church organizations and I am interested to hear what you make of it all, i.e. the religious aspect?

Amal Graafstra: It is actually really interesting. If you believe the Book of Revelation as foretelling the future then that is one thing; that gets one into the realm of "Okay, now let us talk about this seriously- what could constitute the mark of the beast?" I think what people are missing is that RFID has not been the first technology that has been referred to as the "Mark of the Beast". Credit cards and social security numbers all have to do with that issue, the things that we take for granted today have all come under this sort of trial of fire. I think RFID, particularly RFID implants, are a huge issue because the device does actually deal with the body, which is mentioned in the Revelation. A lot of people thought that it could be tattoos from "1984" or tattoos on the neck, that sort of scenario. I think that is really what people are missing, they are minimalizing the passage.

The real message is that people will submit to a system and worship that system rather than God and that system will become more important- so much so, that it will defile the temple of God, which is supposed to be the body, in order to subscribe to that system and worship to its processes. To physically take a "mark" on your body, whether it is an implant or a tattoo, solely for the purposes of trade and to be a member of the system has nothing to do with God. In U.S. it is specifically stated that there is a separation between Church and faith, if it is a National I.D. system that is meant for bartering and trade and security, those things are a matter for the state, that by design have nothing to do with the Church and God. So, it kind of comes full circle to submitting and subscribing to the point of defiling God's temple is to become a member of this other system and eventually worship it. I think that is really the message and to a degree a lot of people are already doing that... I do not want to get into too much trouble but, you know, whole businesses go around religious aspects and it really becomes about the money.

So it is all kind of an interesting thing and I had to talk about this to my Mom at length because she had her concerns. At the time I only had the left hand done, but if I had spoken about the right hand, then it would have been a very literal thing. *And she was like "you know, it is a stepping stone..." We talked for a while and I do not really think my use of this technology has necessarily sold my soul, in the way Revelation is warning us, i.e., I do not use it for buying and selling. The important thing for me is that if the technology became oppressive, where the government was using it to oppress people and to control people's buying behavior, I would remove them and I would be the first to opt out.* I think it is just the option of me using it for my own purposes and not having to deal with those things kind of brings to light a point that the Bible is making, it is not the specific mark that matters, whatever that might turn out to be; it is the act of being involved in that system and worshipping it.

Katina Michael: I have done a lot of research on this topic and found that Christians are not the only ones who have this kind of end-time belief, but a vast range of diverse religious groups, even though they may not articulate it using the same words, also hold to an eschatological view. And there does seem to be an incremental development in thought that the mark has evolved from a bar code, to a mag-stripe, to smart card, to biometrics and now RFID. I am wondering what the religious will now make of nanotechnology, which is like a dot in comparison to silicon; the prospect of us being covered with dots- perhaps not one single mark, but many marks. How will that change the fulfillment of that prophecy, will people then point to nanotechnology and say "that is the mark of the beast"?

Amal Graafstra: Yes, I think anything that is used to identify us will undergo the same fire that RFID tags have undergone. I think what is kind of bizarre, is that nothing much has been

said about straight-out biometrics. Instead of a mark, you just use your hand. Hand and forehead: there are devices where you stick your hand in and it analyses your hand's bone structure and veins for identification purposes. Forehead could easily be looking at a camera or an iris scanner. But for some reason because it is not a mark, it is just a bodily characteristic used to identify you the community has been relatively silent about it. I do not understand why, but I find it is interesting. Again, I think it comes down to symbology and having an actual physical thing and having a tangible thing. So that is the problem with the mark as I see it.

Katina Michael: Amal, were you raised a Christian?

Amal Graafstra: Yes, I was actually.

Katina Michael: And your current philosophical or spiritual orientation is still that?

Amal Graafstra: The more I learn about the universe, the more amazing it is, and the more you learn about everything the more it fascinates. I guess the hardest thing for me is the transition from a rigid spirituality- "this is the way it is and everyone else is wrong"- to more of, "I'm going to have my own relationship with God and that's going to be open and free flowing as I run my life through the course of this amazing universe."

Katina Michael: Amal, how does it make you feel that your wife also opted to have a chip implant in her hand? And how does that make you feel? When I got married, my husband gave me an engraved key-ring with the keys to our home and it has remained a special memory. How do the implants make you feel, that both of you are sharing the same space?

Amal Graafstra: I think that is very interesting- the fact that the keys were so significant to you, not because they were keys, but because they were a symbol of something that was very important to you. The implants for us are not necessarily symbols so it really did not matter too much. My wife asked me about it and I thought, that was kind of interesting, "if you want it, then sure". I had been using mine and she had been watching and asking questions about health issues and things like that and watching me build the projects for the book and saw the excitement that I had. She said, "Well, that might be kind of interesting" so she started using the keycard. And she was always digging in her handbag and looking for it and it became annoying; all the reasons why I did not want to use the card. So eventually she just said, "Well, what is involved in getting this implant done?" and I said, "not a whole lot." And we basically called the doctor that night and he said, "yeah, bring her down." So, we did it.

It was kind of insignificant at the time but other people thought it was very significant. She actually did have some issues with it at first because to her not being able to directly develop and realize the technology, she had major concerns about the permanence of it. A lot of people had said to her, "what if you break up? Would you have to get it removed?" You know even if she does not remove it, I could easily remove her identifier from my authorized list and she could remove my identifier from her front door, without having to take out the chip. But for her obviously not being able to leverage that technology personally it would be more significant and she would probably want to get it removed. So, that for her was a bigger choice "Do I really want to do this? What if I want to take it out later?" So for her it was a little bit more of a symbol than it was for me. For her it became a level of commitment, "did I really believe that my relationship was going somewhere? And am I going to be able to use this technology because Amal is in my life?" So when she did get it, there was a whole lot of reaction from her immediate friends; they thought she was crazy or whatever.

It was a general reaction that people have like an ongoing joke, "you're crazy". So, she could feel herself that it was a step in the relationship. Whereas, I thought, "cool, just another reason that I really love her because she is into this technology" and that she was willing to do it. She joked that it was the "engagement chip". It actually became true because I proposed afterward and we got married on April 7th.

Katina Michael: Congratulations. I have two more questions, Amal. One is how big is the hobbyist community? How many implantees do you think there are in the RFID space?

Amal Graafstra: Everybody asks me that. Of course, there are the two schools. One is the Verichip people who have been marketed to a degree and they've got more implants and use it for whatever they use it for, like VIP rooms. Then there is kind of the Do-it-yourselfers (DIYers) who use glass RFID tags for non-commercial purposes. I think that community is probably around 200 to 1000 people. It is really hard to track. Once word got out, I started talking to a guy in Australia actually, his name is Chris. He started a tag forum and he and I were the first two posts. Just from there, it exploded.

A lot of people wanted to know about the tags and how to do it and what to use it for. The hobby has grown rapidly and now a lot of people are doing it on their own and unaccounted for. The more people that I run into these days, and it has been a little over two years since the first implant, they'll say "yeah, you've got implants" or they might just say "oh, you're one of *those* people". I have met some other people that have had it done. I thought "well, that is strange", then I would ask them if it was in their hand or their arm or their wrist. *There are definitely people getting these implants put in that are not FDA approved and definitely do-it-yourselfers- there is just no way to count them all. Actually I went to a place in Alberta,*

Canada that is doing RFID implants but they are just a tattoo and piercing shop, I thought that is just wild. These are totally non-FDA approved places that are doing these implantations.

Katina Michael: What about suspected health issues related to implants?

Amal Graafstra: Today I got an email from somebody who had cited a few reports of cancerous cells forming around RFID implant sites in pets. They just have different severe issues around the implant sites. So they asked, "what about cancer?" I said, "well, it is definitely not the RFID function, it is not the radiation because it is very minute and temporary, you get more radiation from your house wiring than the RFID tag. So, it is not that. It cannot be the glass wall because it is virtually immersed. The only difference between animal implants and the glass tags that I have is the anti-migration coating, which I suspect will break down chemically and will react chemically in the body. As well as the fact that your skin is perfectly porous and your flesh will grow into those porous areas and pull the implant into place. I think both those factors contribute heavily to the mutated cancerous cells that are forming. Some of them are soft tissue tumors that do not go into full throttle, they form around these implant sites. That is very interesting because we do not know if these pets had strong immune systems or had other possible problems.

I was amazed to find out earlier, that cancer cells form in the body every single day and that is just normal and your body fights them off. Really the only thing that can fight off cancer is the immune system until it becomes malignant and gets out of control, which is when you get "cancer". It is not an abnormal occurrence in the body, it is a daily thing. So if something is wrong in the body, something is helping the cancer mutate much quicker than your immune system can handle or your immune system is really compromised and

then you get cancer. So I thought that was very interesting because the FDA approved Verichip does have this coating, so I am interested to see now what happens long term, with patients who have the Verichip. These pets are very old, they have made it through their lifespan term but in another case with lab rats and mice being implanted and they lived their lifespan and suffered complications right at the end. I am wondering the older these people get, who are now getting these implants very young to get into clubs, I am wondering when they get older if there is going to be issues like these, surrounding implants.

Katina Michael: Do you have any concerns about your own chip?

Amal Graafstra: For myself, not having these chips with coating, I am not experiencing any migration, but my skin is very young. These chips might move around later on in life. Will I have these health issues surrounding my implants? I seriously doubt it. A lot of people have actually brought up the need for anti-migration coating and asked, "do we need this coating at all?" I think that the placement of the chip has a lot to do with it. My chip is just under the skin in that area of the body where the skin is very elastic and can kind of hold onto the chip and not let it move around. From what I understand the Verichip actually is intended for arm tissue, under muscle, under that whole musculatory area. So, there is a concern of migration because there are moving body parts and muscles contract and expand all the time as people move around. I guess time will tell.

Katina Michael: Could I ask you about bodily infections related to implants?

Amal Graafstra: Yes. It is interesting about the infection because a lot of people ask me about the potential of having an infection. Again, for me, just having a smooth glass tag with no coating, it is difficult for an infectious disease to kind of ride along with that tag. *But with a coarse material around it, certainly, there could be all kinds of things "hiding" within that material.* Personally, I always reference the fact that when you are a kid and you fall over and scrape the ground and you get rocks embedded in your skin and you think it is so cool because you have rocks in your skin. That is definitely a buried process and if you have a healthy immune system you will fight infection just like you should.

My question is, if you are embedding these deep tissue implants with this coarse material that is harboring viruses or bacteria what then? There's no circulation through this material and can the immune system fight these infected areas if the tissue is not that deep into the body. These are things I do not know as I am not a medical doctor, but my suspicion is that if you do have infected material in that porous coating it might be much more prone to infection than just a glass tag. Also, a lot of people ask "what if you get an infection later?" In general, people do not have a lot of understanding of how the immune system and the body work. Again, with the sealed glass tags, I just say, "no" because once your skin is healed up, there is no way for bacteria and viruses to get in. I do not know if the coating material serves as kind of a harboring ground for new bacteria to be produced later. These are things I do not know, but they are very interesting questions.

Katina Michael: Finally, because we're actually coming up to the 2 hour mark and you have been very generous with your time- do you have any final comments or anything else that you would like to cover today?

Amal Graafstra: *You know, as I think back now, we have covered a lot of stuff. There is security, there is privacy, what else is there... a lot of people ask me as well if I am ever going to get my tags removed and I do not really see a reason to do that- unless of course they become oppressive in*

some way and my particular brand of tags can be used in that system then I would remove them. People also ask me if I'd ever upgrade my tags. I think so, I think I would. I'd be interested in upgrading my tags but not getting more tags. I'd be interested in getting tags that actually do interact with my body. "Get-well" tags for example, I do not have any health issues that would require, but if I did, biomedics would make my life better. An RFID tag that would allow me to test my blood without having to poke my skin everyday, I'd be into that. Or if they had a temperature sensor in them as well, for animals basically that is how they take their temperature. Being placed into my hand is not going to give me an accurate core temperature. So there is interesting technology that would involve actual interaction with my body and things like that. Depending on what comes out in the future I might do an upgrade. I might do an upgrade if there is better security- that would be interesting to do.

Katina Michael: Do you think people will consider new types of viruses to give implantees? Electronic viruses that may render their transponder useless? Do you think there is a community out there that might be interested in hacking away at the implantee?

Amal Graafstra: There was an article about RFID "viruses" and it had to do with tags that had memory space that you could write to. It made a big splash because it said "RFID tags contain viruses". The concept was that you could put something into a tag, replace the memory block that could overwrite a database or be able to replicate itself on new tags by corrupting the database. But I do not see it happening that way. *One thing that could happen potentially is an implant that uses passive technology to transmit data and power, put next to a much more complex computer like a smart card. The issue of course is data transfer rate and power transfer. These implants as they are now barely have enough power to do what they do.*

But someday in the future you've got something that has actual microprocessor, like a smart card then yes hacking will become an issue. But right now I do not think it is much of an issue.

I think what is more of an issue for implantees would be a high powered EMP pulse (electromagnetic pulse) that would essentially burn out the transponder. The transponders do have an over-voltage protection mechanism built in but there is only so much voltage you can protect against. If you come up against a large enough pulse then, yes, it is going to fry your tag. I was actually just down at the second annual Maker Fair down in San Jose, California and there were a lot of electricals around and I was very tempted to go up and touch one with my left hand because of the EM pulses. I was very tempted to touch it because there were signs that say "Pacemaker wearers stay away! People with hearing aids stay away because it will burn them out". I really wanted to go up and touch one to see what would happen but of course Jenny convinced me that it would be a bad idea. But I think that those types of attacks could happen potentially.

Katina Michael: I guess we can leave it at that Amal, for now at least, and I would just like to thank you again for the giving of your time. It has been a pleasure talking to you and getting to know you through these questions. I think you have quite a balanced perspective based on real-life experience, and I look forward with interest to see where things will go next for you. Good luck with another book perhaps, not just *RFID Toys*. I know many people will be very interested to read what we have spoken about today.

Amal Graafstra: Okay. Thank you very much also.

KEY TERMS

Anti-Migration Coating: A substance, for example parylene, that encourages tissue growth around an RFID implant in a human or animal so that it does not move around the body and make reading the device difficult.

BASIC: A simple interpreted programming language designed for teaching beginners, and the first language made available for personal computers. It was originally designed in 1964.

Biometrics: The measurement of parts of a person's body, for example fingerprints, voice timbre or unique patterns in the iris of the eye, to identify the person for security purposes.

Choice: The act or power of choosing; selection.

Cloned Tags: The theft of an RFID tag identity, commonly referred to as tag cloning. The Electronic Product Code (EPC) tag does not possess any explicit anti-cloning features and as a result is vulnerable to elementary cloning attacks. If the unique IDs in a manufacturer's EPCs are not random, then an attacker can guess or fabricate other valid EPC entries.

Consent: To give assent; agree; comply or yield.

Do-It-Yourself (DIY): The process of doing any project by oneself, as an amateur or as a hobbyist. In the context of RFID implants, it is the act of requesting that the chip implant process be performed by a local medical doctor so that application development is customizable.

Electronic Product Code (EPC): The Electronic Product Code (EPC) is a family of coding schemes created as an eventual successor to the bar code. The EPC was created as a low-cost method of tracking goods using RFID technology. It is designed to meet the needs of various industries, while guaranteeing uniqueness for all EPC-compliant tags.

Eschatology: The doctrines of the last or final things, as death, judgment, heaven and hell.

HITAG: Manufactured by Philips. A remote keyless system (RKE) designed to remotely permit or deny access to premises or automobiles. There are several RKE systems on the market.

Hobbyist: Someone who is engaged in a spare-time activity or pastime, pursued for pleasure or recreation.

International Standards Organisation (ISO): An international, non-governmental organisation founded in 1947 and based in Geneva, Switzerland, which is responsible for creating and promulgating many of the world's most important technical standards. The Greek prefix *iso-* means 'the same.'

Internet Service Provider (ISP): A company that provides internet services, such as hosting web sites, and usually also sells access to the Internet.

Original Equipment Manufacturer (OEM): A maker of computer-related products, normally software companies, which use the term to label versions of their products that are for sale directly to computer manufacturers only.

Patent: A government grant to an inventor, for a stated period of time, conferring a monopoly of the exclusive right to make, use, and vend an invention or discovery.

Public Space: Refers to an area or place that is open and accessible to all citizens, regardless of gender, race, ethnicity, age or socio-economic level.

Radio Frequency Identification (RFID): A technology that incorporates the use of electromagnetic coupling in the radio frequency (RF) portion of the electromagnetic spectrum to uniquely identify an object, animal, or person.

RFID Implantees: A person who has been implanted with one or more RFID devices.

Severe Acute Respiratory Syndrome (SARS): A respiratory disease in humans which is caused by the SARS coronavirus (SARS-CoV). There has been one near pandemic to date, between November 2002 and July 2003, with 8,096 known infected cases and 774 deaths.

Serialization: Implies something that has to be done linearly, one at a time, like people being served in a single check-out line.

Transponder: A combined receiver and transmitter of radio or radar signals that sends an automatic reply upon receiving certain pre-determined signals.

VeriChip: VeriChip is the first Food and Drug Administration (FDA) approved human-implantable radio-frequency identification (RFID) microchip. It is marketed by VeriChip Corporation, a subsidiary of Applied Digital Solutions, and it received United States FDA approval in 2004.

Virus: A small computer program, almost always written with malicious intent that is capable of copying itself from one computer to another, thus emulating a biological virus that infects new hosts.

Wi-Fi: Short for either wireless-fidelity or wide-fidelity; the brand name given to the IEEE 802.11b standard for wireless networking.

Interview 14.3
The Alzheimer's Carer

Mr Kenneth Lea, Wollongong, Australia
Interview conducted by Katina Michael on 11 December 2007.

INTERVIEW

Katina Michael: We are with Mr Kenneth Lea and it's the 11th of December 2007. Kenneth, thank you for accepting to do this interview. Could we begin with a little bit of background, about yourself and your current circumstances, with regards to dementia.

Kenneth Lea: Well, as I have said in previous discussion, it never became apparent that my wife was a sufferer for about five years, until she got very serious variations in her behavior. And for the last 4 years, it's been a sort of *in your face* type of performance, if you get what I mean. It's the way she has been acting but I can honestly say that five years before that she was showing signs but we didn't recognize it.

Katina Michael: And what are some of the tell-tale signs, on looking back, where you could have seen the onset of dementia? What are some of the behavioral traits sufferers might display?

Kenneth Lea: Her falling out with her original doctor, the rejection of the elder daughter, Kay,

was another, which at the time nobody realized, and I did not, that it was actually the onset of the problem, and I guess the other thing was not being keen on housework at the time, things on the cleaning side of the house she began to gloss over. She was doing everything, including ironing, and washing and things like that, but it was only when I started to do it myself I realized how things had slipped. *As you're living with it from day to day, you do not realize it... I didn't realize it, somebody else may have, but I did not...* and the daughters were probably too polite to mention it. But that was the sort of early onset, not realizing what it all meant, at the time. It is only when she had the second CT scan, from the specialist, that we realized. We had our suspicion beforehand, when her doctor said there was deterioration there but there was nothing to worry about, so obviously we didn't really worry about it. It was only when they did the second CT scan, which was the one that started to show that there was some deterioration in the brain, that we realized we had the real problem of Alzheimer's and dementia on our hands (Figure 1). I don't know what the criteria is, but some people refer to it as Alzheimer's disease which is what she really has, which is the dying off of brain cells, as opposed to dementia. But it is one and the same thing, as far as I am concerned. People with Alzheimer's develop this dementia anyway.

Figure 1. The Fisher Center for Alzheimer's Research Foundation. A web site http://www.alzinfo.org/ dedicated to the cause, care, and cure of Alzheimer's disease.

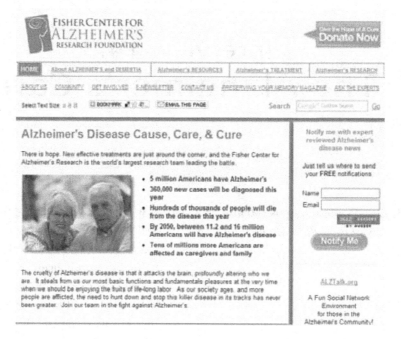

Katina Michael: How did Freda feel at the time? Did she notice a deterioration, or do you think she didn't really understand what was happening to her?

Kenneth Lea: I think, deep down she might have understood. But because she had always really been really personal in her own outlook on life, she wouldn't admit to it. In the early stages, I used to try to explain to her, that she wasn't herself, that she wasn't what she used to be, but it seemed as though it went over her head. *There was no comment either way, she wouldn't say yes or no. You know, she wouldn't disagree or agree, she just kept silent about it. So she never really expressed the way she felt.*

Katina Michael: Do you think she noticed that she was forgetting things?

Kenneth Lea: Oh yes, without a doubt, without a doubt. In the early stages, she would be talking, and then she'd lose the plot so to speak, as though

she didn't know what she was talking about. She'd just stop, and then you'd say "oh yes, what were you going to say?" And she'd say "oh, forget it" because she couldn't recapture what she was talking about, she'd take the easy way out and just say "oh, forget it".

Katina Michael: Mr Lea, you told me earlier you have three children. Could you tell me what their reactions were like when you spoke to them about their mother's condition?

Kenneth Lea: Well, the two daughters both took it the same way. I think they realized, with the conversation side of things with Freda, that something was wrong. And it came as no surprise to them. Both daughters had access to the Internet, and obviously they looked at whether it was hereditary or something like that. And they satisfied themselves with what they got off the Internet, that there was nothing to worry about. This is what the younger daughter said to me, that she realizes that it is not hereditary. And she said that

Kay had done the same thing. That was the first thing they thought about, not that they asked me about it. The Internet was there, and it was easily accessible to them. But the son, in the United Kingdom, when I first told him, he said "oh hell, what sort of a future does that hold for me then". That was his reaction, which I suppose he ought to have had. But straight away, I didn't exactly lose my temper, but I was very firm with him, stressing the point that he had nothing whatsoever to worry about, that it wasn't hereditary. So, no, he sort of did the same I think, because next time he spoke to me on the phone, he said he'd looked it up and got all of the information about it.

Katina Michael: You mentioned that Freda liked to visit Sydney with you, and that one of the first occasions of her wandering was her getting on the train and traveling to Sydney. Could you give us some examples of her capacity to wander and how you reacted to that?

Kenneth Lea: When I was working, quite often she would go to visit Sydney and come back. Now what she did there, I have no idea, but she used to like going to Sydney as a change of scenery for the day. And being on the pension, it was sort of a day out, it was very cheap to travel. After I retired, I used to go up with her once a week, every

Figure 2. The train route (shown in a dotted breadcrumb) taken by Mrs Freda Lea of Thirroul, New South Wales, during several occasions she wandered from her home location. The map of the Sydney metropolitan region train lines is courtesy of CityRail NSW and be found at http://www.131500.com. au/maps/train/. Train commute times are as follows: Thirroul to Wollongong 18 minutes, Thirroul to Unanderra 26 minutes, Thirroul to Sydney 1hr and 30 minutes, Sydney to Wollstonecraft 25 minutes, and Sydney to Westmead 36 minutes.

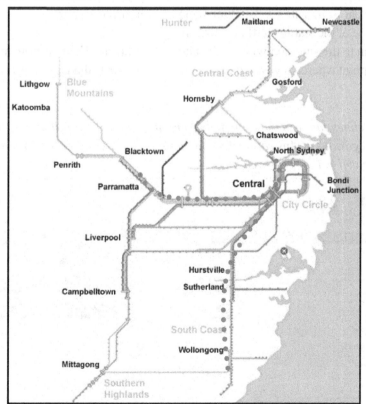

Wednesday actually, and we'd either go to a show or to a film, or even a walk (one of the bushwalks around Sydney). So we always had something to do up there. The first time she really went missing, she went on the train, on the downline, and ended up in Unanderra (Figure 2). And because she had identification at the time, not because I put it in her bag, but she had it on her, they were able to find out who and where she lived. They phoned up and told me. I thought she might have been in Sydney but it turned out she had gone the wrong way. Some security agent found her wandering there. That was the first time she really went astray. After that, there were occasions she would go up to Sydney. The first Sydney-bound occasion, I can't really remember which one it was, but I think she was found during the day and I put this ID card in her handbag and they were able to contact me through that card. And that all happened in an afternoon. And I went up to Sydney and collected her. And I suppose on four or five occasions, afterwards she did the same thing. But one thing with my daughter being friendly with one of the station staff at Thirroul, she alerted them to the situation with Freda, and they got to the point where they would phone me up if she was down at the station and I would go and pick her up. And we did the same with the bus drivers, through the two bus services that ran through Thirroul. We are well-known in the area of Thirroul because we would every day without fail, walk to the seafront and back. Everybody was used to seeing us, walking in the town.

Katina Michael: So community was important to you. Having that contact with locals could help you cope better on occasion.

Kenneth Lea: Well, not really, because I don't think they were really aware that there was anything wrong with Freda. I've still kept the walking up because of health reasons. The doctor said one of the essential things is to keep exercising. And I do a lot of walking. And the amazing thing is that I'll meet up with people there and they'll enquire where Freda is, and I tell them that she had to go into care, and they seem amazed. Most of them just say, they never realized there was anything amiss with her.

Katina Michael: You mentioned an occasion on an Australia Day, that you had the opportunity to

Figure 3. Guidelines for reporting a person "missing" in Australia that can be found on http://www. missingpersons.gov.au. In Australia someone is reported missing every 15 minutes and 95% of those persons are located in the first seven days.

see a vintage car exhibition in inner Sydney, and Freda sat down for a moment and then you lost sight of her. Could you describe what happened on that occasion?

Kenneth Lea: Well, on previous occasions, when she'd gone missing in Sydney, when we got separated, she'd make her way to the station and come home on her own (Figure 3). This happened on two or three occasions, I suppose. And in this particular occasion, it was mid afternoon, and I did a frantic search of the area, and you could imagine what it would be like in that environment, with the Australia Day and with all the crowds around these vintage cars. I went up and down, and then I started moving around Circular Quay and places like that where she might have gone. It was only about 8 o'clock at night that I tried to contact Patricia who lives in Thirroul, to try and find out if Freda had got home. But I couldn't contact her, and so the best thing I thought I could do was to come home. And by that time it was almost the last train. I had a good look round at all the possible places, she could be like the Botanic Gardens… I just didn't want to admit to myself that she had gone missing. And so I finished up coming home and by that time, I was completely whacked out, and I had convinced myself that there was nothing I could do about it because of the previous occasion involving the local police, I vowed never to do it again. So I thought, I'd catch the first train up in the morning and see if I could find her. This is what I did. I just had a quick look round at the places where we'd been and I couldn't find her. This was at 5 o'clock in the morning, the first train, and I decided to report her missing. And the Sydney police put the alert out for her, and that was the time where they located her sitting at a park in Wollstonecraft. So I was able to collect her from there and take her home.

Katina Michael: As a carer, can you tell me some of the emotions you felt, when the person that was in your care, went "missing". What did you feel? And what went through your mind?

Kenneth Lea: Well in my situation. I wasn't worried about Freda's well-being because I've always known she could take care of herself, her experience of all the years, long before I knew her, she was able to look after herself. So I wasn't really worried about her from that aspect, even though she was becoming a little weak with old age, but the main feeling I had was anxiety for her well-being. *She didn't know where she was and she was liable to do anything. There was no telling what she would take it in her head to do. It was just the anxiety of her being "missing" and it was a very stressful situation.* Like I said, when I got home that night before, I was just completely whacked out that I just fell asleep. And I just woke up in time to catch the first train back up to Sydney. I suppose what I should've done, was when she was missing, and I couldn't find her, I should've reported her missing then. But I had this feeling underneath that she probably made her own way home. I didn't want to create a fuss for the police in Sydney if she was at home.

Katina Michael: Can you tell me about the local police involvement a little more, the first time you declared Freda missing and the response by the police and how you felt about it.

Kenneth Lea: Oh, the response by the police was completely over-the-top. I phoned up the police when she didn't turn up on the last train because she was used to going up to Sydney and finding her own way home. And I had this inane sort of hope, that she would turn up right up until the last train. And it was only when she didn't turn up on the last train, that was some time after 12 o'clock in the morning, that I reported her missing. As I said previously, the whole *kabash* and *kaboudl* turned up: the dog squad, the police rescue squad, about three other cars, making one heck of a fuss outside the house at 2 o'clock in the morning, and this is why I would never call them again. If the worst came to the worst, I would never report her missing like that again, to the Wollongong Police because it was that completely over the top.

Katina Michael: What do you think they were looking for- I mean all of that additional force?

Kenneth Lea: A "missing" person.

Katina Michael: What, outside your home?

Kenneth Lea: Yes. And she was up in Sydney… I told them that. I said: "she's probably up in Sydney". As far as I was concerned it was completely over the top. Probably what they are trained to do, you know the normal procedures but they just didn't seem to want to know, what my opinion of what it all was. They just knew what they wanted to do and were doing it, but waking everybody in the neighborhood up in the process.

Katina Michael: Mr Lea, how long were you a full-time carer for your wife, after the dementia was diagnosed?

Kenneth Lea: Well, that would've been when she needed 24-hour supervision, after the second head scan. That was about June 2005 when I had to sort of devote my every hour to her. And it was only the last 2 years that she sort of developed this personal care, and later stages, the problem of incontinence. And then the incontinence was only at night time… She went away for a weekend once, on respite care at one stage, and the person there questioned me about her. "Does she shower herself?" "Yeah, she always has done". Well, I never used to worry about her own personal showering but it was only when one of the people questioned her about her ability to shower that I only took notice that from then on, I'd have to help her shower. And that is what I had to do all the way afterwards. Well, I didn't have to do it, but I did it, to make sure that she was getting a proper shower.

Katina Michael: So you mentioned this notion of "24-hour surveillance", and this requirement to be looking after her, for example if she walked

to your letterbox in the front of your garden or left the house outdoors. How demanding is this constant care because you were on your own as well?

Kenneth Lea: *Well you don't think about it at the time, but looking back on it, it is a bit of a worry and it does wear you down. Because you are constantly thinking "where is she?", "what is she doing?"* Like I would not follow her down, I would let her go and wander around the garden. If I was indoors, I would have to sort of watch what she did, and invariably when she went out the back door she would go down to the post box, and then come back up around the garden. But on the odd occasions, she would take it in her head to go and wander off. And one of the things that I caught onto was that if she had her handbag with her I had to stop her. So it finished up with me sort of hiding her handbags so she couldn't have them. Because she had that thing about it, that if she had her handbag she could get on the train, because she had her money with her. You see I was criticized- she used to carry two and three hundred dollars with her in her handbag- and I always thought if she does get away from me again, and people find her that at least I could tell her to put her into a taxi and she'd have the money to come back home. I used to be criticized for leaving her with so much money, from the family, but I always thought there is that situation that could arise whereby she could be found by someone completely innocently, and they could get in touch with me and I could tell them, well she's got the money in her handbag, could you organize a taxi for her.

Katina Michael: Would she carry a mobile phone? Or she didn't like to carry-

Kenneth Lea: No, she's even worse than me. I don't like mobile phones. I think I am a bit of Luddite with respect to modern technology. I think anything after the HP45 calculator I am lost. And it's only because of this business with her deteriorating to the extent she did, that I got myself a mobile phone, so that people could contact me and get in touch if they needed me.

Katina Michael: So the care was constant. Mr Lea, could you tell us about the time that Freda was found near Westmead.

Kenneth Lea: They found her at the shopping centre near Westmead. Anyway, they took her to Westmead Hospital because she was a "lost person", and yet she had the details in her handbag, obviously. They phoned me up and I went to pick her up at Westmead, and they wouldn't let me take her for a couple of hours, as they said she was dehydrated and she needed to be there because she had been missing overnight. Eventually we got out of Westmead and we caught the train to Central Station, and being a warm day I thought I better get her something to drink before we get on the train again. Being dehydrated and all that, I thought she probably needed some more liquid. Anyway, I went to get a drink off the store on the platform, they didn't have the orange juice there, so like a fool, I did not think, I though she'd just stay there as she was really in just a run-down state, I thought she won't move from there. Anyway, I put her by a certain position next to one of the big pillars, and I just said to her: "just stay here, and I'll nip out and get you an orange drink on the place of the concourse". Anyway, when I got back she had gone. I frantically had a quick look round, I even held up one train while I went through because I thought she might have got on… so I told the guard, let me have a quick look, I've lost my wife. He just laughed and said to me "be quick, we should've left a minute ago". Anyway, I had a quick look through the train, she wasn't on that, and there was one train that was nearby that was leaving… Then I thought, well I better go and report her missing again. So I went to the nearest police on the station, and reported her missing. *They looked at the surveillance*

cameras and eventually saw her on the platform going out towards Liverpool way. So they sort of alerted people along the station route, and she was found at Liverpool. It didn't take long once they knew which way she had gone but it seemed like a lifetime you know. The police asked me what I'd like to do, and I said for them to keep her there, and I'd pick her up. In the meantime, I contacted my daughter Patricia because I knew she was going to be home at that time. When I told her what had happened she said, "well stay at Liverpool, and I'll come and pick you up", to save me coming back all the way on the train. And that is what she did- she got to Liverpool with the car from Thirroul, within ten minutes of me getting there from Central station.

Katina Michael: Mr Lea, you mentioned that Freda wore the MediTrac necklace.

Kenneth Lea: Yes.

Katina Michael: Do you know what technology that was based on?

Kenneth Lea: The FM radio band.

Katina Michael: And did Freda ever object to wearing it?

Kenneth Lea: Only for about the first week, she used to try to get it off but they've got a pretty good clasp on them. She couldn't tear it off but she used to force it over her head. But after a few stern words, chatting to her, trying to explain to her what it was for she just sort of accepted it, and just wore it constantly. It was shower-proof, and of course there was no reason at all to ever take it off.

Katina Michael: Why do you think some dementia sufferers want to take it off? Why is there a reaction to remove the necklace or bracelet (Figure 4)?

Figure 4. The MedicAlert identification bracelet featuring the internationally recognized symbol, a 24 hour telephone hotline, emergency information engraved onto the bracelet and a confidential membership number.

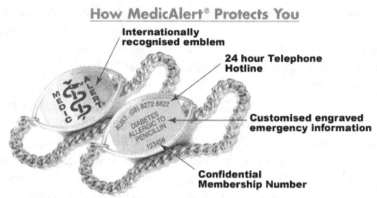

Kenneth Lea: I think, particularly with females, I think it is just that they don't like anything on their neck. You see for males, the other form is as a belt. Although it is better than nothing, as far as I am concerned, anything on the FM band is a waste of time in a built up area. They can be found with the equipment that the police carry in a very short space of time. And if they think you've lost it in the bush, they can put a helicopter up and trace you within 30 kilometers of it. Well, fair enough, if it is in the right sort of environment, it is probably true. But I feel, that if you go into a built-up area where the FM signal would be very weak, because it would be on a pendant and it would depend upon the state of the battery and that sort of thing, I feel it wouldn't be much good unless we're almost on top of the person. As you know, tall buildings and things like that, affect the FM band. It's not so bad nowadays, but in the early days, it used to be that if you drove passed a big building, it would cut out. So I never had any real faith in it, but I utilized it because as far as I was concerned it was better than nothing.

Katina Michael: If there were other types of technologies on the market, for example, watches that had key fobs to ensure that the tracking device wouldn't be removed by the wearer such as a GPS device? What about devices that could be implanted? What are your thoughts for wearable and implantable devices for dementia sufferers?

Kenneth Lea: *Well, I feel that in the specific case of the dementia sufferers, if the carer or the person responsible for the dementia sufferer is willing, if they won't wear a device that is removable, I feel that an implant is the only answer. Not only for the convenience of the carer but also for the subject's safety.* I've got great faith in the GPS system- as it is the best system of locating people over a wide area, whereas the FM band has a limited range on that pendant. GPS is global (Figure 5). It would mean given the right situation, which would be no worse than the FM system, if the situation is right for the GPS, sufferers could be pinpointed within a meter or so and it would involve only sending one police car to pick them up, rather than have the whole force mobilized. Particularly in places like Sydney which is such a vast metropolis with numerous forms of transport where people with dementia could move over kilometers within a very short space of time. You'd never find them unless they were locatable by GPS.

Katina Michael: Why do you think these technologies have not entered the market yet, targeting services at dementia sufferers?

Figure 5. A "locator phone" called Wherifone, marketed by WherifyWireless, that uses a built-in Global Positioning System (GPS). Loved ones can be located quickly and easily, with their position viewable on an online map or via a text message sent to a mobile telephone.

Kenneth Lea: Basically there is no commercial value in it for anybody trying to put it on the market. I don't think the average carer could afford the sort of cost that they would be expected to pay for that sort of system.

Katina Michael: Do you believe those individuals with dementia could have lived at home had these tracking technologies been instituted?

Kenneth Lea: I feel they could, on the proviso that the carers were willing to take on that little bit of responsibility. I feel that most of them would opt for it, in as much as it would bring them back into the family environment.

Katina Michael: Could I ask you something personal now about trust. Seeing you and your wife together today, made me see how strong your relationship was and is. But it became apparent to me that you must've trusted one another a great deal. Can you tell me how significant the idea of

"trust" is today, given Freda's suffering? Do you think for example, that Freda trusted you when you admitted her to the dementia facility? Or trust is not a factor anymore?

Kenneth Lea: I don't think in Freda's case, trust comes into it. She doesn't realize… oh, in one sense she knows. She knows she's in a facility like that but she doesn't realize what it's all about. Because of her placid nature, she just accepts it.

Katina Michael: Can I ask you on a similar note, what kinds of rights to carers of dementia sufferers have in terms of 1) the responsibility to take a patient in; and 2) it's time to go to a facility in consultation with a doctor?

Kenneth Lea: *Ultimately as a carer you have the last word. If you're prepared to live with the problems that is entirely up to you. In most cases in speaking with other carers the last thing any of them want to do is put the relative into care. In* *my case because of pressure from family and the advice from my doctor, I just had to accept she just needed to go into care, and the coincidence of this situation arising that the place became available at Corrimal as all the other places are in Wollongong or South of Wollongong.* I felt that I had to take the opportunity whilst it was there because she was on a waiting list for 18 months to go into care. The advice from other carers was that you've got to get your name down on the list because there is such a long list of waiting. There is always an option to say "I don't want the place yet" but if you do turn it down you go to the bottom of the list again. I often feel, that I was only able to get Freda into Corrimal due to my attendance at carers meetings and advice I received from ACAT representatives that attended these meetings.

Katina Michael: We talked about the carer's rights, what kinds of rights do you think dementia sufferers have? What are their right in this instance?

Kenneth Lea: Well, it's difficult. In Freda's case, she's just not aware of things around her from the point of view of her own well-being- what she should and should not be having. She just accepts everything that happens to her as it comes. So she'd be a poor subject to ask what rights has she got, as she would not know what you're on about.

Katina Michael: On that line of thinking, could you talk about the sufferer's need for privacy while suffering with dementia from the perspective of the surveillance technologies if instituted. And whether you think some things need to remain private still, or the fact that they are suffering with dementia, means that privacy is no longer a right. That safety is more dominant than privacy.

Kenneth Lea: This comes back to the carer, doesn't it? If the carer feels that the need is there for this surveillance, that it would help their life, I don't see why it should not be allowable. It needs to be considered by the carer, and in fact it needs to be emphasized preferably through the local GP (General Practitioner) or specialist that is dealing with the patient, they need to emphasize that it is a means of reducing the stress of the day-to-day happenings when they need constant care.

Katina Michael: Do you think Freda would have objected to a chip implant that could track her, even within the current Facility? If someone was to say to her, "okay Freda, we want to be able to track so you don't get lost, and we are going to inject you with an implant, similar to that of a cat or dog"? Do you think she would undergo that procedure?

Kenneth Lea: It's difficult to know… My own feeling on that is she probably wouldn't object anyway because she wouldn't be aware. She might get that little flash of memory that might cause her to rebel.

Katina Michael: What are the benefits that you could identify of tracking and monitoring devices, beyond the basic MediTrac system that is available today? For example, say the GPS units in the form of a watch. What are some of the benefits that you could list for all stakeholders involved?

Kenneth Lea: From the point of view of the carer, it would be a big stress reliever. If the person went missing, if we could in the ideal situation, get on the phone to a central location say in Sydney, it would be great. I feel it should be the police in charge as they have the existing facilities to carry this sort of thing out. If there was a central point that you could call up and say well "so and so is missing with a certain number and whatever, could you find out where she is", then they could straight away track her and if necessary ask you if you are going to pick her up. It would only take one police car. That is opposed to when you report them missing, you alert the whole police force. It all goes out onto the police network. And you see all this on the television shows. I really feel that it is something that the police ought to be involved in, in as much that the facilities are already there. And it would save the police a heck of a lot of work, in an ideal situation. Obviously there would be situations that it didn't quite work out like that, at the same time, I feel in most cases it would.

Katina Michael: Any other benefits you could identify for the carer or dementia sufferer?

Kenneth Lea: From the carer's perspective the one big saving thing is the removal of most of the stress. It's only when they actually go missing you get that sort of stress, and if you can't turn to somebody that can tell you where she is, it becomes intense. Whereas I feel if you are phoning in to tell somebody that someone is missing, at least you are doing something positive, and hopefully it would resolve itself much quicker than past experience.

Katina Michael: Mr Lea could you describe the ideal tracking system?

Kenneth Lea: *As we've talked about previously, as far as I'm concerned, the GPS system is the ideal solution in as much as it is as good as anything else, like the MediTrac that is on the market. It sort of exceeds that performance. I don't think there are any real disadvantages to it, apart from the fact that it has a limited battery life compared to the 4 months of the MediTrac. So ideally, if it was based on something that could be switched on remotely via a mobile phone network then the battery could operate a lot longer, say for between 4-6 hours, until the individual was located.*

Katina Michael: Would you have any concerns about the location history of an individual being stored anywhere?

Kenneth Lea: Not at all. Put it this way, any organization that is involved in helping to find people, it's all of a benefit. There's nothing detrimental that I can see in that aspect of it.

Katina Michael: And would you consider using the same system? For instance, if authorities wanted to find you and your wife simultaneously if you were out n' bout? Would you adopt the same system? Or you see these sorts of systems being applicable only to sufferers of dementia for instance?

Kenneth Lea: Well, if it is going to help a situation, I have no objection whatsoever because it means that I could probably be informed much quicker if she was found when I didn't know that she was even missing.

Katina Michael: Do you envisage any obstacles or disadvantages pertaining to this technology?

Kenneth Lea: Well, the only disadvantage that I can see is the limited battery life of the device. You know, what is the real optimum performance? For instance, a product may claim to have a battery life of 6 hours, but does it fade after 4 hours, so that you're getting a much weaker signal. I don't know, you know more about this than I do, but this is what comes to mind.

Katina Michael: So which organizations or agencies need to be lobbied to get this type of technology to market to help people who wander away from their homes and carers?

Kenneth Lea: I think I mentioned in one of my letters to you, that I wrote to the police commissioner many moons ago and it was a complete negative reply. Unfortunately, I wrote to him when he was away on a course somewhere. And eventually, after about two or three months, I got a reply from one of his minions, and she told me no more than I already knew. In effect she said the technology was such that it needed a car battery to power it. She was referring to the tracking devices and she said there's no other technology that exists. I don't think they even looked at it properly. They looked it up briefly or spoke to someone briefly and I don't think they got the full picture.

Katina Michael: So the police is one organization. Any others?

Kenneth Lea: Well, I can't think of anybody else that would have the coverage. But one thing I feel that it could go through. I at one stage was considering approaching the local MP. So I feel that it would be a good time to approach him, to see what the police department would like to do to get this system into operation. I strongly feel that because of the nature of the problem, you know in my case, it was in Sydney, but for others it could be anywhere from the remote bush to interstate up in Queensland. In that way the global positioning system would be able to get a location fix on the individual. And the setup exists for them to deal with it quickly. The whole police force is geared to respond, more or less, instantly in anything they are asked to do. And as regards to manpower saving, I mean that night I reported Freda missing, there must've been 20 police at my place, when they could have been dealing with other crimes.

Katina Michael: Finally, are there any other comments you would like to make?

Kenneth Lea: *The only thing that occurs to me about the whole dementia situation is the medical profession, and I am talking now about GPs. You get varying degrees of interest, but a lot of them don't seem to be aware and educated about what dementia for the carer and the sufferer means. It is only after they get some experience with the* *carer and patient that they can appreciate what the whole ordeal is about.*

Katina Michael: Mr Lea, thank you for your time and openness.

Kenneth Lea: Thank you, Katina.

KEY TERMS

24-hr Carer Supervision: One who can watch over an activity or task being carried out by somebody who cannot always perform the task correctly or unaided. The carer is on hand to supervise the patient, 24hrs per day/ 7 days a week, and offer assistance if required.

Alzheimer's Disease: A progressive organic brain disease which appears usually in middle age or old age and which results in confusion, memory failure, disorientation.

Battery Life: The estimated period during which a battery is capable of operating above a specified capacity or efficiency performance level.

Computerized Tomography Scan (CT Scan): A cross-sectional X-ray enhancement technique that greatly benefits diagnosis with high-resolution video images.

Dementia: A state of mental disorder characterized by impairment or loss of the mental powers.

GP: General Practitioner; medical doctor.

Global Positioning System (GPS): A navigational system which relies on information received from a network of satellites to provide the latitude and longitude of an object.

MedicAlert: A non profit organization, that specializes in 24hr personal emergency, medical information and identification services. The

MedicAlert is worn by people who have diagnosed medical conditions, suffer severe allergies (e.g. allergic reaction to penicillin), and/or are taking medications. Form factors include: necklets, sportsband, expandaband, bracelet, and chains.

Missing Person: A person who is declared missing due to a physical or mental disability, to the degree that the person is dependent upon an agency or other individual to ensure their own safety.

MP: Member of Parliament.

Parkinson's Disease: Belongs to a group of conditions called motor system disorders. It occurs when certain neurons which produce dopamine become impaired, or die. The loss of dopamine subsequently causes the nerve cells to fire out of control, leaving patients unable to direct their movement in a normal manner. The disease is both chronic and progressive, with early symptoms being subtle and occurring gradually.

Trust: Reliance and confidence in the integrity, justice, etc., of a person, or on some quality or attribute of a thing.

Wander: To roam or stray without any certain course or object in view.

Chapter XV
Uberveillance

INTRODUCTION

Uberveillance, also überveillance, is an *above* and *beyond*, an *exaggerated*, an almost omnipresent 24/7 electronic surveillance. It is a surveillance that is not only "always on" but "always with you" (it is *ubiquitous*) because the technology that facilitates it, in its ultimate implementation, is embedded within the human body. The problem with this kind of bodily invasive surveillance is that *omnipresence* in the 'physical' world will not always equate with *omniscience*, hence the real concern for misinformation, misinterpretation, and information manipulation (Figure 1).

Uberveillance is an emerging concept, in the full sense of both its application and power it is not yet entirely arrived (Michael & Michael, 2006; Michael, McNamee, Michael & Tootell, 2006; M.G. Michael, 2007; M.G. Michael & K. Michael, 2009; K. Michael & M.G. Michael, 2009). For some time Roger Clarke's (1988, p. 498) *dataveillance* has been prevalent: the "systematic use of personal data systems in the investigation or monitoring of the actions of one or more persons". Almost twenty years on, technology has developed so much and the national security context has altered so greatly (Snow, 2005), that there was a pressing need to formulate a new term to convey both this present reality, and the *Realpolitik* (policy primarily based on power) of our times (Michael & Michael, 2007). It should be said, however, that if it had not been for dataveillance, uberveillance could not be. And for that matter, it must be emphasized that dataveillance will always be- it will provide the scorecard for the engine being used to fulfill uberveillance. The word itself gained entry into the *Macquarie Dictionary* in 2008 and the noun is defined as: "an omnipresent electronic surveillance facilitated by technology that makes it possible to embed surveillance devices in the human body" (Macmillan, 2009; McIlwain, 2009).

Uberveillance takes that which was "static" or "discrete" in the dataveillance world, and makes it "constant" and "embedded". Consider it not only "automatic" and to do with "identification" BUT also about "location"- that is, the ability to automatically locate AND identify- in essence the ability to perform *automatic location identification* (ALI). It has to do with the fundamental "who" (ID), "where" (location), "when" (time) questions in an attempt to derive "why" (motivation), "what" (result), and even "how" (method/plan/thought). Uberveillance can be a predictive mechanism for one's expected behavior, traits, characteristics, likes or dislikes; or it can be based on historical fact, or something in between. The inherent problem with uberveillance is that facts do not always add up to *truth* (ie as in the case of an exclusive disjunction T+T=F), and predictions based on intelligence are not always correct.

Figure 1. Mr Amal Graafstra has two RFID implants, one in each hand, as shown by this x-ray. His left hand contains a 3mm by 13mm EM4102 glass RFID tag that was implanted by a cosmetic surgeon using a scalpel to make a very small cut, into which the implant was placed. His right hand contains a 2mm by 12mm Philips HITAG 2048 S implant with crypto-security features and 255 bytes of read/write memory storage space. It was implanted by a family doctor using an Avid injector kit like the ones used on pets. He can access his front door, car door, and log into his computer using his implants. Courtesy of Mr Amal Graafstra.

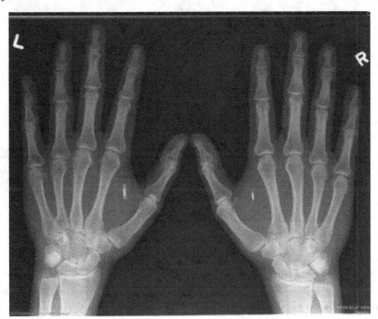

BIG BROTHER ON THE INSIDE LOOKING OUT

Microchip Implants

Uberveillance is more than closed circuit television (CCTV) feeds, or cross-agency databases linked to national identity cards, or biometrics and ePassports used for international travel. Uberveillance is the sum total of all these types of surveillance and the deliberate integration of an individual's personal data for the continuous tracking and monitoring of identity and location in real time. In its ultimate form, uberveillance has to do with more than automatic identification technologies that we carry with us. It has to do with "under the skin" technology that is embedded in the body like microchip implants (Offman, 2007); it is that which cuts into the flesh- a charagma ("mark"). Think of it as Big Brother, on the inside looking out (Figure 2). This charagma is virtually meaningless without the hybrid network architecture which supports its functionality: to make the person a walking online node, beyond luggable mobile phones, PDAs and smart cards. We are referring here, to the lowest common denominator, the smallest unit of tracking- presently a tiny chip in the body of a human being.

Implants cannot be left behind, cannot be lost, 'cannot' be tampered with, they are always on, can link to objects, make the person seemingly otherworldly. This act of *chipification* is best illustrated by the ever-increasing uses of implant devices for medical prosthesis and for diagnostics (Swedberg, 2007;

Figure 2. The Network Operation Centre (NOC) at Yarra Trams in Melbourne, Victoria, Australia. The large panel display shows 8 camera views at a time, refreshing views every 30 seconds. NOCs are reminiscent of Orwell's Big Brother.

Kargl, Lawrence, Fischer & Lim, 2008). Humancentric implants are giving rise to the Electrophorus (Michael & Michael, 2007, p. 313), the bearer of electric technology; an individual entity very different to the sci-fi notion of *Cyborg* as portrayed in such popular television series as the *Six Million Dollar Man* (1974-1978). In its current state the Electrophorus relies on a device being triggered wirelessly when it enters an electromagnetic field; these properties now mean that "systems" can interact with people within a spatial dimension, and for the greater part unobtrusively. And it is surely not just coincidence that alongside uberveillance we are witnessing the philosophical reawakening (throughout most of the fundamental streams running through our culture) of Nietzsche's *Übermensch*– the overcoming of the "all-too-human" (Honderich, 1995b).

That we might establish that chip implants are not mere science-fiction we need to identify a number of sources which add confirmation to the current reality. It is important to do so because the widespread misconception by information and communication technology (ICT) and engineering researchers at international conferences attended by both authors, is that chip implants are not commercially available for a variety of applications, and that the technology is not relevant to national security *per se*. Some researchers even believe that RFID implants have naught to do with "tracking" and can only be used for "identification". The following accounts and background sources should place things into perspective, at least at an overview level (see also, K. Michael, 2007).

THE ETHICAL DEBATE

In March of 2005 the European Group on Ethics (EGE) in Science and New Technologies, established by the European Commission (EC), submitted an Opinion on ICT implants in the human body (Rodotà &

Capurro, 2005). The thirty-four page document outlines a number of legal and ethical issues to do with ICT implants and is premised around the European Union Treaty (Article 6) which has to do with the "fundamental rights" of the individual. Fundamental rights have to do with human dignity, the right to the integrity of the person, and the protection of personal data. From the legal perspective the following was ascertained (Rodotà & Capurro, 2005, pp. 18-19):

"a.   The existence of a recognized serious but uncertain risk, currently applying to the simplest types of ICT implant in the human body, requires application of the precautionary principle. In particular, one should distinguish between active and passive implants, reversible and irreversible implants, and between offline and online implants;

b.   The purpose specification principle mandates at least a distinction between medical and non-medical applications. However, medical applications should also be evaluated stringently and selectively, partly to prevent them from being invoked as a means to legitimize other types of application;

c.   The data minimization principle rules out the lawfulness of ICT implants that are only aimed at identifying patients, if they can be replaced by less invasive and equally secure tools;

d.   The proportionality principle rules out the lawfulness of implants such as those that are used, for instance, exclusively to facilitate entrance to public premises;

e.   The principle of integrity and inviolability of the body rules out that the data subject's consent is sufficient to allow all kinds of implant to be deployed; and

f.   The dignity principle prohibits transformation of the body into an object that can be manipulated and controlled remotely – into a mere source of information."

The conclusion is that ICT implants for non-medical purposes violate fundamental legal principles. From the ethical perspective, ICT implants have numerous issues, including the requirement for: non-instrumentalization, privacy, non-discrimination, informed consent, equity, and the precautionary principle (see also IEEE, 2007; Lewan, 2007a; Burton and Stockhausen, 2005). It should be stated, however, that the EGE while not recommending ICT implants for non-medical applications because they are fundamentally fraught with legal and ethical issues, did state the following (Rodotà & Capurro, 2005, p. 32):

ICT implants for surveillance in particular threaten human dignity. They could be used by state authorities, individuals and groups to increase their power over others. The implants could be used to locate people (and also to retrieve other kinds of information about them). This might be justified for security reasons (early release for prisoners) or for safety reasons (location of vulnerable children).

However, the EGE insists that such surveillance applications of ICT implants may only be permitted if the legislator considers that there is an urgent and justified necessity in a democratic society (Article 8 of the Human Rights Convention) and there are no less intrusive methods. Nevertheless the EGE does not favor such uses and considers that surveillance applications, under all circumstances, must be specified in legislation. Surveillance procedures in individual cases should be approved and monitored by an independent court.

The same general principles should apply to the use of ICT implants for military purposes.

Although this Opinion was entirely comprehensive for its time, we hold growing concerns for the development of the information society, the lack of public debate and awareness regarding this emerging technology, and the pressing need for regulation that has not eventuated commensurate to developments in this domain. For a research note that contains an up-to-date bibliography on the social implications of microchip implants see Michael, Fusco and Michael (2008).

HUMAN RIGHTS AND THE BALANCE BETWEEN FREEDOM, SECURITY AND JUSTICE

One of the methodological weaknesses in the worldwide debate on the "microchipping of people" is the insistent focus by some of the interlocutors in this discussion on *metaethics*. What we must realize, if we are to make any practical progress in our negotiations, is that this subject must first be approached from the perspective of *normative* and *applied ethics*. The lines of distinction between all three of these approaches will at times be unclear, but there are some "litmus tests" (human rights for example) for determining the morality and ultimate consequences of our decisions.

Herein rests the problem of human rights and the "balance" between freedom, security and justice. First, it is a built-in fallacy to speak of a balance. In the microchip implant scenario, there will never be a balance, so long as someone else has the potential to control the implant device or the stored data about us which is linked to the device. Second, we are living in a period where chip implants for the purposes of *segregation* are being discussed seriously by health officials and politicians. We are speaking here of the identification of groups of people in the name of "health management" or "national security." We will almost certainly witness new, and more fixed forms, of 'electronic' apartheid. Whatever the guise of parliamentary speak we are not far from such potentially explosive perils as a global community.

Implants for National Security Applications

Consider the very real case where the "Papua Legislative Council is deliberating a regulation that would see microchips implanted in people living with HIV/AIDS so authorities could monitor their actions" (Somba, 2007). Although this proposal was quashed by human rights advocates some 18 months after it was originally proposed by the government, it points to the very real trajectory of the technology (Williamson, 2008). Similar discussions on "registration" were held regarding asylum seekers and illegal immigrants in the European Union (Hawthorne, 2001). RFID implants or the "tagging" of populations in Asia (eg Singapore) were also considered "the next step" in the containment and eradication of the Severe Acute Respiratory Syndrome (SARS) in 2003 before it subsided (RFID, 2003). Apart from disease outbreaks, RFID has also been discussed as a response and recovery device for emergency services personnel dispatched to terrorist disasters (BBC, 2005), and for the identification of victims of natural disasters, such as in the case of the Boxing Day Tsunami (Channel, 2005). The question remains whether there is a truly legitimate use function of chip implants for the purposes of emergency management as opposed to other applications. 'Definition' plays a critical role in this instance. A similar debate has ensued in the use and application of the Schengen Information System (SIS) II in the European Union where differing states have recorded alerts on individuals based on their definition and understanding of "security risk" (Guild and Bigo, 2002).

Anti-Chipping Laws in the United States

In June of 2006, legislative analyst, Anthony Gad, reported in brief 06-13 for the Legislative Reference Bureau, that: *"2005 Wisconsin Act 482, passed by the legislature and signed by Governor Jim Doyle on May 30, 2006, prohibits the required implanting of microchips in humans. It is the first law of its kind in the nation reflecting a proactive attempt to prevent potential abuses of this emergent technology."* Today a number of states in the United States have passed similar laws, despite the fact that the U.S. Food and Drug Administration (FDA, 2004) at the national level have allowed radio frequency identification implants for medical use in humans. The Wisconsin Act (2006) states: *"The people of the state of Wisconsin, represented in senate and assembly, do enact as follows: SECTION 1. 146.25 of the statutes is created to read: 146.25 Required implanting of microchip prohibited. (1) No person may require an individual to undergo the implanting of a microchip. (2) Any person who violates sub. (1) may be required to forfeit not more than $10,000. Each day of continued violation constitutes a separate offense."*

North Dakota was the next state to follow Wisconsin's example. Governor John Hoeven signed a two sentence bill into state legislature on 4 April 2007. The bill was criticized by some who said that while it protected citizens from being "injected" with an implant, it did not prevent someone from making them swallow it (Songini, 2007). More recently, Californian Governor Arnold Schwarzenegger, signed bill SB 362 proposed by state Senator Joe Simitian barring "employers and others from forcing people to have a radio frequency identification (RFID) device implanted under their skin" (Woolfolk, 2007; Jones 2007). According to the Californian Office of Privacy Protection (2007) this bill *"...would prohibit a person from requiring any other individual to undergo the subcutaneous implanting of an identification device. It would allow an aggrieved party to bring an action against a violator for injunctive relief or for the assessment of civil penalties to be determined by the court."* The bill which will be effective 1 January 2008, did not receive support from the technology industry on the contention that it was "unnecessary".

COMMERCIAL MICROCHIP IMPLANTS

The VeriChip

Interestingly, however, it is in the United States, that most chip implant applications have come to pass despite the calls for caution. This is not surprising given the first human-implantable passive RFID microchip (the VeriChip™) was approved for medical use in October of 2004 by the U.S. Food and Drug Administration (Michael, Michael & Ip, 2007). Today the VeriChip Corporation has over 900 hospitals across the United States that have registered the VeriMed system, and now the corporation's focus has moved to "patient enrollment" including people with diabetes, Alzheimer's and dementia (Diabetes News, 2007). The VeriMed™ Patient Identification System is used for "rapidly and accurately identifying people who arrive in an emergency room and are unable to communicate" (VeriChip, 2007).

In July of 2006 (The Age, 2007), CityWatcher.com reported two of its employees had "glass encapsulated microchips with miniature antennas embedded in their forearms... merely a way of restricting access to vaults that held sensitive data and images for police departments, a layer of security beyond key cards and clearance codes." It is not difficult to see how implants may soon find themselves being applied to the corrective services sector (RFID, 2006). In 2002, 27 of 50 American states were using some form of satellite surveillance to monitor parolees. Similar schemes have been used in Sweden since 1994. In the majority of cases, parolees wear wireless wrist or ankle bracelets and carry small boxes containing the vital tracking and positioning technology. The positioning transmitter emits a constant signal that is monitored at a central intelligence point (Michael & Masters, 2006a). Despite continued claims by researchers that RFID is only used for identification purposes, *Health Data Management* (2005a) disclosed that VeriChip (the primary commercial RFID implant patient ID provider) had enhanced its patient wander application by adding the ability to follow the "real-time location of patients, the ability to define containment areas for different classes of patients, and one-touch alerting. The system now also features the ability to track equipment in addition to patients." A number of these issues have moved the American Medical Association to produce an ethics code for RFID chip implants. Due to copyright restrictions, we cannot quote this code here but it can be sourced online (Sade, 2007; Reichman, 2006; Bacheldor, 2007).

In chip implant cases outside the U.S. we also find a number of diverse applications for humancentric RFID. VeriChip's Scott Silverman had stated in 2004 that 7,000 chip implants had been given to distributors of which it was estimated 1,000 chips had been implanted in humans by year end worldwide (Weissert, 2004). Today the number of VeriChip implantees is estimated to be at about 2,000. So where did all these chips go? Well, they may not be mainstream applications, but they are in operation. As far back as 2004, a nightclub in Barcelona, Spain, the VIP *Baja Beach Club* in Catalan City (Chase, 2007) was offering "its VIP clients the opportunity to have a syringe-injected microchip implanted in their upper arms that not only [gave] them special access to VIP lounges, but also [acted] as a debit account from which they [could] pay for drinks" (Morton, 2004). Microchips have also been implanted in 160 Mexican officials in the law enforcement sector (Weissert, 2004). "Mexico's top federal prosecutors and investigators began receiving chip implants in their arms… in order to get access to restricted areas inside the attorney general's headquarters." In this instance, the implant acted as an access control security device despite the documented evidence purporting to the fact that RFID is not a secure technology at all (see *Gartner Research* report by Reynolds, 2004).

Commercial and Community-Based Wearable Tracking Applications

In the United Kingdom, *The Guardian* (Wilson, 2002), reported that 11-year old Danielle Duval had an active chip (i.e. containing a rechargeable battery) implanted in her. Her mother believes that it is no different to tracking a stolen car, simply that it is being used for another more important application. Mrs Duvall is considering implanting her younger daughter age 7 as well but will wait until the child is a bit older, "so that she fully understands what's happening". In Tokyo, Japan, the Kyowa Corporation in 2004 manufactured a schoolbag with a GPS device fitted into it, to meet parental concerns about crime, and in 2005 Yokohama City children were involved in a four month RFID bracelet trial using the I-Safety system (Swedberg, 2005). In 2007, we now have a company in Lancashire in England, Trutex, which is seriously considering fitting the school uniforms they manufacture with RFID (Meikle, 2007). What might be next? Concerned parents to enforce microchip implants on minors? And what is the difference between this type of parental consent over and against that of compulsory immunization for instance (Ip, Michael & Michael, 2008)? The overriding difference between the former and the latter is that microchipping proposes 24/7 monitoring "control".

Figure 3. Sousveillance is defined as inverse surveillance. Here, displayed round the neck of a glogger is a device, known as the neclacedome, that captures and records an activity in which the person doing the recording is an active participant. Sousveillance was a concept developed and put into practice by Professor Steve Mann. Uberveillance differs to sousveillance in its existentiality axis. Courtesy of Steve Mann, 2009. http://wearcam.org/domewear/neclacedome.jpg

Figure 4. Instructions on how to become a part of the Glogger Community can be found on glogger. mobi. The web service is free and can be linked to social networking, blogging, and other applications on the Internet. Courtesy of Steve Mann, 2009. http://glogger.mobi/about.php

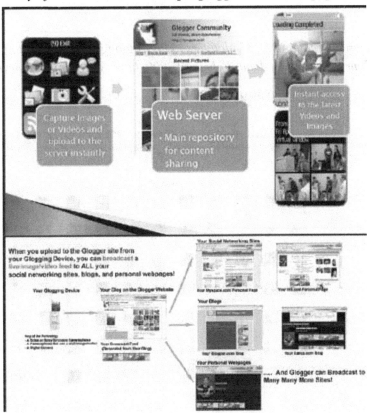

One location based system that inverts the control from another entity, such as an organization that is engaged in the act of surveillance, and asserts the control back to the individual is known as *sousveillance* (Figure 3). "Sousveillance disrupts the power relationship of surveillance when it restores a traditional balance that the institutionalization of Bentham's Panopticon itself disrupted" (Mann, Nolan, Wellman, 2003, p. 347). To be engaged in the act of sousveillance (i.e. invert surveillance) one simply requires to do a first-person recording of an activity they are a participant of using a camera phone or digital camera (Mann, 2009). The glogger.mobi web site is a free web service that allows people to easily broadcast live content from their recording equipment to blogs, personal pages, even social networking sites (Figure 4). As of 1 February 2009, there were 35,500 gloggers in the global community (Figure 5). And while sousveillance does present a counteracting force against surveillance conducted by governments, law enforcement and private organizations, it is not without its challenges either. Although never the intention, *glogger.mobi* takes what *Google Earth* has done at a macro level with satellite imagery and street level digital photographs, and has placed it at a person level. Glogger.mobi does not remove individual faces from its recordings as *Google Earth* has attempted to do via sophisticated algorithms. Creating a cyborglog is premised by the fact that a person walking down the street is in full public view (Figure 6). The advantage of *glogger.mobi*, however, is that the individual also is left with their own factual depiction of events for community policing, although it should not be negated that gloggers can also fabricate evidence. Although the intention of sousveillance is completely at odds with the commercialization of information, there are some risks, even at the community level, that need to be addressed (Michael & Michael, 2009). For Mann (Wikipedia.org, 2009), the main difference between uberveillance and sousveillance is the *existentiality axis* as defined in Mann (2001, p. 97).

Figure 5. There are more than 35,737 gloggers today. A glogger is a cyborglog which is often abbreviated to 'glog. Courtesy of Steve Mann, February 2009. http://glogger.mobi/viewall.php

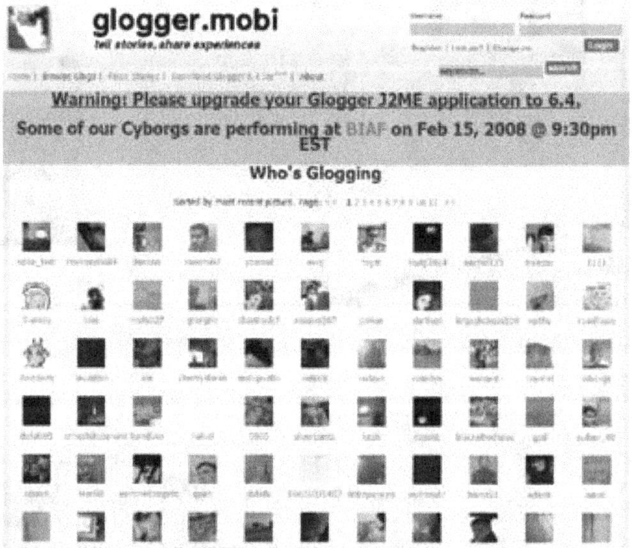

Figure 6. A screenshot of the Glogger.mobi web site. On this occasion, the video streaming depicts protestors demonstrating for a particular cause with police cars on hand. It is a first-person recording of an activity, in which the person doing the recording is a participant in the activity. Courtesy of Steve Mann, 2009.

Are Microchip Implants Safe to be Implanted in Humans?

More recently decade-old experimental studies on microchip implants in rats have come to light tying the device to tumors (Lewan, 2007b). The American Veterinary Medical Association (AVMA, 2007) was so concerned with the report that on 13 September 2007 they released the following statement, quoted here in full:

The American Veterinary Medical Association (AVMA) is very concerned about recent reports and studies that have linked microchip identification implants, commonly used in dogs and cats, to cancer in dogs and laboratory animals. AVMA staff and member veterinarians are actively looking into any potential for this technology to induce tumor formation in dogs, cats, or people but must await more definitive data and test results before taking further action. Based on the fact that a large number of pets have already been implanted with this microchip technology and there has been a relatively small number of confirmed cases of chip-induced tumors, the AVMA advises pet owners against a rush to judgment on the technology. In fact, there is a concern among veterinary medical researchers that some of the research into chip-induced tumors may be flawed, because the animals used were genetically predisposed to cancer. In addition, removal of the chip is a more invasive procedure and not without potential complications. It's clear that there is a need for more scientific research into this technology.

We can see here, already, evidence pointing to the notion of 'no return'- an admittance that removal of the chip is not easy, and not without complications.

Just over a month after the AVMA released their statement on microchip implants, VeriChip reprinted a *Time* article on their web site regarding the safety of implants in animals dated 18 October 2007 (Morrissey, 2008). CEO Scott Silverman provided a list of 34 studies that accompanied VeriChip's FDA application, that showed that less than 1% of 4,279 chipped mice developed tumors as a direct result to the implants. Silverman said that the tumors were "clearly due to the implanted microchips [and that] no clinical symptoms except the nodule on their backs were shown." The argument made by the veterinarian who conducted some of the microchip trials on VeriChip's behalf stated, that if microchips in pets had been a problem that by now the world would have known about it, as approximately 10 million pets over 15 years was a considerable sample. At the conclusion of the article Silverman stated that he hoped that the company's sales would double in 2008 from the "1.7 millions chips sold in 2006." This figure sounds exorbitant, surely not all units of human implantable microchips; but if indeed they are, the question remains, to who and in which market(s) have all these implants gone to, and what is the customer feedback to date, regarding matters related to health (Figure 7)?

Let us for a moment revisit the decade old case of the Norplant System, the *levonorgestrel* contraceptive inserts that over 1 million women in the United States, and over 3.6 million women worldwide had been implanted with through 1996 (AMA, 1997). The implants were inserted just under the skin of the upper arm in a surgical procedure under local anesthesia and could be removed in a similar fashion. As of 1997, there were 2,700 Norplant suits pending in the state and federal courts across the United States alone. Most of the claims had to do with "pain or damage associated with insertion or removal of the implants… [p]laintiffs have contended that they were not adequately warned, however, concerning the degree or severity of these events" (AMA, 1997). While the Norplant system did not use RFID there are many lessons to be gained. Concerns for the potential for widespread health implications caused by humancentric implants have also been around for some time, it should not surprise us. In 2003, Covacio provided evidence why implants may impact humans adversely, categorizing these into thermal (i.e.

Figure 7. A veterinary hospital in Nowra, New South Wales, Australia. In the foreground is a picture of animals large and small, and in the background is a large sign that reads "microchip implant center". In "centers" across the United States, people "large" and "small" have been acquiring microchip implants since late 2003. Time will tell if implants are actually linked to health risks, although for the time being the studies conducted on rats seem to point to a clean bill of health, save for common tumors during such experiments. Photo taken in 2009.

whole/partial rise in body heating), stimulation (i.e. excitation of nerves and muscles) and other effects most of which are currently unknown.

THE FUTURE AS WIRELESS, NANOTECH, AND IMPLANTABLE

The future is here now, and it is *wireless* (Smith, 2007). What is not completely here yet are the formal service level agreements to hand-off transactions between different types of networks owned by a multitude of network providers (few of whom are truly global)- free or commercial. These architectures and protocols are being developed, and it is only a matter of time before existing technologies have the capability to track individuals between indoor and outdoor locations seamlessly, or a new technology is created to do what present-day networks cannot (Identec, 2007). For instance, a wristwatch device with GPS capabilities to be worn under the skin translucently is one idea that was proposed not long ago in 1998. Hengartner and Steenkiste (2005) forewarn that "[l]ocation is a sensitive piece of information" and that "releasing it to random entities might pose security and privacy risks."

In short, there is *nowhere* to hide in this digital society, and nothing remains private (in due course, perhaps, not even our most intimate thoughts). Nanotechnology, the engineering of functional systems at the molecular level, is also set to change the way we perceive surveillance- microscopic bugs (some 50,000 times smaller than the width of the human hair) will be more parasitic than even the most advanced silicon-based *auto-ID* technologies. In the future we may be wearing hundreds of microscopic implants, each relating to an exomuscle or an exoskeleton, and which have the power to interact with literally millions of objects in the 'outside world'. The dangers are not whether state governments will invest in this technology, they are and they will (Ratner & Ratner, 2004), but whether the next generation will idealistically view this technology as super 'cool' and 'convenient' and opt-in without comprehending the full extent of their compliance.

The social implications of these *über*-intrusive technologies will have no restricted limits or political borders. They will affect everything from our day-to-day existence, to our family and community relations. They will give rise to mental health problems, even more complex forms of paranoia and obsessive compulsive disorder. The writer of a perceptive article published in *Newsweek* (10 September, 2007) commenting on the high profile suicides of two internationally recognized digital technologists, Theresa Duncan and Jeremy Blake, put it well when he surmised "for some, technology and mental illness have long been thought to exist in a kind of dark symbiosis." The refusal of some thinkers to admit to a body and mind correlation, i.e. psychophysical interaction, is progressively losing ground with many now agreeing, especially with the support of modern neuroscience, that "the intimate relation between bodily and psychic functions is basic to our personal identity" (Rodotà and Capurro, 2005, p. 3). Even those engaged in religious observances will be affected, especially in the context of their practice of confession and their specific understanding of absolution of 'sin'- we might 'confess' as much as we might want, but the records on the database, 'the slate', will not be wiped 'clean'. The list of social implications is endless; it is an exercise for our imaginations. Whatever our respective –*ism* or not, condition of our mental health or not, this 'peeping Tom' which we will carry on the inside, will have manifest consequences for that which philosophers and theologians normally term *self-consciousness*.

In all of this rest the multiple paradoxical levels of uberveillance. In the first instance, it will be one of the great blunders of the new political order to think that chip implants (or indeed nanodevices) will provide the last inch of detail required to know where a person is, what they are doing, and what they are thinking. Ambient *context* will always be lacking, and this will further aggravate the potential 'pup-peteers' of any comprehensive surveillance system. Marcus Wigan (2007) captures this critical facet of "context" very well when he speaks of "asymmetric information" held by third parties. Second, chip implants will not necessarily make you smarter or more aware (unless you can *afford* it, of course), but on the contrary and under the 'right' circumstances could make us increasingly dumb and mute. Third, chip implants are not the panacea they are made out to be- they can fail, they can be stolen, they are not tamper-proof, and they may cause harmful effects to the body- they are after all a foreign object and their primary function is to relate to the outside world not the body itself (as in the case of pacemakers and cochlear implants). Fourth, chip implants in our present framework in any case, do not give you greater control over your space, but allow for others to control you and to decrease your autonomy and as a result your interpersonal trust at both societal and state levels. *Trust* is inexorably linked to both *metaphysical* and *moral* freedom. Therefore the naive position routinely heard in the public domain that if you have "nothing to hide, why worry?" misses the point entirely. Fifth, chip implants will create a presently unimaginable digital divide- we are not referring to computer access here, or Internet access, but access to another mode of existence. The "haves" (implantees) and the "have-nots" (non-implantees) will not be on speaking terms; perhaps a fresh interpretive approach to the biblical account of the tower of Babel (Gen. 11:9).

At this point of adoption, unless the implant is removed within a short time, the body will adopt the foreign object and tie it to tissue. At this moment, there will be no exit strategy, no contingency plan, it will be a life enslaved to upgrades, virus protection mechanisms, and inescapable intrusion. Imagine a working situation where your computer- the one which has all your personal data stored on it- has been hit by a worm, and becomes increasingly inoperable and subject to overflow errors and connectivity problems, being the only machine you could use; now imagine the same thing happening with an embedded implant. There would be *little* choice other than to upgrade or, the unthinkable, to opt out of the networked world altogether.

CRADLE-TO-GRAVE UNIQUE LIFETIME IDENTIFICATION INFRASTRUCTURE

The first discernible movement towards this escalating and forward-looking scenario, with the potential to entangle us all "both small and great", will be our unique and 'non-refundable' identification number (ID) (Ip, Michael & Michael, 2008). The universal drive to provide us all with cradle-to-grave ULIs (unique lifetime identifiers) which will replace our names is gaining increasing momentum, especially post *September 11*. Philosophers have generally held that our names are the most identifiable expressions of our personhood. Names, they have argued, are the signification of identity and origin; our names possess both sense and reference (Honderich, 1995a, p. 602f). Two of the twentieth century's greatest political consciences (one who survived the Stalinist purges and the other the holocaust) Aleksandr Solzhenitsyn and Primo Levi, have warned us of the connection between murderous regimes and the numbering of individuals. There is no quicker way to dehumanize an individual than by 'removing' someone's name and replacing it with a number. It is far easier to extinguish an individual on every level if you are 'rubbing' out a number rather than a life history.

Aleksandr Solzhenitsyn recounts in one place from his famous anti-Stalinist testament, *The Gulag Archipelago* (1918-56), (2007, p. 346f): *"Then again, they [Corrective Labor Camps] quite blatantly borrowed from the Nazis a practice which had proved valuable to them – the substitution of a number for the prisoner's name, his "I", his human individuality, so that the difference between one man and another was a digit more or less in an otherwise identical row of figures... [i]f you remember all this, it may not surprise you to hear that making him wear numbers was the most hurtful and effective way of damaging a prisoner's self-respect."*

Primo Levi writes similarly in his own well-known account of the human condition in *The Drowned and the Saved* (1989, p. 94f): *"Altogether different is what must be said about the tattoo [the number], an altogether autochthonous Auschwitzian invention... [t]he operation was not very painful and lasted no more than a minute, but it was traumatic. Its symbolic meaning was clear to everyone: this is an indelible mark, you will never leave here; this is the mark with which slaves are branded and cattle sent to the slaughter, and this is what you have become. You no longer have a name; this is your new name."*

And many centuries before both Solzhenitsyn and Levi were to become acknowledged as two of the greatest political consciences of our times, an exile on the isle of Patmos- during the reign of the Emperor Domitian- expressed a disturbingly comparable position when referring to the abuses of the *emperor cult* which was especially practiced in Asia Minor away from the more sophisticated population of Rome (M.G. Michael, 1998, pp. 176-196). He was Saint John the Evangelist, commonly recognized as the author of the *Revelation* (c. A.D. 95): *"Also it causes all, both small and great, both rich and poor, both free and slave, to be marked on the right hand or the forehead, so that no one can buy or sell unless he has the mark, that is, the name of the beast or the number of its name. This calls for wisdom: let him who has understanding reckon the number of the beast, for it is a human number, its number is six hundred and sixty-six (Rev 13:16-18)."*

The technological infrastructures: the software, the middleware, and the hardware for ULIs, are readily available to support a diverse range of humancentric applications, and increasingly those embedded technologies which will eventually support uberveillance. Multi-national corporations, particularly those involved in telecommunications and banking, are investing millions (expecting literally billions in return) in such 'identifiable' technologies that have a tracking capability. At the same time the media which in most instances can yield more sway with people than government institutions themselves, squanders this influence and is not intelligently challenging this auto-ID (automatic identification) trajectory. As if in chorus, block-buster productions from Hollywood are playing up all forms of *biometrics* as not only hip and smart, but also as unavoidable mini-device fashion accessories for the upwardly mobile, and attractive. Advertising, of course, plays a dominant role in this cultural tech-rap. Advertisers are well aware that the market is literally limitless and demographically accessible at all levels (and more tantalizingly from cradle-to-grave consumers). Our culture, which in previous generations was for the better part the van guard against most things detrimental to our collective well-being, is dangerously close to bankrupt (it already is *idol worshipping*) and has progressively become fecund territory for whatever idiocy might take our fancy. Carl Bernstein (1992) of Bernstein and Woodward fame has captured the atmosphere of recent times very well: *"We are in the process of creating what deserves to be called the idiot culture. Not an idiot sub-culture, which every society has bubbling beneath the surface and which can provide harmless fun; but the culture itself. For the first time the weird and the stupid and the coarse are becoming our cultural norm, even our cultural ideal."*

Oddly enough, given this technological fixation with which most of the world is engaged, there is a perceptible mood of a collective disquiet that something is not as it should be. In the face of that, this self-deception of 'wellness' is not only taking a stronger hold on us, but it is also being rationalized and deconstructed on many authoritative platforms and levels. We must break free of this dangerous daydream to make out the cracks that have already started to appear on the gold tinted rim of this seeming 21st century utopia. The *machine*, the new technicized "gulag archipelago" is ever pitiless and without conscience. It can tear sinew; crush bones; break spirits; and rip out hearts without ever needing to take a break.

CONCLUSION

Lest there be any misunderstanding the authors of this study are not anti-government, after all, the alternative is anarchy-; nor are they conspiracy theorists (though we now know better than to rule out *all* conspiracy theories). Nor do they believe that these dark scenarios need necessarily eventuate as precisely as they are describing them. But they do believe that we are close to reaching the critical point of no return. Others believe that point is much closer (ACLU, 2007). It remains for individuals to speak up and argue for, and to demand regulation, as has happened in several states in the United States where Acts have been established to avoid *microchipping* without an individual's consent, i.e. compulsory electronic tagging of citizens. Politicians for a number of reasons will not normally legislate on this issue of their own accord. It would involve multifaceted industry and absorb too much of their time, and the fear they might be labeled anti-technology or worse still, failing to do all that they can in the fight against "terror". This is one of the components of the modern-day *Realpolitik* which in its push for the *transparent society* is bulldozing ahead without any true sensibility for the richness, fullness, and sensitivity of the undergrowth. As an actively engaged community, as a body of concerned researchers with an ecumenical conscience and voice, we can make a difference by trying to downgrade some of the doomsday scenarios.

REFERENCES

ACLU. (2007). Surveillance Society Clock 23:54. *American Civil Liberties Union*. Retrieved 5 October, 2007, from http://www.aclu.org/privacy/spying/surveillancesocietyclock.html

AMA. (1997). Norplant System Contraceptive Inserts. *Report 9 of the Council on Scientific Affairs (I-97)*. Retrieved 5 October, 2007, from http://www.ama-assn.org/ama/pub/category/print/13593.html

AVMA. (13 September 2007). Breaking News: Statement on Microchipping. *American Veterinary Medical Association*. Retrieved 5 October, 2007, from http://www.avma.org/aa/microchip/breaking_news_070913_pf.asp

Bacheldor, B. (17 July 2007). AMA Issues Ethics Code for RFID Chip Implants. *RFID Journal*. Retrieved 4 October, 2007, from http://www.rfidjournal.com/article/articleprint/3487/-1/1/

Ball, E., & Bond, K. (2005). Bess Marion v. Eddie Cafka and ECC Enterprises, Inc., No. 2005-CV-0237. *IT Moot Court*. Retrieved 2 October, 2007, from http://www.itmootcourt.com/2005%20Briefs/Petitioner/Team18.pdf

BBC. (28 July 2005). Implant Chip to Identify the Dead. *BBC News*. Retrieved 10 January, 2006, from http://news.bbc.co.uk/1/hi/technology/4721175.stm

Bernstein, C. (1992, 3 June). The Guardian.

Burton, P., & Stockhausen, K. (22 February 2005). The Australian Medical Association's Submission to the Legal and Constitutional's Inquiry into the Privacy Act 1988. Retrieved 5 October, 2007, from http://www.ama.com.au/web.nsf/doc/WEEN-69X6DV/$file/Privacy_Submission_to_Senate_Committee.doc

Californian Office of Privacy Protection. (23 July 2007). California Privacy Legislation

Office of Privacy Protection, State of California. Retrieved 10 October, 2007, from http://www.privacy.ca.gov/califlegis.htm

Channel. (3 January 2005). Thai Wave Disaster Largest Forensic Challenge In Years: Expert. *Channel News Asia.* Retrieved 10 February, 2005, from http://www.channelnewsasia.com/stories/afp_asiapacific/view/125459/1/.html

Chase, C. (n.d.). VIP Verichip, Baja Beach House- Zona VIP. Retrieved 12 October, 2007, from http://www.baja-beachclub.com/bajaes/asp/zonavip2.aspx

Clarke, R. A. (1988). Information Technology and Dataveillance. *Communications of the ACM, 31*(5), 498-512.

Covacio, S. (2003). Technological Problems Associated with the Subcutaneous Microchips for Human Identification (SMHId). *InSITE-Where Parallels Intersect, June,* 843-853.

Diabetes News. (20 March 2007). 13 Diabetics Implanted With VeriMed RFID Microchip At Boston Diabetes EXPO. *Medical News Today.* Retrieved 9 October, 2007, from http://www.medicalnewstoday.com/articles/65560.php

FDA. (10 December 2004). Medical Devices; General Hospital and Personal Use Devices; Classification of Implantable Radiofrequency Transponder System for Patient Identification and Health Information. *U.S. Food and Drug Administration- Department of Health and Human Services 69(237).* Retrieved 5 October, 2007, from http://www.fda.gov/ohrms/dockets/98fr/04-27077.htm

Gad, A. (June 2006). Legislative Brief 06-13: Human Microchip Implantation. *Legislative Briefs from the Legislative Reference Bureau.* Retrieved 5 October, 2007, from http://www.legis.state.wi.us/lrb/pubs/Lb/06Lb13.pdf

Guild, E., & Bigo, D. (2002). The Schengen Border System and Enlargement. In M. Anderson & J. Apap (Eds.), *Police and Justice Co-operation and the New European Borders* (pp. 121-138): European Monographs.

Hawthorne, M. (13 December 2001). Refugees Meeting Hears Proposal To Register Every Human In The World. *Sydney Morning Herald.* Retrieved 1 July, 2003, from http://www.smh.com.au/breaking/2001/12/14/FFX058CU6VC.html

HDM. (July 2005b). VeriChip Buys Monitoring Tech Vendor. *Health Data Management.* Retrieved 5 October, 2007, from http://healthdatamanagement.com/HDMSearchResultsDetails.cfm?articleId=12458

HDM. (July 2007). Baylor Uses RFID to Track Newborns. *Health Data Management.* Retrieved 5 October, 2007, from http://healthdatamanagement.com/HDMSearchResultsDetails.cfm?articleId=15439

HDM. (May 2005a). VeriChip Enhances Patient Wander App

Health Data Management. Retrieved 5 October, 2007, from http://healthdatamanagement.com/HDM-SearchResultsDetails.cfm?articleId=12361

HDM. (October 2005c). Chips Keep Tabs on Babies, Moms. *Health Data Management*. Retrieved 5 October, 2007, from http://healthdatamanagement.com/HDMSearchResultsDetails.cfm?articleId=15439

Hengartner, U., & Steenkiste, P. (2005). Access Control to People Location Information. *ACM Transactions on Information and System Security, 8*(4), 424-456.

Herold, R. (3 January 2008). More On Überveillance And Privacy. *Realtime-itcompliance.com*. Retrieved 5 January 2008, from http://www.realtime-itcompliance.com/privacy_and_compliance/2008/01/more_on_uberveillance_and_priv.htm

Honderich, T. (1995a). Names. In T. Honderich (Ed.), *Oxford Companion to Philosophy* (pp. 602f). Oxford: Oxford University Press.

Honderich, T. (1995b). Nietzsche, Friedrich. In T. Honderich (Ed.), *Oxford Companion to Philosophy* (pp. 619-623). Oxford: Oxford University Press.

Identech. (2007). RFID Tags Equipped with GPS. *Navigadget*. Retrieved 10 October, 2007, from http://www.navigadget.com/index.php/2007/06/27/rfid-tags-equipped-with-gps/

IEEE. (March 2007). Me & My RFIDs. *IEEE Spectrum, 4*(3), 14-25.

Ip, R., Michael, K., & Michael, M. G. (2008, 25-27 June 2008). *The Social Implications of Humancentric Chip Implants: A Scenario - 'Thy Chipdom Come, Thy Will be Done'*. Paper presented at the Sixth CollECTeR Iberoamérica, Madrid, Spain.

Jones, K. C. (4 September 2007). California Passes Bill To Ban Forced RFID Tagging. *InformationWeek*. Retrieved 10 October, 2007, from http://www.informationweek.com/shared/printableArticle.jhtml?articleID=201803861

Kargl, F., Lawrence, E., Fischer, M., & Lim, Y. Y. (2008). *Security, Privacy and Legal Issues in Pervasive eHealth Monitoring Systems*. Paper presented at the 7th International Conference on Mobile Business, Barcelona, Spain.

Lewan, T. (9 September 2007b). Chip Implants Linked to Animal Tumors. *WashingtonPost.com*. Retrieved 4 October, 2007, from http://www.washingtonpost.com/wp-dyn/content/article/2007/09/09/AR2007090900467.html

Lewan, T. (2007a). Microchips Implanted in Humans: High-Tech Helpers, or Big Brother's Surveillance Tools? *The Associated Press*. Retrieved 5 October, 2007, from http://abcnews.go.com/print?id=3401306

Macmillan. (2009). Uberveillance. *Macquarie Dictionary*. Retrieved 6 January 2009, from http://www.macquariedictionary.com.au/anonymous@9191E5735084/-/p/dict/WOTY08/tech.html

Mann, S. (2001). Can Humans Being Clerks make Clerks be Human? - Exploring the Fundamental Difference between UbiComp and WearComp *Informationstechnik und Technische Informatik, 43*(2), 97-106.

Mann, S. (2009). About: Glogger Community. *glogger.mobi*. Retrieved 31 January 2009, from http://glogger.mobi/about.php

McIlwain, K. (2009). Vote 1 uberveillance: UOW term in running for 2008 Word of the Year. *UOW News and Media*. Retrieved 16 January 2009, from http://media.uow.edu.au/news/UOW053997.html

Meikle, J. (21 August 2007). Pupils Face Tracking Bugs in School Blazers. *The Guardian,* Retrieved 24 August, 2007, from http://www.guardian.co.uk/uk_news/story/0,,2152979,00.html

Michael, K. (2007). Selected Works of Dr. Katina Michael. *University of Wollongong*. Retrieved 5 October, 2007, from http://ro.uow.edu.au/kmichael/

Michael, K., & Masters, A. (2006a). Realized Applications of Positioning Technologies in Defense Intelligence. In D. Essam & H. Abbass (Eds.), *Applications of Information Systems to Homeland Security and Defense* (pp. 164-192): IDG Press.

Michael, K., McNamee, A., Michael, M. G., & Tootell, H. I. (2006). *Location-based Intelligence- Modeling Behavior in Humans using GPS*. Paper presented at the International Symposium on Technology and Society, Piscataway, NJ, USA.

Michael, K., Michael, M., & Ip, R. (2007). *Microchip Implants for Humans as Unique Identifiers: a Case Study on VeriChip*. Paper presented at the 3TU: Ethics, Identity and Technology, The Hague, The Netherlands.

Michael, K., & Michael, M. G. (2006, 28-1 July). *Towards chipification: the multifunctional body art of the net generation*. Paper presented at the Cultural Attitudes Towards Technology and Communication, Tartu, Estonia.

Michael, K., & Michael, M. G. (2007). *From Dataveillance to Überveillance and the Realpolitik of the Transparent Society*. Wollongong: University of Wollongong.

Michael, K., & Michael, M. G. (2007). Homo Electricus and the Continued Speciation of Humans. In M. Quigley (Ed.), *The Encyclopedia of Information Ethics and Security* (pp. 312-318): IGI Global.

Michael, K., & Michael, M. G. (2009). Uberveillance: The official web site. Retrieved 23 January 2009, from www.uberveillance.org

Michael, K. M., A. (2006b). The Advancement of Positioning Technologies in Defence Intelligence. In D. Essam & H. Abbass (Eds.), *Applications of Information Systems to Homeland Security and Defense* (pp. 193-214): IDG Press.

Michael, M. G. (1998). *"Ch IX: Imperial Cult" in The Number of the Beast, 666 (Revelation 13:16-18): Background, Sources, and Interpretation*. Macquarie University, Sydney.

Michael, M. G. (2007, 25-28 September 2007). *Überveillance: 24/7 x 365- People Tracking and Monitoring*. Paper presented at The 29th International Conference of Data Protection and Privacy Commissioners: Privacy Horizons, Terra Incognita, Montreal, Canada.

Michael, M. G., Fusco, S. J., & Michael, K. (2008). A Research Note on Ethics in the Emerging Age of Uberveillance (Überveillance). *Computer Communications, 31*(6), 1192-1199.

Michael, M. G., & Michael, K. (2006). National Security: The Social Implications of the Politics of Transparency. *Prometheus, 24*(4), 359-364.

Michael, M. G., & Michael, K. (2009). Microchipping People and the Assault on Privacy. *Quadrant, in press.*

Morrissey, S. (18 October 2008). Are Microchip Tags Safe? *Time* Retrieved 18 October 2008, from http://www.time.com/time/health/article/0,8599,1672865,00.html?xid=feed-cnn-topics

Morton, S. (2004). Barcelona Clubbers Get Chipped. *BBC News* Retrieved 11 October, 2007, from http://news.bbc.co.uk/2/hi/technology/3697940.stm

Offman, C. (3 December 2007). You are tagged. *National Post* Retrieved 4 December 2007, from http://www.nationalpost.com/news/story.html?id=139966

Ratner, D. R. M. A. (2004). *Nanotechnology and Homeland Security: New Weapons for New Wars.* New Jersey: Prentice Hall.

Reichman, J. H. (2006). RFID Labeling in Humans

American Medical Association House of Delegates: Resolution: 6 (A-06), Reference Committee on Amendments to Constitution and Bylaws. Retrieved 5 October, 2007, from http://www.ama-assn.org/ama1/pub/upload/mm/471/006a06.doc

Reynolds, M. (20 July 2004). Despite the Hype, Microchip Implants Won't Deliver Security. *Gartner Research.* Retrieved 12 October, 2007, from http://www.gartner.com/DisplayDocument?doc_cd=121944

RFID. (4 June 2003). Singapore Fights SARS with RFID. *RFID Journal* Retrieved 10 August, 2005, from http://www.rfidjournal.com/article/articleprint/446/-1/1/

RFID. (22 August 2006). I Am Not A Number - Tracking Australian Prisoners With Wearable RFID Tech

RFID Gazette. Retrieved 11 October, 2007, from http://www.rfidgazette.org/2006/08/i_am_not_a_numb.html

RNZI. (25 July 2007). Papua Legislative Council Deliberating Microchip Regulation for People With HIV/AIDS. *Radio New Zealand International* Retrieved 12 October, 2007, from http://www.rnzi.com/pages/news.php?op=read&id=33896

Rodotà, S., & Capurro, R. (16 March 2005). Ethical Aspects of ICT Implants in the Human Body. *Opinion of the European Group on Ethics in Science and New Technologies to the European Commission N° 20 Adopted on 16/03/2005* Retrieved 4 October, 2007, from http://ec.europa.eu/european_group_ethics/docs/avis20_en.pdf

Sade, R. M. (2007). Radio Frequency ID Devices in Humans, Report of the Council on Ethical and Judicial Affairs: CEJA Report 5-A-07. *Reference Committee on Amendments to Constitution and Bylaws* Retrieved 5 October, 2007, from http://www.ama-assn.org/ama1/pub/upload/mm/369/ceja_5a07.pdf

Schuerenberg, B. K. (February 2005a). Implantable RFID Chip Takes Root in CIO: Beta tester praises new mobile device, though some experts see obstacles to widespread adoption. *Health Data Management* Retrieved 5 October, 2007, from http://www.healthdatamanagement.com/HDMSearchResultsDetails. cfm?articleId=12232

Schuerenberg, B. K. (November 2005b). Patients Let RFID Get Under Their Skin. *Health Data Management* Retrieved 5 October, 2007, from http://healthdatamanagement.com/HDMSearchResultsDetails. cfm?articleId=12601

Smith, R. E. (26 November 2007). Commentary: Scary Stuff. *Forbes Magazine* Retrieved 30 November, 2007, from http://www.forbes.com/2007/11/21/privacy-surveillance-technology-oped-cx_ res_1126privacy.html

Snow, D. M. (2005). *National Security For A New Era: Globalization And Geopolitics*: Addison-Wesley.

Songini, M. L. (12 April 2007). N.D. Bans Forced RFID Chipping, Governor Wants a Balance between Technology, Privacy", *ComputerWorld* Retrieved 10 October, 2007, from http://www.computerworld.com/ action/article.do?command=viewArticleBasic&taxonomyId=15&articleId=9016385&intsrc=hm_topic

Swedberg, C. (16 December 2005). RFID Watches Over School Kids in Japan. *RFID Journal* Retrieved 11 October, 2007

Swedberg, C. (25 May 2007). Alzheimer's Care Center to Carry Out VeriChip Pilot *RFID Journal*. Retrieved 8 October, 2007, from http://www.rfidjournal.com/article/articleview/3340/1/1/

The Age. (22 July 2007). Chips: High Tech Aids or Tracking Tools? *Fairfax Digital: The Age*. Retrieved 4 October, 2007, from http://www.theage.com.au/news/Technology/Microchip-Implants-Raise-Privacy-Concern/2007/07/22/1184560127138.html

Verichip. (11 October 2007). VeriChip Corporation Adds More Than 200 Hospitals at the American College of Emergency Physicians (ACEP) Conference". *VeriChip News Release*. Retrieved 11 October, 2007, from http://www.verichipcorp.com/news/1192106879

Weissert, W. (14 July 2004). Microchips implanted in Mexican officials. *Associated Press*. Retrieved 11 October, 2007, from http://www.msnbc.msn.com/id/5439055/

Wigan, M. (2007). Owning identity- one or many- do we have a choice? In K. Michael & M. G. Michael (Eds.), *From Dataveillance to Uberveillance and the Realpolitik of the Transparent Society* (Vol. 2, pp. 61-70). Wollongong: University of Wollongong.

Wikipedia.org. (2009). Uberveillance. Retrieved 1 February 2009, from http://en.wikipedia.org/wiki/ Uberveillance

Williamson, L. (1 December 2008). Papua mulls microchips for HIV. *BBC News*. Retrieved 5 January 2009, from http://news.bbc.co.uk/2/hi/asia-pacific/7758331.stm

Wilson, J. (2002). Girl to Get Tracker Implant to Ease Parents' Fears. *The Guardian*. Retrieved 15 October 2002, 2007, from http://www.guardian.co.uk/Print/0,3858,4493297,00.html

Wisconsin Act. (30 May 2006). Wisconsin Act 482. Retrieved 4 October, 2007, from http://www.legis. state.wi.us/2005/data/acts/05Act482.pdf

Woolfolk, J. (12 October 2007). Back Off, Boss: Forcible RFID Implants Outlawed in California. *Mercury News*. Retrieved 13 October, 2007, from http://www.mercurynews.com/portlet/article/html/fragments/ print_article.jsp?articleId=7162880&siteId=568

Chapter XVI
Conclusion

THE AUTO-ID TRAJECTORY

This chapter is dedicated to identifying the main outcomes of the study and reflections on the future directions of the technologies that were under investigation. In concluding we have found that first, an evolutionary process of development is present in the auto-ID technology system (TS). Incremental steps either by way of technological recombinations or mutations have lead to revolutionary changes in the auto-ID industry- both at the device level and at the application level. The evolutionary process in the auto-ID TS does not imply a 'survival of the fittest' approach, rather a model of coexistence where each particular auto-ID technique has a path which ultimately influences the success of the whole industry. The patterns of migration, integration and convergence can be considered either mutations or recombinations of existing auto-ID techniques for the creation of new auto-ID innovations. Second, that forecasting technological innovations is important in predicting future trends based on past and current events. Analyzing the process of innovation between intervals of widespread diffusion of individual auto-ID technologies sheds light on the auto-ID trajectory. Third, that technology is autonomous by nature has been shown by the changes in uses of auto-ID; from non-living to living things, from government to commercial applications, and from external identification devices in the form of tags and badges to medical implants inserted under the skin. This does not negate, however, the inherent qualities embedded in auto-ID technologies, predisposing them to be used in certain contexts. What we have witnessed especially in auto-ID is a movement we have termed the auto-ID trajectory: from bar codes to chip implants towards the *electrophorus* who will herald in the age of *uberveillance*. Convergence of embedded automatic identification technologies with location-based services will offer unprecedented capabilities, but these capabilities will come at a high price.

The Evolutionary Paradigm

The evolutionary paradigm has shown us that "history matters". Auto-ID techniques built their foundations on top of past manual ID techniques, the simplest being facial recognition using human memory. By the 19th century fingerprinting techniques were being discovered and by the mid 20th century auto-ID technologies were being prototyped. What has happened since that time has been cumulative technical change at an exhilarating speed. This rapid change, however, would not have been possible if the building blocks had not been cemented by first generation elementary breakthroughs. As more and more technological advancement occurred within the emerging auto-ID industry, and further support infrastructures, skills and tools emerged simultaneously, the use of auto-ID became widespread. Progress fuelled success and success fuelled progress. While the market in the mid 1960s was not ready for auto-ID, decade after decade thereafter, techniques permeated a diverse range of applications. A domino effect of new auto-ID innovations took place, revolutionizing the way people worked and lived. The conditions for entry were increasingly 'right' as ancillary technologies, like networks, storage devices and database software proliferated.

The auto-ID explosion was energized by up-and-coming niche technology providers who had a clear vision for their innovations. Bar codes in retail, for instance, were driven by stakeholders who could see both the potential impact the technology would make and the immediate path ahead. Understanding the sequence of events that shaped auto-ID was a major contribution of this study. Better understanding "what happened" means that efforts can be concentrated in the right places in the future. Rosenberg (1994, p. 23) describes the importance of historical analysis in understanding technologies. He pointed out that this type of analysis is not only relevant to historians but to economists and people in other fields.

Forecasting Technological Innovation

One of the downsides to exploratory predictive studies is that some researchers attempt to outdo one another with radical futuristic scenarios. This is not to discount that some of these scenarios will not happen 'eventually', however they neglect to use the evidence that is set before them to follow the path or direction of a particular technology, or set of technologies. This study puts forward the usefulness of using frameworks- like the systems of innovation (SI) based on evolutionary theory- to synthesize data from multiple disciplines to characterize and predict the auto-ID trajectory. The market today is so complex, that relying solely on one perspective, albeit technological, could prove severely misleading. What is required is an interdependence of sources (Drangeld, 1991, pp. 157-179). It was also intentional that predictions were not numbered or tabulated- they are present throughout the work and more pronounced in the final chapters when the technological trajectory of auto-ID was explored. The narrative style allowed for analysis throughout. None of the predictions venture beyond 2050 and most focus between the years 2010 and 2020.

Individual auto-ID techniques and their applications were considered separately at first, then as a single technology system, bringing together evidence that would indicate the direction of auto-ID in the short-term future. Among the factors explored in each case (in order of their prominence in that particular case) included: social, cultural, organizational, institutional, economic, regulatory, legal, political and technical dimensions. What was apparent was the time lag between auto-ID technical breakthroughs and developments, in for instance global standards, laws and user acceptance. Ethical considerations it was shown, were also consistently marginalized by technology and service providers until after auto-ID diffusion- an almost "let's wait and see what happens" approach. Regardless, the technology is set to become even more ingrained in our day-to-day practices, especially for critical-response applications. New auto-ID innovations are most likely to be variations or combinations of existing auto-ID technologies, although there will be particular leaps in the use of multiapplication smart cards, the accuracy of biometric techniques (especially multimodal biometrics) and RFID transponders for human application. The study has attempted to present the forces at play which will continue to set the course of the auto-ID technology system. Of great significance is the convergence of 'industries', including auto-ID and biomedical.

Technology is Autonomous

That it is possible to map the future course of a technology does not negate that a given technology could be used for another subsequent purpose to what it was originally intended (Westrum, 1991, p. 238). Once a device is released, there is no turning back. As Rummler (2001, p. 3) put it: "the genie simply will not go back into the bottle". The technology possesses intrinsic controls that can be set off with the right commercial conditions. What we assume is that we are in control, when in actual fact the technology has an inherent trajectory (Figure 1). No one ever seriously predicted (outside the apocalyptic and sci-fi genres) for instance, that auto-ID technologies would be inserted under the skin at the time that bar code was invented or when magnetic-stripe cards made their debut. However, today we have this phenomenon occurring- perhaps not at a rapid rate of adoption but at a speed that has made people take note of developments. There is now a company who has hired staff to tour the United Stated in mobile vans, to directly market the advantages of RFID transponder implants for emergency services. Consumers who choose to be implanted can do so at centralized clinics across the country or even at registered hospitals. There are even self-proclaimed "RFIDs" (i.e. *underground* RFID implantees), tech-savvy hobbyists who are building their own applications for interactive spaces. In brief, it is technology that to a large extent shapes society; drives changes to the way we live, to laws, to our attitudes, and our beliefs. Once diffused technology then is molded and shaped by society in specific ways.

While we have the opportunity to consider where the auto-ID trajectory is leading society, especially when it is coupled with leading edge location based services; it is our responsibility to think about the future possibilities. For instance, what if civil unrest through continual terrorist threats/attacks or outbreaks of fatal viruses causes governments worldwide to introduce RFID implants for security and

Figure 1 Compare a historic photo of the ENIAC with Professor Kevin Warwick's Cyborg experiment. It seems somehow that humans have got too close to the machine and somehow become entangled in all the wiring. Who is really in control?

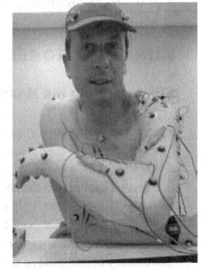

Courtesy: "U.S. Army Photo", from K. Kempf, "Historical Monograph: Electronic Computers Within the Ordnance Corps" The ENIAC, in BRL building 328. Left: Glen Beck Right: Frances Elizabeth Snyder Holberton.
Courtesy of Professor Kevin Warwick.

Figure 2. Courtesy of Steve Mann (1998). In (a) Steve is modelling the `underwearable' signal processing hardware and in (b) is a close up showing webbing for routing of cabling. http://wearcam.org/hi/index.html

 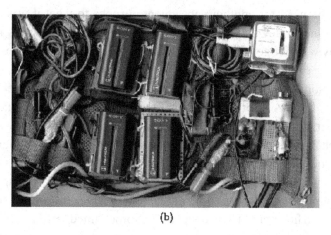

(a)   (b)

Now compare this figure with that of the ENIAC and Kevin Warwick in figure 1.

safety reasons. Would society be ready for such a change? And what types of mechanisms are in place to decide whether this should or should not happen? Already victims of the Boxing Day Tsumani in Thailand were chipped to help in identification later, and European Union officials have on more than one occasion stipulated the use of RFID tags and transponders for helping curb the problem of illegal immigration (Michael and Masters, 2006a; 2006b). There was even the very real suggestion made by the Singaporean government that air travelers to and from the state would have to be tagged if the SARS virus was to continue in duration (Michael et al., 2006). For more national security examples related to auto-ID and location based services see Tootell (2007) and Aloudat, K. Michael and Yan (2007).

WITH AN EYE TO THE FUTURE

Reinterpreting the Meaning of Progress

Progress has often been synonymous with change over time, in a historical context. However, certain types of "progress" are not necessarily advancements. In fact, depending on the perspective taken, some technological progress could actually be considered to have caused social regress. A cochlear implant that gives a deaf person the ability to hear can be viewed as progress without much debate, whereas the proposed 'Soul Catcher' chip implant which will supposedly grant "eternal life" to an individual is surrounded by many unknowns. Consider the motivations for inventing in primitive times. The discovery of rubbing two sticks together to produce fire for warmth and cooking, that of the circular wheel to help move heavy objects, and of sharp stone implements to cut things, were all motivated by a practical need to survive. In contrast, today we seek monetary remuneration for inventing. A lot of money is spent on legal advice and getting an idea patented and this usually happens only when the inventor believes that they will somehow recoup their costs by the resulting royalties. Which leads to another fundamental point, most inventors today are part of corporations whose main goal is profit maximization. Companies measure their "progress" by comparing revenue results and whether these have increased year-to-year. They are driven more by a need to make money to continue viable operations, than by a need to ensure that their product or service offerings are adding real value to human lives. Competition is so fierce in most high-tech areas, and the pace of change so rapid, that economic and commercial discourse takes precedence over moral and ethical reflection.

The *Oxford English Dictionary* defines the word 'ethics' as 'the science of morals; moral principles or 'code' and 'ethical' as 'conforming to a recognized standard'. 'Moral' is that concerned with the distinction between right and wrong" (Brennan, 1996, p. 1/1). *"[E]thics has a positive side which describes the human values which help to specify what one should do... what is the ultimate goal of human life or of society and, thus, what are the priorities for the work to be done within the particular activity or profession" (Brown, 1998, p. 301).* For instance, an auto-ID manufacturer might ask "should this particular auto-ID technology be used in this new application area?" The response would most likely be linked to whether the new innovation would equate to more sales, a better company share price, and subsequently greater investor interest. The reality is that whether the technology will negatively impact individual privacy (or other similar issues) invariably remains somebody else's problem throughout the value chain. Consider the study conducted by K. Michael, McNamee, M.G. Michael (2006) and K. Michael et al., (2006) and the ethics surrounding the precise chronicling of people using GPS-enabled devices, especially those pertaining to social networking issues (Markoff, 2008). The GPS was once used by the U.S. military alone, today it has become a global commodity used for applications like distance running in marathons (Saponas et al., 2006) to prisoners serving their sentences at home.

Managing Technological Innovation

The ability to manage technological innovation assumes that the right social institutions are in place to deal with developments. More often than not however, there is a great divide between technology and society's ability to cope with that technology. The consumer's attempt at resisting change initially coincides with the technology life cycle incubation stage. Eventually, however, widespread adoption is achieved as the technology begins to shape society bit-by-bit, and consumers and service providers succumb to a variety of pressures. It seems that individuals in society are too preoccupied with the ever-increasing pace of life to have the necessary time required to contemplate the far-reaching extensions of technological change, thus leaving the decision making to a small group of people. This results in a type of herd behavior being exemplified. Mass consent in more developed countries (MDCs) to adopt whatever is being flagged as the latest high-tech gadget looks to have overtaken individual reasoning.

Consumers subject themselves to the impacts of these gadgets simply by choosing to adopt them, one after the next. It is almost as if adoption of "new" technology, such as luggables and wearables, is a requirement for a fulfilled existence because our capacity to remain contented with what we have is lacking. In the case of auto-ID however, there is an inherent tyrannical quality about devices like smart cards and biometrics; consumers do not choose to have them, such as in the case of computers and mobile phones, they are imposed on them by service providers. Among the most authoritarian service providers is the government, who has the ability to issue national ID cards (and other similar mandates) to its citizens. As more and more national and international auto-ID and LBS schemes begin to emerge, the need for adequate social institutions for helping society deal with these changes becomes an immediate concern. We cannot rely on a few publicized debates on current affairs television programs to address the fundamental questions. Yet going with the flow seems more effortless than constructive thinking; the masses generally feeling powerless bystanders to these changes, or even worse, indifferent and numb. There is little doubt that as time moves on newer dimensions of Alvin Toffler's (1970) "future shock" will *distress* us (most of us at least) in different ways.

The Need for Safeguard Provisioning

As we prepare for the introduction of fully fledged advanced humancentric location-based applications we need to be mindful of the potential socio-ethical changes that will occur as a result. These "changes" will also include new perspectives to traditional metaphysics as embedded in the flesh technologies challenge us to potentially "updated" definitions of identity and self-consciousness for instance. For the present, technological advancements in this space of research and investigation always seem to take precedence over discussion of the potential detrimental effects to individuals or society at large. There need to be adequate and applicable safeguards 'built-in' if we are to innovate smartly; we cannot hope to 'bolt-on' band-aid solutions on the chance things might go wrong. And things normally do go wrong. One need only refer to the historical events in manual identification to consider the possible effects of a well-orchestrated siege on privacy by any world leader or government. Even as early as 1943 observers realized the potential threats of computerized systems which could be operated for wrong ends by "...an unscrupulous government which sets to work to use that machinery for totalitarian purposes" (Clark, 1943, p. 9). Wicklein (1982, pp. 8, 191f) also wrote that "...[t]he biggest threat of a multifaceted, integrated communications system is that a single authority will win control of the whole system and its contents [and] operate it without adequate restraints".

Who is in Control?

The dynamic nature of the process of innovation indicates that interaction between many different stakeholders leads to the development of a given product or service. It is therefore difficult to single out one particular stakeholder as the primary force for an innovation going from invention to diffusion. Feedback between different stakeholders is a continual process. In the case of auto-ID, it can be argued that the manufacturer of the device is the main instigator, yet this denies the importance of other individual stakeholders like the government, service providers, and infrastructure providers, from being considered as equally key instruments in the creative process. It is possible that the question "who is in control?" only answers the question partially; we should also consider "what is in control?" Is it stakeholders? Is it the technology itself? It is both working together. Humans need to be aware of this when they are considering such future possibilities as creating "spiritual machines" and rejecting in essence part of what it means to be human. Some scientists may believe that doing away with the flesh will grant the individual ultimate freedom- achieving a type of resurrection on Earth. Consider Moravec's idea of doing away with the *sarcous* (i.e. the body) altogether (Dery, 1996, p. 300). But what needs to be foremost in the minds of these visionaries, and the rest of us, is who or what will be in control of this grand scheme? Who or what will be given the responsibility to run this complex network of online brains? A human? A clone? A robot? All of these are subject to failure are they not, leading to the potential extinction of the new genus.

Figure 3. Courtesy of "U.S. Army Photo", from M. Weik, "The ENIAC Story. A technician changes a tube. Caption reads replacing a bad tube meant checking among ENIAC's 19,000 possibilities." Center: possibly John Holberton.

Replacing a bad tube meant checking among ENIAC's 19,000 possibilities.

Figure 4. Professor Kevin Warwick communicating with a computer in the Cyborg 2.0 experiment. It is difficult to comprehend, how 19,000 tubes can now fit on a single pinhead and how a wall-to-ceiling computer that covered a whole room, can now neatly rest within the body of a human being. Compare this photo with the previous figure. Courtesy of Professor Kevin Warwick.

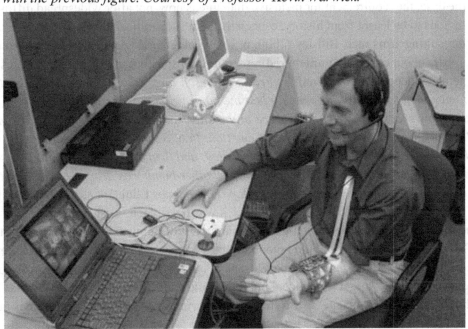

Amnesia

When considering the possibilities of human evolution it is important to ponder on history. In 1946, the public launch of the ENIAC in the United States stimulated people's imagination with some very fantastical thoughts (Figure 2 and Figure 3). However, Kevin Warwick's Cyborg 1.0 project did not receive the same attention. One could observe that society found this breakthrough somewhat lacklustre in comparison. Perhaps what people will find captivating is that next giant leap forward, unwired thought-to-thought communication OR the potential ability to download the human consciousness OR more precisely the means to live "forever" through some technological course. On visiting the Canadian National Art Gallery in Ottawa in 2000, K. Michael took a picture of this artwork that captured this future vision and its ensuing conflicts precisely. It was titled "Amnesia" (1994) and it showed the face of a mature person encased within an external digital storage media unit linked up to an Apple Computer motherboard (Michael and Michael, 2006). It is interesting to note that the person's eyelids were shut. One interpretation of this could have been that the person was asleep (but not dead), another interpretation could be that a future was being followed blindly without enough consideration of what lay ahead. The artwork was reminiscent of the first ENIAC pictures to hit the Sunday papers in the United States. In those famous photos accessible from the University of Pennsylvania, humans are depicted interacting with the room-filled wall-to-ceiling, floor-to-wall computer. It was as if people were about to "enter into" the ENIAC. One could imagine panels and panels of "Amnesia" side-by-side, stacked one on top of the other, i.e. members of a society occupying manifold times more space than the ENIAC and redefining what is meant by such terms as "technological society" and "global village".

NEARING THE POINT OF NO RETURN

The idea of the human electrophorus is one that no longer exists in the realm of the impossible. This being the case, the requirement for inclusive dialogue is now, not after widespread diffusion. There are many lessons to be learnt from history, especially from such radical developments as the atomic bomb and the resulting arms race. Bill Joy (2000, p. 11), chief technologist of Sun Microsystems, has raised serious fears about continuing unfettered research into "spiritual machines". He quotes the following example as evidence. *"As the physicist Freeman Dyson later said, "The reason that it was dropped [the atomic bomb] was just that nobody had the courage or the foresight to say no..." It's important to realize how shocked the physicists were in the aftermath of the bombing of Hiroshima, on August 6, 1945. They describe a series of waves of emotion: first, a sense of fulfillment that the bomb worked, then the horror at all the people that had been killed, and then a convincing feeling that on no account should another bomb be dropped. Yet of course another bomb was dropped, on Nagasaki, only three days after bombing of Hiroshima"* (Joy, 2000, p. 11). Jacques Ellul (1964, p. 99) quotes from a lecture given by Soustelle on the atomic bomb: "[s]ince it was possible, it was necessary".

The question the aforementioned extract raises is, will humans have the foresight to say "no" or "stop" to new innovations that could potentially be a means to a socially destructive scenario? Or will they continue to make the same mistakes? Implants that may prolong life expectancy by hundreds if not thousands of years might sound ideal but they could well create unforeseen devastation in the form of technological viruses, plagues, a different level of crime and violence. The debate is far too complex to enter into here, it is rather a pressing research topic for another work, but if this book has aided to highlight its importance, it has satisfied one of its objectives. Humans may have walked on the moon, and many have dreamed about colonizing other planets but an attempt to "live forever" through the use of technology seems oblivious to the facts: that the Sun has a finite lifetime, that the Earth could be wiped out by an asteroid gone astray, or a full-blown nuclear war could break out between the major powers. These are not fatalistic or apocalyptic considerations, just simple probabilities based on scientific and political fact.

To many scientists of the positivist tradition who are anchored to an empirical world view, the notion of whether something is "right" or "wrong" is redundant and in a way irrelevant. To these individuals a moral stance has little or nothing to do with technological advancement but more with an ideological position. A group of these scientists are driven by an attitude of "let's see how far we can go", not "is what we are doing the best thing for humanity"; and certainly not with the thought of "what are the long-term implications of what we are doing here". The belief is that "science" should not be stopped because it will always make things better. The reality is that it will continue to increase the divide between the "haves" and "have-nots" even further. To the "haves" and "have nots", O'Reilly (1999, pp. 973f) adds the "can-nots". Surely there are more immediate issues at hand than downloading our minds onto hardware. We are not referring here to the medical implant breakthroughs that are helping to save lives but to human extensions. Why not ask the question of whether or not we have directed our resources to solving the greater scientific issues facing the world such as sustainable yield for energy resources, rising water temperatures and ozone layer depletion, soil salinity and fresh water shortages? This is not seeking to be idealistic; these are real and compelling issues with real-time proofs.

CONCLUSION

What we are trying to describe here is the importance of social responsibility, not just for engineers or professionals working on complex problems that possess the knowledge but to all humans. "It has been said that what distinguishes professionals is their possession of "dangerous knowledge." A physician has the means to cure you or kill you. An engineer can design software that is reliable and promotes your safety, or that is critically flawed and precipitates disaster. To repeat an earlier theme, knowledge is power, and the specialized knowledge possessed by professionals gives them power over our lives. Society is rightly concerned, then, that this power is used properly" (Frankel, 1988, p. 199). *"[F]ailure to challenge the 'technological imperative' can pose serious social and moral implications, and that good technical argument, as defined by the values of effectiveness and efficiency, can be accessory to moral abominations, such as those of Hitler's Germany" (Flynn & Ross, 2001, p. 208).* This is not to say that we are against technological development but wary that not all developments will make things better rather than worse. To an extent it is narrow-sighted to be like the Jacobs family who call the debate surrounding chip implants "hullabaloo". The family saw implants as a "gift" and think it is inconceivable that the technology could be used to "do anything but good" (Associated Press, 2002, p. 2). Perhaps Mr Jacobs did not do enough historical research to consider the possibilities... It was a tragic loss to society, and indeed to this critical debate, when young Derek Jacobs lost his life to a motorcycle accident in 2006.

Cohen and Grace (1994, p. 12) investigated the claims that engineers should not pay attention to social responsibility, concluding finally that social responsibility indeed should be seen as integral to the performance of an engineer and that he or she should not only avoid doing harm but seek opportunities to do good. There are *"...five circumstances in which the engineer might choose not to hold the health, safety, and welfare of the public paramount: 1) if the engineer believes that the requirement is internally inconsistent, 2) if the engineer's religious convictions prevent adherence to the requirement, 3) if the engineer believes that the public does not know what is best for it, 4) if the engineer is forced to do otherwise, and 5) if the engineer believes that damage to the environment outweighs short term public interest"* (Vesilind, 2001, p. 162). It seems we are facing an ethical dilemma as a human race, even though the answers to the pressing questions and issues appear seemingly straightforward. What has lead to this analytical displacement? Perhaps it is a preoccupation with short-term "band-aid" solutions rather than looking at the longer-term perspective. Whatever it may be, we all need to actively and responsibly consider what these next steps should be, since generations to come will be living with the monumental and irreversible consequences of our decisions.

Quidquid agas, prudenter agas, et respice finem.- Whatever you do, do cautiously, and look to the end. [*Gesta Romanorum*, cap. 103]

REFERENCES

Aloudat, A., Michael, K., & Yan, J. (2007). Location-Based Services in Emergency Management- from Government to Citizens: Global Case Studies. In P. Mendis, J. Lai, E. Dawson & H. Abbass (Eds.), *Recent Advances in Security Technology* (pp. 191-201). Melbourne: Australian Homeland Security Research Centre.

Associated Press. (2002, 15 October 2002). Chip in your shoulder? Family wants info device. *USA Today: Tech*, from http://www.usatoday.com/life/cyber/tech/2002/04/01/verichip-family.htm

Brennan, M. G. (1996, 7 October). *Ethics and Technology.* Paper presented at the IEE Colloquium on Technology in Medicine.

Brown, W. S. (1998). The interpersonal significance of a fork: what biomedical engineering should do! *IEEE WESCON*, 301-304.

Clark, C. (1943). *The advance to social security.* Carlton: Melbourne University Press.

Cohen, S., & Grace, D. (1994). Engineers and social responsibility: an obligation to do good, *IEEE Technology and Society Magazine* (pp. 12-19).

Dery, M. (1996). *Escape Velocity: cyberculture at the end of the century.* London: Hodder and Stoughton.

Drangeld, K. E. (1991). Characteristics and trends of innovation in electronics and information technology. In B. Henry (Ed.), *Forecasting Technological Innovation* (pp. 157-179). Boston: Kluwer Academic Publishers.

Ellul, J. (1964). *The Technological Society.* New York: Vintage Books.

Flynn, T. R., & Ross, M. S. (2001). Ethical and legal issues related to emerging technologies: reconsidering faculty roles and technical curricula in a new Environment. *International Symposium on Technology and Society*, 203-209.

Frankel, M. S. (1988). Professional ethics and social responsibility. In *Policy Issues in Information and Communication Technologies in Medical Applications* (pp. 199-200).

Joy, B. (2000, April 2000). Why the future doesn't need us. *Wired, 8.04*, from http://www.wired.com/wired/archive/8.04/joy_pr.html

Mann, S. (1998). Humanistic Intelligence: 'WearComp' as a new framework and application for intelligent signal processing, *Proceedings of the IEEE, 86*(11), 2123-2151. Available from http://wearcam.org/hi/index.html

Markoff, J. (29 November 2008). You're Leaving a Digital Trail. What About Privacy? *The New York Times* Retrieved 25 January 2009, from http://www.nytimes.com/2008/11/30/business/30privacy.html?ref=business

Michael, K., & Masters, A. (2006a). The Advancement of Positioning Technologies in Defense Intelligence. In H. Abbass & D. Essam (Eds.), *Applications of Information Systems to Homeland Security and Defense* (pp. 196-220). Hershey, USA: Idea Group Publishing.

Michael, K., & Masters, A. (2006b). Realised Applications of Positioning Technologies in Defense Intelligence. In H. Abbass & D. Essam (Eds.), *Applications of Information Systems to Homeland Security and Defense* (pp. 167-195). Hershey, USA: Idea Group Publishing Press.

Michael, K., McNamee, A., & Michael, M. G. (2006). *The Emerging Ethics of Humancentric GPS Tracking and Monitoring.* Paper presented at the ICMB M-Business Revisited from Speculation to Reality, Piscataway, NJ, USA.

Michael, K., McNamee, A., Michael, M. G., & Tootell, H. I. (2006). *Location-based Intelligence- Modeling Behavior in Humans using GPS.* Paper presented at the International Symposium on Technology and Society, Piscataway, NJ, USA.

Michael, K., & Michael, M. G. (2006, 28-1 July). *Towards chipification: the multifunctional body art of the net generation.* Paper presented at the Cultural Attitudes Towards Technology and Communication, Tartu, Estonia.

Michael, K., Stroh, B., Berry, O., Malhauber, A., & Nicholls, T. (2006). The AVIAN flu tracker- A Location Service Proof of Concept. In P. Mendis, J. Lai & E. Dawson (Eds.), *Recent Advances in Security Technology: Proceedings of the 2006 RNSA Security Technology Conference* (pp. 244-258). Canberra: Australian Homeland Security Research Centre.

O'Reilly, J. (1999). Mind the gap! Electronics and communications in the engineering continuum. *Electronics & Communication Engineering Journal*, 972-979.

Rosenberg, N. (1994). *Exploring the Black Box: technology, economics, and history.* Great Britain: Cambridge University Press.

Rummler, D. M. (2001). Societal issues in engineering [Electronic Version], 1-3. Retrieved 6 March.

Saponas, T. S., Lester, J., Hartung, C., & Kohno, T. (2006). Devices That Tell On You: The Nike+iPod Sport Kit. *University of Washington*, 2007, from http://www.cs.washington.edu/research/systems/privacy.html

Toffler, A. (1981). *Future Shock*. New York: Bantam Books.

Tootell, H. I. (2007). *The Social Impact of Auto-ID and Location Based Services in National Security*. University of Wollongong, Wollongong.

Vesilind, P. A. (2001). The engineer shall hold paramount the health, safety, and welfare of the public. Unless, of course,…. *IEEE International Symposium on Technology and Society*, 162-167.

Westrum, R. (1991). *Technologies and Society: the shaping of people and things*. California: Wadsworth Publishing Company.

Wicklein, J. (1982). *Electronic Nightmare: the home communications set and your freedom*. Boston: Beacon Press.

Wu, X. (2001). *Being ethical in developing information systems: an issue of methodology or maturity in judgment?* Paper presented at the IEEE Proceedings of the 34th Hawaii International Conference on System Sciences.

Acronyms and Abbreviations

2G	Second Generation
3G	Third Generation
4G	Fourth Generation
AA	Aluminium Association
AATA	American Air Transport Association
ABA	American Banking Association
ABC	American Blood Commission
ABS	Acrylonitrile-Butadiene-Styrol (see smart cards)
ADC	Automatic Data Capture
ADFA	Australian Defence Force Academy
ADS	* see ADSX
ADSX	Applied Digital Solutions
AfB	Association for Biometrics
AFDC	Aid to Families with Dependent Children
AFIM	Automated Fingerprint Recognition Machine
AFIS	Automated Fingerprint Identification System (see NAFIS also)
AFIRM	Automated Fingerprint Image Reporting and Match
AFMA	American Furniture Manufacturers Association
AFPA	Australian Federal Police Association
AGV	Automated Guided Vehicles
AHMA	American Hardware Manufacturers Association
AI	Application Identifier (bar code standards)
AI	Artificial Intelligence
AIAG	Automotive Industry Action Group
AIDC	Automatic Identification and Data Collection
AIM	Advanced Informatics Medicine (in the Europe)
AIM	Automatic Identification Manufacturers (in auto-ID)
ALS	Amyotrophic Lateral Sclerosis
AMD	Aged Macular Degeneration
AMEX	American Express
ANA	Article Numbering Association
ANSI	American National Standards Institute
APA	American Pet Association

APACS	Association of Payment and Clearing Services
API	Application Programming Interface (see standards)
API	Automatic Personal Identification (see auto-ID)
API	American Paper Institute (bar code industry association)
APRIL	Army Personnel Rationalisation Individual Listings (in Britain)
APSCF	Asia Pacific Smart Card Forum
AR	Augmented Reality
ARPA	Advanced Research Projects Agency (see ARPANET also)
ARPANET	Advanced Research Projects Agency Network
ASCII	American Standard Code for Information Interchange
ASK	Amplitude Shift Keying
ASR	Artificial Silicon Retina
ATA	Air Transport Authority (see IATA also)
ATA	American Trucking Association
ATM	Automatic Teller Machine
AVID	American Veterinary Identification Devices
AVIS	Automotive Vehicle Identification System
Auto-ID	Automatic Identification
BACS	Bankers Automated Clearing Services (in U.K.)
BART	Bay Area Rapid Transport (in San Francisco)
BCC	Border Crossing Card (in U.S./ Mexico)
BCD	Binary Coded Decimal
BCI	Brain Computer Interaction
BHSUG	Biometrics in Human Service User Group
BIOTEST	Biometric Testing Services
bit	binary digit
bpi	Bits per Inch
BS	Base Station
BSE	Bovine Spongiform Encephalopathy
BSI	British Standards Institute
BT	British Telecom
BWG	Bar Width Growth
C2G	Citizen-to-Government
CAD	Computer-Aided Design
CAFE	Conditional Access for Europe
CANPASS	Canadian Passenger Accelerated Service System
CAO	County Assistance Offices (in U.S.)
CATV	Cable Television
CBA	Canadian Bankers Association
CBD	Central Business District
CBDC	Commercial Biometrics Developer's Consortium
CBEFF	Common Biometric Exchange File Format
CCD	Charge-Coupled Device
CCMIS	Chip Card-based Medical Information System
CCTV	Closed Circuit Television
CD	Cash Dispensers

CDMA	Code Division Multiple Access
CDSA	Common Data Security Architecture
CEC	Chip Electronic Commerce
CEN	Comité Européen de Normalisation
CENELEC	European Committee for Electrotechnical Standardisation
CEPS	Common Electronic Purse Specifications
CEPT	Conférence Européene de Postes et Télécommunications
CFIP	Code of Fair Information Practice
ch.	chapter
CHIPS	Clearinghouse Interbank Payment System
CIBC	Canadian Imperial Bank of Commerce
CITeR	Centre for Identification Technology Research
CITI	Centre for Information Technology Integration
CJIS	Criminal Justice Information Services
COS	Card Operating System
CPR	Central Population Register
CPU	Central Processing Unit
CRC	Cyclic Redundancy Check
CRM	Customer Relationship Management
CRP	Central Register of Persons (Denmark)
CS	Composite Symbology
CTO	Chief Technology Officer
CVM	Centre for Veterinary Medicine
DARPA	Defense Advanced Research Projects Agency
DCC	Distribution Code Centre
DCS	Digital Communication Services (also Digital Cellular System)
DECT	Digital European Cordless Telephone
DERA	Defence Evaluation Research Agency (in UK)
DNA	deoxyribonucleic acid
DNI	Documento Nacional de Identidad (Argentina)
DOD	Department of Defence
dpi	dots per inch
DPSS	Department of Public Social Services
DSD	Direct Store Delivery
DSS	Department of Social Services (in U.S.)
DTE	Data Terminal Equipment
DTR	Data Transfer Rate
E-cash	Electronic Cash
E-commerce	Electronic Commerce
EAN	European Article Number
EAS	Electronic Article Surveillance
EBT	Electronic Benefits Transfer
EC	Electronic Commerce
ECA	Electronic Commerce Association
EDI	Electronic Data Interchange
EDP	Electronic Data Processing

EEG	Electroencephalogram
EEPROM	Electrical Erasable Programmable Read Only Memory
EER	Equal Error Rate
EFT	Electronic Funds Transfer (see EFTPOS also)
EFTS	Electronic Funds Transfer Systems
EFTPOS	Electronic Funds Transfer at the Point of Sale
EIA	Electronics Industry Association
EIN	Event Identification Number (Peru)
ELP	Evaluated List of Products
EMI	Electromagnetic Interference
EMV	Europay, MasterCard, and Visa
ENIAC	Electronic Numerical Integrator and Computer
EPC	Electronic Product Code
EPS	Electronic Payment System
ERMS	Electronic Management System (in Britain)
ERP	Enterprise Resource Planning (in manufacturing)
ERP	Electronic Road Pricing (in Singapore)
ESP	Extra Sensory Perception
ETSI	European Telecommunications Standards Institute
ETTS	European Transport & Telematics Systems
EU	European Union
FACT	Federation of Automated Coding Technologies
FAQ	Frequently Asked Questions
FAR	False Accept Error Rate
FBI	Federal Bureau of Investigation
FCC	Federal Communications Commission (in U.S.)
FDA	Food and Drug Administration (in U.S.)
FedWire	Federal Reserve System
FIN	French Identification Number
FNMT	Fábrica Nacional de Moneda y Timbre
FPA	Flexible Packaging Association
FRAM	Ferroelectric Random Access Memory
FREFLEX	Force Reflecting Exoskeleton
FRR	False Reject Error Rate
FSK	Frequency Shift Keying
FSU	Florida State University
ft	footnote
FTC	Financial Transaction Card
FTC	Federal Trade Commission (see bar codes)
FTTC	Fibre to the Curb
FTTN	Fibre to the Neighbourhood
GA	General Assistance
GAO	General Accounting Office (in U.S.)
GCA	Graphic Communications Association
GHz	Gigahertz
GIN	German Insurance Number

GIS	Geographic Information Systems
GMA	Grocery Manufacturers of America
GMS	Generalised Matching Service (in U.K.)
GP	General Practitioner
GPRS	General Packet Radio Service
GPS	Global Positioning System
GR	General Relief
GSM	Global System for Mobile Communications
HA-API	Human Authentication Application Programming Interface
HCI	Human-Computer Interaction
Hex	Hexadecimal
HIBCC	Health Industry Business Communication Council
HIC	Health Insurance Commission (in Australia)
hico	High Coercivity
high-tech	High Technology
HP	Hewlett-Packard
HRS	Human Recognition Services (in biometrics)
HRV	Heart Rate Variability
HTML	Hypertext Markup Language
IACT	Information and Communication Technology
IAFIS	Integrated Automated Fingerprint Identification System
IAI	International Association for Identification
IATA	International Air Transport Association
IBIA	International Biometric Association
IBG	International Biometric Group
IC	Integrated Circuit
ICC	Integrated Circuit Card (see IC also)
ICMA	International Card Manufacturers Association
ICSA	International Computer Security Association (in U.S.)
ID	Identity; Identification
IDEA	Identification Electronique des Animaux (in Europe)
iDTV	Interactive Digital Television
IEC	International Electronic Commission
IGSANS	Integrated Global Surveillance And Navigation System
IMI	Information Management Institute
IN	Identification Number; Insurance Number
INCITS	InterNational Committee for Information Technology Standards
INS	Immigration & Naturalisation Service (see INSPASS also)
INSPASS	Immigration, Naturalisation Service Passenger Accelerated Service System
I/O	Input/Output
IP	Intellectual Property (in patents)
IP	Internet Protocol
IPN	Insured Persons Number (Switzerland)
IPRP	Information Policy Research Program
IR	Infrared
IRR	Internal Rate of Return
IRS	Internal Revenue Service

IS	International Standard
IS	Information System
ISBN	International Standard Book Number
ISO	International Standards Organisation
ISP	Internet Service Provider
ISV	Independent Software Vendor
IT	Information Technology
ITL	Information Technology Laboratory
IT&T	Information Technology and Telecommunications
IVHS	Intelligent Vehicle Highway Systems
IVR	Interactive Voice Response
JIT	Just-in-Time
JTC	Joint Technical Committee
kHz	Kilohertz
LAN	Local Area Network
LDC	Lesser Developed Countries
LED	Light Emitting Diode
LERTS	Leicester Environmental Road Tolling Scheme
LIS	Local Innovation Systems
loco	Low Coercivity
LOGMARS	Logistic Applications of Automated Marking and Reading Symbols
LoS	line-of-sight
LT	London Transit
m	metres
MAPS	Multimodal Access and Payment System (in transport)
MARC	Multi-technology Automated Reader Card
MDC	More Developed Countries
MEL	MULTOS Executable Language
MEMA	Motor & Equipment Manufacturing Association
MEMS	Microelectromechanical Systems
MFC	MultiFunction Card (IBM™)
mHz	Megahertz
MICR	Magnetic-Ink Character Recognition
MIQR	Minimum Image Quality Requirements
MISC	Magnetics and Information Science Centre
MIT	Massachusetts Institute of Technology
MLI	Multiple Laser Image
mm	Millimetres
MMS	Multimedia Messaging Service
MPEG-3	Moving Picture Experts Group-3
MRT	Mass Rapid Transport (in H.K.)
ms	milliseconds
N-Geners	Net Generation
NAB	National Australia Bank
NAFIS	National Automated Fingerprint Identification System (in U.K., see AFIS also)
NAO	National Audit Office (in U.K.)

NATO	North Atlantic Treaty Organisation
NC	Numerically Controlled
NCP	National ChipCard Platform (NCP)
NCS	National Cash Service (in Japan)
NCSA	National Computer Security Association
NEMA	National Electrical Manufacturer's Association
NETS	Network for Electronic Transfer
NGN	Next Generation Networks
NIC	Newly Industrialised Countries
NIH	National Institute of Health (in the U.S.)
NIN	National Identification Number (in U.K.)
NIS	National Innovation Systems
NOPA	National Office Products Association
NPV	Net Present Value
NRI	National Registry Incorporated
NSA	National Security Agency
OCR	Optical Character Recognition
ODETTE	Organisation for Data Exchange by Tele Transmission in Europe
Oe	Oersted
OEM	Original Equipment Manufacturers
OPCC	Optical Product Code Council
OS	Operating System
OTP	One-Time Programmable
PAM	Pulse Amplitude Modulation
PAN	Personal Area Network
PAN	Primary Account Number (in magnetic-stripe cards)
PARIS	Pennsylvania Automated Recipient Identification System
PBS	Pharmaceutical Benefits Scheme (in Australia)
PC	Personal Computer
PC	Polycarbonate (see smart cards)
PCM	Pulse Coded Modulation
PCMCIA	PC Memory Card Industry Association
PCN	Personal Communications Network
PCR	Polymarase Chain Reaction (in silicon)
PCS	Personal Communications Services
PDA	Personal Digital Assistant
PDF	Portable Data File
PERS	Personal Emergency Response System
PET	Polyethylene Terephthalate (see smart cards)
PIC	Personal Identification Code (Finland)
PID/SS	Personal ID for Social Services
PIN	Personal Identification Number
PIT	Passive Integrated Transponder (see Biomark)
PITO	Police Information Technology Organisation (in U.K.)
PKI	Public-key Infrastructure
PLC	Programmable Controllers

PLD	Personal Location Device (for microchip implants)
PN	Person Number (Norway, Sweden)
PNN	Police National Network (in U.K.)
PORTPASS	Port Passenger Accelerated Service System
POS	Point of Sale (see EFTPOS also)
PR	Public Relations
PSAM	Purchase Secure Application Modules
PSK	Phase Shift Keying
PTT	Post Telephone and Telegraph
PVC	Polyvinyl Chloride
PVV	PIN Verification Value
PWM	Pulse Width Modulation
QR	Quick Response
R&D	Research and Development
RAM	Random Access Memory
RAS	Remote Access Server
RF	Radio Frequency
RF/DC	Radio Frequency Data Communication
RFI	Request for Information (in tender process, see also RFP)
RFI	Radio Frequency Interference
RF/ID	Radio Frequency Identification (also known as RFID)
RFP	Request for Proposal
ROI	Return on Investment
ROM	Read Only Memory
RP	Retinitis Pigmentosa
RSI	Repetitive Strain Injury
RSS	Reduced Space Symbology
RTA	Roads and Traffic Authority (in Australia)
RTLS	Real-Time Locating System (see WhereNet)
RUN	Rol Unico Nacional (in Chile)
SAN	Social Account Number (in Austria)
SARS	Severe Acute Respiratory Syndrome
SC	Smart Card
SC	Sub-committee
SCF	Smart Card Forum
SCIA	Smart Card Industry Association
sci-fi	Science Fiction
SCM	Supply Chain Management
SDK	Software Development Kit
SEIS	Secured Electronic Information in Society
SEMP	Sociedad Espanola de Medios de Pago
SER	Substitution Error Rate
SET	Secure Electronic Transaction
SIBS	Sociedade Interbancaria de Servicos
SI	Systems of Innovation
SIA	Security Industry Association (in U.S.)

SIB	Sociedade Interbancaria de Servicos
SIM	Subscriber Identity Module (see UIM also)
SIN	Single Identifying Number
SIP	Session Initiation Protocol
SIS	Sectoral Innovation Systems
SMS	Short Message Service
SP	Service Provider
SRD	Short Range Devices (in RF/ID)
SSA	Social Security Administration (in U.S.)
SSCC	Serialised Shipping Container Code
SSN	Social Security Number (in U.S.)
SST	Social Shaping of Technology
STAC	Symbol Technical Advisory Committee
SUI	Standard Universal Identifier
SVAPI	Speaker Verification Application Programming Interface
SVC	Stored Value Card
SWIFT	Society for Worldwide Interbank Financial Telecommunications
TA	Technology Assessment
TAB	Tape Automated Bonding (see smart cards)
TAFE	Tertiary And Further Education
TAPA	Terminal Architecture for PSAM Applications (see PSAM also)
TASS	Tarjeta de la Seguridad Social Espanola (in Spain)
TC	Technical Committee
TDI	Teledensity Index
TDMA	Time Division Multiple Access
TFN	Tax File Number (in Australia)
TIN	Taxpayer Identification Number (in U.S.)
TIRIS	Texas Instruments' Registration & Identification System
TS	Technological Systems
U-M	University of Michigan Card
UCC	Uniform Code Council (see also UPCC)
UCC	Uniform Commercial Code (in U.S. legal)
UEPS	Universal Electronic Payment System
UGPCC	Uniform Grocery Product Code Council
UID	Universal Identifiers
UIM	User Identity Module (see SIM also)
UIN	Universal Identification Number
UIS	Unique Identification System
ULI	Unique Lifetime Identifier; Universal Lifetime Identifier
UMI	Universal Multipurpose Identifier
UMTS	Universal Mobile Telecommunications System
UPC	Universal Personal Communications (see UPT)
UPC	Universal Product Code
UPCC	Universal Product Code Council
UPI	Unique Personal Identifier
UPIM	Uniform Personal Identification Mark

UPN	Universal Personal Number
UPT	Universal Personal Telecommunications (known as UPC also)
V	Volts
VAR	Value-added Reseller
VAS	Value-added Services
VGA	Video Graphics Adaptor
VICS	Voluntary Inter-Industry Communications Standards
VOD	Video-on-Demand
VPN	Virtual Private Network
VR	Virtual Reality
VWPP	Visa Waiver Pilot Program (in biometrics)
WISE	Wireless and Internet Infrastructure Software Environment (see Xmarc)
WMATA	Washington Metropolitan Area Transit Authority
WPAN	Wireless Personal Area Network
WWII	World War Two
WWW	World Wide Web

About the Contributors

Dr. **Katina Michael** PhD (University of Wollongong), BIT (University of Technology, Sydney). Senior Member IEEE 2004. Katina is on the IEEE Technology and Society Magazine editorial board, and is the technical editor of the *Journal of Theoretical and Applied Electronic Commerce Research*. Her research interests are in the areas of automatic identification, location-based services, emerging mobile technologies, national security, and their respective socio-ethical implications. Katina is currently a senior lecturer in the School of Information Systems and Technology, Faculty of Informatics, University of Wollongong, Australia. She teaches eBusiness, strategy, innovation, communication security issues, the social impact of technology, and is the research director of the IP Location Based Services Program in the Centre for Business Services Science. Katina has authored over 50 refereed papers, edited three books, and guest edited three special issues in Prometheus, Computer Communications, and JTAER and two special sections in Intelligence and National Security and IEEE Technology & Society Magazine. Select papers can be downloaded from ro.uow.edu.au/kmichael. Katina is also nearing completion of a Masters of Transnational Crime Prevention in the Faculty of Law. She has held several industry positions including as an analyst for United Technologies in 1993, Andersen Consulting in 1996, and a senior network and business planner for Nortel Networks (1996-2001). In her role with Nortel she had the opportunity to consult to telecommunication carriers throughout Asia. More recently Katina was awarded an Australian Research Council grant valued at around $200,000 dollars titled "Toward the Regulation of the Location-Based Services Industry: Influencing Australian Government Telecommunications Policy". Emerging location-based services (LBS) in the Australian telecommunications sector are being deployed without the necessary regulatory provisions in place. The ability to pinpoint a human to a specific geographic location is now possible using a variety of wireless positioning technologies. LBS grants public and private enterprises the ability to track and monitor people for control, care and convenience applications but without the appropriate safeguards and protections for subscribers. The results of this research will direct Australian government telecommunications policy, and specifically address critical gaps in the current telecommunications legislation. Katina has previously been a recipient of other grants valued at $50,000 dollars in the fields of geographic information systems, radiofrequency identification, organizational security and ethics and location based services.

Dr. **M.G. Michael** PhD, MA(Hons), MTh, BTh, BA is a theologian and historian with cross-disciplinary qualifications in the humanities. Michael brings with him a unique perspective on information technology and computer science. His formal studies are in ancient history, theology, philosophy, political sociology, ethics, and government. He has studied at Sydney University, the Aristotelian University of Thessaloniki, the Sydney College of Divinity, Macquarie University, and more recently at the Australian Catholic University. Presently he is an honorary senior fellow in the School of Information Systems and Technology, Faculty of Informatics at the University of Wollongong, Australia. He is currently a member of the IP Location-Based Services Research Program in the Centre for Business Services Science where he provides expertise on ethical issues and the social implications of technology. He is the former coordinator of Information & Communication Security Issues and since 2005 has guest-lectured and tutored in Location-Based Services, IT & Citizen Rights, Principles of eBusiness, IT & Innovation, and Professional Practice and Ethics. The focus of his current research extends to modern hermeneutics and the Apocalypse of John; the historical antecedents of modern cryptography; the auto-ID trajectory; and more broadly the system dynamics between technology and society. Since 2006, Michael has presented papers at numerous IEEE conferences including the International Conference on Mobile Business, the International Conference on Mobile Computing and Ubiquitous Networking, RFID Eurasia, the International Conference on Management of Innovation and Technology, and other venues such as Cultural Attitudes Towards Technology and Communication. Select papers can be downloaded from ro.uow.edu.au/mgmichael. He has guest edited the December 2006 volume of Prometheus on the theme of the "Social Implications of National Security", and the special section on Uberveillance in the IEEE Technology and Society Magazine. He has also co-edited the proceedings of the First Workshop on the Social Implications of National Security on Citizens and Business, the Second Workshop From Dataveillance to Uberveillance and the Realpolitik of the Transparent Society and the third Workshop on Evidence Based Policy in Public Administration- Australia and the New Technologies. He has written papers for Quadrant, Prometheus, the IEEE Symposium on Technology and Society, and the Bulletin of Biblical Studies. In 2007, Michael was invited to speak on the uberveillance concept he developed, in the ubiquitous computing track at the 29th International Conference of Data Protection and Privacy Commissioners' in Montreal, Canada. In 2009 "uberveillance" was voted the most popular "technology" concept in Macquarie Dictionary's Word of the Year competition. Please see www.uberveillance. org. Michael is a member of the Australian Research Council (ARC)-funded Research Network for a Secure Australia, a member of the American Academy of Religion, and an associate member of the Association Internationale d' Études Patristiques. Michael has been the recipient of a number of scholarships and awards.

INTERVIEWEES

Ian Angell has been professor of information systems at the London School of Economics since 1986. His main research work concentrates on organizational and national information technology policies, on strategic information systems, and on computers and risk (both opportunities and hazards), particularly the systemic risks inherent in all socio-technical systems and the security threats posed to organizations by the rapidly diffusing international information infrastructure. His growing reputation comes as the culmination of twenty years work developing a new perspective on information systems, stressing that the social, economic and organizational issues are more important than the technological ones. In particular he emphasizes that even the very best software and investment in the Internet will be a total waste and the cause commercial risks if the complexity caused by societal aspects are not managed properly.Professor Angell acts as a consultant to many national and international organizations and to a number of governments and the EU. Until 2000 he was a personal advisor to the cabinet of the director general of UNESCO (Federico Mayor), he has consulted for the Russian Ministry of Science, presented his ideas to the Malaysian National IT Council and held private advisory sessions with three of the sons of Sheikh Mohammed Al Maktoum, Crown Prince of Dubai. He has also presented his ideas before the Parliamentary IT Committee at the Palace of Westminster to a cross-party group from both Lords and Commons. Undoubtedly it is Angell's radical and controversial views on the global consequences of IT that has brought him such a high-profile reputation as a 'futurologist' in business circles and in the media.

Professor **Allan Brimicombe** is the head of the Centre for Geo-Information Studies at University of East London, UK. He holds BA(Hons) in Geography from Sheffield University and an MPhil in Applied Geomorphology and PhD in Geo-Information Systems both from Hong Kong University. He was employed in the Far East for 19 years first as an engineering geomorphologist with Binnie & Partners International (now Black & Veatch) including being general manager of a subsidiary company – Engineering Terrain Evaluation Ltd. In 1989, Allan joined the Hong Kong Polytechnic University where he founded the Department of Land Surveying and Geo-Informatics. Here he pioneered the use of geo-information systems (GIS) and environmental modeling. In 1995, Allan returned to the UK as Professor and Head of the School of Surveying at the University of East London. His research interests include data quality issues in GIS, the use of GIS and numerical simulation modeling, spatial data mining and analysis, and location-based services (LBS). He is the author of *'GIS, Environmental Modeling and Engineering'* and a new book on *'Location-Based Services and Geo-Information Engineering'* is in press. Email: a.j.brimicombe@uel.ac.uk, Web: www.uel.ac.uk/geo-information

Amal Graafstra is the director of information technology for *OutBack Power Systems*. He is also the author of *RFID Toys*, and one of the most prominent 'do-it-yourselfer' chip implantees in the world. He is the owner of several technology and mobile communications companies. Amal loves thinking up interesting ways to combine and apply various technologies in his daily life. A self-starter, Amal dropped out of community college and started his first company at the age of seventeen. The company was called *The Guild*, and it provided dial-up access to customers, while small set-ups were still feasible. Some years later, Amal started his second company *Morpheus*, which specialized in web hosting and web development. For some time the company did well, but as cheaper hosting services became available, it became more and more difficult to compete in the market. Amal then decided to rebuild *Morpheus* by supplying managed computing services to the medical industry. In parallel, Amal did some work for *WireCutter*, a wireless mobile messaging company that were involved in creating mobile marketing campaigns for various radio stations, sending SMS text messages to mobile phones. Graafstra decided to pour his heart and soul into the company he called *txtGroups* but this too was unable to make ends meet, although he hasn't given up hope on the company's future. His most recent IT adventure is as the head of an IT department where he enjoys fighting typical support fires and watching the business grow.

Mr. **Kenneth Lea** was born in England in 1929 of a coal mining family. He commenced work in coal mining in 1943 in England and married Freda in 1956. He left coal mining in 1964 to go to Africa as a mine surveyor. He worked in Zambia for 5 years (copper mining); in the UK for 1 year (tin mining); 2 years (diamond mining) in Sierra Leone; and 2 years (oil industry) in Nigeria. He returned to England in 1975 and immigrated to Australia with the rest of his family that same year. He worked as a mine surveyor in the coal industry in NSW until his retirement in 1989.

Mrs. **Judith Nachum** (maiden name Lachowitz) was born in Czechoslovakia in Teplice-Sanov (figure 1). Judith was the daughter of Leopold and Hedwig Lachowitz who were born in Slovakia and Austria respectively. In the summer and fall of 1938, the majority of the Jewish community in Teplice-Sanov left due to Czech-German strife and Nazi agitation. At the age of ten, Judith had to move away to Prague. In 1939 Judith's father Leopold tried to get out of Czechoslovakia to go to Palestine but he was unsuccessful and was killed by the Germans in an unknown location in Hungary. Life was difficult and miserable during the years of Jewish persecution. The Jewish children could not go to school, could not go to the playground, could not listen to the radio, they could not even travel on public transport on the weekends. All the Jews had to wear a Star of David stitched to their coats. There was not enough to eat, and the rations the Jews received were always less than the rest of the population. In April 1942, when Judith was 13 years and 8 months, she was sent to Theresienstadt with her mother and older sister.

After 1945 Judith returned to Czechoslovakia. She found it very difficult to assimilate back into her homeland. She did not feel that she belonged. By that stage, she was too old to start her schooling again, and struggled with many complexes. All she knew is that she was a Jew. In 1948 at the age of twenty, Judith left for Israel while her mother and stepfather stayed behind in Czechoslovakia, along with her sister and brother-in-law. Judith's brother-in-law who was a doctor was imprisoned not only by the Germans but also later by the Communist Party in 1952. In the same year, Judith's mother and stepfather migrated to Australia. Judith met her husband Clement on a ship passenger liner where they worked together, and they married before migrating to Australia in 1961.

Coming to Australia was very strange for Judith as she learnt to get used to non-Jewish people. With only ten days of rest after her arrival in Australia, Judith started working and her nine year old son, Thomas, was cared for by others while she worked in the evenings. She later gave birth to her second son whom she named Robert. Both her children were educated at Double Bay Public School. Judith worked in restaurants and later she bought a milk bar with her husband Clement where she worked till her retirement in 1982. Afterward, Judith enrolled at Dover Heights Tafe to fulfill a life-long dream- she sat three HSC courses in Social Studies, English and History achieving an 'A' in her examinations. She has six grandchildren and four great grandchildren and recently she celebrated her 80th birthday with all her family present. She attends her local synagogue every Saturday and every Monday she attends Bible lessons. She is a speaker at the Sydney Holocaust Museum where she has lectured about her experiences to schoolchildren for the last seventeen years. Judith notes that she has never experienced anti-Semiticism in Australia.

Chris tofer Toumazou, PhD, FIEEE, FIET is Professor of Circuit Design and Executive Director of the Institute of Biomedical Engineering at Imperial College London, UK He received his PhD from Oxford-Brookes University in collaboration with UMIST Manchester in 1986. His research interests include high frequency analogue integrated circuit design for RF electronics and low-power electronics for biomedical applications. Chris has made outstanding contributions to the fields of low power analogue circuit design and current mode circuits and systems for radio frequency and biomedical applications. Through his extensive record of research he has invented innovative electronic devices ranging from dual mode cellular phones to ultra-low power devices for both medical diagnosis and therapy. He was made a Professor at Imperial College at 33, one of the youngest ever, in recognition of his outstanding research. He has published over 320 research papers in the field of RF and low power electronics. He holds 23 patents in the field many of which are now fully granted PCT.

Chris is the founder and chairman of four technology based companies with applications spanning ultra low-power mobile technology and wireless glucose monitors (Toumaz Technology Ltd, UK), biomedical devices (Applied Bionics PTE, Singapore), Digital Audio Broadcasting (Future-Waves Pte Taiwan) and DNA Sequencing (DNA Electronics Ltd, UK). These companies employ over 30 RF low power engineers worldwide many of whom are Toumazou's ex graduate students.

Chris is an advisor to many healthcare panels, including the Singapore Government in the field of medical devices. He is a senior Advisor to the Board of Grace Semiconductor in Taiwan, one of the largest Semiconductor Foundries in the World and Senior Advisor to Advanced Nanotech Inc. He was a member of the UK foresight committee on a report for infectious diseases as well as a member of the UK MOD Defense Strategic Advisory Committee on critical technologies. Chris and his colleagues raised £26 million in order to create an Institute of Biomedical Engineering at Imperial College London focusing on Personalized Medicine and Bionanotechnology. This was achieved in 2003 and he became the founding Director and Chief Scientist of the new Institute. Chris is Editor-in-Chief of the IETs Electronics Letters.

Chris has recently been elected to a fellowship of the Royal Society, the national academy of science for the UK and the Commonwealth and the UK's most esteemed scientific organization. Fellowship of the Royal Society is the highest honor in UK science.

Kevin Warwick is professor of Cybernetics at the University of Reading, England, where he carries out research in artificial intelligence, control, robotics and cyborgs.

Kevin was born in Coventry, UK and left school to join British Telecom, at the age of 16. At 22 he took his first degree at Aston University, followed by a PhD and research post at Imperial College, London. He subsequently held positions at Oxford, Newcastle and Warwick Universities before being offered the Chair at Reading, at the age of 33.

As well as publishing over 500 research papers, Kevin's experiments into implant technology led to him being featured as the cover story on the US magazine, *Wired*.

Kevin has been awarded higher doctorates both by Imperial College and the Czech Academy of Sciences, Prague. He was presented with The Future of Health Technology Award in MIT, was made an Honorary Member of the Academy of Sciences, St. Petersburg and in 2004 received The IEE Achievement Medal. In 2000 Kevin presented the Royal Institution Christmas Lectures, entitled "The Rise of the Robots".

Kevin's most recent research involves the invention of an intelligent deep brain stimulator to counteract the effects of Parkinson Disease tremors. The tremors are predicted and a current signal is applied to stop the tremors before they start – this is shortly to be trialed in human subjects. Another project involves the use of cultured/biological neural networks to drive robots around – the brain of each robot is made of neural tissue.

Perhaps Kevin is best known for his pioneering experiments involving a neuro-surgical implantation into the median nerves of his left arm to link his nervous system directly to a computer to assess the latest technology for use with the disabled. He was successful with the first extra-sensory (ultrasonic) input for a human and with the first purely electronic telegraphic communication experiment between the nervous systems of two humans.

Index